*Project Management
for Business
and Engineering*

Project Management
for Business
and Engineering

Principles and Practice
2ND EDITION

John M. Nicholas

Loyola University Chicago

ELSEVIER
BUTTERWORTH
HEINEMANN

Amsterdam   Boston   Heidelberg   London   New York   Oxford
Paris   San Diego   San Francisco   Singapore   Sydney   Tokyo

Elsevier Butterworth–Heinemann
200 Wheeler Road, Burlington, MA 01803, USA
Linacre House, Jordan Hill, Oxford OX2 8DP, UK

Front cover photograph of the Mars rover courtesy NASA/JPL.

Recognizing the importance of preserving what has been written, Elsevier prints its books on acid-free paper whenever possible.

∞
Library of Congress Cataloging-in-Publication Data
Application submitted

British Library Cataloguing-in-Publication Data
A catalogue record for this book is available from the British Library.

This book was previously published by Pearson Education, Inc.

ISBN: 0-7506-7824-0

For information on all Butterworth–Heinemann publications
visit our Web site at www.bh.com

04 05 06 07 08 09 10 10 9 8 7 6 5 4 3 2 1

Printed in the United States of America

To Sharry, Julia, Joshua, and Abigail

Contents

PART IV: ORGANIZATION BEHAVIOR   431

PREFACE

When people see something impressive—a bridge arching high over a canyon, a space probe touching down on a distant planet, a graceful curlicue ramp on a freeway, a motion picture such as *Titanic* (so real you think you're there!), or a nifty computer the size of your hand—they wonder, "how did they do that?" By *they*, of course, they are referring to the creators, designers, and builders, the people who thought up and actually made those things. Rarely do they mean the *managers*, the people who organized and lead the effort that brought those wondrous things from a concept or idea into reality.

This book is about the managers—project managers—and what they do and how they do it. Project managers are the mostly unsung heroes of business and technology, people who, in most cases, stand outside the public eye but without whose talent, skills, and hard work most neat ideas would never amount to anything. Certainly the project manager is but one of the many people who help shape the products, systems, and artifacts of modern life, those things we take for granted as well as those we marvel at. Nonetheless, the project manager is the one who gets all of the others involved, and then organizes and directs them so their combined efforts will come out right. (Sometimes, though rarely, the manager and the creator happen to be the same. Woody Allen, Kelly Johnson, and Gutzon Borglum are examples. Their life work—in motion pictures, supersonic airplanes, and Mount Rushmore, respectively—represent not only creative or technological genius, but leadership and managerial talent as well.)

The pace of change in business and technology is accelerating. The last few decades have seen business be transformed from domestic, nationalistic enterprises and markets into multinational enterprises and a single global market. As a result, no matter what your perspective there is more of everything to contend with—more ideas, competitors, resources, constraints, and, certainly, more people doing and wanting things. The accelerated rate of change in technology means that products or processes are evolving at a more rapid pace, and as a result the life cycles of the things we use and rely on are getting shorter. This accelerated rate of change has a direct impact on the frequency and conduct of projects—whether projects to develop products, systems, or processes that compete in local, domestic, and international markets; projects to create and implement new ways of meeting demand for energy, recreation, housing, communication, transportation, and food; or projects to answer basic questions in science or to resolve problems such as hunger, disease, and pollution. All of this project activity has spurred a growing interest in ways to plan and control projects, and to organize and lead people and groups to meet the needs of customers, markets, and society within the bounds of limited time and resources.

Associated with the growing interest in project management is the growing need to *train* project managers. In the past and still today, project managers were largely persons who had demonstrated some exceptional capability, though not necessarily as a manager. If you were a good engineer, programmer, systems analyst, architect, or accountant, eventually you would become a project manager. Then, presumably, you would pick up the necessary management skills somewhere along the way. The flaw in this approach is that project management encompasses a broad range of skills—managerial, leadership, interpersonal—that are much different than the skills associated with the technology of the particular project. There is no compelling reason to presume that the project environment alone will provide the opportunity for someone to "pick up" the skills necessary for project management.

As a text and handbook, this book is about the "right" way to manage projects. It is intended for advanced undergraduate and graduate university students, and for practicing managers in business and technology. As the title says, it is a book about principles *and* practice, meaning that the topics in it are meant to be applied. It covers the big picture of project management—origins, applications, and philosophy, as well as the nitty-gritty, how-to steps. It describes the usual project management topics of networks, schedules, budgets, and controls as well as the human side of project management.

Why a book on business *and* technology? In my experience, technical specialists such as engineers, programmers, architects, chemists, and so on, often have little or no management training. This book, which includes many technology project examples, provides somewhat broad exposure to relevant business concepts and management specifics to help them get started as project managers.

What about those people involved in product-development, marketing, process-improvement, and related projects commonly thought of as "business projects"? Just as students of technology seldom get management training as part of their formal education, students of business seldom get training about the conduct of projects in technology. For students of business this book reveals not only how "business" projects are conducted, but what happens in a wide variety of engineering, construction, and other kinds of "technical" projects.

Of course, technical projects are *also* business projects because they involve business issues such as customer satisfaction, resource utilization, cost, profits, and so on. Although engineering and development projects may appear different from nonengineering projects, both types are similar in the way they are managed. This book conceptualizes all projects using a single framework called the Systems Development Cycle. This framework serves as a general scheme for illustrating commonalities and differences among projects.

This book is an outgrowth of more than a decade of teaching project management at Loyola University Chicago, preceded by several years of practical experience in business and technology projects, including design and flight test work in the aircraft industry, and software applications development and process improvement projects in banking. From this practical experience I developed an appreciation not only for the business-management side of project management—systems and procedures for planning, scheduling, budgeting, and control—but for the human and organizational side as well. I saw the benefits of good communication, trust, and teamwork on project outcomes, as well as the costs of emotional stress and group conflict. I observed that the most successful projects usually were those where trust, good communications, and teamwork flourished, regardless of the formal planning and control systems in place. This book largely reflects these personal experiences and learnings. Of course, the book reflects much more than my own personal experience. To cover project management in a more general, comprehensive sense, I had to rely on the published works of many other authors, and on the suggestions of colleagues and reviewers.

In this second edition I have revised and added substantial new material to incorporate current examples and reviewers' suggestions, and to take advantage of the growing body of literature in project management. Every chapter has been revised and updated. The most significant changes are as follows: Chapters 1 and 2 have many new examples and case studies of projects and project managers. Chapters 4 and 5 have increased coverage of important front-end topics such as preparation of RFPs and proposals, and definition of user needs, project objectives, requirements, and specifications. Chapter 7 has been revised to cover activity-oriented (rather than event-oriented) scheduling. Chapter 8 has expanded coverage of constrained-resource scheduling and multiple-project scheduling. Chapter 9 includes a new section on the various methods of cost estimating. Chapter 10 is a new chapter that addresses models and practices for assessing and managing project risk. Chapter 11 is expanded to address multiple aspects of project control: scope, quality, schedule, performance, and change control. Chapter 12 is completely revised and covers current software applications and Web-based project management. Chapter 14 is expanded and discusses not only project organization, but mechanisms for project integration including integrated product development teams, concurrent engineering, and quality function deployment. To every chapter I have added new examples and end-of-chapter case studies.

My goal in writing this book has been to provide students and practicing managers of projects the most practical, current, and interesting text possible. I appreciate hearing your comments and suggestions. Please send them to jnichol@luc.edu.

Acknowledgments

Writing a book is a project and, like most projects, reflects the contributions of many people. Here I want to acknowledge and give special thanks to those who contributed the most. First, thanks to my research assistants. In general, research assistants do a lot of work—academic research as well as gofer work, and without their toiling efforts most professors would accomplish far less. I have been fortunate to have had the assistance of two such bright and capable people, Elisa Denney, who reviewed much of the book, helped draft most of Chapter 12, and served as a constant source of energy; and Hollyce James, who helped with revisions and provided editorial competency. Also thanks to Cary Morgan and Louis Schwartzman, my research assistants for the first edition.

I want to express appreciation to Dr. Enrique Venta for reviews and assistance in portions of this and the first edition. Others who deserve special mention and thanks are Dr. Harold Dyck, Dr. Samuel Ramenofsky, Dr. Donald Meyer, Elaine Strnad, Paul Flugel, John Edison, Sharon Tylus, and Debbie Gillespie. I also want to acknowledge the influence of three of my professors, Charles Thompson and Gustave Rath at Northwestern University, and Dick Evans at the University of Illinois, whose philosophy and teachings helped shaped this book.

My appreciation to the following who served as reviewers and provided dozens of helpful suggestions: Thomas B. Clark of Georgia State University; Frank Deromedi of Golden Gate University; Bruce Hartman of the University of Arizona; Joseph L. Orsini of California State University, Sacramento; Peter Papantos of DeVry Institute; and Thomas Tice of California State Polytechnic University, Pomona.

My wife Sharry also gets special thanks. She read the draft for the first edition, provided numerous suggestions, and helped reduce the amount of "techno-jargon" in the book. She also managed the home front, allowed me the time to pursue and complete this project, and was a steadfast source of support.

Thanks also to Tom Tucker, and to the folks at Butterworth-Heinemann, especially to Maggie Smith for her support of this publication.

There are other colleagues, students, and friends, some mentioned in endnotes elsewhere throughout the book, who provided support, encouragement, and reference materials; to them I say thank you. Despite the assistance of so many people and my own best efforts, there are still likely to be omissions or errors. I had final say, and I accept responsibility for them.

John M. Nicholas

ABOUT THE AUTHOR

JOHN NICHOLAS is professor of information systems and operations management, and former associate dean of the Graduate School of Business, Loyola University Chicago. He is an active teacher, writer, and researcher in project management and manufacturing management, and has written extensively about performance issues of teams working in confined, hazardous, stressful environments. He conducts executive seminars and has been a consultant on project management and process improvement.

John is the author of numerous academic and technical publications, including two textbooks, *Managing Business and Engineering Projects* (1990) and *Competitive Manufacturing Management* (1998). He has held the positions of engineer and team leader on aircraft development projects at Lockheed-Martin Corporation, business systems analyst on bank operations at BankAmerica, and research associate on energy-environmental research projects at Argonne National Laboratory. He has a B.S. in aeronautical and astronautical engineering and an M.B.A. in operations research from the University of Illinois, Urbana-Champaign, and a Ph.D. in industrial engineering and applied behavioral science from Northwestern University.

Chapter 1

Introduction

> **project** *(praj' ekt, ikt) n. a proposal of something to be done; plan; scheme 2. an organized undertaking; specif., a) a special unit of work, research, etc., as in school, a laboratory, etc., b) an extensive public undertaking, as in conservation, construction, etc.*
>
> —*Webster's New World Dictionary*

1.1 IN THE BEGINNING . . .

Sometime during the third millennium B.C., workers on the Great Pyramid of Cheops set the last stone in place. Certainly they must have felt jubilant, for this event represented a milestone of sorts in one of humanity's grandest undertakings. Although much of the ancient Egyptians' technology is still a mystery, the enormity and quality of the finished product remains a marvel. Despite the lack of sophisticated machinery, they were able to raise and fit some 2,300,000 stone blocks, weighing 2 to 70 tons apiece, into a structure the height of a modern 40-story building. Each facing stone was set against the next with an accuracy of .04 inch, and the base, which covers 13 acres, deviates less than 1 inch from level (Figure 1-1).[1]

Equally as staggering was the number of workers involved. To quarry the stones and transport them down the Nile, about 100,000 laborers were levied. In addition, 40,000 skilled masons and attendants were employed in preparing and laying the blocks and erecting or dismantling the ramps. Public works were essential to keep the working population employed and fed, and it is estimated that no less than 150,000 women and children also had to be housed and fed.[2]

Figure 1-1
The Great Pyramid of Cheops, an early (circa 2500 B.C.) large-scale project.
[Photo courtesy of Arab Information Center.]

But just as mind-boggling was the managerial ability of the Egyptians—the planning, organizing, and controlling that were exercised throughout the 20-year duration of the pyramid construction. Francis Barber, a nineteenth century American naval attaché and pyramid scholar, concluded that:

> it must have taken the organizational capacity of a genius to plan all the work, to lay it out, to provide for emergencies and accidents, to see that the men in the quarries, on the boats and sleds, and in the mason's and smithies shops were all continuously and usefully employed, that the means of transportation was ample, . . . that the water supply was ample, . . . and that the sick reliefs were on hand.[3]

Building the Great Pyramid is what we today would call a large-scale project. It stands as evidence of numerous such projects from early recorded history that required massive human works and managerial competency. The Bible provides many accounts of projects that required orchestration of thousands of people and the transport and utilization of enormous quantities of materials. Worthy of note are the managerial and leadership accomplishments of Moses. The scriptural account of the exodus of the Hebrews from the bondage of the Egyptians gives some perspective on the preparation, organization, and execution of this tremendous undertaking. Supposedly, Moses did a magnificent job of personnel selection, training, organization, and delegation of authority.[4] The famed ruler Solomon, among other accomplishments, was the "manager" of numerous great construction projects. He transformed the battered ruins of many ancient cities and crude shanty towns into powerful fortifications. With his wealth and the help of Phoenician artisans, Solomon built the Temple in Jerusalem. Seven years went into the construction of the Temple, and after that Solomon built a palace for himself which took 13 more years to complete. He employed a workforce of 30,000 Israelites to fell trees and import timber from the forests of Lebanon.[5] That was almost 3,000 years ago.

With later civilizations, most notably the Greeks and Romans, the number of activities requiring extensive planning and organizing escalated. These societies undertook extensive municipal and government works programs such as street paving, water supply, and sewers. To facilitate their military campaigns and commercial interests, the Romans constructed networks of highways and roads throughout Europe, Asia Minor, Palestine, and northern Africa so that all roads would "lead to Rome." The civilizations of renaissance Europe and the Far East undertook river engineering, construction of canals, dams, locks, and port and harbor facilities. With the spread of modern religions, construction of churches, temples, monasteries, mosques, and massive urban cathedrals was added to the list of projects. The remains of aqueducts, bridges, temples, palaces, fortifications, and other large structures throughout the Mediterranean and China testify to the ancients' occupation with large-scale projects.

With the advent of industrialization and electricity, the projects of humankind took on increasing complexity. Projects for the construction of railroads, electrical and hydroelectrical power facilities and infrastructures, subways, and factories became commonplace. In recent times, research and installation of large systems for communications, defense, transportation, and information technology have spurred different, more complex kinds of project activity.

As long as humankind does things, there will be projects. Many projects of the future will be similar to those in the past. Others will be vastly different either in terms of increased scale of effort or more advanced technology. Representative of the latter are two recent projects, the English Channel tunnel (Chunnel) and the international space station. The Chunnel required tremendous resources and took a decade to complete. The international space station (Figure 1-2) will require new technologies, some that have yet to be developed.

Figure 1-2
The international space station, a modern large-scale project.
[Photo courtesy of NASA/Johnson Space Center.]

From these few examples it is clear that humankind has been involved in project activities for a long time. But why are these works considered "projects" while other human activities, such as planting and harvesting a crop, stocking a warehouse, issuing payroll checks, or manufacturing a product, are not?

What *is* a project? This is a question we will cover in much detail later. As an introduction though, some characteristics will be listed that warrant classifying an activity as a project. They center on the purpose, complexity, uniqueness, unfamiliarity, stake, impermanence, and life cycle of the activity:[6]

1. A project involves a single, definable *purpose, end-item,* or *result,* usually specified in terms of cost, schedule, and performance requirements.
2. Every project is *unique* in that it requires doing something different than was done previously. Even in "routine" projects such as home construction, variables such as terrain, access, zoning laws, labor market, public services, and local utilities make each project different. A project is a one-time activity, never to be exactly repeated again.
3. Projects are *temporary* activities. An ad hoc organization of personnel, material, and facilities is assembled to accomplish a goal, usually within a scheduled time frame; once the goal is achieved, the organization is disbanded or reconfigured to begin work on a new goal.
4. Projects *cut across organizational lines* because they need the skills and talents from multiple professions and organizations. Project complexity often arises from the complexity of advanced technology, which creates task interdependencies that may introduce new and unique problems.
5. Given that a project differs from what was previously done, it also involves *unfamiliarity*. It may encompass new technology and, for the organization undertaking the project, possess significant elements of *uncertainty* and *risk*.
6. The organization usually has something *at stake* when doing a project. The activity may call for special scrutiny or effort because failure would jeopardize the organization or its goals.
7. Finally, a project is the *process* of working to achieve a goal; during the process, projects pass through several distinct phases, called the *project life cycle*. The tasks, people, organizations, and other resources change as the project moves from one phase to the next. The organization structure and resource expenditures slowly build with each succeeding phase; peak; and then decline as the project nears completion.

The examples described earlier are for familiar kinds of projects such as construction (pyramids), development (transportation and information technology), or a combination of both (space station). In general, the list of activities that qualify as projects is long and includes many that are commonplace. Weddings, remodeling a home, and moving to another house are certainly projects for the families involved. Company audits, major litigations, corporate relocations, and mergers are also projects, as are new product development and system implementation efforts. Military campaigns also meet the criteria of projects; they are temporary, unique efforts directed toward a specific goal. The Normandy Invasion during WWII on June 6, 1944, is a good (perhaps the ultimate) example:

The technical ingenuity and organizational skill that made the landings possible was staggering. The invasion armada included nearly 5,000 ships of all descriptions protected by another 900 warships. The plan called for landing 150,000 troops and 1500 tanks on the Normandy coast *in the first 48 hours.* There were large-scale air operations with bombers, gliders, paratroopers, and fighter support. There was PLUTO, the Pipe Line Under the Ocean, to bring the flood of petroleum that the armies would need. And there was Mulberry Harbor. Since the French ports were not large enough to handle the traffic anticipated to follow the invasion (12,000 tons of stores and 2,500 vehicles *per day*), the idea evolved to tow two monstrous breakwaters and floating quays (Mulberries) across the English Channel, each making a complete port the size of Dover.[7]

Most artistic endeavors are projects. Composing a song or symphony, writing a novel, or making a sculpture are one-person projects. The unusual (and somewhat controversial) works of the artist Christo—draping portions of the Grand Canyon, several islands in Biscayne Bay, and 1,000,000 square feet of Australian coastline with colored plastic—are projects also, but on a larger scale. So is the making of motion pictures, whether they are home movies or the releases of major production studios. Some large artistic projects have also involved the skills of many engineers and builders: The Eiffel Tower, and Mount Rushmore, and the Statue of Liberty (both discussed later) are examples.

Many efforts at saving human life and recovering from man-made or natural disasters become projects. Examples are the massive cleanup following the Soviet nuclear accident at Chernobyl, and the rescue and salvage operations following disastrous earthquakes in Mexico City; Turkey; Armenia; and Kobe, Japan.

Figure 1-3 shows generalized project endeavors and some examples of well-known projects. Notice the diversity in the kinds of efforts. The figure shows approximately where projects fall with respect to the degree of complexity and uncertainty involved. Complexity is roughly measured by magnitude of the effort, number of groups and organizations that need to be coordinated, and diversity in skills or expertise needed to accomplish the work. Time and resource commitments tend to increase with complexity.

Uncertainty is measured roughly by the difficulty in predicting the final outcome in terms of the dimensions of *time, cost,* and *technical performance.* In most projects there is some uncertainty in one or two dimensions, at least in the initial stages of planning (e.g., weddings and world fairs). The most complex projects have uncertainty in all three dimensions (e.g., the space station).

Generally, the more often something is done, the less uncertainty there is to doing it. This is simply because people learn by doing and so improve their efforts—the "learning curve" concept. Projects that are very similar to previous ones and about which there is abundant knowledge have lower uncertainty. These are found in the lower portion of Figure 1-3 (e.g., weddings, highways, dams, system implementation). As manned missions to Mars become frequent, they too will move down the uncertainty scale.

The cost curve indicates that the expense of projects increases roughly in proportion to both complexity and uncertainty. Cost, represented in terms of time or economic value, is at the level of tens or hundreds of labor hours for projects with low complexity and uncertainty, but increases to millions and billions of hours for projects with the greatest complexity and uncertainty.

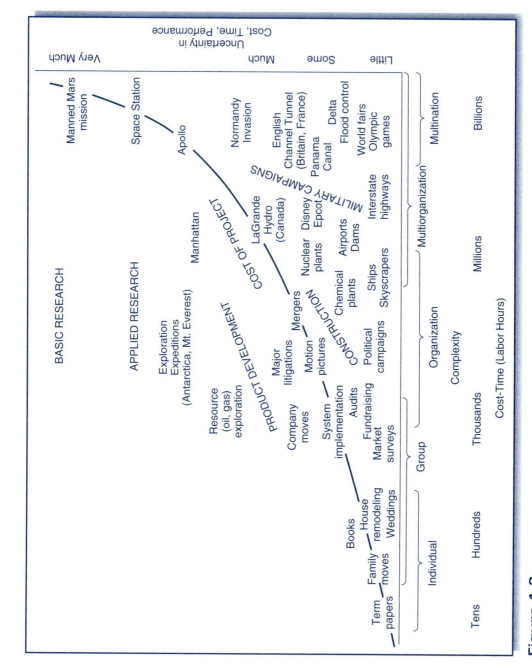

Figure 1-3
A typology of projects.

6

When the uncertainty of a project drops to nearly zero, and when the project effort is repeated a large number of times, then the work is usually no longer considered a project. For example, building a skyscraper is definitely a project, but mass construction of prefabricated homes more closely resembles a scheduled, repetitive task than a project. Admiral Byrd's exploratory flight to the South Pole was a project, but modern daily supply flights to Antarctic bases are not. When (in the future) tourists begin taking chartered excursions to Mars, trips there will no longer be considered projects either. They will just be ordinary scheduled operations.

In all cases, projects are conducted by organizations that, after accomplishment of the project, go on to do something else (construction companies) or are disbanded (Admiral Byrd's crew, the Mars exploration team). In contrast, repetitive, high-certainty activities (prefabricated housing, supply flights, and tourist trips to Antarctica or Mars) are performed by permanent organizations that do the same thing over and over, with little change in operations other than rescheduling. That projects differ greatly from repetitive efforts is the reason they must be managed differently.

1.3   PROJECT MANAGEMENT: THE NEED

Although humankind has been involved in projects since the beginning of recorded history, obviously the nature of projects and the environment have changed. Many modern projects involve great technical complexity and require much diversity of skills. Managers are faced with the problem of putting together and directing large temporary organizations while being subjected to constrained resources, limited time schedules, and environmental uncertainty. To cope with complex kinds of activities and great uncertainty, new forms of project organization and new practices of management have evolved.

Two examples of activities that required project organization and management practice are the Manhattan Project (to develop the first atomic bomb) and the Pathfinder Mission (to land and operate a rover vehicle on the surface of Mars). Projects such as these are not only unparalleled in terms of technical difficulty and organizational complexity, but also in terms of the requirements circumscribing them. In ancient times, project "requirements" were more flexible. If the Pharaohs needed more workers, then more slaves or more of the general population was conscripted. If funding ran out during construction of a Renaissance cathedral, the work was stopped until more money could be raised from the congregation (indeed, this is one reason many cathedrals took decades to complete). If a king ran out of money while building a palace, he simply raised taxes. In other cases where additional money could not be raised, more workers could not be found, or the project could not be delayed, then the scale of effort or the quality of workmanship was simply reduced to accommodate the constraints. There are many early projects of which nothing remains simply because the work was shoddy and could not withstand the rigors of time.

In projects like Manhattan and Pathfinder, requirements are not so flexible. First, both projects were subject to severe time constraints. Manhattan, undertaken during World War II, required that the atomic bomb be developed in the shortest time possible, preferably ahead of the Nazis. For Pathfinder, the mission team was challenged with developing and landing a vehicle on Mars in less than three years time and on a $150 million budget. This was less than half the time and one-twentieth the cost of the last probe NASA had landed on Mars. For the sake of secrecy, the Manhattan Project restricted the informed personnel to a relative few. Both projects involved advanced research and development and explored new areas of science and engineering. In neither case could technical performance requirements be compromised to compensate for limitations in time, funding, or other resources; to do so would increase the risk to undertakings that were already very risky. However, constraints and uncertainty in project work are not restricted to large-scale government science programs. They are common, everyday experiences in business and technology where organizations continually strive to develop and implement new products, processes, and systems, and to adapt themselves to meet changing requirements in a changing world.

Consider, for instance, Company Alpha's development of "Product X", an example representative of new product development efforts that companies everywhere must do to remain competitive, indeed, to survive. In the past, Company Alpha had relied upon trial and error to come up with new products: in essence, whatever worked was used again; whatever failed was discarded. In recent years, Company Alpha had begun to lose market share to competitors. Even though the company had had several innovative concepts on the drawing board, it had lost out because it was too slow to move them into the marketplace. Alpha was now considering development of Product X, a promising, but radically new idea. To move the idea from concept to product would require the involvement of engineers and technicians from several Alpha divisions. Extensive marketing analysis would be needed to establish how best to introduce it. As is typical in product development projects, time was of the essence. Before approving the budget, Company Alpha management wanted assurances that Product X could be introduced early enough to put it well ahead of the competition. It was apparent that the division would need a more efficient means to manage development and marketing of the product.

Another example is Beta Hospital's installation of a new employee benefits plan. The new plan would better suit employee needs, add flexibility and value to the benefits package, and keep costs down. Not only was the new plan dramatically different from the old one, but its installation would require active participation from personnel in human resources, financial service, and information systems, as well as experts from two consulting firms. The project would involve developing new policies, upgrading the training of staff workers and familiarizing 10,000 employees with the plan, and installing a new computer network and database. Hospital management had to approve the resources and capital funding, select the vendors, and choose representatives from participating departments as well as a manager to conduct the project. Although this project was different from anything the hospital had experienced before, it was typical of "change" projects everywhere: The project was initiated in response to changing needs, with the goal of transforming an organization from one way of doing things to another.

As a final example, look at the boom in e-commerce. Every company now has or soon will have a web site. Dot-com addresses appear everywhere on printed and broadcasted advertising as companies scramble to inform customers they are part of the e-business revolution. Behind every dot-com address, however, are multiple projects. To develop or significantly enhance a web site is a project, and to take measures to integrate the concepts of electronic business technology into a company's mainstream marketing and supply-chain operations is also a project. These are examples of projects spurred by the necessity to "change," in this case, to keep pace with the e-commerce revolution.

Efforts such as these defy traditional management approaches for planning, organization, and control. They are representative of activities that require modern methods of project management and organization to fulfill difficult technological or market-related performance goals in spite of severe limitations on time and resources.

As a distinct area of management practice, project management is still a new idea, and its methods are still unknown to many experienced managers. Only 40 years ago, its usage was restricted largely to the defense, aerospace, and construction industries. Today, however, project management is being applied in a wide variety of industries and organizations. Originally developed and applied in large-scale, complex technological projects such as the Apollo Space Program to put a man on the moon, project management techniques are applicable to *any* project-type activities, regardless of size or technology. Modern project management would have been as useful to early Egyptian and Renaissance builders as it is to present day contractors, engineers, systems specialists, and managers.

1.4 RESPONSE TO A CHANGING ENVIRONMENT

Project management arose in response to the need for a managerial approach which could deal with the problems and take advantage of the opportunities of modern society. Three salient characteristics distinguish modern society from earlier periods of history: interdependency, complexity, and rapid, radical change. The challenges and problems of modern society involve risk and uncertainty arising from numerous interacting forces and variables, rapidly changing technology, rising costs, increasing competition, frequent resource shortages, and numerous interest groups and their opposing views about the best course of action.[8]

Project management is a departure from the management of simpler ongoing, repeated operations where the market and technology tend to be predictable, where there is certainty about anticipated outcomes, and where fewer parties or organizations are involved. Situations which are more predictable, less risky, and more stable can be efficiently handled by "mechanistic" organizational forms and management procedures. These forms tend to rely on centralized decision making and adherence to hierarchical authority. When adaptability and rapid response to change are called for, such as in volatile technological or market environments, more "organic" forms of organization and management are required. These forms accommodate the need for diversified technical and managerial competency, and expand the latitude and degree of decentralization in decision making.

1.5 SYSTEMS APPROACH TO MANAGEMENT

Solutions to problems imposed by frequent change and technological complexity must themselves accommodate complexity and be adaptive to change.[9] In response to these demands, new management approaches under the umbrella of the "systems approach" have come into use. They apply the concepts of systems theory and systems analysis to the task of management. More will be said about this in Chapter 3. The systems approach to management recognizes that organizations exist in a universe of forces and are comprised of interrelated units, the goals and effects of which must be coordinated and integrated for the benefit of the organization. Project management is a systems-oriented approach to management because it considers the project as a system of interrelated tasks and work units operating in a changing environment. It seeks to unify the planning and work efforts of numerous organizational units working in a project to efficiently accomplish, with minimal tradeoff, the multiple goals of a project.

1.6 PROJECT GOALS

Virtually every project has three overriding goals: to accomplish work for a client or end-user in accordance with *budget, schedule,* and *performance requirements.* The budget is the specified or allowable cost for the project; it is the target cost of the work to be done. The schedule includes the time period over which the work will be done and the target date for when it will be completed. The performance requirements specify what is to be done to reach the end-item or final result. They include required features of the final product or service, technological specifications, and quality and quantity measures, whatever is important to the client or end-user. As shown in Figure 1-4, the goals can be conceptualized as the axes of a three-dimensional space, and the purpose of project management is to direct the project to a target that satisfies all three goals.[10] Taken together, the three goals represent a contract to deliver a certain something, by a certain date, for a certain cost.

Unfortunately, technological complexity, changing markets, and uncontrollable environmental forces complicate what can be considered as "certain." The three goals are interrelated and must be addressed simultaneously; exclusive emphasis on any one goal is likely to detract from the others. In trying to meet time schedules and performance requirements, costs may be forced to increase; conversely, in trying to contain costs, work quality may erode, schedules may slip, and performance may degrade. In earlier times, one or two of the goals were simply allowed to vary so that the "most fixed" goal could be met. Most projects, as the Manhattan, Pathfinder, Alpha Company, and Beta Hospital examples show, do not have this luxury; time, cost, and performance have to be given equal emphasis. Project management has evolved as an efficient way to maintain focus on all three project goals and to control the nec-

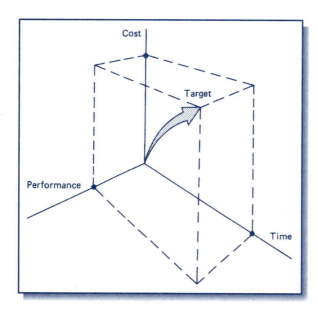

Figure 1-4
Three dimensions of project goals. [Adapted from Milton Rosenau, *Successful Project Management* (Belmont, CA: Lifetime Learning Publications, 1981), 16.]

essary tradeoffs among them. As a systems approach, project management integrates resources and puts emphasis on the "wholeness" of project goals.

1.7   PROJECT MANAGEMENT: THE PERSON, THE TEAM, THE SYSTEM

Three key features distinguish project management from earlier, traditional forms of management: the project manager, the project team, and the project management system.

The Project Manager

The most important element of project management is the project manager, a person whose single, overriding responsibility is to *plan, direct,* and *integrate* the work efforts of participants to achieve project goals. In fast-changing environments it is becoming increasingly difficult for organizations like Company Alpha to relate facts about technology, production methods, costs, and markets, and the number of crucial issues and decisions to be processed is too large for traditional hierarchical organizations to effectively handle. In most organizations, work proceeds along functional lines and the response to change is exceedingly slow. In the role of project manager, the organization has one person who is accountable for the project and is totally dedicated to achieving its goals. The project manager coordinates efforts across the various involved functional areas and integrates the planning and control of costs, schedules, and work tasks.[11]

The Project Team

Project management is the bringing together of individuals and groups to form a single, cohesive team working toward a common goal. Perhaps more than any other human endeavor, project work is teamwork. Project work is accomplished by a group of people, often from different functional areas and organizations, who participate wherever and whenever they are needed. Depending on resource requirements of the project, the size and composition of the team may fluctuate, and the team may disband after the project is completed.

The Project Management System

The project manager and the project team must have available and utilize a "project management system." The project management system is composed of organization structure, information processing, and practices and procedures that permit integration of the "vertical" and "horizontal" elements of project organizations. As shown in Figure 1-5, vertical elements include the breakdown of all tasks in the project; horizontal elements include the functional units and departments involved in the project.

The project management system provides for *integrative planning and control.* According to Archibald, integrative planning and control refers to

the pulling together of all important elements of information related to (1) the products or results of the project, (2) the time, and (3) the cost, in funds, manpower, or other key resources. Further, this information must be pulled

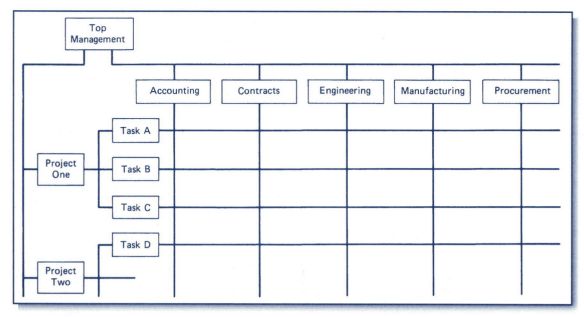

Figure 1-5
Vertical and horizontal elements of project organization.

together for all (or as many as practical) phases of the project. Finally, integrated planning and control requires continual revision of future plans, comparison of actual results with plans, and projection of total time and cost *at completion* through interrelated evaluation of all elements of information.[12]

As projects move from one phase to the next, resource requirements (labor, facilities, capital, etc.) and organizational responsibilities shift. The project management system provides the means for (1) identification of tasks, (2) identification of resource requirements and costs, (3) establishing priorities, (4) planning and updating schedules, (5) monitoring and controlling end-item quality and performance, and (6) measuring project performance.[13]

1.8   ABOUT THIS BOOK

Philosophy and Objectives

Although it has at its foundation traditional management theory and practice, in many ways project management represents a significant departure. A history of the theory and practice of project management would show that its roots touch many disciplines, including management science, systems theory, accounting, operations management, organizational design, law, and applied behavioral science. What has evolved, and will continue to evolve, is a philosophy, approach, and set of practices, the *sum total* of which comprise project management.

As a philosophy and an approach, project management is broader and more sophisticated than traditional management of repetitive activities. Many managers fail to understand this, believing that application of techniques alone, such as "PERT/CPM" or "matrix management" (both explained later) make for successful project management (and successful projects). There is some support for this belief in the literature, much of which focuses rather narrowly on certain methods and procedures of project management.

C. P. Snow wrote an essay entitled "Two Cultures" about the cultural gap that separates scientists from the rest of society. He wrote of the conflict of ideas, the problems of communication, and the lack of understanding between scientists and other intellectuals.[14] Managers and management scholars also tend to see the world from either of two perspectives: some see the world in "hard," quantitative terms; others in "soft," or behavioral terms. The management scientists tend to view projects in terms of economic variables; their approach is to structure problems mathematically and to follow some prescribed set of procedures to arrive at a solution. The behaviorists view problems in terms of human behavior, skills, attitudes, and systems of organization; their solutions are to be found by modifying individual attitudes and behavior, and by altering the processes and structure of groups and organizations. Much of the literature on project management is weighted in favor of one or the other of these perspectives, most often that of the management scientists.

The intent of this book is to give a comprehensive, balanced view that emphasizes both the behavioral and quantitative sides of project management. The philosophy of this book is that for managers to "do" project management, they must gain familiarity with four aspects of it: system methodology; systems development process; management methods, procedures, and systems; and organization and human behavior. All four aspects are essential to project management, and neglect or unbalanced attention to some may render the others ineffective. Correspondingly, the objectives of this book are to

1. Discuss the system principles and philosophy which guide project management theory and practice.
2. Describe the logical sequence of stages in the life of a project.
3. Describe the methods, procedures, and systems for defining, planning, scheduling, controlling, and organizing project activities.
4. Describe the organizational, managerial, and human behavioral issues relevant to project management.

The techniques of management science are important tools in project management, but individual and group skills, the right attitudes, and teamwork are just as essential. Within the four objectives, both the quantitative and behavioral sides of project management are addressed.

This book is intended for "general" project managers. It is comprehensive in the sense that it provides an understanding of project management concepts and techniques widely recognized and of application to virtually any industry or project situation. It is not the intent of this book to dwell on particular methodologies and techniques used only in specific industries or organizations. This would be a difficult task because many industries—construction, defense, computer, product development, social work, and so on—have modified "traditional" project management practices or adopted other approaches to satisfy their unique project needs. Many of these methodologies and techniques are described in texts devoted to construction, product management, software development, research management, and so on.

Just as many of the project management practices described in this book were developed in certain industries to be later recognized and adopted for general use, there are probably many valuable practices currently in use that most of us are ignorant of. These practices remain to be "exposed" and to appear in textbooks like this in the future.

The Study Project

A good way to learn about project management is to actually participate in it or, failing that, to witness it. At the end of every chapter in this book are two kinds of questions: the first kind are the usual chapter review questions, the second are called "Questions About the Study Project." The latter are intended to be applied to a particular project of the reader's choosing. This will be called the "study project." The purpose of these questions is to help the reader relate concepts from each chapter to real-life situations.

The study project questions should be used in the following ways:

For readers who are currently working in projects as either managers or project team members, the questions can be related to their current work. The questions serve both to increase readers' awareness of key issues surrounding the project as well as to guide managers in the organization and conduct of project management.

For readers who are currently full- or part-time students, the questions can be applied either to (1) student projects in which they are currently involved (e.g., group research projects) or (2) outside projects which they are permitted to observe. Many business firms and government agencies are willing to let student groups interview them and collect information about projects. Though secondhand, this is nonetheless an excellent way to learn about project management practice (and malpractice).

Organization of This Book

Beyond this introductory chapter, the book is divided into four main sections. The first section is devoted to the basic concepts of project management. This section describes project management principles, systems methodologies, and the systems approach—the philosophy that underlies project management. Also covered are the origins and concepts of project management, situations where it is needed, and examples of applications. The second section describes the logical process in the creation and life of a system. Called the Systems Development Cycle, it is the sequence of phases through which all human-made systems move from birth to death. The cycle is described in terms of its relation to projects and project management. The third section is devoted to methods and procedures for planning, scheduling, cost estimating, budgeting, resource allocation, controlling, and terminating a project. The topics of resource planning, computer and web-based project management, and project evaluation are also covered. Throughout this section, reference is made to the management and information systems needed to integrate planning and work activities. The fourth section is devoted to project organizations, teams, and the people in projects. It covers structural aspects of project organizations, roles and responsibilities of project managers and team members, styles of leadership appropriate for project managers, and methods for managing teamwork, conflict, and emotional stress.

Thus, the four stated objectives of this book are roughly divided among the chapters in this way:

1. Basic concepts and systems philosophy: Chapters 2 and 3.
2. Systems development and project life cycle: Chapters 4 and 5.
3. Methods, procedures, and systems for planning and control: Chapters 6 through 13.
4. Organization, management, and human behavior: Chapters 14 through 16.

Chapter 17 discusses project success and failure, and ties together the tenets of the book.

The Appendices expand upon three subjects mentioned throughout the book: systems engineering (Appendix A), contracts (Appendix B), and the project plan (Appendix C). All readers should look at Appendices B and C after they have read Chapter 4 and refer to them again whenever they are mentioned in the book. Readers who are, or expect to be, involved in the engineering of large-scale, system integration projects should study Appendix A after they have read Chapter 3.

STUDY PROJECT ASSIGNMENT

Select a project to investigate. You should select a "real" project; that is, a project that has a real purpose and is not contrived just so you can investigate it. It can be a current project or one already completed. It can be a project on which you are currently working. However, it must be a project for which you can readily get information.

If you are not currently involved in a project as a team member, then you must find one that you have permission to study (collect data and interview people, etc.) as an "outsider." The project should include a project team (a minimum of five people) with a project leader and have at least a two or three month duration. The project should also have specific goals in terms of, for example, a target completion date and a budget limit, as well as a specified end-item result or product.

It is also a good idea, if you decide to study a project as an outsider, to do it in a team with three to six people and a project leader (i.e., use a team to perform the study). This, in essence, becomes your *project team*—a team organized for the purpose of studying a project. You can then readily apply many of the planning, organizing, team building, and other procedures discussed throughout the book to see how they work. This "hands-on" experience with your own team, combined with what you learn from the project you are studying, will give you a fairly accurate picture about problems encountered and management techniques used in real-life project management.

MS PROJECT

The Microsoft Project disk included with the book will help familiarize you with many of the project management techniques. MS Project has self helps and tutorials that will enable you to learn and use the software on your own. You might want to use MS Project for creating a work-breakdown structure, responsibility matrix, Gantt chart, network, and other planning aids for the study project or other class project assignments, which will enable you to better understand the actual development and application of project planning and scheduling techniques. These and other techniques, topics of chapters 7 and 8, are readily covered by MS Project.

Chapter 12 includes brief descriptions of MS Project and other popular project management software packages.

REVIEW QUESTIONS

1. Look at newspapers, magazines, or television for examples of items that pertain to projects. Surprisingly, a great number of newsworthy topics relate to the status of current or future projects, or to the outcome of past projects. Prepare a list of these topics.
2. Prepare a list of activities that are not projects. What distinguishes them from project activities? Which activities are difficult to classify one way or the other?

3. Because this is an introductory chapter, not very much has been said about why projects must be managed differently, and what constitutes project management—the subject of this book. Now is a good time to speculate about these: Why do you think that projects need to be managed differently than nonprojects? What do you think are some additional or special considerations necessary for managing projects?

ENDNOTES

1. Peter Tompkins, *Secrets of the Great Pyramids* (New York: Harper & Row, 1976): 233–234; Rene Poirier, *The Fifteen Wonders of the World* (New York: Random House, 1961): 54–67.
2. Ibid., 227–228.
3. Francis Barber, *The Mechanical Triumphs of the Ancient Egyptians* (London: Tribner, 1900) as described by Tompkins, ibid., 233.
4. Claude S. George, *The History of Management Thought* (Upper Saddle River, NJ: Prentice Hall, 1968): 11.
5. Chaim Potok, *Wanderings* (New York: Fawcett Crest, 1978): 154–162.
6. See Russell D. Archibald, *Managing High-Technology Projects* (New York: Wiley, 1976): 19; Jack R. Meredith and Samuel Mantel, *Project Management: A Managerial Approach,* 3rd ed. (New York: Wiley, 1995): 8–9; Daniel D. Roman, *Managing Projects: A Systems Approach* (New York: Elsevier, 1986): 2–10; John M. Stewart, "Making Project Management Work," *Business Horizons* 8, no. 3 (Fall 1965): 54–68.
7. See John Terraine, *The Mighty Continent* (London: BBC, 1974): 241–242.
8. D. I. Cleland and W. R. King, *Systems Analysis and Project Management,* 3rd ed. (New York: McGraw-Hill, 1983): 5–6.
9. Ibid., 4.
10. See Meredith and Mantel, *Project Management,* 3; and Milton D. Rosenau, *Successful Project Management* (Belmont, CA: Lifetime Learning, 1981): 15–19.
11. Harold Kerzner, *Project Management: A Systems Approach to Planning, Organizing, and Controlling* (New York: Van Nostrand Reinhold, 1979): 6.
12. Archibald, *Managing High-Technology Projects,* 6–7.
13. Kerzner, *Project Management,* 7.
14. C. P. Snow, *The Two Cultures and a Second Look* (Cambridge, England: Cambridge University Press, 1969).

Part

Philosophy and Concepts

*T*he two chapters in this section describe the philosophy and concepts that differentiate project management from traditional, nonproject management. Project management is an application of what has been called the systems approach to planning and operating organizations. This section introduces features associated with project management and describes the principles, terminology, and methodology of the systems approach. It forms the foundation of the book and sets the stage for more detailed coverage in later sections.

Chapter 2

What Is Project Management?

The projects mentioned in Chapter 1—the Great Pyramid of Egypt, the Manhattan Project, the international space station, the Chunnel, and the development of Product X—all have something in common with each other and with every other undertaking of human organizations: they all require, in a word, *management.* Certainly the resources, work tasks, and goals of these projects vary greatly; yet without management, none of them could happen. Project management is a special kind of management. This chapter contrasts project and nonproject management and looks at the variety of ways and places where project management is used. It also serves as an introduction to the concepts and topics of later chapters.

2.1 FUNCTIONS AND VIEWPOINTS OF MANAGEMENT[1]

The role of management is to integrate resources and tasks to achieve organizational goals. Although the specific responsibilities of managers vary greatly, all managers—whether they are corporate presidents, agency directors, line managers, school administrators, movie producers, or project managers—have this same role.

Management Functions

The activities of a manager can be classified into the five functions identified in Figure 2-1. First, the manager decides what has to be done; this is the *planning* function. It involves setting organizational goals and establishing means for achieving them consistent with available resources and forces in the environment.

Second, the manager decides how the work will be accomplished; this is the *organizing* function. In this function, the manager (1) hires, trains, and assembles people into a system of authority, responsibility, and accountability relationships; (2) acquires and allocates facilities, materials, capital, and other resources;

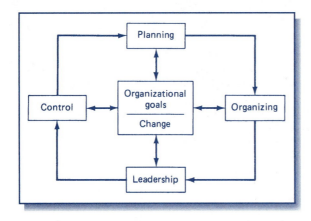

Figure 2-1
The functions of
management.

and (3) creates an organization structure that includes policies, procedures, reporting patterns, and communication channels.

Third, the manager directs and motivates people to attain objectives; this is the *leadership* function. In this function, the manager focuses on workers, groups, and their relationships to influence work performance and behavior.

Fourth, the manager evaluates performance with respect to standards of efficiency and effectiveness and takes necessary corrective action; this is the *control* function. For effective control, the manager relies upon an information system to collect data and report progress with respect to costs, schedules, and specifications.

All four functions are performed to accomplish organizational goals. This implies a fifth function: assessment of the four functions to determine where *change* is needed. The change function recognizes that organizations are open systems (discussed in Chapter 3) and that goals and activities must be adapted to changing forces in the internal and external environment.

On a day-by-day basis, managers rarely perform the functions in Figure 2-1 in strict sequence. Although planning should precede the others, there is always a need to organize activities, direct people, and evaluate work, regardless of sequence. Managers constantly face change, which means that plans, activities, performance standards, and leadership styles must change also. Managers oversee a variety of work tasks simultaneously, and for each one they must be able to exercise any of these functions at a given time.

Different managers' jobs carry varying responsibilities depending on the functional area and managerial level of the job. Some managers devote most of their time to planning and organizing, others to controlling, and others to directing and motivating.

In short, no process or set of prescriptive management functions seems to apply equally well in all cases. Managers must adapt to the situation. This is the modern *contingency viewpoint* of management.

Viewpoints of Management[2]

The current viewpoint about how to manage organizations is but the latest in an evolving series of management propositions and methodologies. The earliest, called the *classical* viewpoint, originated at the start of the 20th century. This held that there was one *best way* to manage with a corresponding set of universal bureaucratic and scientific management principles that applied to all situations. The classical viewpoint established formal principles for planning, organizing, leading, and controlling. In theory, the principles are useful for outlining the kinds of things managers should do. The drawback is that the principles presume much more order and rationality than actually exists in organizations, therefore they provide poor guidance about how managers should practice these principles in different situations.

The 1930s brought the *behavioral* viewpoint in which the emphasis shifted from work principles to the human and social aspects of organizations. One of the early proponents of this viewpoint, Elton Mayo, introduced the concept of "social man"—the worker who is motivated by social needs and relationships with others and is responsive to work group norms and pressures.[3] The contribution of this viewpoint is that it highlighted the importance of leadership style, group dynamics, and social environment, concepts never acknowledged by the classical theorists. The behaviorists, however, like their classical counterparts, tended to look at management rather narrowly. Human and organization behavior are more complex than they presumed, and many behaviorist theories concerning satisfaction, morale, and productivity are too simplistic to be of practical use. In the end, managers still have to rely on their own best judgment.

During World War II the third viewpoint, called the *systems approach,* was introduced. Whereas the first two viewpoints sought to simplify management through concepts that would fit all situations, the systems viewpoint acknowledges complexity and causal relationships. Simply stated, before the manager can prescribe action, she must first understand the system and its relationship with the environment. Rather than give a new set of rote prescriptions about how to manage, the approach suggested ways to understand the elements and dynamics of a situation, and models to help clarify problems and identify courses of action. But even these models were not a panacea. They could not always be relied upon to tell the manager what to do because they could not adequately represent "nonquantifiables" such as human motivations, emotions, and values. Even the systems viewpoint must eventually be supplemented by the judgment of the manager. The systems viewpoint is discussed further in the next chapter.

All three viewpoints represent different perspectives, all make valuable contributions to management theory and practice, and all have limitations. The current *contingency* viewpoint recognizes that none of them alone can guide a manager in all aspects of the job in every situation. The current viewpoint, which includes ideas like situational leadership[4] and the contingency approach to management,[5] stresses that all three views can be applied independently or in some combination, *depending upon the situation.*

The contingency viewpoint suggests that for management practice to be effective, it must be consistent with the requirements of the environment, the tasks to be performed, and the people who perform them. A manager should be familiar with the concepts of the three earlier viewpoints, be able to understand and diagnose each situation, and then choose the most appropriate mix of procedures, leadership styles, and management functions. The contingency viewpoint does not provide solutions to what works in all situations, but does suggest what tends to work best in specific cases.

2.2 PROJECT VIEWPOINT VERSUS TRADITIONAL MANAGEMENT

The practice of project management pays attention to goal-oriented systems, subsystems, their relationships, and environment; this is what makes project management a "systems approach" to management. Nonetheless, project management also relies heavily upon elements of the classical and behavioral viewpoints. It is, in fact, a good example of the contingency approach because it is a management philosophy and methodology oriented toward effective accomplishment of just one type of undertaking—projects.

Characteristics of Projects

Almost universally, the traditional organization has been structured as a pyramidal hierarchy with vertical superior-subordinate relationships and departmentation along functional, product, or geographic boundaries. Authority flows down from the highest level to the lowest level, and formal communication is similarly directed downward along the chain-of-command. The functional units are highly specialized and tend to operate independently. Although these traditional, functional organizations become very efficient in what they do and are often well-suited for work in stable environments (i.e., turning out a uniform product in an unchanging market), they tend to be rigid and, thus, unsuitable for performing work that is unique or requires adaptation to unstable and dynamic environments that characterize project situations. We will elaborate on this in Chapter 14.

A project was defined in Chapter 1 as[6]

1. Involving a single, definable purpose or end-item (product or result). The purpose is specified in terms of cost, schedule, and performance requirements. Purpose and end-item change from project to project.
2. Unique. A project requires doing things differently than before. A project is a one-of-a-kind activity, never to be exactly repeated.
3. A temporary activity. It is undertaken to accomplish a goal within a given period of time; once the goal is achieved, the project ceases to exist.
4. Utilizing skills and talents from multiple professions and organizations. A project often requires multiple skills that rely on task interdependencies which may introduce new and unique problems. Tasks and skill requirements change from project to project.
5. Possibly unfamiliar. It may encompass new ideas, approaches, or technology and possess elements of significant uncertainty and risk.
6. There is something at stake. Failure of the project might jeopardize the organization or its goals.
7. The *process* of working to achieve a goal. A project passes through several distinct phases; tasks, people, organizations, and resources change as the project moves from one phase to the next.

While a particular project might not have all of these characteristics, most have the first three or four of them.

The characteristics that distinguish projects make it necessary to employ a kind of management suitable just for them—thus the emergence of project management.

Characteristics of Project Management

Applying the principles from the classical, behavioral, and systems viewpoints to the unique requirements of projects has led to another set of concepts, the "project viewpoint." This viewpoint has evolved to include new management roles, techniques, and organizational forms. It embodies the following characteristics:[7]

1. A single person, the project manager, heads the project organization and operates independent of the normal chain-of-command. This organization reflects the cross-functional, goal-oriented, temporary nature of the project.
2. The project manager is *the* focal point for bringing together all efforts toward a single project objective.
3. Because each project requires a variety of skills and resources, the actual work might be performed by people from different functional areas or by outside contractors.

4. The project manager is responsible for integrating people from different functional disciplines working on the project.

5. The project manager negotiates directly with functional managers for support. Functional managers are responsible for individual work tasks and personnel within the project; the project manager is responsible for integrating and overseeing the start and completion of activities.

6. The project focuses on delivering a particular product or service at a certain time and cost and to the satisfaction of technical requirements. In contrast, functional units must maintain an ongoing pool of resources to support organizational goals. As a result, conflict may exist between the project and functional managers over the time and talent to be allotted to a project.

7. A project might have two chains-of-command—one vertical and functional, one horizontal and project—and people might report to both the project manager and a functional manager. (There are, of course, problems with this. These are discussed in Chapter 14.)

8. Decision making, accountability, outcomes, and rewards are shared among members of the project team and supporting functional units.

9. Though the project organization is temporary, the functional or subcontracting units from which it is formed are permanent. When a project ends, the project organization is disbanded and people return to their functional or subcontracting units, or are reassigned to new projects.

10. Projects can originate at different places inside or outside the organization. Product development and related projects tend to emerge from marketing, whereas technological applications originate from R&D, and so on.

11. Project management sets into motion numerous other support functions such as personnel evaluation, accounting, procurement, and information systems.

Because projects involve the efforts of different units from within and outside the organization, reliance upon the vertical chain-of-command for authority and communication is time-consuming and causes frequent disruption and delay of work. To get the job done efficiently, managers and workers in different units and at different levels need to associate directly with each other. Even in traditional organizations, the formal lines of communication and authority are frequently bypassed by *informal* lines to cut through red tape and expedite work. In project organizations, the virtue of these informal lines is recognized and formalized through the creation of a *horizontal hierarchy* that augments the vertical hierarchy. This hybrid organizational form enables personnel in different work units to form highly integrated project groups.

Traditional organizations have rigid, unchanging structures and cannot quickly adjust to change. Given the temporary nature of projects, an organization that works on a stream of projects must be flexible and able to alter its structure and resources to meet the shifting requirements of different projects.

Managers in traditional organizations tend to be specialized and have responsibility for a single functional unit or department. This works well for optimizing the efficiency of individual departments, but when projects need the support of many departments there is no one person accountable or responsible for the project's goals. Therefore a project manager is assigned responsibility and is held accountable for the project. This emphasis on project goals versus functional goals is a major distinguishing feature between roles of project and functional managers.

Project managers often depend upon people who are not "under" them but who are "assigned" to them from other parts of the organization as needed. Thus, the task of project managers is more complicated and diverse than for other types of managers.

Project managers must use diplomacy, worker participation, and conflict resolution skills to be effective leaders, but must function without the convenience of a staff that reports to them on a regular basis.

Example 1: Project Management in Construction

Construction projects are often in the news because of problems owing to cost overruns or schedule slippages. Although many factors are cited, such as labor union problems, materials shortages, or inflation, the real cause is frequently poor management and lack of control. The manager of construction projects is usually either the architect or the contractor. This works on small, less complex jobs, but on big construction jobs it is a bad arrangement because architects and contractors each represent the interests of separate "functional areas." When things go wrong and arguments arise, both tend to be self-serving; there is no one who is impartial and can reconcile differences

A better arrangement is when the developer or the building owner appoints an independent construction project manager. The project manager is the owner's agent during the entire design and construction process. The role is similar to that of the ancient master builders whose responsibility covered virtually all aspects of design and construction. This is shown in Figure 2-2. Notice the project manager's central position in the organization. This position enables her to monitor and coordinate all design and building tasks in accordance with the developer's goals. The project manager ensures that the architect's designs are within the developer's cost allowances and building requirements and that the contractor's work is executed according to contract specifications and at a fair price. The project manager is involved throughout the project life cycle: he or she oversees preliminary architectural design, does the subcontracting, and controls site work according to design specification, time, cost, and worker safety.

Several more examples of projects and project managers are described near the end of this chapter.

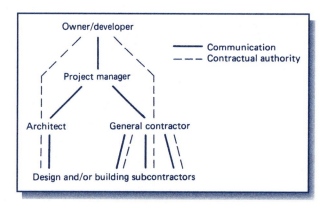

Figure 2-2
The project manager in a construction project.

2.3   EVOLUTION OF PROJECT MANAGEMENT

History

No single individual or industry can be credited with the idea of project management. It is often associated with the early missile and space programs of the 1960s, but clearly its origins go back much earlier. Techniques of project management probably first appeared in the major construction works of antiquity, such as the Pyramids, the Roman aqueducts, and the Great Wall of China. Later, these techniques were improved and modified for usage on other forms of construction projects, such as shipbuilding. The commonality among construction works is that they all require special organizations, labor, facilities, and material resources just for the purpose of doing one job.

Traditional, nonproject management practices work well for high-volume, standardized products, but they are often inefficient on large nonstandard jobs such as production and installation of specialized machinery and tools. Starting in the early twentieth century, industrial managers found that techniques used in construction could also be used for large-scale, nonconstruction "product development" jobs. At the same time, improved techniques for planning were being developed. During World War I, a new production scheduling and monitoring tool called the *Gantt chart* was introduced (examples are in Chapter 6); about 30 years later, the first network-type display for describing industrial processes, called a *process flow diagram*, was developed (see, for example, Figure 5-4). Both are widely used today.

By the 1950s, the size and complexity of many projects had increased so much that even these techniques proved inadequate. In particular, large-scale weapons systems projects—aircraft, missiles, communication systems, naval vessels—were becoming so complex that they defied all existing methods to logically plan and control them. Repeatedly these projects suffered enormous cost and schedule overruns. To grapple with the problem, two new network-based planning and control methods were developed, one by the Navy in 1958 called *PERT,* and the other by DuPont Corporation in 1957 called *CPM.* Both methods (described later in Chapter 8) had originated exclusively for planning, scheduling, and controlling large projects having numerous interrelated work activities. A decade later, these methods were combined with computer simulation in a method called *GERT* to permit more realistic analysis of schedules.

By the mid-1950s, the wide-scale development and installation of computerized data processing systems provided increased capability for handling the immense amount of information necessary to manage large-scale projects. Network methods were refined to integrate project cost accounting with project scheduling. These techniques came into widespread usage in the 1960s when the federal government mandated the use of network scheduling/costing methods, called cost schedule control systems (C/SCS), first with Department of Defense and NASA contracts, then with other large-scale efforts such as nuclear power plants. These methods enabled integrated tracking of costs and project schedules.

Throughout the 1960s, additional methods emerged to help project planners. Some enabled managers to specify the type and quantity of resources needed for each activity in a project, and to plan for and allocate resources among several projects simultaneously. Although the concept had been around for over a decade, it was in the 1970s that the *earned value* concept for planning and tracking came into widespread usage. This concept led to performance measurement systems which kept track of not only expenditures, but also the percentage of work completed. This led to more reliable forecasting of final project costs and completion dates.

The last three decades of the twentieth century witnessed the increased computerization of project management. Initially, project planning and tracking systems were available only for large mainframe computers, then later only for mini's. Most of these systems required investments of $10,000 to $100,000. The cost and size of the organizations needed to operate these systems precluded their usage in all but the largest projects. This all changed in the 1980s with the appearance of the personal computer. Today a large variety of quality project management software programs are available to expand the planning and control capabilities of managers for even the tiniest projects. Relatively low-cost software—between $100 and $2000—makes it possible to apply modern techniques for scheduling, costing, resource planning, performance analysis, and forecasting to virtually all small and medium-sized projects. Some of this software is described in Chapter 12 and elsewhere in this book.

Associated with the development of project planning and control methods was the evolution of project organizational forms and the role of project manager. Project management as a distinct organizational form was not recognized until World War II. In the urgency to develop and deliver sophisticated weapons (such as the atomic bomb) and organize massive task forces (such as the Normandy Invasion), pure project forms of organization evolved. In 1961, IBM became one of the first companies to formally use the project manager role in commercial industry; there, project managers (called "systems managers") were given broad responsibility across functional lines to oversee development and installation of computer models.

Types of Project Managers

In 1962, in one of the first discussions of how project management had evolved, Davis identified four types of project management organization.[8] He noted that organizations tend to evolve from one type to the next as they become more sophisticated and their problems become more complex. Although the correspondence is not exact, Davis' classification can be used to introduce the four types of project managers.

- *Project expeditors.* They are individuals who speed up work and are the communication link to the general manager. Their purpose is to achieve *unity of communications.* They are not really managers, but rather serve as translators of technical concepts into business concepts of costs, schedules, and markets. Because their role is limited to funneling information to executives and making suggestions, the expeditor role is restricted to smaller projects with low risk and little at stake.

- *Project coordinator.* Their purpose is to achieve *unity of control* over project activities. They have authority to control project matters and disburse funds from the budget, but have no actual line authority over workers. Their authority derives primarily through their association with upper-level executives. The construction project manager in Figure 2-2, for example, would be in this position if he coordinated the work but needed the approval of the developer for major decisions such as contracting or reallocation of funds.

- *Matrix managers.* They perform the full range of management functions. Although they serve the same purpose as the first two, they also have authority to plan, motivate, direct, and control project work. Their purpose is to achieve *unity of direction.* Matrix managers direct people located administratively in other, functional departments, and the resulting crisscross pattern of vertical-functional and horizontal-project reporting relationships create what is called a *matrix organization.* The manager of a construction project who is employed by the same company that is both designing and constructing the building is such a manager. She must rely upon managers in the architectural and construction departments for the assignment of personnel to her project. These personnel report to the project manager only in regard to the project and for as long as they are needed on the project; otherwise, they report to their respective department managers. The same personnel may also work on other projects and report to other matrix project managers.

- *Pure project managers.* They direct *pure project* organizations of people who report directly to them. Their purpose is to achieve *unity of command.* These managers are primarily integrators and generalists rather than technical specialists. They must balance technical factors with schedules, costs, resources, and human factors. In the course of a project, they actively deal with top management, functional managers, vendors, customers, and subcontractors. The manager of a large construction project for example, whom the developer has hired and delegated the power to make major decisions (such as letting contracts for architects and builders, or cancelling them) has this role.

Although the last two types are most in keeping with the project management concept, the other two are just as widely found. All four will be discussed further in later chapters.

2.4 WHERE IS PROJECT MANAGEMENT APPROPRIATE?[9]

Project management originated in construction and aerospace because the environments and kinds of activities in those industries demand flexible forms of management. But what about other industries and other environments? Certainly there must be many applications of project management beyond the familiar ones cited. In fact, project management is now used almost everywhere, and there are relatively few industries or situations where project management is not being applied or applicable at least some of the time. This section identifies conditions and situations where it is more applicable (or essential) to use a project-type organization instead of a traditional, functional organization.

Project management can be applied to any ad hoc undertaking. As Figure 1-3 in Chapter 1 showed, "ad hoc undertaking" includes a broad range of activities, such as writing a term paper, remodeling a kitchen, fundraising, or constructing a theme park such as Walt Disney's Epcot center. Some of these undertakings are more appropriate for project management than others. Generally, there are two conditions suggesting when project management should be used: first, the more unfamiliar or unique the undertaking, the greater the need for project management to ensure nothing gets overlooked; second, the more numerous, interdisciplinary, and interdependent the activities in the undertaking, the greater the need for a project manager to ensure everything is coordinated, integrated, and completed.

Frequently, customers such as major corporations or the U.S. government request or require project management because they believe it offers better cost, schedule, and quality control, and they prefer having a single point of contact—the project manager—to deal with. In most cases, however, the contractor has the option of deciding when to use project management. In some cases, project management is inappropriate simply because the nature of the work does not require it, or the effort to implement it would exceed the effort of the undertaking itself.

Criteria

Cleland and King suggest five general criteria to help decide when to use project management techniques and organization:[10]

1. Unfamiliarity

By definition, a project is something different from the ordinary and routine. A project always requires that different things be done, that the same things be done differently, or both. For example, minor changes in products, such as annual automobile design changes, can usually be accomplished without setting up a project team. Modernizing a plant, on the other hand, calls for nonroutine efforts such as revising the facilities hardware and software, replacing equipment, retraining employees, and altering policies and work procedures. So does a corporate relocation or installation of a new employee benefits system. Project management would be needed to plan and coordinate these one-of-a-kind undertakings.

2.   Magnitude of the Effort

When a job requires substantially more resources (people, capital, equipment, etc.) than are normally employed by a department or organization, project management techniques may be necessary. Examples include such undertakings as facility relocation, merging two corporations, or developing and placing a new product on the market. Even when the job lies primarily in the realm of one functional area, the task of coordinating its work with other functional areas might be overwhelming. For example, a corporate software installation might seem to fall within the single functional area of information systems, yet during the course of the project, there will be a continuous meshing of policies, procedures, and resources of all departments affected by the installation. Hundreds of people may be involved, and the required coordination and integration might be more than any one area can tackle.

3.   Changing Environment

Many organizations exist in environments that are rapidly changing. Examples include so-called "high-tech" industries such as computers, electronics, pharmaceuticals, and communications. The environment of these industries is characterized by high innovation, rapid product changes, and shifting markets and consumer behavior. Other industries, such as chemicals, biotechnology, and aerospace, though less volatile, also have highly competitive and dynamic environments. Changing environments present new opportunities that organizations must move swiftly to capture. To survive and succeed, organizations must be creative, innovative, flexible, and capable of rapid response. Project management provides the flexibility and diversity needed to deal with changing goals and new opportunities.

4.   Interrelatedness

Functional areas are sometimes self-serving and work at cross-purposes. When a joint effort is required, project management builds lateral relationships between areas to expedite work and reconcile the conflicts inherent in multifunctional undertakings. The project manager links together and coordinates the efforts of areas within the parent organization as well as those of outside subcontractors, vendors, and customers.

5.   Reputation of the Organization

The risk of the undertaking may determine the need for project management. If failure to satisfactorily complete the project will result in financial ruin, loss of market share, a damaged reputation, or loss of future contracts, there is a strong case for project management. Project management cannot guarantee that any of these will not happen but it does provide better planning and control to improve the odds. The likelihood for successfully completing any activity is increased when a single competent individual is assigned responsibility for overseeing it. The project manager, with the assistance of a technical support group, can do much to reduce the risks inherent in large, complex undertakings.

Where Project Management Is Not Appropriate

The obverse of all of this is that the more familiar the undertaking, the more stable the environment, the less unique and more standardized the end-item, and the lower the stake in any one particular output, the less the need for project management. Production of standardized industrial and agricultural outputs, for example, is generally much more efficiently managed by continuous or lot-size planning and control procedures than by project management. This is because for standardized, repetitive operations, there is greater certainty in the process and outcome, and standardized means of production are well-suited.

2.5 PROJECT MANAGEMENT: A COMMON APPROACH IN EVERYDAY BUSINESS

Though not appropriate for managing every situation, or even every kind of project, project management does apply to a great many situations. It is not only in large-scale, infrequent undertakings that project management applies; it is in all kinds of smaller, more frequent activities as well. As long as the activities are directed to somewhat different, unfamiliar goals that require cooperation from several parties, project management might be appropriate.

For example, consultants in any industry perform work on a project-by-project basis, and whenever these projects call for coordinated participation of several groups, project management applies. The more people or groups involved, the more disparate their tasks and the greater need for coordination, the greater the applicability.

Similarly, any group that works on the development or implementation of anything new (product, system, or service) also works on a project-by-project basis and, again, warrants project management. The larger, riskier, more complex, costly, innovative, or different the thing that is under development or being implemented, the more applicable project management becomes.

Further, any group that performs unique work on a *client-by-client basis* (so-called made-to-order, or made-to-engineer) also performs project work; if the end-item requires coordinated efforts from different parties, project management usually applies.

Think about these various situations for a moment and you will start to realize the many specific cases where project management occurs, or can be appropriately applied.

Managing any kind of work as a discrete project activity is referred to as "managing by project," or MBP.[11] With MBP, an undertaking or set of activities is planned and managed as if it was a project. In particular, MBP implies that the undertaking will have a well-defined scope, a completion date, a budget for the cost of required resources, firm requirements for the objective or end-result, and be reviewed for progress and final results. A project leader, or team leader, is assigned to guide and coordinate the work of a team that is formed for the sole purpose of performing the work. For a large project, top management is kept apprised of progress and may intervene to modify plans and resource allocations. Work progress is carefully tracked and compared to the project plan to assess performance in terms of end results, schedules, and costs. Small jobs can also be done using MBP; however, the team will be small and so will the involvement of top management.

At some time, all organizations use project approaches. Even in stable repetitive industries, small informal projects involving a few individuals are always in progress: New machines are installed, old ones are repaired; the office is remodeled; the cafeteria is relocated. It is only when larger or more special undertakings arise, such as company mergers, major equipment installations, or a company move, that a more formalized project group is formed.

Example 2: Renovating the Statue of Liberty[12]

Ninety-five years after the Statue of Liberty was presented to the American people, its surface and interior structure had become so badly corroded that it was judged structurally unsound. To oversee restoration of the statue and other buildings on Ellis Island, the U.S. Department of Interior established a foundation.

Renovation of the statue involved highly specialized skills, such as erection of scaffolding, construction of a new torch, building of windows for the crown, and replacement of the interior framework, expertise that tends to be found in smaller firms. As a result, the work was accomplished by a legion of over 50 small businesses; many workers were immigrants or descendants of immigrants whom the statue welcomed to America. Very little of the work qualified as "standard."

There were myriad notable features about the job. The scaffolding surrounding the statue never touched it at any point. Constructed of hundreds of thousands of pieces of aluminum, it qualified for the *Guiness Book of World Records* as the largest free-standing scaffolding ever built. To renovate the statue's interior, 1,699 five-foot bars were painstakingly fashioned from 35,000 pounds of stainless steel, then individually installed. Around the crown 25 windows were replaced. Each was handcrafted and had to be treated as a project unto itself. To fashion an entirely new torch, French artisans practiced an ancient copper shaping technique. The project was truly a marriage of art and engineering.

The 30-month, $31 million renovation effort involved thousands of tasks performed by hundreds of people. Most of the tasks were nonroutine and interrelated, and all had to be completed within a tight budget and schedule—certainly the trappings of a situation requiring project management. Indeed, project management was employed and the project was a success. (The company responsible for managing the renovation is discussed in Chapter 16.)

Example 3: Relocation of Goman Publishing Company

Many companies, regardless of size (a headquarters for a multi-billion dollar corporation or a storefront family restaurant), at some point face the decision to relocate. Relocation requires planning and coordination of numerous tasks involving many individuals, departments, and outside contractors. It is a major event that, if done properly, can be an exciting and profitable experience; but, if done poorly, it can lead to financial loss or ruin. It also is representative of innumerable situations wherein a company must do something it does not ordinarily do.

Consider Goman Publishing, a company experiencing a typical event wherein its rapid growth would soon exceed the capacity of its current facility. The initial task of the relocation project was to decide between two options: buying land and constructing a new building, or leasing or buying an existing structure. After deciding to build from scratch, the next task involved selecting a site. The main selection criteria were purchase expense, distance from current location, prestige and size of the new location, and access to major highways. Next came the relocation planning, which had two major aspects: design and construction of the new facility, and the physical move, each involving numerous considerations. For example, Goman wanted to retain its current employees, so to maximize the new facility's appeal, Goman had to have an indoor employee parking area and a large, well-appointed cafeteria. Further, the relocation would have to be scheduled to minimize downtime and interruption of operations. Among the many move-related considerations, decisions regarding furniture procurement, special handling of computer equipment, movers, distribution of information to employees and clients about the move, and maintenance of corporate security were necessary.

To oversee the project and ensure that construction and the physical move went according to plan, Goman appointed a project manager and support staff. The project manager worked with architects and building contractors during the design and construction phases, and later, with moving contractors and representatives from functional departments who kept him abreast of problems and progress. Despite the scope and unfamiliarity of the project, Goman was able to complete both the construction and physical move according to schedule and within budget.

2.6   DIFFERENT FORMS OF PROJECT MANAGEMENT

Project management has been called different names, including systems management, task force management, team management, ad hoc management, matrix management, program management, and others. Regardless of name, all share two features: (1) a *project team* or project organization, created uniquely for the purpose of achieving a specific goal, and (2) a single person—the *project manager*—who is assigned responsibility for seeing that the goal is accomplished. Beyond these, features differ depending on the application.

The following sections highlight differences among the major forms of project management. In the first section, the term "basic" project management refers to what is meant when we say "project management;" in other words, the most commonly understood concept of project management. The others are project management variants or forms of management that are similar to project management.

Basic Project Management

The most common project approach places the project manager and functional managers on the same level so that both report to the same person. The project manager is given formal authority to plan, direct, organize, and control the project from start to finish. The project manager may work directly with any level of the organization in any functional area to accomplish project goals. He or she reports to the general manager and keeps the GM apprised of project status. Although sometimes the project manager has authority to demand resources such as personnel and facilities, more often he or she negotiates with functional managers for assignment of resources.

Basic project management is implemented in two widely used forms—pure project and matrix. In pure project management a complete, self-contained organization is created. Resources are inherent and do not have to be borrowed. In matrix management, the organization is created by using elements allocated from permanent functional units. The project must time share resources with other concurrent projects and with the functional areas from which they borrow. These two project management forms will be described further in Chapter 14 on project organizations.

Although often found in construction and high-technology, the potential for project management extends to smaller, nontechnical activities as well, including the arts and social sciences. Adams, Barndt, and Martin cite these examples where basic project management has yet to be applied:[13]

- Health, Education, and Welfare (HEW), performs much of its social work on the basis of grants allocated through state and local agencies to provide specific services. Associated with each grant are time, cost, and performance requirements; clearly these are project efforts, yet there is little use of project management techniques within HEW.

- When a large advertising firm conducts an advertising campaign it utilizes the support of marketing research, accounting, graphics, sales, and other units. Several projects are usually underway in different stages of their life cycles at any given time. There is much similarity between these operations and project management (and program management, mentioned next).

- A good deal of work performed in education development can be considered project work. Much of this work is funded by grants with target goals and cost and time constraints. The efforts of many educators and researchers must be coordinated—a task for which project management is ideally suited.

The common situations described in Section 2.5 would also employ basic project management.

Program Management

The term "program management" is often used interchangeably with project management due to the similarity between programs and projects: (1) both are defined in terms of goals or objectives about what must be accomplished; (2) both emphasize the time period over which goals or objectives are to be pursued; and (3) both require plans and budgets to be developed for accomplishing specific goals (and not vice versa as in many traditional operations). In short, both work toward a target specified in terms of a desired product or service output, a date of accomplishment, and a related budget.

For definition purposes in this book, programs and projects have technical differences. A program extends over a longer time horizon—5 or more years—and consists of several parallel or sequential work efforts that are coordinated toward program goals. The time scale for projects tends to be shorter, and projects are often the individual "work efforts" of a program. For example, an Urban Development program may include several shorter term projects such as housing rehab, job and skill training, and small business consulting assistance; a planetary exploration program may include projects for unmanned probes to Mars and one of its moons, Phobos, followed by a manned mission to Mars. (Actually, these projects might grow to become so large that they themselves would have to be set up as full-scale programs, such as the Apollo Lunar Program. The Manhattan Project was really a "program.")

Another distinction is that projects are oriented to producing and delivering a product or service, after which the project is dissolved. Though project contracts specify the end-item, cost, and delivery date, the operation of the end-item is someone else's responsibility. Contractors may be concerned about the quality of their products, but they are usually not responsible for maintaining them afterwards. Once the product or service is "out the door," it is up to program management to ensure that it is integrated with other outputs and remains operational for as long as needed. For example, several contractors might produce and deliver a satellite and its booster rocket, but someone else becomes responsible for launching the rocket and satellite, and then monitoring and operating the satellite once in orbit. Program management must arrange for launch support, ongoing satellite monitoring, and so on, so that overall program goals can be achieved.

Most of the concepts and approaches to project management also apply to the management of programs, though some have to be modified to deal with the larger magnitude of programs. For instance, many programs last too long for any one person to be held accountable from start to finish. Thus, the concept of project manager must be modified to include training and replacement to ensure that the role of program manager is occupied throughout the program's life cycle. Also, because programs are composed of teams from various projects, a program structure must be created to coordinate them. This structure is similar to (and overlays) the project structure. Contrast the structure of the typical weapons system development program shown in Figure 2-3 with the project management structure shown in Figure 1-5 in Chapter 1.

New Venture Management

Project management resembles a type of management used in consumer-oriented firms for generating new products or markets, particularly when the product is not well-defined. This is termed *new venture management*. A new venture management team is a team specially created to find new products or markets that fit the organization's specialized skills, capabilities, and resources. Once an idea is defined, the team may go on to design and develop the product, then determine the means for producing, marketing, and distributing it.

There are many similarities between project management groups and venture groups. For example, venture groups[14]

- Focus on a single unifying goal.
- Are multidisciplinary, with skilled experts and managers from various functional areas working together under a single head.

Figure 2-3
Typical aircraft weapons system development program.

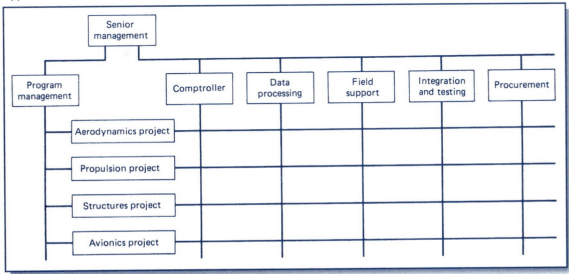

- Are action-oriented and dedicated to change.
- Are temporary. Once a venture group has completed its assignment, members go back to their original departments or to another venture group, or form a new division responsible for the newly developed product or line. The group may become a new division or split off from the parent organization to form a new company.

Product Management

When a single person is given the authority to oversee all aspects of a product's production scheduling, inventory, distribution, and sales, the term *product management* is used. The product manager coordinates and expedites efforts of product development launch, manufacturing, distribution, and sales to ensure uninterrupted flow of the product from its production to its delivery to the customer. Like the project manager, the product manager communicates directly with all levels and functions within and outside the organization. He coordinates the diverse objectives of various functional units so that the total effort is directed at the accomplishment of product goals. The product manager is active in managing conflicts and resolving problems that would degrade manufacturing capability, forestall distribution, alter price, hinder sales, or in any way affect financing, production, and marketing of the product.

For products with long life cycles, the product manager role is filled on a rotating basis. Outgoing product managers work briefly with new product managers, providing on-the-job training and apprenticeship to ensure smooth transition.

Ad Hoc Committees and Task Forces

For many projects, especially those of short duration, a temporary team is usually assembled within a functional department or as a separate organizational arm. These teams, called *task forces* or *interdepartmental committees,* are ad hoc committees with one project leader. (Toffler terms this phenomenon "ad-hocracy.")[15] Both the leader and members are selected by (and the leader reports directly to) the person responsible for the project—a functional manager, vice president, or CEO. Leaders are responsible for expediting and coordinating efforts and may have authority to direct tasks to certain individuals or units, or to contract work out. Usually though, they have little formal authority over team members. Often, team members are not relieved of their other responsibilities, so they must divide their efforts between committees and their "usual" work.

The variety of projects undertaken by ad hoc committees and task forces is unlimited. They include special purpose assignments such as:

Reorganizations
Mergers, acquisitions, or divestitures
Special studies, surveys, or evaluations
Major audits
Efficiency, modernization, and cost reduction efforts
Geographic or marketing expansions
Relocation of facilities or change in facility layout
Management and organization development programs
New equipment or procedures installation

The project team assigned to the corporate relocation in Example 3 is an interdepartmental task force with a full-time project manager.

Projects and project management vary depending on the environment. The environments of projects as classified by author Daniel Roman are: commercial/for profit, government/nonprofit, and military. All of the project forms described previously are found in the commercial environment, an environment wherein product and venture management are found almost exclusively. Program management, however, is most widely used in government and the military. As Roman describes it, there are significant differences in project management practice in these four environments:

Commercial/For Profit Project Management

In commercial projects, the end-item is a clearly defined product or service, often customized to satisfy a customer or an internal requirement. The motivation and success criteria in commercial projects are heavily profit-oriented. The project manager usually guides the project through its entire life cycle, coordinating efforts of the project team with functional areas, subcontractors, and vendors. The project manager maintains close contact with the customer and keeps top management informed of progress toward project and profit objectives.

Once the project has been completed, the group is dissolved and the project manager is out of a job. Thus, project managers are continually working to "perpetuate their existence" through seeking out additional projects and preparing proposals. New projects may be sought in extensions from existing work or in applications of technology developed in other projects.

Government and Nonprofit Project Management

Government and nonprofit projects differ from commercial activities in several ways. First, there is no profit incentive in government and nonprofit work, and economic factors may be of lesser importance in project management. Project managers in these environments are frequently reassigned during projects, which is problematic for administrative continuity. Particularly for government work, continuity of projects depends heavily upon political considerations because funding is legislatively appropriated.

Second, most projects focus on evaluation or testing of products or services because virtually all budgeted funds are spent on procurement of products and services developed by commercial vendors. Due to the fact that design and development work is performed by contractors, the project manager's role is largely administrative. The project manager has little control over technical matters, though he or she is responsible for checking on the contractors' progress. Project managers may oversee and coordinate multiple, related projects that are components of a larger system; in other words, they are program managers.

Military Project Management

Similar to government projects, most military projects involve testing and evaluating hardware developed by contractors. Evaluation is often based on the "weapons systems" approach whereby each project is part of a larger systems program and hardware is evaluated for its contribution to the mission of the overall system. The major criteria for evaluating projects are technical and political; costs are of lesser importance and profit is not a consideration. Project managers are military officers. Because their tour of duty is limited, officers typically do not oversee a project for its full life cycle. Thus the military must train, transfer, or promote people with the administrative and technical competence to carry on the job.

Civilians are often employed to provide technical support and managerial continuity. This arrangement is a source of strife because civilians are not subject to the same rotation of assignments and are often paid more, despite their formal "subordinate" status to military project managers.

Many organizations exist in multiple project environments (such as government/ military and commercial) and utilize a variety of management forms—project, program, matrix, task force and committee. Following are examples of actual projects in industry, the service sector, and the government.

2.8   PROJECT MANAGEMENT IN INDUSTRIAL SETTINGS

The following five cases show typical applications of project management in three industrial settings: product development, manufacturing, and construction. They are intended to portray the diversity in scope and size of typical project management situations in industry.

Product Management: The Development of Product X[17]

Company Alpha, described in Chapter 1, is a firm whose future depends on its ability to continuously develop and market new products. Company Alpha specializes in food and drink additives, but it is representative of all kinds of firms in industries such as pharmaceuticals, food products, biotechnology, home and commercial appliances, computer and entertainment electronics, communications, and numerous others that continuously need new ideas to survive in changing, highly competitive environments.

Company Alpha was concerned about maintaining market share for its products, especially for "Product N," a mainstay that accounted for the majority of its profits. It was known that other companies were developing substitutes for Product N that might be less expensive. To beat the competition, Company Alpha had to develop its own improved substitute, "Product X."

To facilitate the product development process, the company created a department called, appropriately, the New Product Development Department. The department is a "project office" responsible for ongoing management and coordination of this and future internal and external development projects so that successful ideas could be conceived and quickly brought to market. The department has three directors of product development, all of whom are project managers. Each is responsible for managing certain kinds of projects or portions of projects, such as exploration and development, technology-related new business, and new product commercialization. Each director typically manages more than one product. The role of the directors is to facilitate, coordinate, and monitor the efforts of the various departments—Research and Development, Applications Engineering, Marketing, Manufacturing, and Legal.

For each new product concept a project team is created with representatives from functional departments. A director works with the team on a weekly or daily basis to assess the project's progress and requirements. A director is also active in all phases of the project and has the final word over its direction, yet the functional managers make decisions about what is done and how, based on guidelines from upper management.

It is the duty of a director to know the status of the project at all times and convey this to upper management. Problems or delays are reported to upper management so that decisions can be made quickly to minimize losses. Projects showing severe problems or signs of failure are cancelled so resources can be allocated to more promising projects.

For the development of Product X, the following tasks were to be completed: R&D needed to develop a prototype of the product and prepare specifications; Applications Engineering needed to define where and in what ways the product can be used; Marketing needed to define the commercial market and determine how to establish a position in it (including packaging, brand name, advertising, and sales strategies); Manufacturing needed to develop a new, patentable process for making the product to prevent competitors from copying it; Finance needed to determine initial costing of the product, perform forecasts for profit/loss, and note changes to policies for large-scale production and marketing of the product; and Legal needed to obtain regulatory approval and perform patent research.

The director for Product X was involved in the product from its initiation. She worked with R&D scientists and marketing experts to determine the feasibility of the project and she was active in convincing upper management to approve it. She worked with scientists and managers to prepare project plans and schedules. When additional or new equipment, instruments, or raw materials were needed, she wrote requests for funds. When additional personnel were needed, she wrote personnel requests to upper management. In addition to issuing monthly and quarterly progress reports, she also scheduled and planned all project review meetings.

R&D Project Management: LogiCircuit Corporation[18]

Mr. Wilcox is the manager of the Solid State Engineering Department (SSE) of LogiCircuit Corporation. SSE is the firm's R&D support group and receives requests for projects from managers in every area of the corporation. One of Mr. Wilcox's responsibilities is to decide which requests are most urgent. In cases where the speed of completing a project is critical, he does not need to submit the usual cost/benefit analysis to his superiors before starting. Such was the case with a request from a manufacturing division that was experiencing severe quality problems in the production of printed circuit boards. The division had requested that a circuit tester be developed to examine the quality of thousands of components in each board. The request made it clear that a solution was needed quickly.

As with every project, Mr. Wilcox began by estimating the project's total cost. Two engineers "roughed out" a list of components and prepared estimates of how long it would take to do the development work. Mr. Wilcox then prepared cost estimates based upon the component parts list using standard, off-the-shelf prices along with the cost of an outside contractor to provide expertise that SSE did not possess. As in most projects, the greatest single expense was for direct labor hours. Mr. Wilcox estimated that the project would take 5 months.

Once SSE and the requesting division agreed to the problem definition, project cost, and duration, Mr. Wilcox sent requests for assistance to outside contractors. Often in high-technology industries, portions of a project require expertise that is too costly to maintain in-house and must be outsourced. In the circuit tester project, Harmon-Darwood Corp. was contracted to provide developmental assistance.

A project team was organized by Mr. Wilcox with members from SSE, Harmon-Darwood, and the manufacturing division. As project manager, Mr. Wilcox would oversee and coordinate the efforts of SSE with Harmon-Darwood and manufacturing.

All specifications for the tester unit were provided by manufacturing. The project plan called for building six testing units. Once the final design had been completed and the initial unit assembled and tested, the remaining five units would be assembled.

Because of the close cooperation and involvement of manufacturing with SSE and Harmon-Darwood during development, few problems were encountered during installation of the units at the plant. Harmon-Darwood trained the operating personnel on the use of the testers and Mr. Wilcox personally spent 2 weeks at the plant supervising the units' installation. Afterwards, SSE monitored the operation of the units for malfunctions and mistakes. Once it had been agreed that the units were working according to plan, the project was formally terminated by Mr. Wilcox and project personnel were transferred to other assignments.

This project is similar to many R&D projects because the company had no prior examples upon which to base estimates of project time and costs. Every R&D project is unique and, therefore, has to be estimated, planned, and organized from scratch. Although the tester project was accomplished close to its estimated budget and target completion date, it is not unusual for R&D projects to extend months or years beyond original estimates.

Installation Program: GTE Airfone[19]

GTE Airfone provides air-to-ground telephone systems to airlines. Most of its business requires back-of-seat telephone installation in aircraft. Each aircraft installation is unique and therefore considered a project. Timing of the installation is important and requires involvement from many departments within GTE Airfone (GTEAF), the airlines, and subcontractors. GTEAF provides phones at no cost and must remit a share of its call revenue to the airline. It has 11 airline customers, with phones currently installed on over 2,000 aircraft and over 1,500 more under contract to be installed.

A program management department manages the cross-functional groups to achieve schedule, financial, and quality goals. These functional groups include Airline Accounts, FAA Engineering, Seat Engineering, Aircraft Engineering, Operations, Marketing/Sales, Materials, and Product Support. The program manager resolves matters of design, specifications, and schedules for each airline. He or she interfaces with all customers, reviews progress with airline executive staff, and coordinates activities of all functional areas involved in the installation process.

Among the tasks in phone installation are to gather data about the aircraft fleet and interior, document modifications for the FAA, determine the bill of materials and complete purchase requisitions, request price quotes from outside seat installation subcontractors, select the subcontractor, monitor installation, and inspect and test each seat phone unit after installation. Data is gathered for each aircraft to determine the appropriate seatback/cell-phone design. The design must be approved by airline engineers, and a prototype seat (actual working model of a seat modified with a phone) must be constructed and tested. Following tests and approval of the prototype unit, full production of the modified seats is ordered. Outside contractors perform the modification, which is monitored for conformance to GTE standards and airline and FAA requirements for aircraft interiors.

The scheduling for each installation is done by an airline accounts manager, who also takes responsibility for overseeing the installation and keeping it on schedule (hence, he is the project manager for each aircraft installation). Each aircraft installation is supposed to take 4 hours, but sometimes airlines change requirements or do not have the planes ready for installation. Each plane has a slightly different design and seat configuration, and changing requirements or planes on short notice creates problems that the program and accounts managers must resolve.

Ad Hoc Project: R.L. Zept Company[20]

The R.L. Zept Company manufacturers motorized carts and forklift trucks. During a particular growth period, its management faced two problems: (1) production volume had grown to where its existing three-story plant and warehouse were inadequate; (2) how to handle the addition of a new product, called the "Mohac," to their existing line. They decided to undertake an "expansion project" to build a new facility next to the existing plant which could be used both to increase production capacity and to manufacture the Mohac.

The company president called a staff meeting with members from sales, finance, manufacturing, engineering, and accounting to generate ideas about the initiation and execution of the proposed expansion project. At the meeting, the major tasks of the project were defined. They included

- Facilities: Review existing facilities for obsolescence and replacement value; evaluate equipment needed for expansion, competitive equipment prices, trends in equipment development, and advanced manufacturing techniques; determine the relationship between equipment needs and facilities planning.

- Product development: Review the Mohac concept and prepare a development plan for building prototype models, obtain production materials, and set up production.

- Standardization: Revise existing product lines into a standard configuration to which accessories could be added.

- Simplification: Eliminate components and different parts from existing lines to simplify production and reduce inventory investment.

- Labor: Determine the effect of product changes on labor; review shift from semi-skilled to skilled labor; investigate replacing labor with automated equipment.

- Purchasing: Analyze suppliers for quality, fair prices, and prompt delivery.

- Training: Evaluate labor and supervisory training programs; consider wage scales, quality of product and line management, and employee relations.

- Systems planning: Engineer and integrate components and subassemblies for overall design; review information flow necessary for successful company operation.

- Inventories: Determine levels necessary to meet policy and service goals; establish ways to reduce and maintain required inventory level.

Some of the tasks had to be started immediately to determine whether the project was feasible, so the president appointed a project manager to coordinate the activities on the list. The first step was a study and product survey, after which management concluded that the expansion was necessary and the new product development feasible. The project manager then prepared a 6-year plan encompassing the facility expansion and simultaneous development of the new product, in which first shipments were scheduled for midway in the sixth year.

The case illustrates an undertaking which clearly mandates project management. The uniqueness of the project and the scope and magnitude of the effort defined by the list of tasks was unprecedented for the company. Most of the tasks were interrelated, and many required long lead times. Given the complexity, risks, scope, and time involved, it was necessary to appoint one person—a project manager—to plan, coordinate, and direct the effort.

Although this is a somewhat large project, it is representative of all sizes and kinds of "ad hoc" projects—activities which have not been done before, but which suddenly become important to organizational goals and where the means must be found to accomplish them.

Project Management in Small Projects: Delamir Roofing Company

Delamir Roofing Company is in the business of installing and redoing roofs for factories and businesses. It performs work and maintains industrial contracts throughout the United States. Like other businesses associated with the construction industry, Delamir considers each job a project and uses project management to meet work goals.

A project manager is assigned overall responsibility for each job. When a request for work is received from a potential customer, the project manager examines the blueprints to determine how much material and labor time will be needed. (This is called "prepping the job.") He then prepares a budget and drafts a short proposal. After a contract is acquired, the project manager goes to the site ahead of the rest of the crew to make arrangements and accommodations for work to begin. The project manager has discretion in selecting a work crew, dependent upon how many workers are needed and who is available. After work begins, he is responsible not only for supervision of work and delivery of supplies, but for maintaining budget records and reporting progress to the home office. The project manager performs the final inspection with the customer and signs off when the job is completed.

In this example, the project manager ensures that the size and skills of the crew fit the requirements of the job, and that overall, the job is done well.

2.9 PROJECT MANAGEMENT IN THE SERVICE SECTOR[21]

Project management is no longer just a tool for industry. It is a form of management that is employed in a broad range of services, including banking, consulting, and accounting. The major difference between project management in industry and services is that the output of services is not necessarily a tangible product. In the next two examples from two large accounting firms—fictitiously called CPAone and CPAtwo—project management is used to plan and control auditing and management consultation projects. A third example shows project management applied to a nonprofit fundraising campaign.

Improving Auditing Efficiency at CPAone

The auditing division at CPAone generates financial statements to meet generally accepted accounting principles. In large audits, the size of the task and the range of problems require the involvement of many people. In the audit of a national corporation, for example, numerous auditors with diverse specialties are required to investigate all aspects of the operation in various geographic areas. Given the number of people and the variety of skills, expertise, and personalities involved, a project manager is needed to oversee and conduct the audit efficiently. Every audit begins by assigning the client to a partner, usually someone who is familiar with the client's business. The partner becomes the audit's "project director" and is responsible for writing proposals, staffing the audit, delegating tasks, scheduling, and budgeting.

The project director begins by studying the client's income statement, balance sheet, and other financial statements. If the client has a bad financial reputation, the project director can make the decision for CPAone to refuse the audit. If the client is accepted, the director prepares a proposal that explains the general approach for conducting the audit and designates the completion date and the cost estimate.

In determining the general approach for conducting the audit, the project director considers the size of the company including the number of its departments. Auditors are then assigned on a department-by-department basis. The audit team is a pure project team, created anew for every audit, composed of people who have the skills best suited to the needs of the audit. Generally, each audit has one or two staff accountants, one or two senior accountants, and the project director. Before the proposal is even accepted, the director specifies who will be performing each task within a given time frame. Cost estimates are based on estimated labor hours multiplied by employees' hourly wages.

During the audit the project director must ensure that all work strictly adheres to the Book of Auditing Standards and is completed on schedule. Each week the client and project director meet to review progress. When problems cannot be solved immediately, the director may call in people for CPAone's tax or consulting divisions. When the team has trouble interpreting financial documents, the project director may request that the client's own personnel be involved.

Follow-up service may be provided after the audit is completed. Should the IRS request an examination, the project director sees to it that the client is represented.

Management Consulting at CPAtwo

CPAtwo, another large accounting firm, uses project management in its Management Consulting Division (MCD). Projects in the MCD are classified into seven areas: business planning, profit improvement, contract management, systems planning, data security, executive management, and human resources. Project management is used in all of these areas, though specific methods may vary.

In the systems planning area, for example, projects focus on determining the most efficient way for a firm to achieve objectives. Systems analysis methodology (described in Chapter 3) is applied to define system characteristics, evaluate potential benefits, and assign priorities for implementation. A typical project begins by first reviewing the client's present system. A proposal is written summarizing the findings and suggesting options for a new system. If the proposal is accepted, MCD management determines who will be working on the project, when it should be completed, and the cost. A partner or senior manager is assigned as project leader based on his familiarity with the client or the problem. From then on, the project leader has complete responsibility. He selects people from MCD to work on the project team. MCD regularly updates the skill records of employees to help project leaders select the people best qualified for a given project. The project leader then makes up schedules and determines costs based upon employee hourly rates and hours needed to complete the job.

When the division has sufficient internal expertise, a pure project organization of MCD personnel is formed; when it does not, a matrix form of project organization is used with other divisions supplying people with the necessary skills. The project leader plans, coordinates, schedules, and budgets project work, directs the team in project matters, and keeps MCD management informed of progress—much the same role as those of the project directors in CPAone, Alpha Company, and R.L. Zept.

Nonprofit Fund-raising Campaign Project: Archdiocese of Boston[22]

American Services Company, a fund-raising consulting firm for nonprofit organizations, was contracted by the Archdiocese of Boston to manage a 3-year campaign to raise $30 million for education, social and health care services, building renovations, and a retirement fund for clergy. American Services appointed a project manager to prepare the campaign strategy and to organize and direct the campaign staff. The project manager had to deal with issues concerning three groups: donors, the Archdiocese Board of Directors, and campaign volunteers. Potential target donors had to be identified and provided with evidence to show how their financial commitment would benefit the community and the Archdiocese; the board and church leadership had to be involved in and kept apprised of campaign planning and progress; and volunteers had to be identified, organized, and motivated.

One of the project manager's first tasks was to conduct a feasibility study to determine whether there was sufficient leadership capability, volunteer willingness, and "donor depth" within the Archdiocese community to achieve the $3 million goal. Following the study, which indicated that the goal was achievable, pastors were invited to a kick-off luncheon at which time the Cardinal of the Archdiocese introduced the campaign. During the meeting, influential church personnel were signed up and the process of identifying potential donors and volunteers was started.

The project manager provided guidance for establishing a campaign leadership team and project office, enlisting volunteers, forming campaign committees, and recruiting and training volunteers. In addition to procedural and organizational matters, the project manager also was responsible for motivating leaders and seeing that motivation filtered down to other volunteers. He convened several "reality sessions" with chairpersons to remind them of the importance of the campaign and renew their commitment to the campaign goal. He also organized frequent meetings with the volunteers to instill a sense of pride and involvement in the campaign.

2.10   PROJECT AND PROGRAM MANAGEMENT IN GOVERNMENT

The following two cases from the National Park Service and NASA illustrate how project management and program management (as distinguished earlier) are performed in joint government/commercial undertakings.

National Park Service and Friends of the Chicago River [23]

Friends of the Chicago River (FCR) is a nonprofit organization formed to increase awareness about the river's importance and create standards for development along the river and its principle branches. One of FCR's goals is to develop a plan to serve as a general model for clarifying and defining watershed management practices. To assist in studying and developing the plan, FCR called upon the National Park Service (NPS). The NPS provided assistance and funding for a feasibility and definition study of the plan. The study identified the main topics that would be covered by the plan, including achieving a better understanding of the river and its environs, educating policy makers and the public about the importance of watershed management, and specifying possible river-related projects and programs for the future. The last aspect included identification of projects for conservation, recreation, economic development, water quality, and government involvement. The study also cited other organizations to be involved in elements of the plan, including federal agencies such as the USDA Forest Service, U.S. Army Corps of Engineers, U.S. Fish and Wildlife Service, and the EPA, as well as state and local agencies such as the Illinois Department of Energy and the Metropolitan Water Reclamation District of Greater Chicago. Finally, the study also specified particular work activities and budgets for each of these participating organizations.

Needless to say, the broad scope and involvement of so many constituencies to accomplish the goals of the plan required project management. FCR intended to hire a coordinator to oversee the entire project and to work directly with an interagency team of members from NPS, the Fish and Wildlife Service, the Forest Service, and the Army Corps of Engineers. Each of the main activities of the plan was to be managed by a committee with representatives from the principle participating agencies and other constituencies. Activities that required cross-coordination and pooling of resources, and overall scheduling and budgeting would be managed by the project manager and an interagency team. An interagency agreement plan was prepared by the NPS stating work items and funding for each participating agency.

In this example, the FCR and interagency team manage the overall *program* and provide oversight of the numerous subtasks; each subtask is considered a *project* and has its own project manager and team.

NASA Organization and Project Management[24]

NASA was created in 1958 by absorbing the National Advisory Committee on Aeronautics (NACA). NACA had had a long, successful history of working intimately with researchers in universities, industry, and the military, and at NASA there remained a determination to continue a partnership-style of operation. NASA and industry would work closely together on technical problems, but technical initiative and technical decision would be left to NASA field installations.

NASA organization includes (1) top management, (2) functional support for top management, (3) program offices for developing and controlling major programs, and (4) field installations which conduct the programs and their components (on-site, at universities, or at contractors). In 1999, NASA was divided into six operating areas, or offices: Space Flight, Space Science, Aeronautics and Space Transportation Technology, Earth Science, Small and Disadvantaged Business Utilization, and Life and Microgravity Science Applications. NASA's organization is shown in Figure 2-4.

Each office is responsible for development, justification, and management of *programs*—activities which support broad NASA goals. Offices are assigned field installations which report to them for general management. Each field installation has the responsibility to carry out permanent activities in its specific area, but, still, it also carries out projects or tasks under the direction of other offices besides its own. For example, though Ames, Langley, Lewis, and Dryden Centers report to Aeronautics and Space Transportation Technology, all make substantial contributions to projects in Space Flight.

All four kinds of project managers described earlier—expediting, coordinating, matrix, and pure project—are found at NASA, but the latter two are the most common. The matrix is preferred for its efficient use of talent and flexibility. Employees are assigned to the project but remain on the payrolls of their parent organization

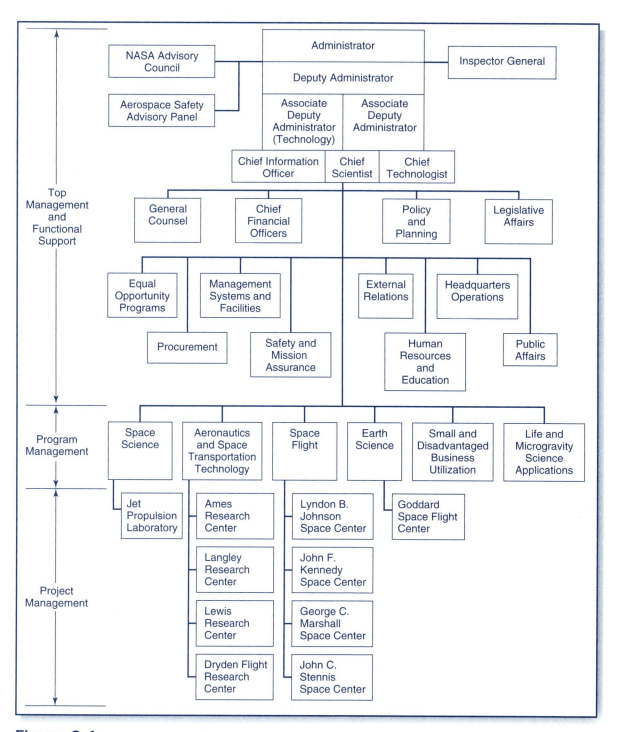

Figure 2-4
NASA program and organization chart, 1999.

and are subject to its merit reviews and promotions. Most stay in the offices of the parent organization. For the largest projects, however, the pure project form is used. It permits better control, quicker location of responsibility, quicker reaction from the project team, and simpler communication patterns. (Despite these advantages, the matrix and pure project forms do cause problems. These are discussed in Chapter 14.)

In a typical (non-NASA) government project, the agency prepares specifications for a program, lets a contract, then depends upon the contractor for results. NASA uses a different approach; they feel that no single company has all of the capability to execute a large space project. Although NASA relies upon industry to build, integrate, and test-flight hardware, it relies upon its own considerable in-house management and technical competence to monitor and work with contractors. Because NASA projects call for a diversity of technical and managerial competency, project management uses the philosophy of "participative responsibility" (discussed in Chapter 16)—an integration of technical and managerial competence in industry, academia, and NASA laboratories. Regardless of location, NASA brings in experts from its own field installations, from universities, and from other government laboratories to assist contractors in tackling difficult problems. This participative team approach avoids the delays caused by working across boundaries which separate government, commercial, and military organizations. The concept utilizes teamwork, central control, and decentralized execution, but respects the semiautonomous status of NASA's field installations.

NASA defines a *program* as a series of undertakings which over several years is designed to accomplish broad scientific or technical goals in NASA's long-range plan. Responsibility for programs is assigned by NASA headquarters. A *project* is an undertaking within a program with a scheduled beginning and end. It normally involves design, construction, or operation of specific hardware items and necessary support.

NASA uses a dual system of responsibility. Perhaps the single greatest contributor to a project's success is the person upon whom final responsibility rests, the *project manager*. He or she is the official responsible for executing the project within the guidelines and controls of NASA. The project director is responsible for day-to-day supervision, execution, and completion of projects, whether conducted by NASA, contractors, or university scientists. Although most of the workers on a project are outside of the administrative authority of the project manager, nonetheless they take directions *on project matters* from the project manager.

The project manager has a counterpart in Washington, the *program manager*, who represents the headquarters' interests. The program manager is the senior NASA staff official responsible for developing and administering the headquarters' guidelines and controls with respect to a given project. He or she must fight the battles for resource allocation within headquarters, monitor project execution, work with organizations participating in the project, relate the project to NASA's broader goals, and testify to or justify authorizations from Congress and the president. On large projects, the program manager might oversee just one project. The success of the project depends on these two people, the project and program manager, and on the quality of their relationship.

2.11 SUMMARY

This chapter addressed the question, "What is project management?" by describing the characteristics that distinguish projects, project environments, and project managers from nonproject forms of activities and managers. All managers "manage" tasks and resources: They translate organizational goals into specific objectives, prepare plans for the tasks and resources needed to achieve objectives, organize the resources, and direct, evaluate, and control work tasks and resources to ensure that objectives are met.

Project management is a systems/contingency approach to organization and management; it applies elements of classical and behavioral management and uses organizational forms and management roles best suited to the unique environment of projects.

The most important role in project management is that of the project manager. This person functions to unify project-related planning, communications, control, and direction to achieve project goals. The project manager is an integrator-generalist who ties together the efforts of functional areas, suppliers, and subcontractors, and keeps top management and the customer apprised of project progress. Project management includes the organizations, systems, and procedures that enable the project manager to perform this function.

Project management applies to any temporary, goal-oriented activity, but it becomes more essential as the magnitude, unfamiliarity, and stake of the undertaking increase. Organizations in rapidly changing environments especially need project management.

Project management takes on a variety of forms: larger efforts typically utilize pure project, matrix, and program management forms; smaller efforts are handled by ad hoc committees and task forces. New venture and product management forms used in consumer-oriented firms are similar to project management. Project management is applied in much the same way in commercial, nonprofit, government, and military projects, with variation to account for differences in the environments.

Project management has been called a "systems approach" to management. The next chapter describes what that means and discusses the systems philosophy and methodologies that underlie a large part of project management theory and practice.

REVIEW QUESTIONS

1. Describe the five functions of management. Are any of these not performed by managers? How do you think each of these functions comes into play in the course of a project?

2. Describe the classical and behavioral viewpoints of management and how they differ from the systems approach. The classical and behavioral viewpoints originated decades ago. Are they still of use today? (For a better idea of how the viewpoints differ and how the contingency approach is applied in general practice, refer to management references such as those cited in endnotes 1, 2, 4, and 5.)

3. Explain what distinguishes the contingency approach to management from the other three viewpoints.

4. List the main characteristics of "projects." How do these features distinguish projects from other, nonproject activities?

5. What are the characteristics of "project management?" Contrast these to functional and other types of nonproject management.

6. What makes project management more suitable to project environments than traditional management and organization?

7. Where did project management methods and organization originate? What happened during the twentieth century that made project management necessary?

8. What are the four types of project management roles? Describe the responsibilities and authority of managers in each role. Are all four roles ever used in the same organization?

9. What are the five criteria that Cleland and King suggest for determining when to use project management? From these, describe briefly how a manager should know when project management is appropriate for the task.

10. When is project management clearly not appropriate? List some "project-type" activities where you think project management should *not* be used. Describe some organizations or kinds of work where you think both project and non-project types of management are appropriate.

11. Briefly compare and contrast the following forms of project management: pure project, matrix, program, new venture, product, and ad hoc committee/task force. Give at least one illustration of an organization where each one is used.

12. What are some of the problems of being a project leader in commercial, government, and military projects? Where do organizations in these environments get project leaders?

13. In the industry, service sector, and government examples in this chapter, what common characteristics of the environment, the project goals, and the project tasks make project management appropriate (or necessary)? Also, what seem to be the common characteristics of the roles and responsibilities of the project managers in these examples? What are the differences?

14. Now that you know a little about projects and project management (with still a long way to go), list some government and private organizations where you think project management might be useful. You might want to check to see if, in fact, they *are* using project management.

QUESTIONS ABOUT THE STUDY PROJECT

1. In the project you are studying, what characteristics of the company, project goals, tasks, or necessary expertise make the use of project management appropriate or inappropriate? Consider the project size, complexity, risk, and other criteria in answering this question.

2. How does the project you are studying fit the definition of a project?

3. What kind of project management is used—program, product, matrix, pure, or other? Explain. Is it called "project management" or something else?

4. What kind of role does the project manager have—an expeditor, coordinator, pure project, or matrix manager? Explain. What is his or her title?

Case 2-1 *Disaster Recovery at Marshall Field's (Another Chicago River Story)*[25]

Early in the morning on April 13, 1992, basements in Chicago's downtown central business district began to flood. A hole the size of an automobile had developed between the river and an adjacent abandoned tunnel. The tunnel, built in the early 1900s for transporting coal, runs throughout the downtown area.

When the tunnel flooded, so did the basements connected to it, some 272 in all, including that of major retailer Marshall Field's.

The problem was first noted at 5:30 A.M. by a member of the Marshall Field's trouble desk who saw water pouring into the basement. The manager of maintenance was notified and immediately took charge. His first actions were to contact the Chicago Fire and Water Departments, and Marshall Field's parent company, Dayton Hudson in Minneapolis. Electricity—and with it all elevator, computer, communication, and security services for the 15-story building—would soon be lost. The building was evacuated and elevators were moved above basement levels. A command post was quickly established and a team formed from various departments such as facilities, security, human resources, public relations, and financial, legal, insurance, and support services. Later that day, members of Dayton Hudson's risk management group arrived from Minneapolis to take over coordinating the team's efforts. The team initially met twice a week to evaluate progress and make decisions and was slowly disbanded as the store recovered. The goal of the team was to ensure the safety of employees and customers, minimize flood damage, and resume normal operations as soon as possible. The team hoped to open the store to customers 1 week after the flood began.

An attempt was made to pump out the water; however, as long as the tunnel hole remained unrepaired, the Chicago River continued to pour into the basements. Thus, the basements remained flooded until the tunnel was sealed and the Army Corps of Engineers could give approval to start pumping. Everything in the second-level basement was a loss, including equipment for security, heating, ventilation, air-conditioning, fire sprin-kling, and mechanical services. Most merchandise in the first-level basement stockrooms also was lost.

Electricians worked around the clock to install emergency generators and restore lighting and elevator service. Additional security officers were hired. An emergency pumping system and new piping to the water sprinkling tank were installed so the sprinkler system could be reactivated. Measures were taken to monitor ventilation and air quality, and dehumidifiers and fans were installed to improve air quality. Within the week, inspectors from the City of Chicago and OSHA gave approval to reopen the store.

During this time, engineers had repaired the hole in the tunnel. After water was drained from the Marshall Field's basements, damaged merchandise was removed and sold to a salvager. The second basement had to be gutted to assure removal of contaminants. Salvageable machinery had to be disassembled and sanitized.

The extent of the damage was assessed and insurance claims filed. A construction company was hired to manage restoration of the damaged areas. Throughout the ordeal, the public relations department dealt with the media, being candid yet showing confidence in the recovery effort. Customers had to be assured that the store was safe and employees kept apprised of the recovery effort.

This case illustrates crisis management, an important aspect of which is having a team that moves fast to minimize losses and quickly recover damages. At the beginning of a disaster there is little time to plan, though companies and public agencies often have crisis guidelines for responding to emergency situations. Afterwards they then develop more specific, detailed plans to guide longer-term recovery efforts.

QUESTIONS

1. In what ways are the Marshall Field's flood disaster recovery effort a project? Why are large-scale disaster response and recovery efforts projects?
2. In what ways do the characteristics of crisis management as described in this case correspond to those of project management?
3. Who was (were) the project manager(s) and what was his or her (their) responsi-bility? Who was assigned to the project team and why were they on the team?
4. Comment on the appropriateness of using project management for managing disaster recovery efforts such as this.
5. What form of project management (basic, program, and so on) does this case most closely resemble?

Case 2-2 Flexible Benefits System Implementation at Quick Medical Center[26]

The management committee of Quick Medical Center wanted to reduce the cost and improve the value and service of its employee benefits coverage. To accomplish this it decided to procure and implement a new benefits system. The new system would have to meet four goals: improved responsiveness to employee needs, added benefits flexibility, better cost management, and greater coordination of human resource objectives with business strategies. A multifunctional team of 13 members was formed by selecting representatives of departments at Quick that would rely most on the new system—Human Resources (HR), Financial Systems (FS), and Information Services (IS). Representation from each department was important to assuring all departmental needs would be met. The team also included six technical experts from the software consulting firm of Hun and Bar Software (HBS).

Early in the project a workshop was held with team members from Quick and HBS to clarify and finalize project objectives and develop a project plan, milestones, and schedules. Project completion was set at 10 months. In that time HBS had to develop and supply all hardware and software for the new system; the system had to be brought on-line, tested, and approved; HR workers had to be trained how to operate the system and load existing employee data; all Quick employees had to be educated about and enrolled in the new benefits process; and the enrollment data had to be entered in the system.

The director of FS was chosen to oversee the project. She had a technical background and, prior to serving as director, had worked in the IS group where she assisted in implementing Quick's patient care information system. Everyone on the team approved of her appointment as project leader, and many team members had worked with her previously. Two team leaders were also selected, one each from HR and IS. The HR leader's task was to ensure that the new system met HR requirements and the needs of Quick employees, and the IS leader's task was to ensure that the new software interfaced with other Quick systems.

Members of the Quick team were committed to the project on a part-time basis. Roughly 50 percent of the time they worked on the project; the rest of the time they performed their normal daily duties. The project manager and team leaders also worked on the project part-time. When conflicts arose, the project took priority. Given specific performance requirements and time deadlines, the Quick top-management committee made it clear that successful project completion was imperative. The project manager was given authority over functional managers and project team members regarding all project-related decisions.

QUESTIONS

1. What form of project management (basic, program, and so on) does this case most closely resemble?
2. The project manager is also the director of FS, only one of the departments that will be affected by the new benefits system. Does this seem like a good idea? What are the pros and cons of her selection?
3. Comment on the team members' part-time assignment to the project and the expectation that they give the project top priority.
4. Much of the success of this project depends on the performance of team members who are not employed by Quick, namely the HBS consultants. They must develop the entire hardware/software benefits system. Why was an outside firm likely chosen for such an important part of the project? What difficulties might this pose to the project manager in meeting project goals?

1. Adapted from Andrew Szilagyi, *Management and Performance,* 2nd ed. (Glenview, IL: Scott, Foresman, 1984): 7–10, 16–20, 29–32.

2. For a comprehensive review of this topic, see Don Hellriegel and John Slocum, *Management,* 4th ed. (Reading, MA: Addison-Wesley, 1986): 25–64.

3. One of the earliest discussions of this viewpoint appeared in F. J. Roethlisberger and W. J. Dickson, *Management and the Worker* (Boston: Harvard University Press, 1939).

4. See, for example, Paul Hersey and Ken Blanchard, *Management of Organizational Behavior: Utilizing Human Resources,* 4th ed. (Upper Saddle River, NJ: Prentice Hall, 1982). This volume presents the "situational leadership" theory and applications.

5. See Don Hellriegel and John Slocum, "Organizational Design: A Contingency Approach," *Business Horizons* 16, no. 2 (1973): 59–68.

6. Russell D. Archibald, *Managing High-Technology Projects* (New York: Wiley, 1976): 19; Jack R. Meredith and Samuel Mantel, *Project Management: A Managerial Approach,* 3rd ed. (New York: Wiley, 1995): 7–9; Daniel D. Roman, *Managing Projects: A Systems Approach* (New York: Elsevier, 1986): 2–10; John M. Stewart, "Making Projects Management Work," *Business Horizons* 8, no. 3 (Fall 1965): 54–68.

7. David Cleland and William King, *Systems Analysis and Project Management,* 3rd ed. (New York: McGraw-Hill, 1983): 191–192.

8. Keith Davis, "The Role of Project Management in Scientific Manufacturing," *IEEE Transactions of Engineering Management* 9, no. 3 (1962): 109–113.

9. Portions of this section are adapted from Richard Johnson, Fremont Kast, and James Rosenzweig. *The Theory and Management of Systems,* 3rd ed. (New York: McGraw-Hill, 1973): 395–397.

10. Cleland and King, *Systems Analysis and Project Management,* 259.

11. Dick Sharad, "Management by Projects, and Ideological Breakthrough," *Project Management Journal* (March 1986): 61–63.

12. Based upon W. Hofer, "Lady Liberty's Business Army," *Nation's Business* (July 1983): 18–28.

13. John Adams, Stephen Barndt, and Martin Martin, *Managing by Project Management* (Dayton, OH: Universal Technology, 1979): 12–13.

14. Szilagyi, *Management and Performance,* 489–490.

15. Alvin Toffler, *Future Shock* (New York: Random House, 1970).

16. This section is adapted from Daniel Roman, *Managing Projects: A Systems Approach* (New York: Elsevier, 1986): 426–429, with the permission of the publisher.

17. Based upon information compiled by Jenny Harrison from interviews with managers in Company Alpha (fictitious name).

18. Based upon information compiled by Cary Morgan from interviews with managers of the LogiCircuit Corporation (fictitious name).

19. Information about this project contributed by Jim Pilcher, Jeff Abbott, Nicole Pontious, Daniel Post, and Melissa Prenger.

20. Adapted from a case in R. L. Janson, *Production Control Desk Book* (Upper Saddle River, NJ: Prentice Hall, 1978).

21. Based upon information compiled by Darlene Capodice from interviews with managers in two accounting firms.

22. Information about this project contributed by Daniel Molson, Mike Billish, May Cumba, Jesper Larson, Anne Lanagan, Madeleine Pember, and Diane Petrozzo.

23. Information about this project contributed by David Banta, Shehadeh Dides, Rachel Murdock, Agnes Rhodes-Rodriquez, and Michael Wood.

24. Portions of this section are adapted from Richard Chapman, *Project Management in NASA: The System and The Men* (Washington, D.C.: NASA SP–324, NTIS No. N75–15692, 1973).

25. Information about this case contributed by Jennifer Koziol, Sussan Arias, Linda Clausen, Gilbert Rogers, and Nidia Sakac. For interesting reading about crisis management following a different crisis, the 1993 bombing of the World Trade Center, see Frank Saladis, "Managing crisis: rebuilding Telecommunications at the World Trade Center," *Pmnetwork* (August 1993): 12–18.

26. Information about this case contributed by Debbie Tomczak, Bill Baginski, Terry Bradley, Brad Carlson, and Tom Delaney. Organizational names are fictitious but the case is factual.

Chapter 3

Systems, Organizations, and System Methodologies

There is so much talk about the system.
And so little understanding.

ROBERT M. PIRSIG
Zen and the Art of Motorcycle Maintenance

A project is a *system* of people, equipment, materials, and facilities organized and managed to achieve a goal. Much of the established theory and practice about what it takes to put together and coordinate project organizations comes from a perspective called "systems thinking" or the "systems approach." At the same time, work done in projects is often done for the purpose of *creating* systems. In projects, especially those in product and software development, engineering, or research in high-technology industries, methodologies such as "systems analysis," "systems engineering," and "systems management" are commonplace. This chapter introduces systems concepts that form the basis for project management and the systems methodologies used in project work.

3.1 SYSTEMS THINKING

Systems thinking is a way of viewing the world. It is the *opposite* of analytical thinking in which things are broken into progressively smaller parts and more highly specialized disciplines. Part of what distinguishes systems thinkers from analytical thinkers is that the former focus on "whole organisms" rather than just the parts. Even when they look at the parts, systems thinkers try to keep the whole organism in mind and attempt to understand the parts by understanding the processes taking place among them.[1]

Systems thinking means being able to perceive the "system" in a situation. It is the ability to take a confused, chaotic situation and perceive some degree of order and interrelationship. Systems thinking is a useful way of dealing with complex phenomena, especially in human endeavors such as large projects.

Although project managers must be familiar with and coordinate the individual parts of the project, most of the responsibility for each of those parts is delegated to managers and technicians who specialize in them. Project managers are concerned with the "big picture," and as such, they must be systems thinkers. This chapter covers fundamental topics for the project manager/systems thinker: Systems concepts, the systems view of organizations, and the systems approach to problem solving, design, and management.

3.2 DEFINITION OF SYSTEM

To some people the word "system" means computer or bureaucracy, yet it is so commonly used that the term seems to refer to almost everything. By definition, a system is "an organized or complex whole; an assemblage of things or parts interacting in a coordinated way." The parts could be players on a football team, keys on a keyboard, or components in a VCR. The parts need not be physical entities; they can be abstract or conceptual entities, such as words in a language or steps in a procedure. Everyday usage of the word is included with such disparate things as river systems, planetary systems, transportation and communication systems, nervous and circulatory systems, production and inventory systems, ecosystems, urban systems, social systems, economic systems, stereo systems, philosophical systems, ad infinitum (and computer systems).

Thus, a system *can* be just about anything. Besides being an "assemblage of parts," the definition of system should include three other features:

1. Parts of the system are *affected* by being in the system and are changed if they leave it;
2. The assemblage of parts *does* something; and
3. The assemblage is of particular interest.[2]

The first feature means that, in systems, the whole is more than the sum of the parts. The human body, for example, can be analyzed in terms of separate components—the liver, brain, heart, nerve fibers, and so on; yet if any of these are removed from the body, both they and the body will change. Parts of the body cannot live outside the body, and without the parts, the body cannot exist either. The name given to a way of viewing things in terms of their "wholeness," or the whole being more than the sum of the parts, is *holism*. Holism is the opposite of *reductionism,* which says that things can be understood by simply breaking them down and understanding the pieces. Certainly many things cannot be understood by simply looking at the pieces. Water, for example, is more than just the characteristics of hydrogen and oxygen combined. The idea of the parts affecting the whole and vice versa is central to systems thinking. (Related ideas appear elsewhere. Psychologists use the term *Gestalt* to describe theories and practices that emphasize the whole person and the surrounding situation. Another term, *synergy*, describes situations where several components work together to produce a combined effect.)

The second feature of systems is that they are dynamic and exhibit some kind of *behavior*; they *do* something. The kind of behavior they exhibit depends upon the particular kind of system at hand. System behavior can usually be observed in the outputs of the system or the way the system converts inputs to outputs, though the conversion process and the outputs may be quite obscure.

Third, systems are conceived by the people looking at them, which means they exist in the eye (or mind) of the beholder.[3] This is not to say that they fail to exist unless someone is there to see them, but rather that the conception of a system can be altered to suit one's purpose. For example, in diagnosing a patient, a doctor may see the whole body as "the system." The doctor may send the patient to a specialist, who sees only the digestive tract as "the system." If the problem is food poisoning and the patient files suit, her attorney may include the restaurant and food manufacturer in "the system."

3.3 SYSTEMS CONCEPTS AND PRINCIPLES

The following concepts, principles, and terms are applicable to all systems.

Elements and Subsystems

Systems can be broken down into smaller and smaller parts. These parts, in combination, form "the assemblage of parts" that constitute a system. The smallest part of a system is an *element*. Systems also can be broken down into parts which are themselves systems, called *subsystems*. A subsystem is a system that functions as a component of a larger system. When it is unnecessary to understand or reveal its inner workings, a subsystem can simply be thought of as an element. Figure 3-1, a common organization chart, illustrates that the production department may be viewed as an element in the company; if we choose to delve into it, however, Production becomes a subsystem with elements of scheduling, manufacturing, and inventory. Each element, such as manufacturing, could in turn be viewed as a sub-subsystem containing elements. In a project, an element could be a unit of work, a person or group doing the work, or a component of the end-item being produced by the project.

Attributes

Systems, subsystems, and elements all have distinguishing characteristics and properties. These *attributes* describe or express the condition of systems, subsystems, and elements in qualitative or quantitative terms. The attributes of a system may be used to monitor and measure system behavior and performance. The most common project attributes are cost and progress, both evaluated at particular points in time.

Environment and Boundary

When someone, called the "decision maker," conceptualizes a system, the term *environment* is used to refer to anything that lies beyond the decision maker's control yet influences the behavior or outcome of the system. The environment can include the

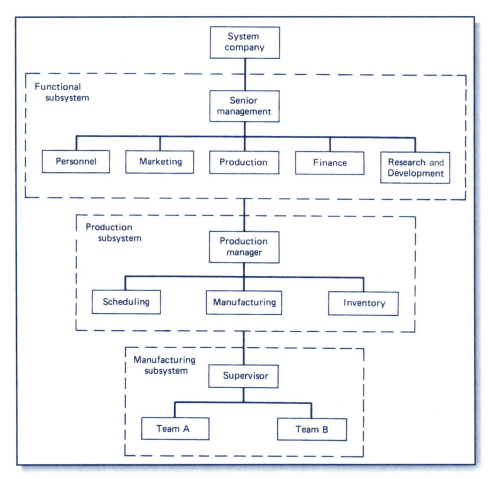

Figure 3-1
A company portrayed in terms of systems, subsystems, and elements.

community we live in, the air we breathe, or the people with whom we associate, though it is not necessarily any of these. A system is separated from its environment by a *boundary*. In many systems the boundary is somewhat obscure, so it is difficult to separate the system from the environment. To determine what is the environment, the decision maker asks the questions "Can I do anything about it?" and "Is it relevant to my situation or objective?" If the answer is "no" to the first question but "yes" to the second, then "it" is part of the environment. The following table shows how to distinguish a system from its environment:

Is it relevant to the system?

		Yes	No
Can the decision maker control it?	Yes	System	The Irrelevant Environment
	No	Environment	

The "irrelevant environment" includes all things that do not influence the system and that do not matter. To a project manager, the planet Jupiter is part of the irrelevant environment—unless the system being produced is an interplanetary space probe, in which case it becomes part of the relevant environment and must be considered in the design of the system. From here on, mention of the environment will always refer to the *relevant* environment—factors that matter to and interact with the system in some way.

Objectives

Human-made systems are designed to *do* something. They have objectives that are conceived by people. One of the greatest aids for conceptualizing, creating, or investigating a system is to begin with a clear, concise statement of the system *objectives.* Frequently objectives are broken down into a hierarchy of objectives, each relating to a subsystem. For instance, the top objective of the project may be defined as "build a space station." Moving down the hierarchy are various activities and subsystems such as "select vehicle configuration," "select prime contractor," "train crew," "launch materials into orbit," "assemble components," and so on. Each activity has objectives which are *subobjectives* for the overall system. The objectives and subobjectives are further broken down into *requirements,* which are specific criteria to which the system or activity must conform.

System Structure

Elements and subsystems are linked together by relationships. The form taken by the relationships is referred to as the *structure* of the system. The functioning and effectiveness of a system is largely determined by the "appropriateness" of the structure to the objective or purpose of the system. Most complex systems have hierarchical structures consisting of organized levels of subelements within elements, elements within subsystems, and so on. The formal organization structure shown in Figure 3-1 is an example of a hierarchical structure.

System structure can also be represented as a *network,* which shows the elements of a functioning system and the way they are interrelated or linked. In a network, often the links between elements represent the *flow* of something. For example, if the system is a physical process (say an automated or manual procedure), the elements represent steps or components in the process, and links represent the flow of material and information between them.

Most systems, including projects, can be conceptualized as both hierarchical and network systems. Figure 3-2a shows a project in terms of hierarchy of tasks and responsibilities. Element X represents the entire project and its management; elements A, B, and C are the major areas of work and management divisions in the project;

Figure 3-2
Ways of conceptualizing project systems.

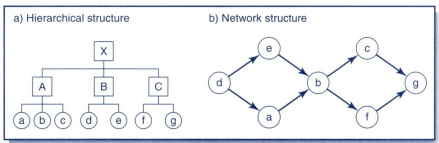

elements a through g are the specific work tasks. The structure implies that tasks a, b, and c are all subsumed under management division A, tasks d and e are under division B, and so on.

Figure 3-2b shows the flow of work in time-oriented progression for the same project. The project will begin with task d; upon d's completion, tasks e and a will be started; upon their completions, task b will be started, and so on. These concepts are fully developed later in Chapters 6 and 7.

Inputs, Process, Outputs

Human-made systems accomplish things by converting *inputs* into *outputs* through a well-defined *process.* This is illustrated in Figure 3-3. Outputs represent the end-result of a system and, generally, the purpose for which the system exists. All systems have multiple outputs, including desirable ones that contribute to system objectives, neutral ones, and undesirable or wasteful outputs that detract from system objectives and/or negatively impact the relevant environment.

Inputs are the raw materials or resources necessary for the system to operate, produce outputs, and meet objectives. Inputs include controllable factors such as labor, capital, energy, and facilities, as well as uncontrollable factors such as weather and natural phenomena. The system input that originates from the system itself is called *feedback.* For example, all systems produce information, and usage of that information for guiding system behavior is *feedback input.*

Process is the means by which the system physically converts or transforms inputs into outputs. An important aspect of system design is to create a process that effectively produces the desired outputs and meets system objectives, yet minimizes production of wasteful outputs and consumption of necessary inputs.

In a hierarchical structure where systems are divided into subsystems, the subsystems each have their own inputs, process, and outputs, which are integrated in some way. In Figure 3-1, for example, the marketing subsystem uses customer surveys and sales reports as input to generate a demand forecast (output), and this forecast, combined with information from the other subsystems, serves as input for the production subsystem.

Constraints and Conflicts

Systems have *constraints* or limitations imposed both from within and by the environment, which may inhibit their ability to reach objectives. Time and money are two universal constraints in projects: Without limitations on one or the other, almost any objective would be attainable. The trouble is that most project objectives are deemed desirable only within a limited time period and budget.

In human organizations, and especially in projects, the objectives of subsystems are frequently in *conflict.* This reduces the chances that any of them or the overall system objective will ever be achieved. Conflict in objectives is especially prevalent between different levels and functions in project systems.

Figure 3-3
Input-process-output relationship.

Open and Closed Systems

Systems can be classified as *open* systems or *closed* systems. Closed systems are viewed as self-contained. Take, for example, a machine: to know its workings, you need only study the machine; it is not necessary to look at anything else. Closed systems thinking focuses on the internal operation, structure, and processes of a system without regard to the external environment. This does not mean that the environment does not affect it; it means that the person looking at the system has chosen to ignore the environment. In fact, for many machines, closed-system thinking works fairly well.

In contrast to machines, biological and social systems are not closed. They are open systems, which means they interact with the environment and have the capability to adapt to environmental changes. To know about them you need to know something about their environment as well. The concept of open systems has been particularly useful in social and organization theory. It has led to the development of a way of viewing organizations in terms of structures, processes, functions, and relationships *among* components. Such a view is a key part of project management.

Integration

For any system to perform effectively, it must be adaptable to requirements and constraints imposed by the environment. For any organization to succeed, it must respond quickly to changing requirements of customers or to resource limitations imposed by suppliers or management. If it does not, the organization will ultimately fail. Similarly, a system's elements and subsystems must perform in a synergistic fashion. All of the elements, the "assemblage of parts," must work in unison. Designing, implementing, and operating a system that adapts to changing environmental requirements and achieves effective, coordinated (so-called "seamless") functioning of its elements and subsystems is called *systems integration*. Project management seeks the integration of project resources to achieve project goals. Especially in technological projects, project management also addresses integration of the physical components and modules that compose the project end-item or output. The subject of systems integration is covered in Chapter 14.

Natural versus Human-Made Systems

Another way of classifying systems is to contrast *natural systems* (e.g., animal organisms and planetary systems) to *human-made systems* (e.g., communication systems and human organizations). Natural systems came into being by natural processes. Human-made systems are designed and operated by people. Projects exist for the purpose of creating human-made systems.

Natural systems can be altered by or become a part of human-made systems. An example is the alteration of a river system and formation of a lake by a dam; another is the alteration of the atmosphere and ecosystems through introduction of human-made pollutants.

Human-made systems are embedded in and utilize inputs from natural systems, and both systems interact in important and significant ways. In recent years the appearance of large-scale human-made systems has had significant, mostly undesirable, impact on the natural world. Examples abound, such as acid rain, toxic contamination of water systems, and air pollution. Such consequences are referred to as "side effects." They arise largely because planners failed to consider or ignored the possibility of their occurrence. It is becoming more and more necessary for designers of systems to adopt a wider systems view which encompasses the elements and interfaces of human-made systems with natural systems.

Organization is a familiar concept. Most people belong to numerous organizations—employers, clubs, congregations, sports teams, and so on. Organizations can be looked at as goal-oriented *systems*—interacting parts, human and nonhuman, generally working toward common (though sometimes vague or uncertain) goals. All organizations have a goal or mission, stated or otherwise; it is the reason they exist.

Organizations as Open Systems

Organizations are *open* systems: They interact with the environment, utilize as inputs people, materials, information, and capital, and produce as outputs goods, services, information, or waste byproducts. Certain features characterize organizational systems; we will consider those relevant to project organizations:

1. Organizations are contrived by humanity, so they can have large numbers of objectives. For just about any "realistic"[5] goal that a person can conceive, a project organization can be developed to work toward it. Unlike biological systems, organizations do not necessarily die; they can be altered and re-formed to sustain life and pursue different objectives. This is certainly true for project organizations because once an objective has been achieved, the organization (its elements, technology, and structure) can be changed to pursue another goal.

2. Given that organizations are open systems, their *boundaries* are permeable and tend to fluctuate with different objectives and types of activities. The boundaries of large project organizations are sometimes difficult to define, especially when one considers all of the contractors, subcontractors, suppliers, customer representatives, and local and government regulatory groups that might be involved. Some of these elements are more involved than others, but all are a part of the project system.

   Project managers are "boundary agents:" they work at the point of contact between subsystems where there is transfer of energy, people, materials, money, and information. Their role is to ensure integration and cooperation among the subsystems within the boundary, and between these and others outside the boundary in the larger environment.

3. Organizations, like all complex systems, are *hierarchical*—they are composed of lower-order subsystems and are part of a higher-order suprasystem. Within an organization, people combine to form organized groups, and groups combine to form departments or project teams. These make up a company, which is part of an industry, which is in an economy, and so on. Hierarchy exists for both structure—units and relationships—and processes—lower level tasks and activities combine to make up higher-level tasks and activities. Much of the planning and scheduling of project work utilizes this concept of hierarchy.

4. To maintain stability in changing environments, organizations depend upon *feedback* of information from their internal elements and the environment. Negative feedback is information signaling that the system is deviating from its objectives and should adjust its course of action. In project organizations, managers continually gather and interpret feedback information and take action to keep the project on course; this is the vital role of project review and control.

Environmental Subsystems

Organizations interact with other, external subsystems such as customers, suppliers, unions, stockholders, and governments. They rely upon the subsystems for inputs of energy, information, and material, and they export to them outputs of goods and services (represented in Figure 3-4).

In establishing goals and methods of operation, organizations are influenced by and must deal with these subsystems. Any organization which challenges others for the same *scarce resources*—customers, raw materials, budget allocations, and so forth—is a competitive subsystem. All organizations compete. Projects organizations rely on technology—equipment, tools, facilities, techniques, and knowledge—that is given or loaned to them by other organizations such as suppliers, consultants, and functional departments. They must compete economically and politically to acquire the resources and technology they need to obtain contracts and accomplish goals, indeed, to survive.

Many organizations try to operate as if they were isolated; they collect too little information about their environment or fail to utilize the information they have. As open systems, organizations must choose goals and conduct their operations in ways that respect the opportunities and limitations afforded by the environment. Cleland and King call this the manager's "environmental problem," meaning that managers must[6]

1. Appreciate the need to assess forces in the environment;
2. Understand the forces that significantly affect their organization; and
3. Integrate these forces into the organization's goals, objectives, and operations.

Although every project is influenced by outside forces, these forces alone should not be allowed to dictate the conduct of the project; that is the role of project management. A project manager must appreciate and understand forces influencing the project, but having done that, must then be able to control the project and guide it to completion. A project that is predominantly influenced or managed by divergent outside forces will go out of control and likely fail, illustrated in the following example.

Example 1: Life and Death of an Aircraft Development Project

Some of the systems concepts described thus far can be related by way of an example based on a study by Law and Callon of a large British aerospace project.[7] The study traces the evolution of the project in terms of two systems: the global system and the project system. The *global system* represents parties and organizations in the environment that influence or initiate a project and provide the necessary resources. This system includes environmental subsystems that have a stake in the project. The *project system* represents the creation and conduct of

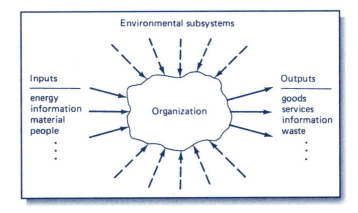

Figure 3-4
Organization as an input-output system.

the project itself. These two systems and their relationships to project management are explained later.

The Global System

The project was initiated by the Royal Air Force (RAF) as a "requirement" for a new military supersonic aircraft with short take-off capability. In addition to the RAF, the principle parties in the global system and their interests include

1. The Ministry of Defence (MOD), which mandated that the aircraft could *not* be a bomber. Because the RAF wanted *some kind* of aircraft, albeit not a bomber, the aircraft was specified to be a tactical strike and reconnaissance fighter, called TSR.
2. The Treasury, which wanted the aircraft to be inexpensive and have market appeal for sale to other nations.
3. The Royal Navy, which wanted to purchase *another* aircraft, but which the RAF hoped would ultimately buy the TSR instead.
4. The Ministry of Supply (MOS), which wanted a project that would consolidate the efforts of several airframe and engine manufacturers into one large consortium.

As typical of most projects, each party in the global system conceptualized the project differently: To the RAF and MOD it would yield an aircraft for a specific mission; To the Treasury it would fit the defence budget and generate revenue; To the Navy it was a competitive threat; and to the MOS it was an instrument of industrial policy. The parties had different interests for contributing resources and support: Some were economic (in return for funds, an aircraft would be built); some political (in return for a demonstrated need, objections of the Navy would be overruled); some technical (in return for engineering and technical effort, the aircraft would meet RAF performance requirements); and some industrial (in exchange for contracts, the aircraft industry would be consolidated).

The Project System

No funding would be approved until features of the project were better defined, including the aircraft's basic design and its likely manufacturer, cost, and delivery date. The RAF and MOD had to begin creating a project system comprised of contractors, tasks, schedules, and so on. They sent requests to the aircraft industry for design ideas, and selected those from two manufacturers; Vickers Corp. and English Electric (EE). RAF and MOD favored Vickers for its integrated "weapons systems" design (aircraft, engine, armaments, and support equipment in a single package) and capability in tackling complex projects, but they also liked EE's design and experience with supersonic aircraft. They decided to contract with both companies and utilize a design that combined features from both designs. The idea was presented to the rest of the global network, which approved it and released funding. The major elements of the project system—major organizations involved, initial designs and costs, and management structure—were now in place, and resources began to flow to it from the global system.

The project system continued to grow as Vickers and EE organized and expanded their design teams, production teams, management teams, subcontractors, and so on. Under the encouragement from MOS, Vickers, EE, and several other contractors merged to form a single new organization called British Aircraft Corporation (BAC).

Designers initially faced two problems: Some wanted to locate the engines in the fuselage to minimize aerodynamic problems, but others worried about fire risks and wanted them on the wings. Also, they could not design a wing that would meet the requirement for both supersonic speed and short take-off capability. Compromises were made, requirements relaxed, and eventually the designs were completed and sent to the factory.

Relationships between the Global System and the Project System

As the project system expanded, so did the problems between it and the global system. MOS wanted centralized control over all aspects of the project and all transactions between the project system and the global system. Although BAC was, in principle, the prime contractor and responsible for managing the entire project, MOS did not vest BAC with much management responsibility. Rather, it formed a series of committees to represent government agencies in the global system and gave the committees much of management responsibility for the project. This led to serious problems:

1. The committees could make or veto any decision related to the project. For example, most important contracts were awarded by MOS, and BAC controlled only 30 percent of project expenditures; often the RAF made decisions and changed requirements without consulting with BAC.
2. With so many interests involved, decisions were hard to reach. Committee members lacked information or knowledge, thus technical committees made decisions without regard to costs, and cost committees made decisions without regard to technical realities. Decisions did not reflect "systems thinking."

Eventually distrust grew between BAC and MOS, and neither could act effectively to integrate the flow of requirements, information, and decisions between parties in the global system and the project system. The project ran into major problems with development of the TSR engine. MOS had specified the engine requirements in general terms and expected the development to be routine, but the new engine needed much greater thrust than anticipated. One of the test engines exploded and it would be 2 years before the cause was understood. Subcontractors were difficult to control. Many ignored BAC and appealed directly to MOS for favorable treatment; some colluded directly with the RAF; and many doubted that the plane would ever fly, overcharged to project, or gave it low priority.

Global System Reshaped

Everyone connected with the project knew it was in trouble. The RAF and MOD recognized that the engine would likely remain unproven for some time, and the treasury, which hoped for an inexpensive aircraft, saw its costs double. The Australian Air Force then announced that instead of the TSR, it was ordering the U.S.-built F-111. Still, RAF and MOD remained strong supporters, and as long as the funding continued, so would the project. However, project opponents were also aware of the project's troubles, and they decided to take them to a broader arena, the Labour Party. A general election was coming, and the Labour Party promised to review the project if it was elected. The emergence of these two new elements in the global system—the F-111 and the Labour Party—clinched the fate of the project. The Labour Party won the election and immediately began assessing the TSR project, which included comparing it with the F-111, considered by now an alternative to the TSR. As cost overruns and schedule delays continued, MOS slowly withdrew support. The RAF also withdrew support when it discovered that the F-111, which was already in production, met all of its requirements. TSR was canceled.

Conclusions

The lesson suggested by this case is that the shape and fate of large technological projects depends on the global system, the project system, and the interface between them as handled by project management. The conclusions of Law and Callon, the study authors, are that[8]

1. The global system provides resources in expectation of some return from the project system. For the project system to perform well, however, the global system must afford it freedom to proceed and make mistakes

without interference. The global system must allow project management the autonomy to make project decisions and control project work.

2. The project system must provide the material, economic, symbolic, and cultural returns expected by parties in the global system. It must be able to experiment, assemble, control, and deliver the benefits or returns that will satisfy parties in the global system.

3. Project management must be the center of transactions (flow of information, resources, decisions) between the two systems. Unless it is, it will not be able to control the resources provided by the global system, which, as a result, will be misused or withdrawn, and it will not be able to claim credit to the global system for any successes the project system achieves.

In the TSR project, project management was not able to exercise control over the project or serve as the agent between the project system and the global system. Project management should have served as the control valve for information and resources flowing between the two systems; in fact, much of the flow completely circumvented project management. Parties in the global system were able to interfere with the structure and management of the project system, and parties in the project system were able to deal directly with parties in the global system, each to maximize its own interests, although usually to the detriment of the project.

Properties of Organizations

Organizations have been called *socio-technical systems*, which means they consist of a social subsystem of individuals with a culture and a mission, as well as a technology subsystem of equipment, facilities, tools, and techniques. An organization cannot be exclusively one or the other because both subsystems are interdependent. Human and social activities must be structured and integrated around the technology because the technology influences the types of inputs and outputs of the organization. Yet it is the social subsystem that determines the effectiveness of the utilization of technology. This is one reason why in project management, it is just as important to be aware of and *manage* the behavioral and social aspects of projects as it is to manage their technology. To the detriment of project goals, some managers behave as if the social subsystem did not exist.

Each organization has a *structure* comprised of the units of the organization and the relationships between them. The structure includes both the formal structure—described by organization charts, job descriptions, procedures, and patterns of authority and communication, as well as the informal structure—procedures and patterns of work and communication that bypass the formal structure.

One way to express formal structure is in terms of functional specializations:

The marketing subsystem
The production subsystem
The personnel subsystem
The financial subsystem
The research and development subsystem
Project subsystems

In much the same way as the circulatory, respiratory, digestive, and other subsystems contribute to the behavior and well-being of an animal organism, *functional subsystems* contribute to the well-being and goals of an organization. Projects are subsystems that, to a large extent, have features similar to, yet beyond, those of all the other subsystems. This is because to accomplish their ends projects take *elements* from other functional subsystems—personnel, financial, and so on—and use them to do things that none of the functional subsystems can do alone.

Project Management System

Of relevance are the *management subsystems* that internally plan and organize the organization and are responsible for its effective performance. All management subsystems are integrated into a larger system that manages the overall organization. Each project has its own management subsystem, hereafter called a *project management system.*

Embedded in the project management system are subsystems for project *control* and project *information collection.* The *project control* subsystem (described in Chapter 11) includes the standards, policies, procedures, decision rules, and reporting requirements to monitor and control a project. Every project has its own control subsystem to monitor activities, compare them to goals and standards, and suggest corrective actions. The *project management information* system (described in Chapter 12) include data requirements, collection procedures, data storage and processing, and information reporting. Its purpose is to collect and summarize data from internal and environmental subsystems to provide managers with information for making decisions.

To be effective, project management must have both information and control subsystems. Timely and pertinent information is necessary to exercise control, and a framework must exist to utilize that information for decision making. In subsequent chapters the concepts of management control and information subsystems will be related to project management.

One way to further explain the position and purpose of project management subsystems in organizations is to consider their relationship to other kinds of management subsystems. In general, management subsystems can be divided according to the three-level hierarchy shown in Figure 3-5:[9]

1. The underlying technical level produces and distributes goods and services. Here, work tends to be standardized or repetitive; decisions are largely programmed according to standards, policies, and procedures.
2. The organizational level organizes and integrates the work at the technical level. This level coordinates inputs and outputs between functional subsystems and disseminates information to and exercises control over activities and outputs at the technical level. Some decisions at this level are programmed, but most are nonprogrammed.
3. The institutional, or highest level, is where organizational activities are related to the environment. This is the realm of the chief executive and board of directors where goals and adaptive, innovative strategies are laid out. Structures and processes are conceived to meet demands of internal and environmental subsystems. Decisions at this level are strictly nonprogrammed.

There is considerable difference in the orientation and tasks of managers at the three levels. At the central, technical level, managers are task-oriented and have a relatively short time perspective. A closed-system perspective is often seen here because the organization closes off the technical "core" from the environment. Much of the work at this level tends to be repetitive and routine, so management's role is largely to guide and control the work.

Managers in the outer, institutional level tend to be conceptual in orientation and have a long-range time perspective. Their principal occupation is planning. They face

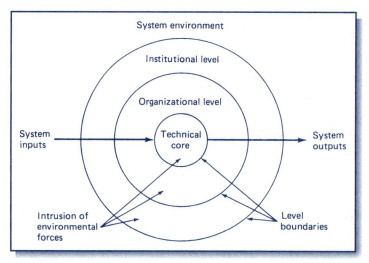

Figure 3-5
Management systems hierarchy. [From Thomas Petit,
"A Behavioral Theory of Management," *Academy of
Management Journal* (December 1967): 346.]

considerable uncertainty in dealing with environmental forces over which they may have little control.

Managers at the middle, organizational level integrate activities and decisions from the technical and institutional levels. They are boundary agents, working at the interfaces between the three levels. They must translate the strategies of the institutional level into procedures and practices for the technical level. Similarly, they must translate decisions by managers at the technical level for interpretation by managers at the institutional level.

Project managers and the project management system usually exist at the organizational level. Important functions of the project management system are to mediate between the institutional and technical levels and to coordinate tasks and functions at the technical level. In carrying out the project goals of top management and coordinating the project work (usually done within various functional areas), project managers do both planning and controlling. They might have only limited knowledge of the functional areas, so they must rely on the expertise of managers at the technical level to get work done.

3.5   SYSTEMS APPROACH

The previous sections described systems thinking as a way to visualize and analyze physical and conceptual systems—but part of systems thinking is what's called the *systems approach*, which is a way of *doing* things rather than just *looking* at them. Three common ways of applying the systems approach, called "system methodologies," will be described later in this chapter: Systems analysis, systems engineering, and systems management. Each has a different purpose and scope, but all share a similar, systems view of the world.

An appreciation of the systems approach is important for project managers because it is the approach that underlines the *process* of project management. Especially in technical projects, many of the steps and procedures are prescribed according to systems methodologies. As will be shown, throughout projects there is often a need to apply a problem-solving approach called "systems analysis;" in large-scale engineering and developmental projects, the approach followed is called "systems engineering;" and most large projects are managed as systems, a process called "systems management." Although methodologies such as these are typically found in technical projects, they are useful for all kinds of problem solving, organizing, and integrating of work tasks, regardless of the type of project. For this reason it is good to know about them even if you do not manage technical projects.

Systems Approach Framework

The systems approach is a framework for conceptualizing problems as systems and for *doing* things—such as solving problems and designing systems. The framework utilizes systems concepts such as elements, subsystems, relationships, and environment. The systems approach formally acknowledges that the behavior of any one element may affect other elements and no single element can perform effectively without help from the others. This recognition of *interdependency* and *cause-effect* among elements is what most distinguishes the systems approach.

For example, as an element of the "world system," the internal combustion engine can be viewed in terms of the multiple chain of effects it has triggered in other world elements and subsystems. They include

- Development of rich economies based entirely on the production and distribution of petroleum.
- Industrialization of previously nomadic societies and redistribution in the concentration of political power among world nations.
- Development of new, improved modes of transportation that have altered patterns of world travel, commerce, markets, and population distribution.
- Alteration of the chemical composition of the atmosphere, causing ecological consequences such as air pollution, altered weather patterns, and the "greenhouse effect."

Managers who use the systems approach recognize the elements in a situation, inputs and outputs among the elements, and the influence of the environment, and they are able to grasp the magnitude of a problem and anticipate consequences of their actions. This leads to better decisions and better management because it reduces the chances that important elements in a situation or consequences of actions will be overlooked.

The systems approach keeps attention on the big picture and the ultimate objective, and shifts the focus away from the parts and toward the whole. For instance, it is possible to view a university system as separate entities of students, faculty, administrators, and alumni, and to take action with respect to each while ignoring their interactions with each other and the environment. Actions that focus exclusively on just parts of the system, however, are likely to be suboptimal because they disregard the negative repercussions on other parts. For example, curtailing the hiring of faculty reduces faculty costs, but it can also result in classroom overcrowding, less faculty research time, fewer research grants, disgruntled students, lower prestige to the university, and ultimately, lower enrollments and less revenue. Similarly, air pollution can be reduced by enacting laws, but such laws might restrict or prohibit industry and damage regional economies.

No problem can be solved in isolation. Every problem is inextricably united to the environment, and attempts to solve it may cause other, more intractable problems. Churchman calls this the "environmental fallacy."[10]

Examples abound of situations where solutions for the parts have led to worse problems for the whole. These examples include trying to improve housing by replacing ghettos with public projects, trying to reduce traffic congestion by adding more highways, trying to eliminate alcohol and drug abuse by outlawing consumption, or trying to increase the "appeal" of wilderness areas by building resorts in national parks. The negative consequences of these problem-solving attempts are well known. The systems approach tries to avoid the environmental fallacy.

Orderly Way of Appraisal[11]

Besides being a way of looking at problems, the systems approach is a *methodology* for solving problems and managing systems. By its holistic nature, it avoids tackling problems narrowly, head-on. It says, "Let's stand back and look at this situation from all angles." The problem solver does this by thinking about the overall system, keeping in mind

1. The *objectives* and the performance measures of the whole system.
2. The *environment* and *constraints* of the system.
3. The *resources* of the system.
4. The *elements* of the system, their functions, goals, attributes, and performance measures.
5. The *management* of the system.

First, the place to start planning for a system is with the overall *objective* of the system. Costly mistakes can be made if the true objective of the system is vague or misconstrued. The systems approach mandates hardheaded thinking about the *real* objective of the system and *real* ways to measure it. Project management uses this kind of thinking: It begins with the mission or objective of the system and, thereafter, all subsequent work is organized and directed to achieve that objective. The stated objective must be precise and measurable in terms of specific performance criteria (the system requirements). Regardless of how intangible the objective—goodwill, quality of life, happiness, or even beauty—performance measures must be established. For system performance to be realistically assessed, performance measures should reflect the many relevant consequences of the system.

The *environment* of the system (relevant subsystems, groups, and persons who affect or are affected by the system) must also be identified—no easy matter because many external forces are hidden and work in insidious ways. The way the system interacts with the environment must be determined, highlighting inputs, outputs, and *constraints* imposed. Looking to the future, questions must be raised about likely changes or innovations in the environment and how they will affect the system.

Internal system *resources* to be used in accomplishing system goals must also be identified. These are assets or the means that the system utilizes and influences to its own advantage; they include capital, labor, materials, facilities, and equipment. Most system resources are exhaustible. The system is free to utilize them only for as long as they are available. When resources are depleted they become *constraints* on the system. The systems approach considers the availability of resources and what happens when resources are depleted.

The fourth concept is *elements* of the system. The systems approach disregards traditional boundaries and definitions for elements. The systems approach to a project, for example, entails viewing the project in terms of many elements, each having performance measures directly related to performance of the overall project. Traditional categories such as functional departments are ignored in favor of basic "work packages" or jobs. By dividing the project into small elements or tasks, the manager can better ascertain if the project is going smoothly and what actions need to be taken.

Finally, the systems approach pays explicit attention to the *management* of the system, that function which takes into consideration all of the other aspects of the system—objectives, environment and constraints, resources, and elements—in the planning and control of the system. This is precisely the role of project management.

The ordering of the above concepts does not mean that they are addressed in sequence. In actuality each concept might need to be dealt with several times before it is completely described and clearly defined. More importantly, each concept serves to suggest numerous open-ended questions that aid in investigating the system. In defining the system along with its elements and environment, the decision maker asks: What cause-and-effect relationships exist among them? What functions need to be performed by each? What tradeoffs may be required among resources once they are defined?[12]

Figure 3-6 illustrates how plans are developed in iterative fashion, utilizing loops and feedback. General objectives are used to define plans, then objectives are refined, plans detailed, and so on. Objectives are used to develop requirements, but as additional data is collected, the requirements (and even the objectives) are refined.

Figure 3-6
The systems approach. [Adapted and revised from P. Thome and R. Willard, in S. L. Optner, ed., *Systems Analysis* (Middlesex, England: Penguin, 1973): 216.]

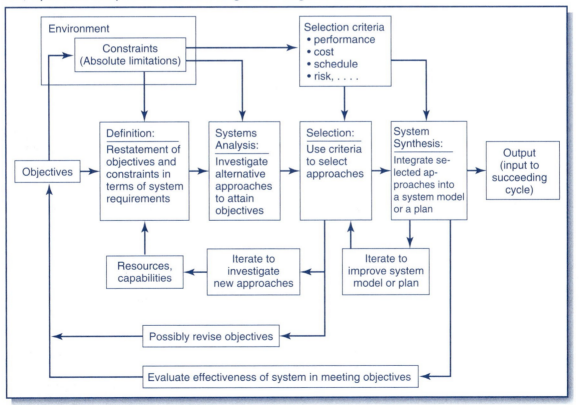

The cycle in Figure 3-6 has a *systems analysis* phase and a *systems synthesis* phase. In systems analysis, each objective is clarified in terms of requirements or criteria, and alternative approaches for attainment are specified. These approaches are weighed and the best ones selected in a tradeoff study. The selected approaches are then synthesized, or integrated together into a system model or plan. The final solution and overall plans are selected and developed based upon criteria compatible with the objectives.[13]

As plans are implemented, *systems management* monitors them to ensure the parts are suitably integrated and carried out. Both the plans' components and their implementation methods and consequences are subsequently evaluated. Management monitors the system and is prepared to modify plans in response to changes in the environment, objectives, resources, or system elements. Because none of these can be known with complete certainty, the best plans incorporate mechanisms for self-evaluation and self-change.

The systems approach can be successfully applied to a wide range of complex, real world problems. It is concerned with the total problem-solving cycle, not just parts of it, which is one reason why it is so important to project management.

Systems Life Cycle

Systems change over time. The changes tend to be systematic and evolutionary, with similar kinds of systems following similar cycles of evolution. One basic cycle, that of living organisms, is the pattern of birth, growth, maturity, decline, and death. Another, that of all nonliving, electro-mechanical systems, is the cycle of burn-in, normal operation, then deterioration or obsolescence. Similarly, all products follow a parallel cycle: They are conceived and introduced, capture market share, then decline and are ultimately discontinued. Some products, such as computer processing chips, have a life cycle of only a few months. Other products last for decades: Kool-Aid and Levi's jeans are examples. Organizations and projects follow life cycles also, with stages characterized by the types of problems they face, the resources they utilize, the formal structures they take on, and the expertise they employ.[14]

The *development* of a system also follows a series of phases, starting with initial conception and ending with final installation or termination. A key feature of the systems approach is recognition of the logical order of thought and action that go into developing systems, whether commercial home products, public works, or military weapons systems. Large-scale design and development projects follow a prescribed process called *systems engineering*. The more general development of a system according to a prescribed series of logical, structured steps is called the *systems development cycle*. These topics will be discussed later in this and the next two chapters.

3.6   SYSTEMS ANALYSIS

Systems analysis is a problem-solving framework to help decision makers select the best alternatives. By one definition, "systems analysis is a systematic examination of a problem in which each step of the analysis is made *explicit*. Consequently, it is the *opposite* of a manner of reaching decisions which is largely intuitive, unsystematic, and where much of the argument remains hidden in the mind of the decision maker or his advisor."[15] Thus, what distinguishes systems analysis from other forms of analysis is its *precision* in defining the elements of the analysis.

As shown in Figure 3-6, systems analysis focuses on only a part of the total systems approach; consequently, it is narrower in scope than the systems approach. However, it is more general than disciplines such as operations research because it covers problem and objective formulation,[16] or economics because it covers all kinds of problems, not just scarce resources. Systems analysis should not be confused with *computer systems analysis,* which is the narrow application of systems analysis to computers and computerized systems.

Elements of Systems Analysis

Systems analysis uses "modeling" to help decision makers understand the system and to measure alternatives against objectives. A model is a simplified representation of the world; it abstracts the essential features of the system under study. It may be a physical model, mathematical formulation, computer simulation, or simple checklist. One example of a *physical model* is a model airplane. It is a scaled-down abstraction of the real system. It includes some aspects of the system (configuration and shape of exterior components) and excludes others (interior components and crew). Another kind of model is a *conceptual model;* it depicts the elements, structure, and flows in a system. The conceptual model in Figure 3-7, for example, helps analysts to understand relationships among the elements contributing to population size and to make limited predictions.[17] Most models for decision making are conceptual and are formulated in terms of mathematical equations.

Models are used to conduct experimentation. Many systems are too expensive or risky with which to do "real life" experiments. The model permits assessment of various alternatives and their consequences before a decision is made. Engineers use model airplanes in wind tunnel tests, for instance, to try out design alternatives and to measure the effect of different design parameters on performance. A good model allows the analyst to ask "what if" questions and to explore the effects of changing various inputs. This exploration is called *sensitivity analysis.*

In doing systems analysis, one must be careful not to catch "modelism"—in other words, not become more interested in the model than in the real world. Modelism

Figure 3-7
A generalized population sector model.

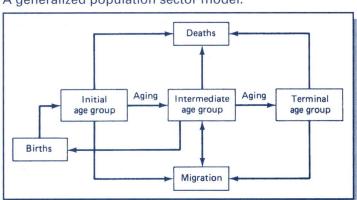

leads to the study of irrelevant or over-idealized questions rather than answers to important questions.[18]

Most models and analytical procedures in systems analysis are quantitative, but this by no means should imply that they are intended to replace qualitative analysis. Indeed, good systems analysis employs both qualitative and quantitative methods. The value of systems analysis is that it explicitly takes into consideration all things that can be quantified, thus permitting decision makers to use judgment on those factors that can only be addressed qualitatively.

The central role of the model is seen in its relation to the other elements of systems analysis in the following list.[19] These elements are present in every systems analysis:

1. Objective(s). The first task in systems analysis is to identify the decision makers and what they expect after the problem has been solved. This expectation is the objective. Objectives must be clear, concise, and—ideally—measurable. To eliminate confusion and misunderstanding about the problem or system, both the decision maker and the systems analyst must agree to the objectives.

2. Criteria. Criteria are performance measures that will enable the analyst to determine the extent to which objectives are being achieved. They are the basis for ranking the performance of alternative solutions or courses of action to the problem. In projects, the criteria are referred to as *requirements* and *specifications.*

3. Alternatives. Alternatives are potential solutions to problems and courses of action for attaining objectives. The common error in many analyses is to focus on the familiar alternatives and ignore innovative solutions. One rule of the systems approach is "Don't prejudge solutions!" Early solutions should serve as guides rather than stopping points. Ideally, a wide range of alternative solutions are considered.

4. Resources and Constraints. Resources are elements of the system—labor, time, capital, materials—available to solve the problem. Constraints are elements of the system or environment that restrict the applicability or usefulness of alternatives. Resources and constraints determine what is feasible and reduce the number of potential solutions to a problem. All resources are limited, so they become constraints when in short supply or exhausted.

5. Analysis Model. The model incorporates *all* of the above elements so that consequences of alternatives can be compared in terms of attainment of objectives. As mentioned, models widely vary, ranging from a set of mathematical equations and computer programs for quantitative analysis, to a verbal description that permits consequences to be assessed using judgment alone.

The model must compare alternatives in terms of both costs and benefits. Costs are resources that, when allotted to alternatives, cannot be used elsewhere; benefits are the worthwhile outcomes of alternatives. It may seem obvious that both aspects must be considered to establish the overall worth of an alternative, but history is replete with cases where benefits and costs were not treated together. For example, there are instances where sophisticated weapons systems have been acquired without adequate funding for maintenance and spare parts (resulting in their being permanently "nonoperational" because of repair backlogs). When decisions are made solely in terms of anticipated system benefits (e.g., a certain type of fighter plane will fulfill a certain mission) without regard to system costs (e.g., "chopping off" maintenance capability to satisfy cost requirements) the outcome likely cancels or greatly diminishes the anticipated benefits. In systems analysis, alternatives yielding the greatest effectiveness (benefits) are examined with respect to current and anticipated resource limitations (costs).

Process of Conducting a Systems Analysis

Systems analysis involves four overlapping phases, shown in Figure 3-8.[20]

In the first phase, *formulation*, fuzzy ideas are translated into clear definitions of the problem, objectives, and criteria measures. Sometimes the decision maker provides a clear problem formulation, though other times she does not know what the problem is and the systems analyst must start from scratch. The problem exists because *needs* of the decision maker are unsatisfied. Thus, one common aspect of problem formulation is identifying and defining needs.

Of course the systems analyst must first establish the identity of the *decision maker*. The decision maker, also called the customer, client, or user, is that party (person or group) which is dissatisfied with the present or prospects for the future and has the *desire* and *authority* to do something about it. Systems analysis is a precursor to action, but unless the true decision maker is involved, it will be to little avail. Many systems analyses have been shelved because they were done for parties *posing* as decision makers rather than the "real" decision makers.

During the second phase, *research,* data about the problem is collected. System components and relationships are identified, specific criteria or performance requirements are defined, resources and constraints are defined, and potential alternative courses of action are identified. Often, the constraints become requirements in the sense that the solution is required *not* to exceed them.

Identifying alternatives is not always straightforward, especially when the obvious ones are inadequate and new ones must be developed. This is where *interdisciplinary teams* are beneficial. The use of interdisciplinary teams to search for broad alternatives is an outgrowth of the early application of systems analysis during World War II. Interdisciplinary teams were found to provide an effective means for combining the knowledge from experts in many fields—physics, mathematics, psychology—and for generating alternatives and solutions that transcended any one person's or one field's area of expertise. Today, teams like this are common in product-development projects. This use of interdisciplinary teams, referred to as "concurrent engineering," is described in Chapter 14.

Figure 3-8
Elements and process of systems analysis.

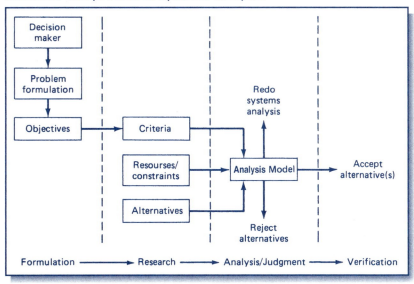

In the third phase, *analysis/judgment*, an analysis model is developed for comparing alternatives and consequences in terms of criteria measures. Conclusions are made and a course of action is selected. The analysis is performed by the systems analyst, but the final judgment is made by the decision maker.

In the final phase, *verification,* the solution is implemented. Empirical evidence is collected to ensure that the alternative selected is the appropriate solution. Any discrepancies between actual performance and system objectives indicate the need for further analysis, revised alternatives, or different objectives.

Systems analysis seldom proceeds smoothly: Objectives may be obscure, in conflict, or difficult to clarify and quantify; none of the alternatives may be adequate to reach the objective; a suitable model may be unattainable; or the decision maker may have changed his mind. One pass through the process is usually not enough and it is necessary to recycle or reformulate the problem, select new objectives and criteria, collect additional data, design new alternatives, build new models, reweigh costs and benefits, and so on until an alternative is chosen.

Example 2: Systems Analysis of a Recycling Program[21]

Following is a hypothetical example to illustrate systems analysis and the main elements as represented in Figure 3-8.

Decision Maker

Corporate senior management group

Statement of Problem

The current paper recycling approach is inadequate. The quantity of paper disposed of as "garbage" is very large. This volume of waste gives the appearance that the corporation is not environmentally responsible. Much of the disposed paper could be reused or recycled into useful products, which would reduce disposal costs and possibly generate revenue.

Objective

Develop and implement a corporate-wide paper recycling program that will

1. Efficiently collect 70 to 90 percent of all paper products used by the corporation and now considered as waste.
2. Effectively channel the collected paper waste to facilities that will sort it into biodegradable and nonbiodegradable categories for recycling into products useful to the corporation and the larger community.

Resources/Constraints

1. **Technology:** The recycling program budget allows for $30 million capital cost and $1 million a year operating cost, maximum. Not all grades of paper can be recycled; the program must take this into account.
2. **Water:** The recycling facility utilizes a maximum of 1 million gallons of water daily and produces 150,000 gallons maximum of effluent, plus solid wastes from ink, staples, tape, and other sources; hence, the facility must be situated in a location with adequate water supply.
3. **Paper:** It can be recycled six or seven times at most before fibers become too short for recycling, depending on the type of paper; the program must take this into account.
4. **Employee support:** The enthusiastic support of employees is necessary for the program to be successful.

Criteria and Requirements

1. Effectiveness of the program in utilizing the greatest percentage possible of paper waste for recycling. *Requirement:* at least 70 percent of all paper products are recycled.
2. Cost of the program to the corporation. *Requirement 1:* The capital cost of the program must not exceed $30 million, which includes equipment and facilities procurement and installation, and one-time start-up costs such as training and promotion. *Requirement 2:* The annual operating cost for collection, sorting, and recycling must not exceed $1 million.
3. Acceptability of the program to corporate management, staff, employees, customers, and the general public. *Requirement 1:* At least 70 percent of each of the above groups as surveyed must approve of the program. *Requirement 2:* At least 75 percent of members in each of the groups within the corporation must participate.
4. Ease of implementing the program with respect to time and similarity to existing recycling programs in use by some departments and divisions. *Requirement:* The program must be fully implemented and requirements 1 and 3 achieved within 1 year of the kick-off date.

Alternatives (Potential Solutions/Courses of Action)

1. Collect, sort, and recycle at corporate plant; local collection and sort; central collection and sort.
2. Collect and sort but sell to contractor for recycling.
3. Contract outside for collection, sorting, and recycling.
4. Use 1, 2, and 3, plus a policy to purchase only recycled paper.
5. Other possible alternatives might be identified and those listed above might be redefined. Such new or revised alternatives will be considered as well.

Analysis Methods/Model

1. Research existing and future requirements, procedures, and opportunities. Consider growth in corporate paper consumption; pending disposal legislation; attitudes of paper suppliers, employees, customers, and the public; list of agencies and organizations dealing with disposal and recovery; and list of corporations with recycling programs.
2. Develop methodology for rating effectiveness of alternatives.
3. Analyze and rate effectiveness of paper collection schemes (wastepaper containers, central waste locations, conveyors, incinerators, compressors/processors); paper removal schemes (trucks, conveyors, incinerators, compressors/processors); paper sorting and recovery (purchasing policies, employee self-sort, central sorting facility).
4. Determine costs associated with collection, removal, sorting, and recovery techniques.

Advantages and disadvantages of each alternative will be considered. Alternatives will be considered feasible if they can achieve the objective stated within the constraints listed. The rating scheme and cost analysis will identify that combination of collection, removal, sorting, and recovery methods that recycle the largest amount of paper for the lowest cost, and provide the greatest acceptance and least difficulty in implementation. The program to be adopted might be a composite and include features of more than one of the alternatives listed.

Systems analysis produces solutions within relatively clearly defined situations. Another methodology, *systems engineering,* produces solutions to problems that are more complex and less clearly defined. Unlike systems analysis, users of systems engineering also consider the elements and subsystems to system solution and how they will be integrated together. Also, they devote much effort to conceptualizing and understanding the overall situation in which a particular solution or system must fit. Within the systems engineering process are smaller, tidier problems, and for these systems analysis is employed repeatedly as a decision making framework.

3.7   SYSTEMS ENGINEERING[22]

Systems engineering has been defined as "the science of designing complex systems in their totality to insure that the component subsystems making up the system are designed, fitted together, checked and operated in the most efficient way."[23] Up through World War II, the term "systems engineering" referred to integrating existing components into a final product. Today it emphasizes instead the conception, design, and development of complex systems where the *components themselves* must be designed and developed from scratch and integrated together to fulfill mission objectives. In contrast to systems analysis, which focuses on *decisions about a system*, systems engineering is a way to actually *bring a system into being*.

All Systems Go

A good example of systems engineering can be seen in the design and operation of a space vehicle. The expression "all systems go," popularized during the early U.S. space flights, means that the overall system of millions of components that make up the vehicle and its support systems, and the thousands of people in its technical and management teams, is ready to "go" to achieve the objectives of the mission. Every component and person is in place, working as prescribed, and ready to contribute to the overall mission.

To get to the point of "all systems go" planners must have first defined the overall system and its *objectives*. Designers must have analyzed the requirements of the system and *broken them down* (analysis) into smaller subsystems so each component could be clearly defined, designed, and put into place. They must then *put together* (synthesis) a total system of rocket boosters, space vehicle, launch facilities, ground support, crew selection and training, and technical and management capability. In the end, every component and person must have a planned role and be *integrated* into a subsystem which is integrated into the overall system.

Systems engineering applies to any system (hardware or software) that must be developed (perhaps from scratch), implemented, and operated to fulfill some temporary or ongoing future purpose. Examples can readily be found in the design and implementation of systems for global telecommunication; metropolitan rail transit; water diversion, purification, and supply; power generation and transmission; customer-supplier communication links (EDI); and office computer networks (LANs).

A central part of systems engineering is design, which includes design of the system architecture, the partitioning of the system into subsystems and components, and often design of the components as well. *System architecture* represents the general characteristics and configuration for a class of systems.[24] For example, the classic architecture for an automobile is four wheels with the engine in front and seating in the middle; for transport aircraft it is the wings located near the center of the fuselage, with the cockpit in front and horizontal and vertical stabilizers at the rear. *System par-*

titioning addresses how the system should be subdivided into parts so that each part can be designed and tested or procured. The system and its parts must be designed so that interfaces between the parts are compatible, and the entire system is compatible with the environment.

Stages of Systems Engineering

Systems engineering includes a much wider role than ordinary "engineering." In fact, it is not even engineering in the same context as other engineering disciplines but, rather is a logical *process* employed in the evolution of a system from the point when a need is first identified, through planning, design, construction, and ultimate deployment and operation by a user. The process, outlined in Figure 3-9, has two parts: One associated with the *development and production* of the system (stages 1 through 4), and the other with the way the system will *work or operate* in its environment (stage 5).

The stages of the systems engineering process are discussed in detail in Appendix A. Briefly, they include the following:

1. System Concept.   Clarify the problem, establish the need and value for the system; set overall mission, objectives, and operational and maintenance requirements for the system.

2. System Definition and Preliminary Design.   Determine major functions of the system; cluster functions to form subsystems; perform systems analysis to evaluate design alternatives; prepare design specifications.

3. Detailed Design and Development.   Describe in detail subsystems, units, assemblies; develop models to test performance and integration of designs; prepare for production of system.

4. System Production or Fabrication.   Maintain construction/production operations and produce the system; prepare for installation of system.

5. System Operation and Support.   Check out and install system within the user environment; provide maintenance, field support, and system enhancement as necessary to ensure continued compliance with objectives; phase out system at the end of its useful life.

Throughout the systems engineering process, *systems evaluation* procedures are repeated to ensure that system requirements satisfy objectives, that design criteria satisfy requirements, that fabricated units meet design criteria, and that the overall system performs within its environment to the satisfaction of users.

Because of its breadth of scope, systems engineering calls for a depth of experience which no single specialist (e.g., manager, physicist, research scientist, computer scientist, engineer, cost accountant, psychologist) can provide. It requires a team effort of specialists from many separate and divergent disciplines. Diverse people from different companies and organizations, spread over a wide geographic area and with no common background, may be involved. The difficult task, largely undertaken by the project manager, is to get them all to work together toward a common purpose. Systems engineering provides the framework without which it would be impossible for teams to effectively communicate and coordinate their efforts.

In summary, systems engineering is a logical sequence of steps for identifying and coordinating the multitude of considerations and tasks in systems development. It provides for identification of overall system requirements and the means for developing and integrating hardware, software, personnel, facilities, and procedures. It

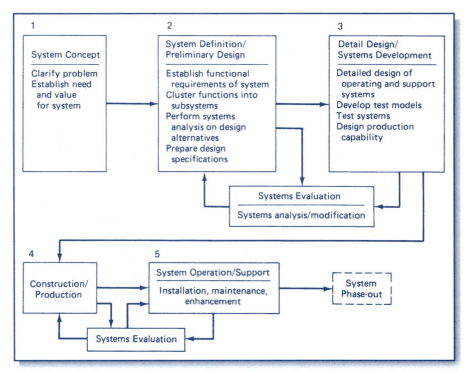

Figure 3-9
Systems engineering process. [Adapted with permission from B. Blanchard and W. Fabrycky, *Systems Engineering and Analysis* (Upper Saddle River, NJ: Prentice Hall, 1981): 238.]

provides checking, cross-checking, and quality control, and thus helps avoid waste, oversights, and redundant effort.

3.8   SYSTEMS MANAGEMENT[25]

Characteristics

A third application of the systems approach is *systems management,* the management and operation of organizations as systems. Three major characteristics distinguish systems management. First, it is total-system oriented and emphasizes achievement of the *overall system* mission and system objectives. Second, it emphasizes decisions that optimize the *overall system* rather than subsystems. Third, it is responsibility-oriented. The manager of each subsystem is given specific assignments so that inputs, outputs, and contribution to *total system* effectiveness can be measured.

Systems management works to ensure that organizations, responsibilities, knowledge, and data are integrated toward achieving overall objectives. Thus, the orientation of the systems manager is to consider the interactions and interdependencies between various subsystems and with the environment. Interdependencies are recognized and plans and actions are made to account for them. This contrasts with the more typical management view, which is to focus on individual functions and tasks, and to enhance the performance of a unit or department, even when at the expense of others or the total organization.

Systems Management, Systems Analysis, and Systems Engineering

The relationship between systems management, systems analysis, and systems engineering can be explained in terms of *when* they are applied during the life cycle of a system. Systems management performs the basic managerial functions of planning, organization, and control throughout the life of a system, but the focus remains on coordinating and integrating work rather than actually performing it.

As Figure 3-10 shows, systems management often works in parallel with systems engineering and utilizes the tools of systems analysis. The purpose of systems analysis is to ask questions about the goal or mission of the system, the kind and nature of resources to use, and the organization of people and facilities. In systems management, systems analysis is used to plan and control activities and materials (scheduling and inventory control), and to evaluate system operation to determine when and why the system is not functioning properly.

Systems management entails identification of total system requirements, control over the evolution of requirements and design, integration of technical efforts, and development of data and documentation. It is applied over the full life cycle of the system. As DeGreene notes, system management serves two broad purposes: *Systems development management* and *systems operations management;* the first applies to the development and growth of a system (the management of the *development* process), and the second to the actual *operation* or use of a system.[26]

Figure 3-10
Application of systems methodologies during the system life cycle.

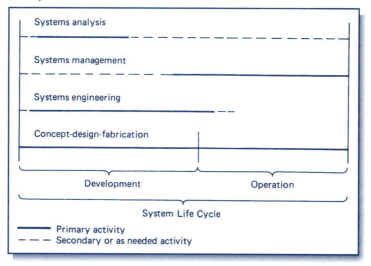

3.9 SUMMARY

Systems thinking is a useful way of dealing with complex phenomena. It implies the ability to view a seemingly confused or chaotic situation in such a way as to discern a degree of order and structure in the situation. A system is defined as an assemblage of parts where (1) the parts are affected by being in the system, (2) the assembly does something, and (3) the assembly is of particular interest. What is called the system depends upon one's point of view and purpose. Projects are systems created for the purpose of making systems.

Human organizations are human-made, open systems. They are sociotechnical systems, meaning they are social systems organized around a technology. They interact with the environment from which inputs are obtained. In establishing goals and methods of operation, managers must deal with subsystems in the environment and account for how these subsystems influence the organization.

Functional subsystems provide the specializations necessary for organizations to achieve their goals. Management subsystems organize these subsystems and are responsible for organization performance. Management systems are hierarchical: Managers at the technical level deal directly with the tasks and technology of the organization; managers at the organization level are responsible for coordinating activities at the technical level and integrating activities across functional areas; managers at the institutional level interface with the environment and develop goals and strategies of the overall organization. Project managers typically are at the organization level.

Systems thinking is a way of conceptualizing and analyzing physical entities, but it is also a way for approaching problems. This is called the "systems approach." The systems approach is action-oriented; it provides a conceptual framework, a process, and a management system to guide the planning, implementing, and managing of solutions and organizations. The methodologies for implementing the systems approach are systems analysis, systems engineering, and systems management.

Systems analysis is the class of approaches concerned with determining whether alternative solutions or elements of a system sufficiently contribute to its desired objective. An essential feature of systems analysis is the use of modeling to perform tradeoff studies in selecting among alternatives. Systems analysis provides a rigorous, logical, and scientific basis for analysis; however, judgment and intuition nonetheless play important roles in formulating objectives, generating and comparing alternatives, and making the final decision.

Systems engineering organizes the process of designing systems to satisfy operational requirements. It refers to the process of translating operational requirements into functional requirements, then expanding these into detailed end-item equipment and support requirements. Requirements refer to the proper mix of mission hardware, software, personnel, training, procedures, and logistics support to achieve integrated, cost-effective system design. The process relates system design and development efforts with other system life cycle requirements for fabrication, installation, test, evaluation, production, maintenance, support, and eventual phase-out of the system.[27]

Systems management is the process of monitoring and controlling a system to ensure fulfillment of overall system objectives. The manager's role is to consider the interactions and interdependencies between various subsystems and with the environment, and to ensure that all necessary disciplines and functional areas are integrated to satisfy system requirements.

The tools of systems analysis, the process of systems engineering, and the concepts of systems management are frequently utilized in the planning, organizing, and execution of projects, especially large-scale and technological projects. In the development of technical systems, management of the systems engineering process is synonymous with project management. Within project management, the systems analysis framework is employed for problem solving. Although project and systems management both emphasize integration of activities to achieve overall goals, one distinction between them is that the former ceases after a project is terminated, whereas the latter continues for the life of the system.[28]

This section of the book has given you an overview of project management, its origins, applications, and underlying systems philosophy. Projects are of finite duration, so of course they always have a beginning and an ending. The activities that go on at the start, the finish, and everything in between comprise the life of the project. In all projects, what "goes on"—the kinds of tasks and activities—tends to follow a sequence of stages, regardless of the kind of project. Some of these activities were alluded to in the examples in Chapter 2, such as doing a feasibility study, preparing a proposal, forming a team, preparing a schedule and budget, and so on. The sequence that activities follow in the life of a project is called the project life cycle. The next section of the book discusses project life cycles and describes a normative approach for conducting projects called the systems development cycle.

REVIEW QUESTIONS

1. What distinguishes systems thinking from analytical thinking? Is systems thinking something new or is it just another perspective? Explain.
2. Define system. What notable features enable you to see something as a system? Describe briefly the American legal or education system in terms of these features.
3. How can several people looking at the same thing see the "system" in it differently?
4. Describe the following concepts and explain how they fit into systems thinking: elements, subsystems, environment, boundary, open systems, objectives, structure, inputs, outputs, process, and constraints.
5. Describe the difference between open and closed systems, and between human-made and natural systems. Are all natural systems open systems?
6. Is a space vehicle an open system? Is an organization an open system? Explain.
7. Why are organizations called socio-technical systems? Are they ever just social systems?
8. What are the limitations of traditional organizational charts? How do "systems models" of organizations differ from these charts?
9. Describe the features and properties that distinguish human organizations from other systems.
10. What is the manager's environmental problem?
11. What are some internal subsystems of organizations? Distinguish between functional subsystems and managerial subsystems.
12. What are the three levels of the management systems hierarchy? How do the roles, perspectives, and time orientation differ between levels? Describe the three levels for a school system; for a religious organization; for a hospital; for the military; for a corporation.
13. What is the relevance of systems thinking to project management?
14. Briefly describe the systems approach. Where does the systems approach apply? In a sentence, explain what a manager does with the systems approach that she might not do otherwise.
15. What things does the problem solver keep in mind when applying the systems approach?
16. Describe how the following elements of the systems approach apply to projects and project management: Objectives, environment, resources, subsystems, and management.

17. Describe the systems approach in Figure 3-6. How does this process vary from situation to situation?

18. What is the systems life cycle? What is the importance of recognizing life cycles in systems design and management?

19. How does systems analysis compare to other types of analysis? If analytical thinking is different from systems thinking, then how is systems analysis a form of systems thinking?

20. Describe the elements and stages of systems analysis shown in Figure 3-8. What is the role of the model in systems analysis?

21. Give some examples of physical models; of graphical models; of mathematical models.

22. Why is systems engineering a systems approach? How does it differ and how is it similar to systems analysis?

23. Describe the stages of systems engineering in Figure 3-9. Think of some projects and describe the stages of systems engineering in these projects.

24. What is the emphasis in systems management? How does it differ from just management? How do systems analysis, systems engineering, and life cycles fit into systems management?

QUESTIONS ABOUT THE STUDY PROJECT

1. Conceptualize the project organization (the project team and the parent organization of the team) you are studying as a system. What are the elements, attributes, environment, and so on? What are its internal subsystems—functional breakdown and management-hierarchy subsystems? What are the relevant subsystems in the environment? Who are the decision makers?

2. Describe the role of the project manager with respect to these subsystems, both internal and external. What is the nature of his or her responsibilities in these subsystems? How aware is the project manager of the project "environment" and what does he or she do that reflects this awareness?

3. Now, conceptualize the output or end-item of the project as a system. Again, focus on the elements, relationships, attributes, subsystems, environment, and so on. All projects, whether directed at making a physical product (e.g., computer, space station, skyscraper, research report) or a conceptual product (e.g., providing a service or giving consultation and advice), are devoted to producing systems. This exercise will help the reader better understand what the project is doing. It is also good preparation for the topics of the next chapter.

4. Has systems analysis been used anywhere in the project? If so, describe where it has been used, the nature of the systems analysis (the problem, objectives, criteria, and so on), the types of models used, how alternatives are evaluated and selected, and who does the analysis. If not, comment about the reasons. What kinds of decision-making and problem-solving approaches are used instead? How are alternatives evaluated?

5. If the study project involves engineering or integration of many components, is the systems engineering process used? Is there a section, department, or task in the project called systems engineering? If so, elaborate. Are there functions or phases of the project which seem to resemble the systems engineering process?

   As described in this chapter, besides the main end-item or operating system (i.e., the output objective of the project), systems engineering also addresses the support system—that system which supports installation, operation, maintenance, evaluation, and enhancement of the operating system. Describe the support system in the study project and its development.

6. What aspects of the project or parent organization appear to use systems management? What aspects do not use systems management? Describe the appropriateness or inappropriateness of systems management in the project you are studying.

Case 3-1   Glades County Sanitary District

Glades County is a region on the Gulf Coast with a population of 600,000. About 90 percent of the population is located in and near the city of Sitkus. The main attractions of the area are its clean, sandy beaches and nearby fishing. Resorts, restaurants, hotels, retailers, and the Sitkus/Glades County economy in general rely on these attractions for tourist dollars.

In the last decade, Glades County has experienced a near doubling of population and industry. One result has been the noticeable increase in the level of water pollution along the coast due primarily to the increased raw sewage dumped by Glades County into the Gulf. Ordinarily, the Glades County sewer system directs effluent waste through filtration plants before pumping it into the Gulf. Although the Glades County Sanitary District (GCSD) usually is able to handle the county's sewage, during heavy rains the runoff from paved surfaces exceeds sewer capacity and must be diverted past filtration plants, directly into the Gulf. Following heavy rains, the beaches are cluttered with dead fish and debris. The Gulf fishing trade also is affected; pollution drives away desirable fish. Recently, the water pollution level has become high enough to damage both the tourist and fishing trade. Besides coastal pollution, there is also concern that as the population continues to increase, the county's primary fresh water source, Glades River, will also become polluted.

The GCSD has been mandated to prepare a comprehensive water waste management program that will reverse the trend in pollution along the Gulf Coast as well as handle the expected increase in effluent wastes over the next 20 years. Although not yet specified, it is known that the program will include new sewers, filtration plants, and stricter anti-pollution laws. As a first step, GCSD must establish the overall direction and mission of the program.

Wherever possible, answer the following questions (given the limited information, it is okay to advance some logical guesses; if you are not able to answer a question for lack of information, indicate how and where, as a systems analyst, you would get it):

1. What is the system? What are its key elements and subsystems? What are the boundaries and how are they determined? What is the environment?

2. Who are the decision makers?

3. What is the problem? Carefully formulate it.

4. Define the overall objective of the water waste management program. Because the program is wide-ranging in scope, you should break this down into several subobjectives.

5. Define the criteria or measures of performance to be used to determine whether the objectives of the program are being met. Specify several criteria for each subobjective. As much as possible, the criteria should be quantitative, although some qualitative measures should also be included. How will you know if the criteria that you define are the appropriate ones to use?

6. What are the resources and constraints?

7. Elaborate on the kinds of alternatives and range of solutions to solving the problem.

8. Discuss some techniques that could be used to help evaluate which alternatives are best.

1. Peter Schoderbek, Asterios Kefalas, and Charles Schoderbek, *Management Systems: Conceptual Considerations* (Dallas: Business Publications, 1975): 7–8.

2. John Naughton and Geoff Peters, *Systems Performance: Human Factors and Systems Failures* (Milton Keynes, Great Britain: The Open University, 1976): 8–12.

3. Ibid., 11. Innumerable systems can be perceived from any one entity. Kenneth Boulding, in *The World as a Total System* (Beverly Hills: Sage, 1985), describes the world as physical, biological, social, economic, political, communication, and evaluative systems.

4. See Fremont Kast and James Rosenzweig, "The Modern View: A Systems Approach." In *Systems Behavior*, 2d ed., John Beishon and Geoff Peters, eds., (London: Harper & Row, 1976): 19–25.

5. "Realistic" is relative, and given greater time and resources, formally unrealistic objectives may become more feasible and realistic. It is possible to uniquely structure an organization that is "best suited" for working toward a particular goal, whether or not that goal is ever achieved.

6. David Cleland and William King, *Management: A Systems Approach*, (New York: McGraw-Hill, 1972): 89.

7. The material in the section is adapted from J. Law and M. Callon, "The Life and Death of an Aircraft: A Network Analysis of Technical Change," in W. Bijker and J. Law, eds., *Shaping Society/Building Technology* (Cambridge, MA: MIT Press, 1992).

8. Ibid.

9. See Talcott Parsons, *Structure and Process in Modern Societies* (New York: Free Press, 1960): 60–96; Herbert A. Simon, *The New Science of Management Decision* (New York: Harper & Row, 1960): 49–50; and Thomas Petit, "A Behavioral Theory of Management," *Academy of Management Journal* (December 1967): 346.

10. C. West Churchman, *The Systems Approach and Its Enemies* (New York: Basic Books, 1979): 4–5.

11. Much of the discussion in this section is based upon C. West Churchman, *The Systems Approach* (New York: Dell, 1968): 30–39.

12. P. G. Thome and R. G. Willard, "The Systems Approach: A Unified Concept of Planning," in *Systems Analysis*, S. L. Optner, ed. (Middlesex, England: Penguin Books, 1973): 212.

13. Ibid., 212–215.

14. The stages of technological products and their impact on competitive markets is eloquently described by Richard Foster in *Innovation: The Attacker's Advantage* (New York: Summit Books, 1986).

15. Malcolm W. Hoag, "An Introduction to Systems Analysis," in *Systems Analysis,* S. L. Optner, ed. (Middlesex, England: Penguin, 1973): 37.

16. Operations research (OR) is problem-solving pertaining to the operations of an organization. OR employs mathematical methods for finding the best solution to satisfy a stated objective under restriction of constrained resources. OR typically is *not* concerned with defining objectives or determining what are the resources and constraints. These, and often the alternatives themselves, must be well-defined before the techniques of OR can be applied to find a solution. See, for example, H. A. Taha, *Operations Research: An Introduction,* 3d ed. (New York: MacMillan, 1982); and W. P. Cooke, *Quantitative Methods for Management Decisions* (New York: McGraw-Hill, 1985).

17. H. R. Hamilton et al., *Systems Simulation for Regional Analysis* (Cambridge: The M.I.T. Press, 1972).

18. See Herman Kahn and Irwin Mann, *Ten Common Pitfalls* (Santa Monica, CA: The RAND Corporation, RM 1937, 1957).

19. E. S. Quade and W. I. Boucher, eds., *Systems Analysis and Policy Planning: Applications in Defense* (New York: Elsevier Publishing, 1968): 11–14.

20. Adapted from C. W. N. Thompson and G. J. Rath, "Making Your Health Systems Work: A Systems Analysis Approach" (Chicago: Annual Meeting of the American Academy of Pediatrics, October 20–24, 1973).

21. Example adapted from Richard Johnson, Fremont Kast, and James Rosenzweig, *The Theory and Management of Systems* 3d ed. (New York: McGraw-Hill, 1973): 135–36.

22. Portions of this section are derived from four sources: Benjamin S. Blanchard and Walter J. Fabrycky, *Systems Engineering and Analysis* (Upper Saddle River, NJ: Prentice Hall, 1981): 18–52; Robert Boguslaw, *The New Utopians: A Study of System Design and Social Change* (Upper Saddle River, NJ: Prentice Hall, 1965): 99–112; Harold Chestnut, *Systems Engineering Methods* (New York: John Wiley & Sons, 1967): 1–41; G. W. Jenkins, "The Systems Approach," in *Systems Behavior,* 2d ed., John Beishan and Geoff Peters, eds. (London: Harper & Row for the Open University Press, 1976): 78–101.

23. Jenkins, ibid., 82.

24. See Walter Beam, *Systems Engineering: Architecture and Design* (New York: McGraw-Hill, 1990).

25. Portions of the discussion on systems management are adopted from Cleland and King, *Management: A Systems Approach,* 171–173; and Johnson, Kast, and Rosenzweig, *The Theory and Management of Systems,* 122–30.

26. Kenyon B. DeGreene, "Systems and Psychology," in *Systems Behavior,* 2d ed., John Beishon and Geoff Peters, eds. (London: Harper & Row for the Open University Press, 1976): 141–143.

27. Wilton P. Chase, *Management of Systems Engineering* (New York: Wiley & Sons, 1974): 125.

28. The term "systems management" sometimes pertains to systems that are designed to operate within defined organization boundaries, whereas project management often extends beyond the boundary of the organization responsible for mission accomplishment. Project management thus relies more upon persuasion than formal authority to coordinate and organize activities (this is discussed in Chapter 15). See Johnson, Kast, and Rosenzweig, *The Theory and Management of Systems,* 395.

Part

Systems Development Cycle

CHAPTER 4

*Systems Development Cycle:
Early Stages*

CHAPTER 5

*Systems Development Cycle:
Middle and Later Stages*

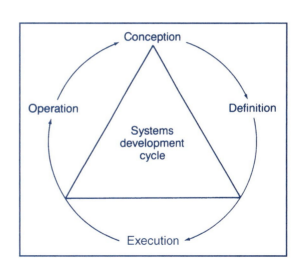

Most systems move inexorably through a process or series of developmental stages. In planned human systems, development occurs through an intentional, logical sequence of prescribed activities called the systems development cycle. Project management takes place within the broader context of systems development and is the function responsible for planning activities and for organizing and guiding their execution. The two chapters in this section outline the process of systems development and describe the role of project management within its stages.

4

Systems Development Cycle: Early Stages

> There is . . . a time to be born, and a time to die; a time to plant, and a time to reap; a time to kill, and a time to heal; a time to break down, and a time to build up . . .

—Ecclesiastes 3:1

An important aspect of the systems approach to management is the concept of "life cycle"—the basic pattern of change that occurs throughout the life of a system. There are two ways of considering life cycles in the systems approach: One is to recognize the *natural process* that occurs in all dynamic systems—that of birth, life, and death; the other is to incorporate such recognition into the planning and management of systems.

The practice of project management occurs within the context of just such a natural process. For any human-made system, the process of developing, implementing, and operating the system involves a logical sequence of activities called the *systems development cycle;* within that cycle is where projects occur. In turn, each project also follows a nominal progression of activities from beginning to end, which is called the *project life cycle.* This chapter and the next describe features of the project life cycle and its relation to systems development. The present chapter focuses on the early stages of the systems development cycle and the role played by project management. The next chapter will consider the middle and later stages of the systems development cycle.

4.1   SYSTEMS LIFE CYCLES

Systems are dynamic—they change over time. Using systems terminology, we say that the state of the system is in *flux*. The flux in system properties is definitely not random; it tends to follow a distinct pattern that is repeated again and again. Mentioned earlier was the obvious life cycle of living organisms—birth, growth, maturity, decline, and death, and the similarity in cycles among virtually all human-made products and organizations. Recognizing this is important because it enables us to create systems, anticipate and guide their actions, and plan appropriately for them.

Project Life Cycle

Projects are undertaken for the purpose of developing systems—either to create new ones or improve existing ones. The natural life cycle of systems gives rise to a similar life cycle in projects called the *project life cycle.* Each project has a starting point and progresses toward a predetermined conclusion during which the state of the project organization changes. Starting with project conceptualization, projects are characterized by a buildup in "activity" that eventually peaks and then declines until project termination—the typical pattern shown in Figure 4-1. This activity in a project can be measured in various ways, such as the amount of money spent on the project, the number of people working on it, the amount of materials being utilized, the percentage of total organizational effort devoted to it, or the amount of conflict generated between project and functional units.

Besides changes in the level of activity, the nature and emphasis of the activity also vary. For example, consider the mix of project personnel: During early stages of the project, users and planners dominate; during middle stages, designers, builders, and implementers are in charge; in later stages, users and operators take over.

Despite changes in level and mix of activity, three measures of activity are applied during the full span of a project: *Time, cost,* and *performance. Time* refers to the progress of activities and the extent to which schedules and deadlines are being met. *Cost* refers to the rate of resource expenditure and how it compares to budget constraints imposed on the project. *Performance* refers to specifications and requirements established for the outputs of the project (for example, the speed and range of an aircraft, the consumer appeal of a new product, the results of polls for a candidate running for office) and how they compare to objectives. Ability to meet the requirements is a measure of the *quality* of the project outputs. Project organizations attempt to achieve time, cost, and performance requirements during successive advances throughout the life of the project.

Managing the Project Life Cycle

The management of project life cycles requires special treatment. In general, management must be *adaptable,* both to changes induced by the life cycle of each individual project as well as to changes induced by the life cycles of multiple, concurrent projects. Unlike nonproject repetitive operations where activities tend to be stable, the

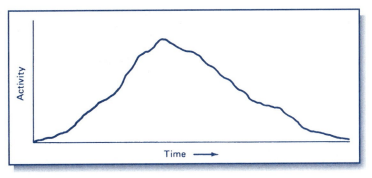

Figure 4-1
Level of activity during the project life cycle.

project life cycle puts resources, costs, and schedules in a constant state of change. To respond, management must be flexible. Little that is done in a project can be considered repetitive or even routine. Work schedules, budgets, and tasks must be tailored to fit the stages of the project life cycle.

All life cycles contain an element of uncertainty. Unforeseen obstacles, which are virtually inevitable, can cause missed deadlines, cost overruns, and poor system performance. Management must anticipate problems and uncertainties and be able to replan activities and shift resources.

Many organizations undertake several projects at once, and at any given time each may be at a different stage of the life cycle. Although some projects are just being started, others have reached maturity or are being phased out. Management must be able to continuously balance resources among these projects so the individual requirements of each are fulfilled and their sum does not exceed the capacity of the parent organization.

4.2   SYSTEMS DEVELOPMENT CYCLE

The life cycle of a human-made system can be segmented into a logical series of phases or stages, each representative of the types of tasks or activities typically conducted during some period in the life of the system. Figure 4-2 shows one way of dividing the life cycle into four phases:

1. Conception phase (Phase A)
2. Definition phase (Phase B)
3. Execution phase (Phase C)
4. Operation phase (Phase D)

This normative four-phase sequence, called the *systems development cycle*, encompasses the total developmental life cycle of systems. The phases overlap and interact, yet are clearly differentiable. They reflect the natural order of thought and action in the development of human-made systems, whether consumer products, space vehicles, computer information systems, company relocations, movie productions, or even political campaigns. For some systems the development cycle overlaps identically with the project life cycle. In others, only portions of systems development are covered in the project life cycle, such as beginning with the definition phase or terminating with the execution phase.

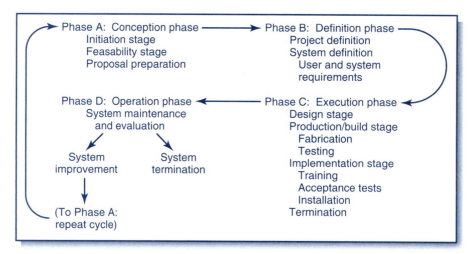

Figure 4-2
Four-phase model of the systems development cycle.

A project typically spans Phases A through C, the conception, definition and execution phases of the cycle. In that context, a project can be thought of as *an organization that exists to develop a system*, and the *project life cycle* as being the first three phases of the systems development cycle. When Phase C is terminated upon implementation of the system, so is the project. At that time the system transits from being the end-result of a project to being an operational entity.

Virtually all projects progress through Phases A, B, and C, though not necessarily through all the activities shown in Figure 4-2. The actual steps in the project life cycle depend on the system or end-item being developed; some stages might receive little emphasis or even be skipped entirely. In general, however, most every project *does* involve at least most of the activities shown in Figure 4-2, even if informally. Many projects do not involve formal proposal preparation, but every project starts as a proposal from *someone*. Similarly, not every project requires design and production as construed in manufacturing and construction, but each does require the designing and bringing together of elements to produce a final result. Even in a consulting project, for example, the investigation of the client situation must be conceptualized and laid out (design), the investigation results compiled and edited to produce the final report (production), and the report presented to the client (implementation).

Each phase of the cycle has specific content and management approaches. Between phases are points at which decisions are made concerning the preceding phase and whether the next phase should be undertaken or the project abandoned. Though the number of phases and details for each are a matter of judgment and differ for every project, the sequence is similar for virtually all projects.

A project can be terminated at the juncture between phases either by prior contractual arrangement or because management decides it is not worth continuing. In large-scale endeavors such as urban renewal, product development, and space and weapons systems development—where the development cycle spans many years, the cycle itself is often treated as a *program* and the phases within it as separate *projects*—sometimes each conducted by a different contracting organization. For example, Phase A would be treated as a project and managed by one organization, Phase B as another project managed by a different organization, and so on. The glue keeping all of the projects and organizations on track throughout is the program manager.

Within the systems development cycle are several main actors (interested parties):

1. System *users,* also called customers or clients. These include
   a. User top management
   b. User operators
2. The system development organization (SDO), also called the *contractor,* developer, promoter, or consultant, includes
   a. Contractor top management (corporate and functional managers)
   b. Project management (project manager and staff)
   c. The doers—professional, trade, assembly, and other workers

Users are the persons or groups for whom the project is being undertaken and who will acquire and/or operate the system when it is completed. User top management pays for and makes decisions about the project, whereas user operators will utilize or become the direct recipients of the project end-item or outputs. The Systems Development Organization or contractor is the group doing the project, that is, studying, designing, and developing the system. It is usually external to the user organization, although, of course, the contractor group might reside within the same organization as the user, which would be the case of an internal consulting/support group. Because in most cases the user *pays* the SDO or contractor to perform the project, the user can also be thought of as the *buyer* and the contractor as the *seller.* Use of these terms makes more sense when you think of a project in the context of being a contract between two parties wherein one party agrees to provide services to the other in return for some payment. The project manager usually works for the contractor, though users may also have project managers to represent their interests.

Besides the individuals or groups listed previously, the cycle usually involves other key actors. These include other individuals, groups, or organizations that have vested interests and/or influence on the conduct of the project or its objectives. They are project *stakeholders,* part of the environmental subsystems or the global system mentioned in Chapter 3. Anyone who is affected by the project who potentially can alter its outcome is a stakeholder.

Phase A: Conception

Every human-made system is an attempt to solve a problem. The first step in solving a problem is recognition and acceptance that the problem exists. The person or group facing the problem—the users (so-called because they become the ones to "use" any proffered solution)—seek out someone who can help. Responding to the call is the contractor (the consultant, developer, or SDO) who believes it can develop a system to solve the problem. (The SDO comprises everyone who will work on the project— top management, project leaders, and others. In big projects it also includes both prime and associate contractors and subcontractors.) When there are multiple users (clients, customers) requesting the services of the contractor, contractor top management must determine which ones they want to respond to or approach for business. Contractor top management makes the preliminary contact with the user and selects the project manager, who in turn selects and organizes the team of workers who will perform the project.

Before the project is undertaken, a sizing up takes place. The contractor (1) examines the user's environment and objectives; (2) identifies alternative solutions, requisite resources, organization, and strategies; and (3) determines the technical, economic, and environmental feasibility of undertaking the project. Having done that, the contractor presents to the user a *letter of interest* or a *formal proposal* that describes the *system concept*—a suggested solution—and the contractor's capability of doing it. The user examines the solution for its appropriateness and for his perception of the contractor's ability to carry it off. Finally, in the case where several contractors have proposed solutions the user makes a choice from among them. All potential systems follow this rite of initiation, but only a relative few are judged to be practical, feasible, or sound enough to progress to Phase B. Most systems die in Phase A.

Phase B: Definition

After the user has decided to accept one of the proposals submitted in Phase A, a commitment is made to the contractor, and the system concept is now investigated and defined in greater detail. The contractor defines and scrutinizes the elements and subsystems of the proposed concept. The project team is expanded and begins to determine the necessary resource and performance requirements, major subsystems, components, support systems, and system interfaces, as well as project costs and schedules. Project management assembles a comprehensive plan indicating the activities, schedules, budgets, and resources necessary to design, build, and implement the system. After being evaluated for acceptability by contractor top management, the plan is forwarded to the user, who similarly evaluates it and decides whether to continue, revise, or cancel the project.

Phase C: Execution

The execution phase is when the work specified in the project plan is put into action. Therefore, this is where most of the project effort is expended. The execution phase is sometimes referred to as the "acquisition" phase because most system resources are acquired here and the user acquires the system at the end of it. It is also variously referred to as "design," "production," or "implementation," all of which refer to the progression the system makes from being an idea to a finished, physical end-item.

All systems have a pattern, configuration, or structure, and it is the *design* that portrays the pattern necessary for the system to fulfill requirements. To ensure requirements are satisfied, various design alternatives are evaluated through the use of models or mock-ups. Once an acceptable detailed design is chosen, the system goes into *production.* Production involves either fabrication of a single item or mass production. The bulk of the work is now handled by personnel in design, development, production, and manufacturing. Project management oversees and controls resources, motivates the workers, and reports progress to the user. Top management is kept apprised of project performance and progress.

Near the end of this phase the system is implemented; in other words, it is moved from the realm of the contractor to that of the user. It is installed and becomes a part of the user's environment. The user is prepared to operate the system through training and technical support.

Phase D: Operation

In the final, operation phase the system is deployed. The user takes charge, operates the system and evaluates its performance and ability to resolve the problem for which it was designed. The contractor may remain involved by providing maintenance support and evaluation services. Some systems are "one-shot" and either succeed or fail. There is no maintenance in these systems, per se, but evaluation of their outcomes is useful for the *next* similar system to be developed. A political campaign, rock concert, or the Mars rover expedition are examples. For such projects, Phase D may be very short (the campaign ends upon election day, the concert lasts only a few hours, and the Mars rover expires within a few months).[1]

However, for ongoing, operational systems such as products, equipment, and systems that people use and rely upon daily, Phase D may last for years or decades. In that case, important activities in Phase D include not only maintenance of the system, but evaluation and improvement.

All systems eventually outlive their purpose or simply wear out. System evaluation identifies when this occurs and suggests a course of action. One course is to phase out or scrap the system. The other is to retain the system but reconfigure or improve it so that it remains useful. In the latter case, system improvement becomes a new "system concept" and the beginning of a new systems development cycle.

One advantage of the systems development cycle is that it enables projects to be taken in steps (called the *phased project planning* approach). Decisions are made stage by stage, and objectives and outcomes are reevaluated between stages at increasing levels of detail. Major resource commitments are never made without thorough management review, so there is no need to commit "all or nothing" in the early stages of the project.

The phases of the cycle as described are not always performed in discrete sequence but are sometimes overlapped in a practice called *fast-tracking*. Before Phase B is completed, elements of Phase C are started, and before Phase C is completed, portions of Phase D are started. Fast-tracking can compress the time for developing and implementing a system; however, unless managed carefully, it presents the risk of overlooking or misdefining tasks and not meeting user requirements.

Also, the phases of the cycle and the steps within the phases are not necessarily performed in strict sequence. Rather, there is a back-and-forth exchange between the stages and phases, with *iterations* occurring within the general sequence. This *iterative* approach, which is especially common in software development projects, is described in the next chapter.

4.3 SYSTEMS DEVELOPMENT CYCLE, SYSTEMS ENGINEERING, AND PROJECT MANAGEMENT

Perhaps you have noticed a similarity between the systems development cycle and the systems engineering process (Chapter 3 and Appendix A). The difference between them is mainly one of scope. Systems engineering focuses on the scientific and technical aspects of systems to ensure that subsystems, components, support subsystems, and environmental subsystems interrelate and interface to satisfy functional requirements.[2] Although it covers the entire systems development cycle, systems engineering is mainly concerned with the conceptual and definition phases—formulating functional requirements, performing system tradeoff studies, and designing systems.

In contrast, the systems development cycle is broader in scope and encompasses virtually *all* considerations in systems development, not just configuration and integration, but also planning, scheduling, budgeting, control, organization, communication, negotiation, documentation, and resource acquisition and allocation—the elements of project management.

Organizational constraints greatly influence the course of the systems development cycle. The project manager is most aware of these constraints because it is he who, regardless of constraints, must guide the project and ensure that the system development is a success. The major constraints in projects are labor, facilities, capital, schedules, knowledge, and technology. They affect the cycle in the following ways:[3]

Sufficient labor (analysts, designers, managers, assembly and other workers) must be available at the right time; otherwise, the work simply cannot be done. Inappropriate or insufficient labor capacity slows the development process, prevents achievement of system objectives, or forces the project to be cancelled.

Even with sufficient labor, there must be *facilities* for them to conduct the work of analysis, design, development, testing, and fabrication. Labor must have the equipment, tools, and a place to work. When new facilities must be built, construction must begin in the systems development cycle long before they are needed.

Similarly, *sufficient capital* must be available to procure facilities, material and equipment, and support the labor force. Clearly, insufficient capital has the same impact on systems development as insufficient labor or facilities: The cycle slows down, system performance is degraded, or the project is cancelled.

Time is always a constraint. The user or management may impose a tight schedule in hopes of speeding up the development cycle, but unless sufficient labor, facilities, and capital are provided the effect will only be to compromise project objectives and system performance.

As the systems development cycle pushes the state of *knowledge,* uncertainty increases and the preceding constraints become more imposing. Requirements of advanced or "leading-edge" systems involve repetitive experimentation that tends to slow the development process and protract the project schedule. Developmental problems may become so difficult that system requirements have to be compromised or the project abandoned.

Even with sufficient knowledge, the contractor must have the *technology* to utilize that knowledge. Archaic or inappropriate technology has the same impact on the systems development cycle as inadequate labor, facilities, capital, or knowledge.

It is obvious that all of these constraints relate to the three dimensions of time, cost, and system performance, and that these three are not only project goals but also constraints that influence the course of the systems development cycle. Throughout the cycle, the project manager must balance the effect of these constraints and negotiate with management to acquire the labor, facilities, capital, and time to achieve system goals. Sometimes the project manager must also negotiate with the user to adjust time, cost, and performance goals to lessen the impact of resource constraints.

Starting in the next section, the phases of the systems development cycle will be examined more closely, emphasizing the activities and outcomes that relate to the role of the project manager. The first phase, conception, is examined in this chapter; the remaining phases, definition, execution, and operation are covered in Chapter 5.

The conception phase nominally comprises two separate stages. The first stage, project initiation, establishes that a "need" exists and that the need is worthy of investigation. The second stage, project feasibility, involves a detailed investigation and choosing a solution.

Project Initiation

The systems development process begins when the user perceives a problem, need, or opportunity. Let us just say that the user has an "idea." Ideas can originate anywhere—in corporate planning, marketing, engineering, manufacturing, or research and development. The user may be in a different organization or in the same organization as the systems development group or contractor. The systems development group may be its own user.

Initiation is the point where the idea for a system is born. Most problems are already being addressed in some way, though the way might be outmoded, inefficient, or otherwise unsatisfactory. At initiation the user perceives a *need,* which is recognition of both a problem and potential solutions for coping with the problem.[5] The user might also see benefits that would accrue should a better way be found. When the need grows out of competitive environmental factors, a decision about the idea must be made quickly.

Example 1: Vision Statement at Microsoft[6]

New product development projects are often initiated internally, starting with a document that outlines a "vision" about the proposed product. For example, at Microsoft each new product development project starts with a vision statement that gives a very short definition of the product and its goals. For a recent version of Excel, it was just five pages long.

The purpose of the vision statement is to communicate the concept and requirements of the product to the development team, other product groups, and management. At Microsoft this includes an executive summary with a one-sentence objective, a list specifying what the product will do and not do, and definitions of the customer and the competitors. The statement might describe product features and priorities in enough detail to begin preparing schedules for development, testing, user education, and preparation of English and nonEnglish product versions. It might also list requirements for the operating system, minimum memory, hardware disk space, processor speed, graphics, and dependencies on printer drivers and components, although usually such details evolve later. In general, the statement informs everyone about what they will do and not do, and gives them a common overview.

Beyond perceiving the need, project initiation requires proving that the need is significant or has merit and can be fulfilled at practical cost. It is easy to identify problems and muse about solutions, but the vast majority of ideas are ephemeral or of small worth. If the users decide to take an idea beyond speculation, they may implement the idea using a "quick and dirty" approach or, alternatively, they may undertake a more protracted, albeit systematic and thorough approach. The latter is the systems development approach. In systems development, only ideas with a reasonably high degree of certainty about success or return on investment are permitted to develop. To cull the few good ideas, the user organization undertakes a brief, initial investigation.

Many users know a problem exists but do not know what it is or how to explain it. During initial investigation, the user tries to clarify the problem and evaluate the merit of solutions. The investigation starts with fact-finding—interviews with upper level and functional managers, background research, and review of existing documentation. A clear statement of the problem is formulated, solution objectives are defined, and a list of alternative, potential solutions is compiled. In considering potential alternatives, emphasis is put on developing a *range* of solutions. No attempt is made yet to work on details of individual solutions. The emphasis is on breadth, not depth. The investigation focuses on the elements of the problem, including

- The environment.
- The needs, symptoms, problem definition, and objectives.
- Preliminary alternative solutions and the estimated costs, benefits, strengths, and weaknesses of each.
- Estimated budgets, wherever possible.
- Affected individuals and organizations.

The user must decide whether or not to proceed. Most ideas never get farther than this; really just "seeds" of ideas, they die before they can germinate. It is obvious why this occurs: although there are endless ideas about needs and potential solutions, resources are scarce and organizations can commit only to those comparative few ideas that provide the most return and seem to have the best chances of success. Only well-founded ideas receive commitment.

To commit to further study, the user must be convinced that

- Potential solutions are consistent with the goals and resources of the organization.
- A real need exists and funding is available to support it.
- The idea has sufficient priority in relation to the opportunity presented by others, present or future.
- The idea has particular value in terms of, for example, applying new technology, enhancing reputation, increasing market share, or raising profits.

The initial investigation is usually conducted by the user and is brief, requiring a few days or a few weeks at most. If, based upon the above criteria, the idea is found to warrant a full-scale, detailed investigation of the alternative solutions, then the idea becomes a "potential project" and is approved for the next stage, project feasibility.

Project Feasibility

Feasibility is the process of investigating a problem and developing a solution in sufficient detail to determine if it is economically viable and worthy of development.

There are several possible perspectives about the feasibility stage—what it entails, when it takes place, and which parties are involved. The initial investigation by users is really a "preliminary feasibility" study. If the users decide to further pursue the idea, they will solicit alternatives for solutions from one or more contractors. Each competing contractor performs its own internal feasibility study to assess the merit of the solicitation and evaluate its capability for submitting a winning proposal and obtaining a profitable contract with the user.

The purpose of the user's solicitation (called a *request for proposal* or *invitation to bid*) might be to find a contractor to perform the feasibility study, in which case the feasibility stage begins after a contractor is selected. Alternatively, the *process* that a contractor follows in responding to the request for proposal may itself be considered a feasibility study. In that case, when the user has evaluated competing responses and decided which, if any, contractor to select, the feasibility stage is completed. Selection of the winning contractor also marks the decision to advance to Phase B, definition.

These different interpretations of the feasibility stage are illustrated in Figure 4-3. The discussion will focus only on Theme A, that is, where the feasibility study is undertaken during the process of responding to a user's request. This is called "proposal preparation process." In general, a similar process is followed under Theme B as well.

Because each project requires allocation of resources and must be coordinated with other, ongoing projects in both user and contracting organizations, it must first be authorized by top management in both the user and contractor organizations. This is the purpose of the feasibility stage—to establish which solution and which contractor, if any, is best. The results of the feasibility study become the basis for determining whether or not the system should be advanced to Phase B.

The specifics of the feasibility stage include the user requesting proposals for solutions, contractors doing feasibility studies and preparing proposals, the user evaluating the proposals, and joint user-contractor negotiations for a project contract. This process of acquiring outside services through soliciting and evaluating proposals and establishing a contractual agreement is part of a process known as *procurement management,*

Figure 4-3
Different paths in the project feasibility stage.

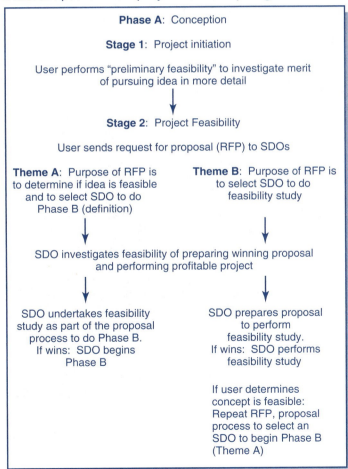

Phase A: Conception

Stage 1: Project initiation

User performs "preliminary feasibility" to investigate merit of pursuing idea in more detail

Stage 2: Project Feasibility

User sends request for proposal (RFP) to SDOs

Theme A: Purpose of RFP is to determine if idea is feasible and to select SDO to do Phase B (definition)

Theme B: Purpose of RFP is to select SDO to do feasibility study

SDO investigates feasibility of preparing winning proposal and performing profitable project

SDO undertakes feasibility study as part of the proposal process to do Phase B. If wins: SDO begins Phase B

SDO prepares proposal to perform feasibility study. If wins: SDO performs feasibility study

If user determines concept is feasible: Repeat RFP, proposal process to select an SDO to begin Phase B (Theme A)

which includes, later, monitoring project work for conformance to the contract and closing out the contract. Details of this process are considered in the following sections and later chapters.

Request for Proposal

Because a feasibility study is usually a time-consuming effort that requires particular expertise, the user typically chooses to bring in a contractor. (Sometimes the contractor is brought in as early as the initial investigation.) The user notifies one or more contractors, internal or external, by sending them a document called an *RFP—a request for proposal* (or a *request for quotation, invitation to bid,* or similar term).[7] The dual purpose of the RFP is to outline the user's idea (problem, need, etc.) and to solicit suggestions (proposals) for solutions—usually with the intent of awarding a contract for the best one. RFP's are sent to companies on the user's *bidders list.* Contractors not on the bidders list can learn about upcoming jobs in newsletters and bulletins. For example, the *Commerce Business Daily* is a daily publication that gives a synopsis of all federal jobs over $10,000. Many smaller contractors scan these and ask for RFP's about jobs they might be interested in bidding on.

The user describes his problems, objectives, and any requirements in the RFP. Contractors choosing to respond send in proposals, and the user assesses and awards a contract to one of them to perform the work. Figure 4-4 shows the contents of a typical RFP.

The user gets just what he asks for, and foul-ups later can often be traced to a poor RFP. The RFP must be clear, concise, and complete; when it is, the user can expect proposals that are clear, concise, and complete. Ultimately, the ability of contractors to *develop* good solutions uniquely tailored to fit the user's needs will depend, in part, on their understanding of the user's requirements (as specified in the RFP). Similarly, the ability of the user to *select* between contractors will depend on the information the contractors provide (again, as specified in the RFP). The appearance of an RFP is illustrated in Example 2.

Figure 4-4
Contents of a Request for Proposal.

Statement of Work
a. Description of problem, need, or general type of solutions to be investigated.
b. Scope of work to be performed by contractor, work to be included, work excluded, and work restrictions; criteria of acceptance for results or end-items.
c. Requirements for the solution, results, or end-item, including specifications and standards; description of how work will be measured; expected relationship between user and contractor; expected completion date; constraints on cost of work to be performed.

Proposal Requirements
Conditions placed on the proposal such as proposal contents and format, data requirements, sample forms to include, and submission location and deadline.

Contractual Provisions
Type of contract to be awarded, sample contract, and nondisclosure provisions.

Technical Information or Data
Any additional data, or name of a contact person for requesting additional data, necessary to develop a solution and prepare the proposal or price quote.

Example 2: RFP for Midwest Parcel Distribution Company

Following is the RFP for the LOGON system that Midwest Parcel Distribution Company sent to contractors chosen as most capable of meeting the requirements. (Only partial entries are shown in each section below to minimize the length of the example. Reference to "Appendix" is for a hypothetical appendix attached to RFP, not to appendices of this book.)

Introduction

After a 4-month search, you have been selected by Midwest Parcel Distribution Company (MPD) as a company capable of meeting our requirements for a new system. You are invited to present a proposal to supply the hardware, software, and support services for the system described in this request for proposal (RFP).

RFP Table of Contents

Section 1. Background
Section 2. Statement of Work
Section 3. Proposal Contents and Format
Section 4. Proposal Submittal
Section 5. Selection Date and Criteria
Section 6. Technical Information

Section 1. Background

MPD seeks to award a contract for the design, fabrication, installation, test, and checkout of a transport, storage, and database system for the automatic placement, storage, and retrieval of standardized shipping containers. The system, referred to as the logistical online system, hereafter referred to as LOGON, will be installed at MPD's main Chicago distribution facility. . . .

(Additional discussion of current environment at the Chicago distribution facility, projected future needs, and purpose and objectives of the new LOGON system).

Section 2. Statement of Work

The contractor's responsibility shall be for furnishing expertise, labor, material, tools, supervision, and services for the complete design, development, installation, check-out, and related services for full operational capability for the LOGON system. All necessary testing of systems and subsystems designed and installed by the contractor, as well as of current facilities, to ensure compatibility with the new system and with local, state, and federal requirements, will be performed by the contractor.

The LOGON system must meet minimal performance requirements, be compatible with existing structural and utility limitations of the facility, and be compliant with packaging and logistical standards and codes, all as specified in Section 6: Technical Information. . . .

(Additional discussion of services, equipment, and material to be provided by the contractor, and a list of specific end-items).

Exclusions

Removal of existing storage, placement, and retrieval equipment will be performed under separate contract and is the responsibility of MPD. The current operation is largely manual, and removal will be completed in time for the new system to be installed. . . . *(Discussion of services, equipment, and material provided by MPD or other contractors and for which the contractor is NOT responsible).*

Chapter 4 Systems Development Cycle: Early Stages 99

Scheduled Delivery Date

LOGON system to be fully operational on or before April 30, 2006. All necessary hardware, software, and support services necessary for full system operation will be supplied and/or completed by April 30, 2006.

Site installation will initiate no later than Nov. 30, 2005.

Subcontractors

Contractor shall submit with the proposal a list of subcontractors and the work to be assigned to each. Subcontractors shall be subject to MPD approval prior to placement of a contract.

Cost and Contract

Price of contract will not exceed $1.5 million.

Contract will be fixed price with a penalty charge of $1,000 per day for failure of the system to meet the target operational completion date of April 30, 2006.

Section 3. Proposal Content and Format

Proposal will include the following sections and conform to the instructions as follows:

Proposal Table of Contents

1. Cover sheet (use Form I provided in Appendix A)
2. Executive summary
3. Statement of work
   a. Background statement
   b. Technical approach, distinguishing features
   c. Project plan and schedule (use Forms II–V provided in Appendix A)
4. Budget (use Form VI provided in Appendix A)
5. Project organization and management plan
6. Prior experience and key personnel
7. Attachments
   a. Signed statement of confidentiality (use Form VII in Appendix A)
   b. MPD supplied confidential information
   c. Letters of commitment for work contracted to third parties.

Specific Instructions

(Details about the purpose, specific content, specific format, and approximate length for each of the sections listed above.)

Section 4. Proposal Submittal

Submittal

Contractor will submit two (2) copies of the completed proposal along with all MPD confidential information to:

Lynn Joffrey
Administrative Assistant (LOGON)
Midwest Parcel Distribution Company
13257 N. Wavelength Ave.
Chicago, IL 60699
(773)773-7733

Deadline

Proposal must be received at MPD by 5 P.M. August 15, 2004.

Section 5. Selection Date and Criteria

Selection and award date

September 5, 2004

Selection Criteria

Completed proposals received by the deadline will be evaluated by the following criteria:

1. Technical ability:
   a. Ability of system to meet performance requirements within the limitations of the existing facility, standards, and codes.
   b. User-friendliness of the system with respect to operation, reliability, and maintenance.
   c. Use of state-of-the-art technology to ensure system remains current into the next decade.
   d. System support services during contract period and available afterward.
2. Contractor's bid price.
3. Contractor experience and qualifications.
4. Project management and project plan.

Section 6. Technical Information

Confidentiality

The attached technical data and any additional requested drawings, specifications, requirements, and addenda shall be treated as confidential and the property of MPD. Information provided in this RFP or requested from MPD will not be duplicated beyond that necessary to prepare the proposal. The original and all duplicates will be returned with the proposal. (See Form VII, Appendix A)

Supporting Technical Data

1. Technical data attached in Appendix C to this RFP:
   a. Technical performance requirements and standards for LOGON system
   b. Facility structural and utility specifications
   c. Facility floor plan
2. For clarification and additional information, contact:
   Mr. Ed Demerest
   Project Director, Facilities
   Midwest Parcel Distribution Company
   13257 N. Wavelength Ave.
   Chicago, IL 60699
   (773) 773-7733

(Attached to the RFP are Appendices A, B, and C containing forms, agreements, and supporting technical data, standards, and performance requirements necessary for preparing and submitting a proposal.)

Each competing contractor must determine if it is capable of preparing a winning proposal and then, should it win, of performing the proposed work. The amount a contractor spends on preparing proposals and the proportion of contracts it wins significantly affect its company overhead because expenses for lost proposals must be charged to overhead. It is only in rare cases, such as major defense contracts, that winning contractors are reimbursed for their proposal expense. The feasibility of winning and concluding a project depend upon numerous factors, including

- Whether competitors have gotten a head start.
- Whether the contractor has sufficient money, facilities, and resources to invest in the project.

- Whether performance on the project is likely to be good for (or damaging to) the contractor's reputation.
- Other criteria, similar to those which the user employed in the initiation stage.

Sometimes contractors will respond to an RFP knowing that they cannot possibly win the project, doing so just to maintain a relationship with the solicitor, remain on the user's bidders list, or keep the field competitive. Sometimes *users* send out an RFP with no intent of ever signing with a contractor; they do it simply to gather ideas. Obviously this is a situation of which respondent contractors must be wary.

Sometimes proposals are submitted to potential users without an RFP. When a project group believes it has a system or solution to satisfy a need or solve a problem, the project manager works with his marketing department to identify prospective customers and then notifies them with an *unsolicited proposal*. Other times the project manager identifies follow-up work related to a current project and submits an unsolicited proposal to the current customer.

The Feasibility Study[8]

The statement of the problem as defined in the initiation stage is frequently incomplete, vague, or even incorrect. If an RFP has been sent out, it will contain such a statement as part of the statement of work. Thus typically one of the first steps of the contractor in responding to an RFP is to develop a more concise, accurate statement of the problem. This is the way to gaining a full and complete understanding of the user's problem situation.

The prime source of information about the problem is interviews with the user or documented information provided by the user. It is thus important that the contractor identify who the *user* really is. Surprisingly, this is not always obvious. The "real" user of the system is often confused with persons of rank and position who only represent the user. If the user is an organization, the contractor must determine the individual parties whose needs are to be met. The contractor will be working closely with the user throughout the feasibility study, so it is important that users be found who are both familiar with the problem and the workings of the organization. Sometimes, however, proposing contractors are required to maintain an "arms-length" relationship with the user to keep the competition "fair," although even then they are usually permitted to make inquiries to or seek additional information from a user contact person.

One way to ensure that the idea, problem, or solution stated by the user is concise and accurate is to start with a list of user needs. Problems originate from needs (Definition: a problem is an unsatisfied need), and so do solutions (Definition: a solution is a way to satisfy a need), so the concern in project management is that the solution adopted for the project fits the right needs. One of the first steps in preparing a proposal or conducting a feasibility study should be defining user needs. Probably one of the best authors on defining needs in the project context and the difficulty of doing it is J. Davidson Frame.[9] For defining user needs that are clear, concise, and accurate, he suggests the following process:

1. Ask the user to state the needs as clearly as possible.   A needs statement might already exist if an RFP has been prepared, though it might be vague or even incorrect because often the user is not clear about the needs.

2. Ask the user a complete set of questions to further elicit the needs.   These are questions that a competent contractor would know to ask. They include:

Are these real needs, or are there other, more fundamental ones?
Are the needs important enough to pursue?

Are we are capable of fulfilling these needs, or is someone else better suited?
If the needs are fulfilled, will they give rise to other needs?
Will satisfying these needs also satisfy others, or instead, would satisfying
   other needs indirectly fulfill these, also?
What effect do the unmet needs have on the organization and the user?
What other parties are affected by these needs and how will they react to
   our efforts?

3. Conduct research to better understand the needs.   "Research" means probing to gain the best understanding possible. It involves gathering whatever information necessary to understand the needs, define the problem, and propose a solution. Sources include interviews, organizational reports and memos, observations, modeling, and analysis of technical data or empirical test results.

4. Based on information from Steps 2 and 3, restate and document the needs.

5. Give the restated needs to the user.   If the user disagrees with the restated needs, repeat the previous steps as often as necessary to reach agreement. The process should conclude with a statement of needs that the user agrees to and that best represents the user's interests (rather than the interests of the contractor or other parties).

Because every project is an effort to fulfill needs, a statement of needs that is unclear, ill-stated, or incorrect will engender a project that is meandering, or worse, irrelevant. Attaining a good definition of needs is not easy. Frame describes the following troublesome aspects.[10]

1. Some needs are ever-changing.   They represent a moving target. Thus, for each need the question must be asked "Is this likely to change?" If the answer is yes, the solutions and plans addressing the need should be flexible and easy to change.

2. Some needs are only vaguely perceived.   It is a fact that most needs are vaguely perceived, at least initially, and the user requires assistance in identifying and clarifying them. Part of the role of the contractor is to help the user turn vague feelings about needs into definitive statements.

3. Solutions are confused with needs.   Attempting to state a need, the user or contractor states a *solution* instead. For example, "We need a new building" is not a statement of the need. True, maybe a new building will be required, but that is only one way of satisfying the need to, for example, overcome a space shortage (other ways include leasing additional space, or reducing the cause of the space shortage.). By confusing solutions with needs, a solution is selected prematurely and other, potentially better solutions, are precluded from consideration.

4. The needs identified are for the wrong user.   *Who* is the user? Is it the party that actually *feels* the need and is most affected by it, or is it the party who *pays* to resolve it? They might be different. The needs statement should reflect the opinion of the party to which the solution will be directed. Do not be content with what one party tells you is the need of another. Talk to the other party, too.

5. There is more than one user, and their needs differ.   When the user embodies several parties, all with valid needs, issues arise such as "Can *all* of their needs be addressed?" and "Do their needs conflict?" When multiple needs exist and are all valid, an attempt must be made to organize and classify them, such as into the needs hierarchy suggested by Frame.[11] For example, suppose the need for "more space" is a composite of the needs of three departments: One department is experiencing rapid employee growth and needs "more space for employees," another is replacing old computer equipment with new equipment and needs "new space for technology," and another is running low on storage space and needs "more room for inventory." These needs might all be handled at once by constructing a new building; however, if resources are limited they might have to be prioritized, restated, and dealt with individually. For example, if the need "more room for inventory" is restated to "reduce inventory," and, if that need is fulfilled, then space is freed-up to contribute toward meeting the need for "more space for employees." Similarly, restating the need from "new space for technology" to "upgraded utilities and hookups" changes the context of the problem and the solution.

6. User's needs are distorted by the "experts." Either inadvertently or intentionally the contractor can lead the user into a distorted statement of needs. This happens in at least three ways.

(a) The contractor suggests that the list of needs is much broader than the user thought. This increases the magnitude of the problem, and, of course, the amount of work the user will have to pay the contractor to do.

(b) The contractor reframes the needs in terms of what he, the contractor is (perhaps uniquely) best suited to do. This increases the likelihood that the user will hire the contractor (the need and contractor are a perfect fit!), and that the contractor will be able to easily fulfill the stated need.

(c) The contractor doesn't bother to ask, but rather *tells* the user what he needs (after all, the contractor *is* the expert).

Any of these cases can result in a muddled or incorrect statement of needs. Sometimes users are resistant to the idea of clarifying needs and expect the contractor to do it. The contractor should insist on the involvement of the user and work with the user until an agreement is reached on the final statement of user needs. This helps both parties to better understand the situation (needs and problems), ensuring that solutions will be appropriate, allowing for better project planning, and engendering user commitment to the solution and the project.

Conceptually, a need arises because of inadequacies within the *present system* or a gap between the output of present system and the desired output. Thus, another step in the feasibility stage is to *document* the present system. Documenting the present system is important because the appropriateness of a proposed system solution depends on how well the proposer understands the present (problem) system. Documentation should identify key system elements (inputs, outputs, functions, flows, subsystems, components, relationships, and attributes) using schematics and charts. The schematic in Figure 4-5, for example, was developed by a consultant in a hospital study to find ways of improving efficiency and reducing procurement and operating costs of surgical facilities and supplies. It shows components and flows in the present (problem) system and was useful for identifying areas of cost and procedural inefficiency.

Good definition of needs and complete documentation of the current system helps in developing a clear formulation of the problem. It also helps the contractor and user determine what the system objectives and user requirements should be. Systems objectives and user requirements delimit the scope of the work to only those areas essential to solving the problem.

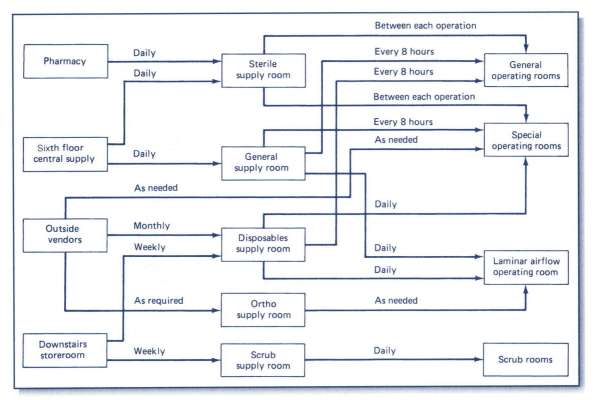

Figure 4-5
System schematic: Flow of supplies to the operating room.

Each contractor develops an approach to meeting the objectives, taking into account what the system must do (operating requirements to satisfy user needs), how it can be done (technical considerations), and the value of it (economic considerations). Alternative solutions may include new systems developed from scratch or modifications of off-the-shelf systems and existing technology. As in the initiation stage, a *range* of solutions should be sought, so project leaders must engender an atmosphere that encourages creativity and stimulates free flow of ideas.

The contractor now has a clear formulation of the problem, objectives and requirements, and alternative solutions to consider, which are the ingredients for conducting a systems analysis as described in Chapter 3. In the analysis, solutions are evaluated and the best ones selected based upon their ability to satisfy objectives and requirements given fixed resources of the contractor (capital, technical expertise, facilities) and constraints imposed by the customer. The requirements specify what the end-result or solution must do to resolve the problem and satisfy the customer. Similar to needs, the statement of requirements must be clear and complete. In the proposal, objectives are high-level requirements for the proposed solution. If the contractor is awarded the project, then it might be necessary to define the requirements in greater depth and technical detail before work can begin. This process of requirements definition is discussed in Chapter 5.

The final feasibility study document includes a summary of the data collected, description of the existing system, statement of the problem, criteria and methods used to evaluate alternatives, preferred solution(s), and reasons for its selection. The analysis procedure might also be included to show the customer the elements and steps that led to the solution. The feasibility study is combined with the project plan, bid price, and contractor qualifications to make up the project proposal.

4.6   THE PROJECT PROPOSAL

Proposal Preparation[12]

Because the contractor may have to commit a significant amount of time and money to preparing a proposal, the proposal preparation process must be first authorized by top management. The proposal effort is itself a project—with cost constraints, a deadline for submittal, and performance requirements—and so it should be managed like one. Upon authorization of the proposal process, a technically competent person is identified to be the project manager. He or she may become sole manager of the proposal effort or, alternatively, may work with a proposal manager who has had experience in conducting proposal-related activities. The project team, or part of it, is selected by the project manager to help prepare the proposal. Usually the rest of the project team cannot be specified until the proposal effort has been completed.

The project manager reviews the requirements of the RFP and then prepares a detailed summary for the project. This summary guides the effort and prevents the focus from shifting to irrelevant technical or managerial considerations.

In preparing the proposal the project team outlines the work to be done for the solution chosen in the feasibility study. This is referred to in the proposal as the *statement of work* (SOW). A similar statement may exist in the RFP that identifies the user's requirements for the technical content of the proposal (see Figure 4-4). The SOW in the proposal might simply repeat the SOW in the RFP, although, more likely (based upon new information culled during the feasibility study) it will be a somewhat expanded and more concise version of it. In cases where the contractor believes that the SOW in the RFP is inaccurate or incorrect, or that a different approach is needed than that suggested by the user, the SOWs in the proposal and in the RFP might be substantially different. The SOW is reviewed with the user for clarity and correctness. In addition to the SOW, the team provides specifications (measurable, verifiable criteria) for the work. Sometimes approximate specifications are given, to be worked out more carefully and precisely later.

The proposal includes both the feasibility study and a plan for conducting the systems development project. The project team performs an economic evaluation to compare development and operating costs of the proposed solution with anticipated benefits. This evaluation will become a major criterion for user management in determining the project's feasibility and priority level among other projects.

During proposal preparation the project team must think through the entire project and prepare a project plan. The project plan addresses the dimensions of time, cost, and performance. A *work breakdown structure* (WBS) is used to determine the work necessary to achieve performance specifications and subsequent work schedules and cost estimates. WBSs, schedules, and cost breakdowns showing how the price was derived are included in the proposal. (These techniques are fully described in Part III of this book.) When more than one system solution is proposed, a plan is worked out for every one.

The proposal is both a sales device and a form of contract: The more detailed it is, the easier it is to work out prices, schedules, and other details, and to convince the user that the contractor is familiar with the work; this is a big help should the contract have to be negotiated.

In complex technical projects, the WBS is a systems engineering effort; it converts system requirements into functional block diagrams and schematic diagrams, which show components, interfaces, and quantitative design specifications for inputs, outputs, and processes. The effort is carried just to the level of detail necessary to satisfy proposal requirements; if the contract is won, the effort is resumed to the level of detail necessary to do the work.

Those contractor functional departments that would be involved in the project, if it is won, should be called upon to provide information for the proposal. This not only increases the accuracy of proposal estimates, it helps build commitment from those who will be doing the work.

During proposal preparation, the contractor should establish a dialogue with the user to determine which requirements are dominant among time, cost, and performance, and which solutions the user prefers. Even when the RFP is clear, there is need to confer with the user about details of scheduling, costing, specifications, reporting, and so on. Dialogue is the best way to ensure that terms in the proposal are clear and satisfy the user's requirements. Sometimes proposal preparation is iterative: The acceptance of one proposal leads to development of another, more detailed proposal. This is illustrated in Example 3.

The feasibility study and proposal preparation may take many weeks or months to complete. Although enough time must be spent to produce an acceptable proposal, not so much time should be spent that it becomes overly time-consuming and expensive. Do not do the entire project while preparing the proposal!

Throughout the proposal preparation, the project manager makes sure that all parts fit together and there is no duplication of effort. To assure nothing is overlooked, project managers typically employ checklists that, over the years, grow to accumulate the most important items on a proposal; they include, for example, key considerations for design, assembly, test, shipment, documentation, facilities, subcontractors, supplies, travel, labor rates, training, and payment.

Contractor top management is briefed about the scope of the proposal and the resources being committed to the project. Prior to submission to the user, the completed proposal is sent to top management for approval.

Proposals range in length from a few statements to many volumes. The content varies depending on purpose, format favored by user, relationship between user and contractor, technical complexity of the work, solicited versus unsolicited proposal, and so on. Figure 4-6 shows the main ingredients of a typical proposal.[13] If the proposal is prepared in response to an RFP, then the content and format of the proposal should conform exactly to any requirements or guidelines stated in the RFP.

Example 3: Writing Proposals for Real Estate Projects at Wutzrite Company

Customers come to the real estate department at Wutzrite Company for help in investigating and choosing real estate investment alternatives. A meeting is set up with the client to establish a clear definition of the investment "problem" and the client's goals. The client and several Wutzrite employees brainstorm about the problem to achieve the clearest, most accurate problem definition. A project "resource director" prepares a proposal that includes the problem definition, the pricing structure, and the steps to be taken in achieving a solution. In proposals that require developing a site or designing and constructing a building, a feasibility

Executive Summary

Perhaps this is the most important section of the proposal because it must convince the user that the proposal is worth considering. It should be more personal than the proposal and briefly state the qualifications, experience, and interests of the contractor, especially drawing attention to the unique or outstanding features of the proposal, the price, and the contractor's ability to do the project. The "contact" person with the contractor also is identified here. This section is important because it is here that user management decides whether or not to examine the rest of the proposal.

Technical Section (Statement of Work)

a. Indicates the scope of the work—the planned approach and the statement of work. It must be specific enough to avoid misunderstandings and demonstrate the method and appropriateness of the approach, yet not so specific as to "give away" the solution. It should also recognize and discuss any problems or limitations inherent to the approach.

b. Describes realistic benefits in sufficient detail to demonstrate that user needs will be fulfilled, but not so specific or enthusiastic as to promise benefits that the contractor may have difficulty in delivering.

c. Contains a schedule of when end-items will be delivered. It should be based upon the work breakdown structure and include the major project phases and key tasks, milestones, and reviews. In developmental projects, portions of this section may have to be negotiated.

Cost and Payment Section

Breaks down projected hours for direct, indirect, and special activities, associated labor charges and materials expenses, and price of project. Preferred or required contractual arrangement (see Appendix B on contracts) and method of payment may also be included.

Legal Section

Contains anticipated, possible, or likely problems and provisions for contingencies; for example, appropriate procedures for handling changes to the scope of the project and for terminating the project.

Management/Qualifications Section

Consists of background of the contractor organization, related experience and achievements, and financial responsibility. Organization of management, and resumes of project manager and key project personnel are also included.

Figure 4-6
Contents of a proposal.

study is included in the proposal. For projects that involve simply evaluating, improving, or determining the value of a site, no feasibility study is needed. If the client likes the proposal, the resource director prepares a second proposal specifying the steps of analysis in greater detail. The second proposal includes a work breakdown structure and a modified CPM network (see Chapters 6, 7 and 8). If approved by the client, the second proposal becomes the project plan. It specifies tasks to be done, dates to be completed, and is the basis for assigning personnel to the project. Usually the second proposal calls for a feasibility study, demographic study, or analysis of financing, tax, accounting, or other ramifications of the alternatives.

The information generated by the study or analysis is then submitted to the client in a third proposal that recommends what action the client should take regarding the alternatives investigated. Although the company does not perform contracting or construction work, if the study favors site development or construction, the real estate department will make recommendations about consultants, contractors, or construction firms.

Selection of Proposal[14]

The user evaluates proposals in a fashion similar to one used by the contractor in deciding which RFPs to respond to. Each proposal is evaluated according to criteria related to system performance, price, and schedule. Generally, priority and selection of projects is based upon considerations of

- Ability of solution to satisfy stated needs
- Return on investment
- Project plan and management
- Reputation of contractor
- Likelihood of success or failure (risks)
- Fit to contractor resources and technological capability

Because many users take it on faith that a competent contractor with a good plan will do a good job, choice of the best proposal is sometimes based more on the project plan, project management, and the qualifications and reputation of the contractor than on the proposed solution or technical approach. Thus, the schedule section of the proposal should include a rudimentary plan clearly indicating the key activities to be performed, start and end dates, and deliverables or end-items for each. Methods for preparing the plan are discussed in chapters 6 to 10.

A variety of methods are used for selecting the best proposals. One is a screening system that rejects proposals that fail to meet minimal requirements, such as rejecting proposals when the estimated rate of return of the suggested solution is less than 15 percent, the contractor has no experience with projects similar to the one proposed, or project team members average less than 5 years of related work experience.

Another method uses a checklist or weighted checklist for rating proposals according to a list of evaluation criteria. The proposal that receives the highest overall score wins. Specifically, each proposal is reviewed and given a score s_j for each criterion j. The overall score for the proposal is the sum of the scores for all criteria,

$$S = \Sigma s_j, \text{ where } j = 1, 2, \ldots, n$$

This method is called *simple rating*. One limitation of the method is that all evaluation criteria are treated as equally important. When some criteria are clearly more important than others, a different method called *weighted rating* should be used. In that method the relative importance of a criterion j is indicated by an assigned weight w_j. After a score has been given to a criterion, the score is multiplied by the weight of the criterion, $s_j \cdot w_j$. The overall score for the proposal is the sum of the $s_j \cdot w_j$ for all criteria,

$$S = \Sigma s_j w_j, \text{ where } j = 1, 2, \ldots, n$$
$$\Sigma w_j = 1, \text{ and } 0 \leq w_j \leq 1.0$$

The procedures for these methods are illustrated in Example 4.

Example 4: Evaluating Proposals at MPD Company

In response to the RFP sent to several contractors (Example 2), MPD received proposals from three companies: Iron Butterfly Contractors, Inc.; Lowball Company; and Modicum Associates. The proposals were reviewed and rated by a group of executives, facility managers, and operations experts at MPD's Chicago and New York offices. The proposals were each rated on five criteria using a five-point scale as follows:

Criteria	1	2	3	4	5
Technical solution approach	Bad	Poor	Adequate	Good	Excellent
Price of contract	>1.8	1.6–1.8	1.4–1.6	1.2–1.4	<1.4
Project organization and management	Bad	Poor	Adequate	Good	Excellent
Likelihood of meeting cost/schedule targets	Bad	Poor	Adequate	Good	Excellent
Reputation of contractor	Bad	Poor	Adequate	Good	Excellent

Simple Rating

The results of the group assessment for the three proposals were as follows.

Criteria	Scores		
	Iron Butterfly	Lowball	Modicum
Technical solution approach	4	2	5
Price of contract	5	5	2
Project organization/management	5	3	4
Likelihood of meeting cost/schedule targets	4	3	5
Reputation of contractor	4	4	5
Sum	22	17	21

Based on the sum of simple ratings, Iron Butterfly was rated the best.

Weighted Rating

Lowball's proposal was clearly the worst, but Iron Butterfly and Modicum were considered too close to make an objective decision. The rating group then decided to look at the criteria more closely and to assign weights to them as follows:

Criteria	Weight
Technical solution approach	0.25
Price of contract	0.25
Project organization and management	0.20
Likelihood of meeting cost/schedule targets	0.15
Reputation of contractor	0.15
	1.00

The weights reflect management's opinion of the relative importance of each of the criteria. Taking the weights into account, the proposals were scored as follows:

Criterion	Weight (w)	Iron Butterfly		Lowball		Modicum	
		s	(s)(w)	s	(s)(w)	s	(s)(w)
Technical solution approach	0.25	4	1.0	2	0.5	5	1.25
Price of contract	0.25	5	1.25	5	1.25	2	0.5
Project organization/ management	0.20	5	1.0	3	0.6	4	0.8
Risks of solution	0.15	4	0.6	3	0.45	5	0.75
Reputation of contractor	0.15	4	0.6	4	0.6	5	0.75
	Sum		4.45		3.4		4.05

Using the sum of the weighted ratings, Iron Butterfly Contractors stands out as having the superior proposal.

Assessment of proposals might also include evaluation of project risk, especially when the proposed solutions and associated levels of risk differ significantly between proposals. Methods for identifying and assessing risks are discussed in Chapter 10, "Managing Risks in Projects."

Proposal finalists are notified when the user has determined that at least one of the proposals is acceptable. Competing contractors may then be requested to provide more data or to make presentations. When a contractor has been selected, the recommendation is submitted to user top management for approval. If management accepts the recommendation, then a contract is awarded to the winner. If several contractors receive equal weight or if some terms in the proposal are unspecified or unquestionable, then negotiation is required to settle upon final terms and a contractor. If none of the proposals are acceptable or the feasibility studies reveal that the systems development process would be too costly, risky, or time-consuming, or have insufficient return, then the project is terminated.

4.7 PROJECT CONTRACTING

Contracting Environment and Contracting Process[15]

Contracting is ubiquitous in project management. The purpose of this section is to give an overall view of important contracting issues in project management. It is not intended to provide legal advice about contracts; for that you need an attorney or contracts specialist. All work in projects is done according to formal or informal contracts. Even in internal projects where users and contractors belong to the same organization, the objectives, requirements, and statements of work are documented such that user expectations are clearly known and that contracted work will conform to them. Most projects, however, involve some degree of external, legal contracting, because most require the user to formally hire an external organization to perform the work. As Figure 4-7 illustrates, this "external organization" might itself be a composite of many organizations linked by numerous contractual agreements. First, the user contracts with a principle party (the prime contractor or SDO) to be responsible for the

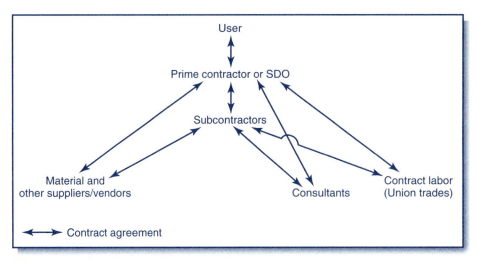

Figure 4-7
Contracting parties in a project.

overall project; in turn, this party might contract with secondary parties—subcontractors, vendors, consultants, material suppliers, and contract labor (union trade professionals) to be responsible for portions of the project; these secondary parties might then contract with tertiary parties.

Project contracting involves several considerations beyond those already discussed. In addition to asking what should be done and how it should be done, the question of *who* will do it needs to be put forth. The *RFP/proposal process* addresses that question, not only for the user as described before, but for any party seeking to hire another to do work. Whether it is the user, the prime contractor, secondary contractor, or anyone else down the line, each follows a process identical or analogous to the RFP/proposal process to document needs, solicit ideas, and choose between potential contractors.

By contracting the work, the customer is not necessarily relinquishing control over the project. In fact, the customer *should* retain part or a large measure of control. To that end, the contract should clearly specify the customer's role in tracking progress and making tradeoff decisions, and identify those project areas where the customer has authority for decisions or supervision over the contractor.

From the time when the contract agreement is reached until the time when the project is completed or terminated, the agreement must be *managed.* This involves ensuring that work performed is in conformance with the contract, and that the contract is up-to-date with respect to ongoing changes in the project, the customer's needs, and the contractor's capability. This process, called *contract administration*, is discussed in the next chapter.[16]

Subcontracting[17]

Each party in Figure 4-7 must decide whether it will do work itself or hire someone else. Some contractors do all the work; others require outside assistance, in which case they subcontract. Construction is an example: A general or prime contractor is hired by a user to manage the overall construction project, and perhaps fabricate and assemble the building structure. For specialized work such as wiring, plumbing, ventilation, and interior details, however, the contractor may subcontract with other organizations to do the work.

Even when a contractor could, conceptually, do all of the work, they may choose to subcontract if they are limited by capacity or facilities, or believe that a subcontractor could do the work at lower expense or higher quality. For development projects of large-scale systems, the prime contractor will usually design the overall system, major subsystems (and possibly assemblies and components), and then decide which elements of the system to produce itself and which to subcontract. When significant portions of project work are to be done by subcontractors, the user will often mandate prior notification about and approval of the subcontractors.

Usually, obligations in subcontracts exist solely between the contractor and subcontractor. That means, for example, that the contractor (not the user) is responsible for ensuring that the subcontractor performs work according to the requirements, and the contractor (not the user) is obligated to pay for the subcontracted work. Similarly, whenever the user wants to change the requirements, communication about those changes is channeled through the prime contractor to the subcontractor. Of course, if you are a subcontractor who has not been paid, you might want to appeal directly to the user and hope he will pressure the contractor into payment.

The specific type of contract agreement appropriate for a subcontract depends on the type of agreement between the user and the prime contractor. If this agreement (the prime contract) is fixed price, then subcontracts should also be fixed price; otherwise, the prime contractor risks being charged more by subcontractors than he will be paid by the user. For prime contracts that are cost-plus or incentive, the contractor has more latitude in using a variety of types of subcontracts.

Negotiating the Contract[18]

The purpose of negotiation is to clarify technical or other terms in the contract and to reach agreement on time, schedule, and performance obligations. Negotiation is not necessary on standardized items for which terms are simple and costs are fairly well known, but it is commonplace on complex systems that require development work and involve considerable uncertainty and risk. Different contractual arrangements offer advantages to the user and contractor, depending on the nature of the project. These are discussed in Appendix B; briefly, they are:

- *Fixed Price*—The price paid by the customer for the project is fixed regardless of the costs incurred by the contractor. The customer knows what the project will cost.

- *Cost-Plus*—The price paid by the customer is based on the costs incurred in the project plus the contractor's fee. The contractor is assured his costs will be covered.

- *Incentive*—The amount paid by the customer depends on the contractor's performance: Beyond an initial specified price, the contractor either receives a *bonus* for exceeding the requirements, or must pay the customer a *penalty* for failing to meet requirements. This arrangement affords the contractor opportunity to make a higher profit and reduces the customer's risk of the contractor not meeting requirements.

Although final negotiation is the last activity before a contractual agreement is reached, the negotiation process actually begins much earlier—during preparation of the proposal—because the proposal must be consistent with the kind of contract acceptable to both user and contractor. During negotiation, terms related to specifications, schedules, and price are converted into legal, contractual agreements. Ongoing negotiation improves communication and helps the user and contractor reach mutual understanding and expectations about the job. Final negotiation is the last opportunity to correct misperceptions that might have slipped through the RFP/proposal process.

Performance, schedule, and cost are interrelated, and a "package" agreement must be reached wherein all three parameters are acceptable to both parties. In highly competitive situations, the user will try to play one contractor against the other, and to raise performance specifications and decrease time and cost. Raising performance requirements, however, may increase corresponding costs to a level unacceptable to the contractor. In that case, each project manager takes on the role of salesperson by pushing the merits of their proposals. Throughout negotiation, their goal is to obtain an agreement to the best advantage of her company. In countering objections to the proposal, the project manager's best defense is a well-thought-out project plan that clearly shows what can or must be done to achieve certain desired parameters. A detailed project plan is often used to define the relatively "fixed" part of the plan—the work and the schedule; the details and final price are often somewhat negotiable.

To be in the most knowledgeable and competitive position, the project manager must learn as much as possible about the user and the competition. The project manager should determine, for example, if the user is under pressure to make a particular decision, needs the system as soon as possible, or faces an impending fiscal deadline. The project manager should determine if the user has historically shown a preference for one particular approach or contractor over others. She should also try to learn about the competition—their likely approach to the problem, costs, and competitive advantages and disadvantages. Information may be derived from historical information about past projects, published material, or employees who once worked for competitors. (Relying on the last source is ethically questionable, and, of course, works against the contractor whenever his employees are hired by a competitor.)

To be able to negotiate tradeoffs, the project manager must be intimately familiar with the technical details of system design, fabrication, and related costs. Sometimes the contract will include incentive or penalty clauses as inducements to complete the project before a certain date or below a certain cost. To competently negotiate such clauses, the project manager must be familiar with the project schedule and time-cost tradeoffs.

The signed contract becomes the binding agreement for the project. Any changes thereafter should follow formal change mechanisms, including change notices, reviews, customer approvals, and sometimes contract renegotiation—topics discussed in Chapter 11. Changes with legal implications should be anticipated and procedures for making changes outlined in the legal section of the proposal.

Contract Statement of Work and Work Requisition

The contract contains a statement of work that is similar to the statement of work in the original RFP or the winning proposal, or is a restatement of either to reflect negotiated agreements. This so-called *contract statement of work* (CSOW) legally defines the expected performance of the project in terms of scope of work, requirements, end-results, schedules, costs, and so on. The CSOW must clearly specify the conditions under which the deliverables or end-results will be accepted by the customer or user. Failure to state these conditions can lead to later disputes and delays in completing the project.

When both the user and the contractor agree on the CSOW, the project is considered to be "approved" and ready to go. Before project work can actually begin, however, it must be divided among different departments and organizations. Requirements that have been specified in the CSOW must be summarized and translated into terminology and expressions understandable to personnel in the SDO and its subcontractors. These translations, themselves SOWs aimed at parties who will perform the work, must have the same interpretation as the requirements or scope of work stated in the CSOW.

The document containing the "personalized" SOW for each work group is called a *work requisition* or *work order*. This document serves two purposes: (1) To notify each party in the project, in language that can be understood, about the work expected; and (2) to authorize the work to begin. This topic is discussed further in Chapter 11, "Project Control."

Signing the contract marks the completion of Phase A and approval to proceed to Phase B. The project is then prioritized with other previously approved projects according to availability of capital funds and resources needed to begin the project. The steps in Phase A are summarized in Figure 4-8.

Figure 4-8
Project initiation, proposal preparation, and project authorization process.

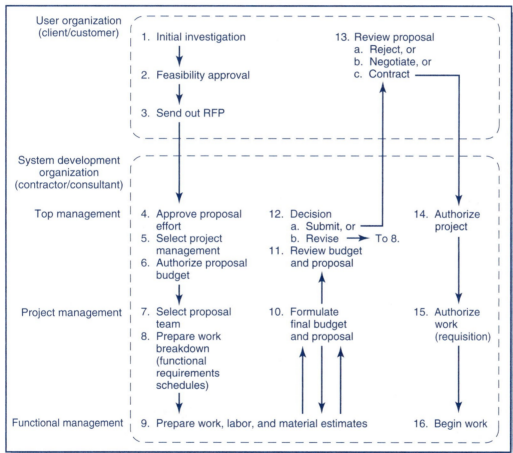

4.8 SUMMARY

The systems approach to management recognizes the life cycle nature of systems. Projects, too, have life cycles that are divided into stages describing their technical and managerial activities. A common theme among project life cycles is the systems development process that divides a project into four phases: conception, definition, execution, and operation.

This chapter focused on the first phase and described the stages of initiating a project and evaluating the feasibility of undertaking it. This phase includes the activities of formulating the problem, defining needs, requirements, and systems solutions, evaluating alternatives, and developing an organization and a proposal to conduct the project. At the start of this phase most activities are in the hands of the user. By the end of the phase, they have been taken over by the contractor or system development organization. The relationship between the user and the contractor is cemented through the process of solicitation (RFPs), proposal preparation and evaluation, and contract negotiation.

Phase A is the "foundation" part of the systems development cycle; it establishes the needs, objectives, requirements, constraints, agreements, and patterns of communication upon which the remaining phases must build. It is a crucial phase, and it is not surprising that most system ideas never get past this phase. Among those that do, the failures often have their roots planted here.

REVIEW QUESTIONS

1. How are projects initiated? Describe the process.
2. How is it determined if the feasibility of an idea should be investigated?
3. Who is the user in the systems development process? Who is the contractor?
4. Besides the user and the contractor, what other parties are involved in the systems development cycle? Give examples for particular projects.
5. What does the term "fast-tracking" imply?
6. How does the contractor (systems development organization) become involved in the project? Describe the ways.
7. What is the role of an RFP? Describe the contents of an RFP.
8. What is a feasibility study? Describe its contents and purpose.
9. What are user needs? Describe the process of defining user needs and the problems encountered.
10. Who is involved in preparing the proposal? Describe the proposal preparation process.
11. What is the statement of work (SOW)? In what documents does the statement of work appear?
12. Describe the contents of the proposal.
13. How is the best proposal selected? Describe the process and the criteria used.
14. Three proposals (W, X, and Y) have been rated on six criteria as follows: $1 = $ poor, $2 = $ average, $3 = $ good. Choose between the three proposals using (a) the simple rating method and (b) the weighted rating method.

Criteria	Weight	W	X	Y
Attention to quality	0.25	2	1	3
Cost	0.20	3	3	1
Project plan	0.20	2	2	1
Project organization	0.15	3	2	3
Likelihood of success	0.10	2	3	3
Contractor's credentials	0.10	2	2	3

15. Describe the different kinds (primary, secondary, etc.) of contractor-user relationships that can exist within a project.
16. What parties are considered subcontractors in a project?
17. Describe the different kinds of contracts (refer to Appendix B). What are the relative advantages and disadvantages of each to the user and the contractor?
18. Discuss the difference between a statement of work, a contract statement of work, and a work requisition or work order.

QUESTIONS ABOUT THE STUDY PROJECT

As appropriate, answer questions 1–13 regarding your project. Also answer the following question: How are contracts negotiated and who is involved in the negotiation?

Case 4-1   *West Coast University Medical Center*

(This is a true story.) West Coast University Medical Center (pseudonym) is a large university teaching and research hospital with a national reputation for excellence in health care practice, education, and research. Always seeking to sustain that reputation, the senior executive board at the Medical Center (WCMC) decided to install a comprehensive medical diagnostic system. The system would be linked to WCMC's computer servers and be available to physicians via the computer network. Because every physician's office at WCMC has a PC, doctors and staff could access the system from these offices as well as from their homes or private-practice offices. By simply clicking icons to access a medical-specialty area, then keying in answers to queries about a patient's symptoms, medical history, and so on, a physician could get a list of diagnostics with associated statistics.

The senior board sent a questionnaire to managers in every department about needs in their areas and how they felt the system might improve doctor's performances. Most managers felt it would save the doctors time and improve their performances. The

hospital computing and information systems (CIS) group was assigned to investigate the cost and feasibility of implementing the system. CIS staff interviewed medical-center managers and software vendors specializing in diagnostic systems. The study showed high enthusiasm among the respondents and a long list of potential benefits. Based on the study report, the senior board approved the system.

The CIS manager contacted three well-known consulting firms that specialized in medical diagnostic systems and invited each to give a presentation. Based on the presentations, he chose one firm to assist the CIS group in identifying, selecting, and integrating several software packages into a single, complete diagnostic system.

One year and several million dollars later the project was completed. However, within a year of its completion it was clear that the system had failed. Although it did everything the consultants and software vendors had promised, the few doctors that did access it complained that many of the system "benefits" were irrelevant, and that certain features they desired were lacking.

QUESTIONS

1. Why was the system a failure?
2. What was the likely cause of its lack of use?

3. What steps or procedures were absent or poorly handled in the project conception phase?

Case 4-2   X-philes Data Management Corporation

X-philes Data Management Corporation (XDM) requires assistance in two large projects it is about to undertake: Agentfox and Mulder. Although the projects are comparable in terms of size, technical requirements, and estimated completion time, they are independent and will have their own project managers and teams. Work for both projects is to be contracted to outside consultants.

Two managers at XDM, one assigned each to Agentfox and Mulder, prepare RFPs and send them to several contractors. The RFP for Agentfox includes a statement of work that specifies system performance and quality requirements, a desired completion deadline, and contract conditions. As an incentive, the contractor will receive a bonus for exceeding minimal quality measures and completing the project early, and will be charged a penalty for poor quality and late completion. The project will be tracked using precise quality measures, and the contractor will have to submit detailed monthly status reports. The RFP for Mulder simply includes a statement of the type of work to be done, an expected budget limit, and the desired completion date.

Based on proposals received in response to the RFPs, the managers responsible for Mulder and Agentfox each select a contractor. Unknown to either manager is that they select the same contractor, Yrisket Systems. Yrisket is selected for the Mulder project because its specified price is somewhat less than the budget limit in the RFP, and Yrisket has a good reputation in the business. Yrisket is chosen for the Agentfox contract for similar reasons—good price and good reputation. In responding to the Agentfox RFP, Yrisket managers had to work hard to get the price down to the amount specified, but they felt that by doing quality work on the project they could make a tidy profit through the incentive offered.

A few months after the projects are underway, some of Yrisket's key employees quit their jobs. Thus, to meet their commitments to both projects, Yrisket workers have to work long hours and weekends. It is apparent, however, that these extra efforts might not be enough, especially because Yrisket has a contract with another customer and will have to start a third project in the near future.

QUESTIONS

1. What do you think will happen?
2. How do you think the crisis facing Yrisket will affect the Mulder project? The Agentfox project?

ENDNOTES

1. It could be argued that Phase D in the election-campaign project will be extended *if* the candidate is elected, whereupon the "operation" phase represents the elected official's full political term—but that would be stretching the analogy! For the Mars rover, however, reducing and interpreting the data that the rover signaled back would likely continue for months or years after the rover has stopped functioning; if analysis and interpretation of data were included in the original system concept for the project, then it would constitute Phase D for the system.

2. Traditionally, the practice of systems engineering has been applied to large-scale, hardware development systems. In concept, however, systems engineering is just as applicable for developing complex software systems or solving difficult problems in social systems.

3. D. Meister and G. F. Rabideay, *Human Factors Evaluation in System Development* (New York: John Wiley & Sons, 1965): 37–39.

4. The initiation stage is covered in greater detail in C. L. Biggs, E. G. Birks, and W. Atkins, *Managing the Systems Development Process* (Upper Saddle River, NJ: Prentice Hall, 1980): 51–59; and J. Allen and B. P. Lientz, *Systems in Action* (Santa Monica: Goodyear, 1978): 41–63.

5. A need is a value judgement that a problem exists. It is a value judgement because different

parties in an identical situation will perceive the situation differently. As a consequence, a need is always identified with respect to a particular party—in our case, the user. See Jack McKillip, *Need Analysis: Tools for the Human Services and Education* (Newbury Park, CA: Sage Publication, 1987).

6. Michael Cusumano and Richard Selby, *Microsoft Secrets* (New York: Free Press, 1995): 210.

7. A request for quotation or bid commonly suggests that selection of the contractor will be based primarily on price; a request for proposal suggests that selection criteria such as nature of the system solution and competency of the contractor are equally or more important than price.

8. Other aspects of the feasibility study are discussed in Biggs, Birks, and Atkins, 59–80; and Allen and Lientz, 65–89.

9. Adapted from J. Davidson Frame, *Managing Projects in Organizations* (San Francisco: Jossey-Bass, 1987): 109–10.

10. Ibid., 111–26.

11. Ibid., 120–22.

12. A thorough description of proposal preparation is provided by V. G. Hajek, *Management of Engineering Projects,* 3d ed. (New York: McGraw-Hill, 1984): 39–57; a good, succinct overview is given by M. D. Rosenau, *Successful Project Management* (Belmont, CA: Lifetime Learning, 1981): 21–32.

13. See D. D. Roman, *Managing Projects: A Systems Approach* (New York: Elsevier, 1986): 67–72; and Rodney Stewart and Ann Stewart, *Proposal Preparations* (New York: John Wiley & Sons, 1984) for comprehensive coverage of proposal contents and the proposal preparation process.

14. Analysis and selection of projects is a broad subject. Models for analysis and selection are discussed in L. Bussey, *The Economic Analysis of Industrial Projects* (Upper Saddle River, NJ: Prentice Hall, 1978); N. Baker, "R&D Project Selection Models: An Assessment," *IEEE Transactions on Engineering Management* EM-21, no. 4 (1974): 165–71; W. Souder, *Project Selection and Economic Appraisal* (New York: Van Nostrand Reinhold, 1984); W. Souder and T. Mandakovic, "R&D Project Selection Models," *Research Management* 29, no. 4 (1986): 36–42; also see issues of *IEEE Transactions on Engineering Management, Management Science,* and *Research Management* for titles regarding project evaluation and selection.

15. See R. Gilbreath, *Winning at Project Management: What Works, What Fails, and Why* (New York: John Wiley, 1986): 196–201.

16. Management of the complete project contracting process, including what and where to contract, soliciting and assessing proposals, reaching the contract agreement, and administration of the contract is called "contract monitoring." For further discussion, see W. Hirsch, *The Contracts Management Deskbook,* revised ed. (New York: American Management Association, 1986): Chapter 6.

17. Ibid., 290–315.

18. See Hajek, *Management of Engineering Projects.,* Chaps. 8 and 9; and Rosenau, *Successful Project Management,* 34–41.

Chapter 5

Systems Development Cycle: Middle and Later Stages

> *When one door is shut, another opens.*
>
> —Cervantes, *Don Quixote*

*T*he result of Phase A is a formalized "systems concept." It includes (1) a clear problem formulation, (2) a rudimentary but well-conceptualized systems solution, (3) an elemental plan for the project, and (4) an agreement between the user and the contractor about all of these. The project is now ready to move on to the "middle" and "later" phases of systems development and to bring the systems concept to fruition.

5.1 PHASE B: DEFINITION

Phase B, definition, can be called the "analysis of the solution" phase because it is here that the *solution* is first scrutinized in great detail. Most of the effort in Phase A was devoted to investigating the *problem*—what is it, is it significant, should it be resolved, and can it be resolved in an acceptable fashion? Despite the effort and expense devoted to initial investigation and feasibility studies, most of the work remained focused on the problem. Any work on the solution was preliminary and rudimentary.

As Figure 5-1 shows, given approval of the project in Phase A, the thrust of the effort is now turned toward definition, design, production, and implementation

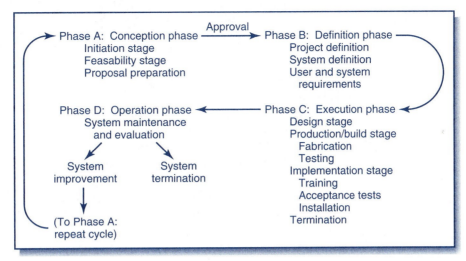

Figure 5-1
Four-phase model of the systems development cycle.

of the solution. In Phase B the system solution is analyzed and defined in sufficient detail so that designers and builders can produce a system with the greatest likelihood of solving the user's problem. The definition phase has two objectives: Determination of final, detailed system requirements and specifications, and preparation of a detailed project plan.

User Requirements

The first step in defining a system is getting the *user requirements*. These describe what the user wants and needs from the finished solution or system. They are the measures by which the user will determine whether or not the final result or system solution is acceptable. Misunderstandings about the requirements are rather common. Consider the following user-contractor exchange:

> USER: "You installed my computer. Why didn't you install the printer, too?"
> CONTRACTOR: "You said you wanted the computer installed."
> USER: "But the computer won't be of much use without a printer. Aren't they usually installed together?"
> CONTRACTOR: "You specified you wanted the *computer* installed. I did just what you requested."

Another exchange:

> CONTRACTOR: "The lighting for the office addition is finished. As we agreed, I wired 20 ceiling lights."
> USER: "But you said there'd be enough lights to make the room bright. The room seems kind of dark."
> CONTRACTOR: "For a room this size, 15 lights are standard. As we agreed, I put in 20 just to be sure."
> USER: "Yes, but you said 20 would make the room bright, and they don't. You'll have to put in more lights."

These cases illustrate user-contractor disagreements about the end-result. In both instances, the user is dissatisfied and expects the contractor to do additional work.

Misunderstandings like this sometimes turn into legal disputes that put outcomes in the hands of the courts; even when these are avoided, completion dates are delayed and costs are driven up.

The project manager has responsibility for making sure that the user is well-informed and that final user requirements are adequate, clear, and accurate. When the project is completed and the contractor says "Here's the system you ordered," the user should be able to say "Yes, it certainly is," meaning "Yes, it satisfies my requirements." User requirements are formally documented and become the ultimate reference for the system solution. They are, in a word, the "quality" measures of the project.

Requirements are the starting points for all systems design activity, and they are the foundation for project planning. Each requirement impacts end-item scope and complexity, and these, in turn, impact the work effort, time, cost, and risk of the project. Requirements must, therefore, be carefully analyzed and settled; otherwise, fully defining the system and creating a viable project plan will be impossible.

In development projects for products and systems in competitive markets, requirements are initially framed in general terms; for example, outperform the F-16, taste better than Joe's beef jerky, construct a commercial building that exceeds 20 percent rate of return, or make the system compatible before the year 2000. General requirements such as these, however, must be expanded before much system design and project planning can be done. Poor requirements definition is a common source of failure in product- and systems-development projects.

Example 1: User Requirements for Product Development

The marketing group for a kitchen appliance manufacturer wrote the requirements for a new food processor. The requirements specified the general size, weight, usage, price, and sales volume of the proposed product, but described nothing about product performance. The engineering design group had to set the performance requirements, a process they accomplished by studying competitors' products. The food processor as developed met all the requirements set by marketing and engineering, yet it was obsolete before it was launched. New products with features that better satisfied customer needs had been released by competitors. In defining the product, both the marketing and engineering groups had ignored the *key* requirements; that is, the user (customer) requirements, and thus, the requirements for a successful product.

User requirements should focus on crucial elements of the end-results and avoid trivial or nonessential elements. They should emphasize *what* is needed, not *how* it will be done. For example, instead of saying, "use brand X component," specify, "the component must have Y properties and perform Z functions". This provides system designers with the necessary flexibility for choosing how to meet performance requirements within project schedule and budget constraints.

Two factors associated with requirements are priority and margin. For each requirement the *priority level* should be specified; for example, high, medium, or low. When two or more requirements conflict so that all cannot be met, a preestablished priority level allows for correct tradeoff decisions. Suppose that although a product is specified to be of a particular maximum height and to perform in a certain way, it is later determined that to achieve the specified performance, the necessary height must exceed the projected maximum. Knowing which requirement has higher relative customer priority—height or performance—guides the system designer to make the right decision. A related matter is the requirements *margin,* or the degree of allowable tolerance or variability in a requirement. For example, "the desired maximum height is 4 feet, but a margin of 6 inches is allowable" tells designers by how much they can exceed the desired height requirement and still meet customer needs.

Defining complete, accurate requirements is not necessarily easy. Among the problems:

- Requirements often must incorporate information from not only the user, but also functional areas such as marketing, engineering, manufacturing, and materials. These parties must interact and share information to jointly establish the requirements.
- All the information needed to define requirements is not available when definition occurs, so it is easy to commit to unnecessary requirements, or to overlook the necessary ones.
- A tendency to use vague terms in the requirements, such as "modern" and "high-tech."
- Inability of the user or contractor to adequately describe requirements in words because the end-result or system is complex, abstract, or artistic.
- Intentional allowance or introduction of ambiguity in the requirements, by the user or contractor, to permit greater latitude of results later in the project.
- Failure to satisfy requirements because of immovable obstacles encountered, or changes in user wants or needs that render original requirements undesirable.

Such problems result in either confused and chaotic project planning or later user-contractor disagreement over whether end-results met the requirements. Following are steps that help reduce such problems associated with requirements definition.[1]

- Convince parties in both the user and contractor groups of the importance of clear, comprehensive definition of requirements. Users and contractors often are reluctant to devote additional time to ensuring that the requirements are clear and complete.
- Review the requirements for ambiguities and inadequacies. Work through ambiguities and redefine the requirements so there can be no misinterpretation.
- Augment written requirements with nonverbal aids such as pictures, schematics, graphics, and visual or functional models.
- Avoid rigid specification of requirements that likely will need to be changed because of high risks or changing environment.
- Treat each requirement as a commitment. Both the user and the contractor must agree to and sign off on each one.
- After the project begins, monitor the requirements and control attempts to change them. Use a change control system for identifying desired or necessary changes, assessing the impact of the changes, and approving and communicating them.

High-level user requirements (summary or bullet points) should fit on one page so that they can be easily referenced. The user reviews them for accuracy and completeness; the contractor reviews them to understand the user's wants and needs. User requirements should be developed anew for each new project.

The requirements, as specific acceptance criteria or expectations, are used to define the project's *scope of work*. Then, as the project nears completion, the customer must determine the acceptability of work results or end-items by comparing them with the scope-of-work requirements. Every requirement's specification must be completed to the customer's satisfaction.

Detailed user requirements come from one source: The user. When an architect-contractor discusses with a client what is wanted in a new home, she is gathering user requirements. The contractor and client work together to discuss needs and formulate requirements. Just as users sometimes require help in determining the problem or need, they also sometimes require help in determining the requirements for the solution. They may not be aware of the cost, schedule, or other ramifications of requirements, nor understand what is needed in a system to fulfill them. The project team should not accept just any requirements from the user, but should help the user to define them. Once the user and contractor agree upon the requirements, the requirements should be documented using the user's own terminology and language.

Preliminary definition of user requirements happens during needs definition and proposal preparation, and summary user requirements are always included in the final contract. In simple systems, user requirements rarely exceed a few sentences. In big systems, however, they might have to be expanded and detailed, and eventually could fill volumes. An example of the former is user requirements for a contract to perform a 1-day management seminar; an example of the latter is user requirements for (what became) the 9-year, multibillion dollar Delta Project to prevent the North Sea from flooding the Netherlands.

System Objectives

System objectives are oriented toward the solution. They specify the contractor's approach and objectives for satisfying the needs and wants spelled out in the user requirements. Although a project must fulfill user requirements, it also has to fulfill contractor needs. For example, besides being profitable, the contractor might also specify objectives to keep skilled workers and costly design and production facilities occupied. The objectives provide an overview of the system or solution approach—the system architecture, principle functions, intended user (customer or market), and resulting end-item (system, solution, or product)—and a common understanding for all involved parties as to what the project must do. Whereas user requirements are stated in the language of the user, system objectives are stated in the technical jargon of the specialists. They are a *translation* of user requirements.

To develop system objectives, the architect, engineer, systems analyst, or consultant thinks about the user's requirements, then translates them into the dimensions, arrangements, quantity, capacity, and so forth of the components and materials necessary to achieve the user's requirements. System objectives identify all of the significant functions to be performed by the system. They identify functions and related components and indicate how functions interface with the rest of the system. They are the *functional requirements* of systems engineering.

The contractor sets the system objectives to comply with the resources that can be mustered for the project—the available people, subcontractors and suppliers, facilities, capital, processes, and their combined capabilities. The objectives might include design criteria such as *design to cost;* that is, the system will be designed so as not to exceed a given cost limit. Such design criteria are more generally referred to as *design for X,* where X can be "specialized or high-volume production," "flexible manufacturing," "testing," "maintenance," and anything else the contractor wants to use as objectives for directing systems design.

System objectives are often stated in terms of required resources (e.g., type, quality, or capacity of engines, materials, systems, personnel, hardware). Following are some examples of system objectives and the user requirements they are derived from:

USER REQUIREMENTS	SYSTEM OBJECTIVES
1. Vehicle must accelerate from 0 to 60 mph in 10 seconds, and accommodate six people.	Vehicle size and weight, engine horsepower, kind of transmission.
2. House must be spacious for a family of four.	Number and size of rooms.
3. House must be luxurious.	Quality of materials; number, quality, and expense of decorative features.
4. Space station must operate life support, manufacturing, and experimental equipment.	Type and kilowatt capacity of power generating equipment; technology for primary system operation; technology for backup operation.
5. Computer system must provide summary reports on a daily basis.	Type of manual and electronic systems, hardware and software; collection, entry, storage, and processing procedures.
6. Aircraft must be "stealthy."	Design of overall configuration and external surfaces; types of materials; usage of existing versus newly-developed components and systems.

Another kind of system objective, called a *performance requirement,* specifies the output of the system in technical terms—miles per hour, miles per gallon, turning radius, decibels of sound, acceleration, percent efficiency, bauds per second, labor turnover rate, operating temperature, BTUs, operating cost, and so on. These are specifications that systems specialists will use to measure performance of the system against the user's requirements. Users may provide a set of system performance specifications as part of the user requirements.

Following are types of specifications placed on the system, its subsystems, and its components:[2]

1. *Compatibility.* Ability of subsystems to be integrated into the whole system or environment and to contribute to objectives of the whole system.
2. *Commonality.* Ability of a component to be used interchangeably with an existing component of a different type. A "high commonality" system is composed of many available (off-the-shelf) components; a "low commonality" system contains many components unique to the system which must be developed (from "scratch").
3. *Cost-effectiveness.* Total cost to which the user *may be subjected* if a particular design is adopted. Cost-effectiveness requires analysis of cost of the design, as well as the user's cost for implementing and operating the design to achieve a given level of benefit.
4. *Reliability.* Ability of a system or component to function at a given level without failing, or to function for a given period of time before failing.
5. *Maintainability.* Ability of a subsystem to be repaired within a certain period of time (i.e., the *ease* with which it can be repaired).
6. *Testability.* Degree to which a subsystem enables systematic testing and measuring of its performance capabilities.
7. *Availability.* Degree to which the system can be expected to operate when it is needed.
8. *Ease of Use.* Amount of physical effort or strain, technical skill, training, or ability required for operating and maintaining the system.
9. *Robustness.* Ability of system to survive in a harsh environment.
10. *Ease of Growth or Enhancement.* Ability of the system to be easily expanded to include new functions or be adapted to new conditions.

System Specifications

System objectives provide direction for the project, but they are high-level and do not actually specify what has to be done or made, a necessity for in-depth project planning and system design. Specifications are needed that tell the project team what it has to do, which is accomplished through *system specifications.* These define in-depth the requirements of the end-item, system, or product, and the involved subsystems, components, and processes.

System specifications reflect and support the system objectives. They are the criteria or procedures that will guide actual project work and are written by and for project specialists—systems analysts, programmers, engineers, product and process designers, consultants, and so on—in their particular technical lingo. System specifications address all areas of the project—system design, fabrication, installation, operation, and maintenance. To retain user involvement, a list of *baseline specifications* also is prepared. These are system specifications defined at a high level design basic enough for the user to understand. The user refers to this list to learn about the details of the system.

In defining technical system specifications, the contractor also refers to the list of baseline specifications. Technical system specifications should be set so as to meet, but *not* exceed, the baseline specifications. This is one way to control against "creeping scope;" which is burdensome growth or enhancements of project requirements that increase project budgets and schedules.

Often, definition of user requirements, system objectives, and system specifications happens iteratively, particularly when the project end-time is complex. The requirements cannot be completely defined without some amount of prior design work, and the design work cannot be completed without some amount of prior fabrication and testing. In such cases, high-level (basic) design of the system must begin soon after the specification definition is started, and be completed before the specifications are approved. The overall process looks like Figure 5-2. Often a *prototype,* which is an early running model of a system or component built for purposes of demonstrating performance, functionality, or proving feasibility, is used to assess and modify specifications. The prototype is built according to the initial specifications and design, and then tested. The test results are used to modify the specifications and the prototype, and the prototype is then retested. This ensures that the basic system design supports the system specifications. The application for software development, called *rapid prototyping,* is discussed in Example 2.

Example 2: Rapid Prototyping for Software Development[3]

When no physical system exists that is similar to the one to be developed, conceptualizing the system may be difficult and confusing. The system the customer "sees" might be very different than the one the developer envisions, yet without a physical or working model, the difference will not be readily apparent. In such instances, the final, delivered system matches the mental picture or conceptualization of the developer, but might not closely correspond to the system conceptualized by the user. The usual approach of requiring the customer to specify and sign-off on requirements early in the project intensifies this problem. It forces the customer and developer to commit to actions before they have reached a mutual understanding about the requirements.

A rapid prototype (RP) is a rudimentary, intentionally incomplete model of the product, and, initially, it is somewhat simple and inexpensive to produce. It represents *key parts* of the system, *not* the complete system, and therefore should be easy to create and modify. The customer experiments with the prototype to assess a system's functionality and determine necessary modifications or addi-

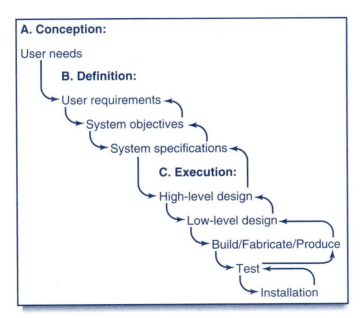

Figure 5-2
Iterative development cycle for complex systems.

tions. Changes are made to the RP, and the customer performs experiments again. After a few iterations, the final requirements and design concept are firmed up. Architects use physical scale models of buildings for the same purpose: To convey to the customer the look, feel, and functionality of the design. For that purpose, a functioning, physical model is always better than drawings, schematics, or lists or requirements. Of course, drawings, schematics, and requirements are necessary to inform the development team of what is expected. In rapid prototyping, however, drawings and requirements are not committed to until the system, as represented by the RP model, has been accepted by the customer. In software development, the RP might be a series of screens or windows with queries to allow the user to "feel" what the system would be like. An RP model should be used wherever there is danger of the project producing a system that fails to meet user requirements or system objectives. Ordinarily, the rapid prototyping process will not speed up definition; instead, it might lengthen the phase. The RP model will likely be incorrect at first, though through experimentation, the customer and developer will learn from it and settle on optimum requirements.

Rapid prototyping is commonly used for requirements definition; however, it also can be employed throughout the full systems development process, in which case the end-item system evolves stepwise, from a simple, incomplete RP model to a full-functioning, operational system. The process progresses through a series of milestones and phases similar to that in the traditional systems development cycle. The first milestone, *definition of preliminary requirements,* represents customer acceptance of a preliminary project plan and user requirements/system objectives document. A high-level (basic) design and functioning RP model are created. Trials and experiments are performed with the model and the results used to modify the requirements, signifying the next milestone, *definition of final requirements.* At this point, two things exist: (1) the approved functioning RP model and (2) its supporting documentation (requirements and objectives, drawings, and schematics). Now the analysis of detailed system specifications can begin. The RP model is tested to reveal further necessary revisions; that is, revisions to details, not the overall concept or system architecture. The final approval by the customer and developer of the detailed design and system specifications signifies the *as-prototyped design* milestone. Next, the expanded RP system is exposed to rigorous testing, and portions of it are replaced, modified, and fine-tuned until it meets user performance requirements. The documentation that emerges during this stage will be used to maintain the system (for a one-of-a-kind system) or to reproduce it (for mass-produced systems). Customer acceptance of the system and its documentation signals the end of this phase and the *as-refined design* milestone. The two remaining milestones are *test acceptance* and *system acceptance.* The former represents approval of the system after the user has put it through a series of exercises that represent the actual *working environment;* the latter, approval of the system after it has been *fully integrated and tested* for operation in the *customer environment.* Passing these milestones is usually somewhat painless, given careful attention to definition of correct requirements and correct basic design in the earliest phases of the process.

Team Involvement in Definition

Problems occur when the parties specifying requirements and objectives do not work together; for example, when one specifies requirements that preclude or complicate meeting those specified by others. Requirements and objectives should be created by a team that includes all parties that have a stake in the project—customers; functional areas such as engineering, marketing, manufacturing, customer service, and purchasing; and even suppliers and outsiders. Because they all have a hand in requirements definition, everyone will be committed to the requirements, and it will not be necessary to later explain or change the requirements as different functional groups enter the project. To ensure that every group works toward the same requirements, there should be one master requirements document to which everyone, regardless of functional specialty, refers during the project. Where additional, more detailed, specific requirements documents are needed, they should be derived from and compatible with this "main" document. At the specification level, this main document is the baseline specifications list noted earlier.

In product development projects, a good place to generate product requirements is at an off-site workshop for the key functional groups and other involved parties.[4] Starting with a statement of customer needs, the team develops the requirements from *scratch.* The workshop is led by a facilitator who has no vested interest in the project; in other words, not by the project manager or any involved functional managers. A procedure called *quality function deployment (QFD)* can be used to provide data for the workshop about critical product elements, and again later to translate requirements from the workshop into specific technical targets. QFD is discussed in Chapter 14.

Detailed Project Planning

Going into Phase B, a portion of the project definition work has already been performed. At minimum, some definition work was necessary in Phase A to prepare project plans and system requirements for inclusion in the proposal. Although the proposal may contain considerable detail, it is still the result of a proposal-sized effort and usually contains only a detailed *outline* of what is to come. During the definition phase the contractor must fill in the outline and expand and elaborate upon details of the project plan. This includes attention to details such as lower-level schedules and networks; cost accounts, budgets, and cost control systems; support documentation about policies, procedures, and job descriptions; the project team, including leaders, supervisors, and workers from functional areas, subcontractors, and project support staff. The work of preparing the project plan parallels that of defining system objectives and specifications because the objectives and specifications affect work activities, schedules, costs, risks and, hence, the project plan.

A full-sized project team begins to evolve from the skeletal group that worked on the proposal. Selection of team members generally follows a cascade pattern. First the project manager selects project team leaders who, in turn, select team members to fill positions under them. The project manager negotiates with functional managers to get specific individuals and the requisite expertise assigned to the project. Sometimes user approval is sought for key members of the project team. This practice is advisable in cases where users and team members must work closely and when it is possible that the user *might* have an objection. Good user-project team rapport is crucial to maintaining a healthy user-contractor relationship.

Once key members of the project team have been assembled, they begin preparing the detailed project plan. The plan includes

1. Detailed user requirements, system objectives, and system specifications
2. Work schedules and deadlines
3. Budgets, cost accounts, and a cost control system
4. Detailed WBS and work packages
5. Areas of high risk, uncertainty, and contingency plans
6. Personnel plans and resource utilization plans
7. Quality plans
8. Plans for testing the system
9. Documentation plans
10. Change control and work review plans
11. Initial plans for implementing the system

Details of the plan and the planning process are discussed in Part III; a sample project plan is given in Appendix C.

Most of the planning on large projects is delegated to subordinate members of the project team. The project manager coordinates and oversees subplanning efforts making sure that all subplans are thorough and tied together. The final plan is reviewed for approval by top management and the user. Contractor management makes sure that the plan fits into existing and upcoming organizational projects and capabilities. User management checks for the plan's conformity with specifications in the contract.

Anxious to get the project underway, many contractors avoid reviewing the project plan with the user. This is shortsighted because the plan may contain elements to which the user may object. A project is not conducted and implemented in isolation but within the user's ongoing system. Everything in the plan must fit: The project schedule must fit the user's schedule; project cash flow requirements must meet the user's payment schedule; personnel and procedures of the contractor must complement those of the user; and materials and work methods must be acceptable to the user. To avoid problems later, it is best to review the plan with the user before starting work.

The planning process continues throughout the project. Although a plan must be developed to cover the project from start to finish, details often are not available until later. As the project moves from one stage to another and new information becomes available, plans are detailed and revised in a rolling wave fashion. The overall plan is adhered to, but the gaps are filled in. The plan enables planners to integrate and coordinate the stages of the project and then, as gaps are found, tells them what other information is needed to develop more detailed plans.

The project plan and system specifications should be reviewed with the user. During review, the user and contractor check for the accuracy and completeness of user requirements, the fit of system objectives to user requirements, the fit of system requirements to time and cost constraints in the project plan, as well as the need to modify, add, or delete specifications. As soon as the project plan and systems specifications have been approved, the project can proceed to Phase C.

Project Quality

Quality is delivering to satisfy the customer. A quality-oriented project has two aims: (1) To produce the correct end-item; (2) to produce it in the correct way. The first aim, which concerns the solution or end-item of the project, is addressed through good definition of user requirements and system objectives; if the requirements and objectives specification from Phase B are accurate, complete, and clear, the project will be headed toward producing the correct end-item. The second aim, which concerns the process of *conducting* the project and ensuring it actually produces the end-item according to requirements, is addressed by a good project *quality plan;* such a plan ensures that the work performed during Phase C will result in an end-item that meets the requirements. Producing an end-item that conforms to prespecified user and system requirements, and continues to do so after the end-item is in operation, is called *quality of conformance.*

Requirements evolve and change throughout the project. Changes in user tastes or needs and in the environment may require periodic modification to the requirements, system objectives, specifications, or design. New competitor products, emerging technology, and intractable barriers can reduce or eliminate the original anticipated project benefits. Changing a project's requirements and objectives midstream is better than sticking to outmoded, obsolete, or unattainable ones. Attention to quality thus requires continuous review of project progress, checking that the system solution is meeting user requirements, and checking that the user requirements and system objectives are satisfying changing customer needs. The quality plan specifies the measures and procedures for monitoring and comparing work output with requirements, and comparing requirements with current needs and realities. The quality plan should specify the role of the customer and contractor during Phase C for making decisions about the adequacy of the requirements and work output in meeting current needs.

Even after the project is completed, attention to quality continues in Phase D by monitoring the end-item for how well it continues to perform and meet customer needs. This monitoring, done by the customer or the contractor, provides information to suggest future designs or solutions that are completely new or are improvements upon existing products or systems. The quality plan specifies the measures and procedures for monitoring operational performance.

One way to ensure that project work during Phase C will be performed according to requirements is to specify the *entry, process,* and *exit* conditions for each work package, stage, or activity.[5] For example, consider the work package "product integration testing." To ensure the work is done right, the plan might specify the following:

- *Entry conditions* (conditions that must exist *before* integration tests *begin*):
  The test plan must have been approved.
  The test procedure must have been inspected, debugged, and be ready to run.
  Testing of all components must have been successfully completed.
  All components must have been approved and certified.
- *Process conditions* (conditions that must exist *while* performing integration tests):
  The test plan and procedures must be followed.

No deviations from the test plan will be allowed without approval from the systems manager and test manager.

Necessary deviations from the test plan will be documented.

Test results must be documented indicating problems, severity of problems, and intended actions (what, who, when).

- *Exit conditions* (conditions that must exist *after* integration tests *end*):

All significant problems identified in the integrated system must have been corrected.

A specific plan for resolving all other problems must have been prepared.

The quality plan is prepared after system objectives have been defined, but before system specifications and high-level design are completed. Parties whose commitment and support are necessary for implementation—that is, key members of the project team—should draft the plan. The customer should review and give prior approval to this plan.

System Defects

People often associate the terms quality and defect. A defect represents a nonconformity—something other than what the customer had expected. The quality plan should address ways for identifying and correcting as many defects, problems, mistakes, or nonconformities as possible, and as soon as possible. In general, the longer a nonconformity is allowed to persist, the more costly it is to remedy. Fixing a defect in an unattached component may be easy and inexpensive, but it becomes expensive after the component has been assembled with others, and more expensive after it has been imbedded inside a system. The defect that causes the greatest expense is the one that results in malfunction or failure of the end-item while in customer use.

But the previous statement, *"correct as many defects as possible,"* requires qualification. The usual presumption is that zero defects equates to high quality, but such is not always the case. Why, you might ask, *not* eliminate all defects? A quality end-item is one that meets many requirements—those that are the most significant. Too much attention devoted to any one requirement, such as eliminating all defects, may detract from meeting other, more important requirements. In any project, there are trade-offs between the dimensions of time, cost, and requirements, and when a problem within one dimension (say, defect requirements) is encountered, and at the same time another dimension (e.g., schedule) must be held constant, the result will be an inevitable increase in the remaining dimension (e.g., cost).[6] In cases such as air traffic control systems and pacemakers for human hearts, there shouldn't be *any* defects, but in others the customer would prefer to have the system delivered on time with a *few* defects rather than one delivered late or at higher cost. Rather than remove *all* known defects from the system, remove only those that enable the system to meet the most important requirements. This is the concept of *"good enough quality"*—where preset priorities on requirements, time, and cost allow the project team to meet the most important ones when constraints preclude satisfying all of them. According to Bach, creating systems "of the best possible quality is a very, very expensive proposition, [although] clients may not even notice the difference between the best possible quality and pretty good quality."[7] The customer, of course, judges what is "good enough." To arrive at that judgment, the customer must be kept apprised of the status of problems, costs, and schedules throughout the project.

The execution phase variously includes stages of *design, development, procurement, construction/production,* and *implementation;* depending on the project, it involves some or all of these activities in sequence. For example, in hardware development projects execution includes stages of design, development, and production; in construction projects it includes stages of design and construction; in consulting projects it includes stages of report outline and compilation. Virtually all projects that have a physical end-item—a product, building, system, or report—also have an implementation stage where the end-item is given to the user. Our discussion will divide the execution phase into three nominal stages: Design, production, and implementation.

Design Stage

During the design stage specifications are converted into plans, sketches, or drawings. The output of design varies depending on the industry and the type of system, but usually it is some form of pictorial representation of the system—blueprints, flow charts, or schematic diagrams showing the system configuration and the relationships, arrangements, and dimensions of components.

In the design process the system is broken into subsystems, then subsystems are divided into tiers of components and parts. Various design possibilities are reviewed for compatibility with each other and with higher level systems, and for their ability to satisfy system specifications and system cost, schedule, and performance requirements. The breakdown of system design into tiers and components uses the block diagramming approach described in Appendix A and the WBS approach described in Chapter 6.

The design process involves two interrelated design activities. The first is preparation of a design that shows the system components and relationships necessary to achieve system objectives. This is essentially the thrust of the systems engineering process described in Chapter 3. The second is preparation of a design that shows what the system will physically look like. This is the "drafting" process or the making of working drawings and schematics.

The purpose of the first design activity is to determine *logically* what functional elements are necessary and how they should be interconnected to achieve the system's purpose. This design is based upon functional analysis of the system and results in block diagrams. Two examples from Schmenner are shown. Figure 5-3 shows the functional design for an automobile assembly line and Figure 5-4 shows the functional design for a paper processing plant.

The second kind of design shows what the actual system will look like, its component parts, their sizes, shapes, and relative location—that is, the *physical* appearance of a system that satisfies the requirements of the functional design. This design activity involves producing engineering, manufacturing, architectural, or other types of drawings. These drawings show details necessary for system fabrication, assembly, and maintenance. Sometimes they reveal places where the functional design is impractical or infeasible because of assembly, maintenance, or appearance considerations. In such cases it is necessary to return to the functional design, revise it, then go back and redo the drawings.

Design often follows an evolutionary, trial-and-error process as illustrated in Figure 5-2. A trial design is prepared, modeled, then tested against system performance specifications. If it fails, the design is modified and retested. This process of iteration

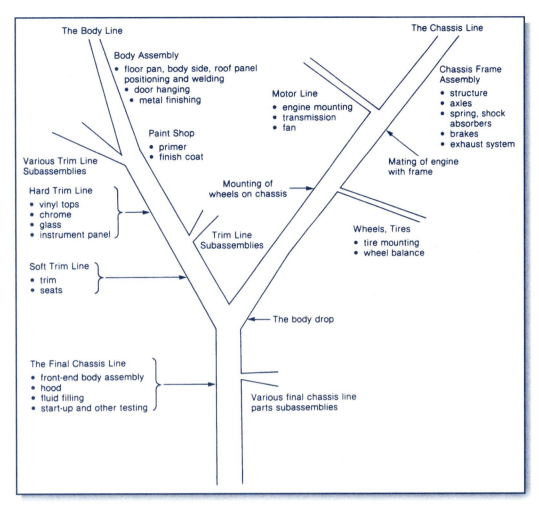

Figure 5-3
Functional design plan for automobile assembly process. [Reprinted with permission of Prentice Hall, Inc., from *Plant and Service Tours in Operations Management*, 5th ed., by Roger Schmenner. Copyright © 1998.]

is followed to varying degrees in virtually all development projects for new or innovative high-technology systems.

When a complex system is being designed, the design-build-test iteration often occurs in many places throughout the system. Changes in one subsystem have a ripple effect on other subsystems. One subsystem may require, for instance, a bigger motor, which takes away space from another subsystem that then must be moved to a different part of the system, which then displaces something else, and so on. Left uncontrolled, each iteration may cause a major system redesign, and, thereby, grossly extend the design stage. Thus, one responsibility of the project manager is to try to minimize the number of design iterations for each subsystem, and to keep redesigns local with minimal interference on other subsystems.

Example 3: Design Complexity in the Chunnel[8]

One change in requirements mandated for the English Channel Tunnel (Chunnel) was that Chunnel trains must be resistant to fire damage for at least 30 minutes; that would enable them, should a fire break out, to continue moving until out of the tunnel. Thus, every train car would have to be capable of continuing along with a fire raging inside. Because the frame of a normal train car would deform from the heat and soon become immobile, special metal alloys would have to be used on Chunnel train cars that are unlike metals used in rapid transit systems everywhere else in the world. This would make the trains heavier, 2,400 tons instead of 1,600 tons, which would require heavier locomotives having six axles instead of four. These locomotives would have to be specially designed. Because the locomotives needed more power, the power system for the tunnel would have to be changed, too.

In many projects, the stages of design and production/build do not occur as discrete, sequential stages. Rather, building or constructing part of the system commences as soon as a portion of the design has been completed, then building of another part starts when more of the design has been completed, and so on. In other words, the system is built as it is designed—a practice referred to as *fast-tracking* or *design-build*. Fast-tracking is common in the construction industry: The foundation is being dug and steel is being cut even though decisions about the roof and interior have not yet been completed. The practice speeds up the work and can save up to 1 year on a major construction project, but it is also risky. Problems with the design often do not appear until the details have been worked out, but by then portions of fabrication or construction will have been completed and have to be reworked, which can diminish quality and increase costs and schedule timelines. The usual sequential or "slow track" method takes longer but allows more time for problems to be spotted and resolved before construction begins. Fast-tracking is a fairly common practice, though because of the risks, it is best handled by project teams that are experienced and have ample budget cushions.

When a system has been designed that finally satisfies system specifications, the result is a physical description, picture, or model. Figure 5-5 shows such a "picture," the blueprint design for the paper processing plant derived from the functional design in Figure 5-4.

Figure 5-4

Functional design for paper manufacturing process. [Reprinted with permission of Prentice Hall, Inc., from *Plant and Service Tours in Operations Management*, 5th ed., by Roger Schmenner. Copyright © 1998.]

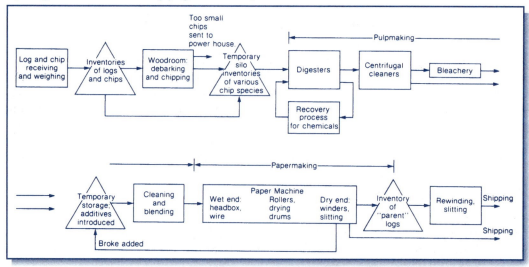

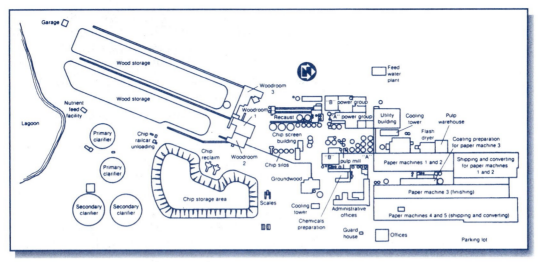

Figure 5-5
Blueprint design for paper manufacturing plant. [Reprinted with permission of Prentice-Hall, Inc., from *Plant and Service Tours in Operations Management,* 5th ed., by Roger Schmenner. Copyright © 1998.]

The Project Manager in the Design Stage

The size of the project team and the level of project activity continually grow as the project moves through Phase C. As the system is defined in greater detail and more activities are identified, the project manager assigns project tasks to group leaders in the systems development organization. Project tasks are broken down into small, clearly identifiable, segments called *work packages.* Each becomes the basis for project scheduling, budgeting, and control for the duration of the project. Work package breakdown, planning, and control are described in Part III.

As the size of the project organization increases, so does the amount of work required of the project manager. Design activities require participation from groups throughout the contractor organization and its subcontractors. The project manager coordinates their efforts to ensure accurate information exchange, effective interfacing, and work that is on schedule and according to budget. Throughout, the project manager keeps the effort directed toward the system objectives to prevent irrelevant or impractical things from sidetracking the project or degrading project performance.

Interaction Design[9]

Why is it that so many software-based products are difficult to use, designed to do things that people don't need, and filled with obscure or irrelevant features that people don't want? As examples, consider all the features of programmable VCRs, PC software products, and digital clocks, watches, and entertainment systems. As an instance of an unwanted feature, you lock your car at the airport with a remote device on your key ring; when you return, you find the car unlocked. What happened? Someone parked nearby with a car of the same make as yours, and when he pressed the button to lock his car, he gave the signal that unlocked yours.

Most commercial software packages have numerous features and functions that most people do not need and never learn to use. Yet in an effort to continuously "improve" the product, developers add more features (a process that leads to "bloatware").

Compare all of the things you presumably could do with word-processing and spreadsheet software with all the features that you actually need. The problem is not having too many features, but that the never-used features are intermixed with the often-used ones, making the whole product seem complex to use and difficult to understand, and the user feel frustrated and stupid. Complexity is in the eyes of the beholder, and for many beholding users, software systems appear too complex.

Complexity in systems has always been around, but in the past, complex systems were operated only by *trained* personnel. Systems such as farm and construction equipment, aircraft, trains, and electrical generators are complex, but designed for use by someone with the special skills for operating them, not for the average person. Commercial software-based products (digital watch, camera, alarm clock, ATM, car console, gas pump, telephone, etc.) also are complex; however, the common person uses them. Developers of these products tend not to think about the common person, or to assume instead that, should a function or feature be added to the product, most people will want to learn about and use it. These days, relatively complex systems are ubiquitous, but they are in the hands of amateurs, not skilled operators.

Complexity and bloatware occur when engineers and programmers control the product design. These people are technically astute, but they pay little attention to "interaction design." Interaction design refers to aspects of the design that ultimately affect the end-user of the product. It includes consideration and selection of behaviors, functions, and information in the system and the way they are presented to the user. The reason engineers and programmers do poorly at interaction design is because they do not consider the interaction between the system and its user as a central design issue. Substandard interaction design also arises from poorly defined product goals and user requirements and no one responsible for guiding the design toward meeting the requirements. Every time a programmer implements a pet function in a product, or a marketing manager insists on another product feature, they are influencing the design; in essence, they are skipping over the definition phase of the project by moving directly from conception to product design.

Interaction design should not be an afterthought, but a major consideration in the creation and design of a product. The first step in product development should be to identify and describe the end-users in detail—their wants, aptitudes, skill levels, and behaviors with the product. After that, everything influencing the function and operation of the product should be designed around the users. The project manager's role is to ensure that the end-users are accurately described, their interaction design requirements are carefully and completely defined, and the final product is designed and produced to meet those requirements.

Controlling Design

During the design stage, reviews are conducted at key milestones to ensure that objectives, requirements, and specifications are being met. Although reviews are planned and scheduled by the project manager, they are, ideally, conducted and chaired by objective "outsiders." Functional and detail designs are approved by the user to ensure that functions, interfaces, and flows satisfy user requirements, and that the final design suits the user's personal tastes, needs, and budget.[10]

As mentioned, during design, development, and review, changes to initial designs may be necessary because of new technology, technical design problems, or new requirements of the user. These inevitably necessitate changes in work activities and significantly affect the project plan, its schedules, costs, and so on. Such changes must be reviewed and approved by project management. Those changes that drastically alter the project plan may require user approval and amendments to, or renegotiation of, the contract.

Project management is responsible for monitoring design changes, determining their impact on the project, communicating the impact to all affected parties, obtaining approvals, and updating schedules, budgets, and plans. Although design changes add to project costs, as shown in Figure 5-6, typical design costs are a small fraction of production costs. Prolonging the design stage to get it right is usually less financially risky than extending the production stage to incorporate omissions or eliminate errors. Still, project management must decide on a date by which all designs are *frozen* so that the project can progress to the next stage.

Project management also is responsible for ensuring that results from design efforts are well documented. Good design documentation is crucial to project success. It informs everyone about the requirements, configuration, detail features, and limitations of the design, and is the precursor and key resource for planning all subsequent work and procedures for system production, operation, and maintenance.

During design, the resources necessary for production, operation, and maintenance of the system are identified. Among these are system *side-items,* defined as such to distinguish them from the main contract end-item of the project. These side-items include special facilities, equipment, tools, and training materials necessary for the production, operation, and maintenance of the end-item. Project management is responsible for ensuring that all the necessary side-items are identified and that work is contracted for their development and production. Because side-items often require special capabilities, their actual development and production is usually subcontracted out. Important to note is that side-items are *no less important* than the main end-item, for without them the production, operation, or maintenance of the end-item will be difficult or impossible to perform. Side-items themselves are simple or complex systems. For example, side-items for a commercial aircraft include, on the one hand, a simple custom hand wrench to facilitate removal of engine parts; and on the other hand, the cockpit flight simulator for the flight crew training, a rather complex system.

Planning for Production

During the design stage, the project manager or production coordinator begins to plan the production stage by dividing it into individual tasks such as tool and machine design, equipment and materials purchasing, metal work, subsystem and final assembly, function testing, component testing, integration testing, packaging, and so on. A

Figure 5-6
Relative costs for design and production.

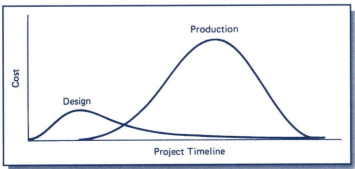

schedule is then prepared for these tasks based upon dates when design inputs are expected. Because the design work might not be completed all at once, production tasks may have to be scheduled in phases. Planning and scheduling of phased production involves considerable coordination of personnel, materials, and facilities. Project leaders and supervisors prepare detailed schedules which are combined and integrated into the master schedule by the project manager and key functional managers.

5.3 PRODUCTION/BUILD STAGE

With detailed designs in hand, the contractor is now ready to begin production of the system. For one-of-a-kind items, this means that the system is ready to be assembled or constructed. For mass-produced items, this means the system is ready for manufacture. In either case, the system is ready to be fabricated.

System Fabrication

Fabrication of the system begins when sufficient design work has been completed for the project manager to authorize fabrication work to begin. The project manager monitors the work, coordinates production efforts among departments, and ensures that expenditures and schedules conform to the project budget and master schedule.[11] The project manager, in conjunction with system, manufacturing or construction managers, is responsible for production planning and control. The control process involves releasing orders; monitoring, inspecting, and documenting progress; and comparing planned versus actual results (the process is described in Chapter 11). Project control and summary reports are released showing budgeted and scheduled work versus actual costs and work completed. These enable managers to make cost and work predictions and take corrective action when they spot deviant trends.

One measure of project performance is the extent to which the system achieves quality specifications. As with most tasks in production, quality control of components and system assembly is not, per se, the responsibility of the project manager. However, because the quality of the final system is the responsibility of the project manager, she must make sure that the system, construction, or manufacturing manager has implemented a quality plan that will achieve the quality objectives of the project.

Concurrent with system fabrication are three other major activities that the project manager oversees and coordinates: System testing, contract administration, and planning for implementation.

System Testing

Throughout Phase C, a variety of tests are performed to ensure that the system meets requirements. In new product development, testing occurs continuously throughout the project. Testing falls into three categories: Tests by the contractor to make sure that (1) the system design is adequate, and (2) that the design is being followed by the producers or builders, and (3) tests by the user to make sure the system meets user requirements and other contractual agreements.

If the system is inadequate because of faulty or poor design, then the design stage must be repeated. If the design problem lies in the specifications, then the definition phase also must be repeated. The most costly situation is where errors or omissions are not found until final integration tests or user acceptance tests near the end of Phase C. The process of repeating stages is costly and time-consuming, so tests should be devised to catch problems as early as possible.

Also, tests are needed to ensure that the design is being correctly implemented by the producers. Even when design is adequate, the system as produced will be inadequate should the builders fail to follow the design or cut corners on materials and procedures. Quality control tests will help determine the acceptability of system components and workmanship. The tests and test criteria as well as conditions are defined in the quality plan, described earlier.

Additionally, verification tests, reviews, and audits should be conducted throughout the project by the user to ensure that system specifications are being met and that test documentation is complete and accurate.

To minimize the chances of having to redesign whole systems because of faulty components, testing should follow the sequence of measuring components first, subsystems next, then the whole system last. Individual parts are tested first to ensure they function individually; parts integrated into components, then are tested to ensure they work together; next, components integrated into subsystems are tested to ensure that subsystems perform; and finally, subsystems integrated into the entire system are tested to guarantee total system performance.

Tests are performed against earlier developed system objectives and systems specifications. In addition, the system might be tested in excess of specifications to determine its actual capacity or point of failure. In *stress tests* an increasingly severe test load is applied to the system to determine its ability to handle heavier than probable conditions. In *failure tests* the system is loaded until it fails so that its ultimate capacity can be measured.

Test criteria are sometimes defined in the contract. In development projects, the contractor establishes design requirements and performance criteria, then specifies, during the design stage, the types of tests needed to verify the system.

The project manager is responsible for overseeing test plan preparation and coordinating the testing effort. A detailed test schedule should be prepared to ensure that tests are done at the right places and to catch problems at the earliest stage possible. The project manager must ensure that the tests are adequate to verify the entire system and its components, that human and facility resources are available to perform tests, and that test results are well documented and filed for later reference.

Contract Administration

In large projects, the work of multiple parties and contractors must be integrated for the development and production of the main end-item and ancillary side-items. Ensuring that the project meets commitments of both the developer/contractor and the customer as specified in the project contract is called *contract administration*.[12] Much of contract administration conduct relates to the more general practice of project control.

Particular tasks in contract administration include giving authorization to begin work; monitoring project work with respect to budgets, schedules, and technical performance; ensuring quality; controlling changes; and receiving payment for work completed. Work tasks are not allowed to begin until they have been authorized, and are not considered complete until end- and side-items have been reviewed and approved. Throughout the project, the project manager tracks ongoing work, comparing it to requirements and the project plan. Work quality, costs, and schedules are monitored simultaneously. Changes to objectives, specifications, designs, or work procedures are permitted only after they have passed through a formal request and review process. As work is completed, requests for payment are issued to the customer in accordance with conditions stated in the contract.

To perform these functions the project manager relies on three systems: (1) task authorization, performance tracking, and reporting; (2) change control; (3) and user payment. These systems, which assist the project manager in collecting data, making decisions, and disseminating information about actions, authorizations, and requests, are discussed in Chapter 11.

Planning for Implementation

Implementation is the process of turning the system over to the user. The two prime activities in implementation are installing the system in the user's environment and training the user to operate the system. Plans and resources for the implementation stage must be developed in advance so that implementation can begin as soon as system fabrication is complete (if not sooner). The plans must ensure that side-items being developed and produced will be available in time for user training, system installation, and operation. Although implementation planning should be started earlier, it must happen no later than during the production/build stage.

While the implementation plan is being prepared, the contractor accumulates materials to enable the user to learn about the system and how to operate and maintain it. Simple systems require only a brief instruction pamphlet and a warranty. Complex systems require much more, such as lengthy manuals for procedures, system operation, repair, and service; testing manuals; manuals for training the trainers; training materials and simulators; and schematics, drawings, special tools, servicing, and support equipment. Much of the information for these manuals is derived from documentation accumulated during the design stage. The difference is that information for user-oriented manuals must be translated into user terms so it is clear, understandable, and *usable* by the user.

The plans to install the system must also be finalized.[13] The project team must develop an implementation strategy which addresses

1. Activities for converting from the old system to the new system.
2. Sequencing and scheduling of implementation activities.
3. Acceptance criteria for the new system.
4. The approach to phasing out the old system and reassigning personnel.

During Phase B an initial implementation plan might have been included as part of the project master plan. In Phase C, a more detailed plan is prepared with the participation of people who will be affected in both the contractor and user organizations. The final implementation plan should contain a user training plan and training schedule; system installation plans (for installation, check out, and acceptance of all central and remote systems); site preparation requirements and schedules (addressing security, access, power, space, equipment, etc.); a conversion plan for phasing the old system out and the new system in; and a systems test plan adequate enough to enable sign off on the system.

Agreement must be reached about when the project will be "completed;" that is, when the system will be considered accepted and the project terminated. Misunderstandings about termination, such as "acceptance only after modification" arrangements, can make a project drag on indefinitely. To prevent that from happening, the user requirements as defined early in the project should include the conditions or criteria for acceptance.

The project manager coordinates preparation of the implementation plan, making sure that all key user and contractor participants are involved or kept informed; that activities are scheduled, budgeted, and adhere to the project plan; that approvals are obtained; and that clear agreement is reached on conditions governing project termination.

5.4 IMPLEMENTATION STAGE

At implementation the system is turned over to the user. In some systems this happens in an instant, such as when purchasing a clock. If the clock is simple, you just plug it in. If it is a digital alarm clock with a radio, you may need to read the instruction booklet to see how to set it. If the clock is a nuclear clock such as the one used by the Bureau of Standards, you may need several manuals and a training program to learn how to use it. If the clock is a replacement for an existing clock connected to a timing device that controls lighting and heating in a large skyscraper, you will have to develop a strategy for substituting one clock with the other in order to minimize disruption and inconvenience to the people in the building. These are some of the issues considered in implementation.

User Training

The purpose of user training is to teach the user how to operate, maintain, and service the system. At one extreme, training is a simple instruction booklet; at the other, it is an extensive, ongoing program with an annual budget of tens of thousands of dollars. The first step is to determine the training requirements—the type and extent of training required. This will dictate the kind of materials needed (manuals, videos, simulators); the personnel to be trained (existing or newly hired personnel); the techniques to be used (classroom, independent study, role plays); the training schedule (everyone at once, in phases, or ongoing); and the staffing (contractor, user, or subcontracted training personnel). Users must be heavily involved in training preparations. They should review and approve all training procedures and documents before training begins and have input afterwards to modify and improve the training.

Frequently the user will take over training after the contractor's trainers have trained user-trainers. In new systems where users may be unfamiliar with training requirements, the contractor should review the user's training program to make sure it is complete.

Good user training addresses the issue of how the newly-installed system fits into the whole system. Training should provide an overview of system objectives, scope, operation, and its interface with other elements of the user organization and environment. This will enable the user to better understand the system as part of the total user environment and to integrate the new system into existing systems.

Training should be aimed at relieving user anxiety. All new systems create fear, stress, and frustration; training should include all people who are affected by the system and address their points of concern.

User Acceptance Testing

The final system test before installation is the user acceptance test. The user relies on the results of this test to determine if the system satisfies requirements sufficiently to warrant (1) adoption or installation as is (2) installation pending modifications or adjustments, or (3) complete rejection.

Sufficient user training enables the user to competently try out the system to determine whether it is acceptable. These tests differ from those conducted by the contractor in the design and production stages because users will have their own kinds of tests. Previous tests conducted by the contractor should anticipate and exceed the test requirements of users. Nonetheless, the contractor should be prepared for the possibility that the system will fail portions of user tests.

Ideally, tests of acceptance will be performed by users with minimal assistance from the project team. When the user is unable to perform the tests, the project team must act as surrogate user and make every effort to view the system *as the user would.* This means putting aside biases or vested interests and assuming a role largely devoid of system-related technical expertise. Lack of user participation in acceptance testing is likely to lead to long-term implementation problems; therefore, even in the role of surrogate, the contractor sees that the user is on hand to witness tests.

The user is likely to discover things about the system that will require modifications or alterations. This is to be expected and, despite the added cost, is preferable and less costly than discovering the need for changes after implementation has been finished. Following modifications, acceptance tests, and tentative user approval, the system is ready to install.

System Installation and Conversion Stage

The system installation and conversion stage is conducted according to the implementation plan. Virtually all new systems are, in a sense, designed to substitute other, existing systems, so a major implementation issue is the strategy to be used for replacing the old system with the new one; This is called *conversion.* Possible strategies include

1. *Parallel installation:* Both new and old systems are operated until the new system is sufficiently proven.
2. *Pilot operation:* The new system is operated in a limited capacity until it is proven, then the old system is phased out as the new one is phased in.
3. *Cold turkey* (Big Bang): In one fell swoop, the new system is moved in and the old one is moved out.

During conversion, equipment must be installed, tested, fine-tuned, and deemed operable to the fulfillment of requirements. Selecting the best conversion strategy is no simple matter; it involves complicated considerations of costs, risks, and logistics. For example, the first strategy seems the safest: If the new system fails there is still the old one. It is also the most expensive because two complete systems must be operated simultaneously. There is also the problem of finding the staff to operate both systems at once. With the second strategy, costs and risks are low, and staff can be trained in stages. As a pilot operation, however, it may not be representative of the full system operation. Often, only after the full system has been phased in (and the old one phased out) will certain critical problems become apparent. The last strategy is the fastest and potentially least costly, but it is also the most risky. Tough questions to be answered are "When will there be time to train the staff?" (they must operate the old system until it is replaced with the new system) and, "What happens if the new system fails?"

Prior to actual installation, implementation plans should be reviewed and updated to reflect the most current conditions. Schedules and procedures for training and conversion should also be reviewed and revised as needed. The project manager must update all plans and schedules, gain approval for revisions, and renew the commitment from involved groups in the contractor and user organizations. Plans must account for the significant increase in user organizational resources required for any conversion. Interpersonal and organizational adjustments are necessary, and enough time must be scheduled to enable careful, thorough, and systematic installation. Implementation is a high-stress stage, particularly for the user, and the project manager must make certain his team is patient and sensitive to the questions, concerns, and fears of the user.

After the system has been installed, its performance in the user's environment must be ascertained. The contractor will continue monitoring the new system and performing tests to ensure that system design is adequate, that the system was installed properly, and that it smoothly interfaces with other systems in the user environment. After a breaking-in period and resolution of discrepancies, the new system is turned over to the user and the remains of the old system are phased out. User management and project management work together in the process.

One of the final tasks of the contractor before termination is to prepare a *post-completion project summary* document. This document is largely for the benefit of the contractor. It should use the project plan as the framework and enumerate everything that happened in the project—bad as well as good. The summary serves two purposes: (1) A learning document to help the contractor know what was right, what was wrong, and how to avoid making the same mistakes twice; and (2) a reference document about details of the system for possible future use. The postcompletion project summary is described further in Chapter 13.

5.5   PHASE D: OPERATION

The conclusion of Phase C marks either (1) the formal termination of the project and the final involvement of the contractor, or (2) the beginning of still another phase: operation. This depends on whether or not the project end-item involves a physical system or procedure that the user must operate or adhere to. Some projects, the *one shot* ones such as rock concerts, company relocations, or corporation mergers and audits, produce no physical system that must be maintained afterward. In such cases, the contractor's last project-related effort is installation. Just as often, however, the project output is a physical system or product that becomes operational; that is, the user must operate it. Virtually all projects for product and systems development result in such a physical system. The contractor sometimes remains involved with both the operational system and the user during this phase, either 1) on a continual basis through contractual arrangement or 2) through a new project with the same system. We will discuss these two cases next.

System Evaluation and Maintenance

The contractor may perform the system evaluation either as part of the original contract agreement or by additional agreement. The evaluation may occur as the last scheduled activity of the contractor in the form of a *postinstallation review,* the purpose of which is to evaluate system performance and to discover any maintenance or design-related problems that arise after the system has become fully operational. The subject of postinstallation review is discussed in Chapter 13.

The involvement of the contractor in system evaluation and maintenance may *extend* thereafter, usually through a contractual agreement to provide periodic review and/or service on a continuing basis. Sometimes the agreement is a warranty type of arrangement where the contractor provides review and maintenance during a pre-specified period as part of the original contract. Other times, it is an "extended" warranty type of arrangement that continues the contractor's involvement for a longer specified time period. The contractor may assign *system representatives* and technicians to the user site to perform periodic, preventive maintenance (parts replacement/ system update at regular intervals) as specified by the agreement. Alternatively, the contractor may perform system repairs or updates, but only when requested by the user and for an additional fee.

Improving the System

System requirements change, either because the user's tastes, needs, or budget change, or because the user's environment changes. In the first case, the user changes his objectives even though the environment is largely the same. In the second case, the user's environment (consumer wants, competition, government regulation, resource availability) changes, whether the user likes it or not. Either way, the system becomes inadequate and must be replaced. Replacement occurs by scrapping the existing system and getting a new one, or by modifying or enhancing the existing system so it satisfies new requirements.

The urgency of deciding what to do depends on the reason for the change. A homeowner-user may decide to add a den simply to acquire more space for leisure and recreation. This is different from the manager-user who is forced to expand production facilities because of rising competition or an increase in product sales. Changes in user tastes and wants are discretionary and, although the existing system may not live up to the new requirements, it will continue to function adequately as originally designed, *without changes.* When the user's environment changes, however, the situation is potentially more critical because these changes can render the system infeasible, inoperable, obsolete, inefficient, or in other ways delimit or incapacitate it. In short, the system *must* be replaced or modified.

For whichever reason, the decision to expand, enhance, or otherwise modify the system from its original requirements marks the beginning of a new systems development cycle. The contractor that originally developed the system may be called back to do the work, or a new contractor may be selected in a competitive bidding process. Mankind engages in few dead-end projects; each one spurs others, and the systems development cycle keeps rolling along. This is represented by the "To Phase A; repeat cycle" arrow in Figure 5-1.

Most projects follow a pattern somewhat similar to the four-phase cycle described in this and previous chapters. Following are examples taken from a variety of settings showing how the cycle is played out in projects of widely differing size and purpose.

5.6   SYSTEMS DEVELOPMENT IN INDUSTRIAL AND SERVICE ORGANIZATIONS

The following four cases illustrate the systems development cycle in projects for new product development (R&D), software product development, a company relocation, and the overhaul of a public agency.

New Product Development[14]

Jamal Industries is a medium-sized, diversified manufacturing firm that produces various products for major retailers under the retailer's own label; for example, Sears and True Value. All of Jamal's development and production work is done in phases similar to the systems development cycle: *Initiation, feasibility, analysis, design,* and *manufacturing.* The R&D director is the project manager for Jamal's development projects. Most projects are initiated and implemented internally, though sometimes development and manufacturing work is contracted out. In such cases, Jamal assumes the role of a user. The following example of the development and production of a computerized lighting timer is such a case.

In this project there was little formal emphasis on the initiation stage. A competitor had just introduced a computerized timer that would have a major impact on Jamal's market share. In essence, the project was initiated by Jamal's competition. To examine project feasibility, Jamal engineers analyzed samples of the competitor's device to see whether they could develop their own version quickly enough to maintain market share. The purpose of the analysis was to see whether a device as good or better could be made and sold with the retailers' private labels for 20 percent less than the competitor's price. As an alternative, Jamal could seek other distribution channels and try to sell the product with its own label. The feasibility study indicated that although Jamal could not design and produce the product in-house and remain 20 percent below the competitor's price, sufficient channels did exist to profitably sell the product with the Jamal label.

An in-depth analysis was made to determine how Jamal could contract out the design and production, which would alleviate the capital investment that the feasibility study had shown Jamal could not afford. For 4 months, the R&D director and his engineering staff analyzed alternatives for contracting out the work. They developed an MRP system to help investigate alternatives. The final decision was to use a general contractor that would be responsible for all tasks of product design, manufacture, and packaging. A foreign contractor was found that could make a competitively superior timer that Jamal could market at a price $12 lower than the competition. Much of the planning, scheduling, and budgeting associated with the project was delegated to this contractor.

A goal was set for design, manufacture, and distribution so that the product could be on store shelves within 1 year. At present, production of the device has just begun and Jamal is involved in monitoring the production progress. As manufacturing progresses, Jamal will devote more of its resources to marketing.

As long as Jamal markets the timing device, the foreign contractor will remain the vendor. The R&D director will continue to monitor the contractor and ensure that quality standards are being maintained. The rest of the Jamal project team will be transferred to other projects.

Software Product Development[15]

Cusumano and Selby describe the product development process at Microsoft in the book, *Microsoft Secrets.* In many companies, the typical product development project follows the three phases of planning, development, and stabilization; however, at Microsoft, the process is not strictly sequential, and steps within phases may go through a series of iterations (as illustrated in Figure 5-2).

The planning phase produces a vision statement, specification document, and plans for marketing, integrating components from other groups, testing, and documentation. The phase runs from 3 to 12 months, depending on whether the product is an upgrade or new application. The vision statement, which guides the entire project, is a short statement about the goals, focus, and priorities of the product. The specification document is a preliminary definition outline of the product's features and packaging that an ordinary user could describe in a single sentence. This document starts out small, but expands by as much as 20 to 30 percent before the project ends. The specification document, along with time estimates from developers and the plans for testing, documentation, and customer support, are used to create the project schedule. The planning phase concludes with management approval of the plans and schedule.

The development phase is nominally subdivided into four subphases with three internal product-release milestones. Each subphase is scheduled to last between 2 to 3 months. The schedule includes time buffers that allow unanticipated problems to be addressed and the subphase to be completed by the milestone date. Each of the first three subphases is devoted to the development (coding), testing for bugs and functionality, and documentation of a set of major product features. The purpose of the subphases is to meet the requirements for a set of product features with zero bugs that could be fully ready to "ship" (except shipping isn't possible at that point, because features have not been integrated into the product). In the event that a competitor threatens to release a similar product, the third, or even second, subphase can be bypassed to cut between 4 to 6 weeks out of the development process. The product would have fewer features, but would beat the competition to launch. During the fourth subphase, product features are further tested and debugged, and a visual freeze is imposed, which means no major changes can be introduced thereafter. This enables the education group to write product documentation that will accurately correspond to the product when released. The development phase ends with "code complete."

The last phase, stabilization, consists of extensive internal and external (beta) testing of the product—the combined, integrated sets of features developed in the previous phase. No new features are added at this time, unless the features of emerging competitive products make such additions essential. "Zero bug release" occurs when there are no more bugs that remain. Either all bugs are fixed, or features with remaining bugs are removed from the product (to be fixed later and included in subsequent product versions). This phase concludes with the release of a "golden master" disk, from which manufacturing will make copies. The project concludes with the project team's preparation of a postmortem report that outlines what worked well and what did not.

Relocation of a Company Division[16]

Over recent years the information systems division of a large corporation had grown at such a rate that relocation to a larger work area became an obvious consideration. The main activities of the relocation closely paralleled the phases of the systems development cycle.

Four phases comprised the project: Phase I, project *concept* (recognize the necessity to relocate); Phase II, project *definition* (find a new location, define facility and equipment needs, and obtain designs and construction drawings); Phase III, *acquisition* (new facility construction and equipment purchase); and Phase IV, *implementation* (relocate the division and monitor it during a settling-in period). Phase I happened by mandate: Either the division would be relocated and survive, or it would not and be "suffocated" out of business. Phase II started with a needs analysis to determine the requirements for the new site, which determined that space would be needed for 100 employees and a new computer room. Preliminary budget figures were prepared for the required square footage of 300,000 square feet for leased and purchased space. It was decided that space should be leased, and three sites were then considered. The company hired a real estate broker and legal consultant to help select the site and conduct contract negotiations. A preliminary space design was prepared for each site, showing location of workstations and work flow. A detailed budget was prepared with leasing arrangements, improvement and construction expenses, furniture, fixture, and telecommunication costs, moving expenses, and plant and office costs. Based upon budget and design considerations, a site was selected.

Later in Phase II, detailed design and construction drawings were obtained for company offices and the computer room. A detailed needs analysis was performed and the space design was analyzed in greater detail. For the computer room, requirements for power, air-conditioning, and both corporate and local data inputs to the system needed consideration. Bids were secured from local distributors and installation groups, and a furniture manufacturer was selected. After the final interior design was selected, bids were taken on general construction drawings for space design, HVAC engineering, electricity, architecture, lighting, telephone, and computer equipment.

Phase III began when the preliminary work was completed and contracts signed. A team of corporate and general contractor personnel was given responsibility to oversee and supervise construction. Phase III involved equipment needs analysis and purchase, vendor selection, and employee training. Numerous vendors performed the electrical, sheet metal, dry wall, painting, HVAC, plumbing, plastering, and carpentry work.

Bids from several moving companies were reviewed, a company was selected, and a moving schedule was prepared. At the same time, bids were received for procurement and installation of plant and office equipment such as computer workstations, photocopy machines, vending machines, and security systems. Bids and maintenance agreements were successfully negotiated.

Under the supervision of the project management team, Phases III and IV (facility construction, relocation to the new site, and equipment installation) were performed according to schedule. Before, during, and after the move an orientation program was conducted for division employees. Following the move, a final check-out was conducted to ensure that all steps had been completed and that all equipment was working properly. During the last phase, management established amicable working relationships with the local municipality and services environment—city hall, the community college, the fire department, and utilities companies.

Overhaul of Human Services Administration

Although small projects in the service sector tend not to follow the exact stages described in this chapter, they do follow a series of phases that is roughly *analogous* to the systems development process. These phases nominally include *initiation, problem definition, analysis of solutions, implementation,* and *operation.* The following example is an illustration.[17]

Human Services Administration (HSA) is a city welfare agency that provides limited financial assistance in the form of money, medical care, and drug rehabilitation treatment to eligible recipients. In administering these services, HSA became plagued by a number of bureaucratic problems, the worst being

- Inefficient control measures that allowed for mismanagement and errors in the payment system.
- High increases in the annual cost of the system.

- Inadequate control in applicant approvals leading to fraudulent client abuse.
- Employee productivity below 40 percent.
- Excessive tardiness and absenteeism among employees.

The city's mayor allotted $10 million annually for the implementation and maintenance of a new administrative system to resolve the problems. A group of outside professionals would be hired as a project team to overhaul the system. After the team had resolved the problems it would become a permanent part of HSA.

The project was to be conducted in four phases. During the first phase, *initiation*, HSA would define overhaul objectives and hire the professionals who would form the project team. In the second phase, *analysis*, the project team would identify problems and related objectives, and recommend solutions. In the third phase, *implementation*, the solutions would be executed, giving priority to the most severe problems. In the fourth phase, *operation*, the project team would be interweaved into the existing organization and become an ongoing staff function.

During the initiation phase, the following project objectives were stated:

1. Create a project management team with clear-cut responsibilities and authority. Conforming to this objective, outside professionals were hired and a project management team was created.
2. Eliminate opposition by some members of the existing organization to the planned overhaul.
3. Produce solutions to smaller problems so confidence could be gained and talent identified for working on larger problems.
4. Gain taxpayer confidence through media attention to the overhaul project.

In the second phase the project management team identified specific problems areas and divided them into five categories: New applications, photo identification, addicts, eligibility, and fraud. It then reorganized HSA to create a task force for each category. Each task force was to define problems, document the system, and suggest long-range recommendations and alternatives to the current system. Problems needing immediate attention were singled out and worked on first.

Parts of the second and third phases overlapped as solutions to some problems were implemented while other, longer-range problems were still being analyzed. Among the changes introduced were a new photo identification system for clients, a more efficient system for processing clients, tighter controls on client eligibility, a computer system for processing procedures and validating payments, tighter auditing controls, greater accountability of personnel, and tighter management controls.

In the final phase, HSA was reorganized again, this time by creating functional departments of roughly the same structure as the original project task forces. Most of the project management team stayed with HSA to assume management and staff positions.

5.7   SYSTEMS DEVELOPMENT IN LARGE GOVERNMENT PROGRAMS

The following illustrate the systems development cycle in two large-scale government programs: NASA planetary exploration and Air Force weapons procurement.

Planetary Exploration Program

A good example of the concepts in the last two chapters is NASA's "phased program planning" approach. This planning and review process is designed to keep projects aligned to NASA goals and within available resources, without premature commitment to a particular course of action.

The NASA system for organizing and managing projects varies from project to project, but common to all are the phases of (A) *conceptualization,* (B) *study,* (C) *design and development,* and (D) *operations.* Throughout a typical spacecraft program the project manager has responsibility for all phases, from initial study and project planning, to fabrication and integration of spacecraft and experiments, to launch and subsequent acquisition and use of experimental data. An example of a typical large scientific space flight project is the hypothetical project "Cosmic," a series of spacecraft for the collection and analysis of geophysical measurements of the planet Mercury.[18]

Phase A, conceptualization, is initiated when, at the urging of scientists, the director for Lunar and Planetary Programs (LPP) at NASA headquarters asks the director of Goddard Space Flight Center to begin preliminary analysis of how NASA might send either a probe or a satellite to Mercury to conduct geophysical experiments. The purpose of Phase A is to determine whether the mission is feasible and should be pursued. This involves looking at alternative project approaches, identifying the best ones for further refinement, defining project elements such as facilities, and operational and logistics support, as well as identifying necessary research or technology development. Phase A is conducted at NASA installations by a study team of NASA scientists and engineers appointed by the director of Goddard. The person chosen as study team leader is someone capable of becoming *project manager* should the concept prove favorable. The person selected is currently the spacecraft manager of a satellite project that is being completed.

At the same time, the director of LPP in Washington assigns a liaison with the Goddard study team. The liaison officer is chosen with the approval of the director of Goddard to assure a smooth working relationship. If the project is approved, the liaison officer will become the *program manager.* (The distinction between project and program managers was discussed in Chapter 2.)

The preliminary analysis is favorable and the study team recommendation to prepare a proposal and proceed to Phase B is approved by Goddard management. Phase B, study, involves detailed study, comparative analysis, and preliminary systems design. The study team leader and the liaison officer draft the project proposal and a project approval document. The approval document outlines resources and the field installation to oversee work (Goddard), specifies project constraints, and defines the number of spacecraft, type of launch vehicle, and allocation of funds and labor. The approval is for Phase B only.

The liaison officer coordinates and receives all necessary approvals from other involved program divisions and operating offices at NASA headquarters. Then the approval document is sent to the top NASA administrator for a decision. With this approval, project "Cosmic" is authorized to begin.

Management formally names the Cosmic program manager (the liaison officer) and the Cosmic project manager (the study team leader). The project manager assembles a skeleton team to develop specifications for study contracts that will provide data to determine whether or not to proceed further. Estimated schedules and resource requirements for the project are developed. The project team works with major project functional groups such as launch vehicle, reliability, data acquisition, and launch operations. Relationships are established to provide the necessary lead time for equipment manufacture, testing, and operations. A detailed project plan is prepared outlining technical specifications, manpower, funds, management plans, schedules, milestones, and launch and tracking requirements to meet project objectives.

The project plan is approved by management at Goddard and NASA headquarters and becomes a contract between them. Headquarters sets up a formal information and control system and makes available the necessary financial resources. The project manager sends monthly (later weekly) reports to the program manager. This is important because, should the project run into difficulties, the program manager can work quickly to obtain or reallocate funds to support it.

The original approval document is updated throughout Phase B and becomes the authorization document for Phase C (design and development) or for both Phase C and Phase D (operations). During Phase B, the appropriate experiments are selected and the number of Cosmic flights is put at three. At the completion of Phase B, project Cosmic appears on NASA information and control systems that permit reviews of financial, schedule, and technical progress. At this point, less than 10 percent of total project costs have been incurred.

During Phase C contractors become involved in detailed engineering design, development of mock-ups, and completion of detailed specifications on all major subsystems of the Cosmic spacecraft. When the project team completes design and supporting studies, it then develops RFPs for design, development, fabrication, and testing of final hardware and project operations.

The project manager has two associates: One facilitates coordination between the project and the experimenters; another coordinates activities for modification of the launch vehicle to meet requirements for the three flights. Members of the project team are also working at Cape Kennedy in preparation of launch, and at Jet Propulsion Laboratory in California which handles data acquisition from deep space probes.

When spacecraft fabrication begins, the project manager travels to the contractor's plants where he spends considerable time in conferences for design and test reviews, quality assurance, components testing, and system integration. Meanwhile the program manager keeps tabs on the project and keeps it "sold" at NASA. Both managers participate in formal reviews to catch errors at critical points in the project. Usual reviews include

1. *Conceptual design reviews* (at end of Phase B) to evaluate preliminary designs and the design approach.
2. *Detailed design reviews* after design is frozen and before assembly begins to evaluate design approach testing.
3. *Flight qualification reviews* to determine hardware status and evaluate tests.
4. *Flight readiness reviews* to assure the appropriate state of completion before the spacecraft is shipped to Cape Kennedy.
5. *Flight operations review* to evaluate orbital operations and spacecraft-ground support interface.
6. Other reviews to determine the state of readiness of communication networks, ground stations, and support facilities and personnel.

Phase D nominally begins with final preparation and launch of the first spacecraft, Cosmic I. The project manager oversees the multiple key teams working in this phase, including the (1) NASA launch team, (2) NASA project management team, (3) NASA program management, (4) scientists whose experiments are on the spacecraft, (5) prime contractors and subcontractors that built the spacecraft and launch vehicle, and (6) the Air Force team that controls the missile range. The spacecraft is "mated" with the launch vehicle and tested. During the last few moments of countdown, only the project manager has authority to make the final irrevocable decision to "go."

Launch data are recorded during the time between rocket lift-off and successful placement of the spacecraft in trajectory to Mercury. Problems are analyzed so as to avoid repetition with the next spacecraft. Once the spacecraft is on its way and communication and instrumentation are verifiably working and returning usable data, the project manager turns attention to Cosmic II—now in the early fabrication stage (Phase C). He continues to monitor Cosmic I operation because lessons from it will be applied to improve the design of Cosmic III, which is, by then, in Phase B.

Air Force Weapons Systems Programs

NASA's four-phase process is an outgrowth of the weapons systems procurement process used by the military. For many years the Department of Defense (DOD) pressed companies in the aerospace industry to develop standardized management, planning, and control tools. When standardization did not occur, the Air Force introduced a series of manuals in 1964 designed to administer consistent management control to all its future systems. A program package concept was designed to relate planning and budgeting to defense requirements.

The program package outlines four phases that a defense system must go through. The phases, as well as the series of manuals, are still in use today. During Phase I, *concept formulation,* experimental and test studies are performed to develop the system concept and establish its feasibility in terms of technical, economic, and military criteria. Each contractor must perform certain steps for the Air Force that, in turn, must do the same for the DOD. When the best technical approach has been selected, the DOD makes sure that the cost-effectiveness of the approach weighs favorably in relation to the cost-effectiveness of competing systems on a DOD-wide basis.

Phase II, *contract definition,* has three stages. Stage A involves screening contractors and negotiating requirements on proposals. DOD finances contract definitions for, usually, two contractors. In Phase B the competing contract definitions are submitted by the contractors; each includes complete technical, managerial, and cost proposals for the proposed system development. In Phase C an advisory committee reviews the competing proposals and selects a contractor.

Phase III and Phase IV overlap. In Phase III, *acquisition,* the system goes through detailed design, development, procurement, and testing. In Phase IV, *operation,* the system is delivered, placed in service, and then evaluated to ensure its effectiveness. After the system has been tested and accepted by the Air Force, it is transferred to a "user command" and made operational with active logistic support.

5.8 SUMMARY

There are good reasons why the systems development cycle appears in so many kinds of projects. First, it emphasizes continuous planning, review, and authorization. At each stage results are examined and used as the basis for decisions and planning for the next stage. Second, the process is goal oriented—It strives to maintain focus on user requirements and system objectives. Review and evaluation help ensure that mistakes and problems are caught early and corrected before they get out of control. If the environment changes, timely action can be taken to modify the system or terminate the project. Third, with the user requirements and system objectives always in sight, activities are undertaken so that they are coordinated and occur at the right time, in the right sequence.

The four-phase systems development cycle of the last two chapters outlines the nominal phases, stages, and activities for projects. It is just an outline, however, and should not be taken as a description of what does or should happen in all projects. As the examples show, it can be altered or simplified so that some phases receive more emphasis, some less, some none. Some even may appear in different sequence, depending on the project. Nonetheless, in preparing for any project it is a good idea to mentally review all of the phases described to make certain that nothing will be missed.

REVIEW QUESTIONS

1. When does the project manager become involved in the project?
2. How is the project team created?
3. What are user requirements, system objectives, and system specifications? Give examples. How are they related?
4. Describe the process of developing user requirements and system specifications.
5. What problems are associated with requirements definition? What are ways to minimize these problems?
6. What is the purpose of specifying priorities and margins in defining requirements?
7. How are the various functional areas and subcontractors involved in the requirements definition and project planning process?
8. Describe briefly the contents of a project master plan.
9. What are the aims of a quality-oriented project?
10. Discuss the preparation and content of a project quality plan.
11. Comment on the statement "a project should strive to produce an end-item with the fewest possible defects."
12. What is the practice of "fast tracking" or "design/build?" What are the associated potential benefits and dangers?
13. What happens during the design stage? Who is involved? What do they do? What is the role of the project manager? How are design changes monitored and controlled?
14. What is a prototype and what is its purpose in design and development?
15. What is rapid prototyping and how is it employed in the systems development process?
16. What happens during the production or building stage? How is work planned and coordinated? Who oversees the work?
17. What is the distinction between the project end-item and project side items? What role does the project manager have regarding each?
18. What is contract administration?
19. How is the project end-item tested and checked out for approval?
20. How is the system implemented? Describe the important considerations for turning the system over to the user.
21. Describe ways of converting to the new system.
22. How are projects "closed out" or terminated?

23. Describe the postcompletion project summary. What is its purpose?
24. Describe the postinstallation review. What is its purpose?
25. Describe what happens during the operation stage. What is the role of the systems development organization?

QUESTIONS ABOUT THE STUDY PROJECT

As appropriate, answer review questions 1–4, 7, 8, 13, 16, 19, 20, 22–25 with regard to your project. Also, answer the following questions:

1. When the end-item is a product, system implementation includes marketing, promotion, and distribution of the product. If the end-item in your project is a product, when does the planning begin for marketing, promotion, and distribution, and who is responsible? Where does the plan fit into the project master plan?

2. If the end-item is a building or other "constructed" item, how is it turned over to the user? Describe the testing, acceptance, training, and authorization process.

3. What happens to the project team when the project is completed?

4. How does the organization get reinvolved in the next project?

Case 5-1   Star-Board Construction/ West-Starr Associates

Star-Board Construction (SBC) is the prime contractor for Gargantuan Project, a large skyscraper project in downtown Manhattan. SBC is working directly from drawings received from the architect, West-Starr Associates (WSA). Robert Starr, owner and chief architect of WSA, had designed similar buildings and viewed this one as similar to the others. However, one difference between this building and the others is in its facing, which consists of very large granite slabs—slabs much larger than traditionally used and larger than anything with which either WSA or SBC has had prior experience.

Halfway into the project, Kent Star, owner and project manager for SBC, started to receive reports from his site superintendent about recurring problems with window installation. The windows are factory units, premanufactured according to WSA's specifications. Plans are to install the granite facing on the building according to specifications that allow for dimensional variations in the window units. The architect provided the specification that a 1/2-inch tolerance for each window space be made (that is, the window space between granite slabs could vary as much as 1/4 inch larger or smaller than the specified value). This created a problem for the construction crew that found the granite slabs too huge to install with such precision. As a result, the spacing between slabs is often too small, making it difficult or impossible to install window units. Most of the 2,000 window units for the building have already been manufactured so it is too late to change their specifications, and most of the granite slabs have been hung on the building. The only recourse for making window units fit into tight spaces would be to grind away or reinstall the granite. It is going to be very expensive and will certainly delay completion of the building.

QUESTION   .

1. What steps or actions should the architect and contractor have taken before committing to the specifications on the window units and spacing between granite slabs that would have reduced or eliminated this problem?

Case 5-2 Revcon Products and Welbar, Inc.

Revcon Products manufactures valves for filling and controlling the level of water in industrial tanks. It had concentrated on products for the construction industry (valves for newly-installed tanks), but now wants to move into the much larger and more lucrative replacement market. Whereas annual demand for new valves is about 100,000, it is about 1 million for replacement valves. The company envisioned a new valve, the Millennium Valve, as a way to gain a share in the tank-valve replacement market. Revcon's objective was to design and produce the Millenium Valve to be of superior quality and lower cost than the competition.

Revcon decided to outsource the development and design of the new valve. It prepared an RFP that included the following objectives and requirements:

Product objectives:

Innovative design to distinguish the Millennium Valve from the valves of competitors.
Be price-competitive but offer greater value.

Market (user) requirements:

Ease of installation
Nonclogging
Quiet operation
Maintain water level with pressure changes
Ease in setting water level
Adjustable height

Revcon sent the RFP to four design/development companies and selected Welbar, Inc., primarily based on it having submitted the lowest bid. Welbar's proposal had been written by its sales and marketing departments and revised by senior management, but received no input from industrial designers, engineers, or anyone else who would work on the project. Welbar had no prior experience with industrial water valves, but the sales team saw Millennium as an opportunity to earn profits and align with a major equipment manufacturer. The marketing department prepared time and cost estimates using standard tasks and work packages from proposals for old projects.

The Welbar design team assigned to the Millennium project was headed by Karl Fitch, a seasoned engineer, and included two industrial designers and two engineers. Because of prior project commitments, the team was not assembled until 5 months after the proposal had been accepted, which became the first time anyone with technical training had looked at the project seriously. It also was at this time that Welbar began to perform industry research on the valve market by talking to contractors, plumbers, and retailers. Karl reviewed the proposal and divided the project into phases and small work packages and prepared a Gantt chart. He concluded that the proposal had omitted several critical processes and steps, and that the requested funding was substantially underestimated. He rewrote the proposal, schedule, and cost estimate.

Throughout the project the design concept, work tasks, and schedules had to be changed many times. Welbar engineers were frustrated at Revcon's constant harping about the need for both low cost and functional superiority. It could be done, but Revcon also wanted a speedy, low-cost development effort. During the project Welbar engineers learned that to design such a valve required more resources than they had been budgeted. Because of all the changes, Welbar exceeded the budgeted amount four times and had to request additional funds from Revcon. One big problem that the project encountered was when Welbar delivered a prototype to Revcon. Because the proposal had not clearly stated what the prototype would be, Revcon expected much more. Revcon thought the prototype would be a virtually finished product with replicable components, whereas Welbar understood it to be a simple working model to demonstrate design and functionality. Extra time and money had to be spent to bring the prototype up to Revcon's expectation. Revcon allotted the additional time and money, but the completed prototype was still over budget and delivered late. To compensate for the delay, Welbar crammed project stages together or executed them out of sequence. When the design stage fell behind because the prototype had not met expectations, Welbar went ahead and started making production-ready models. This was a waste of time and money because the finished prototype showed that the production models could not be produced.

Welbar did design a truly innovative valve; however, the design required substantially new tooling at the factory and would cost Revcon 50 percent more to produce than had been expected.

Revcon canceled the contract with Welbar. The work is estimated to be 90 percent finished, and Revcon is attempting to complete the last 10 percent. However, it looks like completing that last 10 percent will be very challenging. So far, Revcon has spent twice as much time and money on development as expected and still does not have a product to manufacture. Because of development and tooling costs, it is unlikely that the product, once development has been completed (if ever), can be priced low enough to be competitive.

QUESTION

1. What happened to this project? Prepare a list of the factors that contributed to Revcon's failure to obtain the product they wanted. For each factor, discuss what might have been done differently.

Case 5-3 Lavasoft.com

Lavasoft Company, a web site development firm, is developing new site software for one of its corporate clients. The project starts out well. Lavasoft staffers meet frequently with client representatives to produce a document of clearly stated client needs and requirements. There is no question about what the client needs; however, members of the Lavasoft development team disagree about the kind of system that would best satisfy these needs. The project manager, Mary West, is concerned about the time this project will take. She feels that the kind of system that would best satisfy the user needs is more or less obvious, and she asks a few people on the team to help her create some bullet points and general flowcharts to address the requirements. She also creates a project schedule.

She then presents the charts and schedule to the rest of the development team and says that anyone is free to question her about them. Some people are concerned that the approach as stated by the bullet points and the high-level charts are too vague. Mary assures them that the vagueness will be worked out as details of the system are defined.

A team of designers is selected to perform the detailed design and development work. To speed up decision making and reduce outside interference, the team's size is kept small and relatively isolated from other development teams in the company. Daily the team is forced to interpret the bullet points and high-level charts and to make design decisions. Whenever there is disagreement about what should be done, which is frequent, Mary makes the decision.

The design team produces the detailed system specifications on time according to the schedule, so the project is considered in good shape. However, upon looking at the specifications, some reviewers raise questions. For example, it is not clear that all aspects of the system will be compatible with the client's existing site products. Further, the effectiveness of meeting all the requirements is not uniform (some requirements are clearly met; others are questionable); and some of the specifications involve system expertise that isn't the forte of Lavasoft. The original development group does not want to change the general approach; instead they simply change some of the specifications before proceeding.

Many weeks pass as the specifications are reworked, reviewed and approved, but questions persist. Finally, the project manager decides that coding and testing must begin if the project is to stay on schedule. Once coding and testing of elements of the system are completed, however, resistance grows to changing the specifications because that would require recoding and delay the project further. Compromises are made to the specifications. More time passes and the system falls 3 months behind schedule. To meet the deadline, Mary puts more people on the project. Eventually the system is considered ready for installation, but it is 2 months later than the original promised date. Because more people were needed to staff the project, Lavasoft does not make a profit. Also, because the system is not completely compatible with other elements of the client's web site, Lavasoft must continue to work on it and introduce "fixes." The client is not happy with the results and does not contract with Lavasoft again.

QUESTIONS

1. What went wrong with the project?
2. Where were mistakes made in the project initially?
3. How were problems allowed to persist and go uncorrected for so long?

ENDNOTES

1. See J. Davidson Frame, *Managing Projects in Organization* (San Francisco: Jossey-Bass, 1988): 146–51.
2. V. Hajek, *Management of Engineering Projects*, 3d ed. (New York: McGraw-Hill, 1984): 35–37; N. Whitten, *Managing Software Development Projects*, 2d ed. (New York: John Wiley & Sons, 1995): 250–55.
3. John Connell and Linda Shafer, *Structured Rapid Prototyping* (Upper Saddle River, NJ: Yourdan Press/Prentice Hall, 1989).
4. P. G. Smith and D. G. Reinertsen, *Developing Products in Half the Time* (New York: Van Nostrand Reinhold, 1991): 94–96.
5. Whitten, *Managing Software Development Projects*, 197–202.
6. See E. Yourdan, *Rise and Resurrection of the American Programmer* (Upper Saddle River, NJ: Yourdan Press/Prentice Hall, 1998): 157–81.
7. James Bach, "The Challenge of 'Good Enough' Software," *American Programmer* (October 1995).
8. Drew Fetherston, *The Chunnel* (New York: Times Books, 1997): 198–99.
9. Alan Cooper, *The Inmates are Running the Asylum: Why High-Tech Products Drive Us Crazy and How to Restore the Sanity* (Indianapolis: Sams, 1999).
10. Two kinds of design reviews commonly required are the "preliminary review," wherein the preliminary design concept is checked for ability to satisfy the operational requirements (user requirements and system objectives), and the "critical review" wherein details of hardware and software design are checked for ability to execute the preliminary design.
11. The production authorization process is described by Hajek, Management of Engineering Projects, 195–97.
12. For an in-depth discussion of contract administration, see W. Hirsch, *The Contracts Management Deskbook*, rev. ed. (New York: American Management Association, 1986), especially Chapter 6.
13. Portions of this section are derived from C. L. Biggs, E. G. Birks, and W. Atkins, *Managing the Systems Development Process* (Upper Saddle River, NJ: Prentice Hall, 1980): 187–93. This reference focuses on implementation planning for computerized systems but the topics are generalizable to other types of systems.
14. Based upon information collected and documented by Cary Morgen from interviews with managers of Jamal Industries (fictitious name).
15. Michael Cusumano and Richard Selby, *Microsoft Secrets* (New York: Free Press, 1995): 192–207.
16. Based upon an actual company relocation and data collected from interviews with company managers by Pam Paroubek. The title of the division is fictitious.
17. This example is adapted from K. L. Harris, "Organizing to Overhaul a Mess," *California Management Review*, 17, no. 3 (1975): 40–49.
18. Based upon R. L. Chapman, *Project Management in NASA: The System and the Men* (Washington, D.C.: NASA, SP–324, 1973): 13–19.

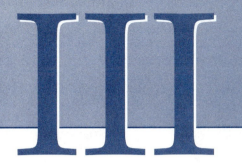

Part III

Systems and Procedures

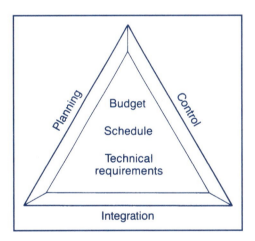

*S*uccessful project management goes beyond coordinating people and groups; it involves defining the goals and work they must accomplish, then providing leadership and direction to ensure the work gets done. Overall project goals need to be articulated into shorter term objectives with carefully plotted plans, schedules, and budgets to accomplish them. Controls are then needed to make sure plans and schedules are carried out as intended.

Over the years an impressive collection of methods has been developed to help project managers collect and use information for defining and directing work. The next eight chapters describe these methods, including techniques and procedures for specifying, scheduling, and budgeting project activities, organizing and keeping records, and monitoring and controlling work to achieve project goals.

Procedures are best conducted within the framework of a system to ensure that all elements are accounted for, properly organized, and executed. The so-called Project Management System and the various structures, activities, and frameworks that comprise it—work breakdown structures, cost accounting systems, management information systems, and many others—are also described in this section.

Chapter 6

Planning Fundamentals

> Big fleas have little fleas
> Upon their backs to bite 'em
> Little fleas have lesser fleas
> And so ad infinitum.

—Old rhyme[1]

*O*ne distinguishing feature of projects is that each is tailored toward some unique end-item or result. That uniqueness implies that every project must be defined anew and a scheme created telling everyone involved *what to do.* Deciding and specifying what to do is the function of *project planning.* Making sure it is done right is the function of *project control.*

Three things occur in the planning and control process: (1) During the conception and definition phases (before project work actually begins) a *plan is prepared* specifying the project requirements, work tasks, responsibilities, schedules, and budgets; (2) during the execution phase the *plan is compared to* actual project performance, time, and cost; if there are discrepancies, (3) *corrective actions are taken* and the requirements, schedules, and budgets updated. Planning and control are essential parts of project management; they enable people to understand what is needed to meet project goals and reduce the uncertainty of outcomes. Planning and control are the subjects of the next six chapters. This chapter gives an overview of the planning process and the initial steps in preparing project plans.

Top management gives the authorization to begin planning shortly after a business need, contract request, or RFP is received. This authorization releases funds so that plans, schedules, and budgets can be prepared. These plans are then used to justify additional funds and authorize work for the remainder of the project.

A project manager, if not already assigned or involved, is now identified to oversee the planning. A *project charter* is created that briefly gives the statement of work, expected end-items or results, and required resources. If the work is being performed under contract, the contract will serve as the charter. The purpose of the charter is to enable the project manager, senior management, and functional managers to reach agreement about the scope of the project and the resources they will commit to it.

Because every project is different, there is never an a priori, established way specifying how each and every one should be done. New projects pose new questions. For starters, the project team needs to answer questions about *what* has to be done, *how* it has to be done, by *whom*, in *what order, for how much*, and by *when*. The formalized way to answer these questions is through the planning process. The process addresses the questions in roughly the following steps:

1. Project *objectives, requirements,* and *scope* are set. These outcome elements specify project end-items, desired results, and time, cost, and performance targets. (What, for how much, and by when?) The scope includes specific acceptance requirements that the customer uses to determine acceptability of results or end-items. Everything specified in these requirements must be completed during the project to the customer's satisfaction.
2. The specific *work activities,* tasks, or jobs to achieve objectives are broken down, defined, and listed. (What?)
3. A *project organization* is created specifying the departments, subcontractors, and managers responsible for work activities. (Who?)
4. A *schedule* is prepared showing the timing of work activities, deadlines, and milestones. (When, in what order?)
5. A *budget* and *resource plan* is prepared showing the amount and timing of resources and expenditures for work activities and related items. (How much and when?)
6. A *forecast* is prepared of time, cost, and performance projections for the completion of the project. (How much time is needed, what will it cost, and when will the project be finished?)

These steps need to be followed each time because every project is somewhat unique, requires different resources, and must be completed to specific time, cost, and performance standards to satisfy users' requirements. Whenever projects are similar, much of the planning relies on past experience and historical records for assistance; when they are first-of-a-kind, much of the planning proceeds from scratch.

Functional areas of the organization assigned to the project should be involved in the planning process. Although each area develops its own plan, all plans are derived from and become a part of a single, overall project plan. This overall plan is referred to as the *project master plan* or project summary plan.

The project is initiated with the preparation of a formal, written master plan. The purpose of this plan is to guide the project manager and team throughout the project life cycle; to tell them what resources are needed, when, and how much they will cost; and, later, to enable them to measure progress, determine when they are falling behind, and know what to do to catch up.

Common sources of project failure such as scheduling and cost overruns could often be avoided if more thought were given to planning. The process of preparing a plan should be thorough and begun early, even before the project is authorized. In most cases, this means that project planning begins during formulation of the project proposal. During proposal preparation, a rudimentary project team is organized and major decisions for resource acquisition are made. The team prepares a summary project plan for inclusion in the proposal using the same (albeit more abbreviated) procedures as they will use later to develop a more elaborate and detailed master plan. The difference between the summary plan in the proposal and the master plan is that the former is intended for the customer, and the latter for the project team. The summary plan need only contain enough detail to give the customer an overview; the master plan must be of sufficient detail to guide the team in the execution of the project. When management approves the plan it gives the project manager tacit authority to conduct the project in accordance with the plan.

Contents of Master Plans

The contents of master plans vary depending on the size, complexity, and nature of the project. Typically, the plan has three major sections:[2]

I. Management Summary. An overview description of the project oriented toward top-level management. It includes a brief description of the project, objectives, overall requirements, constraints, problem areas (and how they will be overcome), and the master schedule showing major events and milestones.
II. Management and Organization Section. Overview of organization and personnel requirements for the project. It includes
    A. Project management and organization: Details how the project will be managed and identifies key personnel and authority relationships.
    B. Manpower: Estimates of workforce requirements in terms of skills, expertise, and strategies for locating and recruiting qualified people.
    C. Training and development: Summary of the executive development and personnel training necessary to support the project.
III. Technical Section. Overview of major project activities, timing, and cost. It includes
    A. Statement of work and scope of work: Generalized description of major project activities and tasks, and results or end-items.
    B. Work breakdown: List of work packages and description of each.
    C. Responsibility assignments: List of personnel and responsibility for work packages and other areas of the project.
    D. Project schedules: Generalized project and task schedules showing major events, milestones, and points of critical action or decision. May include Gantt charts, project networks, and PERT/CPM diagrams.

E. Budget and financial support: Estimates and timing of capital and development expenses for labor, materials, and facilities.
F. Testing: Listing of things to be tested, including procedures, timing, and persons responsible.
G. Change control plan: Procedures for review and decision about requests for changes to any aspect of the project plan.
H. Quality plan: Measures for monitoring quality and accepting results for individual work tasks, components, and end-item assemblies.
I. Work review plan (may be included in quality plan): Procedures for periodic review of work, noting what is to be reviewed, by whom, when, and according to what standards.
J. Documentation: List of documents to be produced and how they will be organized and maintained.
K. Implementation: Discussion and guidelines showing how the customer will convert to, or adopt, the results of the project.
L. Economic justification: Summary of alternatives in meeting project objectives showing tradeoffs between costs and schedules.
M. Areas of uncertainty and risk: Contingency plans for areas of greatest uncertainty in terms of potential work failure or missed milestones. (This section is often excluded because it scares users and management.)

Depending on the client or type of project contract, some plans require additional, special items not outlined here.[3] In small or low-cost projects, it is possible to delete certain sections, taking care not to overlook the crucial ones. It is usually good practice to systematically review every item in the three sections even if only to verify that some of them are "N/A" (not applicable). An example of a project master plan is given for the LOGON project in Appendix C.

You might notice a similarity between the sections of the plan and the contents of the proposal described in section 4.6. Though the format is slightly different, there is indeed a similarity. In many cases the proposal, revised and updated to reflect current agreements and contract specifications, becomes the project master plan. At other times, when the project summary needs to be expanded and defined in greater detail, the proposal serves as an outline. Because the primary audience of the final master plan is the project team and not the user, the technical section is usually larger and in greater detail than what appears in the project proposal.

As the following example illustrates, the development of a project master plan is an evolutionary, multidisciplinary process.

Developing a Project Plan at Master Control Company

The Master Control Company (MCC), a medium-sized engineering firm, was approached by Bier Publishing Company to develop a control unit for tracking the production process of two multistage, high-efficiency printing presses. The Bier engineering department initiated the project by sending MCC a list of requirements for power, wiring, performance, and possible future enhancements for the unit. MCC appointed a project manager to oversee design and development and to prepare a proposal.

MCC's engineering group conceived an initial, theoretical design to cover all specifications and circumvent any design flaws. Throughout the process they consulted with engineers from Bier, and the design was altered and redone several times. The final design consisted of blueprints, a manual of operational specifications, and a bill of materials and parts.

With this design the MCC marketing department performed a detailed analysis of the price of parts and cost of labor. The manager of the production department also examined the design and, together with the project manager, prepared a work breakdown structure and tentative project plan outlining major work tasks.

A meeting was held with representatives from project management, engineering, marketing, and production to review the project plan, costs, and feasibility. The production department supplied information about the kind of labor expertise needed, the availability of parts, and a forecast of the time required to produce the unit. Marketing provided information about the costs of labor, parts and supplies, and the overall project. Having this information, the project manager was able to expand the project plan, develop a bid price, and combine the two into a proposal. Notice that, in terms of the systems-development process, the stages of initiation, feasibility, definition, and most of the design were completed before the proposal was sent to Bier.

Following contract negotiation and signing, the project manager and production manager developed a final, detailed master plan. This plan contained the same information as the proposal did, but was updated and expanded to include a schedule for materials and parts purchases, a schedule of labor distribution for work tasks, a management and task responsibility matrix, and a detailed master schedule.

Seldom does all project planning occur only at one particular point in time. As this example shows, the plan is developed gradually, expanded and modified as information is accumulated and after it has been reviewed, refined, and finally accepted by project participants.

Learning from Past Projects

During development of the project plan, reference should be made to earlier, similar projects (including plans, procedures, successes, and failures) for whatever applications seem relevant. Indeed, when they exist, this is one purpose of the *postcompletion project summary* (described in Chapter 13); that is, to enable planners to avoid reinventing the wheel and repeating past failures. Often projects are approached as *too* unique, and the lessons of history—dilemmas, mistakes, and solutions—are ignored. Simply, this means that in preparing for any project it is important to scrutinize what others have done before. Somewhat common among researchers and scholars, this approach is not as common among persons who consider themselves more "action-oriented."[4]

Tools of Project Planning

Much of the technical content of project plans is derived from the basic tools described in this chapter. They include

1. *Work breakdown structure* and *work packages*—used to define the project work and break it down into specific tasks.
2. *Responsibility matrix*—used to define project organization, key individuals, and their responsibilities.
3. *Events* and *milestones*—used to identify critical points and major occurrences on the project schedule.
4. *Gantt Charts*—used to display the project master schedule and detailed task schedules.

Additional planning tools such as networks, critical path analysis, PERT/CPM, cost estimating, budgeting, and forecasting are covered in subsequent chapters.

6.3   SCOPE AND WORK DEFINITION

Scope Definition

Scope definition is the process of specifying the criteria for determining if important phases of work and the project have been completed. Scope definition results in a document called the *scope statement,* which specifies the user acceptance requirements, project objectives, or high-level specifications for the main end-item and ancillary side items. The document emphasizes the main areas of work to be performed and the intended deliverables or end-items. Given that the definition phase has been substantially completed, most of the necessary information for scope planning should be readily available; all that remains is compilation into a physical document. Sometimes, to ensure clarity about expected outcomes, the scope statement also might specify what is *not* to be included within the project (i.e., exclusions). The scope statement provides a reference source for everyone in the project to review and agree upon the needs, requirements, objectives, and outcomes or end-items, as well as about what individual contributions are expected. It also provides the basis for making decisions about the resources needed to complete the project and about required or requested changes to work tasks or end-items that would alter the project scope.

Example 1: Scope Statement for the LOGON Project

The RFP for the LOGON project (Example 2, Chapter 4), statement of work section, states: "The Contractor's responsibility shall be for furnishing expertise, labor, materials, tools, supervision, and services for the complete design, development, installation, check-out, and related services for full operational capability of the LOGON system." The RFP also specifies exclusions from the expected work (e.g., "Removal of existing storage, placement, and retrieval equipment will be performed under separate contract . . .") as well as technical performance requirements. Iron Butterfly Contractors, Inc., which was awarded the contract, determined that the best system for meeting Midwest Parcel Distribution Company's needs is one that uses robotic transporter units to place and retrieve standard-size shipping containers from racks as instructed by a computerized data base. The key items listed in the LOGON scope statement are as follows (the "reference requirements" are check-off or acceptance criteria listed in a document that would be appended to the scope statement):

1. Basic design of overall system. Reference requirements A and B.
2. Detailed design of racks and storage-bucket system (termed "Hardware A"). Storage system is Model IBS05 modified to meet requirements C.1 through E.14.
3. Detailed design of robotic transporter unit and track system (termed "Hardware B"). Robotic transporter unit is Model IBR04 modified to meet requirements F.1 through G.13.
4. Development of software specifications for the data base and robotic-controller system. Reference requirements H.1 through H.9 and K.3.
5. Procurement of software and subassemblies and components for Hardware A and Hardware B. Reference requirements K.1 through L.9.
6. Final fabrication of Hardware A and Hardware B at Iron Butterfly site. Reference requirement M.
7. Installation and check-out of entire system at MPD site. Reference requirement Y.

The seven items represent deliverables for different stages of the project. As indicated, associated with each deliverable are specific requirements. For example, the detailed designs noted in Points 2 and 3 must, in general, be sufficiently comprehensive so subcontractors will be able to produce all the necessary components and subassemblies for Hardware A and Hardware B. The requirements for these designs (shown above as reference requirements C.1 through E.14 and F.1 through G.13) specify the requisite level of detail for that to happen. The scope statement will also contain exclusions as noted in the RFP or later agreed upon.

Once project objectives and requirements as outlined in the scope statement have been set, they must be translated into specific, well-defined elements of work. A list is needed telling the team what tasks, jobs, or activities must be done to accomplish the project. Particularly for large, new projects it is easy to overlook or duplicate activities. So that activities are not missed and the relationships between them are clearly understood, a systematic, formal approach is used to define the work elements. This is called the "work breakdown structure."

Work Breakdown Structure

Complex projects consist of numerous smaller, interrelated tasks and work elements. As the rhyme at the beginning of the chapter alludes, the goal or end-item of a project is a system that can be broken down into subsystems, which themselves can be broken down, and so on. The procedure for dividing the overall project into subelements is called the *work breakdown structure* or *WBS*. The purpose of a WBS is to divide the total project into small pieces, sometimes called *work packages*. Dividing the project into work packages makes it possible to prepare project schedules and cost estimates and to assign management and task responsibility.

The first step in creating a WBS is to divide the total project into major work categories. These major categories then are divided into subcategories which, in turn, are subdivided, and so on. This level-by-level breakdown continues so that the scope and complexity of work elements is reduced with each level of breakdown. The resulting WBS is analogous to a product structure diagram.

The objective of the analysis is to reduce the project into work elements that are so clearly defined that they, individually, can be thoroughly and accurately defined, budgeted, scheduled, and controlled. The WBS approach helps ensure that, for all elements, even minor ones, an accounting is made.

A typical WBS might consist of the following five levels (in actuality the number of levels varies; the name of the element description at each level is arbitrary):

LEVEL	ELEMENT DESCRIPTION
1	Project
2	Category
3	Subcategory
4	Sub-subcategory
5	Work package

Level 1 represents the total project. At Level 2 the project is broken down into several (usually between 4 and 10) major categories of work. These categories usually conform to the work areas specified in the scope statement. All of the categories' efforts, when taken together, must make up the *total project effort*. Each category, in turn, is broken down into subcategories, the sum of which must comprise the effort of the category. At the lowest level, whatever numbered level that might be, is a work package. Figure 6-1 shows the typical hierarchical structure of a WBS.

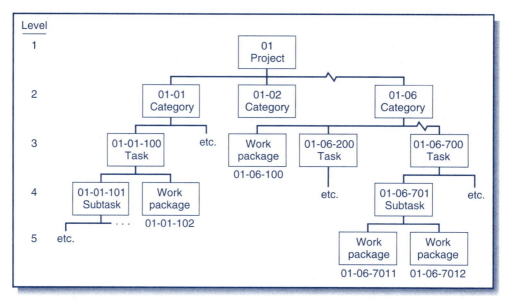

Figure 6-1
Elements of a work breakdown structure.

Figure 6-2 illustrates the WBS for building a house. The top part of Figure 6-2 shows the project objective (Level 1) and the major categories of items (Level 2) necessary to accomplish it. Notice that, for the most part, the items in the breakdown are *hardware-* or *product-oriented*. This makes it easier to assign specific responsibilities and to hold people accountable for specific *units of work* with expected performance, cost, and schedule requirements. As will be demonstrated later, use of a thorough, product-oriented WBS facilitates project scheduling and budgeting.

In contrast to the top WBS in Figure 6-2, the WBS in the middle is *less desirable*, because it is *functionally-oriented*. Thus, associated with each function (e.g., carpentry), are numerous products (such as cabinets, walls, floors, trim, doors, stairs, and windows), all of which require work that must eventually be scheduled at various times in the project. Therefore, planning for the project would necessitate the eventual breakdown of these functions into *products* anyway.

There are, however, a few places in the WBS where a *task-oriented* breakdown might be necessary or desirable. This is the case for tasks such as "design," "engineering," or "management," that are common to more than one element in the WBS or involve *integrating* elements in the WBS into the total system.

Continuing with the example in Figure 6-2, Level 2 items would be further elaborated into a work breakdown at Level 3 (shown at the bottom of Figure 6-2), and each of these items would be further broken down as necessary at Level 4, and so on. Concurrent with the development of the WBS is the process of *work definition*. As each element of the WBS is identified and broken down, project work is further elaborated and more clearly specified. By the time the WBS is completed, all work on the project has been completely defined.

During the WBS process, the questions "What else is needed?" and "What's next?" are constantly being asked. The WBS is reviewed again and again to make sure everything is there. Supplementary or missed items are identified and added to the structure at appropriate levels. For example, nowhere in the WBS in Figure 6-2 are blueprints, budgets, and work schedules indicated, even though construction cannot begin without them. These are items associated with the planning phase of the proj-

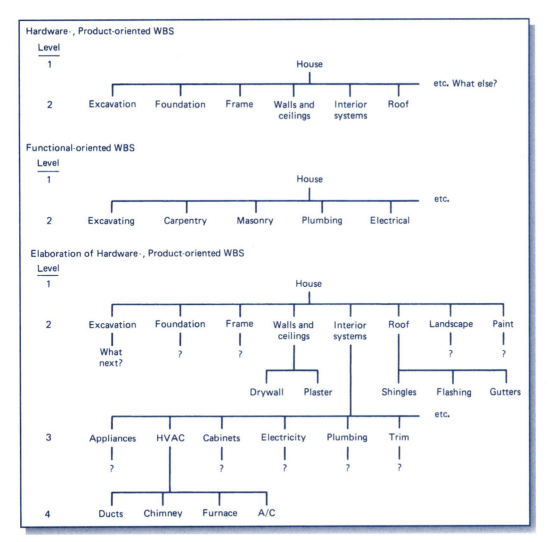

Figure 6-2
Example of WBS for building a house.

ect which must be completed prior to construction. They could be included in the WBS by expanding Level 2 and inserting categories for "design" and "administration and management," then by putting "architectural and engineering blueprints" at Level 3 under "design" and "budget and work schedules" at Level 3 under "administration and management." It might also be necessary to expand Level 2 so that other considerations like site location and building maintenance could be included.

Another example is shown in Figure 6-3. This breakdown subdivides the project according to categories of major system assemblies, then divides the assemblies into subassemblies. Each subassembly would be assigned to a functional work group which would then do a work breakdown to elaborate the items and tasks to produce that subassembly.

The WBS should be checked by the various project participants to ensure that nothing was missed. In cases such as building a house where the work is pretty standardized, the likelihood of overlooking something is remote. However, the larger and less standardized the project, the easier it is to miss something and the more valuable

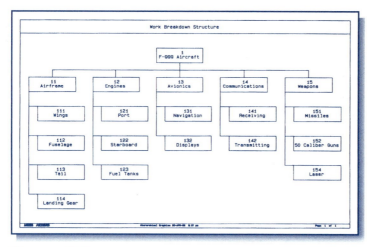

Figure 6-3
Typical WBS based upon primary hardware. [Courtesy,
Metier Management Systems.]

the WBS becomes. Nothing must be overlooked. Training, documentation, and project management activities should all be included.

Example 2: Process of Developing the WBS for the LOGON Project.

The project manager and project staff meet in a brainstorming session to create the WBS for LOGON. Initially they "rough out" the major categories of work according to the scope statement (Example 1) and identify the responsible functional areas. This is the Level 2 breakdown. The project manager then meets with managers from the functional areas identified for approval of the Level 2 breakdown. The functional managers then work with planners and supervisors in their areas to prepare a Level 3 breakdown. Supervisors then prepare a Level 4 breakdown.

The result is shown in Figure 6-4. Level 2 divides the project into the major work elements of basic design, Hardware Part A, fabrication, and so on. At Level 3, Hardware Part A is subdivided into design and drawings. These become the work packages for Hardware Part A because they are the lowest elements in that part of the structure. The resulting WBS is reviewed for final approval by the project manager, functional managers, and supervisors.

To help keep track of project activities, each category, task, and so on should be coded with a unique number. Usually the number at each level is based on the next higher level. For example in Figure 6-1, the six categories in Project "01" were numbered 01–01 through 01–06. Then, for example, in the last category, 01–06, the seven tasks were numbered 01–06–100 through 01–06–700, and so on. The coding scheme is established by managers during development of the WBS. The scheme must be accepted by everyone as being neither "too broad" nor "too detailed." The kind of numbering system varies depending on the control scheme used. It should be emphasized, however, that of paramount importance is the correct partitioning of WBS elements, not the numbering scheme. The numbering scheme shown in Figure 6-3 is another example.

As mentioned, the WBS should be product-, hardware-, or task-, but *not* functionally-oriented. This means that elements on the WBS should correspond to subsystems or components (hardware or software) of the end-item system, or to work tasks (assembly, test, delivery, etc.), but *not* to functional departments such as personnel, finance, engineering, and so forth. Generally there is little or no correspondence between divisions and levels in the WBS and the functional hierarchy of organizations.

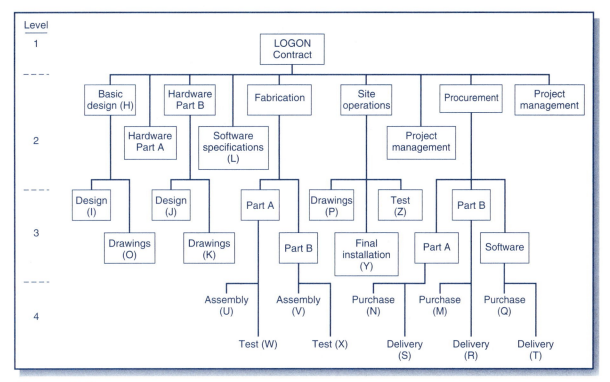

Figure 6-4
Work breakdown structure for the LOGON project. Work packages are lettered H through Z.

How far down does the breakdown structure go? As far as is needed to completely define a work task. Sometimes a Level 2 breakdown will be adequate, though usually a Level 3 or higher level breakdown will be necessary. For a task to be well-defined it must have the following properties:

1. *Clear, comprehensive statement of work:* The task is well-enough defined so the performing parties know exactly what must be done.
2. *Resource requirements:* The labor, skills, equipment, facilities, and materials for the task are identified.
3. *Time:* The time necessary to perform the task is estimated.
4. *Cost:* The costs for the required resources, management, and related expenses for the task are estimated.
5. *Responsibility:* The parties, individuals, or job titles responsible for performing the task and approving it are identified.
6. *Outcomes:* The deliverables, end-items, or results and associated requirements and specifications for the task are identified.
7. *Inputs:* The preconditions or predecessors necessary to begin the task are identified.
8. *Quality Assurance:* The entry, process, and exit conditions to which the task must conform are identified; these are specified in the quality plan (see Chapter 5).
9. *Other:* Additional information is specified as necessary.

If any of the properties listed cannot be defined, then the task is too broad and must be broken down further. In most cases, all of the properties can be eventually determined by breaking tasks down into small-enough pieces. A well-defined piece, which, by definition includes the previously listed features, constitutes a *work package.* The features are summarized in Figure 6-5.

Inputs	*Task*	*Outcomes*
Predecessors	Statement of work	Deliverables
Preconditions	Time	Results
Resources	Cost	
Requirements/	Responsibility	
specifications	Quality assurance	

Figure 6-5
Work package definition.

On the other hand, the breakdown must not continue *so* far that it unnecessarily encumbers the system. Too much breakdown will actually increase the amount of time needed to do the project. A large number of individual tasks require greater time and cost to manage than a few tasks. Each work package is the focal point of management planning and control and, as such, requires paperwork, time, and cost to monitor. Notice that different "branches" on the WBS do not necessarily have the same number of levels; this is because each branch is developed separately.

Companies that specialize in and routinely perform projects that are similar will have roughly the same Level 2 or Level 3 breakdown for every project. In such cases, they can create a work-breakdown "template," which is a standardized WBS for particular kinds of projects. The template is created from experience acquired with many projects, where areas of work common among all of them are recognized. A template simplifies the work-breakdown process and serves as a checklist for the important areas of work. Nonetheless, at some level every project becomes unique, and a WBS for a new project should never be a mere copy of the WBS nor a template for a previous project. No matter how similar projects might seem, adequate care and scrutiny should go into preparing each WBS to identify important differences. Even with a template, uniquely defining the work packages at Levels 3, 4, or greater will be necessary. To reduce oversights, two or more WBSs can be prepared independently, then combined.

WBS in the Planning and Control Process

The WBS becomes the central feature of the project planning and control process. It is used in three ways:

1. During the WBS analysis, functional managers, subcontractors, and others who will be doing the work are identified and become involved. Their approval of the WBS helps ensure accuracy and completeness of work definition, and gains their commitment to the project.
2. The WBS and work packages become the basis for budgeting and scheduling. The cost and time estimates for each work package show what is expected to complete that work package. The sum of work package budgets plus overhead and indirect expenses becomes the target cost of the entire project. These budgets and schedules are the baselines against which actual figures will later be compared to measure project performance.
3. The WBS and work packages become the basis for project control. While the project is underway, actual work completed for each work package is compared to work that was scheduled to have been completed. The result is an estimate of time and schedule variance. Similarly, a comparison of actual expenditures to date with the value of the work accomplished gives an estimate of cost vari-

ance. Schedule and cost variances for the project as a whole are determined by summarizing all schedule and cost data throughout the WBS. These procedures are described in later chapters.

Also, the WBS should be flexible to permit revisions in case of changes in project objectives or scope. Because it serves as the basis for project schedules, budgets, and control mechanisms, even small changes to the WBS can be difficult and costly to make, and cause problems in procurement, staffing, and cash flow. Whenever changes are needed, a systematic "change control" procedure for revision and communication is necessary so that all changes are authorized and communicated to affected parties. This is discussed in Chapter 11.

Work Packages

Within the WBS, work packages should represent jobs of about equal magnitude of effort and be of relatively small cost and short duration compared to the total project. Sometimes, to reduce the proliferation of work packages in large projects, several related activities or small work packages are aggregated to form work packages on the basis of cost and time. For example, DOD/NASA guidelines specify that work packages should be of 3 months' duration and not exceed $100,000 in cost. These guidelines, however, are not strict limits. The dollar size and duration of work packages depend on many factors, including the control practices of the industry, stage of the project (usually design work packages have a longer duration and fabrication work packages have a larger cost), size of the project (smaller projects have smaller work packages), and the detail and shape of the WBS.

Each work package represents either a work subcontract to be performed by outsiders or an "internal contract" for work to be performed by an inside functional unit. Although several functional or subcontracting units might share responsibility for a work package, each work package ideally is the responsibility of only one subcontractor or functional unit. This simplifies work planning and control.

Example 3: Work Package Definition for LOGON Project

The LOGON project was divided into 19 work packages (denoted letters H through Z). Following is work package X (test of robotic transporter unit), an example of a typical work package description.[5]

1. **Statement of work:** Operational test and check-out approval of four Batman robotic transporter units, Model IBR04.
2. **Resource requirements:**
   Labor (full time commitment for 3 weeks): Test manager, two test engineers, three test technicians.
   Procured materials: track for mockup; all other materials on hand.
   Facility: Iron Butterfly test room number 2 for 3 weeks.
3. **Time:** Three weeks scheduled; (time critical) start December 2; finish December 23.
4. **Costs** (Cost account RX0522):

Labor:	Manager, 120 hrs + 25% OH	= $4,500
	Engineers, 240 hrs + 25% OH	= 7,800
	Technicians, 360 hrs + 25% OH	= 10,800
Material:		$930
Subtotal		32,730
10% G&A		3,273
Total		$35,998

5. **Responsibility:**
   Oversee tests, B. J., manager of robotic assembly.
   Approve test results B. O. B., manager of Fabrication Department.
   Notify of test status and results: J. M., project engineer, F. W. N., site operations.
6. **Output:** Four (4) tested and approved Batman robotic transporters, Model IBR04. Refer to specifications (number 9).
7. **Inputs:**
   Predecessor: Assembly of Batman robotic transporter unit (work package V).
   Preconditions: Test room number 2 standard setup for robotic transporter.
8. **Quality Assurance:** Refer to entry, process, and exit conditions for work package X in the LOGON quality plan.
9. **Specifications:** Test specs, refer to test document 2307 and LOGON contract specification sheets 28, 36, and 41; robotic specs, refer to contract requirements G.9 to G.14.
10. **Work orders:** None, pending.
11. **Subcontracts and purchase orders:** No subcontracts; purchase order 8967-987 for track testing material.

Table 6-1 gives partial descriptions of time, cost, and labor requirements for all the work packages in the LOGON project.

Specific start and finish events should be identified for work packages where the output is a tangible result or physical product. Tasks directly related to the project that

Table 6-1 Activities, Time, Cost, and Labor Requirements (Result of Work Breakdown Analysis).

ACTIVITY	TIME (WEEKS)	WEEKLY DIRECT COST ($K)	TOTAL COST ($K)	WEEKLY LABOR REQUIREMENT (WORKERS)
H	10	10	100	5
I	8	8	64	4
J	6	16	96	8
K	4	4	16	2
L	2	18	36	6
M	4	21	84	3
N	4	20	80	2
O	5	10	50	5
P	5	12	60	6
Q	5	16	80	2
R	5	0	0	0
S	3	0	0	0
T	3	0	0	0
U	1	14	14	9
V	5	16	80	14
W	2	12	24	6
X	3	12	36	6
Y	8	13	104	14
Z	6	11	66	5

Total Direct Cost—$990K

have no definable end result—overhead and management are examples—should be delineated in a separate part of the WBS. Other tasks that also have no end product, such as inspection and maintenance, must also be identified as separate work packages. Cost and time figures for these activities are determined as a percentage of other work elements. More will be said about this in Chapter 9.

The concept of the work package is central to project management. All of the major functions of management—planning, organizing, motivating, directing, and controlling—are carried out with reference to individual work packages:[6]

- Projects are planned by subdividing them into work packages and then aggregating the plans of work packages.
- Projects are organized by organizing work packages. This involves assembling resources and delegating responsibility to persons who will manage work packages.
- The project effort is motivated by motivating people who are doing individual work packages.
- Projects are directed by directing activities within work packages.
- Projects are controlled by controlling work packages. This involves monitoring each work package with respect to target costs, performance requirements, and completion dates.

6.4 PROJECT ORGANIZATION STRUCTURE AND RESPONSIBILITIES

Integrating WBS and Project Organization

During its development, WBS is related to the project organization by identifying the areas of the organization that will have functional and budgetary responsibility for each work package. For example, the LOGON project is being conducted by the Iron Butterfly Company. Figure 6-6 represents the integration of the WBS for LOGON with the organizational structure for Iron Butterfly. On the left are company departments and on the top are LOGON work packages. The box at the intersection of a department with a work package, called a *cost account*, represents assignment of responsibility for that work package. Like the work package itself, each account has prespecified start and finish dates, a budget, resource requirements, and a manager or supervisor responsible for overseeing the work. In general, each box represents a "contract" with a department, subcontractor, or supplier to complete a task within work package requirements. Cost accounts are described further in Chapter 9.

Although relationships exist between all levels of the WBS and the project organization, for effective planning and control the accounts should be established at the lowest levels of the WBS—the work package level and possibly lower. Once work package responsibility has been assigned to a department, more detailed subdivisions can be made within the work package by assigning responsibility down to still lower management and technical levels.

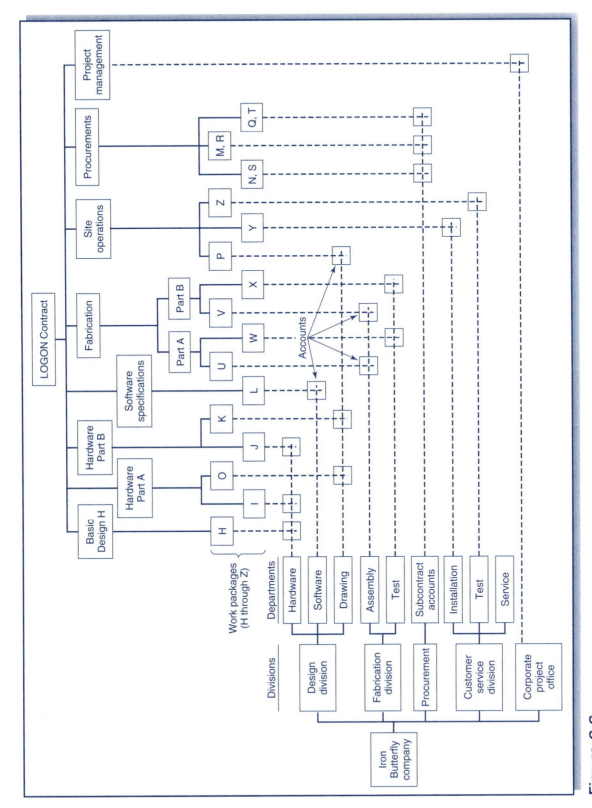

Figure 6-6
Integration of WBS and project organization.

Responsibility Matrix

The intersection of the WBS and the organizational structure is represented by a chart called a *responsibility matrix* or responsibility chart. In Figure 6-7, the responsibility matrix format is shown for one functional position and one work package. The position of project engineer has the responsibility of "approval" for the work package of "basic design." Every work package identified in the WBS should appear on the responsibility matrix.

The responsibility matrix in Figure 6-8 shows the organizational relationships among all work packages and key personnel for the LOGON project. Each row on the responsibility matrix shows all of the persons or functional positions involved in one work package and the type of involvement. Note that for each task, one and only one person is assigned primary responsibility for the tasks. Each column shows all the work tasks or work packages for which a single person or functional position is responsible.

An advantage of the matrix is that project personnel can easily see their responsibilities to work packages and to other individuals on the project. When further breakdown of assignments is necessary, those listed in the matrix can subdivide their respective tasks and make assignments to additional individuals.

The kind of responsibility defined for each organizational position/work package intersection should be determined by mutual agreement of the workers assigned and their managers and other affected parties. This ensures consensus about the nature of responsibilities and enables everyone to share what they think is expected of them and what they expect from others. To prevent confusion or conflict, the matrix can be filled in during a team building session using role analysis or similar techniques described later.

Because the responsibility matrix prescribes how units in the organization *should* perform, it is useful for monitoring and assessing how well responsibilities are being performed. It permits managers and others to know where responsibilities lie and helps avoid "passing the buck." However, it obviously expresses only formal relationships and not necessarily *how* people really interact or other aspects of informal organization. Nonetheless, it is a useful planning device and helps reduce misunderstandings and conflict later on.

Figure 6-7
Structure of a responsibility matrix.

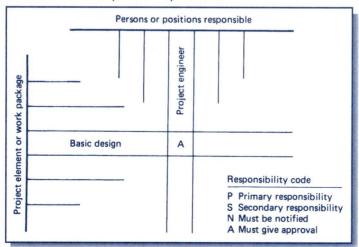

Iron Butterfly, Corp.
Elegant design. Built to last.

Responsibility Code
P Primary responsibility
S Secondary responsibility
N Must be notified
A Must give approval

Persons Responsible

Project Task or Activity	F.W.	J.M.	S.E.H.	R.L.O.	P.J.	D.V.R.	R.I.P.	O.E.M.	P.V.P.R.	D.M.N.	R.L.	L.S.F.	L.L.L.	J.R.S.	D.V.Q.	F.W.N.	J.M.M.	L.O.T.	A.U.A.	D.A.R.	B.O.B.	E.N.	G.G.F.	R.T.T.	B.V.L.	B.J.	T.T.Y.	H.R.D.	B.V.–Purchasing
	Project Manager		Project Engineer														Site Operations					Fabrication Manager							
			Design				Drawing					Software										Assembly A					Assembly B		
Project coordination	P	S	A	P	S	S														S									
Project development	A	P	A	P																N									
Project design	A	A			P	S																							
H Basic design	N		A			A						N			A					N									
I Hardware design A			A			N						N				N				N									
J Hardware design B			A			N						N								A									
K Drawings B	N		A			A	A	S	P																				
L Software specs	N											A	A	P	S	S													
M Parts purchase B	N																			A									
N Parts purchase A	N					A	A			S										A									
O Drawings A						A	A	P		S	P																		
P Installation drawings																N				A									
Q Software purchase	N														N	N				A	A	A							
U Assembly A	N															N				N	A	N	A	A		A		P	
V Assembly B	N															A				N	N			S	S		A	P	
W Test A	N															N	A	P	S	A	A					P			
X Test B	N															N		P		A	A					P			
Y Final installation	N															A	A	P	S	A	P			A	P		A	P	
Z Final test	N															A				A				S			S	P	

Figure 6-8
Sample responsibility matrix for LOGON project (with initials of persons responsible).

6.5   PROJECT MANAGEMENT SYSTEM

The system around which the managerial functions of planning, organizing, communicating, and control are structured and consolidated is called the project management system (PMS). Briefly, the structural elements and activities that jointly comprise the PMS for each project include[7]

1. A *work breakdown structure and work packages* to define all work to be done.
2. An *organization structure* to integrate people and functional areas with the WBS and assign responsibilities.
3. *Project schedules* to provide a basis for work package resource allocation and work timing.
4. *Cost accounts* to provide a basis for project cost aggregation and control.
5. *Budgets* to define expected costs for each cost account and work package.

PMS activities which utilize these structures include

6. Means for collecting and storing *project management information* and performing *evaluation.*
7. Means for *reporting information.*
8. Means for *management direction,* decisions, and corrective action.

These PMS structures and activities will be discussed in later chapters; they are mentioned in this chapter to emphasize the importance of having a thorough, accurate WBS with work packages or other work elements related to the project organization. The WBS, work packages, and project organization become the bases for establishing other structures in the PMS and the focal points around which PMS activities revolve. In Chapter 12, we will look at the project management information systems (PMIS); this is the primary means for consolidating all PMS structures (points 1–5) and accomplishing PMS activities (points 6–8).

6.6   SCHEDULING

Next to the WBS analysis, the *scheduling* of work elements is the most important step in planning because it is the basis for allocating resources, estimating costs, and tracking project performance. Schedules show the timing for work elements and denote when specific events and milestones take place.

Events and Milestones

Project plans are similar to road maps: They show not only how to get to where you want to go, but how much progress you have made along the way. Work packages are what you must do; taken together, they are the road to project goals. Along the way are signposts called *events* and *milestones* that show how far you have progressed. When the last event is passed, the project has been completed.

Events and milestones should not be confused with work packages, activities, or other kinds of tasks. A *task* is the actual work planned (or being done) and represents the *process* of doing something (such as *driving* a car to get somewhere); it consumes resources and time. In contrast, an *event* signifies only a *moment in time,* usually the instant when something is *started* or *finished* (such as beginning a trip or arriving at the destination). On some project schedules, a task is depicted as a line segment (the road) that connects two nodes representing the events of starting and completing that task. For example, in Figure 6-9, the line labeled "Task A" represents the duration or time to do the job (the actual doing of the job), and events 1 and 2 represent moments when the job is started and finished, respectively. Schedules reflect the specific calendar dates (day, month, and year) when events are planned to occur.

There are two kinds of events in project plans: Interface and milestone events.[8] An *interface event* denotes changes in responsibility or the completion of one task and simultaneous start of one or more subsequent tasks. With interface events, tasks are completed and the results, management responsibility, or both are transferred so that subsequent tasks can begin. Important management decisions and approvals, and availability of facilities and equipment necessary for a task to begin are also interface events. Event 4 in Figure 6-9 is an interface event.

A *milestone event* signifies a major occurrence such as completion of several critical or difficult tasks, a major approval, or the availability of crucial resources. Milestone events signify progress and are important measures of project performance. Final approval of a design or successful completion of tests are often designated as milestones because they signify that the project is ready to proceed to another stage of the systems development cycle. Missing a milestone usually signifies that budgets and schedules will have to be revised.

Kinds of Schedules

At least two kinds of planning schedules are commonly used: Project schedules and task schedules. Others may be used in larger projects, but these are usually more detailed versions of project schedules.

One kind of project schedule is the *project master schedule.* It is used by project managers and upper management for planning and reviewing the entire project. It shows the major project activities without too much detail. The project master schedule is developed during project initiation and is continually refined thereafter. Project managers develop the project master schedule in a top-down fashion, making bottom-up refinements as the more detailed task schedules are developed by functional managers.

Task schedules show the specific activities necessary to complete a task. They permit lower-level managers and supervisors to focus on tasks without being distracted by other areas that they have no interaction with. Task schedules are prepared by

Figure 6-9
Relationship between tasks and events.

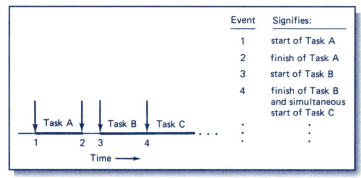

functional managers and incorporate interface and milestone events as shown on the master schedule.

Schedules take many forms including Gantt charts, milestone charts, networks, and time-based networks. All of these should be related to the WBS and account for interrelationships between individual work elements.

6.7   PLANNING AND SCHEDULING CHARTS

Gantt Charts

The simplest and most commonly used scheduling technique is the *Gantt chart* (or bar chart), named after the famous management consultant Henry L. Gantt (1861–1919). During World War I, Gantt worked with the U.S. Army on a method for visually portraying the status of the munitions program. He realized that time was a common denominator to most elements of a program plan and that progress could easily be assessed by viewing each element's status with respect to time. His approach used standardized setup and processing times and depicted the relationship between production jobs planned and completed. The Gantt chart became widely adopted in industry and today has many versions and is used in a variety of ways.[9]

The chart consists of a horizontal scale divided into time units—days, weeks, or months—and a vertical scale showing project work elements—tasks, activities, work packages, and so forth. Figure 6-10 is an example of a Gantt chart for the LOGON project using the work times given in Table 6-1. Work packages are listed on the left-hand side and work weeks are listed along the bottom. The starting and completion times of jobs are indicated by the beginning and ending of each bar.

Figure 6-10
Gantt chart for LOGON project.

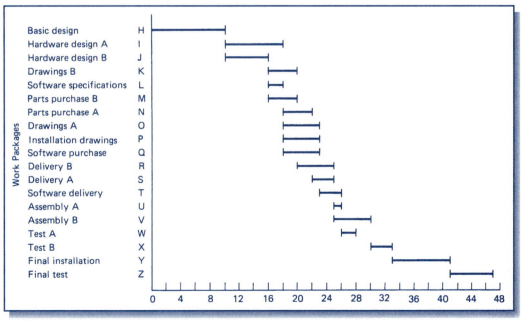

Preparation of the Gantt chart comes after a WBS analysis; the work packages or other tasks are the work elements to be scheduled. During WBS analysis, time estimates are prepared for each work element by functional managers, project planners, or others responsible for the work (as shown in the responsibility matrix). Work elements are then listed in sequence of time, taking into account which elements must be completed before others can be started.[10] Each work package or task from the WBS should appear as a scheduled activity on the Gantt chart.

As an example, consider how the first nine work elements in Figure 6-10 (elements H through P) were scheduled. In any project there is a precedence relationship between the jobs (some jobs must be completed before others can begin), and this relationship must be determined before jobs can be scheduled. These are the "predecessor" inputs mentioned earlier in the discussion of work package definition. Suppose that during the WBS analysis for LOGON it was determined that before elements I and J could be started, element H had to be completed; that before elements K, L, and M could be started, element J had to be completed; and that before elements N, O, and P could begin, element I had to be completed. That is,

THIS MUST BE COMPLETED . . .	BEFORE THESE CAN BE STARTED
H	I, J
J	K, L, M
I	N, O, P

This sequencing logic must be maintained on the Gantt chart. Thus, as shown in Figure 6-11 (using times from Table 6-1), only after week 10—after element H has been completed—can elements I and J be scheduled. After element J has been completed in week 16, elements K, L, and M can be scheduled; finally, after element I has been completed in week 18, elements N, O, and P can be scheduled. When any new work

Figure 6-11
Setting up a Gantt chart.

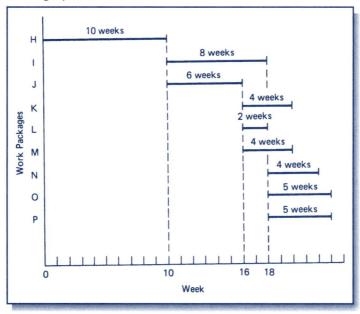

element is added to the chart, care is taken to schedule it only after its predecessor work elements have been completed.

This example uses work packages as the elements being scheduled, but in fact any level of work can be scheduled depending on the level of detail desired.

The big advantage of the Gantt chart is that it gives a clear pictorial model of the project. One reason for its wide use is because of its simplicity for the planner and the user. The Gantt chart is easy to construct and, for everyone else in the project, easy to understand.

After the project is underway the Gantt chart becomes a means for assessing the status of individual work elements and the project as a whole. Figure 6-12 shows progress as of week 20, the posted "status date." Work that has been completed is indicated by the heavy portion of the bars. The thinner part of the bars represents the amount of work unfinished, or the time still needed to complete the tasks.

This method is particularly effective for showing which elements are ahead of or behind schedule. For example, as of week 20, work package N is on schedule and work package O is ahead of schedule. Work packages K, L, M, P, and Q are all behind schedule, with L the furthest behind. This might suggest to the project manager that resources be shifted temporarily from O to L.

The amount of time the project is behind schedule sometimes is assumed to roughly correspond with the element on the schedule that has fallen the furthest behind. Corresponding to the delay in work package L, the project in Figure 6-12 is about 4 weeks behind schedule. As the next chapter will show, however, the project is not *necessarily* 4 weeks behind schedule. More information is needed to say this for certain, information not available on a simple Gantt chart.

When the Gantt chart is used like this to monitor work progress, its accuracy depends upon the reliability of the most current information. Thus, it must be updated

Figure 6-12

Gantt chart for LOGON project showing work progress as of week 20.

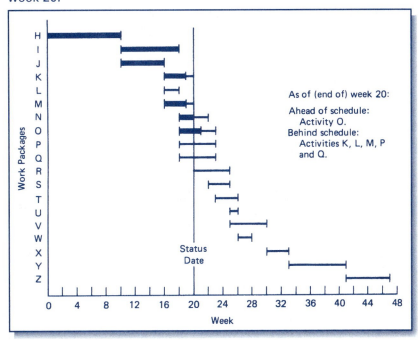

on a daily or weekly basis. Posting the chart to announce progress is one way to help keep the team motivated and the project on schedule.

Expense Charts

Gantt charts can be used for labor planning, resource allocation, and budgeting. Graphs can be constructed based upon information from the Gantt chart to show period-by-period and cumulative figures such as expenditures, labor, and resource requirements. As an example, in Table 6-2 the "activities during the week" column (column 2) was derived from the Gantt chart in Figure 6-10. Summing across activities in a given week gives the weekly labor requirements (column 3), weekly direct expense (column 4), and cumulative expense (column 5).

The information in the last two columns is shown graphically in Figure 6-13. Graphs such as this clearly reveal capital funds, labor, and other requirements and are useful for planning the allocation of resources and for monitoring work progress. Small projects such as the example can be used to reschedule activities so resource requirements are compatible with resource availability. This will be discussed in Chapter 8.

Hierarchy of Charts

As the size of the project increases, it becomes difficult to present, on one chart, sufficient information about all of the project work elements. The problem is resolved by using a *hierarchy* of charts, as shown by the three levels in Figure 6-14. The top level chart, the project master schedule, outlines the principle work packages, or aggregates of work packages, and shows the major milestones and target dates. The summary schedule in Figure 6-15 is another example.

At the intermediate level, charts expand on the detail at the top level. The activities represented are of the cost-account, work package, or subwork package size. The chart in Figure 6-10 is an example. This schedule level is of sufficient detail to permit labor and resource planning by project and functional managers. In a small project, the top-level and intermediate-level schedule is one and the same document.

A more detailed, bottom-level schedule is necessary on many projects. These are derived from intermediate-level schedules as mentioned before. They are used by work package supervisors and technical specialists to plan and control activities on a daily or weekly basis.

Figure 6-15 is a multilevel schedule. It shows both the higher-level phases of the project (denoted by "summary" bars) and the detailed tasks within each phase (denoted by "task" bars).

Disadvantages of Gantt Charts

One disadvantage of the Gantt chart is that it does not explicitly show interrelationships among work elements, meaning that it does not reveal the effect of one work element falling behind schedule on other elements. In most projects, certain work elements must be completed by a specific date to ensure that the project is completed on target; however, others can fall behind without delaying the project. Gantt charts alone provide no way of distinguishing elements that can be delayed from those that cannot.

Gantt charts are often maintained manually. This is an easy task and an advantage in small projects, but it is burdensome and a disadvantage in large projects; it causes apathy and results in charts becoming outdated. Computerized project systems eliminate this problem as long as the input data is frequently and periodically

Table 6-2 LOGON Project Weekly Labor Requirements and Expense.

Week	Activities during Week	Weekly Labor Requirements	Weekly Expense ($K)	Cumulative Expense ($K)
1	H	5	10	10
2	H	5	10	20
3	H	5	10	30
4	H	5	10	40
5	H	5	10	50
6	H	5	10	60
7	H	5	10	70
8	H	5	10	80
9	H	5	10	90
10	H	5	10	100
11	I, J	12	24	124
12	I, J	12	24	148
13	I, J	12	24	172
14	I, J	12	24	196
15	I, J	12	24	220
16	I, J	12	24	244
17	I, K, L, M	15	51	295
18	I, K, L, M	15	51	346
19	K, M, N, O, P, Q	20	83	429
20	K, M, N, O, P, Q	20	83	512
21	N, O, P, Q	15	58	570
22	N, O, P, Q	15	58	628
23	O, P, Q	13	38	666
24	—	0	0	666
25	—	0	0	666
26	U, V	23	30	696
27	V, W	20	28	724
28	V, W	20	28	752
29	V	14	16	768
30	V	14	16	784
31	X	6	12	796
32	X	6	12	808
33	X	6	12	820
34	Y	14	13	833
35	Y	14	13	846
36	Y	14	13	859
37	Y	14	13	872
38	Y	14	13	885
39	Y	14	13	898
40	Y	14	13	911
41	Y	14	13	924
42	Z	5	11	935
43	Z	5	11	946
44	Z	5	11	957
45	Z	5	11	968
46	Z	5	11	979
47	Z	5	11	990

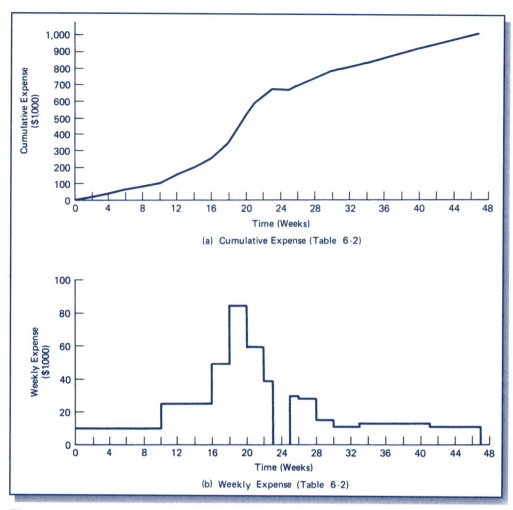

Figure 6-13
Planned weekly and cumulative expenses for the LOGON project.

revised. The computer-generated Gantt chart in Figure 6-16 is an example; notice the display of work completed by the darkened portion of the bars.

6.8 SUMMARY

The purpose of project planning is to determine the way in which project goals will be achieved—what must be done, by whom, when, and for how much. Project planning strives to minimize uncertainty, avoid cost and scheduling overruns, and uphold project performance requirements.

This chapter addresses methods for determining the what/who/when issues of projects. The project scope statement and work breakdown structure (WBS) are ways that managers and specialists answer the question "What must be done?" The scope statement outlines the main areas of work to be done and the deliverables or end-items. The result of the WBS process are work packages or other work elements each small enough to be well understood, planned, and controlled. Virtually all functions

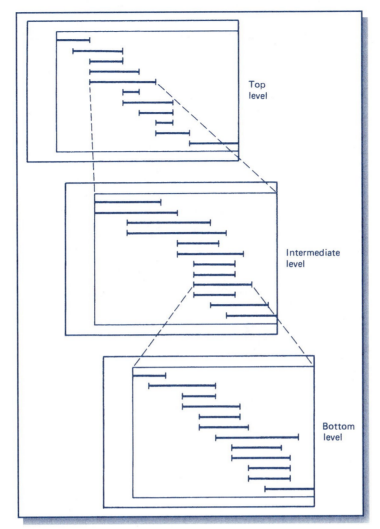

Figure 6-14
A hierarchy of bar charts.

of management and the project management system—scheduling, budgeting, resource allocation, tracking, and evaluation—are subsequently carried out with reference to the WBS and work packages.

The responsibility matrix integrates the project organization with the WBS. It prescribes which units and individuals, both internal and among subcontractors, have project responsibility and the kind of responsibility each one has. It is valuable for achieving consensus, ensuring accountability, and reducing conflict among project participants.

Project schedules show the timing of work and are the basis for resource allocation, cost estimation, and performance tracking. Depending on the amount of detail required, different types of schedules are used. Project-level schedules show clusters of tasks and work packages that comprise the project. Task-level schedules show the jobs needed to complete individual work packages or smaller work elements.

The most common means for portraying schedules is the Gantt chart. As a visual planning device it is effective for showing when work should be done and which work elements are behind or ahead of schedule.

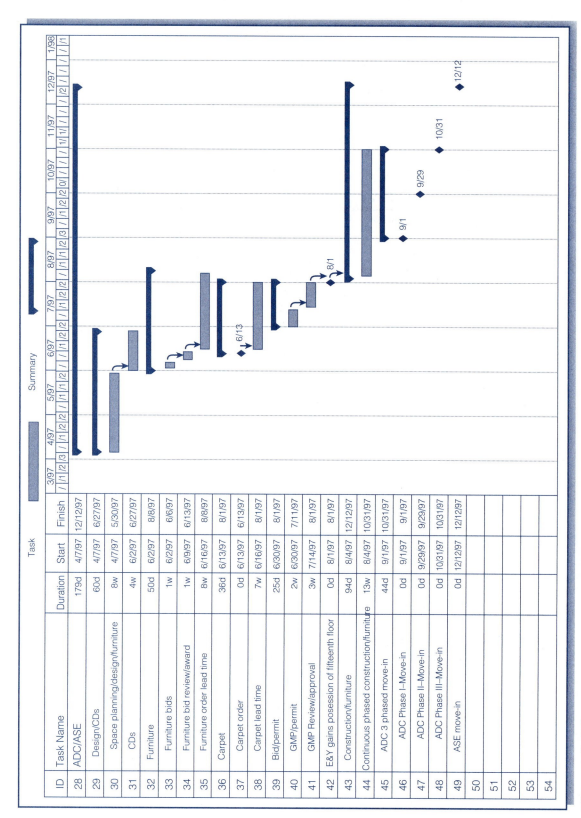

Figure 6-15
Multilevel schedule.

186

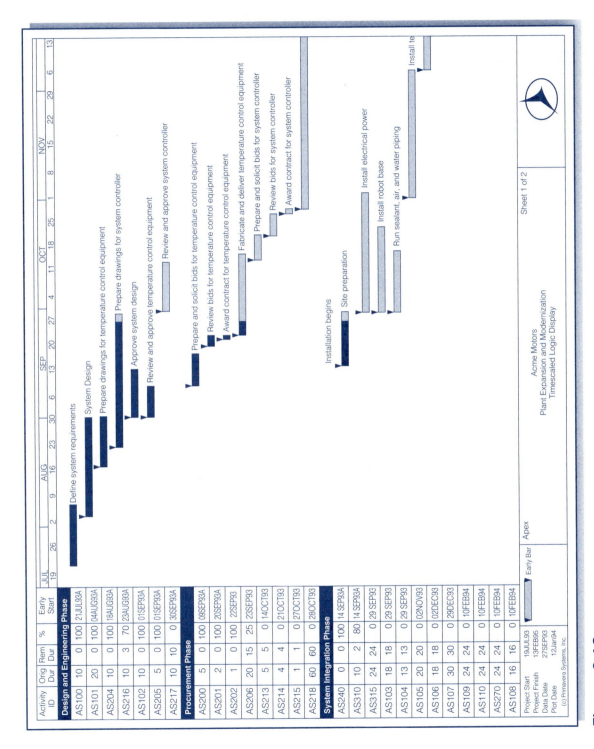

Figure 6-16
Gantt chart showing work progress.

The concepts and techniques in this chapter are foundation tools for planning and scheduling. The next few chapters look at techniques that augment these ideas and compensate for their limitations. Later we will consider the role of WBS, work packages, and project schedules in cost estimating, budgeting, and project control.

REVIEW QUESTIONS

1. What questions must be answered every time a new project is planned? What are the steps in the planning process that answer these questions?

2. What is the purpose of a project master plan? At what stage of the project should this plan be prepared?

3. Can a project be undertaken without a master plan? What are the possible consequences?

4. Which items, if any, could be eliminated from the master plan for projects with small budgets? Which could be eliminated for projects of short duration (a few weeks or months) that have relatively few tasks?

5. The subsection on "Areas of Risk and Uncertainty" is frequently left out of the project master plan. What are the potential pitfalls of doing this?

6. What is the purpose of the project scope statement? What information is used to create the scope statement? How is the scope reflected on the work breakdown structure?

7. Think of a somewhat complicated task with which you are familiar and develop a work breakdown structure for it. (Examples: a wedding, a high school reunion, a questionnaire survey, a motion picture or stage play, etc.). Now do the same for a complicated job with which you are not very familiar. At what point would you need the assistance of "functional managers" or specialists to help you break down subtasks?

8. In a WBS, how do you know when you have reached the level where no further breakdown is necessary?

9. Could the WBS in Figure 6-4 have started with different elements at Level 2 and still ended up with the same work packages? In general, can different approaches to a WBS end with similar results?

10. In what ways is the WBS important to project managers?

11. What is the role of functional managers in developing a WBS?

12. What is the impact of altering the WBS after the project has started?

13. What should a "well-defined" work package include?

14. What is the relationship between the WBS and organization structure? In this relationship, what is the meaning of an "account?"

15. Figure 6-7 shows some possible types of responsibilities that could be indicated on a responsibility matrix. What other kinds of responsibilities or duties could be indicated?

16. Using the WBS you developed in question 7, construct a responsibility matrix. In doing this, you must consider the project organization structure, the managerial/technical positions to be assigned, and their duties.

17. What function does the responsibility matrix have in project control?

18. Do you think a responsibility matrix can be threatening to managers and professionals? Why?

19. Distinguish between an event and an activity. What problems can arise if these terms are confused by people on a project?

20. Distinguish between an interface event and a milestone event. What are some examples of each? When is an interface event also a milestone event?

21. How are project level and task level schedules prepared? What is the relationship between them? Who prepares them?
22. Construct a Gantt chart similar to the LOGON project in Figure 6-10 using the following data:

Task	Start Time (wks.)	Duration (wks.)
A	0	5
B	6	3
C	7	4
D	7	9
E	8	2
F	9	8
G	12	7

When will the last task be completed?
23. How must the Gantt chart you drew in problem 22 be changed if you were told that C and D could not begin until B was completed, and that G could not begin until C was completed? What happens to the project completion time?
24. Is the Gantt chart an adequate tool for planning and controlling small projects?
25. For problem 22, suppose the weekly direct expenses are as follows:

Task	Direct Expense ($1,000/wk)
A	10
B	15
C	25
D	35
E	10
F	20
G	10

Construct charts, as in Figure 6-13, showing weekly and cumulative direct expenses. Use the start dates given in problem 22.
26. Repeat problem 25 using the assumptions given in problem 23. What is the effect on weekly and cumulative expenses?
27. In a hierarchy of charts, how does changing a chart at one level affect charts at other levels?
28. How would you decide when more than one level of charts is necessary for planning?
29. If a hierarchy of charts is used in project planning, explain if there should be a corresponding hierarchy of plans as well.

QUESTIONS ABOUT THE STUDY PROJECT

1. Describe the project master plan for your project (the plan developed at the *start* of the project). What is in the contents? Show a typical master plan.
2. Who prepared the plan?
3. At what point in the project was the plan prepared?

4. What is the relationship between the master plan and the project proposal? Was the plan derived from the proposal?
5. Is there a project scope statement? Who prepared it? Do the major areas of work and deliverables of the project correspond to the scope statement?
6. How, when, and by whom was the work breakdown structure (WBS) prepared? Describe the process used in preparing the WBS.
7. How was project management included in the WBS?
8. Was the concept of work package used? If so, describe what was included in a work package. How was the work package defined?
9. How were ongoing activities such as management, supervision, inspection, and maintenance handled? Was there a work package for each?
10. How were responsibilities in the WBS assigned to the project organization (i.e., how was it determined which functional areas would be involved in the project and which tasks they would have)?
11. How were individual people assigned to the project? Describe the process.
12. Was a responsibility matrix used? Show an example.
13. How were activities in the WBS transferred to a schedule? How were times estimated? Who prepared the schedules?
14. Show examples of project-level and task-level schedules. Who prepared each one? How were they checked and integrated?

Case 6-1   *Barrage Construction Company*

Sean Shawn was recently appointed project planner at the Barrage Construction Company, which specializes in custom-made garages. He had worked for 2 years in the company's human resources department while completing his MBA and was now in the newly created project office. Barrage is considering branching out from building not only custom-designed garages but standard two-car and three-car garages as well. Sean was asked to determine the feasibility of moving into the standard-garage market. Skimming a book on project management, he discovered the work breakdown structure concept, which he thought would be helpful for developing cost estimates for the standardized garages. Even though he had never worked on a garage construction project, he felt he knew the process well enough just from having talked to people in the company. He sat down and drew the WBS in Figure 6-17. To esti-

mate the costs for each work category in the WBS, he reviewed cost records from three recent two-car garage projects that he thought were similar to standard garages and took the average. He then apportioned these costs among the categories in the WBS. For a three-car garage, he increased the cost estimates for the two-car garage by 50 percent. When he tallied the costs for all the categories he arrived at a total of $43,000 for a two-car garage and $64,500 for a three-car garage. Compared to competitors, he discovered, these costs were more than 10 percent higher than their *prices*. However, he believed because his estimates had been based on custom garages, his cost figures were probably at least 20 percent higher than for standard garages. He thus lowered all his estimates by that percentage and concluded that Barrage would be able to price its garages competitively and still make a 10 percent profit.

QUESTION

1. What is your opinion of Sean's approach to creating a WBS and estimating project costs?

Garage			
Site	Construction	Electrical	Finish up
Excavation	Walls	Lights	Paint
Foundation	Roof	Door opener	Clean up
Floor	Windows		
	Doors		

Figure 6-17
Sean's garage project WBS.

Case 6-2 Startrek Enterprises, Inc.

Deva Patel is the project manager at Startrek Enterprises, Inc. for planning and coordinating the move of company offices into a new wing currently under construction. Deva wants the move to commence as soon as the construction supervisor indicates the building is ready for occupancy, which is estimated to be on June 1, still 2 months away. The entire move is to be completed within 1 week. The move will affect four departments and 600 people. Because timing is critical, Deva starts her planning by preparing a Gantt chart. At the project level she draws a bar 1 week (7 days) long, then subdivides it into three major categories: 1) pack office supplies, equipment, and furniture (3 days allotted); 2) move everything (2 days allotted); and 3) unpack and arrange it at new location (2 days). She then prepares an estimate of the total amount of boxes, equipment, and furniture that will have to be moved in 2 days and gives it to the moving contractor, who then gives her a price quote. For assistance in packing and unpacking boxes and equipment, Deva intends to hire workers from a temp agency. She estimates the number of workers needed to complete the move in 1 week and gives it to the agency for a price quote.

Deva gives her manager her complete plan and asks him to review it. The plan consists of the Gantt chart and a budget, which is based on the amount to be charged by the moving company and the temp agency.

QUESTIONS

1. What do you think about Deva's approach to scheduling the move and estimating the costs?
2. If you were Deva's manager, would you consider her plan comprehensive?
3. How would *you* prepare a plan for the move and what would your plan include?

ENDNOTES

1. Cited in Robert Boguslaw, *The New Utopians* (Upper Saddle River, NJ: Prentice Hall): 38.
2. Contents of master plans are listed in D. I. Cleland and W. R. King, *Systems Analysis and Project Management,* 3d ed. (New York: McGraw-Hill, 1983): 461–69; J. Allen and B. P. Lientz, *Systems in Action* (Santa Monica: Goodyear, 1978): 95; H. Kerzner, *Project Management,* 5th ed. (New York: Van Nostrand Reinhold, 1995): 570–73.
3. See, for example, Cleland and King, Systems Analysis and Project Management, 461–69.
4. Seymour Sarason in *The Creation of Settings and The Future Societies* (San Francisco: Jossey-Bass, 1972) argues the importance of knowing the beginnings, origins, and history of any new "setting" before initiating it, especially to learn about and prepare for the struggles, obstacles, and conflicts which will later be encountered.

5. See also R. D. Archibald, *Managing High-Technology Programs and Projects* (New York: John Wiley & Sons, 1976): 147.

6. Cleland and King, *Systems Analysis and Project Management*, 258.

7. F. L. Harrison, *Advanced Project Management* (Hants, England: Gower, 1981): 30–31.

8. Archibald, *Managing High-Technology Programs and Projects*, 65, 156.

9. James L. Riggs, *Production Systems: Planning, Analysis, and Control*, 4th ed. (New York: John Wiley & Sons, 1987): 549–52.

10. Quality function deployment (QFD) methodology can be used to identify the precedence relationship between jobs. QFD is discussed in Chapter 14.

Chapter 7

Network Scheduling and PDM

> *I know why there are so many people who love chopping wood.*
> *In this activity one immediately sees the results.*
>
> —*Albert Einstein*

Gantt charts indicate the general sequence of work tasks, but they do not explicitly show the relationships among tasks, nor the impact of delaying tasks or of shifting resources. Planning and scheduling methods using networks do not have this inadequacy. They clearly show interdependencies among activities and enable planning and scheduling functions to be performed separately. Alternative plans can be analyzed and, afterwards, they can be scheduled according to the availability of resources.

This chapter and the next address the topic of project network development and describe the most widely used network-based approaches to project planning—the precedence diagramming method (PDM), the program evaluation and review technique (PERT), and the critical path method (CPM).

7.1 LOGIC DIAGRAMS AND NETWORKS

The simplest kind of network, called a logic diagram, shows the major elements of a group of tasks and their logical relationship. It clearly exposes those tasks that must be completed before others can be started; this is called the "precedence."

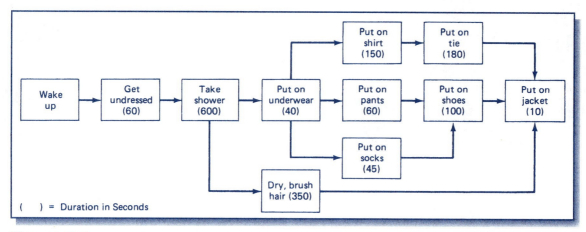

Figure 7-1
Logic diagram for getting up in the morning and getting dressed.

Figure 7-1 is a logic diagram for "getting up in the morning and getting dressed" (for a male). The boxes represent tasks (or activities) and the arrows connecting them show the order in which they should occur (e.g., put on shirt *before* tie, put on pants *and* socks *before* shoes, etc.).

The two common methods for constructing network diagrams are called *activity-on-node (AON)* and *activity-on-arrow (AOA)*. Both were developed independently during the late 1950s—AON as part of the CPM planning method, and AOA in the PERT method. Most of our discussion will center on the AOA method, but we will start with the AON method because it is slightly simpler to explain.

Activity-on-Node Diagrams

Network diagrams describe a project in terms of sequences of activities and events. An *activity* is a work task; it is something to be done. It can be a unit of work at any level of the WBS—a work package, a cluster of work packages, or an individual job smaller than a work package, depending on the desired detail. An activity is something that requires time and utilizes resources. In contrast, as described in section 6.6, an *event* represents an instant in time. It is an "announcement" that something has or will happen. Typically it signifies the start or finish of an activity. A significant event is a *milestone.*

Figure 7-2 shows how an activity is represented using the AON method. The *node* (the circle) represents an activity and its associated events; in this case the activity is "take shower" and the events are the times when the shower is started and finished.

Figure 7-1 is an AON-type diagram for a group of activities. To construct an AON project network such as this, start by drawing the first activity in the project (e.g., "wake up") as the beginning node. From this node, draw lines to the activities that happen next. As shown in Figure 7-1, activities are added one after another, in sequence or parallel, until the last activity is included.

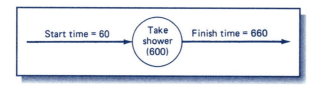

Figure 7-2
AON representation for an activity and its start and finish events.

Before activities can be included in a network, their relationships to each other must be known; in general, this involves knowing for each activity:

- What activities are its predecessors?
- What activities are its successors?
- What activities can be done at the same time as it?

Every activity, except the first one, has *predecessors*, which are activities that must be completed ahead of it. In Figure 7-1, for example, "put on shirt" is a predecessor for "put on tie." Similarly, every activity except the last has *successors*, activities that cannot begin until the current activity is completed. "Put on tie" is a successor of "put on shirt," which is a successor of "put on underwear," and so on.

However, to construct a network it is really only necessary to identify each activity's *immediate predecessors*—those activities that immediately precede it. For example, although "wake up" and "get undressed" are both predecessors for "take shower," only "get undressed" is the immediate predecessor and need be identified. Given the information in, for example, Table 7-1 (and Table 7-1 alone) it is easy to construct the network in Figure 7-1 by starting with the first activity (the one with no immediate predecessors), then linking activities one by one to their respective immediate predecessors.

Once you have constructed the network you can easily see which activities are sequential and which are parallel. Two activities that have a predecessor-successor relationship are *sequential* activities—one follows the other. For example, "take shower," "put on underwear," and "put on shirt" are sequential activities because they occur in that order, one after another. Two or more independent activities that can be performed at the same time are *parallel* activities. For instance, "put on shirt," "put on pants," "dry, brush hair," and "put on socks" are parallel because they can be done in *any* order or (though difficult in this case) *all at the same time.*

The immediate predecessors for a task should be determined during the WBS analysis. Relationships are then checked for completeness and logical consistency when the project network is constructed.

Table 7-1 Activities and Immediate Predecessors.

ACTIVITY	IMMEDIATE PREDECESSORS	DURATION (SECONDS)
Get undressed	—	60
Take shower	Get undressed	600
Put on underwear	Take shower	40
Dry, brush hair	Take shower	350
Put on shirt	Put on underwear	150
Put on pants	Put on underwear	60
Put on socks	Put on underwear	45
Put on tie	Put on shirt	180
Put on shoes	Put on pants Put on socks	100
Put on jacket	Put on tie Put on shoes Dry, brush hair	15

Table 7-2 Activities and Immediate Predecessors.

ACTIVITY	IMMEDIATE PREDECESSOR
A	—
B	A
C	A
D	B, C
E	B, C

A second example is given in Table 7-2. The network diagram for this project begins at Activity A. Because activities B and C both have A as their common immediate predecessor, both are connected directly to A. Then, because D has two immediate predecessors, B and C, it is connected to both of them; similarly, so is Activity E. The result is shown in Figure 7-3. Each node is labeled to identify the activity and its duration time. Nodes labeled "start" and "finish" are included so there is always a single place for the beginning and ending of the project. In Figure 7-3, for example, it would otherwise be difficult to determine if the project was completed with Activity D or Activity E. The "finish" node indicates that *both* D and E must be completed to finish the project.

As another example, Table 7-3 shows the predecessor relationships for the LO-GON project using work packages from the WBS shown in Chapter 6 as activities. Figure 7-4 is the corresponding network.

Activity-on-Arrow Diagrams

The other common method for diagramming networks is the *activity-on-arrow*, or *AOA* technique (for reasons to be evident, it is also sometimes called the activity on line or AOL method). The major feature that distinguishes it from AON is the way activities and events are denoted. Figure 7-5 shows the AOA representation for one activity and its events.

Notice that in the AOA method, the activity is represented as a directed line segment (called an *arrow* or *arc*) *between* two nodes (or circles). As shown in Figure 7-5, the nodes represent the start and finish events for the activity in between them. (The numbers inside the nodes have no significance here. In general, however, they are used to identify each event. The numbers do not need to be in any particular sequence, but every event must have a unique number.)

The direction of the arrow indicates the flow of time in performing the activity. Sometimes the arrowhead is not included, in which case the flow of time is interpreted

Figure 7-3
AON diagram corresponding to project in Table 7-2.

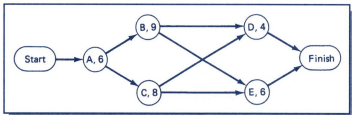

Table 7-3 Activities and Immediate Predecessors for LOGON Project.

ACTIVITY	DESCRIPTION	IMMEDIATE PREDECESSORS	DURATION (WEEKS)
H	Basic design	—	10
I	Hardware design for A	H	8
J	Hardware design for B	H	6
K	Drawings for B	J	4
L	Software specifications	J	2
M	Parts purchase for B	J	4
N	Parts purchase for A	I	4
O	Drawings for A	I	5
P	Installation drawings	I, J	5
Q	Software purchases	L	5
R	Delivery of parts for A	M	5
S	Delivery of parts for B	N	3
T	Software delivery	Q	3
U	Assembly of A	O, S	1
V	Assembly of B	K, R	5
W	Test A	U	2
X	Test B	V	3
Y	Final installation	P, W, X	8
Z	Final system test	Y, T	6

*Work packages from WBS, Figure 6-4.

Figure 7-4
Network diagram for LOGON project.

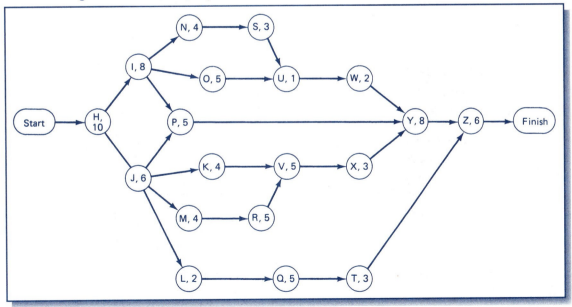

Figure 7-5
AOA representation for an activity and its start and finish events.

as moving from left to right. The *length* of the line has *no* significance (unlike in Gantt charts where it is proportional to the time required). The number over the line is the activity duration.

An activity can be defined in two ways, either by name or by the nodes at the ends. For example, the activity in Figure 7-5 can be referred to as either "Activity Y: Final installation" or as "Activity 14–15."

As in the AON method, a network for a project is developed by drawing arrows and circles in the sequence that the activities must occur. An AOA network is constructed by first drawing a node to represent the *origin* event; this represents the *start* of the first activity in the project. An arrow is drawn from this event to another node to represent the finish of the first activity. Activities to be performed next are then added in sequence or in parallel from the last node. The final or *terminal* node in the network represents the project completion. Every network should have only *one origin* event and *one terminal* event. All arrows must progress toward the right-end of the network and there can be no doubling back or loops.[1]

As with the AON method, the activities must follow the order of precedence as defined by their immediate predecessors. As an example, consider the project in Table 7-4. The diagram for the project, partly shown in Figure 7-6, begins with an arrow and two nodes for Activity A. Because activities B and C both have Activity A as their common immediate predecessor, they are both connected to the finish event of A, as shown in Figure 7-6. Event 2 represents the finish of A and, concurrently, the start of B and C.

When an activity has more than one immediate predecessor, the network must show that it cannot be started until *all* of its immediate predecessors have been completed. This is the purpose of a special kind of activity called a dummy.

Dummy Activities

A *dummy activity* is used to illustrate precedence relationships in AOA networks. It serves only as a "connector," however, and represents neither work nor time. Figure 7-7 indicates a way of diagramming the project in Table 7-4 using dummy activities as represented by the dashed lines. It shows that both B and C must precede D,

Table 7-4 Activities and Immediate Predecessors.

Activity	Immediate Predecessors	Duration (Days)
A	—	6
B	A	9
C	A	8
D	B, C	4
E	B	6
F	D, E	6

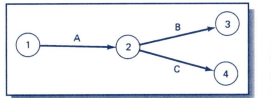

Figure 7-6
Two activities with a common immediate predecessor.

and that both D and E must precede F. Notice that the purpose of the dummy activities is to "connect" activities D and F to their respective immediate predecessors.

To help understand why dummies are necessary, just look at activities B and C: Why couldn't they both be connected directly to D without dummies? The answer is because of the rule followed by the AOA method that says that an arrow connecting any two events can represent at most *one* activity—which means that if two or more activities are performed in parallel, they must be presented by separate arrows. Thus, activities B and C must each be represented by an individual arrow in Figure 7-7 (as must activities D and E). Given that any two parallel activities must be represented by two separate arrows, it follows that the only way a *common* successor can be connected to both of them is to use something similar to a dummy activity.

Another question, then, is why can't we represent two parallel activities as two arrows between two nodes, creating something similar to Figure 7-8? The answer is that the use of several arrows between the same two nodes is confusing and leads to possibly incorrect conclusions. For example, the network in Figure 7-8 is confusing because it leaves out information. It shows Event 3 as representing two things: the ending of Activities B and C as well as the start of D and E. Unless B and C had exactly the same duration, they would be completed at two different times; because node 3 represents one event which—by definition—is *one instant in time,* the implication is that B and C are finished at the same time, which is not true.

The network in Figure 7-8 is also misleading. It implies that both B and C are immediate predecessors for *both* D and E, which according to Table 7-4 is not true. It also implies that D and E are started and completed at the same time, which again is not true.

In practice, dummy activities should be used sparingly to keep the network as simple as possible. The appropriate way to diagram the project in Figure 7-7 using the minimum necessary dummy activities is shown in Figure 7-9. Notice that no information is lost even though there is only one dummy activity. The network still clearly shows that D must be preceded by B and C, and F must be preceded by E and D.

As a second example, consider the project described earlier in Table 7-2. Several possible arrow diagrams for this project are shown in Figure 7-10. Notice in (a) that D

Figure 7-7
Network with dummy activities.

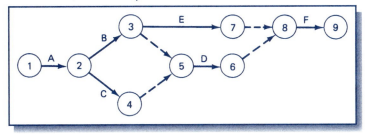

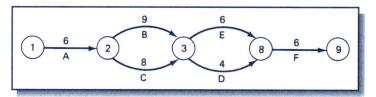

Figure 7-8
Network with no dummy activities (incorrect).

Figure 7-9
Network with minimal use of dummy activities (correct).

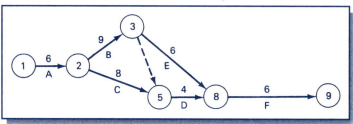

Figure 7-10
Possible and preferred network diagrams for the project in Table 7-2.

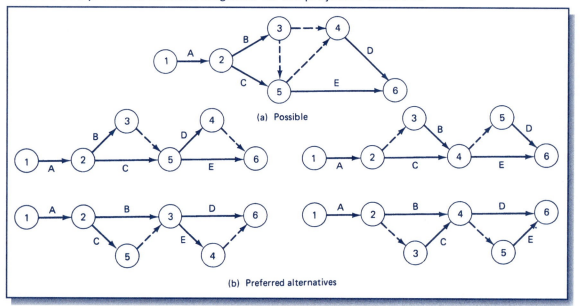

is connected to immediate predecessors B and C with two dummies, and E is connected directly to C and indirectly, with a dummy, to B. In contrast, the four diagrams in (b) all convey the same information, but with one less dummy. In large projects especially, economizing of dummy activities is important because it reduces network "clutter" and helps to improve interpretation of the network.

In constructing networks by hand, as a rule it is easiest to start by putting in dummy activities wherever they seem necessary, then removing them from places where they are not essential. The "overriding rule" is that *dummies cannot be removed whenever it results in two or more activities that run between the same two start and finish nodes.* (An example is Figure 7-8 where activities B and C have the same start and finish nodes, as do activities D and E. This violates the rule.) *As long as they do not result in that rule being violated,* the following rules suggest where to eliminate dummies:[2]

1. If a dummy is the *only* activity emanating from its initial node, it can be eliminated (e.g., dummies 4-5, 7-8, and 6-8 in Figure 7-7).
2. If a dummy is the *only* activity going to its final node, it can be eliminated.
3. If two or more activities have the same identical predecessors, then they both can emanate from a single node connected to their predecessors. (For example, in Figure 7-10a, dummies 3-4 and 5-4 can be eliminated, resulting in something similar to the two alternatives on the left in Figure 7-10b. Dummy 4-6 was added in Figure 7-10b in order not to violate the above "overriding rule.")
4. If two or more jobs have identical successors, they can be joined at their final node and connected with a dummy to their successors. [For example, in Figure 7-10a (as an *alternative* to rule 3 above), dummies 3-4 and 3-5 can be eliminated, resulting in something similar to the two alternatives on the right in Figure 7-10b. Dummy 2-3 was added in 7-10b in order not to violate the "overriding rule."]

Using these rules it is possible to create networks with relatively few dummies. Figure 7-11 shows the network plan for an exaggerated version of changing a flat tire. It indicates, for example, that "jack up car" (Activity 5-8) has immediate predecessors of "set parking brake" (2-5) and "remove tools, tire, and jack" (4-5), and that "put jack, tools, etc., into trunk" (13-14) has immediate predecessors of "tighten lug nuts" (11-12) and "jack down car" (11-13). The last activity "turn on ignition, drive away" (15-17), has immediate predecessors of "close trunk" (14-15), "release parking brake" (13-15), and "replace hub cap" (12-15). The Dummy Activity 16-17 indicates that when "turn off flashers" and "turn on ignition, drive away" are both completed, then the changing flat tire project is completed also.

As a final example, Figure 7-12 shows the AOA network for the LOGON project based on information from Table 7-3 (and corresponding to the AON network in Figure 7-4). Notice the use of dummy activities 3-4 and 5-4. Event 4 could have been connected directly to Event 3 or Event 5, thus eliminating one dummy activity, but the rule of minimal use of activities was relaxed here to clarify the presentation.

Redundant Activities

All activities in a project except the first one have predecessors. Although only the *immediate* predecessors need be known to construct a network, it is easy to accidentally specify *more* predecessors than are necessary. Table 7-5 shows a list of project activities and their predecessors. It shows Activity D as having A, B, and C as predecessors, although listing A is *redundant* because A is the predecessor of B and C. Similarly, listing

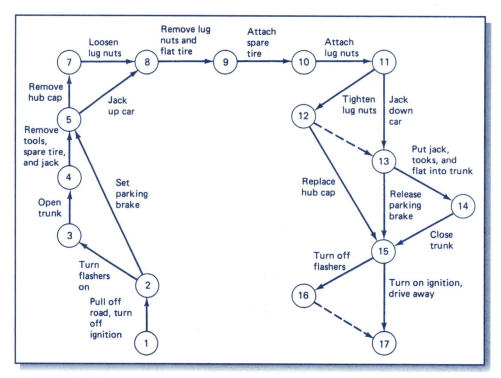

Figure 7-11
Network plan for changing a flat tire.

Figure 7-12
AOA network diagram for LOGON project.

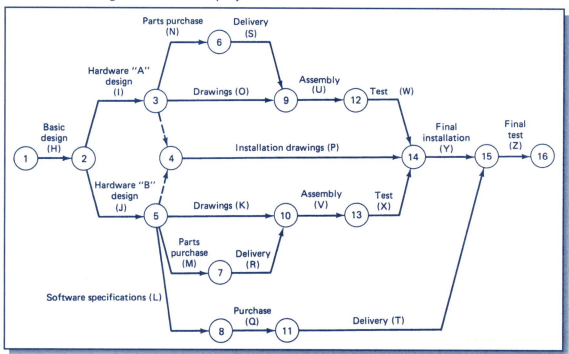

Table 7-5 Redundant and Immediate Predecessors.

ACTIVITY	PREDECESSORS	REDUNDANT PREDECESSORS	IMMEDIATE PREDECESSORS
A	—		
B	A		A
C	A		A
D	A, B, C	A	B, C
E	A, B, C, D	A, B, C	D
F	A, B, C	A	B, C

A, B, and C as predecessors for Activity E is redundant because they are all predecessors of D. As shown in the last column, only the immediate predecessors need to be listed; redundancies can be eliminated without affecting the logic of the network.

Level of Detail

The level of detail in a network must be sufficient to reveal scheduling restraints and important predecessor relationships. This is illustrated in Figure 7-13. The upper

Figure 7-13
Example of level-of-detail requirement for subdividing
Hardware B test (Activity X).

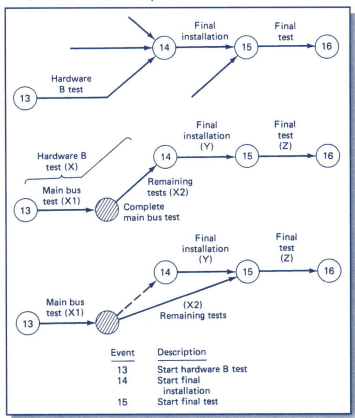

diagram is a portion of the network in Figure 7-12. In the middle diagram, Hardware B test (Activity X) has been divided into two sequential activities, "main bus test"[3] (X1) and "remaining tests" (X2). The shaded node denotes the event "complete main bus test." Should Activity X have been subdivided like this? That depends. If the situation were such that *all* subtasks in Hardware B test must be completed before "final installation" (Activity Y) is started, then there would be no need to subdivide Activity X in two. The event "complete main bus test" would not even be shown.

But suppose we wanted to advance the start of "final installation," and suppose to do so we need *only* to complete the main bus part of the test. In this case, "complete main bus test" should be identified as a separate event because "main bus test" is the immediate predecessor for "final installation." The lower diagram in Figure 7-13 would then be used because it shows "final installation" beginning *as soon as main bus test is completed.* It also shows that although the "remaining tests" (X2) are not needed to begin "final installation," they are needed to begin "final test" (Z).

Although whole work packages are often of sufficient detail to be used as activities in a network, sometimes they must be subdivided to reveal precedence relationships among subtasks within them. In the previous example, it was necessary to subdivide the work package Hardware B test because the work package (X) did not have sufficient detail nor show a precedence relationship permitting "final installation" to be started earlier.

AON versus AOA

The different ways that work activities are represented in AOA and AON results in two kinds of networks. Because AON networks are constructed without use of dummies they are simpler and easier to construct (compare Figure 7-3 with Figure 7-10). Nonetheless the AOA method is used just as often, probably because it was developed first and is better suited for PERT procedures. The PERT model, described in the next chapter, places emphasis on project *events,* and in the AOA method events are specifically designated by nodes. Also, because AOA diagrams use line segments (the arrows) to represent the flow of work and time, it is easy to construct schedules that are similar in appearance to Gantt charts but incorporate the advantages of networks. Most project software packages create AOA networks that look similar to Gantt charts. Still, the AON technique is very popular among certain industries, particularly construction. Many project planning software packages create both AOA or AON networks.

In a particular project, it is best to select one form of technique, AOA or AON, and stick with it. Most examples in this book are in the AOA format.

Event-Oriented Networks

Both AON and AOA formats produce "activity-oriented" networks—they describe projects in terms of tasks or jobs, which makes them especially useful in planning activities in projects. However, for managers who are more concerned with getting activities *completed,* "event-oriented" networks are more useful. Figure 7-14 shows part of an event-oriented network. It is similar to an AOA network except the activity names on the arrows are deleted, and the nodes are drawn large enough to contain event descriptions (in past tense). This kind of network is useful for emphasizing *completion* of activities.

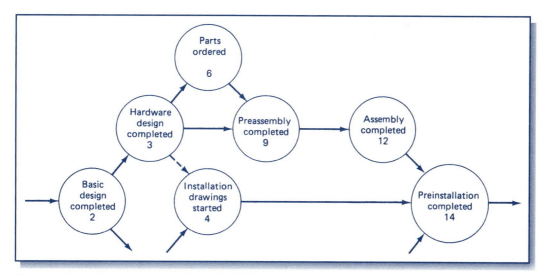

Figure 7-14
Event-oriented network.

Creating a Network

A network is developed by starting with a list of activities (for example, work packages from the WBS) and their immediate predecessors. If done by hand the process is trial and error, and the network might have to be redrawn several times before it is complete and correct. Networks of 50 to 100 activities can be constructed easily by drawing the obvious subnetworks first and then connecting them.

For small projects, computer software packages ease the task; for large projects, they are a must. In large projects, however, before entering the data into a computer, it is a good idea for the project manager to first sketch out the network by hand showing the major clusters of activities. This affords the project manager a better intuitive "feel" for the project. Whenever a computer is used, the resulting network should be reviewed for accuracy, omissions, or mistakes in data entry.

7.2 THE CRITICAL PATH

How are networks used in project planning? The major use of networks is for scheduling—determining *how long* the project will take (the *expected project duration*) and *when* each activity should be scheduled.

The expected project duration, T_e, is determined by finding the *longest path* through the network. A "path" is any route comprised of one or more arrows (activities) connected in sequence. The longest path from the origin node to the terminal node is called the *critical path;* this gives the expected project duration.

These concepts are illustrated in the following example. The firm of Kelly, Applebaum, Nuzzo, and Earl, Assoc. (KANE) is working on the Robotics Self-Budgeting (ROSEBUD) project. Table 7-6 lists the project activities and Figure 7-15 shows the network. The first phase in the project is systems design (Activity J). After that, simultaneously (a) the robotics hardware is procured, assembled, and installed

Table 7-6 Activities for the ROSEBUD project.

ACTIVITY	DESCRIPTION	IMMEDIATE PREDECESSORS	DURATION (WEEKS)
J	System design	—	6
M	Hardware purchase and delivery	J	4
V	Hardware assembly and test	M	6
Y	Hardware installation	V	8
L	Software specification	J	2
Q	Software purchase and delivery	L	8
W	System test	Y, Q	1
X	User test	W	1

(M-V-Y), and (b) the computer software is specified and procured (L-Q). The last phase of the project is system and user testing of the combined hardware and software (W-X).

The first activity J (system design) takes 6 weeks. Notice in Figure 7-15 that after J has been completed, both the "hardware activities" and "software activities" can begin. It will take $4 + 6 + 8 = 18$ weeks to do the hardware activities (Path M-V-Y), and $2 + 8 = 10$ weeks to do the software activities (Path L-Q). Because Activity J takes 6 weeks, the *hardware* will be ready for Activity W (system test) in $6 + 18 = 24$ weeks, and the *software* will be ready in $6 + 10 = 16$ weeks. However, because *both* the hardware and the software activities must be finished before Activity W (system test) can begin, the earliest Activity W can begin is in 24 weeks. Two weeks later, after both Activity W and Activity X (user test) are completed, the ROSEBUD project will be completed. Thus, the project duration is $T_e = 24 + 1 + 1 = 26$ weeks.

Notice that there are two paths from the origin node to the terminal node. The shorter path J-L-Q-W-X is 18 weeks long; the longer path J-M-V-Y-W-X is 26 weeks long. In general, *the longest path gives the duration of the project.* This is called the *critical path,* and the activities that comprise it are called *critical activities.* The path is "critical" in the sense that, should it be necessary to reduce the project completion time, the reduction would have to be made by shortening activities on the critical path. Shortening any activity on the critical path by 1 week would have the effect of reducing the project duration by 1 week.

Figure 7-15
Network for the ROSEBUD project.

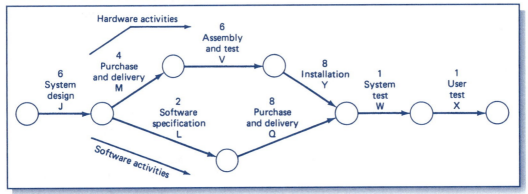

In contrast, shortening activities not on the critical path, L or Q, would have no effect on project duration. If either activity is reduced by 1 week, then the software activities will be completed in week 15 instead of week 16. However, this would not change the project duration because Activity W still has to wait for completion of hardware activities, which is not until after week 24.

The critical path is important for another reason: A delay in any activities along the critical path will result in a delay in the completion of the project. Should any critical activities be delayed by 1 week the project completion will be delayed by 1 week.

Notice, however, that noncritical activities L and Q *can* be delayed somewhat without delaying the project. In fact, together they can be delayed up to 8 weeks. This is because they will be completed in week 16, which is 8 weeks earlier than the hardware. Thus, although the software can be ready at the end of week 16, it is okay if it is not ready until the end of week 24.

As a further example, look at the network in Figure 7-16. This network has four paths leading from origin to termination:

  a. H-J-P-Y-Z
  b. H-J-K-V-X-Y-Z
  c. H-J-M-R-V-X-Y-Z
  d. H-J-L-Q-T-Z

The lengths of the four paths are, respectively: 35, 42, 47, and 32; the critical path is **c**, the longest, and T_e is 47.

Multiple Critical Paths

Can a project have more than one critical path? Why not? Suppose Activity L in Figure 7-15 had a duration length of 10 weeks instead of 2; then the project would have *two* critical paths, J-M-V-Y-W-X and J-L-Q-W-X, both 26 weeks. In that case, a delay along *either* path would *extend* the project beyond 26 weeks. Suppose, however, you wanted to *reduce* the project duration to less than 26 weeks; you would then have to shorten *both* paths. This means you could reduce the time on activities J, W, or X, or, if you reduce either M, V, or Y by a certain amount, then you must *also* reduce either L or Q by the same amount.

Figure 7-16
Example network showing the critical path.

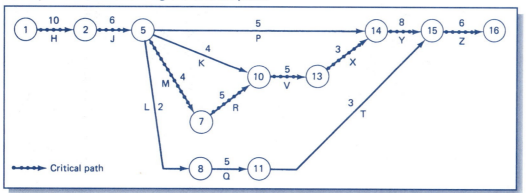

Early Times—ES and EF

Scheduling of activities starts with determining when, at the earliest, the activities can be performed. These are represented on the network by two "early times" for each activity: (1) the *early start time* (ES), and (2) the *early finish time* (EF). These are the earliest possible times that an activity can be started and completed.

The ES of an activity depends on the completion time of an activity's immediate predecessors. It is found by summing the duration of each predecessor activity along the path leading to the activity in question; when more than one path leads to that activity, ES reflects the total time along the *longest path*. This is shown in Figure 7-17. Suppose the ES for the first activity, H, is 0 (meaning that the project starts at time 0). The early finish, EF, of H must then be 10 weeks. That being the case, Activity J will have an ES of 10 weeks and an EF of 16 weeks. Similarly, ES for activities P, K, M, and L will be 16 weeks. Before Activity V can be started, all of its immediate predecessors must be completed. The length of the path going through Activity K is $16 + 4 = 20$; this is the EF for Activity K. The length of the path going through activities M and R is $16 + 4 + 5 = 25$; this is the EF for Activity R. Therefore, the ES for Activity V is 25 weeks because that is the longer of the two paths leading to it and, hence, the earliest time by which *both* of V's predecessors, K and R, will have been completed.

The same happens at Activity Y: ES = 33 weeks is computed using the longest path to Activity Y, which is through Activity X. ES = 33 represents the earliest time that both of Y's immediate predecessor activities will be completed and, hence, the earliest that Activity Y can be started. Finally, for Activity Z, ES = 41 weeks and EF = 47 weeks. Notice that 47 weeks is the same as the expected duration of the project, T_e.

In summary, ESs and EFs are computed by taking a "forward pass" through the network. When an activity has only one immediate predecessor, its ES is simply the EF of the predecessor. When an activity has several immediate predecessors, its ES is the *latest* EF of all its immediate predecessors; this is the latest time when all the immediate predecessors will be completed and, hence, the earliest time the next activity can be started.

Late Times—LS and LF

An activity that is not on the critical path can be delayed without delaying the project. However, by how much can it be delayed? To answer that, we must determine the "late times;" that is, the latest allowable times that the activity can be started and

Figure 7-17
Example network showing ESs and EFs.

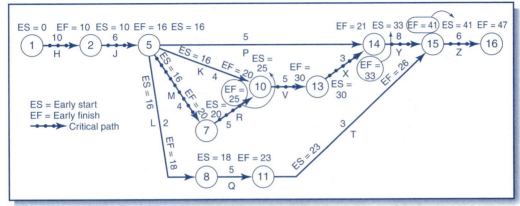

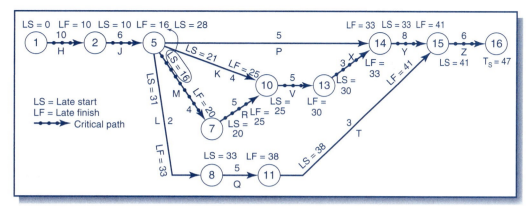

Figure 7-18
Example network showing LSs and LFs.

finished without delaying the completion of the project. As seen in ES and EF, every activity has a *late start* time, LS, and a *late finish* time, LF. Referring to Figure 7-18, we will show that the method for calculating LF and LS is simply the reverse of calculating ES and EF.

Begin by assigning a *target completion date*, T_s, to the terminal node. (Usually T_s is selected to be the same as the expected project duration, T_e; however, a larger value can be used when the project does not have to be completed by the earliest time.) In Figure 7-18, we start at Activity Z and make a "backward pass" through the network. If T_s is 47 weeks (LF at the terminal node is 47), then LS for Activity Z must be $47 - 6 = 41$ weeks. Still moving backwards, for Activity Y, the LF must be 41 weeks, and EF must be $41 - 8 = 33$ weeks. Continue to move backwards through each path, computing LF and LS for each activity.

Whenever an activity is encountered that has *multiple* paths leading back to it (i.e., it has multiple immediate successors), it is the *longest backward path* that becomes the basis for its LF. This is the same as saying that it is the backward path with the *smallest* LS that provides the basis for an activity's LF. For example, there are four paths leading backward to Activity J: for Activity P the LS is $47 - 6 - 8 - 5 = 28$; for Activity K the LS is $47 - 6 - 8 - 3 - 5 - 4 = 21$; for Activity M the LS is $47 - 6 - 8 - 3 - 5 - 5 - 4 = 16$; for Activity L the LS is $47 - 6 - 3 - 5 - 2 = 31$. Notice that the longest path back gives the smallest LS time, which is 16 weeks. Thus, the LF for Activity J is 16 weeks; this is the latest J can be finished and have enough time to complete the longest sequence of remaining activities M-R-V-X-Y-Z by the target date of 47 weeks.

In summary, calculations for LFs and LSs start at the terminal node of the project and work backward. When an activity has more than one path leading back to it, the smallest value of LS among all its immediate successors becomes the activity's LF.

Having completed both forward and backward passes through the network, we now have the earliest possible and latest allowable scheduled times for every activity in the network. The example used in Figures 7-17 and 7-18 is a portion of the LOGON network. The early and late times for the entire project are shown in Figure 7-19.

Total Slack

Referring to Figure 7-19, notice that the ES and LS for an activity are often not the same. The difference between LS and ES (or LF and EF) is referred to as the *total slack* time (or the "slack," or the "float") of an activity. It is the amount of possible variation

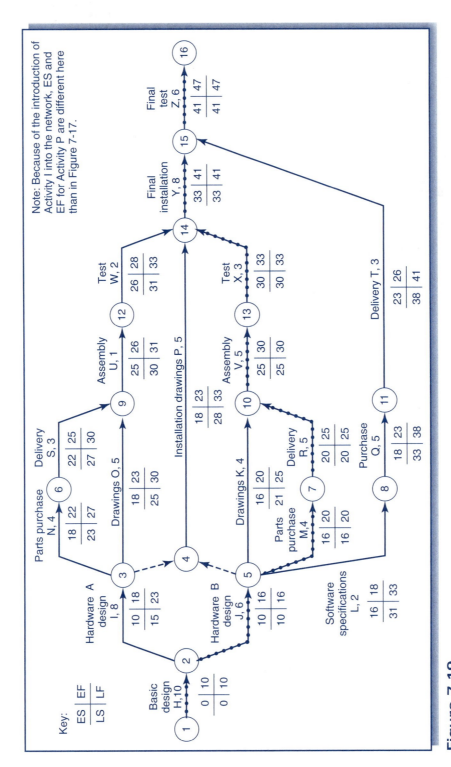

Figure 7-19
Network diagram for LOGON project.

between when an activity *must* take place at the latest and when it *can* take place at the earliest:

$$\text{Total slack} = \text{LS} - \text{ES} (= \text{LF} - \text{EF})$$

In Figure 7-19, the total slack for Activity H is $0 - 0 = 0$ weeks; for Activity I, total slack is $15 - 10 = 5$ weeks; for Activity J it is $10 - 10 = 0$, and so on. Total slack for activities on the critical path (called *critical activities*) is zero; hence, delaying any of these activities will delay the project.

Activities not on the critical path (called *noncritical activities*) can be delayed by their slack time without delaying the project completion. When activities are in sequence on a subpath, delaying earlier activities will also delay the later ones, which thus reduces the slack of remaining activities. In Figure 7-19, for example, activities L, Q, and T are all on a subpath and all have the same total slack of 15 weeks. But if Activity L, the first one in the sequence, is delayed by 5 weeks, then activities Q and T will also be delayed 5 weeks and, thus, will have only 10 weeks of remaining slack. If, in addition, Activity Q is delayed by 10 weeks, then Activity T will have no remaining slack and must be started immediately upon completion of Q.

The total slack time is the maximum allowable delay that can occur for noncritical activities. Once this slack is used up, noncritical activities become critical and any further delays will extend the project completion date.

Free Slack

The term *free slack* refers to the amount of time an activity can be delayed without affecting the start times of any successor activities. The free slack of an activity is the difference between EF for the activity and the ES of its earliest successor:

$$\text{Free slack} = \text{ES (earliest successor)} - \text{EF}$$

For example, in Figure 7-19 Activity I has total slack time of 5 weeks but free slack time of $18 - 18 = 0$ weeks (18 is both the EF of Activity I and the ES of Activity I's earliest successor, P). It has zero free slack because any delay in it will also delay the start of activities N and O (and if N, then S also). Activity O, on the other hand, has free slack of $25 - 23 = 2$ weeks (23 is its EF, 25 is the ES of its successor, U). It can be delayed 2 weeks without affecting the early start of any of its successors.

The importance of knowing free slack is that managers can quickly identify activities where slippage has consequence for other activities. When an activity has no free slack, *any* slippage also will cause at least one other activity to slip. If, for example, Activity L slips, so will Q and T, and work teams in the latter two should be notified. (Specification of who should be notified is indicated in the responsibility matrix.)

As with total slack, the computed free slack for an activity assumes the activity will begin at its ES time. Thus, the free slack for Activity O is 2 weeks only as long as Activity I, its predecessor, is completed at its EF time. If any slack is used up by Activity I, then the free slack of Activity O will be reduced by that amount.

Table 7-7 summarizes these concepts, showing ES, LS, EF, and LF, and total and free slack times for the LOGON project in Figure 7-19. Notice that everywhere on the critical path the total and free slack times are zero.

Changes in Project Target Completion Date

We assumed in discussing total slack time that the target completion date, T_s, was the same as the earliest expected completion date, T_e. In actuality the target completion date can be varied, making it either later to provide for more total slack or earlier to reflect wishes of the client.

Table 7-7 LOGON Project Time Analysis (from Figure 7-19).

ACTIVITY	DURATION (WEEKS)	START NODE ES	START NODE LS	FINISH NODE EF	FINISH NODE LF	SLACK TOTAL*	SLACK FREE**	NOTE
H	10	0	0	10	10	0	0	CP
I	8	10	15	18	23	5	0	
J	6	10	10	16	16	0	0	CP
K	4	16	21	20	25	5	5	
L	2	16	31	18	33	15	0	
M	4	16	16	20	20	0	0	CP
N	4	18	23	22	27	5	0	
O	5	18	25	23	30	7	2	
P	5	18	28	23	33	10	10	
Q	5	18	33	23	38	15	0	
R	5	20	20	25	25	0	0	CP
S	3	22	27	25	30	5	0	
T	3	23	38	26	41	15	15	
U	1	25	30	26	31	5	0	
V	5	25	25	30	30	0	0	CP
W	2	26	31	28	33	5	5	
X	3	30	30	33	33	0	0	CP
Y	8	33	33	41	41	0	0	CP
Z	6	41	41	47	47	0	0	CP
(1)	(2)	(3)	(4)	(5)	(6)	= (6)– = (3) – (2)	[(3) of earliest successor]– (3) – (2)	

*Total slack is the spare time on an activity which, if used, will affect the slack on succeeding jobs (i.e., will delay the jobs and reduce their slack).

**Free slack is the spare time on an activity which, given that previous jobs have been carried out on time, if used up will not affect the early start time of any succeeding activities (i.e., will not affect the total slack nor delay those activities).

Setting the target date *later* than the earliest completion date has the effect of *increasing* total slack for every activity by the amount $T_s - T_e$. All activities will have this amount of slack in addition to what they had when T_s and T_e were the same. Activities on the critical path will now have this additional slack instead of zero slack. Although slack on the critical path is no longer zero, it is still the *smallest* slack anywhere in the network. For example, if the target completion date T_s for the project in Figure 7-19 were increased to 50 weeks, then the total slack in Table 7-7 would be 3 weeks for all critical activities, and 3 weeks more for all noncritical activities.

If the T_s is set *earlier* than T_e, then total slack times throughout the network will be reduced by the amount $T_s - T_e$, and activities along the critical path will have *negative* slack times. Negative slack is an indication that time must be cut from a path to meet the desired target date.

All of this has no influence on free slack times because they depend on early start and finish times, both of which are affected by the same amount when changing T_s.

Using AON Diagrams

How do these concepts apply in AON diagrams? Figure 7-20 is the AON diagram for the LOGON project; it corresponds to the AOA diagram in Figure 7-19. Calculations

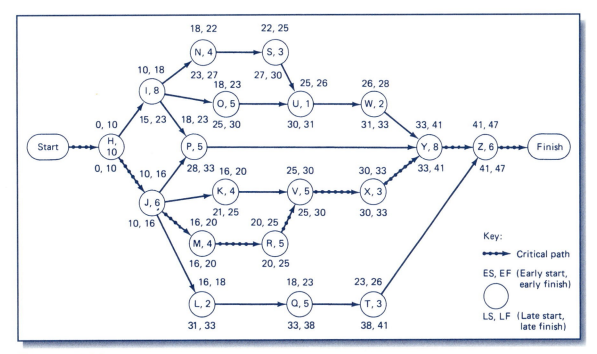

Figure 7-20
An AON diagram for LOGON project showing early and late times.

for the early and late times for both AOA and AON diagrams use the same procedures. As you can see, the resulting scheduled times for the two are identical.

7.3 CALENDAR SCHEDULING AND TIME-BASED NETWORKS

After a project network has been created and finalized the resulting schedule times should be converted into a *calendar schedule* plan—a plan that expresses the schedule in terms of actual calendar dates (day, month, year). Resource constraints such as availability of funds and personnel, and calendar restrictions such as weekends, holidays, and vacations must be taken into account. Some resources may have to be shifted because they are limited or workloads need to be leveled out; this requires shifting and rescheduling of jobs—topics that are discussed in the next chapter.

To complete the calendar schedule, the network is converted into a *time-based network*, such as shown in Figure 7-21. Another example, Figure 7-22, shows the LOGON project time-based network derived from the network in Figure 7-19. On top is a simple Gantt chart altered to show the critical path. The middle figure is the time-based version of the network in Figure 7-19 using the calendar format of the Gantt chart and early times. The bottom figure is the same time-based network using late times.

The schedule in Figure 7-22 uses weeks and assumes no work on weekends. However, it does not indicate holidays and vacations, which would extend T_e beyond 47 weeks. Figure 7-23 shows the LOGON schedule produced by Microsoft Project software and incorporating weekends and holiday time off. Notice the schedule has

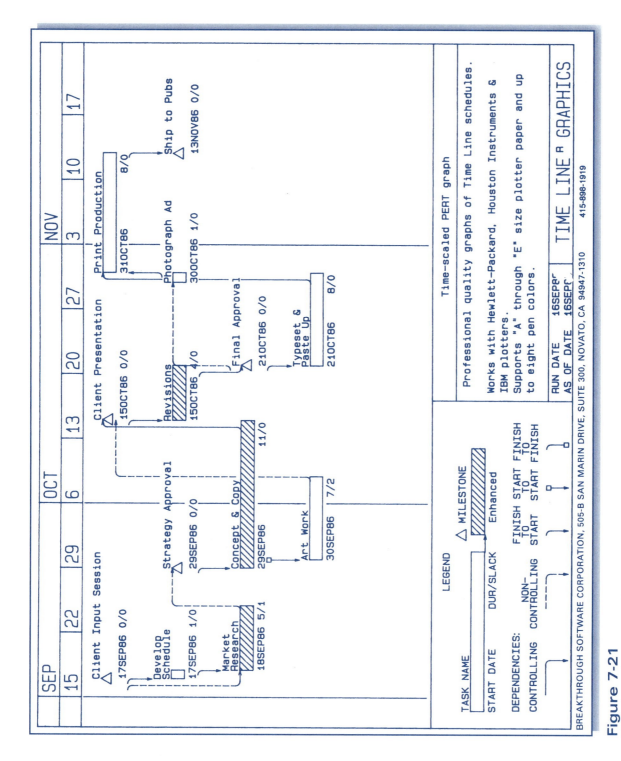

Figure 7-21
Time-based network. (Courtesy of Symantec Corp.)

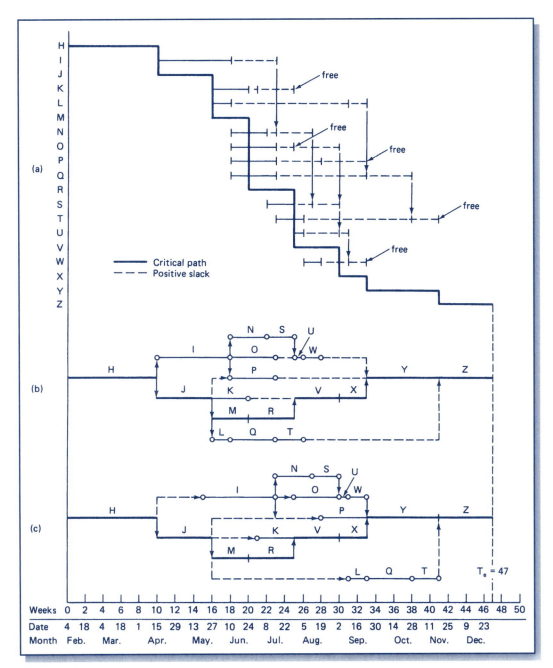

Figure 7-22
LOGON project: (a) Gantt chart, and corresponding time-based networks using
(b) early start times, and (c) late start times.

increased from 47 weeks to approximately 48 weeks. All computerized project scheduling packages use calendar scheduling and generate time-based networks.

Time-based networks have the advantages of both Gantt charts and networks because they show the calendar schedule as well as relationships among activities. As with Gantt charts, once the project is underway the network must be monitored and kept "current."

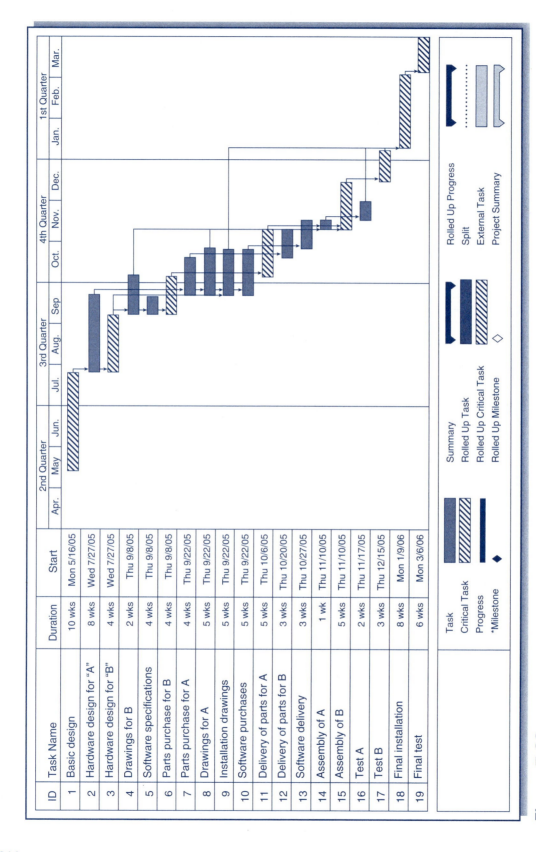

ID	Task Name	Duration	Start
1	Basic design	10 wks	Mon 5/16/05
2	Hardware design for "A"	8 wks	Wed 7/27/05
3	Hardware design for "B"	4 wks	Wed 7/27/05
4	Drawings for B	2 wks	Thu 9/8/05
5	Software specifications	4 wks	Thu 9/8/05
6	Parts purchase for B	4 wks	Thu 9/8/05
7	Parts purchase for A	4 wks	Thu 9/22/05
8	Drawings for A	5 wks	Thu 9/22/05
9	Installation drawings	5 wks	Thu 9/22/05
10	Software purchases	5 wks	Thu 9/22/05
11	Delivery of parts for A	5 wks	Thu 10/6/05
12	Delivery of parts for B	3 wks	Thu 10/20/05
13	Software delivery	3 wks	Thu 10/27/05
14	Assembly of A	1 wk	Thu 11/10/05
15	Assembly of B	5 wks	Thu 11/10/05
16	Test A	2 wks	Thu 11/17/05
17	Test B	3 wks	Thu 12/15/05
18	Final installation	8 wks	Mon 1/9/06
19	Final test	6 wks	Mon 3/6/06

Figure 7-23
LOGON project schedule adjusted for holidays and weekends.

216

7.4 MANAGEMENT SCHEDULE RESERVE

The T_e first computed from the network is usually not the duration specified as the contractual completion time. A *management schedule reserve* is established by setting the required target time T_s at some amount *greater than* the time of the final scheduled event T_e. Generally, the greater the uncertainty of the project, the larger the schedule reserve. The schedule reserve and a management budget reserve, described later, comprise a "safety buffer" that the project manager can use to overcome problems or delays that threaten project performance. Methods for determining the schedule reserve are discussed in Chapter 10.

7.5 PDM NETWORKS[4]

The network scheduling procedures discussed thus far assumed a strict sequential relationship upon which the start of an activity is predicated upon the completion of its immediate predecessors. Such is the case illustrated in the AON (actually, "activity in box") diagram in Figure 7-24. This strict start-only-when-the-predecessors-are-finished relationship is called finish-to-start (FS). The limitation of the FS network representation is that it precludes those kinds of tasks that can be started when their predecessors are only *partially* (but not fully) completed. For example, when a company is being relocated, the "employee move-in" activity can start as soon as *some* of the office furniture has been moved in. Although it might be necessary to have completed "furniture move-in" before completing "employee move-in," the point is that "employee move-in" can begin *before* its immediate predecessor "furniture move-in" has been completed. The *precedence diagramming method (PDM)* allows for this and other situations. Besides the usual FS relationship, PDM permits the relationships of start-to-start, finish-to-finish, and start-to-finish. It also allows for time lags in these relationships, such as a lag between two starts, two finishes, or a start and a finish.

These special relationships in PDM are described next using AON networks.

Start-to-Start, SS

In an SS relationship between two activities A and B, the start of B can occur *n* days, at the earliest, after the start of its immediate predecessor, A. This is diagrammed in Figure 7-25.

Using the example from Figure 7-24, suppose that an "employee move-in" can start no sooner than 5 days after the start of "furniture move-in," the network diagram and associated Gantt chart for the two activities would appear as in Figure 7-26.

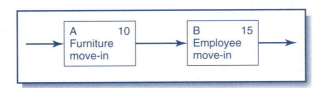

Figure 7-24
Example of FS relationship.

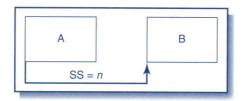

Figure 7-25
PDM representation of SS relationship.

Finish-to-Finish, FF

In an FF relationship between two activities A and B, B will finish n days, at the latest, after A finishes. An illustration is in Figure 7-27 where "paint parking lines" (B) must be finished within 5 days after "lay asphalt" (A) has been finished.

Start-to-Finish, SF

In an SF relationship, the finish of Activity B must occur n days at the latest, after the start of Activity A. For example, "phase-out old system" (B) cannot be finished until 25 days after "test new system" begins. This is shown in Figure 7-28.

Finish-to-Start, FS

In an FS relationship, the start of Activity B can occur n days, at the earliest, after the finish of Activity A. For example, "tear down scaffolding" (B) can start no sooner than 5 days after "plaster walls" is finished. This is shown in Figure 7-29. Note that when $n = 0$, the FS relationship is the same as the one used in traditional AOA and AON network scheduling, wherein the start of a successor coincides with the completion of its latest predecessor, with no lag between them.

Multiple PDM Relationships

Two PDM relationships can be used in combination. Having both SS and FF is a rather common combination. An example is illustrated in Figure 7-30. Notice in the figure that because B must be finished no later than 10 days after A is finished, the start of B must occur at day 10. Suppose B is an *interruptable* activity (i.e., the work in B does not have to be performed contiguously). In that case, B could instead be started 5 days after the start of A *and* be finished 10 days after A is finished. This is represented in Figure 7-31. The assumption is that the 15 days of work required for B will be performed sometime within the 20 days allowed for B between day 5 and day 25.

Notice that the 20 days scheduled for Activity B gives two possible slack values for that activity, LS − ES = 5 or LF − EF = 0. In PDM, usually the smallest slack value is observed, in this case 0.

Figure 7-26
Example of SS relationship.

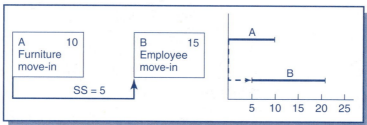

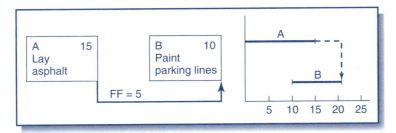

Figure 7-27
Example of FF relationship.

Figure 7-28
Example of SF relationship.

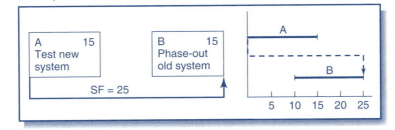

Figure 7-29
PDM representation of FS relationship.

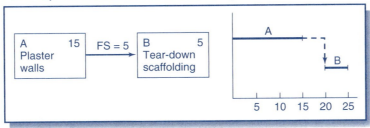

Figure 7-30
Schedule for noninterruptable Activity B.

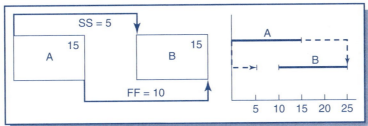

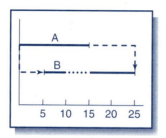

Figure 7-31
Schedule for interruptable
Activity B.

The ROSEBUD project will be used as an example.

Example: PDM in ROSEBUD Project

Figure 7-32 shows the AON diagram for the ROSEBUD project and Figure 7-33 shows the corresponding time-based network.

The network will now be altered to permit the following special relationships:

1. Activity L can begin 3 days after Activity G begins, but it cannot be finished until G is finished also.
2. Activity Y can begin 2 days after Activity V begins, but it cannot be completed until at least 6 days after V is completed.
3. Activity W can begin 5 days after Activity Y begins, but it cannot be completed until Y is completed also.
4. Activity X cannot be started until at least 1 day after Activity W is completed.

The PDM network in Figure 7-34 shows these relationships. Figure 7-35 shows the time-based network assuming earliest start dates and allowing for interruptions in activities.

Although a traditional AON or AOA network can handle relationships where FS > 0 by creating artificial activities, it has no way of incorporating SS, FF, or SF. The obvious advantage of PDM is that it permits a greater degree of flexibility. The trade-off is that PDM networks are more complex and require greater care both in their creation and interpretation. Because activities do not follow a neat start-to-finish sequence, finding the critical path and slack times is not so simple. The complex precedence relationships also cause counterintuitive results. For example, in a simple CPM network, the way to reduce the project completion time is to reduce the time of activities along the critical path; however, doing the same thing in a PDM network does not necessarily produce the same results. In the previous example, the critical path is path G-M-V-Y-W-X. Suppose we decide to reduce the time on Activity Y. Because the precedence requirement is that Y cannot be finished sooner than 6 days before V is finished, the completion date of Y cannot be changed. Thus, any shortening of the duration of Y serves to *move back* the start date of Y. Because of the precedence requirement, mov-

Figure 7-32
AON diagram for ROSEBUD project.

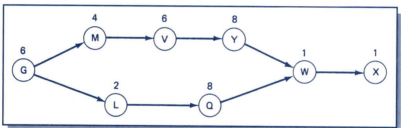

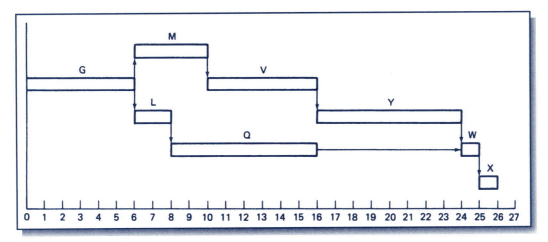

Figure 7-33
Time-based network for ROSEBUD project.

ing back the start date of Y results in moving back the start date of W and, as a result, the start date of X. In other words, shortening critical Activity Y actually causes an *increase in the project duration.*

In general, interpreting PDM networks requires more care than ordinary AON/AOA networks. However, these and other difficulties are relatively less of a burden now that PDM is included in a number of computerized project management software routines.

Criticisms of Network Methods

Network methods have been criticized since their inception because they incorporate assumptions and yield results that sometimes are unrealistic or pose problems to their users.

Network methods assume that a project can be completely defined as a sequence of identifiable, independent activities with known precedence relationships. In many projects, however, the work cannot always be anticipated, and not all activities can be clearly defined. Rather, projects "evolve" as they progress.

Figure 7-34
PDM network for ROSEBUD project.

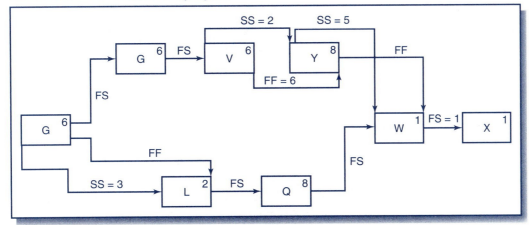

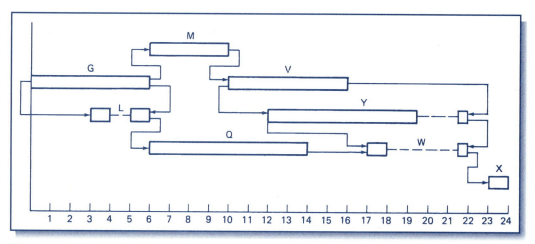

Figure 7-35
Time-based network for ROSEBUD revised for PDM.

Also, it is difficult to demarcate one activity from the next, and the point of separation is more or less arbitrary. Sometimes successors can be started before predecessors are finished, so the two "overlap" in the sequence. Although overlap of activities shortens the estimated project duration, the arbitrariness of demarcating the activities increases its variation. PDM helps overcome this problem.

Precedence relationships are not always fixed, however, and the start of one activity may be contingent upon the outcome of an earlier one which may have to be repeated. The results of a test activity, for example, may necessitate redoing analysis and design, which in a network is a "loop back" to activities that preceded the test. The GERT method discussed in the next chapter deals somewhat with these inadequacies.

Many of these criticisms are problems with *any* planning scheme, not just network methods. It can be argued, and innumerable project managers will attest, that network methods, even if not perfect, are still helpful for getting the best schedule estimates possible. To allow for contingencies of outcomes, the methods can be applied to several alternative networks to reflect various possible project outcomes.

7.6   SUMMARY

This chapter introduced network methods and PDM for scheduling project activities. The advantage of networks is that they clearly display the interconnectedness of project activities and show the scheduling impact that activities have on each other. This feature enables planners to determine critical activities and slack times, both essential variables in project planning. The PDM method allows for a variety of relationships between project activities and better reflects the realities of project work than simpler AOA or AON methods.

The next chapter describes PERT and CPM, two other well-known network scheduling methods. It also introduces the concept of scheduling under constrained resources, and an advanced project modeling and scheduling method called GERT.

Summary List of Symbols

T_e **Expected Project Duration:** the expected length of the project.

T_s **Target Project Completion Date:** the contracted or committed date for project completion.

ES   **Early Start for an Activity:** the earliest feasible time an activity can be started.

EF	**Early Finish for an Activity:** the earliest feasible time an activity can be completed.	
LS	**Late Start:** the latest allowable time an activity can be started to complete the project on target.	
LF	**Late Finish:** the latest allowable time an activity can be completed to complete the project on target.	
t	**Activity Time:** the most likely, or best guess of the time to complete an activity.	
FS = *n*	**Finish-to-Start:** an activity can start no sooner than *n* days after its immediate predecessor has finished.	
SS = *n*	**Start-to-Start:** an activity can start no sooner than *n* days after the start of its immediate predecessor.	
SF = *n*	**Start-to-Finish:** an activity can finish no later than *n* days after its immediate predecessor has started.	
FF = *n*	**Finish-to-Finish:** an activity can finish no later than *n* days after its immediate predecessor has finished.	

Summary Illustration Problem

I. AON representation:

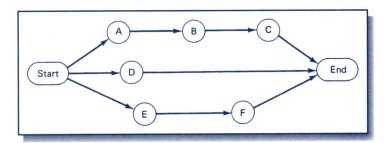

II. AOA representation, same example:

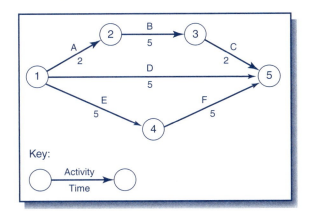

						SLACK	
ACTIVITY	TIME	ES	EF	LS	LF	TOTAL	FREE
A	2.0	0	2.0	0	3.0	1.0	0
B	5.0	2.0	7.0	3.0	8.0	1.0	0
C	2.0	7.0	9.0	8.0	10.0	1.0	1.0
D	5.0	0	5.0	5.0	10.0	5.0	5.0
E*	5.0	0	5.0	0	5.0	0	0
F*	5.0	5.0	10.0	5.0	10.0	0	0

*Activities on critical path

REVIEW QUESTIONS AND PROBLEMS

1. What are the advantages of networks over Gantt charts?
2. How is a WBS used to create a network?
3. Can a Gantt chart be created from a network? Can a network be created from a Gantt chart? Explain.
4. Why is it vital to know the critical path? Explain the different ways the critical path is used in network analysis and project planning.
5. Explain the difference between total and free slack.
6. Explain the difference between AOA and AON diagrams.
7. Explain the difference between event oriented and activity oriented diagrams.
8. Explain the difference between ES, EF, LS, and LF.
9. Consider each of the following projects:
   a. Composing and mailing a letter to an old friend.
   b. Preparing a five-course meal (you specify the course and dishes served).
   c. Planning a wedding for 500 people.
   d. Building a sundeck for your home.
   e. Planning, promoting, and conducting a rock concert.
   f. Moving to another house or apartment.
   g. Developing, promoting, manufacturing, and distributing a new packaged food item.
   h. Developing and installing a computerized information system, both hardware and software.

   Now, answer the following questions for each project:
   1. Using your experience or imagination, create a WBS.
   2. List the activities or work packages.
   3. Show the immediate predecessors for each activity.
   4. Draw the network diagram using the AOA scheme.
   5. Draw the network diagram using the AON scheme.
10. Draw the AON network diagrams for the following projects:

a.

Activity	Immediate Predecessor
A	—
B	A
C	A
D	B
E	D
F	D
G	D
H	E, F, G

b.

Activity	Immediate Predecessor
A	—
B	A
C	A
D	B
E	B
F	C
G	D
H	D
I	G
J	E, F, H, I

Activity	Immediate Predecessor
A	—
B	A
C	—
D	—
E	D
F	B, C, E

Activity	Immediate Predecessor
A	—
B	—
C	—
D	C
E	A
F	B
G	E
H	F, G, J
I	A
J	D, I

11. Redraw the networks in Problem 10 using the AOA method.
12. Redraw Figure 7-11 using the AON method.
13. Redraw the following networks, eliminating unnecessary dummy activities.

a.

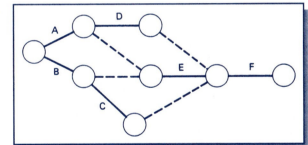

b.

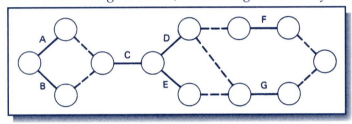

c.

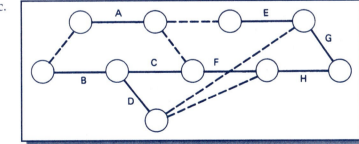

14. Eliminate redundant immediate predecessors from the following lists.

a.

Activity	Immediate Predecessor
A	—
B	—
C	—
D	B
E	C
F	A
G	B, D, C, E
H	A, B, C, D, E, F, G

b.

Activity	Immediate Predecessor
A	—
B	A
C	A
D	A, B
E	A, B
F	A, C
G	A, B, C, D, E, F
H	A, B, C, D, E, G

c.

Activity	Immediate Predecessor
A	—
B	—
C	A
D	A
E	B
F	B
G	A, C
H	A, B, D, E
I	B, F
J	C, D, E, F, G, H, I

15. For each of the following AOA networks
    Compute ES and EF for each activity.
    Compute LS and LF for each activity.
    Find the critical path.
    Determine the total slack and free slack.

a.

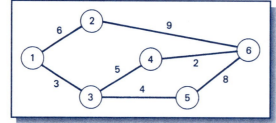

b.

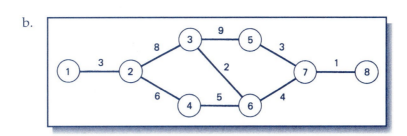

c.

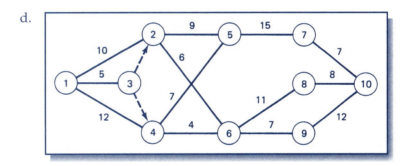

d.

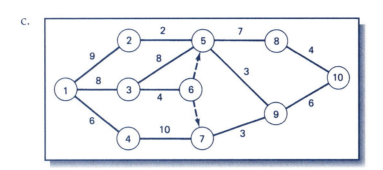

16. For each of the following AOA networks
    Compute ES and EF for each activity.
    Compute LS and LF for each activity.
    Find the critical path.
    Determine the total slack and free slack.

a.

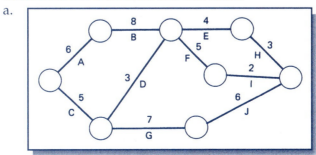

b.

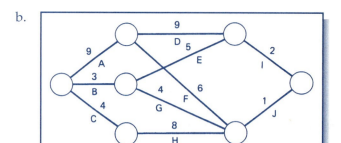

c.

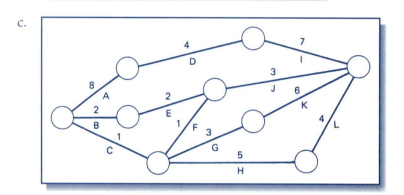

17. What limitations of AOA and AON networks does PDM overcome? What limitations does it not overcome?

18. Give examples of applications of PDM. Take a project you are familiar with (or invent one) and create a PDM network.

19. For the PDM network in Figure 7-34, calculate ES, EF, LS, and LF for all activities.

20. Suppose in Figure 7-34 everything is the same except Activity Y can start 4 days after Activity V starts, but cannot be finished until 6 days after Activity V is finished. Show how this changes the values for ES, EF, LS, and LF.

QUESTIONS ABOUT THE STUDY PROJECT

1. Were networks used for scheduling? If so, describe the networks. Show examples. What kind of computer software system was used to create and maintain them? Who was responsible for system inputs and system operations? Describe the capabilities of the software system.

2. At what point in the project were networks created? When were they updated?

3. How was the schedule reserve determined and included into the schedule?

4. Were AOA, AON, or PDM networks used? Describe the applications and show examples.

ENDNOTES

1. Loops are permitted in a special form of network analysis called GERT. This is discussed in the next chapter.

2. See J. D. Weist and F. K. Levy, *A Management Guide to PERT/CPM*, 2d ed. (Upper Saddle River, NJ: Prentice Hall, 1977): 20–22.

3. A "bus" is a connector that runs through lots of devices, each one taking something from the bus or putting something into it. An electrical circuit is a form of bus.

4. For more about PDM scheduling, see J. B. Dreger, *Project Management: Effective Scheduling* (New York: Van Nostrand Reinhold, 1992).

Chapter 8

PERT, CPM, Resource Allocation, and GERT

> *Look beneath the surface: never let a thing's intrinsic qualities or worth escape you.*

—MARCUS AURELIUS,
Meditations

*T*he planning methods described so far ignore the influence that limited resources such as capital, labor, and equipment have on project scheduling. They disregard the availability of resources and assume that whenever an activity is scheduled the requisite resources will be on hand. The fact is, necessary resources are not always available, so activities must be scheduled around when they can be obtained. Also, project cost and project duration are interdependent variables. Altering project schedules influences costs, and it is possible to alter schedules to achieve the optimum project-cost, completion date trade-off.

This chapter covers the topics of program evaluation and review technique (PERT), critical path method (CPM), and constrained resource planning—methods that enable project managers to assess the impact of time and cost uncertainty on project completion, and to weigh trade-offs between project schedules, costs, and resource utilization. First we look at PERT, which is a way of incorporating uncertainty into schedule estimates, then CPM—a similar method except that it explicitly includes cost as a scheduling consideration. We then consider activity scheduling, taking into account the utilization and allocation of limited resources. The chapter ends with a brief discussion of GERT, a method that surmounts some of the problems and limitations of PERT/CPM.

8.1 PROGRAM EVALUATION AND REVIEW TECHNIQUE (PERT)

In addition to the network methods described in Chapter 7, two other commonly used network methods for project planning and scheduling are the *program evaluation and review technique (PERT)* and the *critical path method (CPM)*. Other network techniques such as PERT/Cost, GERT, and Decision CPM are largely extensions and modifications of these original two. Both PERT and CPM are termed *critical path methods* because both use the critical path to compute expected project duration, early and late times, and slack. The two are frequently described under one term, *PERT/CPM.* Despite their similarity, PERT and CPM were developed independently in different problem environments and industries. The subject of PERT will be introduced here. CPM will be discussed in the next section.

PERT was developed for application in projects where there is uncertainty associated with the nature and duration of activities. It originated in the late 1950s during the U.S. Navy's Polaris Missile System program. In complex research and development programs such as this one, there are questions about the kind of research to be done, how long it will take, what stages of development are necessary, and how fast they can be completed—largely because of the uncertainty about the exact nature of the final outcomes. Such projects are contracted as new developments unfold and before problems in technology, materials, and processes can be identified and resolved. Thus, the duration of the project is uncertain, and there is considerable risk that the project will overrun the target completion time.

To accelerate the Polaris program a special operations research team was formed in 1958 with representatives from the Navy's Special Projects Office, the consulting firm of Booz, Allen, and Hamilton, and the prime contractor Lockheed Missile Systems. As a way of handling uncertainties in the estimating activity times, the team developed PERT.[1]

Three Time Estimates

The AOA, AON, and PDM methods compute the critical path and slack times using *best* estimates for activity duration times. PERT, however, addresses uncertainty in the duration by using three time estimates—*optimistic, most likely,* and *pessimistic.* These estimates then are used to calculate the "expected time" for an activity. The range between the estimates provides a measure of variability, which permits statistical inferences to be made about the likelihood of project events happening at particular times.

As seen in Figure 8-1 the *optimistic time, a,* is the minimum time an activity could take—the situation where everything goes well; there should be little hope of finishing earlier. A normal level of effort is assumed with no extra shifts or personnel. The *most likely* time, *m,* is the normal time to complete the job. It is the time that would occur most frequently if the activity could be repeated. Finally, the *pessimistic* time, *b,* is the maximum time an activity could take—the situation where bad luck is encountered at every step. The pessimistic time includes likely internal problems in develop-

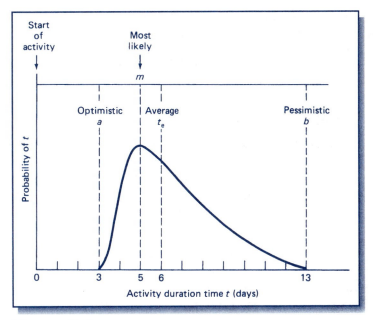

Figure 8-1
Estimating activity duration time.

ment or fabrication, but not environmental snags such as strikes, power shortages, bankruptcy, fire, or natural disasters. The three estimates are obtained from the people most knowledgeable about difficulties likely to be encountered and about the potential variability in time—expert estimators or those who will actually perform or manage the activity.

The three estimates are related in the form of a *Beta* probability distribution with parameters a and b as the end points, and m the modal, or most frequent, value (Figure 8-1). The PERT originators chose the Beta distribution because it is unimodal, has finite end points, and is not necessarily symmetrical—properties that seem desirable for a distribution of activity times.

Based on this distribution, the *mean* or *expected* time, t_e, and the *variance, V,* of each activity are computed with the three time estimates using the following formulas:

$$t_e = \frac{a + 4m + b}{6}$$

$$V = \left(\frac{b - a}{6}\right)^2$$

The expected time, t_e, represents the point on the distribution in Figure 8-1 where there is a 50-50 chance that the activity will be completed earlier or later than it. In Figure 8-1

$$t_e = \frac{3 + 4(5) + 13}{6} = 6 \text{ days}$$

The variance, V, is a measure of variability in the activity completion time:

$$V = \left(\frac{13 - 3}{6}\right)^2 = (1.67 \text{ days})^2 = 2.78$$

The larger V, the less reliable t_e, and the higher the likelihood that the activity will be completed much earlier or much later than t_e. This simply reflects that the farther apart a and b, the more dispersed the distribution and the greater the chance that the actual time will be significantly different from the expected time, t_e. In a "standard job" estimates of a and b are close to each other, V is small, and t_e is more reliable.

Probability of Finishing by a Target Completion Date

The expected time, t_e, is used in the same way as the estimated activity duration time was used in the networks in Chapter 7. Because statistically the expected time of a sequence of independent activities is the sum of their individual expected times, the expected duration of the *project*, T_e, is the sum of the expected activity times along the critical path:

$$T_e = \sum_{CP} t_e$$

where t_e are expected times of the activities on the critical path.

In PERT, the project duration is not considered a single point estimate but an estimate subject to uncertainty owing to the uncertainties of the activity times along the critical path. Because the project duration T_e is computed as the sum of average activity times along the critical path, it follows that T_e is an average time. Thus, the project duration can be thought of as a probability distribution with an average of T_e. So the probability of completing the project prior to T_e is 50 percent, and the probability of completing it later than T_e is 50 percent.

The variation in the project duration distribution is computed as the sum of the variances of the activity durations along the critical path:

$$V_P = \sum_{CP} V$$

where V are variances of activities on the critical path.

These concepts are illustrated in the network in Figure 8-2.

The distribution of project durations is approximated using the familiar bell-shaped, normal distribution.[2] Given this assumption, the probability of meeting any target project completion date T_s that does not coincide with the expected date T_e can be determined.

As examples, consider two questions about the project shown in Figure 8-2: (1) What is the probability of completing the project in 27 days?; (2) What is the *latest* likely date by which the project will be completed? Both questions can be answered by determining the number of standard deviations that separate T_s from T_e. The formula for the calculation is:

$$z = \frac{T_s - T_e}{\sqrt{V_P}}$$

To answer the first question, use $T_s = 27$ because the question asks the probability of finishing within a target completion date of 27 days. From the network, the expected project duration, T_e, is computed as 29 days. Therefore

$$z = \frac{27 - 29}{\sqrt{6}} = -0.82$$

The probability of completing the project within 27 days is equal to the area under the normal curve to the left of $z = -0.82$. Referring to Table 8-1 and interpolating, the probability is 0.207, or about 21 percent.

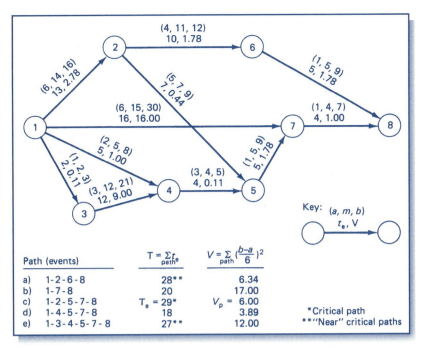

Figure 8-2
PERT network with expected activity times and activity variances.

To answer the second question, suppose we rephrase it to ask: At what date is there a 95 percent probability that the project will have been completed? Again, using the table and interpolating, a probability of 0.95 is seen to have a z value of approximately 1.645. As before, we calculate

$$1.645 = \frac{T_s - 29}{\sqrt{6}}, \text{ so } T_s = 33.03 \text{ days}$$

In other words, it is "highly likely" (95 percent probable) that the project will be completed within 33 days.

Near-Critical Paths

PERT statistical procedures have been criticized for providing overly optimistic results.[3] The criticism is well-justified. First, notice in the example in Figure 8-2 that there are two paths "near" the critical path in length. The variance of these paths is large enough that, should things go wrong, either one could easily become critical by exceeding the 29 days on the original critical path. In fact, as you may wish to verify using the statistical procedure described previously, the probability of not completing Path A and Path E within 29 days is 33 percent and 28 percent, respectively. So there is more than a slight chance that these paths could become critical. Putting too much emphasis on the critical path can lead managers to ignore other paths that are near-critical or have large variances, and which themselves could easily become critical and jeopardize the project.

Furthermore, the 50 percent probability of completing the project in 29 days, as presumed with the normal distribution, is overly optimistic. Because *all* activities in the network must be completed before the project is finished, the probability of completing the project within 29 days is the same as the probability of completing *all* five

Table 8-1 Z values for the normal distribution.

Z	PROBABILITY OF COMPLETING PROJECT BY T_s*
3.0	.999
2.8	.997
2.6	.995
2.4	.992
2.2	.986
2.0	.977
1.8	.964
1.6	.945
1.4	.919
1.2	.885
1.0	.841
.8	.788
.6	.726
.4	.655
.2	.579
0.0	.500
−.2	.421
−.4	.345
−.6	.274
−.8	.212
−1.0	.159
−1.2	.115
−1.4	.081
−1.6	.055
−1.8	.036
−2.0	.023
−2.2	.014
−2.4	.008
−2.6	.005
−2.8	.003
−3.0	.001

*Based on the area under a standard normal curve

paths within 29 days. Although the probability of completing Paths B and D within 29 days is close to 100 percent, the probabilities of completing Paths A and E within that time is 67 percent and 72 percent, respectively, and the probability of completing C, the critical path, is only 50 percent. So the chance of completing all paths within 29 days is the product of the probabilities $(1.0 \times 1.0 \times 0.67 \times 0.72 \times 0.5)$, which is less than 25 percent.[4]

Meeting the Target Date

When there is negative slack on the critical path or when the probability of completing the project by a certain target date is low, planners must consider moving the target date back and/or revising the project network to shorten critical and near-critical paths. When the original activity time estimates are considered good, they should not be shortened merely to meet the target date. Some possible actions that could shorten the project include:[5]

1. Look for activities on the critical path that could be removed from the path and put in parallel with it.
2. Add more resources, or transfer resources from activities having large slack times to critical and near-critical activities.
3. Substitute activities that are less time-consuming or delete activities that are not absolutely necessary when time is of the utmost importance.

Each project must be scrutinized to determine whether any of these are feasible.

Putting activities in parallel that normally lie in sequence can be risky, especially when failure of one would jeopardize the value or intent of the other. For example, promoting a new product at the same time it is under development risks building customer expectations despite the possibility that the development effort might fail.

Adding more resources to speed up activities or transferring resources between activities usually increases the cost. In addition to the added expense of overtime wages and additional shifts, there is the cost of making changes to plans and schedules. Also, managers tend to resist temporary buildups of resources because, besides the direct cost, they pose problems regarding what to do with the resources—labor and facilities—after work has been completed. Ideally, managers desire work schedules that maintain uniform utilization of resources, and they resist changes that result in over- or underutilization. (This is the "resource leveling" approach described later.)

The final alternative, substitution or elimination of activities, can jeopardize project performance. Elimination or substitution means making "cuts" with the potential consequence of degraded end-item performance, failure to meet requirements, or poor quality of work.

Simulating a PERT Network

Monte Carlo computer simulation is a procedure that takes into account the effects of near-critical paths becoming critical. Times for project activities are randomly selected from probability distributions and the critical path is computed from these times. The procedure is repeated thousands of times to generate a distribution of project durations. The procedure gives an average project duration and standard deviation that is more realistic than simple PERT probabilistic analysis.[6] It also gives the probabilities that other paths might become critical.

Simulation allows the use of a variety of probability distributions besides Beta, including distributions based upon historical data. These generated project durations are more likely to represent the range of time to be expected. The method also avoids some limitations of PERT assumptions, such as independence of activities and normality of the project duration distribution. A simulation procedure is described in the following example; another called GERT is described later.

Example: Simulation to Determine Project Completion Times

The following example from Evans and Olson illustrates usage of the three time estimates in a simulation to assess the likelihood of project completion time.[7] The project activities and time estimates are in Table 8-2, and the project network is in Figure 8-3.

The critical path is B-F-G-H-I-K-M-N-O-P-Q; summing t_e and V on this path gives a project duration of 147.5 days with a variance of 56.63 days.

Table 8-2 Activities and Time Estimates.

	ACTIVITY	PREDECESSORS	MINIMUM	MOST LIKELY	MAXIMUM	t_e	V
A	Select steering committee	—	15	15	15	15	0
B	Develop requirements list	—	40	45	60	46.67	11.11
C	Develop system size estimates	—	10	14	30	16	11.11
D	Determine prospective vendors	—	2	2	5	2.5	0.25
E	Form evaluation team	A	5	7	9	7	0.44
F	Issue request for proposal	B, C, D, E	4	5	8	5.33	0.44
G	Bidders' conference	F	1	1	1	1	0
H	Review submissions	G	25	30	50	32.5	17.36
I	Select vendor short list	H	3	5	10	5.5	1.36
J	Check vendor references	I	3	3	10	4.17	1.36
K	Vendor demonstrations	I	20	30	45	30.83	17.36
L	User site visit	I	3	3	5	3.33	0.11
M	Select vendor	J, K, L	3	3	3	3	0
N	Volume sensitive test	M	10	13	20	13.67	2.78
O	Negotiate contracts	M	10	14	28	15.67	9
P	Cost-benefit analysis	N, O	2	2	2	2	0
Q	Obtain board of directors' approval	P	5	5	5	5	0

Suppose the customer would prefer that the project be completed within 140 days. Using the method described before, the probability of completing the project within 140 days is found by computing

$$z = \frac{140 - 147.7}{\sqrt{56.65}} = -0.996$$

Referring to Table 8-1, the probability is about .159, or 15.9 percent. This estimate assumes that the activity times have a Beta distribution, that the project completion time has a normal distribution, and that the noncritical paths have small enough variances such that they will not become critical.

Using a simulation technique called Crystal Ball[8] to generate the completion times for 1,000 replications of the project yields the distribution in Figure 8-4.

The simulation distribution has a mean of 155 days and gives a probability of completing the project in 140 days of about 6.9 percent (the sum of the probabilities to the

Figure 8-3
Project network.

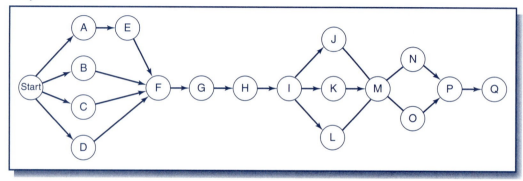

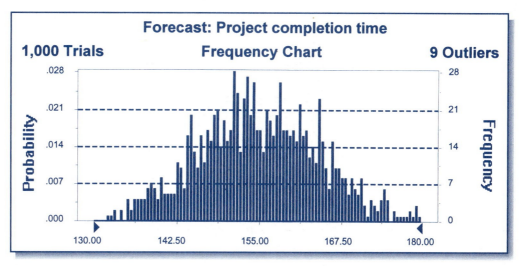

Figure 8-4
Crystal Ball simulation results for project completion times.

left of 140 on Figure 8-4). It is thus unlikely that the project will be finished in less than 140 days, and only 50 percent likely that it will be completed within 155 days.

Criticisms of PERT

The PERT method has been criticized because it is based upon assumptions that sometimes yield results that are problematic.[9]

PERT assumes that activity times can be accurately estimated and are independent. Getting three estimates instead of one adds to the work involved, and unless there is good historical data, all three are still *guesses*, which is not much of an improvement over a single "best" guess. However, time estimates are usually subjective and reflect the estimators' personal biases. This problem is compounded when the people planning the project and making the estimates are not the same as those who implement the plans—problems that are not unique to PERT. Ideally, estimates are made by persons knowledgeable about the tasks and best qualified to make estimates—usually seasoned experts or the workers themselves. With PERT, the pessimistic estimate removes the burden of having to make a single estimate that cannot account for possible setbacks.

If a "history" can be developed of similar activities from previous projects, activity time estimates can be improved. In fact, the requirement for good historical data upon which to base estimates makes PERT more appropriate for projects that are somewhat "repeatable," not for the research and first-time kinds of projects for which it was originated. For this reason the three time estimates are used primarily in construction and standardized engineering projects, but seldom elsewhere.

Contractual arrangements also influence time estimates. Fixed-price-type contracts can lead to overestimating of times; cost-plus contracts can lead to underestimating of times. However, these problems are not the fault of PERT.

The assumption of activity times' independence also has been criticized. The duration of an activity is influenced whenever resources originally planned for it are transferred to other activities that need expediting. In other words, activities are not independent because one's gain is the other's loss. This problem, a conflict of necessary resources, can be minimized if dealt with early enough in the planning and scheduling phases of the project.

Two other criticisms of PERT are that it leads to overly optimistic results and that the Beta distribution gives large errors in estimating T_e. As mentioned, looking only at the critical path to determine expected project duration can be misleading, and the influence of near-critical paths must also be considered. About the Beta distribution: other formulas have been suggested to reduce statistical error but with relatively little consequence. The reason is because in practice most of the errors in T_e come from faulty time estimates, not the Beta distribution.

PERT is the most well-known approach for incorporating time uncertainty into project scheduling. Other methods are discussed in Chapter 10.

8.2   CRITICAL PATH METHOD (CPM)

The *critical path method (CPM)* originated in 1957 through an effort initiated at the DuPont Company and expanded to include Remington Rand and Mauchy Associates.[10] CPM was developed in an industrial setting (a plant construction project for DuPont) and gives relatively more emphasis to project costs. It contrasts to PERT, which was developed in a research and development setting and gives greater emphasis to uncertainty but none to cost.

Although both CPM and PERT employ networks and use the concept of critical path, the methods have two points of divergence. (1) CPM is a "deterministic" approach: Only one time estimate is used for each activity, and there is no statistical treatment of uncertainty. Variations in activity times can be included as planned variations instead of random variations as presumed in PERT. (2) CPM includes a mathematical procedure for estimating the trade-off between project duration and project cost. CPM features analysis of reallocation of resources from one job to another to achieve the greatest reduction in project duration for the least cost.

Time-Cost Relationship

The critical path method assumes that the estimated completion time for a project can be shortened by applying additional resources—labor, equipment, capital—to particular key activities. It assumes that the time to perform any project activity is variable, depending on the amount of effort or resources applied to it.

Unless stated otherwise, any given activity is assumed to be performed at a *normal* (usual and customary) work pace. This is the "normal" point shown in Figure 8-5. Associated with this pace is the *normal time*, T_n—how long the activity will take under normal work conditions. Also associated with the normal pace is the *normal cost*, C_n, the price of doing the activity in the normal time. (Usually the normal pace is assumed to be the most efficient and thus *least costly* pace. Extending the activity beyond the normal pace will not produce any additional savings and might well increase the cost.)

To reduce the time to complete the activity, more resources are applied in the form of additional personnel and overtime. As more resources are applied, the duration is shortened, but the cost rises. When the maximum effort is applied so that the activity can be completed in the shortest possible time, the activity is said to be *crashed*. The crash condition represents not only the shortest activity duration, but the *greatest* cost as well. This is the "crash" point shown in Figure 8-5.

As illustrated in Figure 8-5, the time-cost of completing an activity under normal conditions and crash conditions theoretically defines two extreme points. The line connect-

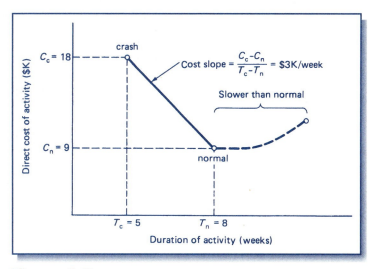

Figure 8-5
Time-cost relationship for an activity.

ing these points, called the *cost slope,* represents the time-cost relationship, or marginal trade-off of cost-to-time for the activity. Every activity has its own unique time-cost relationship. The relationship can be linear, curvilinear (concave or convex), or a step function. Because the shape of the actual time-cost relationship is often not known, a simple linear relationship is assumed.[11] Given this assumption, the formula for the cost slope is

$$\text{cost slope} = \frac{C_c - C_n}{T_c - T_n}$$

where C_c and C_n are the crash and normal costs, respectively, and T_c and T_n are the crash and normal times for the same activity. The cost slope shows by how much the cost of the job would change if activities were sped up or slowed down. In general, the steepness of the cost slope increases as an activity is accelerated.

Using the formula, the cost slope for the activity in Figure 8-5 is $3K per week. Thus, for *each week* the activity duration is reduced (sped up) from the normal time of 8 weeks, the additional cost will be $3K. Completing the activity 1 week earlier (in 7 weeks) would increase the cost of the activity from the normal cost of $9K to the "sped up" cost of $9K + $3K = $12K; completing it another week earlier (in 6 weeks) would increase the cost to $12K + $3K = $15K; completing it yet another week earlier (in 5 weeks) would increase the cost to $18K. According to Figure 8-5, this last step puts the activity at the crash point, the shortest possible completion time for the activity.

Reducing Project Duration

The cost-slope concept can be used to determine the most efficient way of shortening a project. Figure 8-6 illustrates this with a simple example. Start with the preliminary project schedule by assuming a normal pace for all activities: therefore, the project in the figure can be completed in 22 weeks at an expense of $55K. Suppose we want to shorten the project duration. Recall from Chapter 7 that the project duration is the length of the critical path. Because the critical path A-D-G is the longest path (22 weeks), the way to shorten the project is to simply shorten any critical activities— A, D, or G. Reducing an activity increases its cost, but because the reduction can be made *anywhere* on the critical path, the cost increase is minimized by selecting the

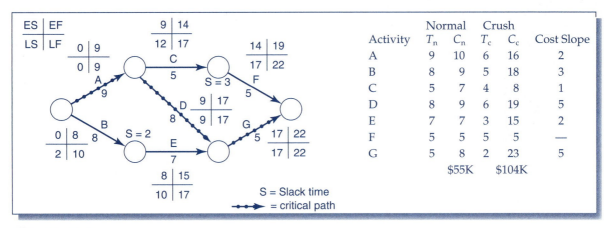

Figure 8-6
Time-cost tradeoff for example network.

activity with the smallest cost slope. Thus, Activity A would be selected because it has the smallest cost slope. Reducing A by 1 week shortens the project duration to 21 weeks and adds $2K (the cost slope of A) to the project cost, bringing the project cost up to $55K + $2K = $57K. This step does not change the critical path so, if need be, an additional week can be cut from A to give a project duration of 20 weeks for a cost of $57K + $2K = $59K.

With this second step the nature of the problem changes. As the top network in Figure 8-7 shows, all of the slack on Path B-E has been used up, so the network now has two critical paths: A-D-G and B-E-G. Any further reduction in project duration must be made by shortening *both* paths because shortening just one would leave the other at 20 weeks. The least costly way to reduce the project to 19 weeks is to reduce both A and E by 1 week, as shown in the bottom network in Figure 8-7. The additional cost is $2K for A and $2K for E, so the resulting project cost would increase to $59K + $2K + $2K = $63K. This last step reduces A to 6 weeks, its crash time, so no further reductions can be made to A.

If a further reduction in project time is desired, the least costly way to shorten both paths is to reduce G. In fact, because the slack time on the noncritical path C-F is 3 weeks, and because the crash time for G is 2 weeks (which means, if desired, 3 weeks *can* be taken out of G), the project can be reduced to 16 weeks by shortening G by 3 weeks. This adds $5K per week, or 3 × $5K = $15K to the project cost. With this last step, all slack is used up on Path C-F, and all paths through the network (A-C-F, A-D-G, and B-E-G) become critical.

Any further reductions desired in the project must shorten *all three critical paths* (A-C-F, A-D-G, and B-E-G). As you may wish to verify, the most economical way to reduce the project to 15 weeks is to cut 1 week each from E, D, and C, bringing the project cost up to $86K. This step reduces the time of C to its crash time, which precludes shortening the project completion time any further. The sequence of steps is summarized in Table 8-3.

Shortest Project Duration

The time-cost procedure as discussed thus far determines, step-by-step, which activities to speed up so as to reduce the project completion time. This stepwise reduction of the project duration eventually leads to the shortest possible project duration and

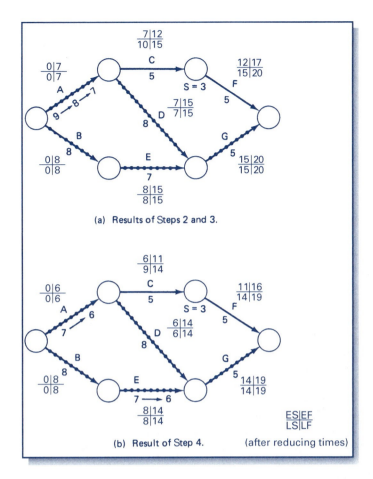

(a) Results of Steps 2 and 3.

(b) Result of Step 4.   (after reducing times)

$$\frac{ES|EF}{LS|LF}$$

Figure 8-7
Reducing project completion time.

its associated cost. However, if we want to directly find the *shortest possible project duration* and avoid the intermediate steps, a simpler procedure is to simultaneously crash *all* activities at once. This, as Figure 8-8 shows, also yields the project duration of 15 weeks. However, the expense of crashing all activities, $104K (table in Figure 8-6) is an artificially high amount because, as will be shown, it is *not* necessary to crash every activity to finish the project in the shortest time.

Table 8-3   Duration Reduction and Associated Cost Increase.

Step	Duration (T_e, wks)	Activities on CP with Least Cost Slope	Cost of Project (K$)
1*	22		$55
2	21	A ($2)	$55 + $2 = $57
3	20	A ($2)	$57 + $2 = $59
4	19	A ($2), E ($2)	$59 + $2 + $2 = $63
5, 6, 7	18, 17, 16	G ($5)	$63 + $5 + $5 + $5 = $78
8	15	E ($2), D ($5), C ($1)	$78 + $2 + $5 + $1 = $86

*Time-cost using normal conditions

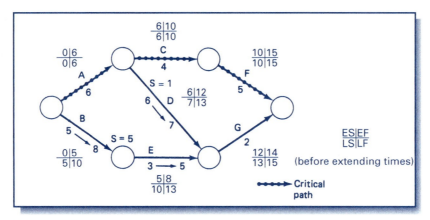

Figure 8-8
Example network using crash times.

The project completion time of 15 weeks is the time along the critical path. Because the critical path is the longest path, other (noncritical) paths are of shorter duration and, consequently, have no influence on project duration. So it is possible to "stretch" or increase any noncritical activity by a certain amount without extending the project. In fact, the noncritical activities can be stretched until all the slack in the network is used up.

Just as reducing an activity's time from the normal time increases its cost, so stretching time from the crash time *reduces* its cost. As a result, the project crash cost of $104K can be reduced by stretching noncritical jobs. To do so, start with those noncritical activities that will yield the greatest savings—those with the greatest cost slope. Notice in Figure 8-8 that because Path B-E-G has a slack time of 5 weeks, activities along this path can be stretched by up to 5 weeks without extending the project. Three weeks can be added to Activity B (bringing it to the normal time of 8 weeks) without lengthening the project. Also, 2 weeks can be added to E and 1 week to D, both without changing the project duration. The final project cost is computed by subtracting the savings obtained by stretching B 3 weeks, E by 2 weeks, and D by 1 week from the initial crash cost.

$$\$104K - 3(\$3K) - 2(\$2K) - 1(\$5K) = \$86K$$

In general, start with all activities crashed, then stretch the noncritical activities with the greatest cost slope to use up available slack and obtain the greatest cost savings. An activity can be stretched up to its normal time, which is assumed to be its least-costly time (Figure 8-5).

Total Project Cost

The previous analysis dealt only with direct costs—costs immediately associated with individual activities and that increase directly as activities are expedited. But the cost of conducting a project includes more than direct activity costs; it also includes *indirect* costs such as administrative and overhead charges. (The distinction between direct and indirect cost is elaborated upon in the next chapter.) Usually indirect costs are a function of, and increase proportionately to, the duration of the project. In other words, indirect costs, in contrast to direct costs, *decrease as the project duration decreases.*

The mathematical function for indirect cost can be derived by estimation or by a formula as established in an incentive type contract. As an illustration, suppose indirect costs in the previous example are approximated by the formula

$$\text{Indirect cost} = \$10K + \$3K(T_e)$$

where T_e is the expected project duration in weeks. This is represented by the indirect cost line in Figure 8-9. Also shown is the *total project cost,* which is computed by summing indirect and direct costs. Notice from the figure that by combining indirect costs and direct costs it is possible to determine the project duration that gives the lowest total project cost. Figure 8-9 shows that from a cost standpoint, 20 weeks is the "optimum" project duration.

In addition to direct and indirect costs, another cost that influences total project cost (and hence the optimum T_e) is any *contractual incentive* such as a *penalty charge* or a *bonus payment.*[12] A penalty charge is a late fee imposed on the contractor for not completing a facility or product on time. A bonus payment is a reward—a cash inducement—for completing the project early. The specific terms of penalties and bonuses are specified in incentive type contracts such as described in Appendix B.

Suppose, in the previous example, the contract agreement is to complete the project by Week 18. The contract provides for a bonus of $2K per week for finishing before 18 weeks, and a $1K per week penalty for finishing after 18 weeks. Figure 8-10 shows these incentives and their influence on total project cost. Notice that even with incentives, the optimum completion time (for the contractor) is at 19 or 20 weeks, not the contractual 18 weeks. This example reveals that a formal incentive agreement alone is not necessarily enough to influence performance. For the incentive to motivate the

Figure 8-9
Total time-cost tradeoff for the project.

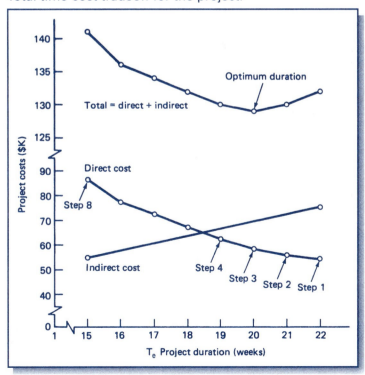

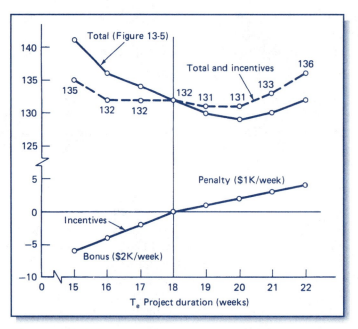

Figure 8-10
Time-cost tradeoff for the project with incentives.

contractor it must have "teeth;" in other words, it should be of sufficient magnitude with respect to other project costs to affect contractor performance. Had the penalty been raised to an amount over $2K (instead of $1K) per week for finishing after 18 weeks, the contractor's optimum completion time would have shifted to 18 weeks.

8.3   SCHEDULING WITH RESOURCE CONSTRAINTS

Until now the discussion of work scheduling has assumed implicitly that any resources needed to do the work would always be available. The only scheduling restriction was that predecessor activities must be completed first. A different, additional restriction will now be considered: Constrained resources. A resource refers to working capital or a particular kind of labor, equipment, or material needed to perform activities in the project. Although many resources are available in sufficient quantity so as not to pose scheduling problems (such as air, unless the project is being conducted under water or in outer space where air is limited), all resources are finite and many are scarce. In many cases, limited availability of skilled workers, machinery, equipment, and working capital dictate that activities must be scheduled at times other than the early, or even late, start date. This is especially true when multiple activities requiring the same resources are scheduled for the same time. When resources are not adequate to satisfy the requirements of them all, some will have to be rescheduled.

The same problem occurs in multiproject organizations such as the matrix which depends upon resources from a common pool. To schedule activities for any one project, managers must take into account resource requirements of other concurrent projects. The result is that project schedules are largely determined by when resources will be freed from other higher priority projects.

In the following sections, two resource-related problems will be considered. The first concerns scheduling of activities so that utilization of a given resource is somewhat balanced throughout the project. The objective is to reduce the extreme highs and lows of resource requirements typical in project life cycles. The second concerns the scheduling of activities so that strict constraints placed on the availability of a resource are not violated.

Resource Loading and Leveling

Resource loading refers to the amount of a resource necessary to conduct a project. Because this amount depends on the requirements of the individual activities, the resource loading will change throughout a project as different activities are started and completed. This results in variable loading for a certain resource over time. The usual resource loading pattern in a project is a steady buildup, then a peak, then a gradual decline. Most projects require relatively few resources during the early and late stages compared to the many resources needed in the middle. This is problematic for functional managers who have to support a stable, uniform pool of workers and equipment, regardless of project requirements.

The process of scheduling activities so that the amount of a certain required resource is somewhat balanced or "smoothed" throughout the project is called *resource leveling*. The goal of resource leveling is to alter the schedule of individual project activities such that the resultant resource requirements for the overall project are maintained at a fairly constant level.

Consider, for example, the important resource of labor. Figure 8-11 shows the labor or *worker loading* for the LOGON project. This diagram was created with the project schedule and the weekly labor requirements shown in Table 8-4, using a procedure similar to that for creating the costs schedules in Chapter 6. For example, activity H is the only activity scheduled for the first 10 weeks, so the loading stays at five workers. Over the next 6 weeks, activities I and J are scheduled so the loading becomes $4 + 8 = 12$, and so on.

The loading for the LOGON project is potentially a problem because it varies from a maximum of 23 workers in Week 26 to a minimum of zero workers in Weeks 24 and 25. The question facing the manager of LOGON is what to do with excess workers during slow periods and where to get additional workers during busy periods. To reduce the problems of frequent hirings and layoffs, it is desirable to try attaining a balanced work effort so that the worker loading is somewhat uniform over the duration of the project.

The problem can be reduced by "juggling" activities around. This is done by taking advantage of the slack time and delaying noncritical activities so that the resulting shifting of resources will cause loading peaks to be leveled and valleys to be filled. A smoothed worker loading, achieved by delaying activities P and Q each 2 weeks and U and W each 5 weeks, is shown in Figure 8-12. Of course, it should be recognized that in reality, rarely can projects attain the ideal leveling.

In the previous example, an even more uniform loading could be achieved if each activity could be split and pieces scheduled at different times. Whether this is feasible depends upon whether the work, once started, can be interrupted and then restarted later. As we have seen, the designation of work packages takes place during the process of creating the WBS, and the final breakdown is used to establish schedules, cost accounts, and so on. Once an activity is defined as an "activity" in the WBS, it is difficult later to divide it because this might also require changing the cost account structure, budgets, schedules, and other control mechanisms. Consequently, the usual

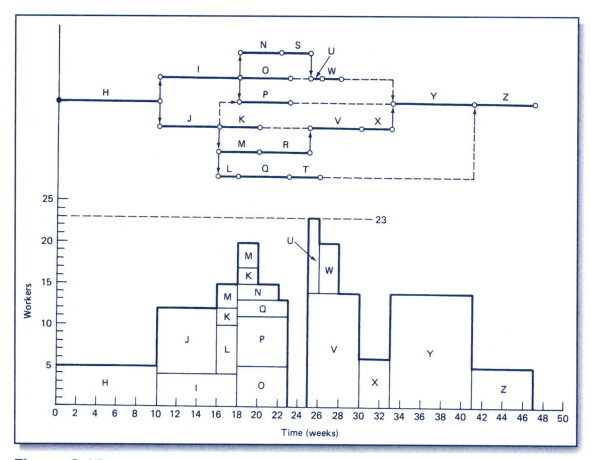

Figure 8-11
Schedule and corresponding worker loading for the LOGON project.

assumption in network scheduling is that once started, an activity must be carried out uninterrupted. However, many project software packages and PDM do permit splitting activities.

Leveling can easily be applied to any single resource, but it is difficult when several resources must be balanced simultaneously. Because work packages often require resources from more than one functional unit or subcontractor, a schedule that provides a smooth loading for one organizational unit may cause problems or hardships for others. Also, projects require numerous resources, and a schedule that levels one resource inevitably produces irregular loadings for others. For example, based on the

Table 8-4 LOGON Project Weekly Labor Requirements.

Activity	H	I	J	K	L	M	N	O	P	Q	R	S	T	U	V	W	X	Y	Z
Duration (weeks)	10	8	6	4	2	4	4	5	5	5	5	3	3	1	5	2	3	8	6
Weekly Labor Requirements (workers)	5	4	8	2	6	3	2	5	6	2	0	0	0	9	14	6	6	14	5
Weekly Equipment Requirements (hours)	8	2	6	1	2	2	0	0	6	0	4	4	0	8	8	8	8	8	8

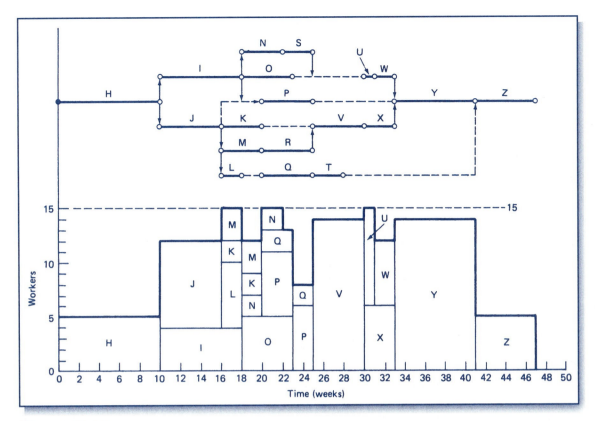

Figure 8-12
Smoothed worker loading for the LOGON project.

weekly equipment requirements for LOGON shown in Table 8-4, the schedule in Figure 8-12 (which provides for a level worker loading) yields the erratic equipment loading shown in Figure 8-13. Any attempt to smooth this equipment loading by adjusting or delaying the schedule will result in disrupting the loading of workers and other resources. (As you can verify—the schedule in Figure 8-11 that produced the erratic worker loading yields a relatively balanced equipment loading.)

It is impossible to level requirements for all resources. The best results arise from applying the scheduling equivalent of the "Pareto optimum;" in other words, schedule the activities in the best interests of the project, but among organizational units try to minimize the number of conflicts and problems caused by the schedule. When considering multiple resources simultaneously, schedules are adjusted to provide a level, smooth loading for those "priority" resources where irregular loadings would be the most costly to the project or demoralizing to workers. The high financial and social costs associated with hiring, overtime, and layoffs often dictate that "human resources"—the workers—be given the highest priority. Some project software packages perform scheduling analysis with simultaneous leveling of multiple resources.

Delaying activities is one method of leveling resource utilization. Three other methods are to

- Eliminate some work segments or activities.
- Substitute less resource-consuming activities.
- Substitute resources.

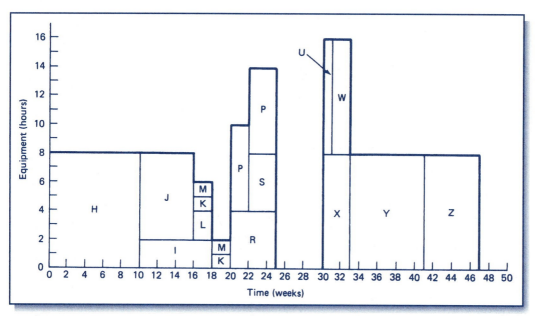

Figure 8-13
Equipment loading for the LOGON project.

These methods eliminate or alter work segments, or tasks, to consume fewer or different resources. For example, when the most qualified workers are not available, work requiring their expertise can be eliminated from the plan, or less qualified workers can be called in. These options are compromises that reduce the scope or quality of the work. When employing any of these alternatives there is always the attendant risk of not meeting project performance requirements.

Constrained Resources

What happens when the number of personnel, pieces of equipment, or working capital available restricts what can be scheduled? This is called the *constrained resource* problem: Activities must be scheduled so that the allocation of a particular resource to project activities does not exceed a specified maximum. It differs from resource leveling in that less attention is given to the variability in resource utilization than to the *maximum availability* of resource. As each activity is to be scheduled, the sum of its required resources plus the resource requirements for activities already scheduled must be checked against the amount available. This problem is more than just leveling resources; rescheduling jobs, often delaying them until such time when resources become available is necessary.

In the LOGON project, for example, suppose only 14 workers are available in any given week. The "leveled" schedule in Figure 8-12 results in a maximum loading of 15 workers. It is not possible to reduce the maximum loading to any number less than this and still complete the project in 47 weeks. To reduce the loading to the 14 worker maximum, some activities will have to be delayed beyond their late start dates. This will delay the project. With problems such as this something has to give: It is infeasible to both satisfy the resource restriction and to complete the project by the earliest completion time. Figure 8-14 shows a schedule which satisfies the 14-worker constraint. This schedule was determined by trial and error, making certain to violate neither the precedence requirements nor the loading constraint of 14 workers. Notice that

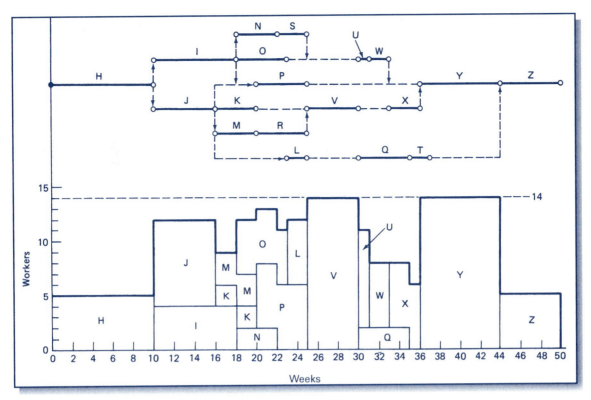

Figure 8-14
Schedule and corresponding worker loading for the LOGON project with 14-worker constraint.

the project now requires 50 weeks to complete because Activity X had to be delayed 3 weeks beyond its late start date.

As the example in Figure 8-14 shows, utilization of a resource by multiple activities can dictate the project completion time and override the critical path time. Consider another example, again from the LOGON project. Suppose one very important project resource is a technical inspector for the prime contractor, Iron Butterfly. This employee is unique with experience and knowledge that make her ideal for inspecting and approving a variety of project activities. However, her work is quite exacting, preventing her from working on more than one activity at a time. Suppose the activities in which she will be working are H, J, P, K, L, V, and X. These activities are highlighted in Figure 8-15. Because the same person to work on all of the activities highlighted can only work on one of them, the activities must be done sequentially. Adding the durations of these activities gives the time required for the technical inspector to complete her work, 36 weeks. Add to this time the durations for the last two activities, Y and Z, and the total is 50 weeks. Therefore, the project duration will be 50 weeks, not the 47 weeks determined by the critical path. Goldratt distinguishes the path connecting activities that require the same constrained resource (here, H-J-P-K-L-V-X) from the critical path (H-J-M-R-V-X) by calling the former the *critical chain*.[13] As illustrated, the significance of the critical chain is that when activities must be delayed and performed sequentially due to constrained resources, and when the sum of the durations of these activities exceeds the critical path, then it is these activities—the critical chain, *not* the critical path—that sets the project duration.

Scheduling with constrained resources involves decisions about which activities should be scheduled immediately and receive resources, and which should be delayed

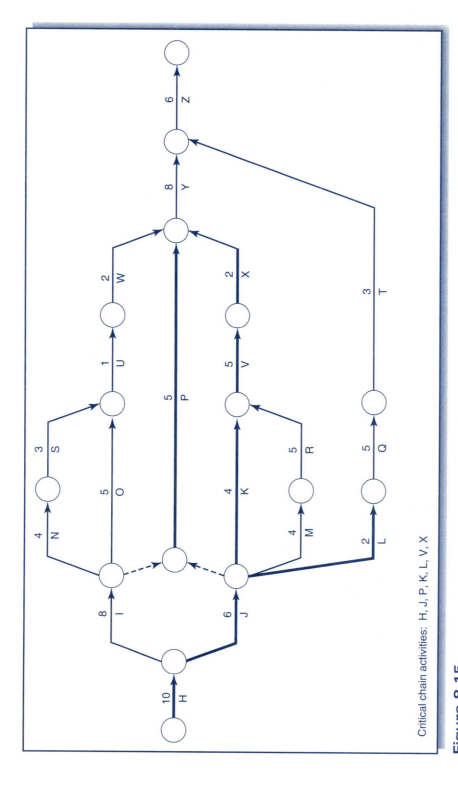

Critical chain activities: H, J, P, K, L, V, X

Figure 8-15
Activities in the LOGON project involving the constrained resources of technical inspector.

until resources are available. Most project management scheduling software use *heuristics* for making the decisions. A heuristic is a procedure based upon a simple rule. Scheduling of activities to meet a project completion deadline given constrained resources can be difficult even for projects of moderate size. Although heuristics often do not provide optimal schedule solutions, they can provide solutions that are, nonetheless, good. A heuristic starts with early and late times as determined by traditional network methods, then analyzes the schedule in terms of the required resources (that is, the resource loading). Whenever a resource requirement exceeds the constraint, the heuristic determines which activities are high priority and should receive resources, and which are low priority and should be rescheduled to a later date. Among the different heuristic rules for determining scheduling priority are:

a. **As soon as possible:** Activities that *can* be started sooner are given priority over (will be scheduled ahead of) those that must be started later.

b. **As late as possible:** Activities that can be finished later are given lower priority than those that must be finished earlier.

c. **Most resources:** Activities requiring more resources are given priority over those requiring fewer resources.

d. **Shortest task time:** Activities of shorter duration are given priority over those of longer duration.

e. **Least slack:** Activities with less slack time are given priority over those with more slack time (critical path activities thus have highest priority).

All of these rules are subordinate to precedence requirements, which means whatever the rule, the resulting schedule will not violate the necessary predecessor-successor relationships.

Some examples of the influence that different rules have on final schedules are shown in Figure 8-16. Most project management software employ some combination of these rules (for example, using "shortest task time," then using "as soon as possible" as a tie breaker) or offer a choice of rules. The goal is always to complete the project within the scheduled target completion date; sometimes, however, that is not possible regardless of the priority rule, in which case the project completion must be delayed. For example, suppose the target completion date for the project in Figure 8-16 is the critical path length of 9 weeks. Given the constrained-resource level of 10 workers, none of the heuristics in the example enable this completion time, although one of them ("as late as possible") results in 10-week completion.

In general, no single heuristic rule works universally better than the others, so the best way to determine a constrained-resource schedule is to use a variety of methods in combination, then go with the method that yields the best schedule. However, this option is usually not available because popular commercial scheduling software use only one or a few methods. (In one study containing several of these software packages, the resulting project schedules yielded project completion dates that averaged 5 percent to 9 percent longer than the known optimal schedules.)[14]

In addition to using heuristics, other ways to account for resource constraints in project scheduling include:

- **Reduce the level of resources per activity.** This technique assumes that work *can* be performed with fewer resources than specified, although the usual consequence is to lengthen the duration of the activity. For example, an activity that requires 10 workers per day for a 2-week period might be assumed doable with only five workers per day, but it would take perhaps twice as long (4 weeks).[15] The trade-off between workers and time is similar to the trade-off between cost and time in the CPM method.

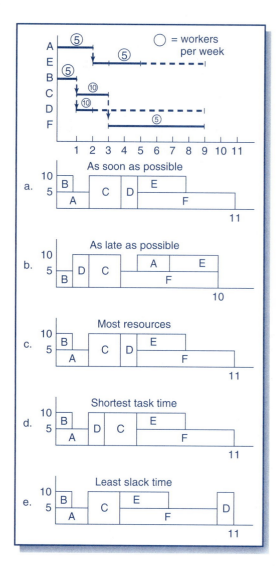

Figure 8-16
Results of several priority rules (heuristics) on project schedule and completion times.

- **Split activities.** Shorter-duration activities are easier to schedule with constrained resources than are longer-duration activities. Thus, whenever feasible, an activity is split into smaller activities; these subactivities are scheduled (maintaining the precedence relationships) when sufficient resources are available. For example, suppose in Figure 8-16d that Activity A can be split into two 1-week subactivities. After completing Activity B and the first segment of A, activities D and C are then performed; upon completing D and C, the remainder of Activity A is performed concurrent with Activity F. The resulting project schedule is compressed by 1 week.

- **Alter the network.** Often resources exceed constraints because multiple activities are scheduled in parallel, and the slack times are insufficient to meet the constraint by delaying activities. A possible alternative to delaying activities is to start them *earlier,* which can be accomplished whenever an FS relationship can be changed to an SS relationship. In general, constrained-resource scheduling is much easier with PDM and activity-splitting than with ordinary FS-type networks and no activity-splitting.

Multiple Project Scheduling

Related to the topic of resource allocation is planning and scheduling of multiple concurrent projects. The scenario of multiple, concurrent projects that draw upon a common resource pool is typical. Organizations that perform construction, consulting, or systems development and maintenance projects commonly rely on a pool of shared equipment and skilled workers from which all projects must draw resources. In matrix organizations (see Chapter 14), it is expected that all projects will share resources from the same functional departments.

When multiple projects share resources, the mix of projects must be planned and scheduled such that they not only satisfy their individual objectives and requirements, but in combination do not exceed resources available in the shared pools. Although the projects might in other ways be entirely independent, the fact that they share resources means that they cannot be managed and scheduled independently.

As you might expect, the problem of scheduling multiple, concurrent projects is somewhat analogous to scheduling multiple, concurrent activities within a single project, but with modification for the economic, technical, and organizational issues that arise when dealing with multiple projects.

First, each project has its own target completion date, and the projects must be scheduled so as to meet these dates or minimize delays. Delayed completion can result in deferred payments, penalty costs, or lost sales and revenues. Further, when projects are dependent—for example, the completion of a telecommunications project depends on the successful completion of a satellite development and launch project— then delays in one project have ripple effects on other, subsequent projects. In any case, scheduling of multiple projects first requires determining the priority of the project to enable decisions about how to allocate scarce resources among them.

Also, because for most organizations it is desirable to maintain a minimum, uniform level of personnel and other resources, ideally the schedules for multiple projects should result in a uniform utilization of these resources. In other words, the resource loading for a combination of projects should be somewhat uniform. In theory, projects are scheduled so that as resources are released from one project, they are assigned to other projects. This minimizes costs associated with hirings, layoffs, and idle workers and facilities, and helps ensure efficient use of resources as well as worker job security.

The following section introduces another network scheduling method called GERT. This is a relatively more advanced technique developed to handle limitations and shortcomings of PERT/CPM. The purpose of this section is to make you aware of this method; more thorough coverage, necessary to apply this technique, is beyond the scope of this book. Interested readers should refer to the references in the endnotes.

8.4   GERT[16]

All of the network scheduling methods described thus far, including PDM, PERT, and CPM, are limited as tools in their capacity to model projects realistically. Among the limitations are:

1. All immediate predecessor activities must be completed before a given activity can be started.
2. No activity can be repeated, and no "looping back" to predecessors is permitted.

3. The duration time for an activity is restricted to the Beta distribution for PERT and a single estimate (deterministic) for CPM.

4. The critical path is always considered the longest path even though variances include the likelihood of other paths being longer.

5. There is only one terminal event and the only way to reach it is by completing all activities in the project.

Although these are only minor limitations for some projects, for others they are major drawbacks. Take the situation, for example, of a product development project which involves the stages of research, design, assembly, and test. At a given time, multiple research groups might be in pursuit of a product "breakthrough," and success of any one of them would lead to a go-ahead for the rest of the project. Although there are several research activities taking place at once, not all of them need to be completed to begin successor activities (Limitation 1).

In some situations it is necessary to repeat activities. Product tests can reveal inadequacies in performance and dictate changes to design or fabrication. Especially in development-oriented projects, tests likely will reveal places where improvements or adjustments are necessary and the project must "loop back" to repeat the stages of design or assembly (Limitation 2).

Depending on the nature of the activity, its duration might follow any of a variety of distributions other than the Beta (Limitation 3).

Because of the variance in path durations, there is a high likelihood that "near critical" paths will become critical and extend the project duration. Even in relatively less complex projects, it is difficult to accurately assess the impact of path variability on project completion times (Limitation 4).

Just as individual activities such as tests can have multiple outcomes, so also an projects. In a research and development project, the result can be failure, partial success leading to further product development, or complete success leading to manufacture and distribution of any one of numerous different products. Different outcomes of activities lead to different paths of successors and, ultimately, to different outcomes for the project (Limitation 5).

The GERT technique (graphical evaluation and review technique) overcomes these limitations. It is similar in many ways to PERT except that it permits alternative time distributions (in addition to Beta) and allows looping back so previous activities can be repeated. The major distinction of GERT, however, is that it utilizes complex "nodes." In PERT, a node is an event that represents the start or finish of an activity. A node cannot be realized until all of its immediate predecessors have been realized (e.g., a "start event" cannot occur until the "finish event" has been reached for *all* of its immediate predecessors). Also in PERT, once a node is reached, *all* of its successor nodes must then be realized (e.g., reaching the "finish event" for an activity signals the "start event" for successor activities).

GERT utilizes *probabilistic* and *branching* nodes that specify both the number of activities leading to them that must be realized, as well as the potential multiple branching paths that can emanate from them. For example, the node in the following figure represents that

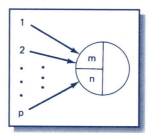

the node will be reached if *any* m of its p immediate predecessors are completed. The node can be reached more than one time (through looping), but in subsequent times it will require that *any* n of its immediate predecessors be completed. When an "A" is inserted in the node, all predecessors (m or n) must be completed to reach it (as in conventional PERT).

The node in the next figure represents a probabilistic output where any of q outputs or branches are possible. Each branch has an assigned probability; the sum of the probabilities over all the branches is 1.0. When no probabilities are given for the branches, the probability is assumed to be 1.0 for *each one* (as in traditional networks, where every branch must be taken).

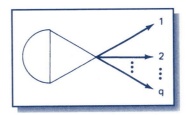

The symbols may be combined to represent a large variety of situations, such as the two shown in the next figure. The first represents a node that can be reached the first time by completing any two of the input activities a, b, or c; subsequently, only one of the possible inputs need be completed. This node also represents that upon reaching it, both d and e can be started. The second node represents that both a and b must be completed before the node can be reached. The infinity means that it cannot be reached subsequently; in other words, no loops are permitted back to it. It also shows that upon being reached, activities c, d, or e will start with probabilities of 0.3, 0.4, and 0.3, respectively. This discussion covers only a few of the available nodal representations. Several other options are available in GERT; these are discussed in the endnotes.[17]

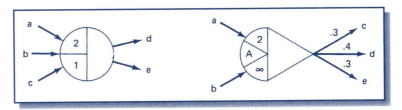

A simple example follows to illustrate the application of GERT. A basic network diagram for the ROSEBUD project is shown in Figure 8-17. It is similar to the diagram for ROSEBUD in Chapter 7 except it has been expanded to include the possibility of failure following each of three tests for hardware, system, and the user. Specifically:

1. A failure in the hardware test would require adjustments to the equipment.
2. A failure in the system test would require either adjustments to the installation, minor redesign of the hardware, or minor respecification of the software, depending on the nature of the failure.
3. A failure in the user test would require either minor or major system adjustments followed by a new system test.

The example is greatly simplified, and you can probably see numerous other places where loops and branches would likely occur in a project such as this. For example, there could be multiple branches at each of the activities for design, delivery, and adjustments.

Figure 8-18 illustrates the corresponding GERT network for the project. Notice that for probabilistic nodes the probabilities are given for the output branches. For example,

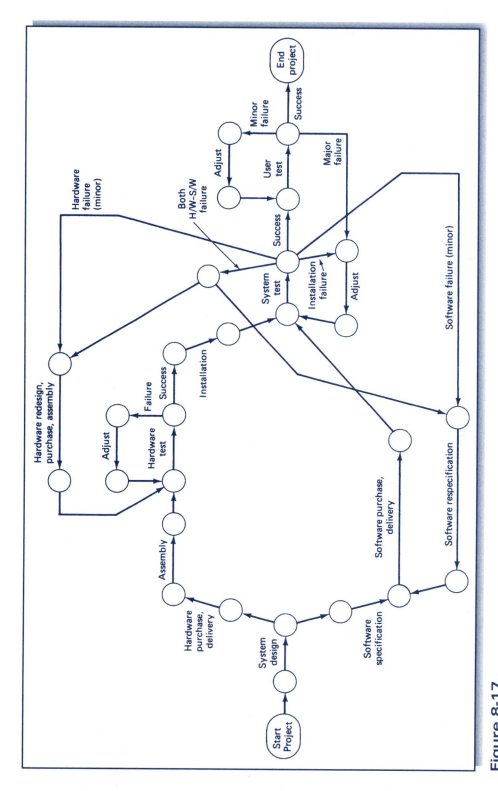

Figure 8-17
Expanded network for the ROSEBUD project.

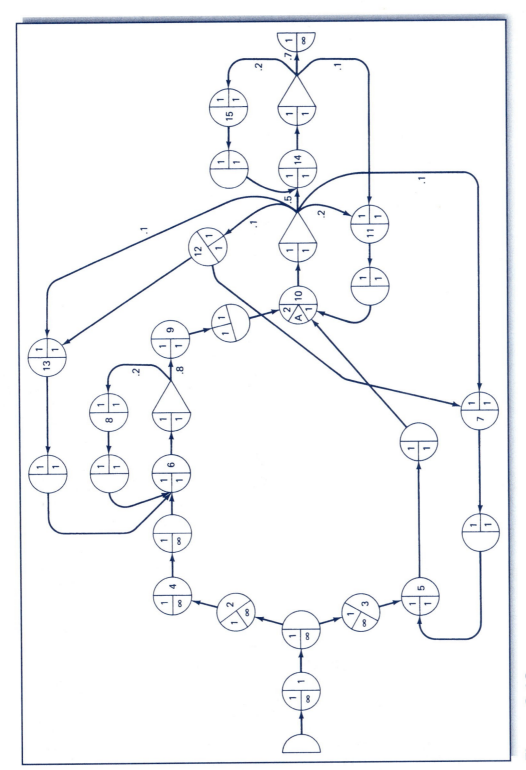

Figure 8-18
GERT network for the ROSEBUD project.

257

the node for complete user test (the node following Node 14) ends with success, 0.7; minor adjustments, 0.2; and major adjustments, 0.1. Also notice Node 12 represents failure in both hardware and software and the need to redesign both. Although not indicated on the figure, each activity would also have an assigned probability distribution type (e.g., normal, Beta, Erlang, uniform, constant, and so on) as well as distribution parameters (mean, variance, maximum, and minimum).

Given the network and distributions, a Monte Carlo computer simulation model can be prepared to derive statistics about the project. For example, the project could be simulated 1,000 times to gather statistics on the mean, variance, and distribution of times to successfully assemble the hardware, administer the system test, and complete the project. Similar information can also be gathered and tallied for other nodes in the network. It is also possible to collect information about the distribution of failure times (the time when failures are most likely to occur)—an important item of information for estimating the ultimate cost of the project. As the network stands, there is the possibility, though small, that it could loop back infinitely without ever reaching an end.

8.5 DISCUSSION AND SUMMARY

The PERT method is a statistical network-based scheduling procedure developed to help project managers account for the uncertainties in conducting project activities. CPM is a network-based method developed to help managers analyze the effect of project duration on cost. Project cost is just one constraint that prescribes project schedules; scarce resources such as labor, equipment, materials, and capital required over the duration of the project must also be considered. The resource loading and leveling techniques in this chapter are helpful for reconciling conflicts between project time schedules and scarce resources, and for balancing resources to reduce fluctuations. When activities require more resources than are available, some activities must be delayed until those resources can be made available.

Despite the advantages of CPM, PERT, and related applications described in this chapter, such methods have gained only marginal acceptance outside the construction and aerospace industries. In contrast, simpler techniques such as Gantt charting are in widespread usage. Probably the reason for this lies in the fact that network methods require considerably more data and computation than Gantt charts. On large projects the amount of time spent planning and managing the *network itself* can be large. When PERT/CPM methods were first developed they received much fanfare and acquired numerous advocates. Many organizations eagerly attempted to utilize the techniques, often without considering the appropriateness of the application or the best way to go about it. For a while, PERT was *required* of all contractors of the U.S. government. In either case, the techniques were frequently poorly understood, misapplied, and fell into disfavor with managers.

Nonetheless, the merits of PERT/CPM methods stand. Most of the computational difficulties are no longer a problem with the widespread availability of user-friendly project management software systems. Dozens of software packages are available suitable for projects ranging in size from hundreds to tens of thousands of activities.[18]

PERT/CPM and related methods must be understood for what they are: planning tools for grappling with the problems of arranging and scheduling work. They are not substitutes for other planning and control techniques; Gantt charts, WBSs, responsibility matrices, and additional planning and scheduling tools are still necessary.

As with other management methods, managers must first understand the logic behind the method and its costs and limitations before they decide when and where to apply PERT/CPM and related methods. PERT/CPM methods should be adopted when the potential benefit of their application is estimated to be greater than the time and cost of using them. It is likely that the widespread availability of easy-to-use, inexpensive, quality software will increasingly put these methods back in favor.

The next chapter rounds out our coverage of planning techniques. It focuses on the "accountant's" perspective of project planning; namely, the subjects of cost estimating and budgeting.

Summary List of Symbols

t_e **Expected Activity Time:** In PERT, the mean time to complete an activity, based on optimistic (a), most likely (m), and pessimistic (b) estimates of the activity duration.

V **Variance of an Activity:** The variability in activity completion time.

V_p **Variance of the Project Duration:** The variability in the expected project completion time.

C_n **Normal Activity Cost:** The direct cost of completing an activity under normal work effort; usually, the lowest cost for completing an activity.

C_c **Crash Activity Cost:** The direct cost of completing an activity under a crash work effort; usually, the highest cost for completing an activity.

T_n **Normal Activity Duration:** The expected time to complete an activity under normal work effort; usually, assumed to be the longest time the work will take.

T_c **Crash Activity Duration:** The expected time to complete an activity under a crash work effort; the shortest possible time in which an activity can be completed.

Summary Illustration Problem

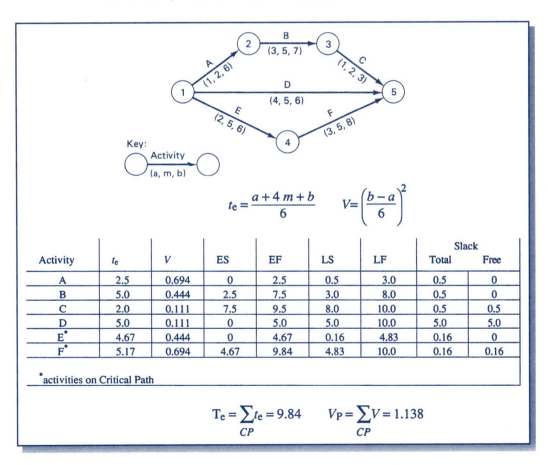

Key:
Activity
(a, m, b)

$$t_e = \frac{a + 4m + b}{6} \qquad V = \left(\frac{b-a}{6}\right)^2$$

Activity	t_e	V	ES	EF	LS	LF	Slack Total	Slack Free
A	2.5	0.694	0	2.5	0.5	3.0	0.5	0
B	5.0	0.444	2.5	7.5	3.0	8.0	0.5	0
C	2.0	0.111	7.5	9.5	8.0	10.0	0.5	0.5
D	5.0	0.111	0	5.0	5.0	10.0	5.0	5.0
E*	4.67	0.444	0	4.67	0.16	4.83	0.16	0
F*	5.17	0.694	4.67	9.84	4.83	10.0	0.16	0.16

*activities on Critical Path

$$T_e = \sum_{CP} t_e = 9.84 \qquad V_P = \sum_{CP} V = 1.138$$

REVIEW QUESTIONS AND PROBLEMS

1. How do CPM and PERT differ? How are they the same?
2. Define crash effort and normal effort in terms of the cost and time they represent. When would a project be crashed?
3. What does the cost slope represent?
4. The cost slope always has a negative (−) value. What does this indicate?
5. Time-cost tradeoff analysis deals only with direct costs. What distinguishes these costs from indirect costs? Give examples of both direct and indirect costs. (The answer to this question is covered in detail in the next chapter, but take a guess now.)
6. What are the criticisms of CPM? How and where is CPM limited in its application?
7. Distinguish resource loading from resource leveling.
8. Why is leveling of resources preferred to large fluctuations?
9. Discuss the implications of resource allocation for organizations involved in multiple projects.
10. For the following networks, given a, m, b for each activity, compute:
    a. t_e and V for each activity
    b. ES, EF, LS, and LF for each activity.
    c. T_e and V_p for the project.

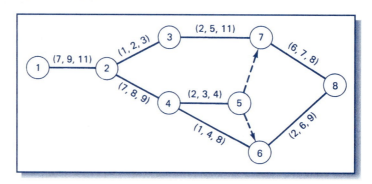

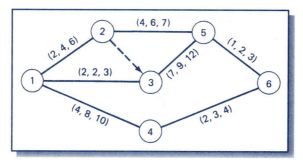

11. Referring to problem 10a above
    a. What is $P(T_e < 23)$?
    b. What is $P(T_e < 32)$?
    c. For what value of T_s is the probability 95 percent that the project will be completed?
12. Referring to the network shown in Figure 8-2 of this chapter, what is the probability of completing each of the five paths within 30 days? What is the probability of completing *all* five paths within 30 days?

13. The following project network and associated costs are given (*T* in days, *C* in $1,000s)

	Normal		Crash		
Activity	T_n	C_n	T_c	C_c	Cost slope
A	4	210	3	280	70
B	9	400	6	640	80
C	6	500	4	600	50
D	9	540	7	600	30
E	4	500	1	1100	200
F	5	150	4	240	90
G	3	150	3	150	—
H	7	600	6	750	150

a. Verify that the normal completion time is 22 days and that the direct cost is $3,050.
b. What is the least costly way to reduce the project completion time to 21 days? What is the project cost?
c. What is the least costly way to reduce the completion time to 20 days? What is the project cost?
d. Now, what is the *earliest* the project can be completed and what is the least costly way of doing this? What is the project cost?

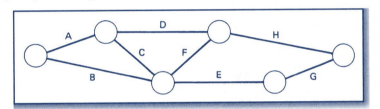

14. The following project network and associated costs are given (*T* in days, *C* in $1,000s)

	Normal		Crash		
Activity	T_n	C_n	T_c	C_c	Cost slope
A	6	6	3	9	
B	9	9	5	12	
C	3	4.5	2	7	
D	5	10	2	16	
E	2	2	2	2	
F	4	6	1	10	
G	8	8	5	10	

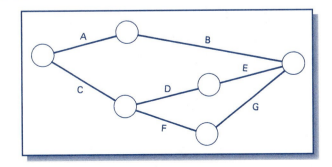

a. What is the earliest the project can be completed under normal conditions? What is the direct cost?
b. What is the least costly way to reduce the project completion time by 2 days? What is the project cost?
c. What is the *earliest* the project can be completed and what is the least costly way of doing this? What is the project cost?

15. The following table gives information on a project (T in days, C in $1000s)

Activity	Immediate predecessors	Normal		Crash	
		T_n	C_n	T_c	C_c
A	—	6	10	2	38
B	—	4	12	4	12
C	—	4	18	2	36
D	A	6	20	2	40
E	B, D	3	30	2	33
F	C	10	10	6	50
G	F, E	6	20	2	100

a. Draw the project graph. Under normal conditions, what is the earliest the project can be completed? What is the direct cost? What is the critical path?
b. What is the cost of the project if it is completed 1 day earlier? Two days earlier?
c. What is the earliest the project can be completed? What is the lowest cost for completing it in this time?
d. If overhead (indirect) costs are $20,000 per day, for what project duration are total project costs (direct + indirect) lowest?

16. The network and associated requirements for systems analysts and programmers for the GUMBY project are as follows:

Activity	J	M	V	Y	L	Q	Z
Duration (weeks)	6	4	6	8	2	8	2
Systems Analysts (weekly)	8	5	3	2	5	3	5
Programmers (weekly)	3	4	2	3	3	2	3

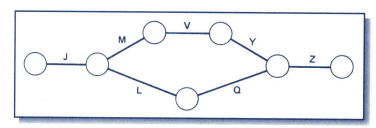

a. Compute ESs, LSs, and total slack times.
b. Then show the separate resource loadings for systems analysts and programmers, assuming early start times.
c. Suppose the maximum weekly availability is eight systems analysts and five programmers. Can activities be scheduled to satisfy these constraints without delaying the project?

17. Describe how GERT overcomes the limitations of PERT/CPM.

18. Give some examples of projects where GERT could be used.

19. Take an existing network (such as for LOGON); using your imagination (and the rules of GERT), redraw it as a GERT network.

1. In the project you are studying, discuss which of the following kinds of analysis were performed:
   a. PERT
   b. time-cost tradeoff analysis
   c. scheduling with resource constraints
   d. GERT
2. Discuss how they were applied and show examples. Discuss those applications which were not applied but which seem especially applicable to the project.

Case 8-1   Petersen General Contractors[19]

Petersen General Contractors was an established construction company doing work in several states in New England. Petersen generally handled small- to medium-sized commercial and industrial construction projects. Some recent projects that the company had completed were a 20,000-square-foot factory building, a four-story office building, and a water filtration plant.

TELEVISION TOWER BID

The company was now in the process of preparing a bid for a television station for the erection of a 225-foot-high television antenna tower and the construction of a building adjacent to the tower that would be used to house transmission and electrical equipment. Petersen was bidding only on the tower and its electrical equipment, the building, the connecting cable between tower and building, and site preparation. Transmission equipment and other equipment to be housed in the building were not to be included in the bid and would be obtained separately by the tele-vision station. The site for the tower was at the top of a hill, with the building to be constructed at a slightly lower elevation than the base of the tower and near a main road. Between the tower and building was to be a crushed gravel service road and an underground cable. Adjacent to the building a fuel tank was to be installed above ground on a concrete slab. A sketch of the tower and building site is shown in Figure 8-19.

PREPARATION OF COST ESTIMATES

Prior to preparing the detailed cost estimates, Petersen's estimator met with the company's general supervisor to go over the plans and blueprints for the job. In addition to preparing a cost estimate, the estimator was to prepare an estimate of the time it would take to complete the job. The television station management was very concerned about the time factor and it had requested that bids be prepared on the basis of the normal time and costs for completing the job and also for the fastest time for completing the job and the additional costs that this would entail. The result of the conference between the estimator and general supervisor was to determine that the activities shown in Table 8-5 would be necessary to complete the job. It was agreed that the estimator would prepare time and cost estimates for these activities.

In addition to determining the list of activities, the estimator and supervisor discussed in some detail how these activities could be sequenced as the list of activities in Table 8-5 did not necessarily indicate the order in which the work could be performed. In the course of the discussion, the estimator made the following notes.

Survey work and procurement of the structural steel and electrical equipment for the tower can start as soon as contract is signed.

Grading the tower and building sites can begin when survey is completed.

After tower site is graded, footings and anchors can be poured.

After building site is graded and basement excavated, building footings can be poured.

Septic tank can be installed when grading and excavating of building site is done.

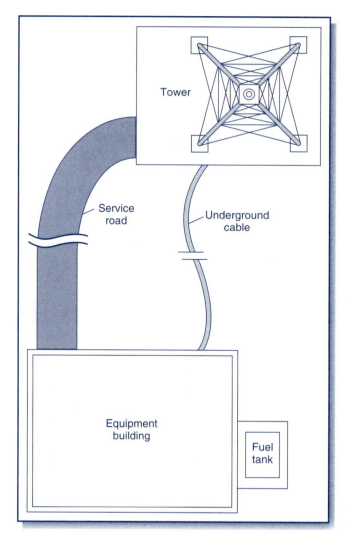

Figure 8-19
Television tower and building site plan.

Construction of connecting road can start as soon as survey is completed.

Exterior and interior basement walls can be poured as soon as footings are in.

Basement floor and fuel tank slab should go in after basement walls.

Floor beams can go in after the basement walls and basement floor.

Main floor slab and concrete block walls go in after floor beams.

Roof slab can go on after block walls are up.

Interior can be completed as soon as roof slab is on.

Put in fuel tank any time after slab is in.

Drain tile and storm drain for building go in after septic tank.

As soon as tower footings and anchors are in and tower steel and equipment are available, tower can be erected.

Connecting cable in tower site, drain tile, and storm drain can be put in as soon as tower is up.

Main cable between building and tower goes in after connecting cable at tower site is in and basement walls are up.

Tower site can be backfilled and graded as soon as storm drain, connecting cable, and main cable are in.

Clean up tower site after backfilling and grading is done.

Backfill around building and grade after main cable is in and after storm drain is in.

Table 8-5 Television Tower and Building Construction Time and Cost Estimate.

Activity Code	Activity	Normal Time Days[1]	Normal Time Cost[2]	Fastest Time Days[1]	Fastest Time Cost[2]
a	Sign contract and complete subcontractor negotiations	5		5	
b	Survey site	6	$3,270	4	$ 4,680
c	Grade building site and excavate for basement	8	3,900	6	5,490
d	Grade tower site	30	19,050	21	26,970
e	Procure structural steel and guys for tower[3]	85		85	
f	Procure electrical equipment for tower and connecting underground cable[3]	120		120	
g	Pour concrete for tower footings and anchors	42	24,930	25	35,010
h	Erect tower and install electrical equipment	38	34,050	25	46,860
i	Install connecting cable in tower site	8	5,220	4	5,850
j	Install drain tile and storm drain in tower site	35	10,800	18	15,300
k	Backfill and grade tower site	8	2,790	4	4,350
l	Pour building footings	29	9,090	21	12,300
m	Pour basement slab and fuel tank slab	14	3,150	11	4,620
n	Pour outside basement walls	34	7,650	30	8,430
o	Pour walls for basement rooms	9	2,400	7	2,880
p	Pour concrete floor beams	11	2,940	10	3,330
q	Pour main floor slab and lay concrete block walls	12	5,580	10	6,720
r	Pour roof slab	15	5,220	13	5,880
s	Complete interior framing and utilities	42	29,250	30	35,400
t	Lay roofing	3	810	2	1,020
u	Paint building interior, install fixtures, and clean up	19	2,760	13	4,050
v	Install main cable between tower site and building	35	13,080	25	13,620
w	Install fuel tank	3	540	2	660
x	Install building septic tank	12	1,890	8	2,250
y	Install drain tile and storm drain in building site	15	1,590	10	2,490
z	Backfill around building, grade, and surface with crushed rock	9	2,040	7	2,550
aa	Lay base for connecting road between tower and building	15	7,680	13	8,910
bb	Complete grading and surface connecting road	8	4,800	5	7,020
cc	Clean up tower site	5	720	3	1,500
dd	Clean up building site	3	630	2	1,200
ee	Obtain job acceptance	5		5	
Total			$206,280		$269,340

[1]Working days only

[2]For direct labor and rental of equipment only.

[3]Costs are included in Table 8-6.

Clean up building site after backfilling and grading is done.

Following his meeting with the general supervisor, the estimator prepared cost estimates and time estimates for completing the various portions of the job. Estimates for both the normal time in which the work could be completed and the fastest possible time along with the corresponding costs were made as shown in Table 8-5. The cost figures in Table 8-5 are for the direct labor and equipment use costs only. Estimated costs of materials used in construction and

Table 8-6 Estimated Cost of Materials and Equipment.

ITEM	COST
Structural steel and guys for tower	$ 70,800
Tower electrical equipment and connecting cable	21,780
Sand, gravel, crushed rock, and cement	15,330
Lumber and millwork	19,200
Drain tile and dewer pipe	10,800
Septic tank, plumbing fixtures, fuel tank, and other hardware	9,900
Other miscellaneous materials	9,960
Total	$157,770

purchased equipment to be installed in the tower are shown in Table 8-6. Company experience had shown that for this kind of job indirect labor and other overhead costs could be expected to amount to 65 percent of the direct labor and equipment use cost. The company also customarily added 15 percent to the total estimated cost for contingencies. Using this information, the estimator prepared analyses for the job: One for the cost of doing the work at the normal rate and one for the cost of doing the job in the shortest possible period of time.

QUESTIONS

1. Working at a normal rate, in how many days can the job be completed? What should the bid be on this basis if Petersen attempted to obtain a profit of 10 percent before federal income taxes?
2. What is the shortest possible time in which the job can be completed? What should the bid be on this basis if Petersen attempted to obtain a profit of 10 percent before federal income taxes?
3. If the job is obtained and the work is to be completed working at a normal rate, what portions of the work should be supervised most carefully to ensure that the job is completed on time? What portions of the work should be supervised most carefully if the contract is let on the basis of completing the job in the shortest possible time?
4. If television station management felt that the estimated time for completing the job in the shortest possible period of time was still too long, what could be done?

ENDNOTES

1. The method first appeared in the article by the originators of PERT: D. G. Malcolm, J. H. Roseboom, C. E. Clark, and W. Fazar, "Application of a Technique for Research and Development Program Evaluation," *Operations Research 7*, no. 5 (1959): 646–70.
2. This approximation is inferred from the Central Limit Theorem which specifies that the sum of a large number of independent random variables will be normally distributed no matter what the distribution of the individual random variables. Strictly speaking, this implies the requirement for a "large number" of activities on the critical path—but the approximation is always used, regardless of the number of activities.
3. See A. R. Klingel, "Bias in PERT Project Completion Time Calculation for Real Networks," *Management Science* 13 (1966): 194–201.
4. This computation assumes that paths are independent, which, in fact, they are not because portions of paths overlap (e.g., Paths a and c both contain Activity 1-2; c and d both contain 5-7-8; and so on). This fact makes the computation of the probability of finishing within a given time period very difficult, so difficult that it is never done. Nonetheless, the

criticism that PERT gives overly optimistic results still holds.

5. See R. W. Miller, *Schedule, Cost, and Profit Control with PERT* (New York: McGraw-Hill, 1963): 58; and Harold Kerzner, *Project Management: A Systems Approach to Planning, Scheduling, and Controlling,* 5th ed. (New York: Van Nostrand Reinhold, 1995): 653–91.

6. See R. M. Van Slyke, "Monte Carlo Methods and the PERT Problem," *Operations Research* 11, no. 5 (1963): 839–60.

7. Adapted with permission from J. R. Evans and D. L. Olson, *Introduction to Simulation and Risk Analysis* (Upper Saddle River, NJ: Prentice Hall, 1998): 111–20.

8. Crystal Ball is a registered trademark of Decisioneering, Inc., 1515 Arapahoe, Suite 1311, Denver, CO, 80202; www.decisioneering.com.

9. See M. Krakowski, "PERT and Parkinson's Law," *Interfaces* 5, no. 1 (November 1974); and A. Vazsonyi, "L'Historie de la grandeur et de la decadence de la methode PERT," *Management Science* 16, no. 8 (April 1970) (written in English). Other problems of PERT/CPM are described by Kerzner, *Project Management,* 679–80; Miller, *Schedule, Cost, and Profit Control with PERT,* 39–45; and J. D. Weist and F. K. Levy, *A Management Guide to PERT/CPM,* 2d ed. (Upper Saddle River, NJ: Prentice Hall, 1977), 57–58, 73, 166–173.

10. CPM first appeared in the article by its originators: J. E. Kelley and M. R. Walker, "Critical Path Planning and Scheduling," *Eastern Joint Computer Conference* (Boston, MA: 1959): 160–73.

11. A piece-wise approximation can be used for nonlinear relationships. See Wiest and Levy, *A Management Guide to PERT/CPM,* 81–85.

12. See Miller, *Schedule, Cost, and Profit Control with PERT,* 123–24.

13. E. M. Goldratt, *Critical Chain* (Great Barrington, MA: North River Press, 1997).

14. For the following popular project management software, the average difference between the optimal and software-produced schedules in terms of project completion times are: Timeline, 5.03 percent; Superproject 2.0, 5.94 percent; MS for Windows 3.0, 6.20 percent; Primavera, 9.07 percent. See R. V. Johnson, "Resource constrained scheduling capabilities of commercial project management software," *Project Management Journal* 22 (December 1992): 39–43.

15. As Brooks points out, the relationship between number of workers and activity duration is usually nonlinear; that is, cutting the number of workers in half will not necessarily double the time but might increase it by, say, only 50 percent, or maybe as much as 150 percent, depending on the task. See F. P. Brooks, *The Mythical Man Month: Essay on Software Engineering* (Reading, MA: Addison-Wesley, 1995): 13–36.

16. E. R. Clayton and L. J. Moore, "PERT Versus GERT," *Journal of Systems Management* 23, no. 2 (February 1972): 11–19; L. J. Moore and E. R. Clayton, *GERT Modeling and Simulation: Fundamentals and Application* (New York: Petrocelli/Charter, 1976); and Wiest and Levy, *A Management Guide to PERT/CPM,* 150–58.

17. Ibid.

18. For example, see *Project Management Software Survey* (Newton Square, PA: Project Management Institute, 1999).

19. From R. C. Meier, R. A. Johnson, W. T. Newell, and A. N. Schrieber, *Cases in Production and Operations Management* (Upper Saddle River, NJ: Prentice Hall, 1982): 213–18.

Chapter 9

Cost Estimating and Budgeting

A billion here and a billion there. Pretty soon it starts to add up to real money.

—SENATOR EVERETT DIRKSEN

Besides work definition and scheduling, the other major focal points of project planning are cost estimating and budgeting. The concepts described in Chapters 6, 7, and 8 are used in this chapter to show how estimates and budgets are combined with WBSs and schedules into a single, integrated plan.

Cost estimates, budgets, WBSs, and schedules are interrelated concepts. Ideally, estimates for project costs are based upon elements of the WBS and are prepared at the work package level. When the cost of a work package cannot be estimated because it is too complex, the work package is broken down further until it can. When the cost cannot be estimated because of uncertainties about the work, the estimate is initially based upon opinions and judgement, and is then refined as information becomes available. Project schedules dictate rates of expenditures and cash flows, but, as described in the last chapter, the converse is also true: limited resources and working capital dictate the scheduling of activities.

It is necessary in projects to put practical constraints on costs so that realistic budgets can be established. Failing to do so results in projects that are prematurely terminated for lack of funds, or are completed but at exorbitant expense. Both occurrences are relatively commonplace.

Cost estimating, budgeting, and cost control sometimes are thought to be the exclusive concerns of project planners and accountants, but in projects they should be a concern to everyone. Project participants who have the best understanding of the work—the engineers, scientists, systems specialists, architects, or others who are the closest to cost sources—should be involved in the estimating and budgeting process (it is common, however, for these same people to be disdainful of budgets or ignorant of why they are necessary and how they work). Also, project managers must be involved. They do not have to be financial wizards, but they should have an accountant's skill for organizing and using cost figures.

This chapter describes cost aspects with which project managers should be familiar including the cost estimating and budgeting process. Even with this knowledge, it is a good idea for the project manager to have a cost accountant on the project staff.

9.1 COST ESTIMATING

The initial cost estimate can seal a project's financial fate. When project costs are overestimated (unrealistically high), chances are good that the contract will be lost to a lower bidding competitor. Just as harmful is when the cost is underestimated. A $50,000 bid might win the contract, but obviously the project will lose money if it ends up costing $80,000. Underestimates are often accidental, the result of being overly optimistic; however, they are sometimes intentional as a result of trying too hard to beat the competition. In a practice called *buy in*, the contractor takes an initially realistic estimate and reduces it just enough to win the contract, hoping to cut costs or renegotiate higher fees after the work is underway. The practice is risky, unethical, and, sadly, relatively commonplace.

A very low bid signifies more than the desire to get a contract. It may imply that the contractor cut corners, left things out, or was just sloppy. The consequences for both client and contractor can be catastrophic, from operating at a loss to going bankrupt.

Cost estimates are used to develop budgets and become the baseline against which project performance is evaluated. The rate of actual cost expenditure compared to the estimated rate of expenditure (as indicated on the budget) is an important measure of project work performance; thus throughout the project actual costs are continuously compared with estimated, budgeted costs. Without good estimates it is impossible to evaluate work efficiency or to determine how much the finished project will cost.

9.2 COST ESCALATION

Accurate cost estimating is sometimes a difficult task, largely because it begins during project conception, well before all necessary, final information about the project is available. The less well-defined the project, the less information there is, and the greater the chances that the estimated costs will substantially differ from final, actual figures. As a rule, the difference will be on the side of a cost overrun. The amount by which actual costs increase to overrun the initial estimated costs is referred to as *cost escalation*.[1]

Some escalation can be expected; up to 20 percent is relatively common. Usually the larger and more complex the project is, the greater the *potential* for escalation. Cutting edge, high-technology, and R&D projects frequently show cost escalations upwards of several hundred percent. The Concorde supersonic airliner cost more than five times its original estimate, nuclear power plants frequently cost two to three times their estimates, and NASA spacecraft often exceed estimates by a factor of four to five. How does this happen? The following reasons are listed—many are avoidable, some are not:

- Uncertainty and lack of accurate information
- Changes in design or requirements
- Economic and social variables in the environment
- Work inefficiency, poor communication, and lack of control
- Ego involvement of the estimator
- Kind of project contract

Uncertainty and Lack of Accurate Information

Much of the information needed to make accurate estimates is simply not available when early cost figures are first developed. In NASA, for example, lack of well-defined spacecraft design and unclear definition of experiments is the principal reason for cost overruns. Not until later, when the design is finalized and work activities are well-defined (usually during the definition phase or later) can material and labor costs be accurately determined. In most research and development projects the activities are unpredictable, of uncertain duration, or must be repeated.

To minimize escalation from uncertainty, management must strive for the most definitive scope of work and the *clearest, most specific project objectives.* The clearer the objectives, scope, and work definition, the better the requirements definition, and the easier it is to make accurate cost estimates.

Whenever major changes in product design or project schedule are needed due to, for example, changes in state of the art or product concept, developmental barriers, strikes, legal entanglements, or skyrocketing wage and material costs—then the original cost estimate should be updated. This revised estimate then becomes the new baseline for controlling project costs.

In large projects that involve substantial technical uncertainties, work can be divided into successive phases where each one is estimated, budgeted, and evaluated for performance. As each phase is completed, the decision is made to proceed or terminate the project. This process is referred to as *phased project planning.* Sometimes competitive bids are received and new contracts negotiated for each phase.

To make allowances for uncertainty, an amount called a *contingency fund* or *budget reserve* is added to the original estimate.[2] This is the budget equivalent of the *schedule reserve or buffer* mentioned earlier. A contingency amount can be added to individual work packages or activities, or to the project as a whole. The amount is proportionate to the uncertainty of the work, so work with greater uncertainty is allotted a higher contingency amount. When possible, the percentage contingency is derived from historical records of similar tasks and projects.

Contingency funds are intended to offset small variations arising from estimating errors, small omissions, minor design changes, small schedule slippages, and so on. Each time the cost estimate is updated, so is the contingency fund. The contingency fund is not a "slush" fund. When no longer needed as intended, it should be cut from the project cost in order not to be used elsewhere; otherwise, there is a tendency for costs to rise to expend whatever remains in the fund. Contingencies are discussed later as an aspect of the cost estimating process.

Changes in Requirements or Design

Another major source of cost escalation is discretionary, nonessential changes to system requirements and plans. These changes come from a change in mind, not from oversights, mistakes, or environmental changes that would make them imperative. The routine tendency is for users and contractors alike to want to continually modify systems and procedures—to make "improvements" to original plans throughout the project life cycle. These kinds of changes are especially common in the absence of exhaustive planning or strict control procedures.

Many contracts include a *change clause* which allows the customer to make certain changes to contract requirements—sometimes for additional payment, sometimes not. The clause gives the customer flexibility to incorporate requirements not envisioned at the time of the original contract agreement. The clause can be exercised at any time and the contractor is obligated to comply. Any change, however, no matter how small, causes escalation. To implement a change requires some combination of redesigning or reorganizing work, acquiring new or different resources, altering previous plans, and undoing or scrapping earlier work. The more work completed on the project, the more difficult and costly it is to make changes.

When accumulated, even small changes have substantial effect on schedules, costs, and performances. In many projects, formal mechanisms such as a *change control system* and *configuration management* procedures are used to reduce the number of discretionary or imperative changes, and to contain their influence on escalation. These topics are discussed in Chapter 11.

Economic and Social Factors

Even with good initial estimates and few changes, cost escalation occurs because of social and economic forces beyond the contractor's or user's influence. Variables such as labor strikes, legal action by consumer and public interest groups, trade embargoes, and materials shortages can neither be precisely anticipated nor factored into plans and budgets, but they all serve to stifle progress and increase costs. Whenever project work is suspended or interrupted, administrative and overhead costs continue to mount, interest and leasing expenses continue to accrue on borrowed capital and equipment, and the date when payback begins and profit is earned is set back. Rarely can such problems be anticipated and their impacts incorporated into the contingency fund.

One economic factor that has major influence on cost escalation and project profitability is *inflation*.[3] The contractor can try to offset increases from inflation by inflating the price of the project, but often the actions of competitors or federal restrictions on price increases is confining. Some protection from inflation may be gained by including clauses in the contract that allow increases in wages or material costs to be appended to the contract price,[4] but the protection may be limited. Inflation is not one-dimensional; it varies depending on the labor, materials, and equipment employed, the geographical region, and the country. Subcontractors, suppliers, and clients use different kinds of contracts that have different inflation protection clauses and which may be to the advantage or disadvantage of other parties in the project.

Inflation also causes cash flow difficulties. Even when a contract includes an inflation clause, payment for inflation-related costs is tied to the publication of inflation indices, which always lags behind inflation. Although contractors pay immediately for the effects of inflation, it is not until later that they are reimbursed for these effects.

Trend analysis of inflation in the industry and the economy can improve the accuracy of cost estimates. In long-term projects especially, wage rates should be projected to indicate what they will be at the time they must be paid. This is done by starting with best estimates of labor hours and wage costs in current dollars, then applying inflation rates over the project's length.

Initial cost estimates are based upon prices at the time of estimating. After that, whenever actual costs are compared with initial estimates, inflation adjustments must be included so there remains a common basis upon which to identify variances and take corrective action. Either the estimates must be adjusted upward or actual expenses adjusted downward.

Inefficiency, Poor Communication, and Lack of Control

Another source of cost escalation is work inefficiency, the result of poor management, lack of supervision, and weak planning and control. In large projects especially, poor coordination, miscommunication, and sloppy control lead to conflicts, misunderstandings, duplication of effort, and mistakes. This is *one* source of cost escalation where management can have a substantial influence. Meticulous work planning, tracking and monitoring of activities, team building, and good control all help improve efficiency and keep (at least this source of) cost escalation to a minimum.

Ego Involvement of the Estimator

Cost escalation also comes from the *way* people estimate. Most people are overly optimistic and habitually underestimate the amount of time and cost it will take to do a job, especially in areas where they have little experience. Have you ever estimated how long it would take for *you* to paint a room, tile a floor, or replace a tire? How long did it *really* take? Most people think of an estimate as an "optimistic prediction." They confuse estimates with incentives or goals, and see the estimate as a reflection upon themselves, not an honest prediction of what it will take. The more "ego involvement" of the estimator in the job, the more unreliable the estimate.

The problem can be lessened by having professional estimators, or people different than those who will actually do the work. Remember the earlier contention about the necessity of involving project participants in planning the project? Most experienced workers are much better at estimating tasks, materials, and schedules than they are at costs. Although the doers (those who do the work) should *define* the work—the WBS, work packages, tasks and schedules—and provide *initial* estimates of time and costs, professional estimators should review the estimates for accuracy, check with the doers, and then prepare *final* cost estimates.[5]

A cost estimate should not be something to strive for; it should be a reasonable prediction of what will happen. Estimators must be, organizationally, in a position where they will not be coerced to provide estimates that conform to anyone's desires.

Project Contract

Chapter 4 and Appendix B describe the relative merits of different forms of contracts. Some of the merits are related to the contract's influence on cost escalation.[6]

Consider, for example, differences between the two basic kinds of contracts: Fixed-price and cost-plus. A fixed-price agreement gives the contractor incentive to control costs because, no matter what happens, the amount paid for the project remains the same. In contrast, in a strictly cost-plus contract there is only slight incentive to control costs. In fact, in cases where profit is computed as a percentage of costs, cost-plus agreements tend to motivate contractors to "allow" controllable costs to escalate. Other forms of legal agreements, such as the incentive contracts described in Appendix B, permit cost increases but at the same time encourage cost control and provide some motivation to try to reduce escalation.

9.3 COST ESTIMATING AND THE SYSTEMS DEVELOPMENT CYCLE[7]

Development of the cost estimate is closely tied to the first three phases of the systems development cycle:

A. Conception: initiation/feasibility
B. Definition: detailed planning/analysis
C. Execution: design/fabrication/implementation

The first cost estimate is made during project conception. At this time very little hard cost information is available so the estimate is the least reliable that it will ever be. Uncertainty about the cost and duration of the project may be large, as illustrated by the largest "region of time-cost uncertainty" in Figure 9-1. How much the project will *really* cost and how long it will *really* take are questionable. The project is compared to other, similar projects, and adjustments made for differences. Typically the

Figure 9-1
Time-cost graph showing cumulative project cost and regions of time-cost uncertainty.

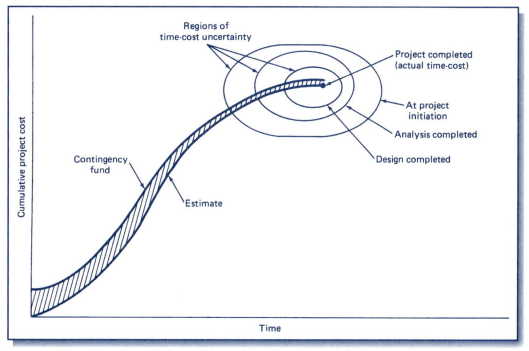

estimate is based upon standards of what it should take—labor time, materials, and equipment—to do a certain job. This approach is less useful when there is much development work involved because fewer of the tasks can be classified as "standard" and no other projects are similar. On large development projects the initial estimates are largely "guesstimates" and might end up being nowhere close to actual costs.

Unless the project is somewhat routine and well-defined, uncertainty in estimates dictates that contracts awarded during the conception phase be of the cost-plus form. Only after much of the definition phase is finalized, material costs become known and reliable estimates of labor requirements and rates can be made. It is then possible to obtain solid cost estimates for fabrication and installation. This is illustrated by the shrinking time-cost uncertainty regions in Figure 9-1.

By the time design work is half completed, cost estimates may be reliable enough to award incentive-type or (in well-defined situations) fixed-price contracts. In fact, the awarding of contracts is sometimes put off until well into the design stage so that the cost estimate can be more certain. This requires contractors to do a lot of front-end work without assurances that they will be awarded the job. When contractors are required to bid before the design phase is reached, they usually include substantial contingencies to cover the uncertainty of their estimates.

As the project moves into the middle and later phases, with work actually being completed and funds expended, cost estimates become more certain. Often, to control usage of the contingency fund, the amount in the fund is decreased as the project progresses. For example, a project starting out with a contingency of 15 percent of the base estimate might be decreased to a contingency of 8 percent when the project is half completed, then to 3 percent when it is three-fourths completed, and then to just 1 percent to cover small corrections during the final stages of installation and completion sign-off. This is illustrated in Figure 9-1.

Once the cost estimate has been developed and approved, it is used to establish the budget and becomes the baseline against which progress and performance will be evaluated. Thus, it is bad practice to change the estimate frequently during the project life cycle because it destroys the purpose of having a baseline. However, sometimes escalation factors render the initial estimate obsolete and require it to be revised periodically.

9.4   COST ESTIMATING PROCESS

Classifying Work Tasks and Costs

The cost estimating process begins by breaking the project down into work phases such as design, engineering, development, fabrication, and so on, or into work packages from the WBS. The project team, including representatives from the involved functional areas and contractors, meet to discuss the work phases or work packages, and to receive specific work assignments.

The team tries to identify tasks in the project similar to existing designs and standard practices that can readily be adopted. Work is classified either as *developmental* or as an adaptation of existing or *off-the-shelf* designs, techniques, or procedures. Because developmental work requires considerable effort in design, testing, and fabrication cost estimating is thus more difficult due to the greater uncertainty about what needs to be done. Overruns for developmental work are common, especially because of the difficulty in estimating labor hours. Estimation for standard, off-the-shelf work is more straightforward because it is based upon records of material and labor costs for similar systems or tasks. It is thus beneficial to try to make use of existing designs and technology in as many work packages as possible; this helps reduce estimating errors and may produce cost savings.

Estimated costs are classified as *recurring* and *nonrecurring*.[8] Recurring costs are those that happen more than once; they are associated with tasks periodically repeated and include costs for labor, materials, tooling, quality assurance, and testing. Nonrecurring costs happen only once and are associated with unique tasks or procurement of special items; they include development, fabrication, and testing of one-of-a-kind items.

In the pure project form of organization the project manager assigns responsibility for estimating, directs the estimating effort, and combines the estimate results for presentation to management. In a matrix organization, estimating is the joint responsibility of the project and functional managers, though the project manager coordinates the effort and accumulates the results. Close coordination and communication during the estimating effort is crucial for reducing redundancies and omissions—especially for estimates from groups working jointly on interfacing work packages.

Although this typifies the cost estimating process, the actual method used to estimate cost figures will depend on the required accuracy and the information available to make the estimate. Estimated cost figures are determined using four basic techniques: expert opinion, analogy, parametric, and cost engineering.

Expert Opinion

An *expert opinion* is an estimate provided by an expert— presumably someone who, from breadth of experience and expertise, is able to provide a reasonable, ball-park estimate. It is a "seat of the pants" estimate used when insufficient information precludes a more-detailed, in-depth cost analysis. Expert opinion is usually limited to cost estimating done in the conception phase, or for a project that is poorly-defined or is unique and for which there are no previous, similar projects available for comparison.

Analogy Estimate

An *analogy estimate* is an estimate developed by reviewing costs from previous, similar projects. The analogy method can be used at any level: Overall project cost can be estimated from the cost of an analogous project; work package cost can be estimated from other, analogous work packages; task cost can be estimated from analogous tasks; and so on. The cost for a similar project or work package is analyzed and adjusted for differences between it and the proposed project or work package. The adjustment takes into account factors such as dates, project scale, location, complexity, exchange rates, and so on. If, for example, the analogy project was performed 2 years ago and the proposed project is to commence 1 year from now, costs from the analogy project must be adjusted for inflation and price changes during the 3-year interim. If the analogy project was conducted in California and the proposed project will be in New York, costs must be adjusted for site and regional differences. If the "size" (scope, capacity, or performance) of the proposed task is twice that of the analogy task, then the costs of the analogy task must be "scaled" up. However, twice the size does not mean twice the cost, and the size-cost relationship must be determined empirically from several analogies, or from formulas based on physical principles.

So-called process industries such as petrochemicals, breweries, and pharmaceuticals use the following formula to estimate the costs of proposed projects:

Cost (proposed) = Cost (analogy)[Capacity (proposed)/Capacity (analogy)]$^{2/3}$

where "proposed" refers to a new facility and "analogy" refers to an analogous facility. In practice, the exponent varies from 0.35 to 0.9, depending on the kind of process and equipment used.[9]

Suppose a proposed plant is to have a 3.5 million cum (cubic meter) capacity. Using an analogy project for a plant with 2.5 million cum capacity and a cost of $15 million, the cost formula gives the estimated cost for the proposed plant as

$15 million [3.5/2.5]$^{2/3}$ = $15 million [1.2515] = $18.7725 million

Because the analogy method involves comparisons to previous, similar projects, it requires an extant database with information about prior projects. Companies that are serious about using the analogy method require good project cost documentation and a database that classifies cost information according to type of project, work package, task, and so on. When a new project is proposed, the data base is accessed to reveal prior projects or work packages that are similar, and provide cost details.

Parametric Estimate

A *parametric estimate* is an estimate derived from an empirical or mathematical relationship. The parametric method can be used with an analogy project (the case in Example 1) to scale costs up or down, or it can be applied directly—without an analogy project—when costs are a function of system or project "parameters." The parameters can be physical features such as area, volume, weight, or capacity, or performance features such as speed, rate of output, power, or strength. Parametric cost estimating is especially useful when preliminary design characteristics are first being set and a cost estimate is needed quickly. Example 2 is an application of parametric cost estimating.

Warren Eisenberg, president of Warren Wonderworks, Inc., a warehousing facilities contractor, wants a quick way to estimate the material cost of a facility. The company's engineers investigate the relationship between several building parameters and the material costs for eight recent projects comparable in terms of general architecture, layout, and construction material. Using the method of least squares (beyond our scope, but covered in textbooks on mathematical statistics), they develop the following formula—a multiple regression model that relates material cost (y) to floor space (x_1, in terms of 10,000 sq. ft.) and number of shipping/receiving docks (x_2) in a building:

$$y = 201,978 + (41,490)x_1 + (17,230)x_2$$

The least squares method also indicates that the standard error of the estimate is small, which suggests that the model provides estimates fairly close to actual costs for the eight projects.

Suppose a proposal is being prepared to construct a new 300,000 sq. ft. facility with two docks. The estimated material cost using the model is thus:

$$y = 201,978 + (41,490)(30) + (17,230)(2) = \$1,481,138.$$

Cost Engineering

Cost engineering refers to detailed cost analysis of individual cost categories at the work package or task level. It provides the most accurate estimate of all the methods, but also is the most time-consuming, requiring considerable work-definition detail and design information—both of which might not be available until later in the project. The method starts by first breaking down the project into activities or work packages, then further dividing these into cost categories such as labor, material, and equipment. For small projects the approach is simple and straightforward, as shown in Example 3.

Example 3: Cost Engineering Estimate for a Small Project

Ralph Lorn, Iron Butterfly Corp. project manager for the DMB project, is preparing a project cost estimate. He begins by breaking the project into eight work packages and preparing a preliminary schedule. For each of the work packages, he estimates the number of labor hours per week for each of the three labor grades assigned to the project. Hours per week per labor grade are shown in Figure 9-2.

For each work package he also estimates the cost of material, equipment and supplies, subcontracting, and other nonlabor expenses such as freight charges and travel. Table 9-1 is a summary of the labor hours and nonlabor costs.

Figure 9-2
Schedule showing hours allocated to work packages by labor grade.

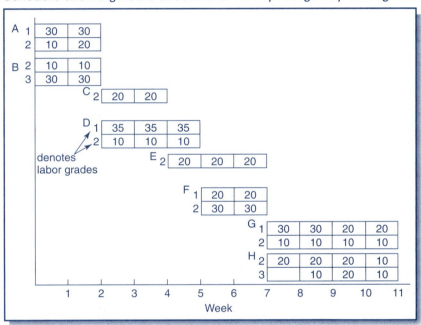

Table 9-1 Labor Hours and Nonlabor Costs.

WORK PACKAGE	HOURS BY LABOR GRADE			NONLABOR COSTS			
	1	2	3	MATERIAL	EQUIPMENT	SUBCONTRACTS	OTHER
A	60	30		$ 500			
B		20	60		$1,000		
C		40			500		$ 500
D	105	30			500		
E		60				$4,500	
F	40	60		8,000	1,000	5,000	500
G	100	40		1,500			500
H		70	40		1,000		1,500
Total	305	350	100	$10,000	$4,000	$9,500	$3,000

Total nonlabor cost (material, equipment, etc.) is thus $26,500. For labor grades 1, 2, and 3, suppose the hourly rates are $10, $12, and $15, respectively, and the overhead rates are 90 percent, 100 percent, and 120 percent, respectively (overhead rate is the amount to be *added* to the labor cost; overhead rates are discussed later). Therefore, labor-related costs are:

$$
\begin{array}{lll}
\text{Grade 1:} & 305(\$10)(100\% + 90\%) & = \quad\$5,795 \\
\text{Grade 2:} & 350(\$12)(100\% + 100\%) & = \quad8,400 \\
\text{Grade 3:} & 100(\$15)(100\% + 120\%) & = \quad\underline{3,300} \\
& & \quad\$17,495
\end{array}
$$

The preliminary estimate for labor and nonlabor cost is $17,495 + $26,500 = $43,995. Suppose Iron Butterfly Corp. routinely adds 10 percent to all projects to cover general and administrative expenses, which puts the cost at $43,995(1.1) = $48,395. To this Ralph adds another 10 percent as a project contingency, giving a final cost estimate for the DMB project of $48,395(1.1) = $53,235.

At the task level, detailed estimates are sometimes derived with the aid of *standards manuals*. Standards manuals contain time and cost information about labor and materials to perform particular tasks. In construction, for example, the numbers of labor-hours to install an electrical junction box or to install a square foot of wall forms are both standard times. To determine the labor cost of, say, installing junction boxes in a building, the estimator first determines the required number of junction boxes, then multiplies this by the labor standard per box, then multiplies that by the hourly labor rate.

For larger projects with larger work packages, the procedure is roughly the same as illustrated in Example 3, though more involved. First, the manager of each work package breaks the work package down into more fundamental or "basic" areas of work. For example, a work package might be divided into two basic areas, "engineering" work and "fabrication" work. The manager of the work package then asks his supervisors to estimate the hours and materials needed to do the work in each basic area. The supervisor overseeing engineering might further divide work into the tasks of structural analysis, computer analysis, layout drawings, installation drawings, manuals, and reproduction, then develop an estimate for each task duration and the labor grade or skill level required. In similar fashion, the fabrication supervisor might break the work down into fabricated materials (steel, piping, wiring), hardware, machinery, equipment, insurance, and so on, then estimate how much (quantity, size, length, weight, etc.) of each will be needed. The supervisors' estimates of time and materials are determined by reference to previous, similar work, standards manuals, reference documents, and rules of thumb ("one hour for each line of code"). The more developmental and the less standardized the task, the more guesswork involved; even with routine, off-the-shelf items, good estimating is an art. The supervisors submit their estimates to the work package manager who checks, revises, and then passes them on to the project manager.

The project manager and independent estimators or pricing experts in the project office should review the time and material estimates to be sure that no costs were overlooked or duplicated, estimators understood what they were estimating, correct estimating procedures were used, and allowances were made for risk and uncertainty.[10] The estimates are then aggregated, as shown in Figure 9-3, and converted into dollars by multiplying by standard wage rates and material costs (current or pro-

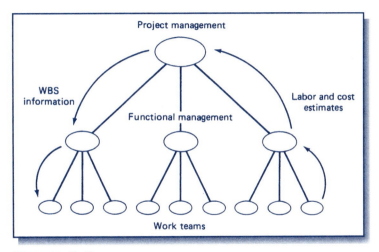

Figure 9-3
The estimating process.

jected). Finally, the project manager tallies in any project-wide overhead rates (to cover project management and administrative costs) and company-wide overhead rates (to cover the burden of general company expenses) to come up with a cost estimate for the total project.

Contingency Amount

Throughout the estimating process, contingency amounts might be added to estimates to offset uncertainty. Adding a contingency reduces the probability that actual costs will overrun the estimates. In general, the less well-defined or complex the situation, the greater the contingency amount.

Contingency amounts can be added to individual activities or work packages, or to the project as a whole. *Activity contingency* is an amount added by the estimator to the initial estimate of an activity or work package to account for "known unknowns," which are sources of cost increases that experience indicates as possible or highly likely; they include scrap and waste, design changes, increases in the scope, size, or function of the end-item, and delays due to weather. The total project cost, including activity contingencies, is called the *base estimate.* To the base estimate the project manager might add another amount, called a *project contingency,* to account for "unknown unknowns"—external factors that affect project costs but cannot be pinpointed or estimated. Examples include fluctuation in exchange rates, shortages in resources, changes in the market or competitive environment. The project contingency added to the base estimate gives the *final cost estimate,* which is the *most likely cost.* The likelihood that the actual project cost will fall above or below the final cost estimate is 50/50. The project manager has direct control over usage of the project contingency. Computing the amount for the project contingency is covered in Chapter 10.

Besides the activity and project contingencies, the corporation might also set aside an additional allowance to cover overruns. This amount, the *overrun allowance,* is added to the most likely cost to yield a cost where the probability of it being exceeded is less than 10 percent. The overrun allowance is controlled by corporate managers and is ordinarily not available to the project manager without approval.

Reconciling Estimates

The final cost estimate and project schedule are reported to company management. The project manager may also include forecasts showing time and cost effects of likely, potential escalation factors such as inflation, project risks, and so on. Management then decides to accept the estimate or have it revised.

This upward accumulation of work package estimates to derive the project estimate is called the "bottom-up" approach. The resulting total estimate is compared against the "top-down" or gross estimate from top management. If the gross estimate is substantially larger, the project manager reviews each work package estimate for oversights or overoptimism (the ego involvement of estimators). If the gross estimate is much smaller, the work package estimates are examined for incorrect assumptions or padding.

In general, cost estimating and the application of the estimating techniques listed previously occurs in two ways: top-down and bottom-up. Top-down refers to estimating the cost by looking at the project as a whole. A top-down estimate is typically based upon an expert opinion or analogy to other, similar projects. Bottom-up refers to estimating costs by breaking the project down into elements—individual project work packages and end-item components. Costs for each work package or end-item element are estimated, then these estimates are aggregated to derive the total project cost. Example 3 illustrates a bottom-up approach; Example 2 illustrates a top-down approach. The two approaches can also be used in combination, depending on the available data. For example, portions of a project that are well-defined can be broken down into work packages and estimated bottom-up; other portions less well-defined can be estimated top-down. In turn, the cost of each work package can be estimated by either breaking it down into smaller elements and estimating the cost of each (bottom-up), or by a gross estimate from analogy or expert opinion (top-down). The bottom-up method provides a more accurate estimate of project costs than the top-down method, but it requires more data and a project that is well-defined.

To reconcile differences between estimates, top management sometimes exercises an across-the-board cut on all estimates. This is poor practice because it fails to account for judgmental errors or excessive requests on the part of just a few units. It also unfairly penalizes unit managers who tried to produce fair estimates and were honest enough not to pad them. Such indiscriminate, across-the-board cuts induce everyone to pad estimates for their own protection.

Mistakes in estimation run in both directions. The project manager should approve bottom-up estimates for work packages, but functional units should approve top-down estimates for the work expected of them. Final estimates should be mutually agreed upon by both project and functional managers.

Reducing Costs

What happens if competition or insufficient funding force upper management to reduce costs? Managers will want to retain their share of the project and none will want to see their budget or staff reduced. Nonmanagement professionals such as engineers, scientists, or systems analysts, unless actively involved in the budgeting process, are often unaware of budget constraints and resist cuts. Here is where effective communication, negotiation, and diplomacy between project management, functional management, and staff is necessary to get project team members to accept a share of budget reductions. When this fails, the project manager must try to alter the work plan to reduce labor requirements. The final resort is to appeal to top management.[11]

The extent to which a contractor is willing to cut costs depends partly on the existing and projected work load. A company with current or expected excess capacity is usually much more willing to take on projects with little or no profit just to absorb its fixed overhead costs.

Suppose you are the project manager and it is clear that management wants to buy in with a budget too low to perform the work. There are only two courses of action: Either undertake the project and attempt wholeheartedly to meet the budget, or hand it over to another manager.[12] If you decide on the former, you should document your disagreement with the budget and report it to top management; later, the client might agree to changes in the project that would enable it to be completed within budget. If the contract is cost-plus, then the risk is low because additional costs will be reimbursed. If, on the other hand, the contract is fixed-price, and the budget is so grossly underfunded as to result in cutting corners or an uncompletable project, then you should try to get the project cancelled or step down as project manager. Not only is this good business practice, it is the only ethical alternative.

9.5 ELEMENTS OF BUDGETS AND ESTIMATES

The similarity between budgets and estimates is that both state the cost of doing something. The difference is that the estimate comes first and is the basis for the budget. An estimate may have to be refined many times, but once it is approved, it becomes the budget. Organizations and work units are then committed to performing work according to the budget: It is the agreed-upon contracted amount of what the work should cost and the baseline against which expenditures will be compared for tracking and control purposes. Project budgets are similar to fiscal operating budgets with the difference that the former covers the life of the project, but the latter covers only a year at a time.

Estimates and budgets share most or all of the following elements:

Direct labor expense
Direct nonlabor expense
Overhead expense
General and administrative expense
Profit
Total billing

Direct Labor Expense[13]

Direct labor expense is the charge of labor for the project. For each task indicated on the project schedule, an estimate is made of how many people will be needed in each labor grade and for how many hours or days of work. This gives the distribution of labor hours or days required for each labor grade. The labor hours for the various grades are then multiplied by their respective wage rates. The work package in Figure 9-4 is an example, showing the wage rates for three labor grades and the associated labor hours time-phased over a 6-month period.

When the wage rate is expected to change over the course of the work, a weighted average wage rate is used. In Figure 9-4, suppose the initial rate for assistant is expected to increase from $20 to $25 in months 3, 4, and 5. The labor cost for assistant in months 2, 3, 4, and 5 would then increase from $8000 to $100(\$20) + 100(\$25) + 100(\$25) + 100(\$25) = \$9500$. (The average wage rate would thus be $\$9500/400$ hours $= \$23.75$/hour.) Notice that the average wage rate changes whenever the distribution of hours changes. In the example, had the work been evenly distributed 100 hours/month over months 1 through 4 (instead of over months 2 through 5), the average wage for assistant would have been $\$9000/400$ hours $= \$22.50$/hour.

Project CASTLE Date April 1, 1592

Department Excavating Work Package Moat

Charge	Rate	Months⁺						Totals	
		1	2	3	4	5	6	Hours	Cost
Direct labor									
Professional	$35/hr	50				50		100	3,500
Associate	$30/hr								
Assistant	$20/hr		100	100	100	100		400	8,000
Direct labor cost		1,750	2,000	2,000	2,000	3,750			11,500
Labor overhead	75%	1,312	1,500	1,500	1,500	2,813			8,625
Other direct cost*			100						100
Total direct cost		3,062	3,600	3,500	3,500	6,563			20,225
General/adminstration	10%	306	360	350	350	657			2,023
Total costs		3,368	3,960	3,850	3,850	7,220			22,248
Profit	15%								
Billing total									

⁺Should extend for as many months as required by the project.
*Should be itemized to include costs for materials, freight, subcontracts, travel, and all other nonlabor direct costs.

Figure 9-4
Typical 6-month cost report for a work package.

Direct Nonlabor Expense

Direct nonlabor expense is the total expense of nonlabor charges applied directly to the task. It includes subcontractors, consultants, travel, telephone, computer time, material costs, purchased parts, and freight. In Figure 9-4 this expense is represented by the line "other direct cost." Material costs include allotments for waste and spoilage and should reflect anticipated price increases. Material costs and freight charges sometimes appear as separate line items called *direct materials* and *overhead on materials,* respectively; computer time and consultants may appear as *support.*

Direct nonlabor expenses also include items necessary for installation and operation such as maintenance manuals, engineering and programming documentation, instruction manuals, drawings, and spare parts. Note that these are costs incurred only for a specific project or work package. Not included are the general or overhead costs of doing business, unless those costs are tied to the specific project.

On smaller projects all direct nonlabor expenses are individually estimated for each work package. In larger projects, a simple percentage rate is applied to cover travel and freight costs. For example, 5 percent of direct labor cost might be included as travel expense and 5 percent of material costs as freight. These percentages are estimated in the same fashion as the overhead rates discussed next.

Overhead, General, and Administrative Expenses

Direct expenses for labor and materials are easily charged to a specific work package. Many other expenses cannot be easily allocated to specific work packages, nor even to a specific project. These expenses, termed *overhead* or *nondirect expenses* are the cost of doing business. They include whatever is necessary to house and support the labor, including building rents, utilities, clerical assistance, insurance, and equipment. Usually overhead is computed as a percentage of the direct labor cost. Frequently, the rate is around 100 percent but it ranges from as low as 25 percent for companies that do most of their work in the field to over 250 percent for firms with laboratories and expensive equipment.

The actual overhead rate is computed by estimating the annual business overhead expense, then dividing by the projected total direct labor cost for the year. Suppose projections show that total overhead for next year will be $180,000. If total anticipated direct labor charges will total $150,000, then the overhead rate to apply is 180,000/150,000 = 1.20. Thus, for every $1.00 charged to direct labor, $1.20 is charged to overhead.

Although this is the traditional accounting method for deriving the overhead rate, for project management it results in a somewhat arbitrary allocation of costs. This is counterproductive for project control because the sources of many overhead costs are independent of project performance. Overhead costs in projects should thus be treated differently. They should be divided into two categories: *Direct overhead*, which can be allocated in a logical manner; and *indirect overhead*, which cannot. Direct overhead costs can be traced to the support of a particular project or work package, so these costs are allocated only among the specific activities for which they apply. If a department is working on four projects, then its overhead is apportioned among the four projects based on the percentage of labor time it devotes to each. Department overhead should not be allocated to projects in which it is not involved.

Indirect overhead includes general expenses for the corporation. Usually referred to as *general and administrative* expense, or *G&A*, it includes taxes, financing, penalty and warranty costs, accounting and legal support, proposal expenses on lost contracts, marketing and promotion, salaries and expenses of top management, and employee benefits packages. These costs are not tied to any specific project or work package, and are allocated across all projects, to certain projects, or parts of projects. For example, corporate or company-level expenses are allocated across all projects, project management costs are allocated on a per project basis, and departmental overhead is allocated to specific project segments in which the department did work. Overhead expenditures are allocated on a time basis so that as the duration of a given project is extended, so is the period over which G&A is charged.

The actual manner in which indirect costs are apportioned varies in practice. The example for the SETI Company in Table 9-2 shows three methods for distributing indirect costs between two projects, MARS and PLUTO.[14] Notice that although company-wide expenses remain the same, the cost of each project differs depending on the method of allocating indirect costs.

Clients want to know the allocation method used by the contractor, and the contractor should know the allocation method used by subcontractors. For example, Method I is good for the client when the project is labor (DL) intensive, but bad when it is direct nonlabor (DNL) intensive. Method III is the opposite and gives a lower cost when the project is relatively nonlabor intensive (i.e., when labor costs are low but material and parts expenditures are high). This can be seen in Table 9-2 by comparing MARS (somewhat nonlabor intensive) to PLUTO (somewhat labor intensive).

Profit and Total Billing

Profit is the amount left over for the contractor after expenses have been subtracted from the contractual price. It is an agreed-to fixed fee or a percentage of total expenses. (Different ways of determining profit are discussed in Appendix B.) Total billing is the sum of total expenses and profit. Profit and total billing are included for estimates of the project as a whole, for large groups of work packages, and for subcontracted work. They usually do not appear on budgets for lower-level work elements.

Table 9-2 Examples of Indirect Cost Apportionment.

SETI Company Company-wide (indirect costs)
Overhead (rent, utilities, clerical, machinery)   OH   120
General (upper management, staff, benefits, etc.)   G&A   40

Indirect Total   160

Project costs	MARS Project	PLUTO Project	Total
Direct labor (DL)	50	100	150
Direct nonlabor (DNL)	40	10	50
	90	110	

Direct Total   200

Direct and Indirect Total   360

Some methods for apportioning indirect costs:

I. Total indirect proportionate to total direct costs

	MARS	PLUTO	Total
DL and DNL	90	110	200
OH and G&A	72	88	160
	162	198	360

II. OH proportionate to direct labor only; G&A proportionate to all direct costs

	MARS	PLUTO	Total
DL	50	100	150
OH on DL	40	80	120
DNL	40	10	50
G&A on (DL and DNL)	18	22	40
	148	212	360

III. OH proportionate to direct labor only; G&A proportionate to DL and OH and DNL

	MARS	PLUTO	Total
DL and OH and DNL	130	190	320
G&A	16.25	23.75	40
	146.25	213.75	360

9.6 PROJECT COST ACCOUNTING AND MANAGEMENT INFORMATION SYSTEMS

A project is a complex system of workers, materials, and facilities, all for which the cost must be estimated, budgeted, and controlled. Hundreds or thousands of items may be involved. To reduce confusion, improve accuracy, and expedite procedures, a system is needed to compute estimates, store and process budgets, and track costs. The term *project cost accounting system (PCAS)* refers to a structure and methodology, manual or computerized, that enables systematic planning, tracking, and control of project costs. The PCAS is set up by the project manager, project accountant, and involved functional managers. Although the PCAS emphasizes project costs by relating project costs to schedules and work performance, it also permits tracking and control of schedules and work progress. When combined with other project planning, control, and reporting functions, it more generally is referred to as a *project management information system (PMIS)*.

During project planning, costs estimates of work packages are accumulated through the PCAS to produce a total project estimate. These estimates later become the basis upon which total project and work package budgets are created.

After work on the project begins, the PCAS enables total project and subactivity costs to be accumulated, credited, and reported. Time-phased budgets are created to help managers monitor costs to ensure they are allocated against appropriate work, and to verify that work has been completed and charged. The system also provides for revision of budgets.

The functions of the PCAS are reviewed in Figure 9-5.

Example 4: Using a PMIS for Estimating Labor Requirements and Costs[15]

Sigma Associates is a moderately large architectural/engineering firm with a staff of over 100 architects, engineers, and draftsmen supported by 40 information system and office personnel. The firm has developed its own PMIS which, in addition to planning and scheduling functions, stores information about all Sigma projects since 1978.

The project manager begins planning a project by creating a WBS to identify the major work activities (e.g., architectural schematics, design administration, construction cost estimating). Using a menu in the PMIS, she then reviews the history of similar work activities in previous projects and the kind and amount of labor required to do them. By entering factors related to relative project size, relative construction costs, and type of clients, the project manager can forecast the labor requirements for every activity in the project.

The PMIS combines these labor requirements with requirements for existing projects to make a 1-year, manpower loading forecast. The forecast enables the project manager to determine whether or not sufficient labor is available. If it is not, the system aids the project manager in reviewing options, including modifying the original schedule, scheduling overtime, and so on, using resource loading procedures as discussed in Chapter 8.

The labor requirements plan is then given to the comptroller for establishing a budget. The comptroller uses the PMIS to apply one of two hourly rates to each activity in the plan. The first is the average hourly rate of all employees who might work on the activity, and the second is the average rate associated with all hours

Figure 9-5
Elements of project cost accounting system.

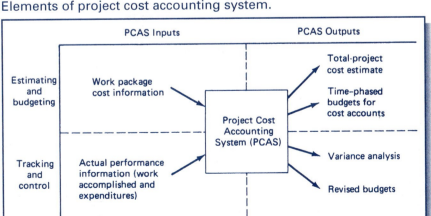

charged to that kind of activity in the last 90 days. The second rate is used more often because it reflects the actual mix of personnel currently employed in similar work. The comptroller then applies factors to account for employee benefits and labor overhead. The result is a budget for direct labor cost.

With information from the company general ledger, the comptroller computes the overhead rate in terms of overhead amount per labor dollar. The project then is charged with this rate for its share of company-wide expenses. Project related, nonlabor expenses that will not be reimbursed by the client (e.g., travel, reproduction, communications) are forecasted and through the PMIS rolled up into the total budget.

When the forecasted total budget is completed, the comptroller analyzes the project plan for profitability. If the plan shows a reasonable profit, the project is accepted. If not, a more profitable plan that maintains the same high-quality standards is sought. When both the comptroller and project manager agree to a plan, the project is accepted.

Time-Phased Budgets

In most projects it is difficult to simultaneously control work schedules and cost expenditures. The project manager needs some way of knowing how the project is progressing, when expenses are occurring, and where problems are developing.

The two primary tools for controlling projects, the project schedule and the project budget, can be consolidated using a cost equivalent to the project schedule called a *time-phased budget.* This is a scheme roughly showing how budgeted costs are distributed over time according to project schedules. Figure 9-4 is an example showing the distribution of costs over one 6-month period. Throughout the duration of the project the PCAS would generate time-phased reports similar to Figure 9-4 for every work package. This allows managers to review planned expenditures on a monthly basis and to compare them with actual expenditures. The reports also are used to perform variance analysis of costs (discussed in Chapter 11) to ensure that work is completed and accurately charged, and to revise estimates and budgets as needed.

9.7   BUDGETING USING COST ACCOUNTS[16]

On small projects, planning and performance monitoring is done using one simple budget for the project as a whole. This budget, perhaps similar in appearance to the one in Figure 9-4, is used as the basis for comparison with actual costs throughout the project.

On larger projects, however, a single, project-wide budget is too insensitive; once the project is underway, should the actual costs begin to exceed budgeted costs it would be difficult to quickly locate the source of the overrun. To overcome this problem the project-wide budget is broken down into smaller budgets called *cost accounts* where each budget is monitored individually. On very small projects there is only one cost account—the budget for the project as a whole. Larger projects have tens of cost accounts; very large projects have many hundreds.

The cost account is the basic project tracking and control unit of the PCAS. A system of cost accounts is set up in a hierarchy, similar or identical to the WBS. Although the lowest level cost account usually corresponds to a work package, cost accounts may also be formed on the basis of several work packages, especially when the number of work packages in a project is very large. A multilevel numerical coding scheme is used to organize, communicate, and control the accounts. For example,

LEVEL	NUMERICAL ASSIGNMENT (COST ACCOUNT NUMBER)
1	01-00-0000....
2	01-01-0000....
3	01-01-1000....
3	01-01-2000....
2	01-02-0000....
3	01-02-1000....
4	01-02-1010....

Cost accounts and work packages are analogous. Each cost account includes

- A description of the work.
- A time schedule.
- Who is responsible.
- Material, labor, and equipment required.
- A time-phased budget.

Notice that with the exception of the time-phased budget, these points are all determined from the WBS analysis. The time-phased budget is derived from the work schedule and shows the distribution of costs throughout the period of the work. In practice, both the schedule and time-phased budget should be developed simultaneously to account for resource and cash flow limitations.

Cost accounts also are established for *nondirect* project costs—costs not readily attributable to any work packages or specific tasks. For example, monies allocated to a project for general purpose items, materials, or equipment that can be used by anyone on any task, or for jobs nonspecific to activities such as administration, supervision, or inspection jobs that apply across the project, are budgeted to separate cost accounts, or, where appropriate, to special work packages for general project items. These accounts are usually set up for the duration of the project and extended, period by period, as needed or as funds are appropriated.

With the PCAS and the cost-account structure, cost performance can be monitored for a work package, groups of work packages, and the project as a whole. As an example consider again the Robotics Self-Budgeting (ROSEBUD) project. Figure 7-15 in Chapter 7 is the project network; Figure 9-6 is the WBS and organization chart for the ROSEBUD contractor, KANE & Associates. The shaded boxes represent locations of cost accounts. Notice that each represents all or part of a work package for which a single functional area is responsible.

The WBS for ROSEBUD results in nine work packages performed by four functional departments plus an additional work package for project management. During the estimating phase each department submits a cost estimate for its part of the project. Through the PCAS these estimates are accumulated upward to derive the total project estimate. Upon approval, with additions for overhead and G&A, each departmental estimate becomes a budget.

In Figure 9-6 the shaded boxes represent where initial estimates were made and budgets will be set up. In this example, they also represent cost accounts. The total project budget is the sum of the 10 budgets. In particular, Figures 9-7 and 9-8 show, respectively, the time-phased budget portions of the cost accounts for the programming department and for work packages L and W.

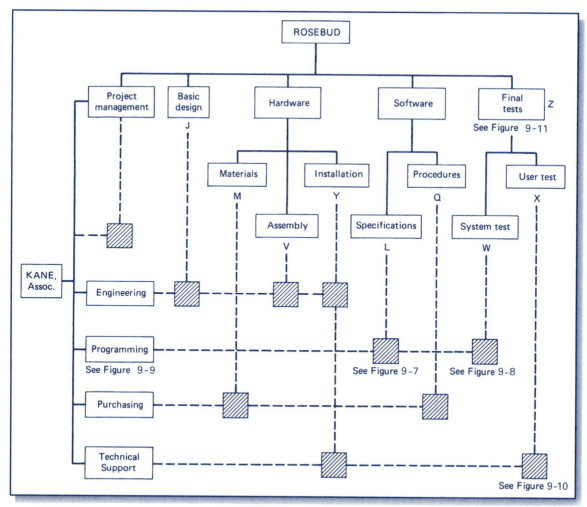

Figure 9-6

Integration of WBS and organization structure showing cost accounts. (See Figures 9-7 to 9-11 for details.)

9.8 Cost Summaries[17]

The cost account structure can be a matrix. If desired, higher-level summary accounts can be developed by consolidating cost accounts through the WBS and organizational hierarchies. Cost-summary accounts are obtained with a computerized PCAS although for small projects they also can be developed manually.

Consolidating basic cost-account information is useful for monitoring the performance of individual departments and segments of the project. For example, consolidating accounts horizontally in Figure 9-6 results in a cost account for each functional department. Figure 9-9 shows this in the time-phased budget summary for the programming department, which is the sum of the programming costs for work packages L and W (Figures 9-7 and 9-8). This is the budget for the ROSEBUD cost account for the programming department.

Cost accounts also can be consolidated vertically through the WBS. This information is useful for tracking and controlling individual work packages, clusters of work

Figure 9-7
Budget for programming department for Work Package L.

Project ROSEBUD					Date					
Department Programming					Work Package L- S/W Specifications					

Charge	Rate	Months+						Totals	
		1	2	3	4	5	6	Hours	Cost
Direct labor									
Professional	$35/hr.		130					130	4,550
Associate	$30/hr		50	100				150	4,500
Assistant	$20/hr			100				100	2,000
Direct labor cost			6,050	5,000					11,050
Labor overhead	75%		4,538	3,750					8,288
Other direct cost*									0
Total direct cost			10,588	8,750					19,338
General/administrative	10%		1,059	875					1,934
Total costs			11,647	9,625					21,272

+ Should extend for as many months as required by the project.
* Should be itemized to include costs for materials, freight, subcontracts, travel, and all other nonlabor direct costs.

packages, or the project as a whole. Figure 9-11 illustrates this with the budget summary for final tests, which sums the costs from work packages W (Figure 9-8) and X (Figure 9-10).

The highest-level cost accounts are for the project and the company. Figure 9-12 shows how costs are aggregated vertically and horizontally to derive these costs. Through the PCAS and cost-account structure, any deviation from budget at the

Figure 9-8
Budget for programming department for Work Package W.

Project ROSEBUD					Date					
Department Programming					Work Package W- System Test					

Charge	Rate	Months+						Totals	
		1	2	3	4	5	6	Hours	Cost
Direct labor									
Professional	$35/hr						20	20	700
Associate	$30/hr						50	50	1,500
Assistant	$20/hr								0
Direct labor cost							2,200		2,200
Labor overhead	75%						1,650		1,650
Other direct cost*							0		0
Total direct cost							3,850		3,850
General/administrative	10%						385		385
Total costs							4,235		4,235

+ Should extend for as many months as required by the project.
* Should be itemized to include costs for materials, freight, subcontracts, travel, and all other nonlabor direct costs.

Charge	Rate	1	2	3	4	5	6	Hours	Cost
Project ROSEBUD — **Department** Programming — **Date** — **Work Package** All									
Direct labor									
Professional	$35/hr		130				20	150	5,250
Associate	$30/hr		50	100			50	200	6,000
Assistant	$20/hr			100				100	2,000
Direct labor cost			6,050	5,000			2,200		13,250
Labor overhead	75%		4,538	3,750			1,650		9,938
Other direct cost*									0
Total direct cost			10,588	8,750			3,850		23,188
General/administrative	10%		1,059	875			385		2,319
Total costs			11,647	9,625			4,235		25,507

+ Should extend for as many months as required by the project.
* Should be itemized to include costs for materials, freight, subcontracts, travel, and all other nonlabor direct costs.

Figure 9-9
Budget summary for programming department.

project level can readily be traced to the work packages and departments responsible. Chapter 11 describes specifically how this is done.

Most PCASs can be used to create a variety of cost summaries, depending on the purpose. Table 9-3 is an example, showing the allocation of certain budget elements—direct labor, overhead, materials, and G&A—among the four departments and seven work packages that comprise the ROSEBUD project.

Figure 9-10
Budget summary for user test work package.

Charge	Rate	1	2	3	4	5	6	Hours	Cost
Project ROSEBUD — **Department** Technical Service — **Date** — **Work Package** X- User Test									
Direct labor									
Professional	$35/hr						10	10	350
Associate	$30/hr						40	40	1,200
Assistant	$20/hr								
Direct labor cost							1,550		1,550
Labor overhead	75%						1,163		1,163
Other direct cost*						1,200	2,107		3,307
Total direct cost						1,200	4,820		6,020
General/administrative	10%					120	482		602
Total costs						1,320	5,302		6,622

+ Should extend for as many months as required by the project.
* Should be itemized to include costs for materials, freight, subcontracts, travel, and all other nonlabor direct costs.

| Charge | Rate | Months[+] | | | | | | Totals | |
		1	2	3	4	5	6	Hours	Cost
Project ROSEBUD									
Department All									

Project: ROSEBUD
Department: All
Date:
Work Package: (W + X) Final Tests

Charge	Rate	1	2	3	4	5	6	Hours	Cost
Direct labor									
Professional	$35/hr						30	30	1,050
Associate	$30/hr						90	90	2,700
Assistant	$20/hr								0
Direct labor cost							3,750		3,750
Labor overhead	75%						2,813		2,813
Other direct cost*						1,200	2,107		3,307
Total direct cost						1,200	8,670		9,870
General/Administrative	10%					120	867		987
Total costs						1,320	9,537		10,857

[+] Should extend for as many months as required by the project.
* Should be itemized to include costs for materials, freight, subcontracts, travel, and all othe nonlabor direct costs.

Figure 9-11
Budget summary for final tests.

Figure 9-12
Aggregation of cost account information by project and organization.

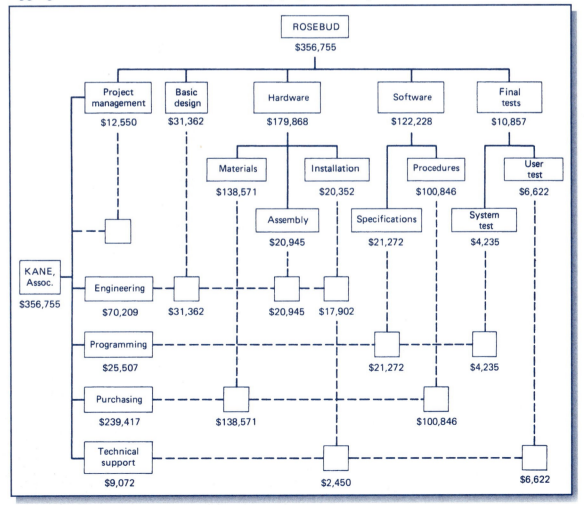

Table 9-3 Cost Summary for ROSEBUD project.

	LABOR ($)				OVERHEAD ($)						
	ENGINEERING	PROGRAMMING	PURCHASING	TECHNICAL SUPPORT	ENGINEERING	PROGRAMMING	PURCHASING	TECHNICAL SUPPORT	MATERIALS	GENERAL AND ADMINISTRATIVE	TOTAL COST
Total project	22,800	13,250	2,230	2,850	22,800	9,938	1,673	2,138	235,236	31,290	356,755
Project management										12,550	12,550
Activity J	7,200				7,200				14,111	2,851	31,362
Activity L*		11,050				8,288				1,934	21,272
Activity M			1,100				825		124,050	12,596	138,571
Activity Q			1,300				818		89,700	9,168	100,846
Activity V	8,200				8,200				2,641	1,904	20,945
Activity Y	7,400			1,300	7,400			975	1,427	1,850	20,352
Activity W		2,200				1,650				385	4,235
Activity X				1,550				1,163		602	6,622

*Refer to Figure 9-7 to see, for example, how costs in this row were developed

Questions arise during planning and budgeting about what the rate of project expenditures will be, which periods will have the heaviest cash requirements, and how expenditures will compare to income. To help answer these questions and others, the project manager analyzes the "pattern of expenditures" using work package cost estimates and cost forecasts derived from the project schedule. Following are some examples.

Cost Analysis with Early and Late Start Times

One simplifying assumption used in cost forecasts is that costs in each work package are incurred uniformly. For example, a 2-week, $22,000 work package is assumed to have a weekly cost of $11,000 per week. With this assumption, a *cost schedule* for the project can be easily created by adding costs, period by period, for the work packages scheduled in each period. As an example, look again at the LOGON project and Figure 9-13, which shows the time-based network using early start times. Table 9-4 shows LOGON work packages and, for each, the corresponding time, total cost, and resulting average weekly direct cost (derived using the simplifying assumption). For example, the average weekly direct cost for Activity H is computed as $100K/10 weeks = $10K/week.

Using the early start schedule in Figure 9-13, the total weekly project cost can be computed by summing the weekly cost for all activities on a week-by-week basis. The procedure is the same as that described in the last chapter for determining resource loading. In the first 10 weeks, only Activity H is scheduled, so the weekly cost stays at $10K. Over the next 6 weeks only activities I and J are scheduled, so the weekly cost is their sum total, $16K + $8K = $24K. Further along, in weeks 17 and 18, four work packages—I, K, L, and J—are scheduled, so the weekly expense is their sum total, $8K + $4K + $18K + $21K = $51K. These weekly expenses, summarized in Table 9-5, represent the cost schedule for the project. Table 9-5 also shows the cumulative project expense, which can be interpreted as the forecasted project cost as of a given week. These costs are shown graphically in Figure 9-14.

Figure 9-13
Time-based network for the LOGON project using early start times.

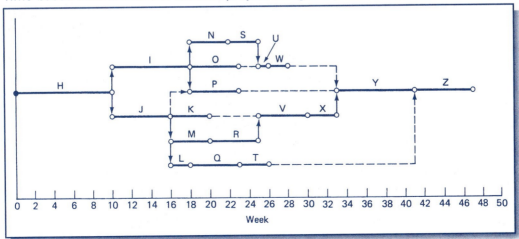

Table 9-4 Activities, Time, Cost, and Labor Requirements (Result of Work Breakdown Analysis).

ACTIVITY	TIME (WEEKS)	TOTAL COST ($K)	WEEKLY DIRECT COST ($K)	WEEKLY LABOR REQUIREMENTS (WORKERS)
H	10	100	10	5
I	8	64	8	4
J	6	96	16	8
K	4	16	4	2
L	2	36	18	6
M	4	84	21	3
N	4	80	20	2
O	5	50	10	5
P	5	60	12	6
Q	5	80	16	2
R	5	0	0	0
S	3	0	0	0
T	3	0	0	0
U	1	14	14	9
V	5	80	16	14
W	2	24	12	6
X	3	36	12	6
Y	8	104	13	14
Z	6	66	11	5

Total Direct Cost—$990K

Project cost schedules and cost forecasts can be prepared in the same fashion using late start times. Figure 9-15 is the time-based network for LOGON using late start times, and Table 9-6 is the associated weekly and cumulative costs.

Given the two cost profiles in Tables 9-5 and 9-6 it is possible to analyze the effect of delaying activities on project costs and budgets. The cost and budget implications of using early start times versus late start times is shown in Figure 9-16. Even if escalation factors are disregarded, changes in the project schedule that significantly influence project cost are apparent. The shaded area in the top figure represents the *feasible budget region,* the range of budgets permitted by changes in the project schedule. The lower part of the figure shows the weekly impact on the cost schedule of delaying activities.

When budgetary restrictions put constraints on project expenditures, cost schedules reveal places of conflict. For example, Figure 9-16 shows a peak weekly expense of $82,000 in Weeks 18 and 19. What if the budget ceiling is only $60,000? In that case the late start times would be preferred because they provide a more "leveled" cost profile and a peak expense of only $54,000. (The general method for leveling resources discussed in Chapter 8 also is applicable to minimizing variation in costs. Costs are treated just as any other resource.)

The forecasts in the previous example were based upon the total budgeted costs for each work package. Similarly, cost schedules and forecasts can be prepared for other specific kinds of costs or portions of budgets—such as direct labor or materials. Table 9-7 shows the labor cost schedule for the ROSEBUD project using early start times. This kind of cost schedule is useful for spotting periods where scheduling

Table 9-5   LOGON Project Weekly Expense Using Early Start Times ($1000).

Week	Activities during Week	Weekly Expense	Cumulative Expense
1	H	10	10
2	H	10	20
3	H	10	30
4	H	10	40
5	H	10	50
6	H	10	60
7	H	10	70
8	H	10	80
9	H	10	90
10	H	10	100
11	I, J	24	124
12	I, J	24	148
13	I, J	24	172
14	I, J	24	196
15	I, J	24	220
16	I, J	24	244
17	I, K, L, M	51	295
18	I, K, L, M	51	346
19	K, M, N, O, P, Q	83	429
20	K, M, N, O, P, Q	83	512
21	N, O, P, Q	58	570
22	N, O, P, Q	58	628
23	O, P, Q	38	666
24	—	0	666
25	—	0	666
26	U, V	30	696
27	V, W	28	724
28	V, W	28	752
29	V	16	768
30	V	16	784
31	X	12	796
32	X	12	808
33	X	12	820
34	Y	13	833
35	Y	13	846
36	Y	13	859
37	Y	13	872
38	Y	13	885
39	Y	13	898
40	Y	13	911
41	Y	13	924
42	Z	11	935
43	Z	11	946
44	Z	11	957
45	Z	11	968
46	Z	11	979
47	Z	11	990

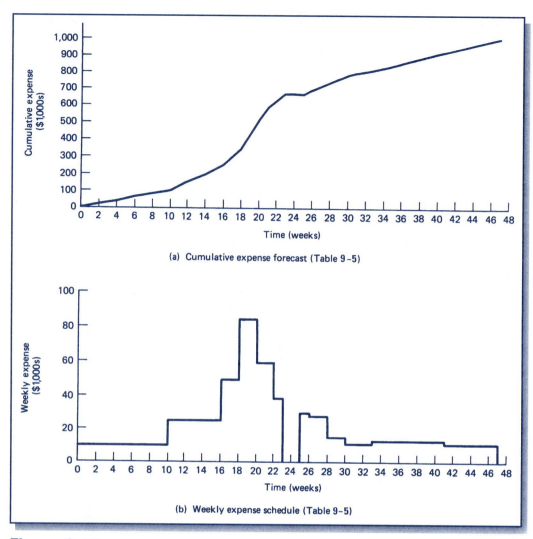

(a) Cumulative expense forecast (Table 9-5)

(b) Weekly expense schedule (Table 9-5)

Figure 9-14
Planned weekly and cumulative expenses for the LOGON project.

Figure 9-15
Time-based network for the LOGON project using late start times.

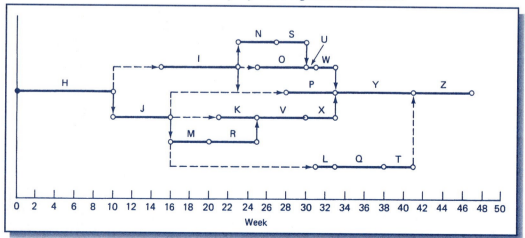

Table 9-6 LOGON Project Weekly Expense Using Late Start Times ($1000).

Week	Activities during Week	Weekly Expense	Cumulative Expense
1	H	10	10
2	H	10	20
3	H	10	30
4	H	10	40
5	H	10	50
6	H	10	60
7	H	10	70
8	H	10	80
9	H	10	90
10	H	10	100
11	J	16	116
12	J	16	132
13	J	16	148
14	J	16	164
15	I, J	24	188
16	I, J	24	212
17	I, M	29	241
18	I, M	29	270
19	I, M	29	299
20	I, M	29	328
21	I, R	8	336
22	K, I, R	12	348
23	K, R	4	352
24	K, R, N	24	376
25	K, R, N	24	400
26	N, O, V	46	446
27	N, O, V	46	492
28	S, O, V	26	518
29	S, O, P, V	38	556
30	S, O, P, V	38	594
31	U, P, X	38	632
32	W, P, X, L	54	686
33	W, P, X, L	54	740
34	Y, Q	29	769
35	Y, Q	29	798
36	Y, Q	29	827
37	Y, Q	29	856
38	Y, Q	29	885
39	Y, T	13	898
40	Y, T	13	911
41	Y, T	13	924
42	Z	11	935
43	Z	11	946
44	Z	11	957
45	Z	11	968
46	Z	11	979
47	Z	11	990

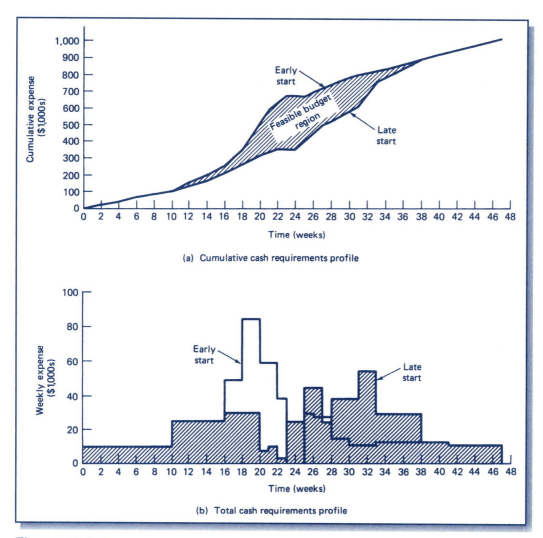

Figure 9-16

Comparison of cash requirements, early versus late start times.

Table 9-7 Labor Cost Schedule, ROSEBUD Project.

DEPARTMENT	MONTHLY COST ($)						TOTAL COST
	1	2	3	4	5	6	
Engineering (Project)	7,200	4,800	3,300	5,100	2,100	300	22,800
Programming*		6,050	5,000			2,200	13,250
Purchasing		1,100	580	550			2,230
Technical service				800	500	1,550	2,850
Total direct labor cost	7,200	11,950	8,880	6,450	2,600	4,050	41,130

*Refer to Figure 9-9, for example, to see how costs in this row were obtained

changes may be necessary to meet payroll ceilings (i.e., when the monthly total direct labor cost cannot exceed a payroll ceiling).

Effect of Late Start Time on Project Net Worth

The time value of money results in work that is done farther in the future having a lower net present value than the same work done earlier. Delaying all activities in a lengthy project can thus provide substantial savings because of differences in the present worth of the project. For example, suppose the LOGON project had a long duration, say 47 *months* instead of the 47 weeks used so far. If an annual interest rate of 24 percent were used, compounded monthly at 2 percent per month, the present worth for the project would be $649,276. This is computed by using the monthly expenses in Table 9-5 (again, assuming the weeks shown to be months instead) and discounting the amounts back to time zero. Now, when the late start times are used instead, the present worth is only $605,915—a savings of $43,361.

Does this mean that activities should always be delayed until their late start date? Not necessarily. Remember, delaying activities uses up slack time and leaves nothing for unexpected problems. If a problem arises, slack is needed to absorb the delay and keep the project on schedule. Thus, whether or not an activity should be delayed depends on the *certainty of the work*. Activities that are familiar and unlikely to encounter problems can be started later to take advantage of the time value of money. However, intentionally eliminating slack in schedules of uncertain activities is risky. Activities that are less familiar, such as research and development work, should be started earlier to retain valuable slack that might be needed to absorb unanticipated delays.

Also, whether or not to delay activities will depend on the schedule of customer payments. If payments are tied to completion of *stages* of the project, then activities essential to their completion cannot be delayed.

Material Expenditures and Cash Flow

Cost schedules and forecasts are also used for estimating cash requirements to meet payments for materials, parts, and equipment.[19] There are several ways to prepare such a cost forecast depending on purpose. The forecast, for example, might represent the cost of materials "when needed;" that is, the cost of materials corresponding to the date when the materials must actually be on hand for use. Alternatively, the forecast might represent the date when actual payments for materials must be made. This forecast will be different from the "when needed" forecast because often a portion of the payment must accompany the order—in other words, the expense *precedes* when the material is needed. Other times payment can be delayed until after the order is received—in other words, the expense *follows* when the material is needed. The costs shown in the time-phased budget usually reflect costs of materials when needed and not when actual payments are due. Because the times when actual expenditures occur seldom correspond to the times shown on time-phased budgets, forecasts should be made to reveal major discrepancies. Figure 9-17 illustrates this point.

A problem often facing the project manager is maintaining a positive cash flow. Throughout the project, differences between cash in and cash out will ideally be small.[20] The project manager must do a juggling act to hold income from the client in balance with expenses for labor, subcontractors, materials, and equipment. To help keep the cash flow in balance, management can, for example, take advantage of the time lag between when materials are needed and when payment for them is required.

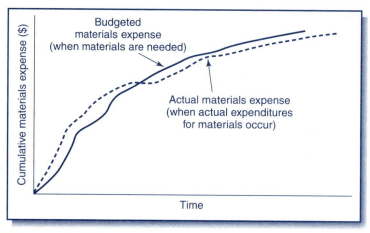

Figure 9-17
Material expenses showing budgeted versus actual expenditures.

Figure 9-18 shows an example of forecast cash flow. All sources of income over the life of the project based on contractual agreements are compared to all foreseeable expenditures—direct and indirect, as well as any penalty costs should the project have to be completed late or terminated. The deficit between forecasted income and estimated expenditures represents the amount of invested or working capital needed to meet payment commitments. Once such a cash flow forecast has been completed, a *funding plan* must be created to ensure that sufficient working capital will be available.[21]

9.10 SUMMARY

Cost estimation and budgeting are part of the project planning process. Cost estimation logically follows work breakdown and precedes project budgeting. Accurate cost estimates are necessary to establish realistic budgets and to provide standards against

Figure 9-18
Balancing project income and expenditures.

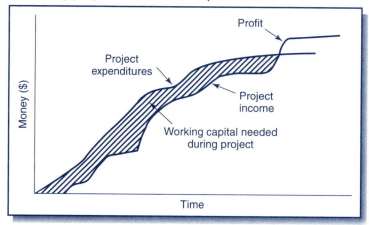

which performance will be measured; they are thus a prerequisite for project tracking and control, and crucial to the financial success of the project.

Costs in projects have a tendency to escalate beyond original estimates. The accuracy of estimates can be improved and cost escalation minimized by using good management, employing skilled estimators, and anticipating the effects of escalation factors such as inflation.

Accuracy of estimates is partly a function of the stage in the systems development cycle during which the estimates are prepared; the further along the cycle, the easier it is to produce accurate estimates. However, good estimates are needed early in the project. Clearly defining project scope and objectives as early as possible, subdividing the project into activities and work packages, and employing standard technology and procedures are ways to improve the accuracy. In general, the smaller the work element being estimated and the more standardized the work, the greater the precision and certainty of the estimate. The aggregate of cost estimates for all subelements of the project plus overhead costs becomes the cost estimate for the overall project. Approved estimates become budgets.

The project budget is subdivided into smaller budgets, called cost accounts. Cost accounts are derived from the WBS and project organization hierarchies and are the financial equivalent to work packages. In larger projects a systematic methodology, or project cost accounting system (PCAS), is useful for aggregating estimates and for maintaining a system of cost accounts for budgeting and control.

Cost schedules show the pattern of costs and expenditures throughout the project. They are used to identify cash and working capital requirements for labor, materials, and equipment.

The last four chapters described steps in the project planning process—things that should be done largely *before* the project begins. Planning precedes action, but only in the simplest sense. The greater the uncertainty in the project, the more that actions will dictate changes be made to the plan. This is to be expected because planners do not have perfect information. Still, under the circumstances, planners work with the intent of creating the best possible plan. The better the plan, the easier it is for participants to communicate intentions, the more prepared they are for contingencies, and the easier it is for them to successfully complete the project.

REVIEW QUESTIONS AND PROBLEMS

1. Why are accurate cost estimates so important, yet so difficult, in project planning? What are the implications and possible consequences of overestimating costs? Of underestimating costs?
2. Define cost escalation. What are major sources of cost escalation?
3. What is the purpose of a contingency fund (management reserve)? How is the contingency fund used and controlled?
4. Describe what the term "phased project planning" means.
5. How do changes in requirements cause cost escalation?
6. How does the type of contractual agreement influence the potential for cost escalation?
7. What is the relationship between phases of the project life cycle and cost escalation?
8. For each of the following estimating methods, briefly describe the method, and discuss when it is used and the likely estimate accuracy it provides:
   a. Expert opinion
   b. Analogy

c. Parametric
d. Cost engineering

9. Describe the process of using the WBS to develop cost estimates. How are these estimates aggregated into total project cost estimates?
10. What is the role of individual functional and subcontracting units in cost estimating?
11. Describe the different kinds of contingency amounts and the purposes each serves.
12. Describe the project cost accounting system (PCAS). What is its purpose and how is it used in project planning?
13. What is a time-phased budget? What is the difference between a budget and a cost estimate?
14. Distinguish recurring costs from nonrecurring costs.
15. What are six cost elements shared by most estimates and budgets?
16. How are direct labor expenses determined?
17. What expenses are included under direct nonlabor?
18. How is the overhead rate determined?
19. What is a cost account and what kinds of information does it contain? How does a cost account fit into the structure of the PCAS?
20. How are cost accounts aggregated horizontally and vertically? Why are they aggregated like this?
21. How are time-based forecasts prepared and how are they used?
22. What are the reasons for investigating the influence of schedules on project costs? What is the feasible budget region?
23. What might happen if top management submitted a bid for a project without consulting the management of the areas to be involved in the project?
24. Refer to Case 1, the Barrage Construction Company, in Chapter 6. In the case the project manager Sean Shawn employed the analogy method with an adjustment to estimate the cost of constructing a three-car garage. Specifically, he started with the cost of an average two-car garage, $43,000, and increased it by 50 percent to $64,500. Comment on the accuracy of the three-car garage estimate. Suggest a different approach that would probably yield a more accurate cost estimate, then use this approach and made-up time and cost figures to compute the estimate. Argue why your estimate is better than Sean's. Figure 9-19 is Sean's WBS.

Figure 9-19
Sean's garage WBS.

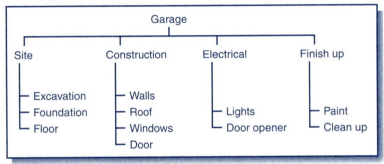

25. The example in Table 9-2 shows three possible ways of apportioning total direct costs. Suppose, using the same example, the direct nonlabor (DNL) cost and G&A are broken down as follows:

Direct Nonlabor

	MARS	PLUTO		G&A
Materials	30	5	Freight	8
Other	10	5	Other	32
	40	10		40

Assuming all remaining costs shown in Table 9-2 are unchanged, compute the project costs for MARS and PLUTO using the following apportioning rules:
   a. Overhead (OH) is proportionate to direct labor (DL).
   b. Freight G&A is proportionate to materials.
   c. Other G&A is proportionate to DL, OH, DNL, and freight.

26. Chapter 8 discussed the impact of crashing activities and the relationship of schedules to cost. The assumption was that as activity duration was decreased, the direct cost increased owing to the increase in direct labor rates from over-time. Overhead rates also may vary, although the overhead rate is often *lower* for overtime work. For example, the overhead rate may be 100 percent for regular time but only 20 percent for overtime. In both cases, the overhead rate is associated with the wage rate being used.

   Suppose that in the MARS project in Table 9-2, 1,000 direct hours of labor are required at $50 per hour, and the associated overhead rate is 100 percent for regular time. Now suppose for overtime, the wage rate is time-and-a-half and the overhead rate is 10 percent.

   Compare the project cost if it were done entirely on regular time with the cost if it were done entirely on overtime. Which is less expensive?

27. Use the following table and network in Figure 9-20 to answer questions about the ARGOT project:

Activity	Time (wks)	Weekly Cost ($K)	Total ($K)
A	4	3	12
B	6	4	24
C	3	5	15
D	4	5	20
E	8	3	24
F	3	4	12
G	2	2	4
			111

   a. Compute the ESs and LSs for the project. Assume T_s is the same as the earliest project completion date.
   b. Construct a time-based network for the project such as Figure 9-13 (use early start times).
   c. Construct two diagrams similar to those in Figure 9-14 showing the weekly and cumulative project expenses.

28. Using the data in problem 27, repeat Steps b and c using late start times. Then identify the feasible budget region using the cumulative curves.

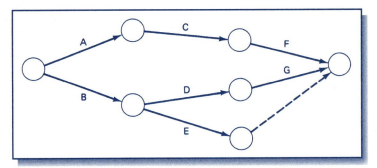

Figure 9-20
ARGOT project.

QUESTIONS ABOUT THE STUDY PROJECT

1. How were project costs estimated? Who was involved? Describe the process.
2. When did estimating take place? How were estimates checked and accumulated? How were they related to the WBS?
3. What, if any, were the principle causes of cost escalation in the project?
4. How often and under what circumstances were cost estimates revised during the project?
5. How were overhead costs determined? What basis was used for establishing overhead cost rates?
6. How were cost estimates tallied to arrive at a total project cost estimate? Who did this?
7. What kind of project cost accounting system (PCAS) was used? Was it manual or computerized? Describe the system and its inputs and outputs. Who maintained the system? How was it used during the project?
8. Describe the process of creating the project budget. Show a sample budget (or portion thereof).
9. How were management and supervisory costs handled in the budget?
10. Was the project budget broken down into cost accounts? If so
    a. How were they related to the work packages and WBS, and
    b. How were they tied into the PCAS?
11. What kinds of costs summaries were prepared? Who were they sent to? How were they used? Show some examples.
12. Did the PCAS produce time-phased cost schedules and forecasts? Show some examples. How were they used by the project manager?

Case 9-1 Estimated Tunnel Costs for the Chunnel Project[22]

Before construction began on the English Channel Tunnel (Chunnel) Project, the banks underwriting the project hired engineering consultants to review cost estimates prepared by the contractors. The consultants concluded that the tunneling estimates were 20 percent too high. Their analysis was based on com-parisons of costs from recent European tunnel projects, including 50 German railroad tunnels ranging in length from 400 m to 11 km, to the Chunnel, which would be 49 km in length. The costs of the tunnels ranged from £55 to £140 per cum (cubic meter) of open tunnel; the cost of the Chunnel was estimated at £181 per cum on the British side of the channel and £203 on the French side (the difference owing to more difficult conditions on the French side). The Chunnel is actually three interconnected tunnels—one for trains going in each direction and a smaller service tunnel in between them. Note, however, that the cost estimates are per cubic meter of tunnel, so *presumably,* differences in tunnel lengths and diameters are not major factors. Why might the estimates for the Chunnel be so much higher per cum than the costs for the analogy projects? Discuss possible, logical adjustments to the analogy tunnel project costs to arrive at a cost estimate for the Chunnel tunnel.

ENDNOTES

1. See F. L. Harrison, *Advanced Project Management* (Hants, England: Gower, 1981): 147–48.
2. See R. D. Archibald, *Managing High-Technology Programs and Projects* (New York: John Wiley & Sons, 1976): 167–68.
3. See Harrison, *Advanced Project Management,* 148–52.
4. Ibid., 172–73, gives an example of an escalation clause.
5. Politically, how independent should the estimators be? So independent, says DeMarco, that the project manager has "no communication with the estimator about how happy or unhappy anyone is about the estimate." See Tom De-Marco, *Controlling Software Projects* (New York: Yourdon Press, 1982): 19.
6. A more complete discussion is found in Harrison, *Advanced Project Management,* 162–71.
7. Ibid., 154–61.
8. Archibald, *Managing High-Technology Programs and Projects,* 171.
9. J. Dingle, *Project Management: Orientation for Decision Makers* (London: Arnold/John Wiley & Sons, 1997): 105.
10. A complete discussion of the pricing review procedure is given by Harold Kerzner, *Project Management: A Systems Approach to Planning, Scheduling, and Controlling,* 5th ed. (New York: Van Nostrand Reinhold, 1995): 724–28.
11. See Milton Rosenau, *Successful Project Management* (Belmont, CA: Lifetime Learning, 1981): 91.
12. Ibid., 91–92.
13. A thorough discussion of labor pricing is given by Kerzner, *Project Management,* 728–32. This example is derived from Kerzner.
14. This example is derived from a similar one in Rosenau, *Successful Project Management,* 89–91.
15. This example is derived from Thomas Wilson and David Stone, "Project Management for an Architectural Firm," *Management Accounting* (October 1980): 25–46.
16. See Harrison, *Advanced Project Management,* 199–202 for further discussion of cost accounts.
17. The kinds of cost summaries used often depends on what is available in the software, though many software packages permit customizing of reports.
18. J. D. Wiest and F. K. Levy, *A Management Guide to PERT/CPM,* 2d ed. (Upper Saddler River, NJ: Prentice Hall, 1977): 90–94.
19. See Kerzner, *Project Management,* 396–98, for an example of a material expenditure forecast.
20. Harrison notes that keeping cash in balance in foreign contracts is especially difficult because foreign currency use must be managed: "In many cases, the profits from [currency dealings] can exceed the profits from the project; in others, if this is not managed effectively, the losses from foreign currency commitments can bring about large losses on a project and lead to bankruptcy." See Harrison, *Advanced Project Management,* 185.
21. See Archibald, *Managing High-Technology Programs and Projects,* 168.
22. Drew Fetherston, *The Chunnel* (New York: Times Books, 1997): 141–42.

Chapter 10

Managing Risks in Projects

> Life "looks just a little more mathematical and regular than it is; its exactitude is obvious, but its inexactitude is hidden; its wildness lies in wait."
>
> G. K. CHESTERTON[1]

> When our world was created, nobody remembered to include certainty.
>
> PETER BERNSTEIN[2]

Every project is risky, meaning there is a chance things won't turn out exactly as planned. Project outcomes are determined by many things, some that are unpredictable and over which project managers have little control. Risk level is associated with the certainty level about technical, schedule, and cost outcomes. High-certainty outcomes have low risk; low-certainty outcomes have high risk. Certainty derives from knowledge and experience gained in prior projects, as well as from management's ability to control project outcomes and respond to emerging problems.[3] This chapter discusses how sources of risk in projects are identified, how risks are assessed or measured in terms of likelihood, impact, and consequences, and appropriate ways of dealing with risks.

10.1   RISK CONCEPTS

In general, risk is a function of the uniqueness of a project and the experience of the project team. When activities are routine or have been performed many times before, managers can anticipate the range of potential outcomes and manipulate aspects of the system design and project plan to achieve the outcomes desired. When the project is unique or the team is inexperienced, the potential outcomes are more uncertain, making it difficult to know what could go wrong and how to avoid problems. Even in routine projects there is risk because outcomes may be influenced either by factors that are new and emerging, or those beyond anyone's control.

The notion of project risk involves two concepts:

1. The *likelihood* that some problematical event will occur.
2. The *impact* of the event if it does occur.

Risk is a joint function of the two; that is,

$$\text{Risk} = f(\text{likelihood, impact})$$

Given that risk involves both likelihood and impact, a project will be ordinarily considered risky whenever at least one factor—either the likelihood or the impact—is large. For example, a project will be considered risky where the potential impact is human fatality or massive financial loss even when the likelihood of either is small.

Though risk cannot be eliminated from projects, it can be reduced. That is the purpose of risk management. There are three major aspects of risk management: risk identification, risk assessment, and risk response planning.

10.2   RISK IDENTIFICATION

Before you can manage something, you must first know about it. Thus, risk management begins with identifying the risks and predicting their consequences. If a risk and its consequences are significant, ways must be found to avoid the risk or reduce it to an acceptable level. What is considered acceptable risk depends on the *risk tolerance* of project stakeholders and managers. Often, experienced managers and stakeholders are somewhat more careful (and risk averse) because they understand the risks and their consequences, whereas less experienced stakeholders tend to be greater risk-takers (more risk tolerant) because they don't know of the risks or are ignorant of the consequences.

Risk in projects is sometimes referred to as the risk of *failure*, which implies that a project might fall short of schedule, budget, or technical goals by a large margin. There is also the risk of *opportunity*, which are events that could lead to rewards, savings, or benefits. The main emphasis of risk identification is usually on determining the risk of failure.

There are many ways to identify project risks. One method proceeds according to project chronology; that is, the risks associated with phases and events throughout the project life cycle such as project feasibility, contract negotiation, engineering concept, or system definition, design, and development are separately identified. Each phase presents unique hurdles and problems that may ruin the project immediately or lead to later failure. For instance, in product development projects the number of hurdles and risk of failure tend to be high during the early stages of preliminary design and testing, but diminish as the project progresses. Some risks that remain may lead to project failure at any time; two examples include loss of funding and management commitment.

Risk can also be classified according to type of work or technical function, such as engineering risks associated with product reliability and maintainability, or production risks associated with the ability to manufacture a product, the availability of raw materials, or the reliability of production equipment.

Identifying project risks should start early in the conception phase. The emphasis at that time is on identifying the high risks—factors that might make the project difficult to execute or destine it to failure. High risks in projects typically stem from

- Using an unusual approach.
- Attempting to further technology.
- Training for new tasks or applying new skills.
- Developing and testing of new equipment, systems, or procedures.

The areas or sources of high risk must be studied and well-understood before deciding to approve a project and commit funds to it. Although risks identified in the conception phase are often broadly defined and assessed subjectively, they might also be subject to detailed quantitative analysis using methods discussed later. When multiple, completing projects are under consideration, a comparative assessment should be performed. The result can help managers to decide which of them, based upon trade-offs of the relative risks, benefits, and available funding, should be approved.[4]

Sources of Risk

Any factor with an uncertain probability of occurring that can influence the outcome of a project is considered a *risk source* or *risk hazard.* Identifying hazards involves learning as much as possible about what things could affect the project or could go wrong, and what the outcome for each would be. The purpose of such deliberation is to identify all sources of significant risk, including sources yet unknown. (The most difficult part of risk identification is discovering things you don't already know.)

Risk in projects can be classified as internal risks and external risks.

Internal Risks.   *Internal* risks originate inside the project. Project managers and stakeholders usually have a measure of control over these. Two main categories of internal risks are market risk and technical risk.

Market risk is the risk of not fulfilling either market needs or the requirements of particular customers. Sources of market risk include

- Incompletely or inadequately defined market or customer needs and requirements.
- Failure to identify changing needs and requirements.
- Failure to identify newly introduced products by competitors.

Market risk can be reduced by thoroughly and accurately defining needs and requirements at the start of the project, and continuously monitoring and updating requirements as needed throughout the project.

Technical risk is the risk of not meeting time, cost, or performance requirements due to technical problems with the end-item or project activities. Technical risk tends to be high in projects involving activities that are unfamiliar or require new ways of integration. It is especially high in projects that involve new and untried technical applications. Technical risk is low in projects that involve mostly familiar activities done in customary ways.

One approach to expressing technical risk is to rate the risk of the project end-item or primary process as being high, medium, or low according to the following features:[5]

- *Maturity.* How ready is the end-item or process for production or use? An end-item or process that is preexisting, installed and operational, or based on experience and preexisting knowledge entails less risk than an end-item or process that is in the early stages of development, new and cutting edge, or trend-setting.

- *Complexity.* How many steps, elements, or components are in the product or process, and what are their relationships? An end-item or process with numerous interrelated steps or components is more risky than one with few steps or components that have few, simple relationships.

- *Quality.* How producible, reliable, and testable is the end-item or process? In general, an end-item or process that is known to be completely producible, reliable, or testable is less risky than one that has not yet been produced or has low reliability or testability.

- *Concurrency,* or *Dependency.* To what extent do multiple, dependent activities in the project overlap? In general, risk increases the more that activities overlap one another: Sequential, dependent activities with no overlap are much less risky than those with much overlap.

External Risks. The other main risk category is *external* risks, which includes only risks that stem from sources outside the project. Project managers and stakeholders usually have little or no control over these. External risk hazards include changes in:

Market conditions	Customer needs and behavior
Competitors' actions	Supplier relations
Government regulations	Weather (adverse)
Interest rates	Labor availability (strikes and walkouts)
Decisions made by senior management or the customer regarding project priorities, staffing, or budgets	Material or labor resources (shortages)
	External control by customers or subcontractors over project work and resources

Although the success of a project can be affected by any of these, the question remains: To *what extent* can any of these affect project success? A project where success depends heavily on external factors such as market conditions or facilities controlled by a customer or vendor is beset with much more external risk than one with few dependencies on external factors.

Identification Techniques

Project risks are identified from analysis of the numerous documents reviewed or prepared during project conception and definition. These documents include reports from past projects, lists of user needs and requirements, WBSs, work package definitions, cost estimates, schedules, and schematics and models of end-items. Among the techniques for pinpointing risks are analogy, checklists, WBS analysis, process flowcharts, and brainstorming.

The *analogy* technique involves looking at records, postcompletion summaries, and project team members' notes and recollections from previous, similar projects to identify risks in new, upcoming projects. The better the documentation (more complete, accurate, and well-catalogued) and the better peoples' memories, the more useful the information is for identifying potential problems and hazards in future, similar projects. Of course, the technique requires more than just information about past projects; it also requires a history of past projects that are similar, in significant ways, to the new project for which risks are being assessed.

Documentation from prior projects also is used to create risk *checklists*—lists of factors that can affect the risk in a project. Risk checklists can be created for the overall project or for specific phases, work packages, or tasks within the project. They might also specify the *levels* of risk thought to be associated with risk sources. The levels specified are based on personal judgment and assessments of past projects.

To illustrate, the checklist in Table 10-1 shows three categories of risk sources: (1) status of implementation plan, (2) number of module interfaces, and (3) percentage of components requiring testing, and the risk level associated with each. Suppose, for example, that an upcoming project will use a standard completed plan, have eight modules, and test 15 percent of the system components. According to the checklist, the project will be rated as low risk, low risk, and medium risk, respectively, for the three risk sources.

The greater the relevant experience from past projects, the more comprehensive the checklist and valid the assessed levels of risk. As experience grows with completed projects, the risk checklists are expanded and updated. A good checklist is never considered complete: Its composers acknowledge that not all the risks are known, and that other risks will be discovered over time. Although using checklists cannot guarantee that all significant risk sources in a project will be identified, it does help ensure that important areas of risks are not overlooked.

Another way to identify sources of risk is to analyze the *WBS*. Every work package is scrutinized for potential problems with management, customers, suppliers, equipment and resource availability, and technical hurdles. Within each work pack-

Table 10-1 Risk Checklist.

Risk Sources	Risk Level
Status of implementation plan	
1. No plan required	None
2. Standard plan, existing, complete	Low
3. Plan being prepared	Medium
4. Plan not started	High
Number of interfaces between modules	
1. Less than 5	None
2. 5–10	Low
3. 11–20	Medium
4. More than 20	High
Percent of system components requiring tests	
1. 0–1	None
2. 2–10	Low
3. 11–30	Medium
4. Over 30	High

age, processes or end-items are assessed for internal risk in terms of the features described before—complexity, maturity, quality, and concurrency or dependency. Each work package also is assessed for external risks; for example, work package tasks to be performed by a subcontractor with little contractor oversight.

Project risks can also be identified with process *flowcharts*. A flowchart illustrates the steps, procedures, and flows between tasks and activities in a process. The functional process designs in Figures 5-3 and 5-4 are examples. Examination of a flowchart can pinpoint potential trouble spots and areas of risk. Similarly, scrutiny of the precedence relationships and concurrent or sequential scheduling of activities in a *project network* can reveal potential problems and risks.

In addition to these techniques, risks can be identified from the collective experience of project team members. Team members meet in a *brainstorming* session to share opinions and generate ideas about possible problems or hazards in the project. Ideas can be recorded on a *cause-and-effect diagram* as shown in Figure 10-1. Brainstorming and cause-and-effect diagrams are used in two ways: (1) Given an identified, potential outcome (*effect*), they can identify potential *causes* (hazards); (2) Given a risk hazard (*cause*), they can identify outcomes that might ensue (*effects*). Figure 10-1 illustrates the first use: For the outcome "completion delay," it shows the potential hazards that could lead to delay.

The diagram in Figure 10-1 is divided into the generic risk categories (hazards) of problems with software, hardware, and so on. (Other generic categories not shown are poor time and cost estimates, design errors or omissions, changes in requirements, and unavailability or inadequacy of resources.) Each generic risk hazard might be

Figure 10-1
Cause-and-effect diagram.

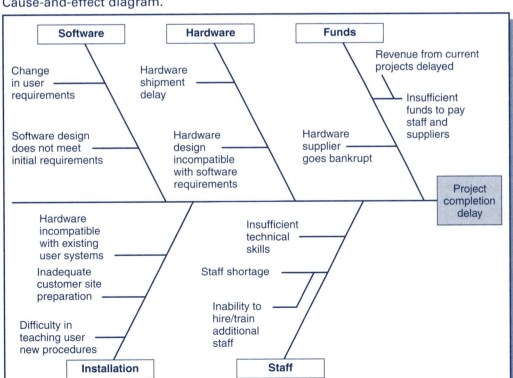

broken down into more fundamental sources of risk (i.e., factors leading to the hazards). In Figure 10-1, for example, the hazard "staff shortage" is shown as caused from inability to hire and train additional workers.

As the sources and outcomes of each risk are identified, so are the *symptoms* and warning signs. These are visible indicators that a given risk has materialized. They serve as *triggers* to initiate counteractions or contingencies. For example, a warning sign for the risk of "failure to meet project technical requirements" might be "failure during test of component X," which might trigger the action "modify the system design or its requirements." As another example, a warning sign for the risk of "delayed installation" might be "failure to complete on-site preparation by June 1," which might trigger the action "initiate overtime work."

10.3   RISK ASSESSMENT

Risks are commonplace, but it is only the notable ones that require attention. What is considered notable depends on three things: risk likelihood, risk impact, and risk consequence.

Risk Likelihood

Risk likelihood is the probability that a hazard or risk factor will actually materialize.[6] It can be expressed as a numerical value between 1.0 (certain to happen) and 0 (impossible) or as a qualitative rating such as high, medium, or low. Numerical values and qualitative ratings are sometimes used interchangeably. Table 10-2 shows an example of qualitative ratings and the associated numerical percent values for each. When, for example, someone says, "the likelihood of this or that risk is low," the estimated probability of its happening is 20 percent or less. Alternatively, if someone feels that the probability of risk is between 20 and 50 percent, the risk can be equivalently expressed as "medium."

Table 10-2 is for illustration only. The association between qualitative ratings and particular values is subjective and depends on the experience of the project team and the risk tolerance of stakeholders. For example, Table 10-2 might represent a project with high economic stakes; therefore, a risk likelihood greater than 50 percent equates to "high risk" whereas in another project (one with low economic states), a risk likelihood of 75 percent or higher might equate to "high risk." People often have difficulty agreeing on the appropriate qualitative rating for a given likelihood value, even when they have common information or experience.

Table 10-3 is a checklist that gives numerical likelihood for five potential sources of failure in computer systems projects.[7] It is interpreted as follows: looking just at the

Table 10-2   Risk Likelihood: Qualitative Ratings for Quantitative Values.

QUALITATIVE	NUMERICAL
Low	0–0.20
Medium	0.21–0.50
High	0.51–1.00

Table 10-3 Sources of Failure and Likelihood.
[Adapted from W. Roetzheim, *Structured Computer Project Management* (Upper Saddle River, NJ: Prentice Hall, 1988): 23–26.]

M_S	failure likelihood due to immaturity of software
C_S	failure likelihood due to complexity of software
M_H	failure likelihood due to immaturity of hardware
C_H	failure likelihood due to complexity of hardware
D	failure likelihood due to dependency on external factors

Note: "failure" refers to not meeting technical goals.

LIKELIHOOD	M_H	M_S	C_H	C_S	D
0.1 (low)	Existing	Existing	Simple design	Simple design	Independent
0.3 (minor)	Minor redesign	Minor redesign	Minor complexity	Minor complexity	Schedule dependent on existing system
0.5 (moderate)	Major change feasible	Major change feasible	Moderate complexity	Moderate	Performance dependent on existing system
0.7 (significant)	Complex design; technology exists	New, but similar to existing software	Significant complexity	Significant complexity	Schedule dependent on new system
0.9 (high)	State of the art; some research done	State of the art; never done	Extreme complexity	Extreme complexity	Performance dependent on new system

M_S column, the likelihood of failure is low for existing software, but high when the software is state-of-the-art. Again, the numerical values are illustrative and would be tailored to each project depending on prior project experience or the opinion of stakeholders. In assigning likelihood values or ratings to risk factors, it is best to use collective judgment, including as much knowledge and experience as possible. A likelihood estimate based upon several individual's opinions (assuming all have relevant experience) is usually more valid than one based on only a few people's opinions.

When a project has multiple, independent risk sources, they can be combined and expressed as a single *composite likelihood factor,* or *CLF.* For example, using the sources listed in Table 10-3 the CLF can be computed as a weighted average,

$$\text{CLF} = (W1)M_H + (W2)C_H + (W3)M_S + (W4)C_S + (W5)D \qquad (1)$$

where W1, W2, W3, W4, and W5 each have values 0 through 1.0 and together total 1.0.

Example 1: Computation of CLF

The ROSEBUD project involves development of hardware and software with characteristics as follows: The hardware is existing and of minor complexity; the moderately complex software involves a minor redesign of current software; the performance of the overall system depends on how well it can be integrated into another, larger system. Therefore, from Table 10-3, $M_H = 0.1$, $C_H = 0.3$, $M_S = 0.5$, $C_S = 0.3$, and $D = 0.5$. Assuming all sources are rated equally at 0.2, then

$$\text{CLF} = (0.2)0.1 + (0.2)0.3 + (0.2)0.5 + (0.2)0.3 + (0.2)0.5 = 0.34$$

The application of this CLF is discussed later.

Note that the computation in equation (1) assumes that the risk sources are independent. Often they are *not* independent; for example, when the failure likelihood due to software complexity depends on the failure likelihood due to hardware complexity, the individual likelihood for each cannot be summed. In such a situation, the sources would be subjectively combined into one source ("failure due to a combination of software and hardware complexity"), and a single likelihood value can be assigned.

The risk factors in a project may be interrelated, and one way to show that is with an *influence diagram* such as Figure 10-2.[8] To construct a diagram, start with a list of previously identified risks and space them apart as shown in Figure 10-2. Then look at each risk and ask whether it is influenced by, or has influence on, any of the other risks. If the answer is yes, draw lines between the related risks. The arrows indicate the direction of influence (for example, S.1 influences S.2 and I.2). To minimize confusion, keep the number of risks on the diagram to 15 or fewer.

Risks with the most connections are the most important. Notice in Figure 10-2 that risks I.2, S.1, and S.2 are each influenced by other risks, which would increase their failure likelihood.

Risk likelihood also is affected by the future: *ceteris paribus*, activities planned further in the future have a greater likelihood of failure than those that are closer at hand.[9] That is because activities planned for farther in the future possess greater chances of being influenced by unknowns. After the project has been executed and activities progressively completed, the likelihood of failure diminishes. As project completion approaches, the likelihood of failure becomes very small. (That doesn't mean, however,

Figure 10-2
Influence diagram.

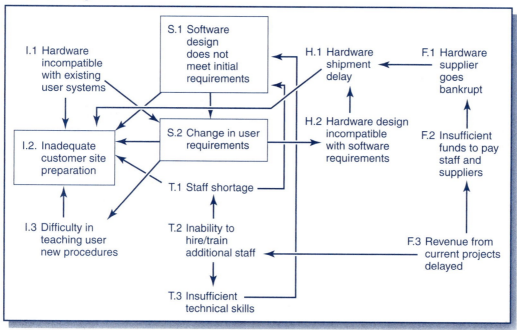

that concern for risk disappears. There is a trade-off: Although failure likelihood diminishes with time, the *stake* in the project—the amount of human and financial capital sunk into it—increases, which means that the loss suffered from project failure is greater with time. Hence, risk remains important throughout the project.)

Risk Impact

What would happen if a risk hazard materialized? The result would be called *risk impact*. A poorly marked highway intersection is a risk hazard; the risk posed is that of collision with the impact of injury or death. Risk impact in projects is specified in terms of time, cost, and performance measures. For example, insufficient numbers of skilled labor to staff a project has the impact of extending the schedule or preventing the project from meeting user requirements. The exact amount by which the schedule or requirements would be affected are based on opinions of project managers and staff.

Risk impact can be expressed as a qualitative rating such as high, medium, or low. The rating is subjective and depends upon the opinion of managers about the importance of the risk. For example, a risk leading to a schedule delay of 1 month or less might be considered "low impact," whereas a delay of 3 months or more might be deemed "high impact."

Risk impact also can be expressed as a numerical measure between 0 and 1.0, where 0 is "not serious" and 1.0 is "catastrophic." Again, the rating is subjective and depends on opinion. Table 10-4 is an example of project technical, cost, and schedule impacts and suggested qualitative and numerical ratings associated with them.[10] The ratings represent the impact of failure to meet technical goals on technical performance, cost, and schedule.

Just as the likelihoods for multiple risks can be combined, so can the impacts from multiple risk sources. A composite impact factor (CIF) can be computed using a simple weighted average,

$$\text{CIF} = (W1)TI + (W2)CI + (W3)SI \qquad (2)$$

where W1, W2, and W3 are valued 0 through 1.0, and together sum to 1.0. CIF will have values between 0.0 and 1.0, where 0 means "no impact" and 1.0 means "the most

Table 10-4 Impact Values for Different Technical, Cost, and Time Situations.
[Adapted from W. Roetzheim, *Structured Computer Project Management* (Upper Saddle River, NJ: Prentice Hall, 1988): 23–26.]

IMPACT VALUE	TECHNICAL IMPACT (TI)	COST IMPACT (CI)	SCHEDULE IMPACT (SI)
0.1 (low)	Minimal impact	Within budget	Negligible impact; compensated by scheduled slack time
0.3 (minor)	Small reduction in performance	1–10% cost increase	Minor slip (<1 month)
0.5 (moderate)	Moderate reduction in performance	10–25% cost increase	Moderate slip (1–3 months)
0.7 (significant)	Significant reduction in performance	25–50% cost increase	Significant slip (>3 months)
0.9 (high)	Technical goals might not be achievable	Cost increase in excess of 50%	Large schedule slip (unacceptable)

severe impact." Equation (2) assumes that risk impacts are independent. If they are not, then they must be treated jointly as, for example, the impact of both a 20 percent increase in cost and a 3-month schedule slip.

Example 2: Computation of CIF

Failure in the ROSEBUD project to meet certain technical goals is expected to have minimal impact on technical performance and be corrected within 2 months at an additional cost of 20 percent. Therefore, from Table 10-4:

$$TI = 0.1, CI = 0.5, SI = 0.5$$

Suppose the most important criteria is technical performance, followed by the schedule, then cost, so that the weights assigned to them are 0.5, 0.3, and 0.2, respectively. Therefore, from equation (2):

$$CIF = (0.5)(0.1) + (0.3)(0.5) + (0.2)(0.5) = 0.22$$

Application of this CIF is discussed later.

Still another way to express risk impact is in terms of what would be necessary to *recover* from, or compensate for, resulting damages or undesirable outcomes. For example, suppose there is a risk of being unable to meet system performance requirements using a proposed technology. The project will apply the proposed technology, but if tests reveal inadequate performance, then the technology will be abandoned and an alternative, proven approach used instead. The impact of the risk is the cost of switching to the second technology, which would be to, for example, delay the project by 4 months and increase the cost by $300,000.

Risk impact should be assessed for the entire project and expressed with the assumption that no response or preventive measures are taken. In the above instance, $300,000 is the anticipated expense under the assumption that nothing will be done to avoid or prevent the failure of the proposed technology. This assessed impact will be used as a measure to evaluate the effectiveness of possible ways to reduce or prevent risk hazards.[11] This is discussed later in the section on risk analysis methods.

Risk Consequence

The notion of risk was defined early in the chapter as being a function of risk likelihood *and* risk impact. This notion is referred to as the *risk consequence*.

There are two ways to express risk consequence. First, it can be expressed as a simple numerical rating with a value ranging between 0 and 1.0. In that case, the risk consequence rating, RCR, is

$$RCR = CLF + CIF - CLF(CIF) \qquad (3)$$

where CLF and CIF are previously defined in Equations (1) and (2). The risk consequence derived from this equation measures how serious the risk is to project performance. Small values represent unimportant risks that might be ignored, large values represent important risks worth attending to.

Example 3: Risk Consequence Using Subjective Rating

For the ROSEBUD project, the assessed CLF was 0.34 (Example 1) and the CIF was 0.22 (Example 2). Thus, the risk consequence rating is

$$RCR = 0.34 + 0.22 - (0.34)(0.22) = 0.48$$

The consequence rating value is interpreted subjectively. In general, a value over 0.7 would usually be considered a high-risk project, whereas a value under 0.2 would be low risk. A value of 0.48 in most cases would be considered moderate-level risk and, therefore, important enough to merit attention. Management would thus take measures to reduce the risk or prepare contingency plans. Other possible responses to risk are discussed later.

Another way to express risk consequence is as an *expected value.* Expected value can be interpreted as the average outcome if the project was repeated a large number of, for example, 100, times. The risk consequence expected value is computed as

$$\text{Risk consequence} = (\text{Impact}) \times (\text{Likelihood}) \tag{4}$$

Example 4: Risk Consequence Using Expected Value

Suppose the likelihood associated with a risk is 0.40. Also, should this risk materialize, it would set the project back 4 months and increase the cost by an estimated $300,000. The expected risk consequences for time and cost are thus

Risk consequence time (RT) = (4 months)(0.40) = 1.6 months = 6.4 weeks
Risk consequence cost (RC) = ($300,000)(0.40) = $12,000

Expected value is further discussed later in the supplement section on risk analysis methods.

PERT

The PERT method, discussed in Chapter 8, was intended by its originators to account for risk in project scheduling. It is a way to warn managers of the need to compensate for the consequence of a risk on project duration.

The PERT method incorporates risk into project schedules by using three estimates for each project activity: a, m, and b (optimistic, most likely, and pessimistic times, respectively). Greater risk in an activity is reflected by a greater spread between a and b, and especially between m and b. For an activity with no perceived risk, a, m, and b would be identical. If, however, hazards are identified, the way to account for them is to raise the values of b and m. In general, the greater the perceived consequence of risk hazards on time, the further b is from m.

With PERT, recall, it is the average time, not m, that is the basis for scheduled times, where the average time is the mean of the Beta distribution, which is

$$t_e = \frac{a + 4m + b}{6}$$

Thus, for a particular activity with given optimistic and most-likely values (a and m), using a larger value of b to account for greater risk will result in a larger value of t_e, which logically would allow more time to complete the activity and compensate for things that might go wrong (risk hazards). In addition, however, the larger value of b also results in a larger time variance for the activity because variance is

$$V = \left[\frac{b - a}{6}\right]^2$$

This larger V will result in a larger variance for the *project* completion time, which would spur the cautious project manager to add a time buffer or reserve to the project schedule.

Consider a simple example, a project that consists of only one activity and has a target completion time of 8 months. Suppose the activity has little risk and the values of a, m, and b are estimated as 5, 6, and 7 months, respectively. From the formulae, the values of t_e and V are thus 6 months and 0.111 months. Using a normal approximation for project duration and the method discussed in Chapter 8, we can compute the probability of completing the project in 7 months thus:

$$z = \frac{7 - 6}{\sqrt{0.111}} = 3.00$$

and from Table 8-1, this z-value yields a probability of over 99 percent. Assuming management trusts the time estimates, they would likely proceed with the project without worry.

Now, take the same one-activity project and suppose a major risk is identified that would increase the estimate of the pessimistic value from 7 to 12 months. In that case, t_e and V would be 6.83 months and 1.362 months, and z would be

$$z = \frac{7 - 6.83}{\sqrt{1.362}} = 1.00$$

Looking at Table 8-1, this z-value yields a probability of about 84 percent. Given the lower probability of meeting the 8-month target time, management might add a time buffer to the schedule (extend the target time), or take action to reduce the risk (which would allow a lower value for b). In short, assuming that the estimates for a, m, and b are credible, the PERT method provides a way for measuring the consequence of risk on project completion times.

Risk Priority

Projects are subject to numerous risks, yet only a few are important enough to merit attention. Once the risk consequences for a project have been computed, they are rank-ordered and those with moderate-to-high consequences are given a second look. Project team members, managers, subcontractors, and customers review them to ensure everyone's awareness so that the appropriate risk responses can be planned. To better assess the risks, sometimes activities or work packages must be broken down further. For example, before the full consequences and magnitude of the risk of a staffing shortage can be comprehended, the risk must clearly be defined in terms of the specific skill areas affected and the amount of the shortage.

To decide which risks to focus on, management might specify a level of expected value risk consequences, and address only risks at that level or higher. For example, in Table 10-5 if risks with expected consequences of a 2-day or longer delay deserve attention, then only risks S1, F1, T1, T3, I1, I2, and I3 would be addressed.

One drawback with specifying risk priority using expected value is that very low likelihood risks are sometimes ignored even when they have potentially severe, even catastrophic, impact. Suppose, for example, the impact of a project failure is 1,000 fatalities. If the risk likelihood is infinitesimal, then the expected value consequence (tiny likelihood of many fatalities) will be very small and, hence, the risk relegated a low-priority.[12]

In a complex system with a large number of relationships where joint failures in several would lead to system failure, it is common to ignore joint failures in the hope they will not occur or be of only insignificant consequence. Usually the likelihood of joint failure is very low. Very low, however, is not the same as impossible, and a failure with terrible impact should never be ignored, regardless of how small the expected value. For example, the chemical plant accident at Bhopal, India has been attributed to over 30 separate causes, their joint probability being so small as to be beyond consideration. Yet they *all* did happen, causing an accident that resulted in between 1,800 to 10,000 deaths and 100,000 to 200,000 more injuries.[13] Similarly, the

Table 10-5 Risk Likelihood, Risk Impact, and Expected Value Consequence.

	LIKELIHOOD (%)	IMPACT: DAYS LATE	CONSEQUENCES
Software			
S1 Software design does not meet initial requirements	20	10	2
S2 Change in user requirements	30	5	1.5
Hardware			
H1 Hardware shipment delay	5	5	0.25
H2 Hardware design incompatible with software requirements	5	10	0.5
Funds			
F1 Hardware supplier goes bankrupt	5	40	2
F2 Insufficient funds to pay staff and suppliers	5	15	0.75
F3 Revenue from current projects delayed	30	5	1.5
Staff			
T1 Staff shortage	10	20	2
T2 Inability to hire/train additional staff	15	10	1.5
T3 Insufficient technical skills	10	30	3
Installation			
I1 Hardware incompatible with existing user systems	5	60	3
I2 Inadequate customer site preparation	20	10	2
I3 Difficulty in teaching user new procedures	20	20	4

nuclear meltdown at Chernobyl was the result of *six errors* in human action, any one of which, if removed, would have precluded the accident. Despite the minuscule likelihood of all six happening, they did happen with the immediate outcome being an accident that caused several dozen deaths, several hundred hospitalizations, and 135,000 evacuations. More disturbing is the long-term impact: an estimated 5,000 to 24,000 additional cancer deaths in the former Soviet Union, and more throughout Europe and Asia.[14] The lesson: Any risk with severe impact should be carefully considered, no matter how small the likelihood.

10.4   RISK RESPONSE PLANNING

Risk response planning addresses the matter of how to *deal* with risk. In general, the ways of dealing with an identified risk include transferring the risk, altering plans or procedures to avoid or reduce the risk, preparing contingency plans, or accepting the risk.

Transfer the Risk

Risk can be transferred partly or fully from the customer to the contractor, or vice versa, using contractual incentives, warranties, or penalties attached to project performance, cost, or schedule measures. The contractor and customer may decide to split the risk through a contractual agreement in which each manages the risks they can handle best. Different types of contracts split the risks in different ways: In fixed-price contracts, the contractor assumes almost all of the risk for cost overruns; in fixed-price with incentive fee, the contractor accepts roughly 60 percent of the risk, the customer 40 percent; in cost plus incentive fee, the contractor assumes roughly 40 percent, the customer 60 percent, and with cost plus fixed fee (CPFF), the customer assumes almost all of the risk.

Of course it is impossible to entirely transfer the risk to one party or another. Even with a fixed-price contract, where ostensibly the contractor takes all the risk, the customer still incurs damages or hardship should the project exceed the target schedule or the contractor declare bankruptcy. The project still must be completed and someone has to pay for it. Coming along with the transfer of risk usually is a transfer of authority, so that a customer agreeing to a CPFF contract also will almost certainly argue for a large measure of management oversight on the project.

Transfer of one kind of risk often means inheriting another kind of risk. For example, to minimize the financial risk associated with capital cost of tooling and equipment for production of a large, complex system on a mass scale, the manufacturer might subcontract the production of major portions of the system to suppliers who must then assume the financial risk of tooling and equipment. However, the prime manufacturer must now rely on many suppliers, increasing the risks associated with managing quality control and production scheduling. Should the manufacturer feel more capable of handling *management* risks than financial risks, however, the trade-off will be accepted.

Avoid Risk

Risk can be avoided by altering the original project concept (e.g., eliminating risky activities, minimizing system complexity, and reducing end-item quality requirements), changing contractors, incorporating redundancies and safety procedures, and so on. Even though many risk factors can be avoided, not all can be eliminated, especially in large, complex, or leading edge projects. Attempts to eliminate risk usually entail adding innumerable management controls and monitoring systems that increase system complexity and introduce new sources of risk. Also, avoiding risk can diminish the payoff opportunities. Research projects and innovative, new-product development projects are inherently risky, but they offer potential for huge benefits later on. Because the potential benefit of such a project is proportionate to the size of the risk, it is better to reduce risk to an acceptable level rather than completely avoid risk.

Reduce Risk

Among the many ways to reduce risk associated with technical performance are to[15]

- Employ the best technical team.
- Base decisions on models and simulations of key technical parameters.
- Use mature, computer-aided system engineering tools.
- Use parallel development on high-risk tasks.
- Provide the technical team with adequate incentives for success.
- Hire outside specialists for critical review and assessment of work.
- Perform extensive tests and evaluations.
- Minimize system complexity.
- Use design margins.

The last two points deserve further explanation. In general, system risk and unpredictability increase with system complexity. Thus, minimizing complexity through reorganizing and modifying project tasks as well as the end-item design can reduce risk in a project. By *decoupling activities* and subsystems, that is, making them independent of one another, the failure of any one activity or subsystem is contained and will not spread to others.

Incorporating margins into design goals can reduce the risk of meeting technical requirements.[16] A *design margin* is a quantified value that serves as a safety buffer to be held in reserve and allocated by management. In general, a target design value is set that is stiffer or more rigorous than the design requirement. In particular:

$$\text{Target value} = \text{Requirement} - \text{Design margin}$$

By aiming for the target value, any designer error can miss by as much as the design margin amount and still satisfy the requirement. By striving to meet target values that are stiffer than the requirements, the risk of not meeting the requirement is reduced.

Example 5: Design Margin Application

Suppose the weight requirement for an aircraft navigation system is 900 pounds. To allow for the difficulty of reaching the requirement (and the risk of not meeting it), the design margin is set at 10 percent or 90 pounds. Thus, the *target weight* for the navigation system becomes 810 pounds.

A design margin can also be applied to each subsystem or component within the system. If the navigation system is entirely composed of three major subsystems, A, B, and C, then the three together must weigh 810 pounds. Suppose that C has a weight of 10 pounds, which is fixed and cannot be modified. Further, suppose the design goal for A is a weight of 500 pounds, and for B, a weight of 300 pounds. If a 12 percent design margin is imposed on both subsystems, then the *target weights* for A and B are 500 (1.0 − 0.12) = 440 pounds, and 300 (1.0 − 0.12) = 264 pounds, respectively.

Design margins provide managers and engineers a way to flexibly meet the problems in an evolving design. Should the target value for one subsystem prove impossible to meet, then portions of the margin values from other subsystems or the overall system can be reallocated to it. If subsystem B cannot possibly be designed to meet the 264 pound target, but assuming subsystem A *can* be designed to meet *its* target value, then the target value for B can initially be increased by as much as 36 pounds (its margin value) to 300 pounds; if that value also proves impossible to meet, the target can be increased by another 60 pounds (the margin value originally allocated to subsystem A) to 360 pounds; if even that value cannot be met, the target can be increased again by as much as another 90 pounds (the margin value for the entire system) up to 450 pounds. Even with these incremental additions to B's initial target value, the overall system would still be able to meet the 900 pound weight requirement.

Design margins not only help reduce the risk in meeting requirements, they encourage designers to exceed requirements, to design a system that weighs less than required. Of course, design margins must be set carefully so as to reduce the design risk yet not increase design cost.

Among ways to reduce risks associated with meeting schedules are[17]

- Create a master project schedule and strive to adhere to it.
- Schedule the most risky tasks as early as possible to allow time for failure recovery.
- Maintain close focus on critical and near-critical activities.

- Put the best workers on time-critical tasks.
- Provide incentives for overtime work.
- Shift high-risk activities in the project network from series to parallel.
- Organize the project early and be careful to adequately staff it.

To reduce the risk associated with meeting project cost targets[18]

- Identify and monitor the key cost drivers.
- Use low-cost design alternative reviews and assessments.
- Verify system design and performance through modeling and assessment.
- Maximize usage of proven technology and commercial off-the-shelf equipment.
- Perform early breadboarding, prototyping, and testing on risky components and modules.

The last way, *use of breadboards* and *prototypes*,[19] which are test models for verifying designs, is an especially powerful way to reduce risk. They enable ideas to be tested through trial and error so that designs can be corrected very early in the project, which greatly reduces the likelihood of necessary changes later on with accompanying schedule delays and budget increases.[20] Breadboards and prototypes are discussed in Appendix A.

Example 6: Managing Schedule and Cost Risk at the Vancouver Airport Expansion Project[21]

The expansion of facilities at Vancouver International Airport involved constructing a new international terminal building (ITB) and a parallel runway. The project budget for $355 million was approved in January 1993; the project schedule called for full operation of the ITB by June 1, 1996, and the new runway by November 2, 1996. The project team identified the following as major risk areas in meeting the budget and schedule constraints:

1. *Risk in Structural Steel Delivery and Erection.* Steel is the most critical aspect of big construction projects in Canada. Long procurement lead times from steel mills and difficulties in scheduling design, fabrication, and erection make big-steel projects problematic. Recognizing this, the project team awarded the structural steel contract very early in the project so there would be ample time to design, procure, fabricate, and erect the 10,000 tons of steel required for the ITB. As a result, the ITB was completed on time.
2. *Material Handling Risk.* Excavation, moving earth, and material handling comprised the second critical area. Millions of cubic meters of earth had to be moved, and over 4 million cubic meters of sand were required for concrete runways, taxiways, and so on. The project team developed an advance plan to enable coordinated movement of earth from one locale to another, and they used local sand as a component in the concrete. This saved substantial time and money, and the runway was completed 1 year ahead of schedule.
3. *Environmental Risk.* Excavations and transport of earth and sand by barges threatened the ecology of the Fraser River estuary. The environmental risks were mitigated by advance planning and by constantly identifying and handling problems as they arose through cooperative efforts of all stakeholders.
4. *Functionality Risk.* Because new technology poses risk, the project team adopted a policy of using only proven components or technology. Whenever

a new technology was in doubt, its use and success at other existing sites was evaluated. Consequently, all ITB systems were installed and operational according to schedule, with few problems.

One additional way to reduce the risk of failing to meet budgets, schedules, and technical performance is to retain focus on meeting the minimum requirements, which means to do whatever necessary for achieving the requirements, and *nothing* more.[22] The project team might be aware of many things that could be done beyond the stated requirements, but they will consume additional resources and add time and cost. Unless the customer approves the added time and cost, these things should be avoided. Avoiding nonessentials reduces the risk of failing to provide for the essentials.

Contingency Planning

With contingency planning you identify the risks, anticipate whatever might happen, then prepare a detailed plan of action to cope with it. The initial project plan is followed, yet throughout execution the risks are closely monitored. Should a problem arise as indicated by an undesired outcome or risk symptom, then the contingency course of action can be adopted. The contingency action can be a post-hoc remedial action to compensate for the risk impact, an action taken in parallel to the original plan, or a preventive action initiated by preliminary risk symptoms to mitigate the risk impact. Multiple contingency plans can be developed based upon "what-if" analyses of possible outcomes for multiple risks.

Accept Risk (Do Nothing)

Not all impacts are severe or fatal, and if the cost of avoiding, reducing, or transferring the risk exceeds the benefit, then "do nothing" might be advisable. Of course, this response would not be chosen for risks where the impacts or consequences are potentially severe.

10.5 PROJECT MANAGEMENT *Is* RISK MANAGEMENT

Risk management supplements and is a part of other project management tools and practices, such as requirements and task definition, scheduling, budgeting, configuration management, change control, and performance tracking and control. With these tools, managers know and assess the risks so they can proactively reduce them or plan for the identified consequences. If, for example, a project must be completed in 9 months but knowledgeable people estimate that it might take closer to 12 months, a multitude of actions may be taken to increase the likelihood of it being finished in 9 months.

Not all projects need comprehensive risk analysis and risk management. On small projects, a small, highly paid and motivated staff can usually overcome difficulties associated with the risks, and, if not, the consequences are usually small anyway. In larger projects where the stakes and/or the risks of failure are high, however, risk management is especially important. These projects require awareness and respect for all significant risks involved—safety, legal, social, and political, as well as technical and financial. Application of risk management principles can make the difference between project success and project failure.

Risk Management Principles

Following are general principles for managing risks:[23]

- Create a *risk management plan* that specifies ways to identify all major project risks, and then create a risk profile for each identified risk. The plan should specify the person responsible for managing risks as well as methods for allocating time and funds from the risk reserve.

- The *risk profile* for each risk should include likelihood, cost and schedule impact, and contingencies to be invoked. It should also specify the earliest visible symptoms (trigger events) that indicate the risk is materializing. In general, high-risk areas should be visible and have lots of eyes watching closely. Contingency plans should be kept up-to-date and reflect project progress and emerging risks.

- A person whose principle responsibility is risk management should be appointed to the project. This is the *risk officer*. The risk officer should not be the same person as the project manager because the role involves matters of psychology and politics. He should *not* be a can-do person, but instead, to some extent, a devil's advocate identifying, assessing, and tracking all the reasons why something might not work even when everyone else in the project believes otherwise.

- The budget and schedule should include a calculated *risk reserve,* which is a buffer of money, time, and other resources for dealing with risks as they materialize. The risk reserve is used at the project manager's discretion to cover risks not specifically detailed in the risk profile. The reserve may be the RT or RC values (described later) or other amounts. It is usually not associated with a contingency plan, and its use might be constrained to particular applications or areas of risk. The size of the risk reserve should be estimated carefully because a reserve that is *too large* can actually increase the time and cost of the project. (There is the tendency to consume whatever time-cost resources are available, even if in reserve form).

- Risks must be *continuously monitored* and the risk management plan updated to account for emerging or potential risks. The project manager must be alert to emerging problems from unknown hazards. Even known risks may take a long time before they begin to produce problems, so they need to be carefully monitored. Sometimes the response is to do nothing; however, doing nothing should be a conscious choice (not an oversight) followed up by close tracking to ensure it was the right choice and that no further problems are developing.

- Establish *communication channels* (perhaps anonymous) and candor within the project team to ensure that bad news quickly gets to the project manager.

- Specify procedures to ensure accurate, comprehensive project *documentation.* Documentation includes proposals, detailed project plans, change requests, summary reports, and postcompletion summaries. In general, the better the documentation of past projects, the more information available for planning future, similar projects, estimating necessary time and resources, and identifying possible risks and associated outcomes.

Expect the Unexpected

Risk management involves identifying and analyzing myriad risk hazards and possible consequences, and often responding with all kinds of controls and safeguards in the project plan. Having done that, everyone might be led to believe that everything that could possibly go wrong has been anticipated and covered. Then when something *still* goes wrong, it catches them completely off guard. Although it's true that most risks can be covered in risk planning, it is rare that all of them can. Thus, risk planning should be tempered with the concept of "nonplanning," or Napoleon's approach, which is to expect that something surely will go wrong, and that it will be necessary to find a way to deal with it *as it emerges*. Expecting the unexpected is often better preparation for coping with risk than preparing extensive plans and believing that the unexpected has been eliminated.[24]

Example 7: Successful Management of Risks as They Arise— Development of the F117 Stealth Fighter[25]

A good example of how to manage risk in R&D is the F117 Stealth Fighter program, aimed at developing a revolutionary new weapons system notable as the first operational "low observable" (difficult to detect with radar) combat aircraft capable of high precision attacks on enemy targets. The success of this program gave the United States a minimum 15- to 20-year lead over other nations in low observable fighter technology. The F117 involved high risk because many lessons had to be learned throughout this program, one that provided significant challenges to be overcome. In the F117 program, however, challenges were *expected* at all phases of the program, from design and test, through evaluation and deployment. To handle the risks, numerous decisions were made on the spot between program managers for Lockheed (contractor) and the Air Force (customer). The program was set up for rapid deployment of resources to solve problems *as they arose*. Managers from the customer and the contractor were closely involved to minimize bureaucratic delay. Schedules were optimistic and based on assumptions that everything would work, however everyone throughout the management chain knew the risks and the significant challenges to overcome, so problems and delays did not come as a surprise or threaten program support. This is a good example of *managing* risk as opposed to *avoiding* risk, and it illustrates how to pursue aggressive, revolutionary advances when a technological opportunity exists.

Risk Management Caveats

For all the good it can provide, risk management itself can *create* risks. Most every philosophy, procedure, or prescription has exceptions and caveats, and that is true of risk management as well. Misunderstanding or misapplication of concepts associated with risk management can stymie a project by fooling people into thinking they have nothing to worry about, and actually leaving project personnel worse prepared for dealing with emerging problems.

Having created a risk management plan, project managers and supporters might be emboldened to charge ahead and take risks they might not take otherwise. Much of the input to risk analysis is subjective; after all, a likelihood is just that—it does not indicate what *will* happen, only what *might* happen. Data analysis and planning gives people a sense of having power over events, even when the events are chancy. Underestimating the risk likelihood or impact can make consequences seem insignificant, leading some people to venture into dangerous water that common sense would have disallowed. For example, the security of seat belts and air bags encourages some drivers to take risks such as driving too close behind the next car or accelerating through yellow lights. The result is an actual *increase* in the overall number of accidents (even though the seriousness of injury is reduced).

Repeated experience and good documentation are important ways to identify risks, but they cannot guarantee that some important risks will not remain unknown. Same and similar outcomes that have occurred repeatedly in past projects eventually deplete peoples' capacity to imagine anything else happening. As a result, some risks become unthinkable and are never considered. Even sophisticated computer models are worthless when it comes to dealing with unthinkable risks because a computer cannot be instructed to analyze events that have never occurred and are beyond human imagination. Risk analysis models are based on the occurrence frequency of past events in a finite number of cases. History provides a sample, not a population of infinite possibilities.

Managing risk does not mean eliminating it, although the management in some projects makes it seem as though it was the goal. The prime symptom of "trying to eliminate risk" can be management overkill or micromanagement: excessive controls, unrealistic requirements for documentation, and trivial demands for the authorization of everything. By definition, projects inherently entail uncertainty and risk. Micromanagement is never appropriate, and may prove disastrous for some projects, particularly for product development and R&D. When management tries to eliminate risk, it stifles innovation and, say Aronstein and Piccirillo, "forces a company into a plodding, brute force approach to technology, which can be far more costly in the long run than a more adventurous approach where some programs fail but others make significant leaps forward."[26] The appropriate risk management approach, particularly for development projects, is not to try to avoid or eliminate risk altogether, but to accommodate and mitigate risk by reducing the cost of failure.

10.6   SUMMARY

Project risk management maximizes areas of the project over which internal stakeholders control the outcomes, and minimizes areas over which stakeholders have absolutely no control. It involves identifying the risks, assessing them, and then planning the appropriate responses.

Identifying project risks starts early in the project conception phase. Areas of high risk are important considerations in assessing and approving the project. Any uncertain factor that can significantly influence project outcomes presents a hazard to be dealt with. Risks in projects stem from internal and external sources. Internal risks include failure to define and satisfy customer needs or market requirements, or technical problems arising in the work. External risks include weather, labor and supplier problems, competitors' actions, or changes imposed by outside parties. Risk hazards are identified from experience with past projects and careful scrutiny of current projects.

Projects have innumerable risks, but only the important ones need be addressed. Importance depends on the likelihood, impact, and overall consequence of the risk. Likelihood is the probability a risk will occur as determined by knowledgeable, experienced people. Risk impact is the effect of the risk, its seriousness or potential influence on project schedule, cost, or performance outcomes. Risk consequence is a combination of both likelihood and impact, a way of expressing the two concepts as one. Risk consequence measures are used to decide which risks should receive attention and which can be ignored. As a safety measure, every risk with severe impact should be carefully considered, even when the likelihood of occurrence is very small.

Risk response planning addresses the way identified risks will be dealt with. Some risks can be transferred to other parties or spread among many stakeholders or subcontractors. Some risks can be avoided, and should be. On the other hand, a higher risk might be associated with greater benefits, so trying to eliminate such a risk might also reduce the payoff. Thus, better than trying to avoid risk is to try to reduce it to a manageable level. Risk can be reduced by employing an experienced team, minimizing project complexity, implementing careful planning and scheduling, using proven methods and technology, and monitoring critical-path and high-risk activities closely. For areas of high risk, contingency plans with alternatives for dealing with new problems should be developed.

Good risk management accommodates or mitigates risk, and reduces the cost of failure. Principles for risk management include having a risk management plan that specifies the risks, their symptoms and backup plans, a risk officer responsible for identifying and tracking the risks, and a budget and schedule reserve. The plan must specify the ways that risks will be monitored and emerging problems will be communicated to the project manager. Good project documentation furnishes insurance against perilous situations in the future because lessons learned about risks can be referenced. No amount of preparation can anticipate all risks, therefore project managers should expect the unexpected and be prepared to find ways to deal with risks as they arise.

The last several chapters focused primarily on aspects of project planning—work definition, scheduling, and budgeting. This chapter discussed how risk could be dealt with during project planning and project execution. The next several chapters move more fully into the area of project execution and, in particular, methods for tracking and controlling project performance, creating and sharing information, and bringing the project to successful completion. The following section discusses common analytical methods for assessing risk consequences and deciding between alternative risk responses. It is a supplement to the analytical methods covered earlier.

10.7   SUPPLEMENT: RISK ANALYSIS METHODS

Four common methods for risk analysis are expected value, decision trees, payoff tables, and simulation.

Expected Value

Selection of the appropriate risk response is sometimes based on analysis of risk consequences in terms of the expected value of project costs and schedules.

In general, expected value is the average or mean outcome of numerous repeated circumstances. For risk assessment, expected value represents the average outcome of a project, if it were repeated many times, accounting for the possible occurrence of risk. Mathematically, it is the weighted average of all the possible outcomes, where the respective likelihoods of the possible outcomes are the weights, that is

$$\text{Expected value} = \Sigma[(\text{Outcomes}) \times (\text{Likelihoods})]$$

To account for risk, the risk project time and cost consequences are determined using expected value. The risk consequence on project duration is called the *risk time, RT*. It is the expected values of the estimated time required for risk correction, computed as

$$RT = (\text{Corrective time}) \times (\text{Likelihood}) \tag{6}$$

The risk consequence on project cost is called the *risk cost, RC*. It is the expected value of the estimated cost of correcting for the risk, computed as

$$RC = (\text{Corrective cost}) \times (\text{Likelihood}) \qquad (7)$$

For example, suppose the baseline time estimate (BTE) for project completion is 26 weeks and the baseline cost estimate (BCE) is $71,000. Assume that the risk likelihood for the project as a whole is 0.3, and, should the risk materialize, it would delay the project by 5 weeks and increase the cost by $10,000. Also, because the probability of the risk materializing is 0.3, the probability of it *not* materializing is 0.7. If the risk does not materialize, no corrective measures will be necessary, so the corrective time and cost will be nil. Hence

$$RT = (5)(0.3) + (0)(0.7) = 1.5 \text{ weeks, and}$$
$$RC = (\$10,000)(0.3) + (0)(0.7) = \$3,000$$

These figures, RT and RC, would be included as reserve or buffer amounts in the project schedule and budget to account for risk. RC and RT are the *schedule reserve* and *project contingency* (budget reserve), respectively, as mentioned in Chapters 7 and 9.

Accounting for the risk time, the *expected project completion time, ET,* is

$$ET = BTE + RT = 26 + 1.5 = 27.5 \text{ weeks}$$

and accounting for the risk cost, the *expected project completion cost, EC,* is

$$EC = BCE + RC = 71,000 + 3,000 = \$74,000$$

When the corrective time and cost cannot be estimated, then ET and EC are computed as

$$ET = BTE(1 + \text{likelihood}) = 26(1.3) = 33.8 \text{ weeks} \qquad (8)$$
$$EC = BCE(1 + \text{likelihood}) = \$71,000(1.3) = \$92,300 \qquad (9)$$

These examples account for risk factors that affect the project as a *whole*. Another way to determine risk consequence is to first disaggregate the project into work packages or phases and then, *for each* element, estimate the risk likelihood and corrective time and cost. These individual corrective estimates are then aggregated to determine ET and EC for the entire project. This approach tends to give more credible RT and RC estimates than do Equations (6) through (9) because risks so pinpointed to individual tasks or phases can be more accurately assessed. Also, it is easier to identify the necessary corrective actions and estimate the time and costs associated with particular tasks.

For example, a project has eight work packages, and for each the baseline cost estimate (BCE), risk likelihood, and corrective cost have been estimated. The following table lists the information for each work package and gives EC, where EC is computed as

$$EC = BCE + [(\text{corrective cost}) \times (\text{likelihood})]$$

WBS ELEMENT	BCE	CORRECTIVE COST	LIKELIHOOD	EC
J	$10,000	$ 2,000	.2	$10,400
M	8,000	1,000	.3	8,300
V	16,000	4,000	.1	16,400
Y	10,000	6,000	.2	1,200
L	8.000	2,000	.3	8.600
Q	9,000	2,000	.1	9,200
W	5,000	1,000	.3	5,300
X	5,000	1,500	.3	5,750
Total		$71,000		$75,150

Therefore, the project EC is $75,150. Because this is only 5.8 percent above the project BCE of $71,000, the overall cost consequence of project risks is small.

Now, for the same eight work-package project, assume the baseline time (BTE), risk likelihood, and corrective time have been estimated for each work package. These figures are listed below along with ET, computed as

$$ET = BTE + [(Corrective time) \times (Likelihood)]$$

WBS ELEMENT	BTE	CORRECTIVE TIME	LIKELIHOOD	ET
J	6	1	.2	6.2
M	4	1	.3	4.3
V	6	2	.1	6.2
Y	8	3	.2	8.6
L	2	1	.3	2.3
Q	8	1	.1	8.1
W	1	1	.3	1.3
X	1	1	.3	1.3

The project network is used to determine ET for the overall project. Suppose the network looks similar to Figure 10-3. Without considering the risk time, the critical path would be J-M-V-Y-W-X, which gives a project BTE of 24 weeks. Accounting for risk consequences, the critical path does not change but the duration is increased to 27.9 weeks. This is the project ET.[27]

Although activities on critical and near-critical paths should be monitored carefully, in general, *any* activity that poses a high-risk consequence (high likelihood and/or high impact) should also be monitored carefully, even if not on the critical path.

Increasing the project schedule and budget to account for the expected risk time and expected risk cost cannot guarantee adequate protection against risk. Expected value is equivalent to the long-run average, which results from repeating something many times. Project activities are never identical or repeated over and over, but even if they were, that would not preclude a bad outcome in a particular instance. The point: No attempt to prepare for risk using expected value criteria offers any guarantee—such is the nature of risk.

Decision Trees[28]

A decision tree is a diagram wherein the "branches" represent different chance events or decision strategies. Decision trees can be used to assess which risk responses among alternatives yield the best-to-be-expected consequence.

Figure 10-3
Project network, accounting for risk time.

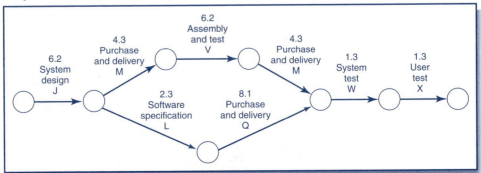

One application of decision trees is in weighing the cost of potential project failure against the benefit of project success. Assume a project has a BCE of $200,000 and a failure likelihood of 0.25. If the project is successful, it will yield a net profit of $1,000,000.

The expected value concept can be used to compute the average value of the project assuming it could be repeated a large number of times. If it were repeated many times, then the project would lose $200,000 (BCE) 25 percent of the time, and generate $1,000,000 profit the other 75 percent of the time. The average outcome or expected value would be

$$\text{Expected outcome} = (-\$200,000)(0.25) + (\$1,000,000)(0.75) = \$700,000.$$

This suggests that although there is potential to net $1,000,000 maximum, it is more reasonable to use $700,000 for the BCE. It also implies that any action taken to reduce or eliminate the failure risk should not exceed $700,000.

Another application of decision trees is in deciding between alternative risk responses. Suppose a project has a BCE of $10 million, risk failure likelihood of 0.6, and a risk impact of $5 million. Two strategies are being considered to reduce the risk likelihood (but not the risk impact):

Strategy 1 will cost $2 million and will reduce the failure likelihood to 0.1.
Strategy 2 will cost $1 million and will reduce the failure likelihood to 0.4.

The decision tree and resultant expected project costs are shown in Figure 10-4. The analysis suggests Strategy 1 should be adopted because it has the lowest expected cost.

Uncertainty and Payoff Tables

When no prior experience or historical data exists upon which to estimate likelihood, then the expected-value risk consequence cannot be computed; hence, other criteria must be used to assess courses of action in the face of risk. This situation is referred to as *uncertainty*, which implies no information is available about what may occur. To determine the best strategy under uncertainty, begin by identifying possible alternative routes the project could take in response to factors over which management has no control. These different routes are called *states of nature*. Consider different possible strategies or actions, and then indicate the likely outcome for each state of na-

Figure 10-4
Decision tree.

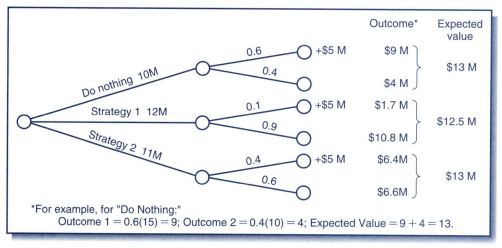

*For example, for "Do Nothing:"
Outcome 1 = 0.6(15) = 9; Outcome 2 = 0.4(10) = 4; Expected Value = 9 + 4 = 13.

ture. The outcomes for different combinations of strategies and states of nature are represented in a matrix called a *payoff table.*

For example, suppose the success of a project to develop a new product, "Product X," depends on market demand that is a known function of particular performance features of the product. The development effort can be directed in any of three possible directions, referred to as strategies A, B, and C, each of which will result in a product with different performance features. Also, assume that another firm is developing a competing product that will have performance features similar to those under Strategy A. One of three future states of nature will exist when the product development effort ends: N1 represents no competing products on the market for at least 6 months, N2 represents the product competing with Product X introduced between 0 and 6 months later; N3 represents the product competing with Product X introduced first. The *payoff table* shown in Table 10-6 gives the likely profits in millions of dollars for different combinations of strategies and states of nature.

The question is: Which strategy should project sponsors follow? The answer is: It depends! If project sponsors are optimistic, they will choose the strategy that maximizes the potential payoff. The maximum potential payoff indicated in the table is $90 million, which happens for Strategy C and State of Nature N1. If project sponsors are optimistic, they will thus adopt Strategy C. The strategy choice that has the potential of yielding the largest payoff is called the *maximax decision criteria.*

Now, if project sponsors are pessimistic, they instead will be interested in minimizing their potential losses; they will use the *maximin* decision criteria by adopting the strategy that gives the best outcome under the worst possible conditions. For the three strategies A, B, and C, the worst-case payoff scenarios are −$20 million, $50 million, and $40 million, respectively. The best (least bad) of the three is $50 million, or Strategy B. Pessimistic sponsors would thus adopt Strategy B.

Any choice of strategy other than the best one will cause the decision maker to experience an opportunity loss called *regret.* If, for example, Strategy A is adopted, and the state of nature turns out to be N2, the sponsor will regret not having chosen Strategy C, which is the best for that state of nature. A measure of this regret will be the difference between the unrealized payoff for Strategy C and the realized payoff for Strategy A, or $70 − $30 = $40 million. This way of thinking suggests another criteria for choosing between strategies, the *minimax regret* decision criteria in which a strategy is chosen that minimizes the *regret* of not having made the best choice.

Regret for a given state of nature is the difference in the outcomes between the best strategy and any other strategy. This is illustrated in a *regret table,* shown in Table 10-7. For example, given the payoffs in Table 10-6, for state of nature (N1) the highest payoff is $90 million. Had Strategy C, the optimal strategy, been selected, the regret would have been zero, but had strategies A or B been selected instead, the regrets would have

Table 10-6
Payoff Table.

	STATES OF NATURE		
STRATEGY	N1	N2	N3
A	60	30	−20
B	60	50	60
C	90	70	40

Table 10-7
Regret Table.

STRATEGY	STATES OF NATURE		
	N1	N2	N3
A	30	40	80
B	30	20	0
C	0	0	20

been $30 million each (the difference between their outcomes, $60 million, and the optimum, $90 million). The regret amounts for states of nature N2 and N3 are determined in similar fashion.

To understand how to minimize regret, first look in the regret table at the largest regret for each strategy. The largest regrets are $80 million, $30 million, and $20 million for strategies A, B, and C, respectively. Next, pick the smallest of these, $20 million, which occurs for Strategy C. Thus, Strategy C is the choice to minimize regret.

Another approach for selecting a strategy is to assume that every state of nature has the same likelihood of occurring by using the *maximum expected payoff* criteria. Referring back to the payoff table, Table 10-6, where the likelihood of each state of nature is assumed to be one-third, the expected payoff for Strategy A given outcomes from the payoff table is

$$1/3(60) + 1/3(30) + 1/3(-20) = 23.33, \text{ or } \$23.33 \text{ million}$$

The expected payoffs, computed similarly for strategies B and C, are $56.66 million and $66.66 million, respectively. Thus, Strategy C would be chosen as giving the maximum expected payoff. Notice in the previous examples that three of the four selection criteria point to Strategy C. This in itself might further convince decision makers about the appropriateness of selecting Strategy C.

Simulation

Application of simulation to project management was illustrated in Chapter 8. In general, simulation gives the probability distribution of outcomes, which can be used to determine the probability (or likelihood) of a particular outcome such as completion time or cost. Simulation of, for instance, project completion time can be used to establish an appropriate target completion date or to prepare contingency plans. Although the simulation in the critical path example illustrated in Chapter 8 indicated that the project would be completed in 147 days, the simulated completion time distribution (Figure 8-4) indicated instead that it would be 155 days, *on average*. Thus, at the *earliest*, the target completion should be set at 155 days, although the likelihood of not meeting the target would remain at 50 percent. Using the probability distribution, a target completion date could be set such that the associated probability of failure (i.e., of not meeting the target date) is an acceptable level. Alternatively, given a prespecified date by which the project must be completed, management could use simulation to estimate the likelihood of failure and, hence, to decide whether they should either prepare contingency plans or change the requirements, activities, or the network.

1. Should risks that have low likelihood be ignored? Explain.
2. How does a person's risk tolerance affect whether a risk is rated as high, medium, or low?
3. What is meant by risk of failure?
4. What factors make a project high-risk?
5. Discuss the difference between internal risk and external risk. List sources of risk in each of these categories.
6. Describe each of the following sources of technical risk: maturity, complexity, quality, and concurrency or dependency.
7. Briefly describe the following risk identification techniques: analogy, checklists, WBS analysis, process flowcharts, and brainstorming.
8. Describe a cause-and-effect diagram. Pick a problem (effect) of your own choice and use a cause-and-effect diagram for illustration.
9. A project involves development of a system with state-of-the-art hardware and software, both of which are very complex, and where system performance depends on another, external system being concurrently developed. Based on Table 10-3, and assuming all risk factors are independent and equally weighted, what is the CLF for the project?
10. What is an influence diagram? How is it used to identify and analyze risk sources and to assign priorities to those sources?
11. Tables 10-3 and 10-4 are for illustration purposes. Discuss the general applicability of these tables to rating risks in projects. Would *you* use these tables to assess the risk likelihood and impact in a project of your choice? Why or why not?
12. In your opinion, do equations (1), (2), and (3) present good ways for rating the overall likelihood, impact, and consequences of risk? Discuss pros and cons of using these equations.
13. Discuss briefly each of the following ways to handle risk: transfer risk, avoid risk, reduce risk, do contingency planning, and accept risk.
14. Think of a project you are familiar with and problems the project encountered. List some ways that risk could have been reduced in the project and explain each of them.
15. What is a design margin? How does its application reduce risk?
16. One requirement of a power-generating system states that it must provide 500 kwh minimum output. The system has three power-generating subsystems, X, Y, and Z. Constraints on physical size indicate that the output capacity of overall system will be split among the three subsystems in the approximate ratio of 5:3:2. Suppose a design margin of 3 percent is applied to the system and the subsystems. Note that because the power requirement is stated as *minimum* output, the design margin would set the target output at 3 percent *higher than* the requirement.
    a. What is the target requirement output for the overall system?
    b. What are the target requirement outputs for each of the subsystems? (Remember, subsystem margins are *in addition to* the system margin.)
    c. Suppose that, at best, Subsystem X can be designed to meet only 47 percent of the power output requirement for the overall system. Assuming the Subsystems Y and Z can be designed to meet their respective design targets, will the output requirement for the overall system be met?
17. List and review the principles of risk management.

18. How does risk planning serve to increase risk-taking behavior?
19. Risk management includes being prepared for the unexpected. Explain.
20. Can risk be eliminated from projects? *Should* management try to eliminate it?
21. How and where are risk time and risk cost considerations used in project planning?
22. Where would criteria such as minimax, maximin, and minimax regret be used during the project life cycle to manage project risk?
23. The network for the Largesse Hydro Project is shown:

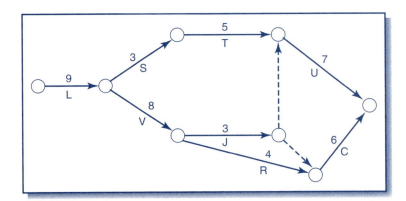

The following table gives the baseline cost and time estimates (BCE and BTE), estimates of the cost and time to correct for failure, and the likelihood of failure for each work package in Largesse.

WBS Element	BCE	BTE (wk)	Corrective Cost	Time	Likelihood
L	$20,000	9	$ 4,000	2	.2
V	16,000	8	4,000	2	.3
T	32,000	5	8,000	2	.1
U	20,000	7	12,000	3	.2
S	16,000	3	4,000	1	.3
J	18,000	3	4,000	1	.1
R	10,000	4	4,000	3	.3
C	15,000	6	5,000	2	.3

a. Determine the risk time and risk cost for the project.
b. Consider the risk times on noncritical paths. Which activities and paths should be watched carefully as posing the highest risks?
c. What is the project expected cost (EC) and expected time (ET)?

24. Because of its geographical location, the Largesse Turbo project is threatened with delays and costs associated with bad weather. The likelihood of bad weather is estimated at 0.30 with a potential impact of delaying work by 10 weeks and increasing the cost by $20,000.
a. Ignoring the time and cost risks in Problem 23, what are the expected project completion time and completion cost considering the weather risk?
b. What is the estimated expected project completion time and cost considering the weather risk *and* the risks listed in Problem 23?

25. Softside Systems has a $100,000 fixed price contract for installation of a new application system. The project is expected to take 5 weeks and cost $50,000. Experience with similar projects suggests a 0.30 likelihood that the

project will encounter problems that could delay it as much as 3 weeks and increase the cost by $30,000. By increasing the project staff 20 percent for an additional cost of $10,000, the likelihood of problems would be reduced to 0.10, and the delay and cost would be 1 week and $8,000, respectively. Set up a decision tree to determine whether Softside should increase the size of the project staff.

26. Corecast Contractors has been requested by a municipality to submit a proposal bid for a parking garage contract. In the past, the cost of preparing bids has been about 2 percent of the cost of the job. Corecast project manager Bradford Pitts is considering three possible bids: cost plus 10 percent, cost plus 20 percent, and cost plus 30 percent. Of course, increasing the "plus percent" increases the project price, decreasing the likelihood of winning the job. Bradford estimates the likelihood of winning the job as follows:

	Bid Price	P(win)	P(lose)
P1	$C + 0.1C = 1.1C$	0.6	0.4
P2	$C + 0.2C = 1.2C$	0.4	0.6
P3	$C + 0.3C = 1.3C$	0.2	0.8

In all cases, the profit (if the bid is won) will be the bid price minus the proposal preparation cost, or $0.02C$; the loss (if the bid is not won) will be the proposal preparation cost.

Prepare a decision tree for the three options. If Bradford uses the maximum expected profit as the criterion, which bid proposal would he select?

27. Iron Butterfly, Inc. submits proposals in response to RFPs. The outcome of submitting a proposal is one of three cases: N1, Iron Butterfly gets a full contract; N2, Iron Butterfly gets a partial contract (job is shared with other contractors); N3, Iron Butterfly gets no contract. Iron Butterfly is currently assessing three project RFPs code named P1, P2, and P3. The customer for P3 will pay a fixed amount for proposal preparation; for P1 and P2 Iron Butterfly must absorb all of the proposal-preparation costs, which are expected to be high. Based upon project revenues and proposal-preparation costs, the expected profits ($ thousands) are as shown:

	N1	N2	N3
P1	500	200	−300
P2	300	100	−100
P3	100	50	25

To which RFPs would Iron Butterfly respond using the various uncertainty criteria?

28. The Iron Butterfly Corporation project manager for the Logon project, Frank Wesley, is concerned about the development time for the robotic transporter. Although the subcontractor, Creative Robotics has promised a delivery time of 6 weeks, Frank knows that the actual delivery time will be a function of the number of other projects Creative Robotics is working on at the time. As incentive to speed up Creative Robotic's delivery of the transporter, Frank is considering the following actions:

S1: Do nothing.
S2: Promise Creative Robotics a future contract with Iron Butterfly.
S3: Threaten to never contract with Creative Robotics again.

He estimates the impact of these actions on delivery time would be as follows:

Payoffs: Strategy	Creative Robotics Workload		
	Slow	Average	Busy
S1	4	6	8
S2	3	4	7
S3	3	6	6

What strategy should Frank adopt based upon uncertainty criteria? Use criteria similar to the maximax, maximin, minimax regret, and maximum expected payoff, except note that the criteria need to be adapted because here the goal is to *minimize* the payoff (time), which contrasts to the usual case of maximizing the payoff (profit).

QUESTIONS ABOUT THE STUDY PROJECT

1. What did the project manager and stakeholders believe were the major risks in the project?
2. In your own judgment, was this a risky project? Why or why not?
3. Was formal risk analysis performed? When was it done (during initiation, feasibility, planning, etc.)?
4. Was a formal risk management plan created? Discuss the plan.
5. Was there a risk officer? Discuss her duties and role in the project.
6. How were risks identified?
7. How were risks dealt with (through risk transfer, acceptance, avoidance, reduction, etc.)?
8. Discuss the use of contingency plans and budget and schedule reserves to cover risks.
9. What risks materialized during the project and how were they handled?

Case 10-1   The Sydney Opera House[29]

The Sydney Opera House (SOH) is a top tourist attraction and landmark for Sydney and all of Australia. It has become a major arts center (although, owing to the design, it is not necessarily the best place to hear opera). The SOH is visually spectacular and a magnificent structure (Figure 10-5), but designing and building it was somewhat nightmarish.

The original concept for the SOH was a sketch submitted by Danish architect, Jorn Utzon. Judges selected it from an open competition that ended with 233 entries from 11 countries. Though happy to win the competition, Utzon was mildly shocked. Although his concept had caught the attention of the judges, it consisted only of simple sketches with no plans or even perspective drawings. Utzon faced the task of converting the concept into a design from

which a structure could be built, but he had no prior experience in the design and construction of such a large building. Because of his lack of plans, detailed design drawings, and estimates of materials, little existed from which cost could be determined. Interestingly, because the design was *so* unique, some people presumed it would also be inexpensive to build. No one knew how it would be built, and some experts questioned that it could be built at all. Despite all the uncertainty, the initial project cost estimate was put at $7 million. The government would use profits from a series of state-run lotteries to pay for the project.

Engineers who reviewed the concept noted that the roof shells were much larger and wider than any shells seen so far. Further, because they stuck up so

Figure 10-5
Sydney Opera House. [Photo courtesy of Australian Information Service.]

high, they would act like sails in the strong winds blowing up the harbor. Thus, the roof would have to be carefully designed and constructed to prevent the building from blowing away.

The government was worried that people scrutinizing the design might raise questions about potential problems that would stall the project. They thus quickly moved ahead and divided the work into three main contracts: the foundation and building except the roof, the roof, and the interior and equipment.

As feared by many experts, the SOH project became an engineering and financial debacle, lasting 15 years and costing $107 million ($100 million over the initial estimate). Hindsight is 20/20, yet from the beginning this should have been viewed as a very risky project. Nonetheless, risks were either downplayed or ignored, and not much was done to mitigate or keep them under control.

QUESTIONS

1. Identify the obvious risks.
2. What early actions should have been taken to reduce the risks?
3. Discuss some principles of risk management that were ignored.

Case 10-2   Infinity & Beyond, Inc.

Infinity & Beyond, Inc. is a producer of high-tech fashion merchandise. The company's marketing department has identified a new product concept through discussions with potential customers conducted in three focus groups. The marketing department is excited about the new "concept" and presents it to top management who gives its approval for further study. Lisa Denney, senior director of new product and Web site development, is asked to create a plan and cost breakdown for the development, manufacture, and distribution of the product. Despite the enthusiasm of top management and the marketing department, Lisa is unsure about the product's market potential and the company's ability to develop it at a reasonable cost. To Lisa's way of thinking, the market seems ill-defined, the product goals unclear, and the product and its production technology uncertain. Lisa asks her chief designer to create some product requirements, a rough design that would meet the requirements and marketing concept, and to propose how the product might be manufactured and marketed.

After a few weeks the designer reports back with requirements that seem to satisfy the marketing concept. She tells Lisa that because of the newness of the technology and the complexity of the product design, the company does not have the experience to develop the product on its own, let alone manufacture it. Lisa checks out several design/development firms, asking one, Margo-Spinner Works Company, to review the product concept. Margo-Spinner Works assures Lisa that although the technology is new to them, it is well within their capability. Lisa reports everything to top management who tells her to ignore any misgivings and go ahead with the development.

Lisa sets a fixed-price contract with Margo-Spinner and gives them primary responsibility for the entire development offer. Margo-Spinner management had argued for a cost-plus contract, but when Lisa stipulated that the agreement had to be fixed-price, Margo-Spinner said okay, only under the condition that it be given complete control of the development work. Lisa, who has never worked with Margo-Spinner, feels uncomfortable with the proposal, but knows of no other design company qualified to do the work, so she agrees. Several people from Infinity & Beyond, Inc. will be assigned to work at Margo-Spinner during the development effort, and during that time they will determine whether Infinity & Beyond, Inc. will be able to make the product or will have to outsource production.

QUESTIONS

1. Discuss the major sources of risk in this project.
2. What do you think about Lisa's handling of the project so far? If you were her, what would you have done differently?
3. Discuss the handling of stages of the project—product concept, definition, development, and production—and what Lisa and other parties did that served to increase or decrease the risks.

ENDNOTES

1. Quoted in Peter Bernstein, *Against the Gods: The Remarkable Story of Risk* (New York: John Wiley & Sons, 1996): 331.
2. Ibid., 207–208.
3. Asked once to define certainty, John Von Neumann, the principle theorist of game theory and mathematical models of uncertainty, answered with an example: To design a house so it is certain the living room floor never gives way, "calculate the weight of a grand piano with six men huddling over it to sing. Then triple the weight." That will guarantee certainty! Source: Bernstein, *Against the Gods*, 233.
4. See Robert Argus and Norman Gunderson, *Planning, Performing, and Controlling Projects* (Upper Saddle River, NJ: Prentice Hall, 1997): 22–23.
5. Adapted from Jack Michaels, *Technical Risk Management* (Upper Saddle River, NJ: Prentice Hall, 1996): 208–50.
6. The term "likelihood" is sometimes distinguished from "probability." The latter refers to values based on frequency measures from historical data; the former to subjective estimates or gut feel. If 2 of 3 previous attempts met with success the first time, then *ceteris paribus,* the probability of success on the next try is 2/3 or 0.67 (and the probability of failure is 1/3). However, even without numerical data, a person with experience can, upon reflection, come up with a similar estimate that "odds are two to one that it will succeed the first time." Although one estimate is objective and the other subjective, that does not imply one is better than the other. Frequency data does not necessarily give a more reliable estimate because of the multitude of factors that influence outcomes; a subjective estimate, in contrast, might be very reliable because humans often can do a pretty good job of assimilating lots of factors.

7. W. Roetzheim, *Structured Computer Project Management* (Upper Saddle River, NJ: Prentice Hall, 1988): 23–26; further examples of risk factors and methods of likelihood quantification are given in Michaels, *Technical Risk Management*.

8. See J. Dingle, *Project Management: Orientation for Decision Makers* (London: Arnold, 1997).

9. See Robert Gilbreath, *Winning at Project Management: What Works, What Fails, and Why* (New York: John Wiley & Sons, 1986).

10. Roetzheim, *Structured Computer Project Management*, 23–26.

11. Michaels, *Technical Risk Management*, 40.

12. Statistics make it easy to ignore risks by de-personalizing the consequences. For example, it is less distressing to state that there is a 0.005 likelihood of someone being killed than to say that 5 people out of 1000 will be killed.

13. I. Mitroff and H. Linstone, *The Unbounded Mind* (New York: Oxford, 1993): 111–35.

14. Ibid.

15. Howard Eisner, *Computer-Aided Systems Engineering* (Upper Saddle River, NJ: Prentice Hall, 1988): 335.

16. See Jeffrey Grady, *System Requirements Analysis* (New York: McGraw-Hill, 1993): 106–11.

17. Eisner, *Computer-Aided Systems Engineering*, 336.

18. Ibid.

19. A breadboard is a working assembly of components. A prototype is an early working model of a complete system. The purpose of both is to demonstrate, validate, experiment, or prove feasibility in a concept or design.

20. Roetzheim, *Structured Computer Project Management*, 96.

21. Henry Wakabayashi and Bob Cowan, "Vancouver International Airport Expansion," *PM Network*, Sept. 1998, 39–44.

22. Neal Whitten, "Meet Minimum Requirements: Anything More is Too Much," *PM Network*, Sept. 1998, 19.

23. Tom DeMarco, *The Deadline* (New York: Dorset House, 1997): 83; Edward Yourdan, *Rise and Resurrection of the American Programmer* (Upper Saddle River, NJ: Prentice Hall, 1998): 133–36.

24. Dietrich Dorner, *The Logic of Failure* (Reading, MA: Addison-Wesley, 1997): 163.

25. D. Aronstein and A. Piccirillo, *Have Blue and the F117A: Evolution of the Stealth Fighter* (Reston, VA: American Institute of Aeronautics and Astronautics, 1997): 79–80.

26. Ibid., 186–90.

27. For other approaches to risk time analysis, see Michaels, *Technical Risk Management*.

28. This section and the next address the more general topic of decision analysis, a broad topic that receives only cursory coverage here. Most textbooks on production/operations management and quantitative analysis for management cover the topic in depth. A classic book on the subject is R. D. Luce and H. Raiffa, *Games and Decisions* (New York: John Wiley & Sons, 1957).

29. Adapted from O. Kharbanda and J. Pinto, *What Made Gertie Gallop: Learning from Project Failures* (New York: Van Nostrand Reinhold, 1996): 177–91.

Chapter 11

Project Control

> *The rider must ride the horse, not be run away with.*
>
> —DONALD WINNICOTT,
> *Playing and Reality*

It is impossible at the onset of a new project to foresee all problems or to anticipate all changes that the project might need. Still, every effort is made throughout the project to regulate work, minimize changes to the plan, and guide the project toward preestablished performance, cost, and schedule objectives. The process of keeping the project moving toward objectives and as close to plan as possible is the subject of *project control*.

This chapter discusses the overall process, specific steps, and analytical methods of project control. It addresses the questions:

- What is project control and how does it differ from traditional cost control?
- Who controls the project?
- What are the steps and areas of emphasis in project control?
- How is project performance tracked and analyzed?
- What changes occur in projects and how are they controlled?

11.1 THE CONTROL PROCESS

As author Daniel Roman states, the control process

> is concerned with assessing actual against planned technical accomplishment, reviewing and verifying the validity of technical objectives,

340

confirming the continued need for the project, timing it to coincide with operational requirements, overseeing resource expenditures, and comparing the anticipated value with the costs incurred.[1]

In general, the process is achieved in three phases: (1) setting performance standards, (2) comparing these standards with actual performance, then (3) taking necessary corrective action.

In the first phase, *performance standards* are defined and expressed in terms of technical specifications, budgeted costs, schedules, and resource requirements. Performance standards are derived from the user requirements, the project plan, and the statement of work. These standards precisely define the cost, schedule, and technical factors to be regulated and the boundaries within which they must be maintained.

In the second phase, the standards are compared with the actual project *performance to date.* Schedules, budgets, and performance specifications are compared to current expenditures and work completed. The time and cost of work still remaining are estimated and used to forecast the anticipated date and cost of the completed project.

Finally, whenever actual performance significantly deviates from standards, *corrective action* is taken. Either the work is altered or expedited, or the plans and standards revised. When work performance is deficient, resources are added, shifted, or altered. When original estimates or expectations prove unrealistic, then project goals are changed and the performance standards themselves revised. The project control system and the project organization itself might have to be restructured.

To keep the project close to plan, obviously there must first be a plan. Thus the initial step in project control is project planning, though, in a sense, the two are interrelated and it is sometimes difficult to tell where planning stops and control begins. In contrasting the two, Roman notes that planning *anticipates* action, whereas control *initiates* action.[2] Both work toward similar ends:[3]

- Planning concentrates on setting *goals* and *directions;* control *guides* the work toward those goals.
- Planning *allocates resources;* control ensures effective, ongoing *utilization* of those resources.
- Planning *anticipates* problems; control *corrects* the problems.
- Planning *motivates* participants to achieve goals; control *rewards* achievement of goals.

11.2   INFORMATION MONITORING

To enable timely and effective project control, the project must be systematically tracked and observed. This requires setting up a project *monitoring function.* The monitoring function is composed of two activities: data collection and information reporting.

It is during the first phase of the control process—while performance standards are being set—that a data collection and information reporting system is established. Data for monitoring the project must be directly related to the project—its plans, outputs, schedules, budgets, and standards. Typical data sources include materials purchasing invoices, worker time cards, change notices, test results and expert opinion. A balance must be struck between gathering too much data and too little. Too much data is costly to collect and process, and will be ignored; too little does not capture the project status and allows problems to go unchecked.

The monitoring function must ensure that management receives reports in sufficient detail and frequency to enable them to identify and correct problems while they are small. It must guarantee that significant deviations from the plan, called *variances,* will be flagged.[4]

The timing of measurement and reporting—daily, weekly, or monthly—is also important. Data can be collected periodically or topically, and reported periodically or by exception. The distinction is crucial to the effectiveness of the monitoring function. At minimum, reports should coincide with significant project milestones and be available in sufficient time to permit problems to be spotted while they are still small.

11.3   INTERNAL AND EXTERNAL PROJECT CONTROL

Both internal and external control systems are used to monitor and regulate project activities. *Internal control* refers to the contractor's systems and procedures for monitoring work and taking corrective action. *External control* refers to the additional procedures and standards imposed by the client, including taking over project coordination and administration functions. Military and government contracts, for example, impose external control by stipulating the following of the contractor:

- Frequent reports on overall project performance.
- Reports on schedules, cost, and technical performance.
- Inspections of work by government program managers.
- Inspection of books and records of the contractor.
- Strict terms on allowable project costs, pricing policies, and so on.[5]

External controls can be a source of annoyance and aggravation to the contractor because, superimposed on internal controls, they create management turmoil and increase the cost of the project. Nonetheless, they are sometimes necessary to protect the interests of the client. To help minimize conflicts and keep costs down, contractors and clients should work together to establish agreed-upon plans, compatible specifications, and joint methods for monitoring work.

11.4   TRADITIONAL COST CONTROL

In traditional cost control, the method for measuring performance is called *variance analysis.* This involves comparing actual costs with planned costs to see if the amount spent was more or less than budgeted. In project management, cost variance analysis is, by itself, inadequate because it indicates neither how much work has been completed nor what the future expenses are likely to be.

Consider the following weekly status report for a software development work package:

Budgeted cost for period = $12,000	Actual cost for period = $14,000	Period variance = $2,000
Cumulative budget to date = $25,000	Cumulative actual costs to date = $29,000	Cumulative variance = $4,000

The report indicates apparent overruns for both period and cumulative costs, with to date cumulative costs running $4,000 (16 percent) over budget. However, because we do not know how much work has been completed for the $29,000, it is impossible from this data to determine if the project is really over budget.

Suppose that the $25,000 indicated was the amount budgeted for completing 50 percent of software development work. That is, as of the week of this report, 50 percent of the work package should have been completed. Therefore, as of the week of the report, if only 30 percent of the work had been completed, then the project would be over budget and behind schedule, and additional cost overruns could be expected just to get caught up. If 50 percent of the work had been completed (as intended), then the project would be on schedule but still over budget. Something would have to be done to reduce future expenditures and eliminate the $4,000 overrun. If, however, as of the week of the report, 70 percent of the work had been completed—20 percent beyond what was scheduled—then the project would actually be ahead of schedule; future expenditures would probably be less than budgeted, possibly reducing or eliminating the $4,000 variance by project completion. In other words, in the last case the project is probably not over budget because substantially more work has been completed than was planned for this date.

This example shows that cost variance information alone is inadequate; it is also necessary to have information about *work progress*—information such as percentage of work completed, milestones achieved, and so on—to be able to assess the status of the project and suggest a course of action. In project management, work progress as of a given status date is expressed using the concepts of *percent complete* and *earned value.* These concepts will be discussed later.

There are times when even work progress information is not enough. Whenever large developmental problems, schedule delays, or changes to the scope of work arise, then the original plans, schedules, and budgets are invalidated. It is then necessary to modify the plans and update the budgets and schedules themselves. Effective project control thus requires comparisons not only of actual costs and work completed to budgets and work plans, but of budgets and work plans to *revised estimates* of the costs and work necessary to complete the project.

11.5 COST ACCOUNTING SYSTEMS FOR PROJECT CONTROL

PERT/Cost Systems

The previous section showed that traditional cost variance analysis alone is insufficient; information also is needed on work progress. Early attempts to correct for this using PERT/CPM went to the opposite extreme by ignoring costs and focusing entirely on work progress. If PERT/CPM users wanted to integrate cost control with network planning methods they had to develop their own systems.

In 1962 the U.S. government developed a PERT-based system which combined cost-accounting with scheduling. Called *PERT/Cost,* the system became mandatory for all military and R&D contracts with the Department of Defense and National Aeronautics and Space Administration (DOD/NASA).[6] Any contractor wanting to bid to DOD/NASA had to demonstrate the ability to use the system and to produce the necessary reports. Although this mandate increased usage of PERT/Cost, it also created resentment. Many firms found the project-oriented PERT/Cost system an expensive duplication of, or incompatible with, existing functionally oriented accounting systems. Interestingly, many firms not involved in DOD/NASA bidding voluntarily adopted PERT/Cost with far fewer complaints.[7]

PERT/Cost was a major improvement over traditional cost-accounting techniques because it blended costs with work schedules. Just as important, it spurred the development of other more sophisticated systems to track and report work progress and costs on a project rather than a fiscal/functional basis. PERT/Cost was the original network-based PCAS. Hereafter the term PCAS will be used to refer to any network-based cost-accounting system that incorporates PERT/Cost principles.

Most PCASs integrate work packages, cost accounts, and project schedules into a unified project control package. They permit cost and scheduling overruns to be identified and causes to be quickly pinpointed among numerous work packages or cost accounts. Rapid identification and correction of problems are the greatest advantages of modern PCASs. Two elements common to most of these systems are use of work packages and cost accounts as basic data collection units, and the concept of earned value to measure project performance.

Work Package and Cost Account Control

Earlier chapters described the importance of work packages and cost accounts as planning tools. It is no coincidence that they are also major elements of project control. Each work package is considered a contract for a specific job, with a manager or supervisor responsible for overseeing costs and work performance. A cost account consists of one or more work packages. Both include information such as work descriptions, time-phased budgets, work plans and schedules, people responsible, resource requirements, and so on. During the project, work packages and cost accounts are the focal point for data collection, work progress evaluation, problem assessment, and corrective action.

Early PERT/Cost systems were inadequate for two reasons. First was the problem of how to handle *overhead* expenses. Typically, work packages are identified in either of two ways: (1) as *end products* when they result in a physical product and have scheduled start and finish dates, or (2) as *level of effort* when they have no physical end product and are "ongoing"—such as testing or maintenance. Given that there is usually no direct connection between company overhead and either of these kinds of work packages, there is a problem with arbitrarily allocating overhead expenses to them. Any arbitrary allocation of expenses reduces expense control and distorts the apparent performance of work packages. Work package managers have little influence on overhead, yet such costs are a frequent source of overruns.

In current PCASs the problem is resolved in two ways. First, any expenses such as supervisory and management overhead that can be traced to specific work packages are allocated directly to them. Second, any overhead that cannot be traced to specific work packages is separated by using either an "overhead" work package for the entire project (lasting for the duration of the project) or a series of shorter duration overhead work packages. Overhead work packages are kept "open" for the duration of the project and extended as needed if the project is delayed.

Another problem with some early PERT/Cost systems was that they consolidated and reported information *only* at the project level, making it difficult to sort through hundreds of work packages to locate sources of cost or schedule overruns. Other systems reported information *only* at the work package level, which was fine for project control but conflicted with the functionally organized cost and budgeting systems that most organizations use. In modern project management the individual work package remains the central element for control, but PCASs now permit consolidation and reporting of information for *any* level of the project, from the individual cost account or work package up to the project level. Additionally, most also permit consolidation and reporting of project information using a functional breakdown.

For instance, when cost accounts are established for work packages, the PCAS can aggregate them vertically through the WBS or horizontally through the project-functional organization. Figure 9-11 in Chapter 9 is an example of how cost-account information was aggregated for the ROSEBUD project. Because higher-level accounts in the cost-account structure are built up through the WBS and organizational hierarchies, variances in costs and schedules at any project level can be tracked through the structure to identify the work packages causing the variances. Similarly, cost or schedule variances observed at the project level can be traced back through the account structure to find the functional departments responsible for the variance.

Earned Value Concept

Costs are budgeted period-by-period for each work package or cost account (time-phased budgeting). Once the project begins, work progress and actual costs are tracked every period and compared to these budgeted costs. Managers measure and track work progress using the concept of *earned value*. Roughly, earned value represents an estimate of the "percentage of work completed" thus far. (The variable "BCWP," discussed later, is the identical concept.)

Example 1: Earned Value

The earned value of work completed in a project is determined by the combined status of all work packages at a given time. It is computed by taking (1) the sum of the budgeted costs of all work packages thus far completed, plus (2) the sum of the earned value (costs or subjective estimates) of all "open" (started but not yet completed) work packages. If, for example, as of June 30 work packages A, B, and C had been completed, and if they had been budgeted to cost $20K, $10K, and $12K, respectively, and if, additionally, Work Package D had been budgeted to cost $20K and was only 75 percent completed, then the earned value for the project on June 30 would be:

$$\$20K + \$10K + \$12K + (0.75)\ \$20K = \$57K$$

Like expense data, the earned value for the project, individual work packages, or levels in between can be summarized and reported through the PCAS. The application of earned value to project performance analysis will be discussed later.

11.6 PROJECT CONTROL PROCESS

Project control means keeping the project on track according to the project plan. This section focuses on three major aspects of the project control process: work authorization; collecting cost, schedule, and work progress data; and scope, quality, schedule, and cost control.

Work Authorization

As shown in Figure 11-1, *work authorization* begins with upper management, moves down through middle management, and ends with the work teams. Before they accept responsibility, each level should review tasks they are authorized to perform according to the specified statement of work, schedule, and budget.

Authorization formally occurs upon top management's acceptance of the project plan. This authorizes the project manager, functional managers, and supervisors to begin expending project funds for labor and materials. Similar authorization is extended to subcontractors and suppliers.

On large projects, authorization is subdivided into the stages of *contract release,* *project release,* and *work order release* or *requisition.* After a contract has been awarded, the contract administrator prepares a contract release document that specifies contractual requirements and gives project management the go-ahead. The comptroller or project accountant then prepares a project release document that authorizes funding for the project.

Actual work begins when a department or work unit receives a *work order* or requisition, which might be an "engineering order," "shop order," "test order," or similar document, depending on the kind of work. Each work order is a small but crucial part of project control; it specifies how requirements are to be fulfilled, the permissible resources to be expended, and the time period over which the work should span. Work orders include:[8]

- Statement of work.
- Time-phased budget of direct labor hours, materials, and other direct costs.
- Schedules, milestones, and relationships to other work packages.
- Position of the task in the WBS.
- Specifications and requirements.
- Cost-account number and position in the cost-account structure.
- Signatures of person authorizing and person accepting responsibility.

Before any task can begin, a work order requisition or other such order is required. As the start date for a given task draws near, the project office releases authorization to begin work using the work order document. Each work order is assigned to a cost account and is updated as new information is available or new requirements

Figure 11-1
Project work authorization process.

arise. Other authorization documents such as purchase orders, test requests, and tool orders are released as needed.

Collecting Cost, Schedule, and Work Progress Data

Work orders and their cost accounts are the fundamental elements of project control. For each work order, data about *actual* costs and work progress is periodically collected and entered into the PCAS. The PCAS tallies and summarizes information up through the WBS and project organization structure in a process similar to creating the budget summaries described in the last chapter. Using work order information, the PCAS generates performance reports on a period-by-period basis for every work package, the entire project, every department or section, and at various levels of the WBS.

Assessing the impact of work progress on work schedules is the responsibility of the functional manager or team supervisor in charge of the work order. Each week the supervisor tallies the labor hours for each task as indicated on time cards. She notes tasks completed and tasks still "open," and estimates the time still needed to complete open tasks. Progress is recorded on a Gantt chart showing completed and open tasks. Figure 11-2 is an example showing the status of the LOGON project as of Week 20. Notice that work packages K, L, M, and Q are all behind schedule.

How is work progress measured? Certainly costs and time elapsed are measured easily, but neither say much about the actual progress made toward completing the project. There are few instances in project work where performance can be measured precisely or reliably. Because for many tasks finding quantitative measure of progress is difficult or impossible, managers typically rely on the subjective estimates of people involved in the tasks. Although resulting measures are not accurate, their approximation to reality comes close enough to improve project control efforts.

Figure 11-2
Gantt chart showing work status as of Week 20.

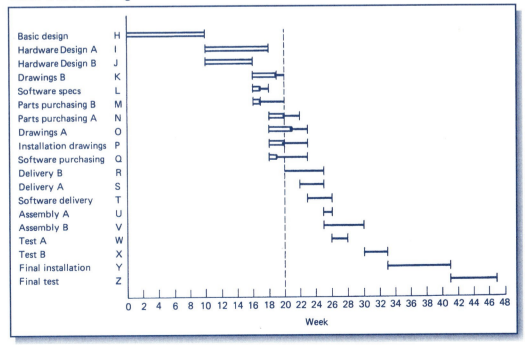

In a survey of conventional ways to measure ongoing project performance, Thompson identified the following.[9]

1. *Supervision.* Managers and supervisors assess progress by direct observation, asking questions, and reviewing written reports and project documentation.
2. *Milestones.* Milestones are easily measured end-points of tasks or transition points between tasks. Milestones, usually considered critical to the project, represent achievement of a desired level of performance, including, for example, completion of drawings, reports, design documents, or solution specific technical problems.
3. *Tests and demonstrations.* These can range from simple testing of system elements and components to full-system and user acceptance testing. They are a good way of obtaining periodic, objective measures of technical systems' progress at intermediate stages of the project.
4. *Design reviews.* These are review meetings with managers and technical personnel (engineers, systems analysts, designers, etc.) to review the state of progress of a design or system against the plan.
5. *Outside experts.* The project manager or other stakeholder invites a person or "expert panel" with experience to review project status. Such experts assess project status by observation, talking to project personnel, and reviewing documentation.
6. *Status of design documentation.* Experienced project managers can determine when a design is nearly finished by the "completeness" of documentation such as drawings, schematics, functional diagrams, manuals, and test procedures.
7. *Resource utilization.* A request for or change in resources may reflect progress; for example, tasks nearing completion often require special testing or implementation facilities, personnel, and equipment.
8. *Telltale tasks.* Certain tasks such as concept design, requirements and specification definition, feasibility analysis, and repeated testing should be completed early or midway through the project; they may signify a *lack* of progress when occurring later in the project.
9. *Benchmarking or analogy.* Certain tasks, or the entire project, may be compared to similar tasks or projects as a crude way to weigh relative progress.
10. *Changes, bugs, and rework.* The rate of changes to the plan (design, schedule, budget), number of system bugs, and amount of rework also are measures of progress. Because, ordinarily, the number of changes, bugs, and so forth, should decrease as the project nears completion, a sustained high number may *indicate* lack of progress.

The work package supervisor documents any changes in estimates or schedules for remaining work and submits it to the project manager for approval. Using network methods, the impact of current work on remaining work is reassessed.

Each week the work package supervisor also tallies current expenses. Labor hours reported on time cards are converted into direct labor cost. The supervisor adds direct labor, material, and level-of-effort costs for completed and open tasks to the cost of work done in prior periods, then applies the overhead percentage rate to applicable direct charges. Late charges and outstanding costs (a frequent source of cost overruns) are also included.[10]

As each task is completed its cost account is closed to prevent additional, unauthorized billing. Each week a revised report is prepared showing costs of all work completed in prior periods plus work accomplished in the current period. This is reviewed, verified, and signed by the supervisor before forwarding it to the project manager. Once work package information has been validated by the project manager it is entered into the PCAS so that costs to date can be accumulated across all work packages and summary reports prepared. Periodically the project manager reviews the summary reports to reassess the project and prepare estimates of the work and cost still needed to complete the project. These estimates plus the record of project costs and work progress to date provide a forecast of the completion date and project cost at completion. This forecast of the cost of work and time needed to complete the project is described later.

11.7   PROJECT CONTROL EMPHASIS

In project control, the emphasis is on scope, quality, schedule, and cost.

Scope Change Control

A change in project scope is an alteration to the original, agreed-upon scope statement defined in the project plan and specified in the WBS. Projects have a natural tendency to grow over time because of changes and additions in the scope, a phenomenon called "creeping scope." Changes or additions to the scope reflect changes in requirements and work definition that usually result in time and cost increases. The aim of scope change control is to identify where changes have occurred, ensure the changes are necessary and/or beneficial, contain or delimit the changes wherever possible, and manage the implementation of changes. Because changes in scope directly impact schedules and costs, controlling scope changes is an important aspect of controlling schedules and costs. Scope change control is implemented through the *change control system* and *configuration management*, described later.

Quality Control

Quality is synonymous with ability to conform to the requirements of the end-item and work processes and procedures. Quality control is managing the work to achieve the desired requirements and specifications, taking preventive measures to keep errors and mistakes out of the work process, and determining and eliminating the sources of errors and mistakes as they occur.

Part of project quality control is the *quality management plan* mentioned in Chapter 5. The quality plan describes necessary "quality conditions" for every work package; that is, prerequisites or stipulations about what must exist before, during, and after the work package to ensure quality. The quality plan should specify the measures and procedures (tests, inspections, reviews, etc., as discussed earlier) to assess conditions and progress toward meeting requirements.

Another part of quality control is tracking project performance with respect to technical requirements, and modifying the work or the requirements as necessary. A methodology for doing this called *technical performance measurement, TPM,* is described later.

A variety of methods are employed for testing and inspection to eliminate defects and ensure that end-items satisfy requirements. Tests and inspections should be ongoing so that problems or defects are identified as early as possible. In general, the earlier in the development cycle that problems are found, the less costly it is to remedy them. The following illustrates an inspection approach appropriate for use in design engineering and software development projects.

Example 2: Team Inspection Process[11]

The purpose of the team inspection process is to improve quality, shorten development time, and reduce costs by avoiding defects. The process occurs in a team meeting of four or five people who inspect requirements documents, design documents, and software code. The roles of the team members are:

- *Moderator:* The person who oversees the inspection and records defects spotted in the document or code.

- *Reader:* The individual who reads the document or code, line by line, during the inspection meeting.

- *Inspector(s):* The person who is the most knowledgeable, with the most information, and best able to detect errors in the documentation or code.

- *Author:* The engineer or programmer who created the document or code.

The process works like this:

Upon completing the requirements document, design document, or code, the author schedules an inspection meeting. To hold the meeting, every member of the inspection team must have a copy of the material being inspected and all supporting documentation at least 2 days in advance.

Each inspection meeting lasts for about 2 hours. During that time a team can usually inspect 10–15 pages of text or 400 lines of code. Defects are documented, and, at the end, the team decides whether it should meet again after the defects have been corrected. When the inspector signs off on the document or code, the inspection can be considered completed and the material approved.

As part of a continuous improvement effort (discussed next), the identified defects or mistakes can be entered into a database. Reference to the database during other projects can reduce the chances of similar mistakes occurring again.

In assisting project managers to meet conditions, achieve requirements, and eliminate defects, quality control identifies *why* requirements or conditions are not being met; that is, the *sources* of defects, mistakes, or problems, as well as ways to eliminate the sources so the same problems won't reappear. Although projects are unique entities, they often consist of repeating tasks or processes that may incubate sources of errors, mistakes, or defects. To deal with quality problems that are both unique and repetitive, the project manager can appoint a *quality-improvement team,* which is a small group of individuals responsible for identifying and eliminating the sources of quality problems. On a small project, one cross-functional team might serve the function; on a large project, several specialized teams might be needed to address particular problems in certain phases or technical areas of the project. To help eliminate problem sources and improve processes in future projects, the contractor or customer can incorporate the findings of these quality-improvement teams into larger, ongoing continuous improvement efforts.

Schedule Control

The intent of schedule control is to keep the project on schedule and minimize schedule overruns. One cause of project schedule overruns is poor planning and, especially, poor definition and time estimating. However, even when projects are carefully planned and estimated, they can fall behind schedule from causes beyond anyone's control, including, for example, changes in project scope, weather problems, and interrupted shipments of materials. Other, more controllable, causes of schedule overruns are as follows.[12]

1. Multitasking. Working on many tasks or projects dissipates focused energy, causing some tasks to be delayed. For example, a contractor has three independent projects, X, Y, and Z, each of which are anticipated to take 10 weeks to complete; further, assume that the contractor is anxious to finish *all* of them as soon as possible.

Instead of giving any project priority, the contractor divides each into small pieces so that, in a sense, work on all three can occur at the same time. If the projects were scheduled sequentially, without interruption, and, if X was given top priority, Y secondary importance, and Z last place, then, as shown in Figure 11-3, Schedule (a), Project X could be finished at Week 10, Project Y at Week 20, and Project Z at Week 30. However, when the projects are broken up into smaller pieces, say, in 5-week periods, so that work alternates among projects, then the *elapsed time* for each of the projects becomes 20 weeks. This is illustrated in Figure 11-3, Schedule (b). The net result is that two of the projects are actually delayed: Project X finishes in Week 20, and Project Y finishes in Week 25. In general, the more tasks or projects are broken up to be worked on concurrently, the greater the elapsed time necessary to finish each of them.

2. Procrastination.   Given a choice between two scheduled times, one early and one late, the human tendency is to *wait* until the late time to begin. This, of course, automatically eliminates any slack time for a task, puts it on the critical path, and increases the likelihood of project delay.

3. Task variability.   The time to complete a task is variable: Some tasks will be completed sooner than expected; others later. In projects, however, the effect of early tasks and late tasks on the project schedule do not average out, and it is only the *late* tasks that count. For example, a task takes 8 days to complete. If the task is actually completed in 10 days, the 2-day delay will be passed on to succeeding tasks. If, however, the task had been completed in 6 days, the 2-day savings usually will not be passed on to succeeding tasks because they are not *scheduled* to start until Day 8. In most cases, those responsible for initiating later tasks either will not know that they *could* have started earlier or, if informed they can start sooner, won't have the resources to do so.

With parallel activities the effect is the same, even when some tasks finish early and some late. Figure 11-4 shows Task D with three predecessors. Suppose tasks A and B finish 10 days ahead of their late finish dates, and that Task C finishes 10 days *after* its late finish date. On average, the three tasks are finished $(10 - 10 - 10)/3 = -3.33$, which means 3.33 days early. Only Task C counts, however, and as a result, Task D is delayed 10 days.

The following are guidelines for controlling schedule variability and keeping projects on schedule.

1. *Fight the tendency to multitask.* Do not interrupt work on particular tasks or projects by interspersing work on other tasks or projects. Assign priorities; then work continuously on one task or project at a time until completed. Not only does this reduce the total elapsed time to complete the task (Schedule (a), Figure 11-3), it also tells workers on what to concentrate.

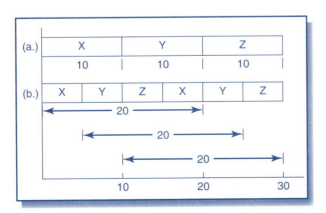

Figure 11-3
Effect of multitasking on elapsed and completion times.

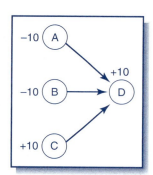

Figure 11-4
Influences of early and late predecessors.

2. *Include time buffers in the schedule.* A time buffer is a schedule reserve, an amount of time included in the expected duration to account for variability in completion times. To implement a time buffer, start with the late finish date and advance it (move it up) by the buffer amount. If the late finish date is July 31 and the desired time buffer is 4 weeks, the late finish date on the schedule is set for 4 weeks earlier. Goldratt suggests that, in general, time buffers should be located at two places; (1) at the end of every subpath in the project network that leads into the critical path, and (2) at the end of the critical path for the entire project.[13] This is illustrated in Example 3. The size of the time buffer depends on the perceived variability or uncertainty in project tasks. It can range from a small percentage of the total time estimate to well over 50 percent.[14]

Because of people's tendency to procrastinate or slack off when they perceive excess available time, the project manager does not *broadcast* the time buffers, but enforces the advanced schedule. Of course, the project manager can further increase the likelihood of finishing on time by circulating only *one* set of dates—the *early* start and finish times for the advanced schedule.

Example 3: Time Buffers in a Project Schedule

The contract for the Aroma project specifies completion in 35 weeks. The project manager wants to include time buffers to ensure the project is done within that time frame. She begins by determining the usual early and late times, shown in Figure 11-5(a). The network Critical Path B-F-J-K-L indicates that the project duration will be 27 weeks. Next, she picks the buffer times. For example, the project manager believes from experience that for a project of this type and duration, a buffer of 4 weeks is adequate to ensure completion by the target date, 35 weeks later. She also believes that 2-week buffers in the upper and lower noncritical subpaths are adequate to ensure their completion. To include the 4-week buffer on the critical path, she advances (moves up) the late times everywhere in the project by 4 weeks. This is shown in Figure 11-5(b). Then, using these advanced times, she moves up the time on the two noncritical subpaths by an *additional* 2 weeks. This is shown in Figure 11-5(c).

Assuming the present time is zero, the times in Figure 11-5(c) become the scheduled weeks when activities in the Aroma project should start and finish.

Goldratt suggests using a project time buffer that is 50 percent of the original time estimate.[15] This is because often the time estimates for project activities are "low-risk estimates," meaning they are set (intentionally or not) high enough so there is little risk of not finishing them on time. Therefore, if instead you ask for a "50/50 estimate," the number you will get is about one-half the typical (low-risk) estimate. For example, suppose a project is estimated to take 28 weeks to complete. Reducing this by half gives 14 weeks. Thus, instead of 28 weeks, the scheduled completion time would be set to 14 weeks, while the remaining 14 weeks

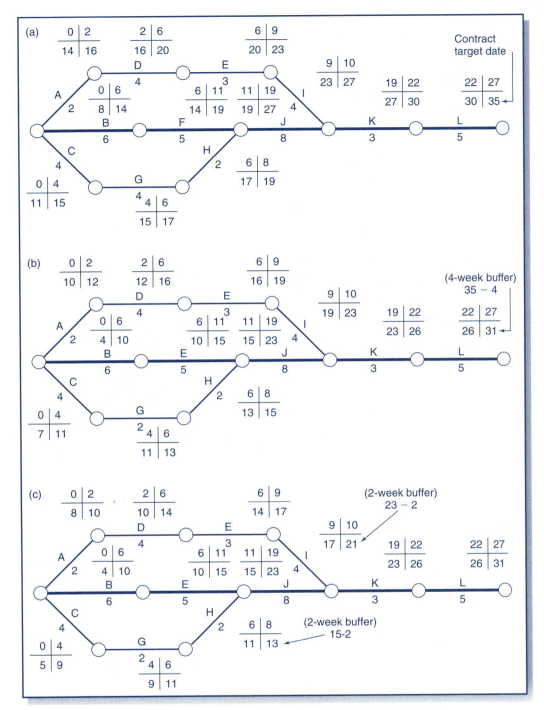

Figure 11-5
Inclusion of time buffers in the Aroma project schedule.

would be held in the project schedule reserve. Should any activity run over its scheduled duration (which would now be one-half the original estimated duration), the overage amount would be subtracted from the buffer. Although a 14-week completion time might be considered quite aggressive—and have a good chance of being overshot, because everyone is striving to achieve it the project nonetheless has a high likelihood of finishing well ahead of the originally estimated 28-week completion time.

Including time buffers in this manner is one way to reduce the risk of not meeting target completion dates, an alternative to *adding in* "corrective times" as explained in the supplement in Chapter 10. The following example illustrates how the time buffer (or schedule reserve) in a large project is controlled and allocated.

Example 4: Doling Out the Reserves in the Mars Pathfinder Project[16]

The goal of the Pathfinder project was to land on Mars a skateboard-sized, self-propelled, six-wheel rover that would move over terrain and send back photos and scientific data (See Figure 11-6.) The project had a budget reserve, or contingency, of $40 million, which represented 30 percent of the total project budget (a large percentage common to risky technological projects), and a schedule reserve of 20 weeks, which was included in the 37-month schedule for system design, building, and testing.

Once the project was underway the question arose: How should the reserves be used? Use them too freely and too early and you have nothing left for later when reserves might be critical. Be too stingy and you stifle progress, increase risk, and end up with leftover reserves that might have been put to better use.

The guideline adopted for allocation of reserves was to set hard limits as to how much to release in each period of the project. For example, *none* of the schedule reserve was to be used (no slippage allowed) until the start of system assembly and test, which was planned at the halfway point in the project. (Time was a strategic consideration because the launch date had been set to coincide with a certain relative position of Earth and Mars.) But when problems arise, something has to give way to prevent the project from falling behind; hence the

Figure 11-6
The Mars Pathfinder rover vehicle.

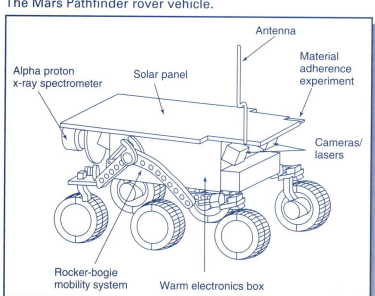

decision was made to commit whatever budget reserves were necessary to keep the project on schedule.

The project was a success. Pathfinder landed on July 4, 1997, and the little rover sent back thousands of pictures. The project established a new standard for space exploration in its use of imaginative new technology to design, build, and land a spacecraft in half the time and at one-twentieth the cost of previous Mars missions.

3. *Frequently report the expected completion times.* For adequately preparing activities to start at the earliest possible time, information on the progress on their predecessors is necessary. Especially in extremely time-sensitive projects, reports on every activity should be delivered on a daily basis indicating the expected number of days remaining to complete and the earliest date by when subsequent activities will be expected to begin. In priority projects, the expectation is that as soon as the immediate predecessor is completed, the work group next in line will stop doing whatever else it is doing to begin work on the project activity. The continual reporting about progress gives work groups time to acquire additional resources they might need, and to quickly finish up whatever else they are doing.

4. *Publicize the consequences of schedule delays.* All project team members, subcontractors, and suppliers should be informed about the consequences of overrunning the schedule, and of the possible benefits of beating the schedule. Often the project manager is unaware of the consequences, so he and other stakeholders are not especially concerned about schedule overruns. The project contract might include incentive payments to the contractor to complete the project early or on time, though regardless of contract type the project manager might be able to add money to the budget for making bonus payments to workers as incentives to deliver on schedule.

A variety of measures in combination can be used to keep projects on schedule, as the following example illustrates.

Example 5: Meeting Launch Deadlines at Microsoft[17]

Microsoft meets product launch dates by utilizing visual freeze, internal target ship dates, and time buffers in schedules. A "visual freeze" is a halt imposed on a product's aspects that affects its visual appearance to customers. The freeze date usually occurs at approximately the 40 percent mark of the schedule. Upon reaching that date, developers lock into the product its major features. After that, few, if any, changes are allowed in major interface features (menus, dialog boxes, and document windows). Any change requests that arise must be negotiated with the program manager, lead developer, and product manager. The freeze enables the user education group to prepare training and system documentation in parallel with product final debugging and testing so the documentation will be ready at the time of product release. Despite the apparent benefits of this tactic, managers admit that sticking to the visual freeze date is difficult, that late changes still happen, and that often many hours are spent redoing the documentation so that it conforms with late changes in the product.

Microsoft also sets "internal targets dates" that it tries to fix. Internal target dates pressure developers to decide which product features must absolutely be included and which may be forgone. Without fixed ship dates, developers tend to add product features and ignore product schedules. Given fixed ship dates, they must determine in advance which features can be included so the product can be released to market in time.

To account for overlooked or poorly understood tasks, very difficult bugs, and unforeseen changes in features, Microsoft also includes time buffers in project schedules. The buffers are used exclusively for uncertainties, not for routine or planned tasks. A time buffer can range from 20 percent of the total schedule time for application projects, to 50 percent for totally new projects. Schedules for project teams do not include time buffers. These schedules show only the internal ship dates, the launch dates announced to the public minus the time buffer.

Cost Control

Cost control tracks expenditures versus budgets to detect variances. It seeks to eliminate unauthorized or inappropriate expenditures, and to minimize or contain cost changes. It identifies why variances occur, where changes to cost baselines are necessary, and what cost changes are reflected in budgets and cost baselines.

Cost control is accomplished at both the work-package level and the project level using the cost account structure and PCAS described earlier. Through the PCAS, actual expenditures are tallied, validated, accumulated, and compared to budgeted costs. Periodically the project manager reviews actual and budgeted costs, compares costs to assessments of the work completed, and prepares estimates of the completion cost and completion date of the project. The methods for assessing performance and forecasting cost and time outcomes are described next.

11.8   PERFORMANCE ANALYSIS

Data collected through the PCAS is used to assess project work, schedule, and cost performance. Analytical methods for assessing performance are described next.

Cost and Schedule Analysis with Budgeted Cost of Work Performed

The status of the project or any portion of it can be assessed with three variables: BCWS, ACWP, and BCWP.

1. *BCWS* is the *budgeted cost of the work scheduled*—the sum cost of all work, plus apportioned effort, scheduled to be completed within a given time period as specified in the *original budget.* It is the same as the time-phased budget mentioned before. For example, Table 9-5 in Chapter 9 shows the cumulative and weekly BCWS for the LOGON project. In Week 20, for example, to date BCWS is $512,000 and weekly BCWS is $83,000.

2. *ACWP* is the *actual cost of the work performed*—the actual expenditure incurred in a given time period. It is the sum of the costs for all completed work packages plus all "open" work packages and overhead.

As one measure of project performance, ACWP can be compared to BCWS. Suppose in the LOGON example that the ACWP as of Week 20 is $530,000. This is $18,000 more than the budgeted amount of $512,000 (Chapter 9, Table 9-5). Remember, however, that whether or not this represents a cost overrun depends on how much work has been completed. The additional $18,000 might have resulted from some tasks being performed ahead of schedule, meaning that the project is not overbudget but rather is ahead of schedule. As mentioned before, project work progress must be known before project performance can be judged. This is where the next variable comes in.

3. *BCWP* is the *budgeted cost of the work performed.* This variable is the same as the *earned value* concept mentioned earlier. It is determined by looking at work tasks

already performed (completed and open work packages, plus overhead) as well as their *corresponding budget* to see what they were *supposed* to cost. Then,

- The BCWP for a completed task is the same as the BCWS for that task.
- BCWP of a partially completed work package is estimated more subjectively, using formulas or an actual tally of the work completed so far. It is sometimes computed by taking 50 percent of BCWS when the work package is started, then the remaining 50 percent when it is completed at the finish.

Following is a simple example illustrating how to compute BCWP.[18]

Example 6: BCWP versus BCWS in the Parmete Company

The Parmete Company has a $200,000 fixed-cost contract to install 1,000 new parking meters. The contract calls for removing old parking meters from their stands and replacing them with new ones. The cost for this is $200 per meter.

Parmete estimates that 25 meters can be installed each day. On this basis, the budgeted cost of the work scheduled (BCWS) for any given day in the project is determined simply by multiplying the number of working days completed by the cost of installing 25 meters ($200 times 25). For example, as of Day 18,

$$BCWS = 18 \text{ days} \times (25 \text{ meters}) \times (\$200) = \$90,000.$$

Another way of saying this is that the $90,000 represents what the project *was budgeted, or supposed to have cost as of the eighteenth day*. Notice that cumulative BCWS is always associated with a specific date on the schedule. At a rate of 25 meters per day and a cost of $200 per meter, the project should take 40 working days to finish and have a final BCWS of $200,000.

In contrast, the budgeted cost of the work performed (BCWP), or the *earned value*, shows, for any day in the project, how much work has *actually* been done in terms of the budgeted costs. In this project, it is the number of meters *actually* installed to date times the $200 budgeted for each. Suppose, for example, that as of the eighteenth working day, 400 meters had been installed; thus,

$$BCWP = (400 \text{ meters}) \times (\$200) = \$80,000$$

In other words, as of the eighteenth working day, $80,000 worth of work has been performed. Now, given that $90,000 was the amount of work that was *supposed* to have been performed, the project is $10,000 worth of work behind schedule. Notice that the $10,000 does not represent a cost savings, but rather that the project is *behind schedule*. $10,000 represents 50 parking meters, or 2 days worth of work, which means that as of Day 18 the project is 2 days behind schedule. (The 2 days is referred to as the *time variance*, or *TV.*) Thus the concept of BCWP enables project cost to be translated into project work progress. As of Day 18, this project has made only 16 days worth of work progress. This is represented on the graph for BCWS and BCWP in Figure 11-7.

As stated before, besides completed tasks, the BCWP must also reflect tasks started but not yet completed (open tasks). For example, suppose that before quitting at the end of the eighteenth day the meter installer had just enough time to remove an old meter but not to put in a new one. Therefore, the work on that task was 50 percent completed. If this was the four hundred and first meter, then BCWP would be the full cost for the first 400 meters plus 50 percent of the cost for the four hundred and first:

$$BCWP = \$80,000 + (0.50)(\$200) = \$80,100$$

Thus, as of Day 18 the BCWP would be $80,100, which is slightly more than 16 days of work completed. (Actually, it represents $80,100/(25 \times \$200) = 16.02$ days of

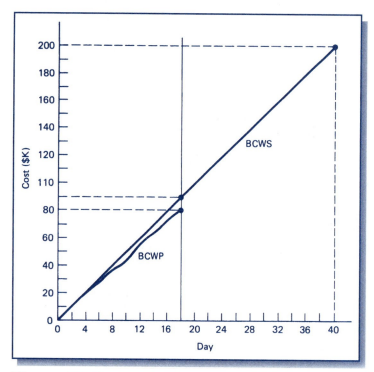

Figure 11-7
BCWS and BCWP graph.

work, which puts the project 1.98 days behind schedule, but such precision is usually unwarranted.)

When taken together, the variables BCWS, ACWP, and BCWP can be used to compute variances which reveal different aspects about the status of a project. For example, assume for the LOGON project as of Week 20, shown in the graph in Figure 11-8,

$$BCWS = \$512,000$$
$$ACWP = \$530,000$$
$$BCWP = \$429,000$$

Then with these figures, four kinds of variances can be determined: accounting, schedule, time, and cost.

1. AV = BCWS − ACWP (accounting variance) = − $18,000
2. SV = BCWP − BCWS (schedule variance) = −$83,000
3. TV = SD − BCSP (time variance) = [SD is the "status date" (here Week 20) and BCSP is the date where BCWS = BCWP (here, about Week 19)] = about 1 week
4. CV = BCWP − ACWP (cost variance) = −$101,000

The accounting variance (AV) of −$18,000 is the difference between the current budget and current actual expenditures. As Figure 11-8 reveals, as of Week 20, actual expenses were $530,000 even though only $512,000 was budgeted.

The schedule variance (SV) shows that the total work completed as of Week 20 is −$83,000 less than planned, suggesting that the project is behind schedule.

The time variance (TV) shows approximately how much the project is behind schedule, about 1 week. This is because only $429,000 worth of work has been com-

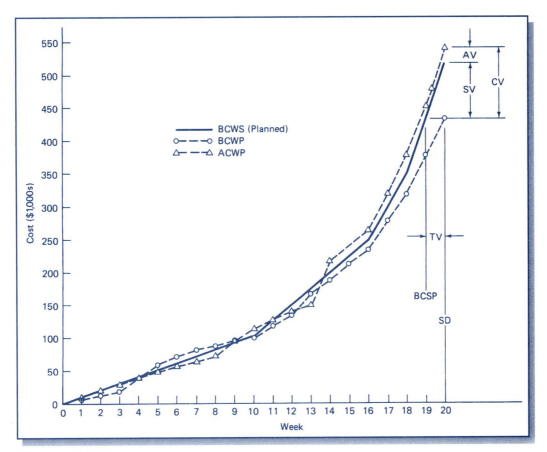

Figure 11-8
LOGON project status as of Week 20.

pleted (BCWP), which is roughly the amount of work scheduled (BCWS) to have been completed a week earlier.

The cost variance (CV) of −$101,000 also takes into account the status of work indicating, again, that LOGON is behind schedule. Given that it compares actual work completed with actual costs, it is a more valid measure of cost performance than SV.

However, taken alone, even CV can be misleading. Sometimes a negative CV (overrun) arises because of factors that are outside of project control, such as overhead rates. Sometimes a positive CV (underrun) occurs because bills have not yet been paid (or are paid in periods other than when expenses are incurred). In the end, individual cost sources should be scrutinized.

Work Package Analysis and Performance Indices

For the project manager to know the status of the project, she needs information on the performance for all work packages and participating functional areas. With information from the PCAS, graphs similar to Figure 11-2 and Figure 11-8 can be prepared for every work package and cost account.

Consider the status of the LOGON project as of Week 20. Referring to Figure 11-2, activities H, I, and J have been completed and are closed accounts, activities K through Q are "open" and in progress. This Gantt chart gives a general *overview* of work package and project status, but to determine the origins of project problems it is necessary to assess each work activity in more detail. For this, two kinds of *performance indices* are used to assess the schedule and cost performance of work packages and the relative size of problem areas:

1. SPI = BCWP/BCWS (schedule performance index), and
2. CPI = BCWP/ACWP (cost performance index).

Values of SPI and CPI greater than 1.0 indicate that work is ahead of schedule and underbudget, respectively; values less than 1.0 represent the opposite.

Table 11-1 shows cost and variance information for all LOGON activities as of Week 20. The performance indices CPI and SPI show trouble spots and their relative magnitude. Notice that L, M, and Q have fallen the most behind schedule (they have the smallest SPIs) and that L and M have had the greatest cost overruns relative to their sizes (they have the smallest CPIs). The overall project is "somewhat" behind schedule and over cost (SPI = 0.84; CPI = 0.81).

Focusing on *only* the project level or *only* the work package level to determine project status can be misleading, and the project manager should scan both, back and forth. If the project manager looks only at the project level, good performance of some activities will overshadow and hide poor performance in others. If she focuses only on individual work packages, the cumulative effect from slightly poor performance on many activities can easily be overlooked. Even small cost overruns on many individual work packages can add up to large overruns for the project.

The importance of examining detailed variances at both project and work package levels is further illustrated in the following two examples. The SV = $83,000 in Figure 11-8 would suggest that the LOGON project is behind schedule; this project level analysis says it is about 1 week behind (TV = 1). However, scrutinizing Figure 11-2 reveals that one of the work packages behind schedule, Activity M, is on the critical path (see Chapter 7, Figure 7-19). Because this activity appears to be about 3 weeks behind schedule, the project must also be 3 weeks behind schedule, *not* 1 week as estimated by the project level analysis.

The importance of monitoring performance at the work package level is further illustrated by the following example from the ROSEBUD project. Figure 11-9 is the cost report for Work Package L for Month 2. This report would likely be available to

Table 11-1 LOGON Performance Report Week 20 Cumulative to Date.

Activity	BCWS	ACWP	BCWP	SV	CV	SPI	CPI
H*	100	100	100	0	0	1.00	1.00
I*	64	70	64	0	−6	1.00	0.91
J*	96	97	96	0	−1	1.00	0.99
K	16	12	14	−2	2	0.88	1.17
L	36	30	18	−18	−12	0.50	0.60
M	84	110	33	−51	−77	0.39	0.30
N	40	45	40	0	−5	1.00	0.89
O	20	28	24	4	−4	1.20	0.86
P	24	22	24	0	2	1.00	1.09
Q	32	16	16	−16	0	0.50	1.00
Project	512	530	429	−83	−101	0.84	0.81

*Completed

	Current Period					Cumulative to Date				
Charge	BCWS	BCWP	ACWP	SV	CV	BCWS	BCWP	ACWP	SV	CV
Direct labor Professional Associate Assistant										
Direct labor cost Labor overhead Other direct cost	6,050 4,538	4,840 3,630	6,050 5,445	−1,210 −908	−1,210 −1,815	6,050 4,538	4,840 3,630	6,050 5,445	−1,210 −908	−1,210 −1,815
Total direct cost General/adminstrative	10,588 1,059	8,470 847	11,495 1,150	−2,118 −212	−3,025 −303	10,588 1,059	8,470 847	11,495 1,150	−2,118 −212	−3,025 −303
Total costs	11,647	9,317	12,645	−2,330	−3,328	11,647	9,317	12,645	−2,330	−3,328

Project ROSEBUD

Department Programming

Date Month 2

Work Package L Software specifications

Note: BCWP is for 80 percent of work scheduled and labor overhead is increased
to 90 percent of labor cost.
SPI: BCWP/BCWS = .80   CPI: BCWP/ACWP = .74

Figure 11-9
Cost chart as of Month 2.

managers about 2 or 3 weeks into Month 3. The numbers in the BCWS columns are derived from the Month 2 column in the budget plan in Figure 9-7, Chapter 9. Current and cumulative numbers are the same because Work Package L begins in Month 2.

The performance indices (total costs) for Work Package L are

$$SPI = BCWP/BCWS = 0.80, \text{ and}$$
$$CPI = BCWP/ACWP = 0.74$$

which indicate both schedule and cost overruns as of Month 2. Suppose the project manager investigates the costs for Work Package L and finds the following:

First, although ACWP and BCWS for direct labor are equal, BCWP reflects the estimate that only 80 percent of work scheduled for the period was actually performed (BCWP = BCWS × SPI = 6050 × 0.80 = 4850). Second, although ACWP and BCWS for direct labor are equal, the corresponding labor overheads are different. Suppose in this example that the difference was due to a rate increase in labor overhead from 75 percent to 90 percent during Month 2 because of changes in company workload. If other projects required fewer direct labor hours than planned, projects such as ROSEBUD would have to carry a larger percentage of overhead expenses. The project manager has no control over factors such as this, yet they affect his costs.

Now look at Figure 11-10, the cost report for the same work package for Month 3. The performance indices for cumulative total costs are

$$SPI = BCWP/BCWS = 1.00, \text{ and}$$
$$CPI = BCWP/ACWP = 0.92.$$

Notice that, first, direct labor AWCP for the month is the same as direct labor BCWS, but more work was performed than expected for the month (BCWP > BCWS). The result is that the task was completed on schedule, as indicated by the cumulative SPI = 1.00. Also notice that there was a negative cost variance, but the project manager

	Current Period					Cumulative to Date				
Charge	BCWS	BCWP	ACWP	SV	CV	BCWS	BCWP	ACWP	SV	CV

Direct labor
  Professional
  Associate
  Assistant										

Direct labor cost Labor overhead Other direct cost	5,000 3,750	6,050 4,538	5,000 4,500	1,050 788	1,050 38	11,050 8,288	11,050 8,288	11,050 9,945	0 0	0 1,657
Total direct cost General/administrative	8,750 875	10,588 1,059	9,500 950	1,838 184	1,088 108	19,338 193	19,338 193	20,995 2,100	0 0	1,657 166
Total costs	9,625	11,647	10,450	2,022	1,196	21,272	21,272	23,095	0	1,823

Project __ROSEBUD__ Date __Month 3__

Department __Programming__ Work Package __L Software specifications__

Note: BCWP is for 121 percent of work scheduled, but for cumulative it is 100 percent (made up for delay in Period 2). $1,823 CV reflects increase in overhead rate.

Figure 11-10
Cost chart as of Month 3.

knows that it is not the project's fault, because the contributing factor is the increased overhead rate, which remained at 90 percent during months 2 and 3.

Of the numerous factors that affect project work progress and costs, some are simply beyond the project manager's control. Thus, to determine the sources of variance and places where action can or must be taken requires close scrutiny of costs and performance at the work package level. A project level analysis is simply inadequate.

Updating Time Estimates

Work progress should be reviewed and reported frequently. In general, time elapsed between reviews should be less than the average length of work packages. A good rule of thumb is to review work every 1 to 2 weeks. For small projects, a weekly review will ensure that even small work packages—those lasting only 2 to 3 weeks—are reviewed at least twice. For large projects with lengthy work packages of several months, a review conducted every 2 to 3 weeks might be adequate. The goal is to review work often enough to be able to spot problems early, measure progress accurately, and forecast outcomes, yet not so often that it is overly time-consuming or burdensome.

Following each progress review, it might be necessary to update scheduled completion dates of each task or work package based upon estimates of current progress. In general, the forecast finish date for a task is the start date plus the time remaining. The *time remaining* is determined in two ways. One way is to compute time remaining as a function of current progress and the days worked so far, that is:

$$\text{Time remaining} = \frac{\text{Percent of task remaining}}{\text{Percent progress per day}}$$

where

$$\text{Percent progress per day} = \frac{\text{Percent of task completed so far}}{\text{Days worked on task so far}}$$

The other way is to simply get the estimate from an experienced, reputable source ("it'll take another 5 days to finish the job"). The latter often yields a more accurate estimate than the former because it accounts for possible recent changes in the rate of work progress.

Example 7: Revising the Task Completion Date

A task is planned to start on July 3 and requires 12 days of work. Assuming work continues during weekends, the last day of work will be July 14.

Suppose the actual start date for the task is July 10. After 5 working days (end of July 14), the job leader reviews the work, estimating that the task is 20 percent complete. If the rate of progress stays the same, what is the forecast completion date of the task?

After 5 days of work, the estimated percent complete for the task is 20 percent, so the work progress is 20 percent/5 = 4 percent per day. Thus, completing the remaining 80 percent of the task should take 0.80/0.04, or 20 working days, and the revised scheduled completion date would be August 3. Now instead, assume that the job team leader believes that the remainder of the task will proceed much faster than 4 percent per day because of an accelerated work pace, and that, at most, only 10 more working days will be required. If the team leader's estimate is considered more credible than the computation, then the revised completion date would be July 24.

Either method results in a delayed completion date. If the task is on the critical path, or will become critical as a result of the delay, then the completion date of the project must be revised also.

Technical Performance Measurement

Besides costs and schedules, project performance depends on how well the project is meeting technical requirements of the end-item. *Technical performance measurement* (TPM) is a methodology for tracking the history of a set of technical objectives or requirements over time. It provides management with information about how well the system development process is progressing with respect to particular system objectives, targets, or requirements. TPM's intent is to monitor progress in performance measures and their relationship to goals or targets by providing (1) a best estimate of current technical performance or progress to date, and (2) an estimate of technical performance at project completion. Both kinds of estimates are based upon results from modeling, simulation, or tests and demonstrations.[19]

To perform TPM, it is necessary to specify certain technical performance measures that are key indicators of program success. These measures should be tied to user needs and represent major performance drivers. A large-scale program might involve a dozen or so high-level measures, in which case it is necessary to define certain design parameters upon which the measures depend, and to place required values on these parameters. Examples of performance measures include:

Availability	Capacity	Size or space
Back-up utility	Response time	Reliability
Safety	Security	Power
Speed	Setup time	Interface compatibility
Survivability	Durability	Interoperability
Maintainability	Range	Simplicity/complexity
Flexibility	Variance	Signal-to-noise ratio
Cycle time	Cost	Trip time
Efficiency	Utilization	Idle time
Output rate	Error/defect rate	

Periodically during the project, current (actual) performance estimates are computed or measured and then compared to objectives. Initially these estimates are based upon results from modeling and simulation activities, then later upon test and demonstration results using actual hardware and software. Current estimates and the technical objective are charted on a time-phased TPM chart, which simplifies determining the extent of progress made toward achieving the objective. If actual performance for one part of the system *exceeds* the target or objective by some margin, then that margin can be traded-off against other parts of the system where performance is lacking or at risk. This is illustrated in Example 8.

Example 8: Technical Performance Measurement for Design Tradeoff Decisions

Example 5 in Chapter 10 discussed design margins. In the example, design target weight values for two subsystems of an aircraft navigation system were put at 440 pounds for Subsystem A and 264 pounds for Subsystem B. To cover the risk associated with meeting the requirements, design margins were established for the two subsystems. These represent amounts by which the target values *could* be increased and still achieve system requirements.

Figure 11-11 gives two TPM charts showing the design progress (actual versus target values) for the two subsystems following the critical design review. Charts such as this assist managers and engineers in assessing progress toward design targets, and in determining where design tradeoffs or changes in targets are necessary. Figure 11-11 shows current performance and design targets at three project milestones:

Figure 11-11
Time-phased TPM charts for subsystems A and B.

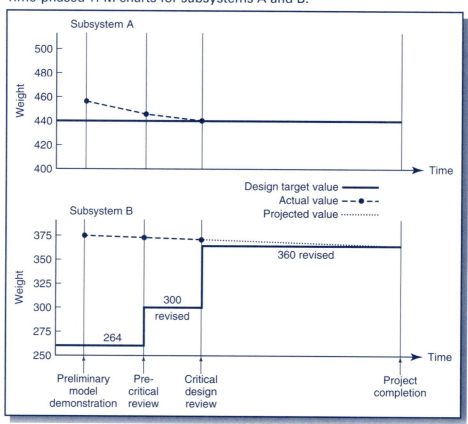

1. At the time of the *preliminary model demonstration,* the actual design values for both subsystems were too high, although Subsystem A was relatively much closer to its design target value than was Subsystem B.
2. By the time of the *precritical review,* Subsystem A had been improved and was very close to its design target, but work on Subsystem B had resulted in little improvement. At this point it was apparent that Subsystem A would be able meet its design target of 440 pounds, but that Subsystem B would *not* be able to meet its target of 264 pounds. The decision was made to remove 36 pounds from Subsystem A's unused design margin and apply it to Subsystem B's new design target of 300 pounds.
3. As of the *critical design review,* Subsystem A had met its target value, but Subsystem B still lagged behind its target value; further, it was anticipated that only limited additional improvement was possible. The decision was therefore made to allocate 60 pounds more from Subsystem A's unused design margin to increase the target value for Subsystem B to 360 pounds. The dotted line for Subsystem B indicates the necessary improvement beyond its current point to achieve B's revised target value by the end of the project.

11.9   FORECASTING "TO COMPLETE" AND "AT COMPLETION"

As the project moves along, the project manager reviews not only what has been accomplished so far, but what remains to be done. Throughout the project, the expected final cost and completion date might have to be revised repeatedly, depending on its current status and direction. Significant schedule and cost overruns or underruns early in a project often indicate that the planned completion date and final cost estimate will have to be revised. In the LOGON example, large cost and schedule overruns as of the twentieth week would likely lead the project manager to wonder when the project will actually be completed and at what cost.

Estimate at Completion

Each month the project manager should prepare what is called a *to complete* forecast. This is a forecast of the time and cost remaining to complete the project. This forecast plus the current actual status of the project provide a revised estimate of the date and cost of the project *at completion.*

The following formulas are used to estimate the cost remaining to complete the project (the to complete cost) and the approximate final project cost (the at completion cost):

$$\text{ETC (Forecasted cost to complete project)} = (\text{BCAC} - \text{BCWP})/\text{CPI}$$

where BCAC is the budgeted cost at completion for the project. This is the same as the BCWS as of the target completion date.

$$\text{EAC (Forecasted cost at completion)} = \text{ACWP} + \text{ETC}$$

Example 9: Forecasting ETC and EAC for LOGON

In the LOGON project at Week 20,

$$\text{CPI} = 429{,}000/530{,}000 = 0.81$$

thus,

$$ETC = (990,000 - 429,000)/0.81 = \$692,593, \text{ and}$$
$$EAC = 530,000 + 692,593 = \$1,222,593.$$

As shown in Figure 11-12, the revised project completion date is estimated by extending the BCWP line, keeping it parallel to the BCWS line, until it reaches the level of BCAC, $990,000. The *horizontal* distance between the BCWS line and the BCWP line at BCAC ($990,000) is roughly the amount the project will be delayed. On Figure 11-12 this is roughly 1 to 3 weeks, meaning the project completion date should be revised from Week 47 to between weeks 48 and 50.

The estimated revised completion date remains to be verified because the actual delay depends on whether any of the activities behind schedule are on the critical path. (From the previous discussion we know that because Activity M is on the critical path, 50 LOGON is almost 3 weeks behind schedule; the revised completion date should thus be Week 50.)

As shown in Figure 11-12, another line, the "Forecast ACWP" can be drawn by extending the current ACWP line up to the level of EAC ($1,159,630) at the revised completion date. In effect, this gives a running estimate of what the "actual" costs should be until project completion.

The forecast completion cost and completion date assume that conditions and resources will not improve (nor, of course, will they worsen either). The proj-

Figure 11-12
Project status chart and forecasts as of Week 20.

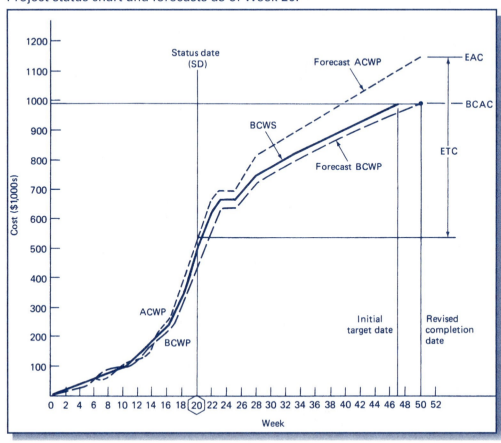

ect manager should question the validity of these assumptions in light of the project environment. In LOGON, for example, given the size of the current overrun ($101,000 as of Week 20), he should question the reasonableness of the forecast completion cost of $1,159,530. Given that the project is less than half finished, is it likely that all remaining work will be completed for only $692,593 more without *additional* overruns? If the answer is no, the figure should be revised further according to best guess estimates. Thus, instead of using the EAC formula given previously, EAC might instead be the actual cost (ACWP) plus the best-guess estimate of the cost of remaining work.

If the *schedule performance* does not improve, it is likely that the project will be completed somewhat later than the current revised estimate of between Weeks 48 and 50. As of Week 20, the BCWP is equivalent to the BCWS at Week 19. This means, in terms of budgeted cost, there are still

$$47 \text{ weeks (target date)} - 19 \text{ weeks} = 28 \text{ weeks}$$

to go. However, given the current schedule performance index SPI = 0.84, it is more likely that there are 28/0.84 = 33.3 weeks to go. Because we are now in Week 20, the revised completion date is 20 + 33.3 = 53.3; that is, the project will be completed sometime in Week 54. This revised estimate takes into account current levels of schedule performance and is probably a more realistic estimate than the graphical estimate of Weeks 48 to 50 in Figure 11-12.

Effect of Uncertainty

The EAC is based upon a single-value assessment of progress, the earned value or BCWP as of the status date. This assessment of the BCWP often is based upon opinions about the percent complete, which means it is subject to uncertainty. If the BCWP is subject to uncertainty, then so is the EAC. A way to account for this uncertainty is to consider a *range* of EACs.[20] The range would consider optimistic, pessimistic, and most likely values of EAC and be interpreted probabilistically. This is illustrated in the following example.

Example 10: Uncertainty in Forecast EAC and Completion Date

Using the LOGON project example from before, the total BCWP as of Week 20 is $429,000. With a project budget of $990,000, the BCWP at Week 20 means that 43.3 percent of the project is completed. Suppose that an expert looks at the project and concludes that, in actuality, it is somewhere between 35 percent and 48 percent completed. These represent the pessimistic and optimistic scenarios, respectively. The corresponding BCWPs are:

Pessimistic	0.35($990,000) = $346,500
Most likely	(given) $429,000
Optimistic	0.48($990,000) = $475,200

Given that as of Week 20 the ACWP = $530,000 and BCWS = $512,000, the range of possible CPIs, SPIs, EACs, and forecast completion dates are:

	CPI	EAC ($)	SPI	Week, BCWP Scheduled*	Revised Week of Completion**
Pessimistic	0.65	1,322,308	0.68	18	62.6
Most likely	0.81	1,222,593	0.84	19	53.3
Optimistic	0.90	1,102,222	0.93	19.5	49.6

*Approximate week where BCWS = current BCWP (see BCWS curve, Figure 11-8).
**20 weeks + [47 weeks − (BCWP, scheduled)]/SPI.

Figure 11-13 shows three points representing the forecast costs (EAC) and revised completion times, and the associated EAC and completion-time probability distributions.

The estimated completion times do not reflect which, if any, of the current behind-schedule activities are on the critical path and, if so, by how much. The estimates reflect only the current rate at which the work is being done and do not distinguish critical from noncritical activities. The assumption is that the pace of work is uniform everywhere in the project, on critical and noncritical tasks alike.

The three measures (optimistic, most likely, pessimistic) for cost and time can be forecast at periodic intervals throughout the project. The procedure for getting the forecasts at Week 20 (demonstrated in Example 10) may be repeated to produce forecasts at later dates; for instance, at weeks 30, 40, 50, and so on. Figure 11-14 shows the plots of pessimistic, most likely, and optimistic EAC forecasts made at 10-week intervals starting in Week 20. (Similar plots of periodic forecasts for optimistic, most likely, and pessimistic completion *times* can also be constructed.) The convergence of the pessimistic and optimistic forecasts as the project moves toward completion indicate a

Figure 11-13
Forecasted cost (EAC) and time estimates at completion.

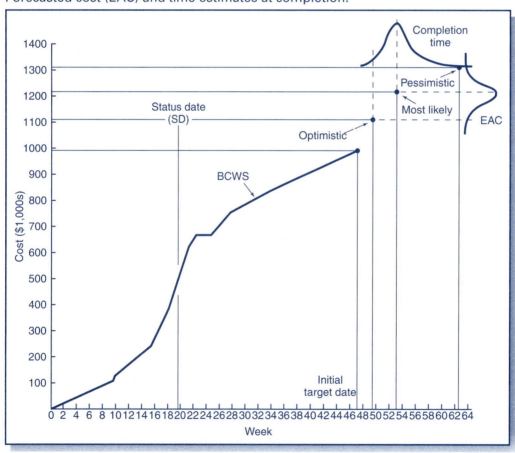

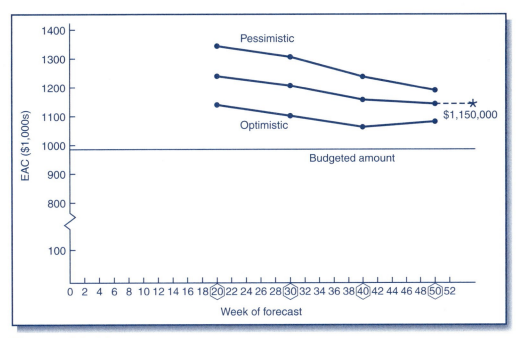

Figure 11-14
Plots of pessimistic, most likely, and optimistic EACs at four review periods.

reduction in uncertainty about the EAC, and suggests that the EAC is heading toward a most likely value of $1,150,000.

11.10 PERFORMANCE INDEX MONITORING

Although project managers should analyze individual work packages to validate project forecasts, in large projects they frequently have to rely more on analysis at the project level. This is because, quite simply, there are so many work packages that it is impossible to investigate every one on a frequent basis.

Project level forecasts may be somewhat inaccurate, but at least they provide the manager with a quick, periodic "ballpark" estimate of project performance. It is better to get this slightly inaccurate information in time than to receive very accurate information too late.

One way for the project manager to track project status and performance trends is to follow a plot of SPI against CPI. The plot in Figure 11-15 is an example. It shows performance for the LOGON project as starting out somewhat poor, recovering, then drifting disturbingly back to and *remaining* in the poor region. In a case such as this the project manager has to rely on the appraisal and judgment of functional managers to help identify causes of problems at the work package level. Plots similar to Figure 11-15 for individual work packages and cost accounts can also be maintained to help the project office recognize the sources of trouble.

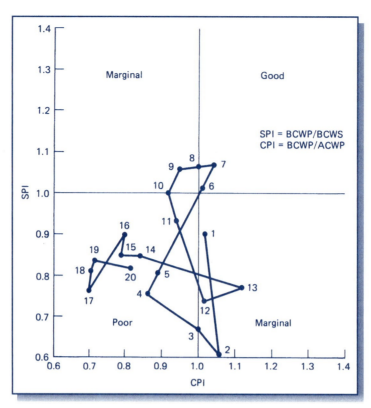

Figure 11-15
Cost/schedule performance index plotted for months 1 to 20.

11.11   VARIANCE LIMITS

Seldom do actual and planned performance measures coincide, and as a result, non-zero variances are more often the rule rather than the exception. This leads to the question: What amount of variance is acceptable before action must be taken? Such is the purpose of *variance limits*.

At each level of the project organization—work package, departmental, and project—critical values are established as "acceptable." When a variance falls outside this acceptable range it is necessary to take measures of corrective action. Some variance limits, similar to those shown in Table 11-2, are set at the beginning of the project

Table 11-2 Example of Variance Boundaries

Work Package A	Variances greater than $2,000
Work Package B	Variances greater than $18,000
Department C	Variances greater than $6,000
Department D	Variances greater than $38,000
Project	Variances greater than $55,000

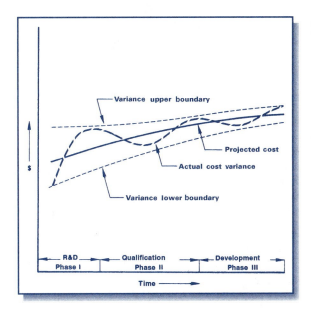

Figure 11-16
Variance tolerance
boundaries.
[Source: H. Kerzner,
*Project Management:
A Systems Approach to
Planning, Scheduling, and
Controlling* (New York:
Van Nostrand Reinhold,
1979): 439. Reprinted with
permission.]

and remain constant for its duration. For jobs where there is considerable uncertainty, such as in a research project, variance limits are varied to permit a larger acceptable range during earlier, riskier phases, and a smaller acceptable range during later, less risky, phases. This is shown in Figure 11-16.

Note that lower as well as upper variance limits can be used. This is as expected because there should be both maximum and minimum acceptable standards. Upper limits are necessary on technical parameters—not to keep performance down, but to minimize costs from excessive or unnecessary development. Upper and lower limits are important for cost and schedule control, also. A project running far ahead of schedule and under budget—an apparently desirable situation—should be scrutinized for oversights, corner cutting, and shoddy workmanship. Variance limits help point out places where cost and schedule underruns might be hurting work quality.

11.12   CONTROLLING CHANGES

No project goes entirely according to plan. Changes to the initial plan and, often, to the end-item system are inevitable because of planning oversights, new opportunities, or events or problems no one could have anticipated. Changes to the plan involve modifying the work, reorganizing or adding personnel, and making time, cost, and performance tradeoffs. Changing the system often involves altering specifications and sacrificing technical performance to meet time and cost restrictions.

Whenever a project manager has to revise the project plan or reschedule work, the two most common constraints are:

- The project *must* be finished by a certain date.
- Resources are strictly *limited*.

With the first constraint it is likely that additional resources will have to be employed so deadlines can still be met. With the second constraint, however, the project usually will be delayed or the project scope altered. In either case, resources are a central issue and problems associated with rescheduling constrained resources, as described in Chapter 8, must be addressed.

The Impact of Changes

It is a fact that any project plan will have to be changed before the project is completed; generally, the larger and more complex the project, the larger the number of changes and the greater the deviation of actual costs and schedules from original objectives. However, there is a reverse causality: Not only do emergent project problems require that the plan be changed, but changes to the plan *cause* problems to the project. In fact, changes to the project plan are a chief cause of cost and schedule overruns, low worker morale, and poor relationships between project and functional managers and clients.

In general, the further along the project, the more detrimental the effect of these changes. The more work that already has been done, the more that will have to be undone. Because changes in the design of one system or component require redesign of other interrelated systems and components, changes in designs made after the design stage has past usually have the effect of significantly increasing the scope and cost of the project and delaying its completion.

Changes made still later, during construction or installation, are even more detrimental. Work is disrupted, things must be torn down and started again, materials are scrapped, and so on. Morale is affected also. People see their work being dismantled, discarded, and redone, usually on a rush basis to try to reduce overruns.

Reasons for Changes

Harrison lists the typical kinds of changes sought or required during a project. They include[21]

1. Changes in project scope and specifications during the early stages of development. The greater the uncertainty of the work, the more likely that the scope and specifications will have to be altered during development. Such changes must be evaluated carefully because they are expensive to implement once the plan has been approved.
2. Changes in design, necessary or desirable, because of errors, omissions, afterthoughts, or revised needs. Mistakes, errors, and omissions must be corrected, but "desirable" changes requested by clients should be questioned, especially when they alter the original, contractual scope of the project. Customer representatives sometimes try to squeeze in changes (for the same price) that are beyond original specifications.
3. Changes imposed by government mandate (health, safety, labor, or environmental codes), labor contracts, suppliers, the community, or other parties in the environment. There is usually no choice but to alter the plan to incorporate these.
4. Changes that are believed to improve the rate of return of the project. Such changes often cannot be justified because of the difficulty in estimating rate of return. Decisions of this nature should be referred to upper management.
5. Changes perceived as improvements upon original requirements. People have a tendency to want to improve upon their work. Apparently desirable, these changes can lead the project beyond its original intended scope and requirements. The project manager should distinguish "necessary" from "nice" changes and resist the latter.

Examples of the project changes include: (Type 1) After development has begun, increasing the payload requirements on a space probe to allow for necessary, additional hardware; (Type 2) after work is well along, modifying a computer software package or a building floor plan to give the user room for expansion; (Type 3) interrupting work because of labor problems or violations of municipal environmental codes; unexpected large increases in the cost of materials; (Type 4) increasing the capacity of a refinery under construction to speed up its payback; (Type 5) adding more and more refinements to an already acceptable product design.

Change Control System and Configuration Management

Because of their adverse effect on project cost and schedule objectives, project managers usually resist changes. As a result, disagreements over the necessity for changes and the impact of changes on project scope, cost, and schedule are a common source of conflict with functional managers and clients. Often these disagreements have to be resolved by upper management and require renegotiation of contracts.

One way to reduce the number of changes and their negative impact on project performance is to employ a formal system for change review and control. Because changes, like other aspects of project work, must be defined, scheduled, and budgeted, the process of drafting and implementing changes is similar to the original planning process. To quickly process and communicate the many changes a large project can generate, a formal *change control system* is used. The purposes of this system are to review and authorize design and work changes, weed out all but the necessary ones, and make sure that related work also is revised and authorized. According to Harrison,[22] such a system should:

1. Continually identify changes as they occur.
2. Reveal their consequences in terms of impact on project costs, project duration, and other tasks.
3. Permit managerial analysis, investigation of alternative courses of action, and acceptance or rejection.
4. Communicate changes to all parties concerned.
5. Specify a policy for minimizing conflicts and resolving disputes.
6. Ensure that changes are implemented
7. Report monthly a summary of all changes to date and their impact on the project.

Early in the project, preliminary baseline specifications are established to be used as a means for identifying changes and measuring their consequences. In projects with considerable uncertainty, initial estimates for technical specifications are based on rough approximations, to be revised and improved as more information becomes available. Throughout the project, the change control system should enable managers to trace the sources of differences between estimates to specific changes or to appraise the impact of proposed changes on current estimates and project plans. In some industries, the formal process of systematic change control and coordination integrated into the systems development cycle is referred to as *configuration management*.

The frequency and necessity for changes can be controlled and minimized through a configuration management approach, which emphasizes such strict procedures as[23]

- Ensuring that original work scope and work orders—with specific schedules, budgets, and statement of work—are clearly stated and *agreed to* by persons responsible.
- Close monitoring of the work to ensure it is *meeting* (not exceeding) specifications.

- Careful screening of tasks for cost or schedule overruns (which may signify increase in work scope) and quick action to correct the problem.
- Requiring that all discretionary changes be subject to a prespecified request and approval process.
- Requiring similar control procedures of all subcontractors and for all purchase orders, test requests, and so on.
- At a predefined phase, freezing the project against all nonessential changes. The freeze prohibits changes and allows the design to be finalized so the next stage (procurement, fabrication, construction, or coding and testing) can begin. The freeze point must be agreed to by management; the sooner the plan can be frozen, the less chance that changes will adversely affect scheduling and cost.

All engineering and work changes should be (1) documented as to their effect on work orders, budgets, schedules, and contractual prices; (2) formally reviewed; and (3) assessed and accepted or rejected. This process is summarized in Figure 11-17. An essential part of the process is the change request document (Figure 11-18), which provides the data and rationale for the proposed change.

Often, the process is handled by a committee called a *change control board*. In larger projects, the change board consists of the project manager and managers from engineering, manufacturing, purchasing, contract administration, and other areas, and meets weekly to review change requests. Prior to the meeting, the effects of proposed changes are estimated to help the board decide which to reject and which to accept.

Any proposed or enacted change that impacts the time, cost, or nature of work of a single task or other related tasks must be documented. Because everyone involved in the project has the potential to recognize or originate changes, everyone must watch for changes and be held accountable for bringing them to the attention of the appropriate stakeholders.

Figure 11-17
The change request process.

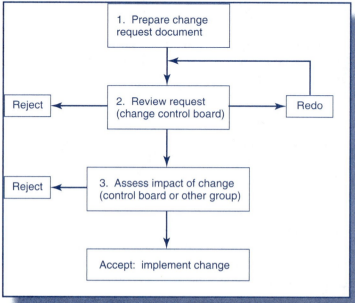

Iron *Butterfly, Corp.*

Change Request	Page of

Title			

Project no.	Task no.	Revision no.	Date issued

Reason for change

Description of change

Documentation attached

Schedule Start date:	Completion date:

Originated by:			

Originated by:	Date:	Accepted by:	Date:
Approved by:	Date:	Approved by:	Date:
Approved by:	Date:	Approved by:	Date:

Figure 11-18
Example of a change request document.

11.13 CONTRACT ADMINISTRATION

Project control also includes aspects of contract administration, including the ongoing comparison of project activities, changes, and accomplishments to the requirements as stipulated in the contract, as well as invoicing of customers and payment of bills. The project control system should assess change requests against conditions stated in the project contract and specify where modifications to the contract are necessary before proceeding. It should assure that all necessary approvals are secured before the contract is modified and the change implemented.

When a contract stipulates customer requirements for project monitoring and reporting, the control system should incorporate the specified measures within the usual performance tracking and progress reporting system. The control system should also ensure that external subcontractors and suppliers are being paid, and that external clients are being invoiced for services and materials in the manner specified in the contract. Certainly, timely billing and receipt of payment are aspects of contract administration of particular importance to the contractor. For a simple project, billing and payment tracking is done through the contractor's accounts receivable system. Large, complex projects often have dedicated billing and tracking systems of their own.

11.14   CONTROL PROBLEMS

No matter how thorough and control conscious the project manager is, and no matter how sophisticated the control systems are, control problems still occur. Roman notes the following common kinds of project control problems:[24]

1. Only one factor, such as cost, is emphasized; yet others such as schedule and technical performance are ignored. This happens when control procedures are issued by one functional area, such as accounting or finance, and other areas are left out. Forcing compliance to one factor alone, such as cost, distorts the control process and usually results in excesses or slips in other areas, such as schedule delays or shoddy workmanship.

2. Control procedures are resisted or do not receive compliance. Individuals who do not understand the benefits or necessity of using formal controls resent attempts at evaluating and controlling their work. Management encourages noncompliance with control procedures when it fails to exercise sanctions against people who defy the procedures.

3. Information is inaccurately or partially reported. The people first aware of a problem may not understand the situation or, if they do, they may be hesitant to reveal it. The information reported may be fragmented and difficult to piece together.

4. Self-appraisal kinds of control systems force people to act defensively and cannot provide unprejudiced information. Bias is one of the biggest obstacles to achieving accurate control.

5. Managers are diffident on controversial issues, believing that with time problems resolve themselves. This gives some workers the impression that management doesn't care about the control process, an attitude likely to spread to others throughout the project.

6. Managers in charge of several projects sometimes misrepresent charges so that poor performance in one is offset by good performance in others. The practice is common in organizations with multiple government contracts as a means of avoiding the bureaucracy and, overall, satisfying the requirements on all contracts. Not only does this distort the overall control process, it is unethical because clients are mischarged for the work.

7. Information reporting and accounting mechanisms are misleading. For example, subjective measures such as the earned value of open work packages can suggest that more work was completed than actually was. Similarly, by altering accounting procedures, a bad situation can be made to look favorable.

To minimize these problems, upper management, functional managers, and project managers must actively support the control process, and all project workers must be shown the relevance of the control process and how it benefits them and the project. To be effective, control procedures must be impersonal, objective, and uniformly applied to all people, tasks, and functional areas.

11.15   SUMMARY

Project control is intended to guide work toward project goals, ensure effective utilization of resources, and correct problems. Project control assesses actual against planned accomplishments, confirms the continued need for the project, and updates expectations about project outcomes and requirements. It requires an effective system for collecting and disseminating information.

Project control utilizes cost, schedule, and work progress variance information. Using the concept of earned value and BCWP, project progress is assessed from the progress of all work packages at a given time.

The focal point of control is the work package and cost account. All activities—authorization, data collection, work progress evaluation, problem assessment, and corrective action—occur within the work package or cost account. Because higher level cost accounts are built up through the WBS and organizational hierarchies, project cost and schedule variances can be traced through the cost account structure to locate the sources of problems.

The control process begins with authorization, specifying time, cost, and technical specifications against which work will be evaluated. Once work begins, the project is continually tracked, with reference to the project plan, for conformance to scope and quality requirements, schedules, and budgets. Data is collected period-by-period for each work package. All projects have a tendency to grow, so keeping the work within the original scope statement is one way to contain cost and schedule overruns. Work quality is monitored against requirements for work tasks and end-items. To assess progress toward meeting project objectives, certain key technical measures are tracked.

As part of a larger quality improvement process, quality-improvement teams identify the sources of mistakes and defects, and implement measures to prevent their recurrence. Work progress and cost data are collected and compared to schedules and budgets. Performance to date is reviewed, and estimates of project cost and completion date are revised.

Variances in costs and schedules are compared to preestablished limits. Whenever variances move beyond acceptable limits, or when new opportunities or intractable problems arise, the work must be replanned and rescheduled. Changes are inevitable, but every effort is made to reduce their impact on cost and schedule overruns. A formal change control system minimizes the frequency and scope of changes, and configuration management ensures that all changes are authorized, documented, and communicated.

A formal PCAS or, more generally, project management information system (PMIS) is required to accumulate, store, integrate, process, and report project information. The next chapter describes the customary requirements and features of PMISs and reviews some software systems for computerizing the tasks of project management.

Summary of Variables

BCWS = budgeted cost of work scheduled
ACWP = actual cost of work performed
BCWP = budgeted cost of work performed (the earned value)

$$AV = \text{accounting variance} = BCWS - ACWP$$
$$SV = \text{schedule variance} = BCWP - BCWS$$
$$CV = \text{cost variance} = BCWP - ACWP$$
$$BCAC = \text{total budgeted cost of project}$$
$$SPI = \text{schedule performance index} = BCWP/BCWS$$
$$CPI = \text{cost performance index} = BCWP/ACWP$$
$$ETC = \text{forecast cost to complete project} = (BCAC - BCWP)/CPI \text{ where BCAC is the budgeted cost at completion}$$
$$EAC = \text{forecast cost of project at completion} = ACWP + ETC$$

REVIEW QUESTIONS AND PROBLEMS

1. What are the three phases of the project control process?
2. Explain the differences between internal and external project controls.
3. How are overhead expenses allocated in work packages?
4. If a cost or schedule variance is noticed at the project level, how is it traced to the source of the variance?
5. Describe the typical pattern of work authorization. What is usually included on a work order?
6. Describe the process of collecting data about the cost, schedule, and work accomplished.
7. Discuss different ways of measuring ongoing work progress.
8. Why is scope change control an important part of the project control process?
9. Discuss quality control as applied to projects.
10. What are the principle causes of project schedule overruns? Discuss at least four practices that may be used to reduce schedule variability and keep projects on schedule.
11. Explain BCWS, ACWP, and BCWP, and how they are used to determine the variances AV, SV, CV, and TV. Explain the meaning of these variances.
12. What does it signify if cost or schedule index figures are less than 1.00?
13. Explain TPM, its purpose, and how it is conducted.
14. Explain what is meant by a forecast "to complete," and how this forecast is related to the "at completion" forecast.
15. Discuss reasons why the project manager frequently resists project changes.
16. What should a change control system guarantee? Describe procedures that minimize unnecessary changes.
17. What aspects of project control fall under contract administration?
18. What are some difficulties encountered when attempting project control?
19. Use the information on the networks in Figure 11-19 to determine ES, LS, EF, and LF for all activities using time buffers (numbers on activities indicate duration in days). For Part (a) use a 3-week time buffer for the critical path, a 1-week time buffer for every other path that connects to the critical path, and a project target completion time of 29 weeks. For Part (b) use a 4-week time buffer on the critical path, a 2-week time buffer for every path that connects to the critical path, and a target completion of 45 weeks.
20. In the LOGON project suppose the status of the project as of Week 22 is as follows:

$$BCWS = \$628,000$$
$$ACWP = \$640,000$$
$$BCWP = \$590,000$$

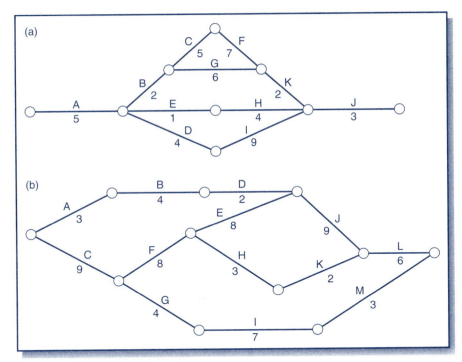

Figure 11-19
Two project networks.

Answer the following questions:
a. What is the earned value of the project as of Week 22?
b. Compute AV, SV, and CV.
c. Using a graph similar to Figure 11-8, plot BCWS, ACWP, and BCWP. Show AV, SV, and CV. Determine TV from the graph.
d. Compute SPI and CPI. Has the project performance improved or worsened since Week 20?
e. Using BCAC = $990,000, compute ETC and EAC. How does EAC compare to the Week 20 estimate of $1,222,593? Draw a status chart similar to Figure 11-12 and use it to determine the revised completion date. How does it compare to the revised date (Week 48–49) as of Week 20?
f. Are the results from Part (e) consistent with the results from Part (d) regarding improvement or deterioration of project performance since Week 20?

21. For a particular work package, the budgeted cost as of April 30 is $18,000. Suppose, as of April 30, the supervisor determines that only 80 percent of the scheduled work has been completed and the actual expense is $19,000. What is the BCWP? Compute AV, SV, CV, SPI, and CPI for the work package.

22. Using the status chart in Figure 11-20:
a. Estimate AV, SV, CV, and TV, and compute SPI and CPI for Week 30. Interpret the results.
b. Compute ETC and EAC. Estimate the revised completion date and sketch the lines for forecast ACWP and forecast BCWP.

23. Assume for the following problems that work continues during weekends.
a. A task is planned to start on April 30 and takes 20 days to complete. The actual start date is May 3. After 4 days of work the supervisor estimates that the task is 25 percent completed. If the work rate stays the same, what is the forecast date of completion?

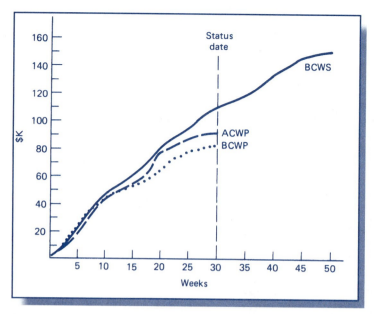

Figure 11-20
Project status chart.

b. Task C has two immediate predecessors, tasks A and B. Task A is planned to take 5 days to complete; Task B is planned to take 10 days. The early start time for both tasks is August 1. The actual start dates for tasks A and B are August 2 and August 1, respectively. At the end of August 4, Task A is assessed to be 20 percent completed and Task B, 30 percent completed. What is the expected early start time for Task C?

24. Refer back to Problem 20. Assume the $590,000 indicated for Week 22 is the most likely BCWP. Given a BCAC of $990,000, this represents 59.6 percent of the project completed. Suppose an expert assesses the LOGON project at that time using various measures and concludes that LOGON is between 50 percent and 65 percent completed. Let these represent pessimistic and optimistic scenarios. Compute the corresponding pessimistic, most likely and optimistic scenarios. Compute the corresponding pessimistic, most likely, and optimistic CPIs, SPIs, EACs, and forecast completion dates for the project.

25. Refer back to the networks in Figure 11-19 (Problem 19).
    a. For Network (a), suppose after 7 weeks, activities A, B, and E have been completed, D is 50 percent completed, and C is 80 percent completed. What is the revised early completion date for the project?
    b. For Network (b), suppose after 25 weeks, activities A, B, C, F, E, G, and I have been completed, and D and H are ready to begin in Week 26. What is the revised early completion date for the project?

QUESTIONS ABOUT THE STUDY PROJECT

1. What kinds of *external* controls, if any, were imposed by the client on the project?
2. What kinds of internal control measures were used? (For instance, work package control, cost account control, etc.) Describe.
3. Describe the project control process:
   How was work authorized to begin? Describe and show examples of work authorization orders.

How was data collected to monitor work? Explain the methods and procedures (time cards, invoices, etc.)
How was the data tallied and summarized?
How was the data validated?

4. Was the concept of earned value (budgeted cost of work performed) used?
5. How was project performance monitored? What performance and variance measures were used? Who did it? How often?
6. How were problems pinpointed and tracked?
7. Were the concepts of forecasting "to complete" and "at completion" used? If so, by whom? How often?
8. Were variance limits established for project cost and performance? What were they? How were they applied?
9. When cost, schedule, or performance problems occurred, what action did the project manager take? Give examples of problems and what the project manager did.
10. What changes to the product or project goal occurred during the project? Describe the change control process used in the project. How were changes to the project plan and systems specifications reviewed, authorized, and communicated? Show examples of change request and authorization documents.

Case 11-1   The Cybersonic Project

The Cybersonic project is off to a good start. Careful attention was given to preparing detailed objectives and requirements, well-defined work packages, assignments and responsibilities, a schedule, and a budget.

The project manager, Miles Wilder, considers himself a "project manager's project manager." He claims to know and use the principles of good project management, starting with having a good plan and then carefully tracking the project. He announces to his team leaders that status meetings will be held on alternating Mondays throughout the duration of the year-long project. All 18 project team leaders are instructed to attend these and give a run down on the tasks on which they are currently working.

At the first status meeting, all of the team leaders show up. Seven of them are currently managing work for the project and are scheduled to give reports; the other 11 are not yet working on the project (as specified by the project schedule), but attend because Miles wants to keep them informed about the project progress. The meeting is scheduled for 3 hours, during which the team leaders are to give oral reports about whatever they think is important. After almost 5 hours of reports by five of the leaders, Miles ends the meeting. Several major problems are reported that Miles tries to resolve at the meeting. Specific actions to resolve some of the problems are decided,

and Miles schedules another meeting for the afternoon 2 days later to address remaining problems and hear the remaining two reports. Some of the team leaders are miffed because they will have to change their schedules to attend this new meeting.

Miles arrives an hour late at the next meeting, which, after 3 hours, gives the team only enough time to resolve the problems raised at the first meeting. There is not enough time for two team leaders to give their first reports. Miles asks these leaders whether any major issues or problems with their tasks have occurred. When they respond, "no," he lets them skip their reports, promising to start with them at the next meeting in 2 weeks. A few of the team leaders are assigned actions to address current problems. Some of the attendees feel the meeting was a waste of time.

Before the next status meeting, a few of the team leaders inform Miles they cannot attend and will send representatives. This meeting becomes problematic for three reasons. First, several new problems about the project are raised and, again, the ensuing discussion drags out so that there is not enough time for everyone to give a status report. Second, during the 5-hour long meeting, only six team leaders of a scheduled eight give their reports. Also, some of the team leaders disagree with Miles about actions assigned at the previous meeting. Because no minutes had been taken at that meeting, each leader had followed his/her own notes about actions to take, many of which now conflict with Miles' expectations. Further, people at the meeting who are "representatives" are not fully aware of what was discussed at the previous meetings, do not have sufficient information to give complete reports or answer questions, and are hesitant to commit to action without their team leaders' approval.

The next several meetings follow the same pattern. They run longer than scheduled. Fewer team leaders and more representatives attend. Some status reports are not given because of inadequate time. Attendees disagree over problems identified and actions to be taken. Some meetings are rescheduled or canceled because Miles cannot attend. The project

falls behind scheduled because problems are not addressed adequately or quickly enough.

Miles feels that too much time has been wasted on resolving problems at the meetings and that many of them should, instead, be resolved entirely by the team leaders. He instructs the leaders to work out solutions and changes on their own, and to report at status meetings only the results. This reduces the length of the meetings, but it creates other complications: Some of the team leaders take actions and make changes that ignore project dependencies and conflict with the schedules and work tasks of other team leaders. Even though everyone is working overtime, the Cybersonic project falls further behind schedule.

QUESTIONS

1. Why is Miles' approach to tracking and controlling the Cybersonic project ineffective?

2. If you were in charge, what would you do?

ENDNOTES

1. Daniel Roman, *Science, Technology, and Innovation: A Systems Approach* (Columbus, OH: Grid Publishing, 1980): 369.
2. A. D. Szilagyi, *Management and Performance,* 2d ed. (Glenview, IL: Scott, Foresman, 1984): 507–08.
3. Roman, *Science, Technology, and Innovation,* 382.
4. Here the terms "variance" and "deviation" are used interchangeably, although it should be noted that in some contracts, variance refers to small changes in the project plan for which compensation or correction is expected, whereas deviation refers to large changes that require a formal contractual response.
5. Roman, *Science, Technology, and Innovation,* 383.
6. *DOD & NASA Guide, PERT Cost Accounting System Design* (Washington, D.C.: U.S. Government Printing Office, June 1962).
7. J. D. Wiest and F. K. Levy, *A Management Guide to PERT/CPM* (Upper Saddle River, NJ: Prentice Hall, 1977): 86.
8. Russell Archibald, *Managing High-Technology Programs and Projects* (New York: John Wiley & Sons, 1976): 184.
9. The following list is adapted from Charles Thompson, "Intermediate Performance Measures in Engineering Projects." Proceedings of the International Conference on Management of Engineering and Technology, Portland, OR, July 27–31, 1997.

10. Archibald, *Managing High-Technology Programs and Projects,* 195.
11. Information for this application provided by Elisa Denney and Jennifer Brown.
12. Portions adapted from Eliyahu Goldratt, *The Critical Chain* (Great Barrington, MA: North River Press, 1997). This book, written as a novel, gives insight into scheduling problems and solutions.
13. Ibid.
14. An approach to sizing time buffers is discussed in K. Hoel and S. G. Taylor, "Quantifying Buffers for Project Schedules," *Production and Inventory Management Journal,* 40, no. 2 (Second quarter, 1999): 43–47.
15. Goldratt, *The Critical Chain,* 151–60.
16. From Brian Muirhead and William Simon, *High Velocity Leadership: the Mars Pathfinder Approach to Better, Faster, Cheaper* (New York: HarperBusiness, 1999): 40–42.
17. Michael Cusumano and Richard Selby, *Microsoft Secrets* (New York: Free Press, 1995): 204, 221, 256–57, 417.
18. A good explanation of ways of determining BCWP is given in T. G. Pham, "The Elusive Budgeted Cost of Work Performed for Research and Development Projects," *Project Management Quarterly* (March 1985): 76–79. For additional explanation of the earned value approach, see Q. W. Fleming and J. M. Hoppleman, *Earned*

Value Project Management (Upper Darby, PA: Project Management Institute, 1996).

19. For examples of analytical models used for TPM see Howard Eisner, *Computer-Aided Systems Engineering* (Upper Saddle River, NJ: Prentice Hall, 1988): 297–326.

20. See Arild Sigurdsen, "Method for Verifying Project Cost Performance, *Project Management Journal* 25, no. 4 (December 1994): 26–31.

21. F. L. Harrison, *Advanced Project Management* (Hants, England: Gower, 1981): 242–44.

22. Ibid., 245–46.

23. Ibid., 244; Archibald, *Managing High-Technology Programs and Projects*, 187–90.

24. Adapted from Roman, *Science, Technology, and Innovation*, 327–28, 391–95.

Project Management
Information Systems

> *An individual without information cannot take responsibility;*
> *an individual who is given information cannot help*
> *but take responsibility.*

—Jan Carlzon,
Riv Pyramidera!

> *If this is the best of possible worlds, what then are the others?*

—Voltaire

*T*he formal methods for planning, budgeting, and control in the last six chapters might seem too sophisticated, complicated, or time-consuming to be practical. Whether that is true or not depends upon *how* they are implemented. Those chapters illustrated the kind of information needed to manage projects, but they presume that the project manager is "organized" and has the means for collecting, storing, and processing the information. Generally, formal methods for planning and control do not require any more input data or information than is, or *should be*, available in any project. What they *do* require, however, is a framework and methodology, a *system*, for collecting, organizing, storing, processing, and disseminating that information. Here, we refer to such a framework and methodology as a *project management information system (PMIS)*.

The term "PMIS" can pertain to a manual or computer-based system, but most commonly it refers to the latter. With the growing importance of computers in management and the proliferation of computer-based PMISs, it is important that project managers understand the kinds of computer-based PMI software and hardware systems available, and appreciate the issues in selecting and implementing these systems. These are the topics covered in this chapter.

12.1 FUNCTIONS OF THE PMIS

It is almost impossible for any contemporary manager to do her job adequately without using some kind of manual or computer-based *management information system* (MIS). Virtually all managers use information systems for functions such as payroll, billing, ordering, accounting, and inventory control. Project managers also use these systems. The major difference between these and PMI systems is that the latter are dedicated solely to the function of project management. They are utilized by project managers and staff to fulfill the unique requirements of project management.

PMISs have capabilities that assist project managers in planning, budgeting, and resource allocation. Many PMISs additionally perform assorted analyses such as variance, performance, and forecasting for any level of the WBS and project organization. A good PMIS enables facile control of changes to system configuration and project plans as well. These PMISs allow for quick review and easy periodic updating; they filter and reduce data to provide information on summary, exception, or "what if" bases. With an effective PMIS the project manager does not have to wait for days or comb through reams of data to identify problems and determine project status.

12.2 COMPUTER-BASED TOOLS

If you think about it, methods such as earned value analysis, forecasting, change control, and configuration management for large projects can involve processing and integrating great quantities of information. These methods "roll up" work package information to the project level (or start at the project level and tunnel down information to the work package level) so problems can be traced to their source. However, they also presume the capability to process lots of information in a short time. As computers are good at this, they have become essential tools not just for planning but for control as well. In fact, without computers it would be difficult to do much of the analysis necessary to control large projects.

Benefits of Computer-Based PMISs

The benefits of computer PMISs over manual systems are speed, capacity, efficiency, economy, accuracy, and ability to handle complexity.

The major benefit is speed. Once data have been collected and entered, practically any manipulation can be done more rapidly by computers. To create or revise printed plans, schedules, and budgets takes days or weeks with a manual system, but seconds or minutes with computers. This is especially true of Internet and intranet project management systems. Computer-based PMISs store large amounts of information that is easily accessed, prioritized, and summarized.

Manual systems for large projects are tedious to maintain, difficult to access, and provoke people to try to work around them or avoid them. They require the efforts of numerous support personnel to maintain and use their outputs for analysis. In contrast, computer-based PMISs can perform much of this analysis, reduce the requirement for clerical personnel, and relieve managers and support personnel from having to do computations. This frees them to use analysis results for making decisions.

The speed, capacity, and efficiency of computers afford still another benefit: economy. In most cases, computers offer a significant cost advantage over manual systems for storing and processing information. Assuming input data are correct, computers produce fewer computational errors and reduce the cost of correcting mistakes.

Finally, computer-based PMISs are much better at handling and integrating complex data relationships. Large projects with thousands of work tasks, hundreds of organizations, and tens of thousands of workers cannot be managed efficiently without computers. For managing large projects, a computer-based PMIS is a virtual necessity, but even in small projects it simply makes the work easier to manage.

Project managers have dozens of kinds of project software packages to choose from. Software packages vary greatly in capability and flexibility; generally, as the size and capability increase, so does the price. The degree of technical support accompanying software packages also varies, which means sometimes it is difficult to get help or assistance from the software developer when needed. As if choosing the right software were not enough of a problem, the project manager also must determine the right combination of computer and peripheral devices—processors, monitors, printers, plotters, modems, and database and web servers.

Generally, a computer system's outputs are only as good as its inputs. To perform well, the computer system must be given adequate and accurate input, stored data must be periodically updated, and information outputs must be distributed to the people who need them. In short, any computer system needs a good manual support system.

Because satisfaction depends on how well system capabilities match user expectations, it is important at the start to have the "right" expectations. Simpler PMISs have limited capability, but they usually are good at what they can do, and they *can* be of tremendous benefit. Also, once mastered, it is easy to upgrade to more sophisticated systems.

Computer Applications in Project Management

There are myriad hardware/software configurations with various applications in project management. For a project manager to be able to assess how satisfactory a given computer application is, he must first know both the information requirements of the project and the capabilities of the computer application. Often, to satisfy all information requirements—data, text, and graphics—it is necessary to use more than one kind of software.

We will discuss these applications and requirements in the following sections.

12.3   COMPUTER-BASED PMI SYSTEMS

A computer-based PMIS *should* be able to

- Create and update project files containing information necessary for planning, control, and summary documents.

- Enable data from other information files to be transferred to the project database.
- Integrate work, cost, labor, and schedule information to produce planning, control, and summary reports for project, functional, and upper-level managers.

Among the many available PMISs, not all have these capabilities. Some do not even perform the most essential functions of project management. The following sections discuss the kinds of features and options available in computer-based PMISs and their appropriateness for planning and control functions.

Features of PMISs

Here is a list of the kinds of analytical capabilities, outputs, and other features offered by various PMI systems.

Scheduling and Network Planning. Virtually all project software systems do project scheduling using a network-based procedure. These systems compute early and late schedule times, slack times, and the critical path. Among the capabilities a user must assess are the type of procedure (PERT, CPM, PDM, or multiple types), event or activity-oriented outputs (or multiple types), and use of probabilities. Capabilities also vary with regard to the maximum number of allowable activities, the way activities and events are coded (some use a WBS scheme), the quality and clarity of the output format (e.g., network, Gantt chart, tabular reports, or multiple types) and whether only single or simultaneous multiple projects can be planned and tracked. The kind of calendar also varies: Most systems allow input of nonwork periods such as weekends, holidays, and vacations, and produce schedules accordingly, but details of input and output differ greatly.

Resource Management. Most project systems also perform resource loading, leveling, allocation, or multiple functions, although the analytical sophistication and quality of reports vary between systems. The major considerations are the maximum number of resources permitted per activity or project; the kind of resource loading/scheduling techniques used (resource-limited, time-limited, or both); split scheduling (stopping activities, then starting later); interchangeable usage of different resources; and using resources which are consumed.[1]

Budgeting. In many project systems it is possible to associate cost information with each activity, usually by treating costs as resources. However, software systems vary greatly in the way they handle fixed, variable, and overhead costs, and in their ability to generate budget and cost summary reports. In many systems cost and expense information are not treated explicitly; in others, cost accounting is a major feature. The ability of a system to handle cost information and generate budgets is a significant variable in the system's usability for both planning and control.

Cost Control and Performance Analysis. Here is where project system capabilities differ the most. To perform the control function, a system must be able to compare actual performance (actual costs and work completed) to planned and budgeted performance. Among the features to consider are the system's ability to compute and report cost and schedule variances, earned values (BCWP), and various performance indices, as well as to forecast by extrapolating past performance. The most sophisticated PMIS software "roll up" results and allow aggregation, analysis, and reporting at all levels of the WBS. They also permit modification and updating of existing plans through input of actual start and finish dates and costs.

The most comprehensive PMISs *integrate* network, budget, and resource information and allow the project manager to ask "what if" questions under various scenarios while the project is underway. They allow the system user to access, cross-reference, and report information from multiple sites or databases linked via the Internet or an intranet.

Reporting, Graphics, and Communication. Project software systems also vary greatly in the number, kind, and quality of reports they produce. This is an important consideration because it affects the speed with which PMIS outputs are communicated and the accuracy of their interpretation. Many systems provide only tabular reports or crude schedules; others generate networks and resource histograms; still others offer a variety of graphics including pie charts and line graphs. The main features to consider are the number, quality, and type of available reports and graphics. Many systems generate only a few standardized types of reports; others generate a wide range, including customized ones created to satisfy any format or information requirement including company-specific features such as background information and logos. The quality often depends on the system's ability to use different output devices. All systems produce reports on standard printers and show reports on the monitor as well; the highest quality reports and graphics are produced on plotters.

With the trend toward decentralized teams and multisite projects, more projects now have team members that are geographically dispersed, which poses a problem for project tracking and control. One way around this problem is use of the World Wide Web to gather and distribute project information. The Web allows team members everywhere to have easy access to project information, and to store and retrieve it in a common place. The software enables team members to communicate via e-mail, and retain e-mail information on a project database. This is discussed later.

Interface, Flexibility, and Ease of Use. Some systems are compatible with and can tie into existing databases such as payroll, purchasing, inventory, MRP, ERP, cost-accounting, or other PMISs. Some can be used with popular DBMS and spreadsheet systems. They also can be used to provide input data for systems that do modeling and risk analysis.

Many larger PMISs allow data from different projects to be pooled so *multiproject* analysis can be performed. This feature enables organization-wide administration of projects and combining of information from several, simultaneous projects to form a picture of the overall state of the organization. Some software allows the user to "click" on a particular project in order to view more detailed, project specific information. Managers can readily distinguish the work functions or projects performing as expected from those experiencing problems or overruns.

The capability of a PMIS to interface with other software from which existing data files have been created is an important selection criterion. Many firms have had to spend considerable time and money developing interfaces to link a commercial PM package with existing data and other PMI systems. Most small, inexpensive systems are stand-alone and have limited interface ability.

Systems also vary widely in flexibility. Many systems are limited and perform a narrow set of functions which cannot be modified. Others allow the user to develop new applications or alter existing ones depending on needs. Among the potential additional applications and reports sometimes available are change control, configuration management, responsibility matrixes, expenditure reports, cost and technical performance reports, and technical performance summaries. Many software systems utilize Internet technology and protocols that enable easy access through a browser to a wide variety of management applications and databases.

Finally, there is also the consideration of user friendliness: How easy is it to learn and operate the system? Systems vary greatly in the style of system documentation, thoroughness and clarity of tutorials, ease of information input, clarity of on-screen presentation and report format, helpfulness of error messages, and the training and operating support offered by the developer.

Functions of PMIS

Because the purpose of a PMIS is to support project management decisions and to provide information necessary to conduct the project, the functions of PMISs closely parallel those of project management. In most projects, these are

1. Planning and scheduling.
2. Budgeting.
3. Work authorization and control.
4. Control of changes.
5. Communicating all of these functions.

It is important to note that currently many computer-based PMIS software systems are able to support only the first, and to a limited extent, the last functions on this list. As Levine notes, this is because software that is able to perform the control function requires several features beyond those for planning; these include the ability to[2]

1. Save an old version of the baseline database for comparison with current status and actual costs.
2. Accept actual start and finish dates, and revise task durations without having them override the plan dates.
3. Accept actual costs incurred, for comparison to budget.
4. Track actual resource usage.

Popular project management software systems that lack these capabilities may be useful in the early project phases of planning and definition, but *once the project begins* they provide little assistance in the place where, perhaps, it is needed most—project control. This is unfortunate because project control is an area where computers offer a tremendous advantage over manual systems. For procedures that require the capability to integrate time, cost, and performance information, to "roll up" this information through the WBS, and to do it quickly and efficiently, computers are the only practical means.

12.4   REPRESENTATIVE COMPUTER-BASED PMISs[3]

Most PMIS software are designed for usage on desktop computers, either individually or with client-server systems, centralized databases, and Internet and/or intranet capabilities. The following sections provide a sampling of six popular PMIS software covering the gambit of available products. These descriptions are intended as basic introductions and are not product endorsements. Software products change rapidly, and no description remains current for long. For the most up-to-date descriptions, visit the Web sites of the individual software manufacturers. Many sites provide downloads and free limited trial usage of the products.

Microsoft

Microsoft Project (MS Project) dominates project management software systems. The software system carries its own database and is compatible with SQL Server or Oracle databases. Although it requires installation on every user's computer, it is fully compatible with Microsoft Office so team members can easily save to the database documents created in any Office application. In addition, because it has the same toolbars as MS Office applications, most users become quickly familiarized with it. MS Project provides the ability to publish to the Internet or the company intranet, topics that will be discussed later. There are no limits to the number of tasks or projects the software can handle.

Interesting features of MS Project include its ability to distribute resources among multiple projects from a common resource pool; use existing e-mail infrastructure to communicate with team members; "flag" certain tasks or phases as reminders; split tasks and drag and drop tasks on the Gantt chart; analyze project completion given "worst" and "most likely" cases; and incorporate hyperlinks into the database to access supporting documents and Web sites. Gantt and PERT charts from MS Project are shown in Figures 12-1 and 12-2.

Project Scheduler

Project Scheduler works with an SQL database and is MS Office compatible. Information from multiple projects or subprojects can be merged or consolidated to reveal company-wide resource utilization. The report writer enables a wide range of standard and customized reports, which can be output in HTML format. Data can be located on shared disk drives and accessed only by users with the appropriate password. A Project Scheduler resource screen is shown in Figure 12-3.

Welcom

Welcom has three software products: *Open Plan, Cobra,* and *Spider.* Open Plan has advanced scheduling and modeling tools for resource management. It integrates company-wide information and enables information sharing across multiple projects. Team members can work on pieces of the project, then roll-up information for composite reporting. Cobra is a cost-management tool designed to manage and analyze budgets, earned value, and forecasts. Spider is a multiuser, multiproject web-based tool for viewing and updating project data from Open Plan user Web browsers. Figures 12-4 and 12-5 show screen reports from Welcom Cobra.

Trakker

Trakker offers a variety of interesting products including, for example, tools for risk management (Figure 12-6), activity-based costing, earned value management (Figure 12-7), as well as the usual planning, budgeting, and tracking tools. These tools interface with commercial accounting systems and can be Web-enabled for use on the Internet or intranet with browsers.

Primavera

Primavera offers four software products.

SureTrak Project Manager. This software enables modeling and scheduling of simultaneous projects of up to 10,000 activities per project. Activities can be inserted or rearranged on Gantt charts and PERT charts (Figures 12-8 and 12-9) with a mouse click. Actual completion dates and costs can be compared with targets, progress estimated for each activity or for the entire project, and forecasts produced of resources necessary to get a project back on track. If resources exceed supply, SureTrak can reassign

Figure 12-1
MS Project Gantt chart.

ID	ⓘ	Task Name	Duration	Start	Resource Names
1		**1 Introductory Activity**	**0.03 days**	**Wed 9/1/99**	
2		1.1 Formation of team	0.25 hrs	4/7/97	all
3					
4		**1 Introductory Activity**	**14.13 days**	**Wed 9/1/99**	
5		**2.1 Guidelines**	**9.13 days**	**Wed 9/8/99**	
6		2.11 Discuss Guidelines	1 day	Wed 9/8/99	all
7		2.12 Draft Guidelines	2 hrs	Wed 9/8/99	Kathy
8		2.13 Review Guidelines	1 hr	Mon 9/13/99	all/Dr. Nicholas
9		2.13 Finalize Guidelines	1 hr	Tue 9/21/99	Kathy
10		**2.2 Cover Page & TOC**	**1 day**	**Wed 9/1/99**	
11		2.21 Draft Cover Page	1 day	Wed 9/1/99	Girish
12		2.22 Finalize Cover Page	1 day	Wed 9/1/99	Girish
13		2.23 Table of Contents	1 day	Wed 9/1/99	Jinwen
14		**2.3 Objectives**	**9.13 days**	**Wed 9/8/99**	
15		2.31 Discuss Objectives	2 hrs	Wed 9/8/99	all
16		2.32 Draft Objectives	1 hr	Mon 9/13/99	Patty
17		2.33 Finalize Objectives	1 hr	Tue 9/21/99	Patty
18		**2.4 WBS (MS Project)**	**2.06 days**	**Fri 9/17/99**	
19		2.41 Draft WBS	2 hrs	Fri 9/17/99	Kathy, John
20		2.42 Edit WBS	2 hrs	Mon 9/20/99	all
21		2.43 Finalize WBS	0.5 hrs	Mon 9/20/99	Kathy, John
22		**2.5 Timeline (MS Project)**	**2 days**	**Fri 9/17/99**	
23		2.51 Draft Timeline	3 hrs	Fri 9/17/99	Kathy, John
24		2.52 Edit Timeline	1 day	Mon 9/20/99	all
25		2.53 Finalize Timeline	2 hrs	Mon 9/20/99	Kathy, John
26		**2.6 Assign Responsibilities**	**1.06 days**	**Mon 9/20/99**	
27		2.61 Discuss Responsibilities	1 hr	Fri 9/17/99	all
28		2.62 Draft Responsibilities	1 hr	Mon 9/20/99	Kathy, John
29		2.63 Finalize Responsibilities	0.5 hrs	Mon 9/20/99	Kathy, John
30		**2.7 Compile and Edit**	**2 hrs**	**Mon 9/20/99**	all
31		**2.8 Submission of Proposal**	**0.25 hrs**	**Wed 9/22/99**	
32					

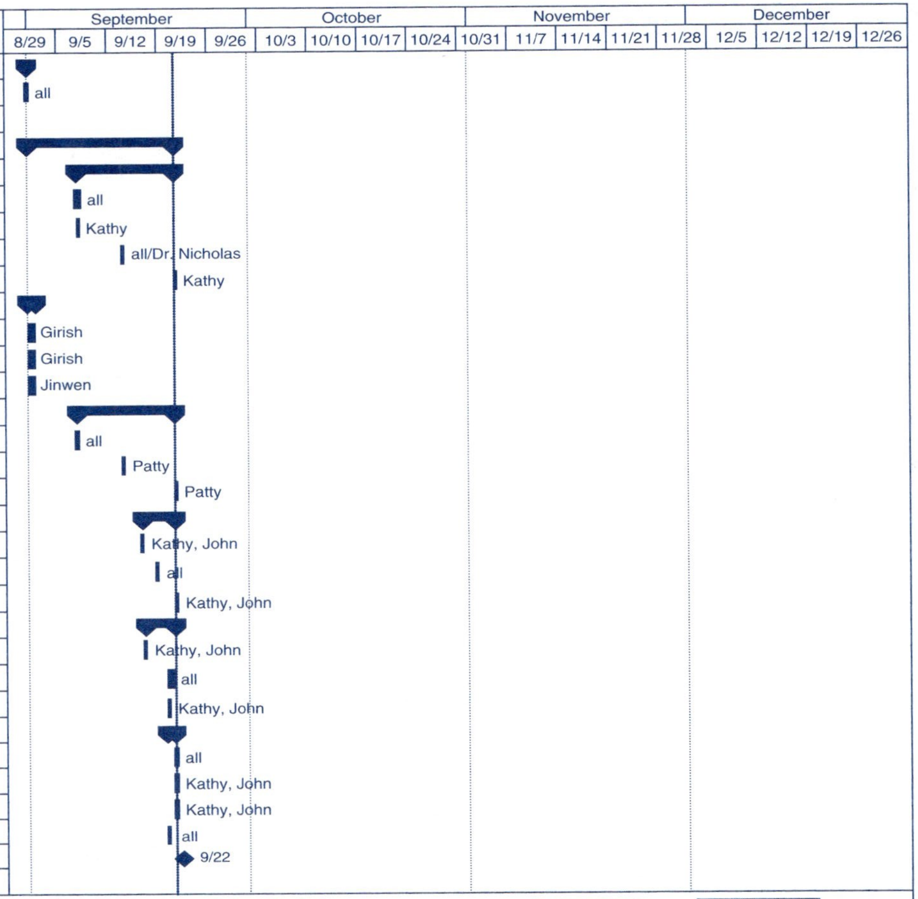

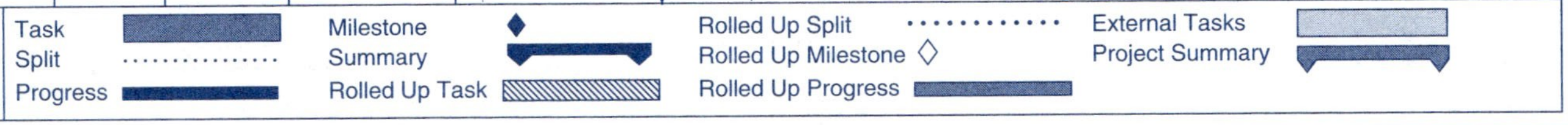

Legend:

Task   Split   Progress   Milestone   Summary   Rolled Up Task   Rolled Up Split   Rolled Up Milestone   Rolled Up Progress   External Tasks   Project Summary

Figure 12-2
MS Project PERT network diagram.

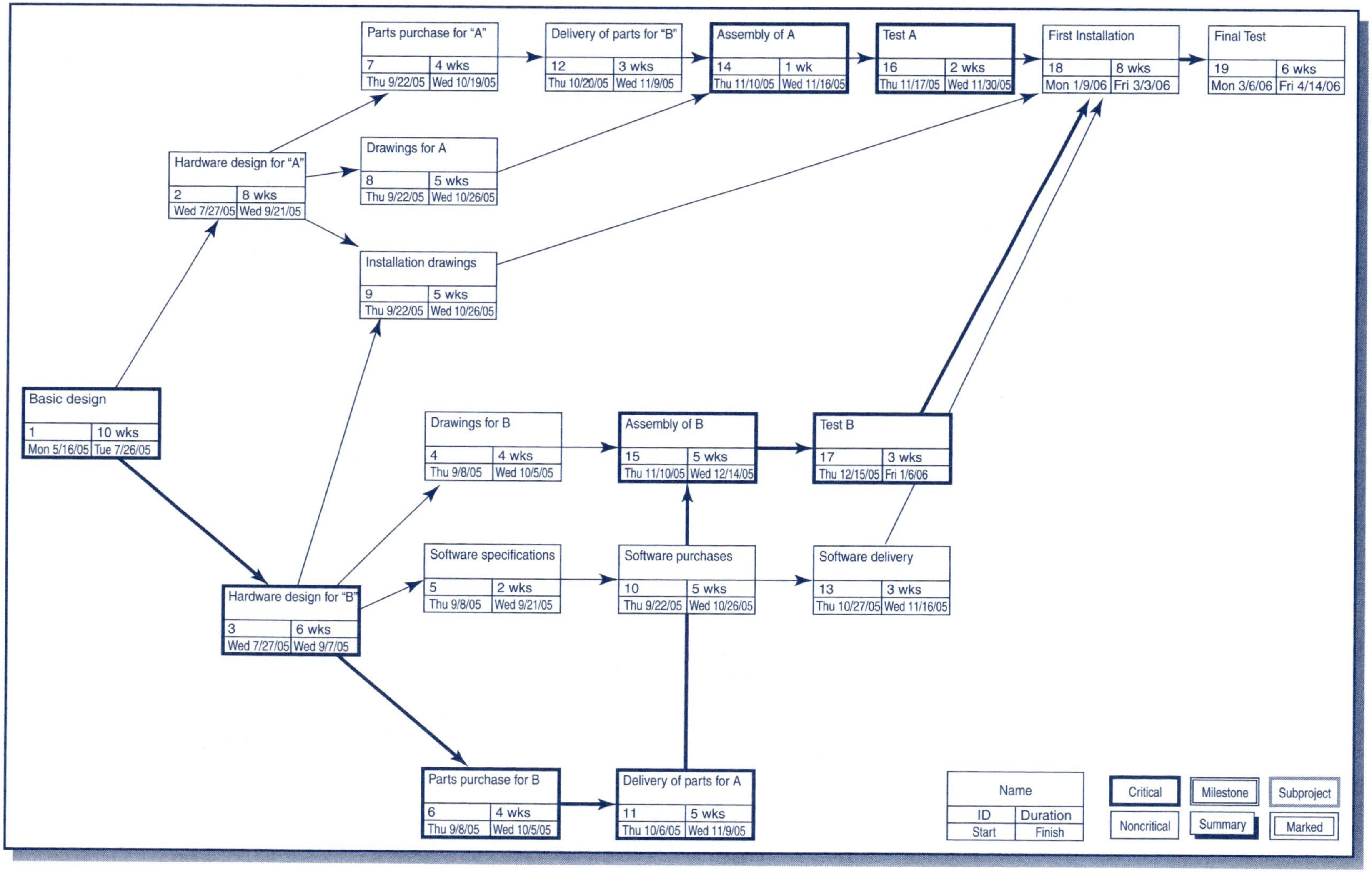

Figure 12-3
Project Scheduler resource screen.

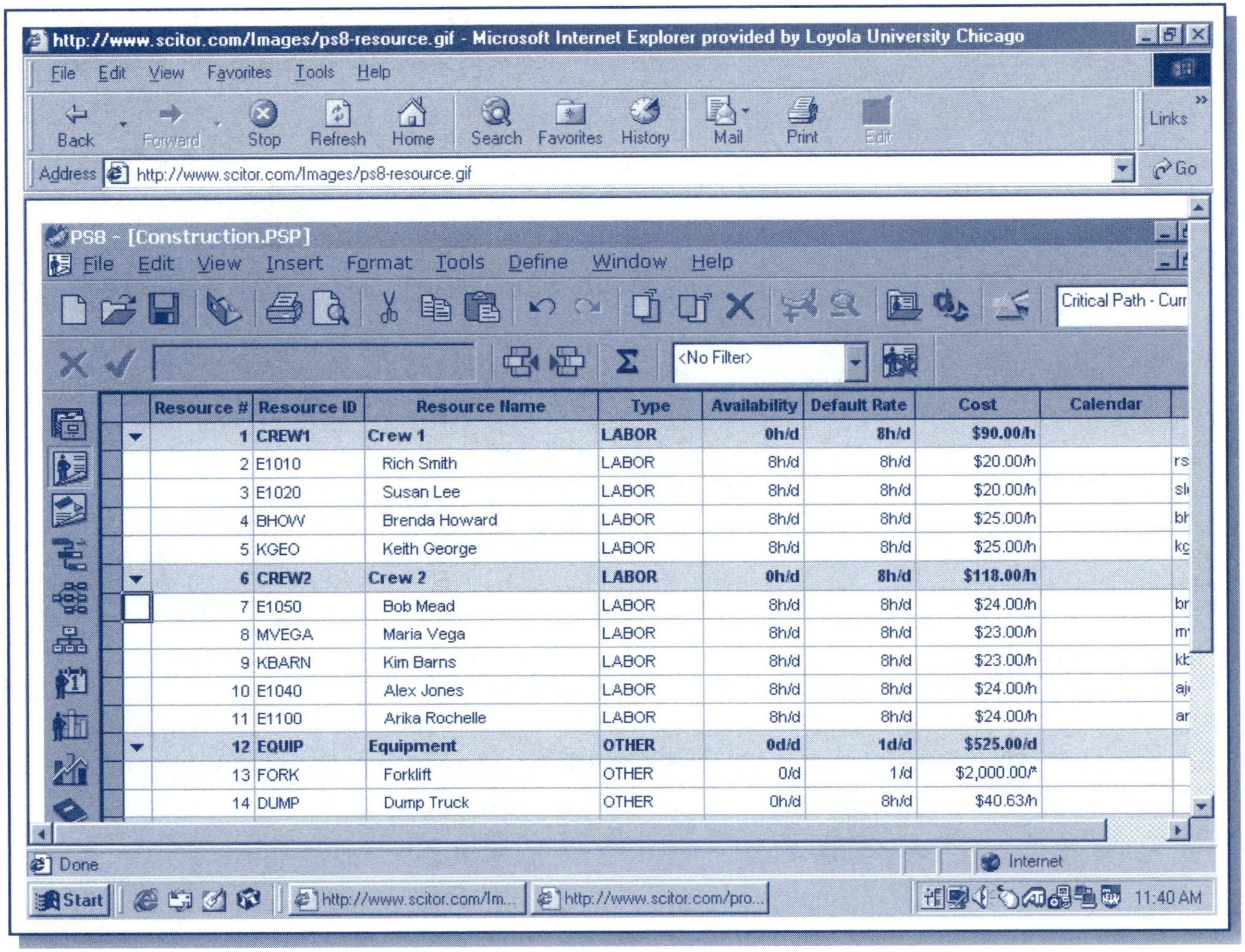

Resource #	Resource ID	Resource Name	Type	Availability	Default Rate	Cost	Calendar
1	**CREW1**	**Crew 1**	**LABOR**	**0h/d**	**8h/d**	**$90.00/h**	rs
2	E1010	Rich Smith	LABOR	8h/d	8h/d	$20.00/h	sl
3	E1020	Susan Lee	LABOR	8h/d	8h/d	$20.00/h	br
4	BHOW	Brenda Howard	LABOR	8h/d	8h/d	$25.00/h	kc
5	KGEO	Keith George	LABOR	8h/d	8h/d	$25.00/h	
6	**CREW2**	**Crew 2**	**LABOR**	**0h/d**	**8h/d**	**$118.00/h**	br
7	E1050	Bob Mead	LABOR	8h/d	8h/d	$24.00/h	m
8	MVEGA	Maria Vega	LABOR	8h/d	8h/d	$23.00/h	kt
9	KBARN	Kim Barns	LABOR	8h/d	8h/d	$23.00/h	aj
10	E1040	Alex Jones	LABOR	8h/d	8h/d	$24.00/h	ar
11	E1100	Arika Rochelle	LABOR	8h/d	8h/d	$24.00/h	
12	**EQUIP**	**Equipment**	**OTHER**	**0d/d**	**1d/d**	**$525.00/d**	
13	FORK	Forklift	OTHER	0/d	1/d	$2,000.00/*	
14	DUMP	Dump Truck	OTHER	0h/d	8h/d	$40.63/h	

Figure 12-4
Welcom Cobra progress graphic.

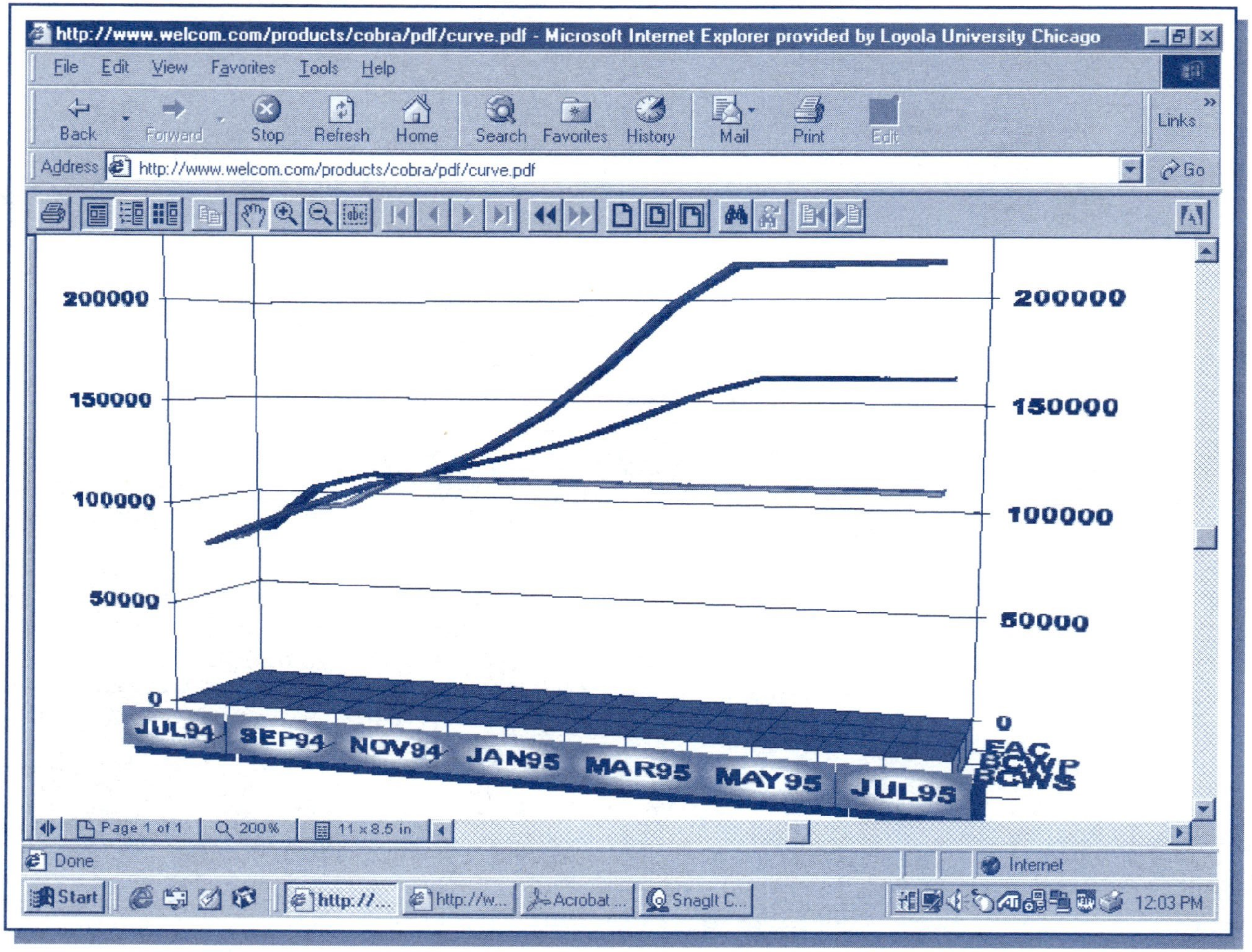

Figure 12-5
Welcom Cobra earned value report.

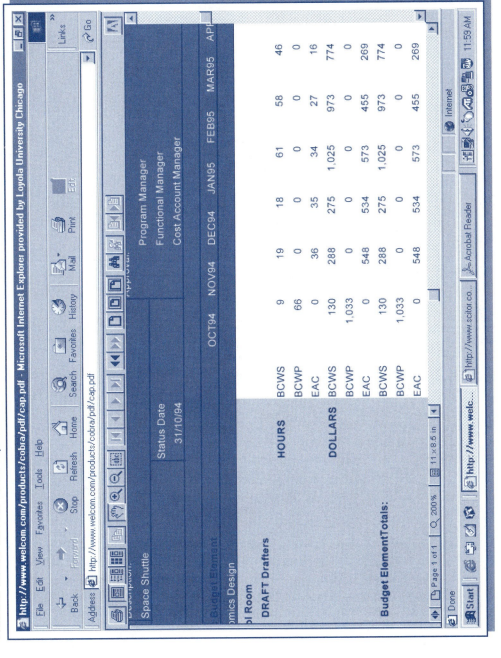

Figure 12-6
Trakker risk analysis screen.

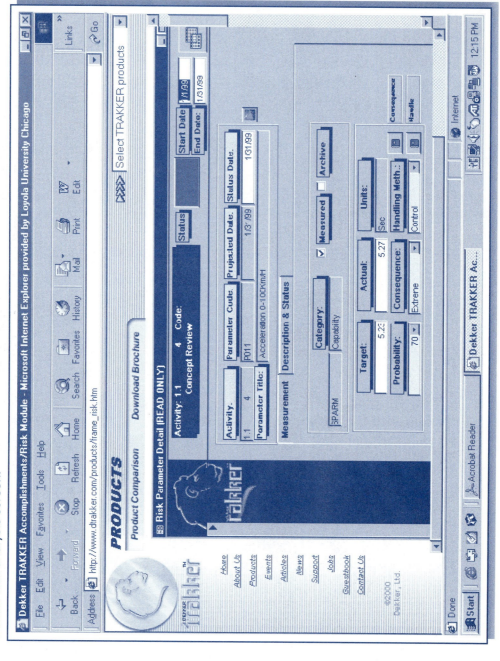

Figure 12-7
Trakker earned value analysis screen.

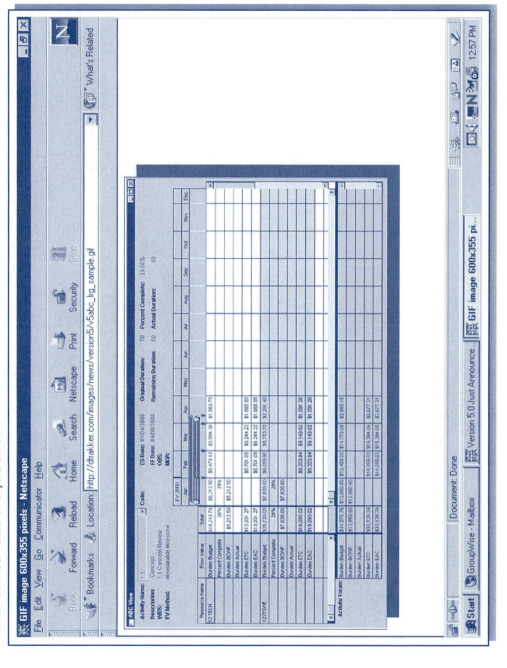

Figure 12-8
Primavera SureTrak® Gantt chart.

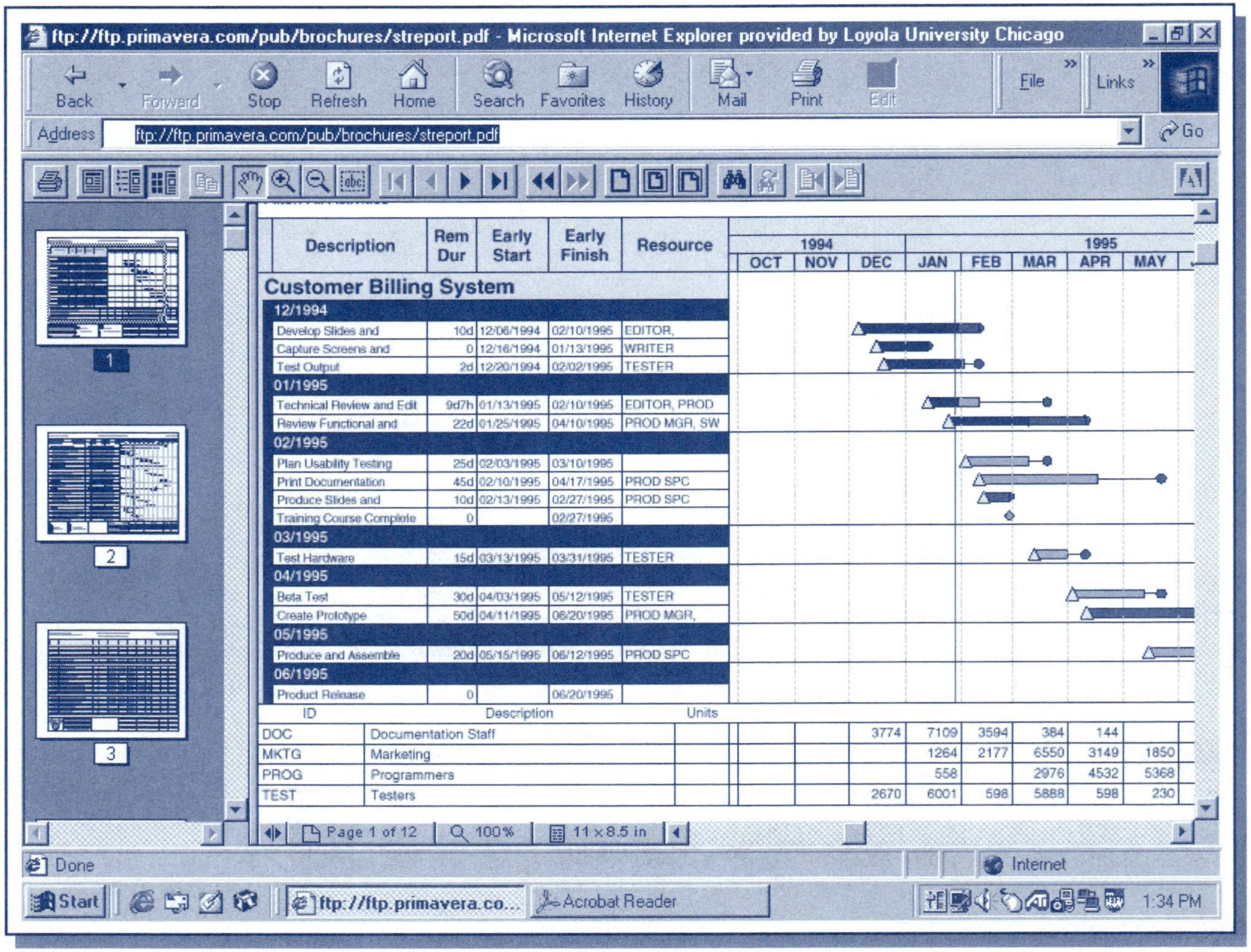

Figure 12-9
Primavera SureTrak® PERT chart.

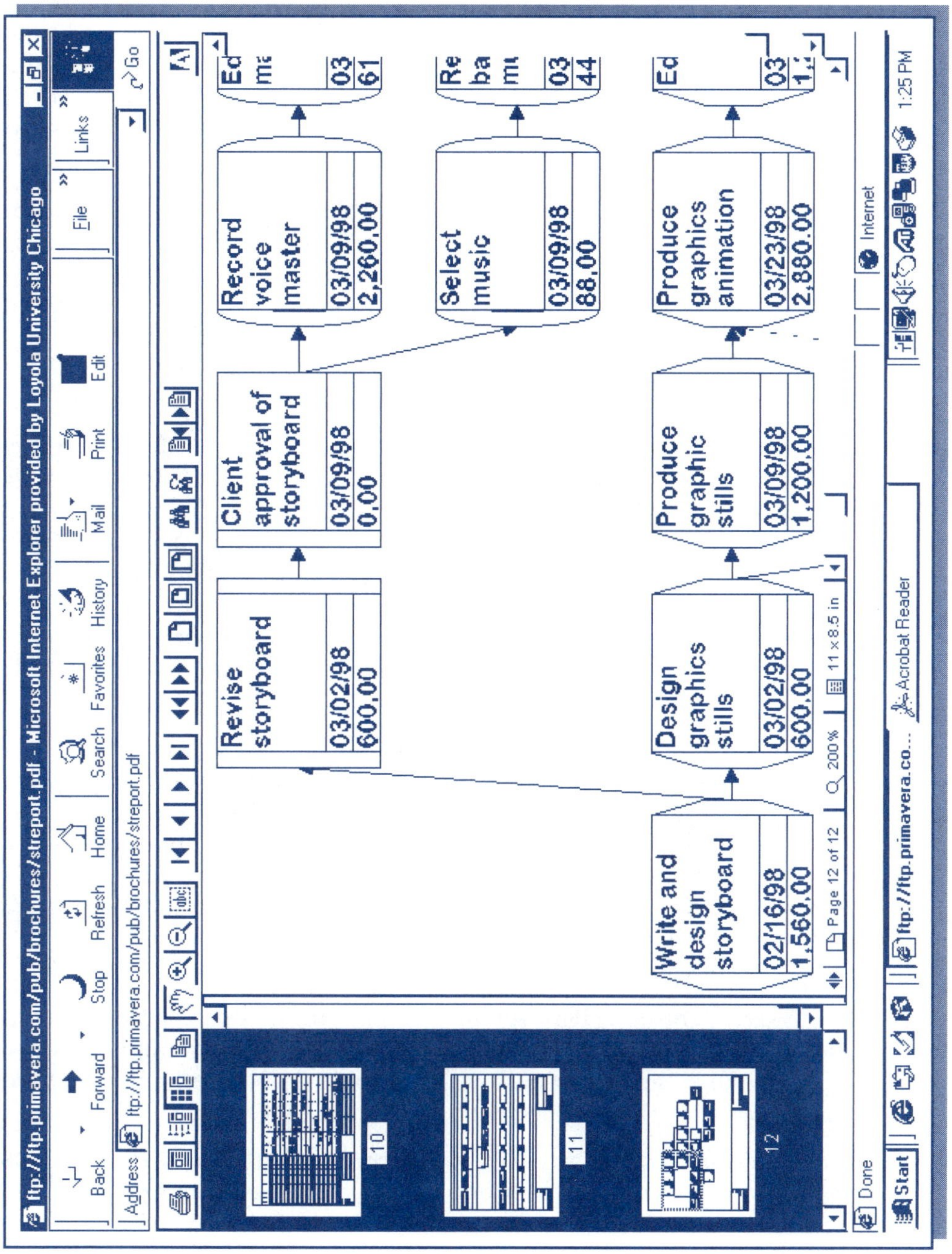

them from low-priority activities. Assignments, deadlines, and status can be shared with project participants at all levels and locations using the Web publisher.

Primavera Project Planner®, (P3®). This program provides for unlimited projects, up to 100,000 activities per project, concurrent, multiuser accessibility, and scheduling options similar to SureTrak. P3 can create fragments of networks to store for later use as templates or building blocks for creating other project plans. Also, P3 supports cost accounts and allows tracking of costs and exchange of information with cost-accounting systems. e-mail addresses can be embedded into the project to automatically route status information to individuals who need to know. A Web publisher enables team members with Web browsers to review, update, and return project activity status data (Figure 12-10).

Primavera Expedition® Contract Control Software. This software assists in change management and tracking of contracts and purchase orders. It enables users to view the latest submittals and schedule changes from P3 or SureTrak in real time. It ensures that everyone who needs drawing revisions gets them. It also has a change management feature to assess the impact of changes on costs and schedules, and to identify where additional equipment is needed and the contractors affected (Figure 12-11). It also automatically distributes requisitions and RFPs.

Webster for Primavera®. This software provides access to the project database, time-card activities, and project information from SureTrak and P3. Team members can see assignments and can report accomplishments and time needed to complete assignments.

Artemis

Artemis offers a suite of project management software solutions; all work in conjunction with SQL Server, Oracle, or Sybase databases. All are compatible with each other, and are independently functional.

Track View. This application tracks resources and worker time. It enables team members to review activities for which they are responsible, and managers to set approval levels, generate reports, and maintain records of project progress for future use. Track View is a LAN-based intranet application with an optional Internet Explorer browser interface, which allows managers to assign, approve, and track staff activity anywhere, from across the hall to around the world. Users can enter and update timesheet information, as well as download scheduled activities and timesheets from MS Project or ProjectView databases (Figure 12-12).

Cost View. This is a client-server-based application designed to provide managers and controllers with tools for planning and budgeting multiple projects, reviewing contracts, and managing finances. It has tools for progress analysis, variance analysis, and earned value management control and reporting.

Project View. This is a powerful enterprise multiuser, multiproject management application created for project and resource managers and project planners. It has capabilities for scheduling, cost control, multiuser planning, resource assignments (Figure 12-13), and graphical reporting. Users can access their project information anytime, anywhere via the Internet using complementary browser-based Web View. Project View can be easily integrated with MS Project and with popular ERP (enterprise resource planning) applications. It is scalable to thousands of projects and users and maintains up to 99 versions of a project. It also allows multilevel, multiproject consolidation, analysis, and reporting.

Figure 12-10
Primavera Post Office activity status screen.

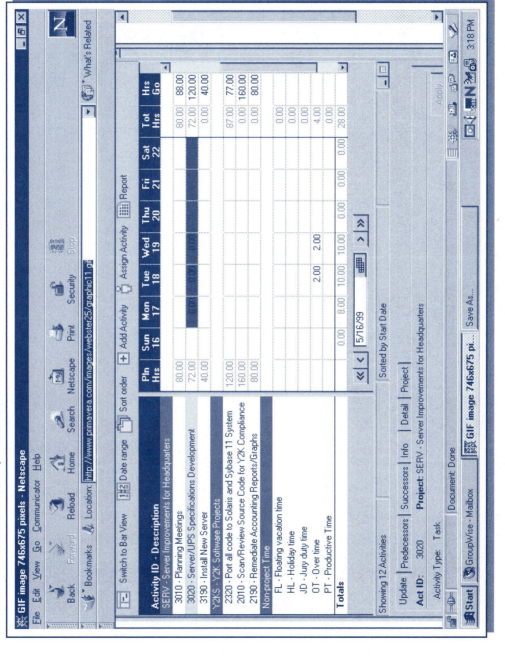

Figure 12-11
Primavera Expedition® change request screen.

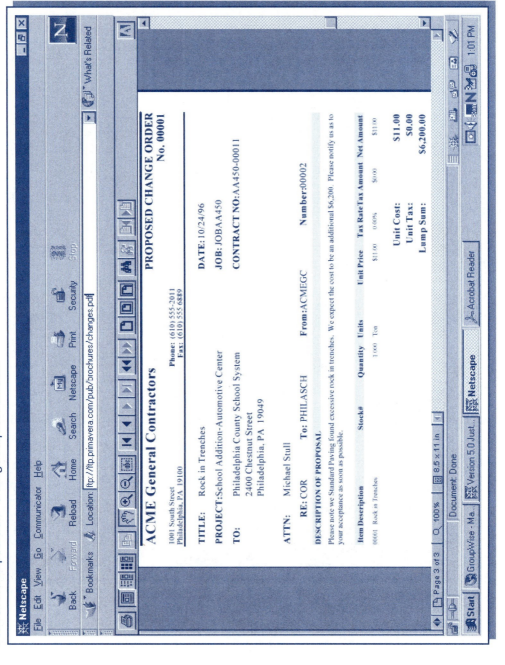

Figure 12-12
Artemis Track View timesheet screen.

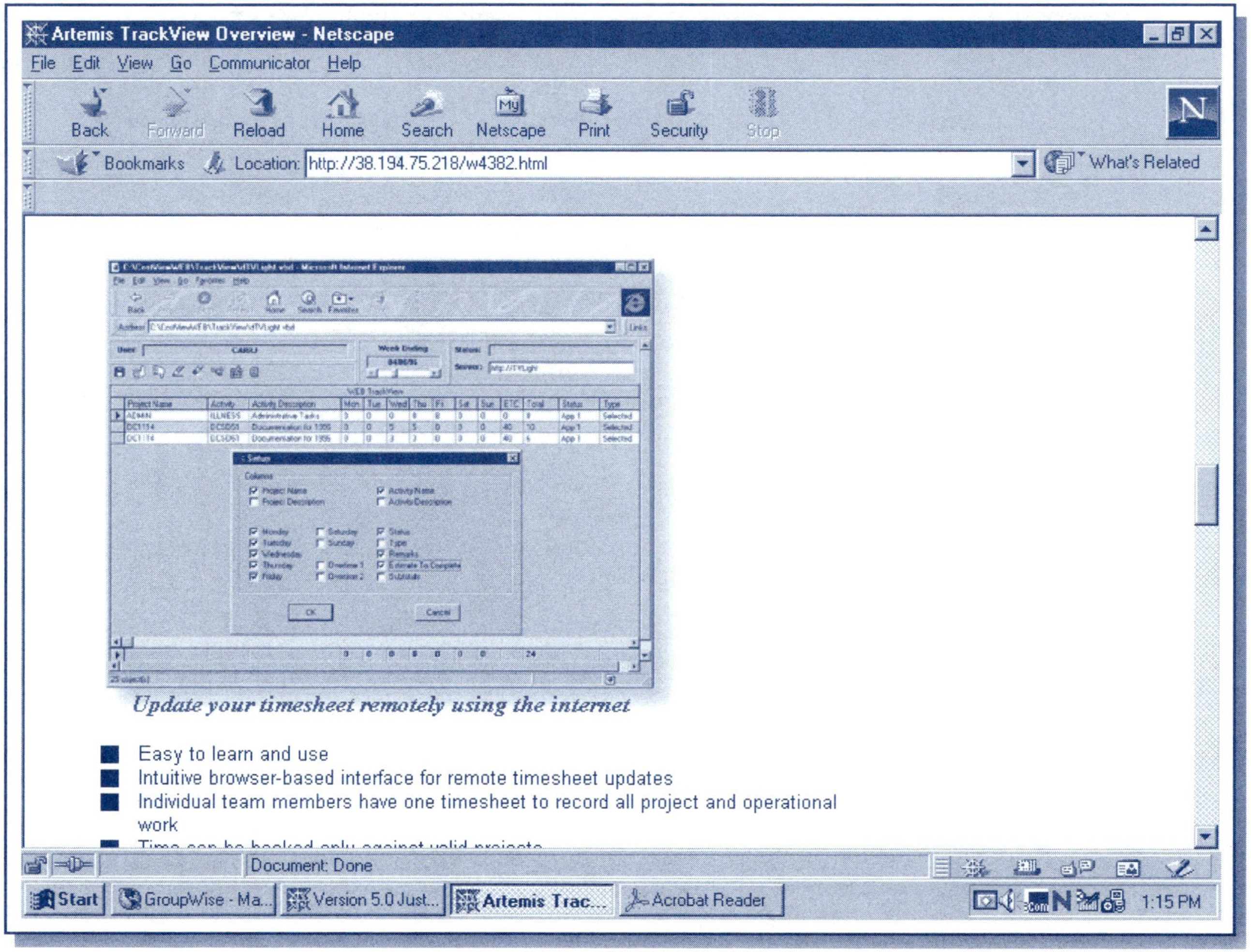

Figure 12-13
Artemis Project View resource assignment screen.

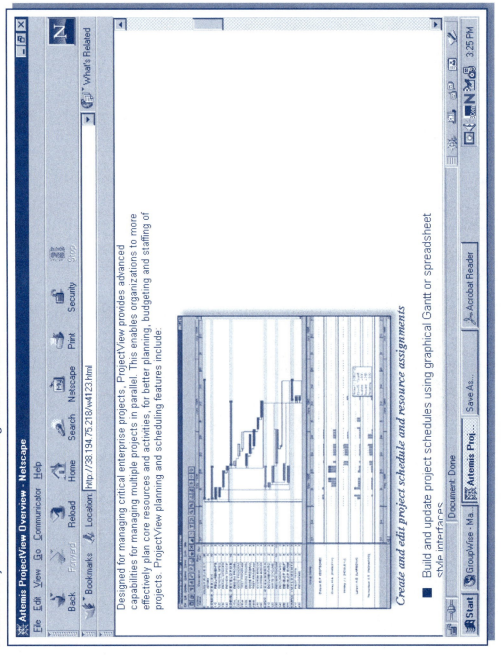

Designed for managing critical enterprise projects, ProjectView provides advanced capabilities for managing multiple projects in parallel. This enables organizations to more effectively plan core resources and activities, for better planning, budgeting and staffing of projects. ProjectView planning and scheduling features include:

Create and edit project schedule and resource assignments

■ Build and update project schedules using graphical Gantt or spreadsheet style interfaces.

Global View. This software is designed for high-level managers. It is an OLAP (on-line analytical processing) tool that can be used on an intranet or the Internet. Global View provides point-and-click access to cost, resource, and schedule status for multi-project analysis. Problem areas can be identified, projects ranked according to the most over budget, and activities within projects identified as principle sources of cost overruns. Users can navigate, filter, sort, and explore information over the Internet using Web browsers. Reports can be prepared in HTML format for inclusion in memos, e-mails, presentations, or Web sites.

12.5   WEB-BASED PROJECT MANAGEMENT[4]

It should be clear from the previous section that virtually all project management software products include the capability to take advantage of Web-based technology. This is because the benefits of Web technology are very well suited to the needs of project management.

Benefits

A project Web site and Web-based project software are especially helpful in situations where project team members are located at different sites. Putting project information on the Internet or other networks utilizing Internet standards expedites projects that might ordinarily be delayed because team members are dispersed. Benefits of Web-based project management include immediate availability of project information, efficiency and accessibility for communicating with workers, ease of learning and usage, and reliability and currency of information because it is entered and communicated in real time.

Web-based project management fills the information needs of project stakeholders at all levels; from individual teams, team members, and project managers working on a particular project; to high-level managers who want information about every project in the organization.

With Web-browser integrated project management software, each team member can have her own individual Web page on which to report progress and retrieve assignments. Web pages for team members at scattered work sites enable everyone to easily send information to the project manager, and vice versa. The project manager can then aggregate the provided information to create an overview of the entire project.

Web-based tools are easy to learn, understand, and use. Because the training and learning required for Web-based tools are minimal, team members can concentrate on their job rather than spend time in training, or in trying to figure out the software.

In most cases, the necessary tools are already at hand. Web-based software requires one thing: access to a Web browser, such as Internet Explorer or Netscape, which is available on any computer with Internet access. Internet and intranet networks are easy to use and learn, and therefore team members are likely to use them more frequently for status reporting. Special Web site administration is unnecessary when team members, who enter up-to-date information, maintain their own sites. Web-based communication not only provides management with a current view of projects, but it demands low overhead and frees management from worry associated with system updates and maintenance.

Intranets, Virtual Private Networks, and Security

Security of information on a network is an important matter for organizations using Web-based project management. Project Web sites may contain information that an organization does not want to share with outsiders, in which case the company should use an intranet or a virtual private network.

An *intranet,* a private computer network, uses Internet standards and protocols to allow communication among people within an organization. This internal network provides access to a common pool of information from computers within organizational walls. The intranet is owned by the organization it serves, to be accessed only by organizational members and other authorized persons. Access can be extended to include trusted external organizations, partners, or clients through direct, private line connections, or through the Internet. Either type of extended network is called an *extranet.* Unless the network is connected to the Internet, it is very difficult for outsiders to break into the system.

Organizations take steps to keep unauthorized people out of their intranet systems by using firewalls and other mechanisms that either block unauthorized access or make internal information unreadable to unauthorized computers that gain access. When employees are allowed to access the Internet from inside the company's property, the company can keep its stored information secure with the use of firewalls and virtual private networks. A *virtual private network* allows access by authorized users to an organization's intranet from the Internet.

Every computer connected to the Internet has a numerical or Internet protocol (IP) address which serves as its unique "identification number." A *firewall* compares the IP address of a computer attempting to access the protected network with a list of authorized IP addresses. The firewall acts as a sort of gatekeeper that requests from all visitors the key to access, and either allows or denies entrance to the network. When the firewall permits access, the requesting computer is connected to the company's intranet. Otherwise, access is denied and the computer rejected. However, when an unauthorized computer finds a "hole" in the firewall to gain access, it will encounter a second security level, "authentication," which requires entry of an authorized user name and password combination. Without the right combination, access will be denied.

If the system operates as a virtual private network, a third security level, called "encryption," exists. If you have ever entered a credit card number on a Web site to make a purchase, you have encountered this type of security. When an individual enters a credit card number on a Web site, usually a key appears on one side of the browser window. The key indicates that the site is secured with an encryption technique that will jumble the information into an indecipherable status until the receiver provides appropriate information for "unencryption."

Group Productivity[5]

Intranets use browser-based software for enabling users to move easily among different kinds of software tools and perform a wide variety of functions. With an intranet it is very easy to access *group productivity software* and to store reports, profiles, calendars, and schedules. It is also easy for internal users to locate information in these documents using special search tools. This information can be shared and revised by team members in different locations using *document-sharing tools* such as newsgroups, chat rooms, and electronic whiteboards. These tools are especially useful for sharing pictorial information about product design requirements and descriptions.

One of the most common ways that project managers use intranets is for collecting and reporting information about time spent on projects. Time information is collected and retained in a project database, then accessed by project management software to report and tally time spent on projects, and track time needed to complete the project.

Another important tool for project managers is *e-mail.* More than just a means of dashing off a note, teams send multiple copies of memos back and forth over e-mail to share information and resolve problems.

Other means for collectively sharing information about issues and problems include *discussion forums* and *chat areas.* By completing an e-mail form, a person can initiate or contribute to a topic for a discussion forum. Everyone in the discussion group list can view others' contributions and add comments. Chat areas are similar to e-mail although, unlike e-mail and discussion forums in which the transmission is time-delayed, they permit almost immediate response by participants to incoming messages.

It used to be that to hold a team meeting in which the members are geographically dispersed, special video-conferencing facilities were necessary—no longer. Video, voice, and data can be shared over the intranet or Internet at desktop locations. The information conveyed over a network can be spreadsheet, word document, Power Point presentation, chart, graphic, photo, engineering design, or video files. At Boeing, all designs and changes are electronic, so the status of any design, including the most recent changes, is always accurate and available immediately to everyone. Specific notification of any change can be sent via an e-mail list-serv to everyone who needs to know. The names on the list-serv are specified on a responsibility matrix (each person involved in a particular work package that has "N" responsibility).

As long as team members have access to a computer and browser, they can participate in a meeting. For example, engineers in Seattle having trouble assembling a mock-up can send video images to a design team in New York. The design team can *see* what the mock-up looks like, assess the problem, and make a decision. Without this technology the design team would actually have to *go* to Seattle.

12.6   APPLYING COMPUTER-BASED PROJECT MANAGEMENT SYSTEMS

PMIS in the Project Life Cycle

A computer-based PMIS can assist the project manager throughout all phases of the project life cycle. Figure 12-14 shows the range of managerial tasks and functions where a PMIS can help. Following are ways a PMIS is applied during the project life cycle.

Conception.   During the conception phase, mathematical/statistical and "thought organizer" software are employed for feasibility analysis, cost-benefit studies, and project development. PMI software is used to model variations of the end-item, to create a work breakdown structure, preliminary budget and schedule, and to prepare documents and presentations to management. Integrated software combining design and management analyses are used for performing tradeoff and feasibility studies and preparing proposal and contract documents.

Definition.   Objectives and work tasks defined in conception are input to PMI software to check precedence relationships and to produce networks and Gantt charts with schedule dates, slack times, and critical path. These outputs are used for further analysis to determine necessary resources and to prepare more detailed schedules and

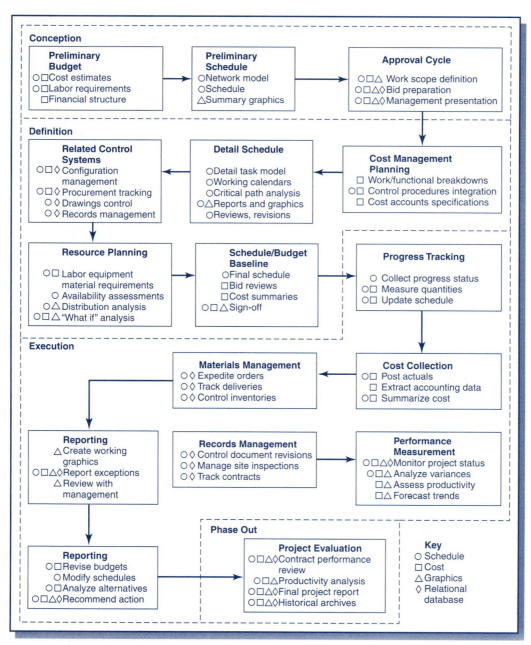

Figure 12-14
PMIS functions in the project life cycle. (*Source:* Project/2.)

budgets. A PMIS is used to perform "what if" analysis to evaluate the interactive effects of altering project scope, resources, and schedules, and to prepare a final baseline plan specifying the cost-account structure, detailed work tasks, labor/equipment/material requirements, and final schedules down to the work task level. In projects with dispersed work teams, data is gathered via the Internet or an intranet to maximize the scope and validity of information used to prepare the project plan.

Execution.   Once the project is underway, current information from all project sites is entered into the project database and is compared to the baseline plan to track project progress. Computer-generated reports and graphics help facilitate comprehension and communication of progress information. Key parameters held in the system monitor performance and give warnings whenever variances move outside tolerable limits. The PMIS provides cost and schedule forecasts to help the project manager develop scenarios about alternative, corrective strategies. It also helps her identify and investigate opportunities to reduce costs or finish early. A PMIS linked to purchasing and inventory files assists in expediting orders, tracking deliveries, and controlling inventories.

The PMIS enables the project manager to take quick corrective action by providing timely, accurate reports of deviations from cost, schedule, or technical performance objectives. When critical decisions affecting project objectives, scope, and resources must be made, information can be rapidly reported to upper management and the user. Computer-based systems are especially useful when decisions must be evaluated about resource transfers which affect multiple projects. Mathematical and statistical packages are used to model problems and assess alternatives.

Whenever changes must be made to the plan, PMI systems that integrate time, cost, and resources help managers revise schedules, budgets, and plans, and report changes to project participants. Design changes and their effects on project plans are swiftly communicated via Internet or intranet.

Termination Phase-Out. During phase-out (described in Chapter 13) the PMIS is used for reviewing requirements to ensure contract commitments have been fulfilled. Throughout the project, information—from original studies and the baseline plan, to the most recent plan for completion—has been entered into the project database. This information, properly organized, provides a complete set of project archives. Maintaining such archives is an important, though often neglected, function of project management. If the database is indexed by date, critical information about any stage or element of the project can be retrieved and sequenced into a series of "snapshots" to outline the project's history. This information forms a major portion of the project postcompletion summary (described in the next chapter).

Example 1: Sigma Associates' PMIS for Project Planning and Control

Sigma Associates, the architectural/engineering firm mentioned in Example 4, Chapter 9, relies on a computer-based PMIS for most planning and control functions. So ubiquitous is Sigma's PMIS that employees think of it as a member of the team; they call it "Sally." Recall from Chapter 9 that each project manager uses Sally, the PMIS, to help estimate project labor requirements, to create original project schedules, and to adjust schedules according to labor availability. The comptroller uses Sally to forecast labor expenses, overhead costs, and to prepare project budgets. Information combined from the two constitutes the project plan.

Once a project is approved, Sally's function changes from planning assistance to monitoring and control. Sally's major purpose is to routinely compare the project plan with actual performance, to raise warnings about discrepancies, and to forecast project outcomes (schedule and cost at completion). Sally "knows" the original project plan because labor hours, labor cost budgets, schedules, and activity completion dates are entered at the beginning of the project.

Each week, information about current costs is input to Sally. Estimates of weekly time spent on each activity are accumulated from all project participants. Nonlabor expenses and client reimbursements are input through the company's general ledger system.

Project managers make biweekly estimates of hours anticipated to complete each activity. Sally converts the anticipated hours-to-complete into a percentage completed for each activity. The system multiplies budgeted labor hours by the percentage completed to determine the estimated labor hours intended to bring the activity to its current level of completion (a form of BCWP). By comparing this estimate with actual labor expenditures from time cards, the project manager can determine whether the activity is moving at its budgeted pace.

Sally makes actual-to-plan comparisons and reports discrepancies. Project managers employ these reports to spot problems and locate causes. Sally also revises and reports the cost and date of the project at completion.

When project managers fail to make the biweekly estimates of anticipated hours, Sally makes its own estimates based upon the amount of labor hours that were charged since the last time anticipated hours were input. It also prompts managers about the missing estimate entries.

Sally uses the anticipated hours-to-complete to prepare estimates of labor requirement loads for the remainder of the project. These estimates are used to adjust the remaining labor loadings and to make necessary revisions to schedules.

The comptroller also uses Sally to forecast the timing and amounts of client billing, and the timing of expected payments according to each client's payment history. Based on the percentage of work completed, the system computes an estimate of earned client fees. These fees are compared to actual labor costs, overhead costs, and nonlabor expenses in a monthly profit/loss analysis. Sally does the computations and generates monthly reports of net profit for project-to-date and year-to-date, summarized by office, department, and project manager. It also combines net profit for all projects to give a picture of the company's financial health.

Sally also is able to satisfy one-time needs. If a project manager sees costs running higher than expected because of an improper personnel mix, he can request a report showing the personnel assigned to the project and the extent of their involvement. The comptroller can delve deep into cost details by requesting special reports, such as one showing the printing expenses for a building design. Though not a part of Sally's standard output, these reports are easy to produce because of the system's versatile data retrieval capabilities.

Sally also checks much of the data entered; for example, that the number of hours charged on time cards is correct. Hours charged are compared with dates on the schedule. A card with discrepancies is withheld and a memo describing the error is sent to the employee. A summary report of rejected or uncorrected cards is sent each week to the comptroller.

Sally is an example of a sophisticated, comprehensive PMIS: it serves all the functions (and more) that might be expected of a high-end PMIS.

Fitting the PMIS to the Project

Though most computer-based PMI packages are no match for the capabilities of Sally, that is not a problem when such capabilities are not required. Just as the project team should carefully plan and define the project before it begins, so too should it plan and define the information requirements of the PMIS; then it should choose the PMIS that satisfies these requirements most economically and effectively.

The idea of having a computer PMIS is, in the words of Palla, to "get the right information to the right person at the right time so the right decision can be made for the project."[6] Whatever PMIS is able to do this is the right one. However, as alluded to earlier, deciding which is the right one is not necessarily easy. When a computer-based PMIS is being chosen and implemented for the first time, it is a good idea to start out with a small-scale project and a limited PMIS application—a "prototype" system that can be developed quickly and at low cost to test its feasibility. The project staff should evaluate the system to determine how well it fulfills the information requirements of the test project. The evaluation should indicate what features need to be added or enhanced, or if the system should be discontinued and a new system tried instead.

Choosing, developing, and implementing a PMIS is a *project* and so it is very appropriate to apply the project management principles espoused in this book to ensure that its goals are fulfilled and its users are satisfied.

Many firms use more than one kind of PMI package—for example, Microsoft Project for smaller projects and Artemis for large ones. Some firms rely on a highly user-friendly package to help clients feel comfortable with the output data, then transfer the data to a more powerful package for planning and control. For a comprehensive review of PMIS software, see the *Project Management Software Survey* (Newtown Square, PA: Project Management Institute, 1999); see also the Project Management Forum at www.pmforum.org, and www.gantthead.com.[7]

12.7 SUMMARY

Modern methods of project planning and control require a system, manual or computerized, to handle information efficiently. Some kind of system is necessary for integrating multifunctional tasks and for tying schedules, costs, and work performance together. Such a system is the project management information system or PMIS.

For most projects, major project management functions of scheduling, budgeting, and control are greatly facilitated by using computer-based PMI systems. For managing medium- and large-scale projects, computers have become essential. In recent years, PCs and low-cost, high-quality software have made computer PMISs commonplace.

Most PMIS software offer such features as network scheduling, resource management, budgeting, and to a lesser extent, cost control and performance analysis. The capabilities of PMIS software vary greatly, although all can be used for project planning, many cannot be used for project control. A sophisticated PMIS should be able to assist in numerous planning and control tasks throughout the entire project life cycle, from conception to close out. Software that make use of Internet technology further expand upon these capabilities. Among commercially available PMISs, there is considerable variation in technical capabilities, flexibility, ease of use, and interface and integration capability. As a result, their usefulness varies greatly.

Most smaller computer PMISs, such as the ones described in this chapter, assist in scheduling, budgeting, resource allocation, and, to a lesser extent, project control. Most larger computer PMISs provide integrated planning, scheduling, costing, control, and reporting functions. These systems utilize practically all of the planning and control techniques described in this book.

This chapter concludes the discussion of project planning and control. The next chapter discusses the topics of project evaluation and reporting, and the last stage of the project life cycle, termination.

REVIEW QUESTIONS

1. What is the role of the PMIS in project management? What is the difference between a PMIS and an ordinary MIS?
2. What are some of the information requirements of projects?
3. Why has the computer become an essential tool in project planning and control? What kinds of managerial functions are better performed using a computer-based PMIS?

4. What are the major advantages of computer-based PMISs over manual PMISs?

5. List the major features available on commercial PMIS software.

6. Discuss the applications and benefits of Web-based project management.

7. What capabilities must a PMIS have so that it can be used for the function of project control?

8. Discuss the uses of the PMIS throughout the phases of the project life cycle.

9. Discuss the considerations in selecting and implementing a computer-based PMIS

QUESTIONS ABOUT THE STUDY PROJECT

1. Describe the PMIS used in the project you are studying. Was it the same one used for cost-accounting (PCAS) and project scheduling? Does it combine scheduling, budgeting, authorization, and control, or were several different systems used? If several systems were used, how were they integrated?

2. What are the strong and weak points of the system? Does the system adequately satisfy the information requirements needed to plan and control the project? Is a Web-based system used? Are inadequacies in the system the fault of the computer PMIS, or of the manual support system that provides inputs and utilizes the outputs? What improvements would you suggest to the system?

3. If a computer-based PMIS is not being used, why? How effective is the current manual system and what parts of it could be supplemented or replaced by a computer system? Given the information requirements of the project, what kinds of available PMIS software might be appropriate? How would you suggest going about implementing a computer-based PMIS for this organization?

ENDNOTES

1. D. Roman, *Managing Project: A Systems Approach* (New York: Elsevier, 1986): 181, 184; L. F. Suarez, "Resource Allocation: A Comparative Study," *Project Management Journal* 18, no. 1 (March 1987): 68–71.

2. H. A. Levine, *Project Management Using Micro-computers* (Berkeley, CA: Osborne McGraw-Hill, 1986): 7.

3. Portions of this section were prepared with the assistance of Elisa Denney.

4. This section was prepared by Elisa Denney.

5. Much of this discussion is based upon Tyson Greers, *Understanding Intranets* (Redmond, WA: Microsoft Press, 1998); For discussion of project intranets, see Stephen Mead, "Project-Specific Intranets for Construction Teams," *Project Management Journal* (September 1997): 44–51.

6. R. W. Palla, "Introduction to Micro-computer Software Tools for Project Management," *Project Management Journal* (August 1987), 61–68.

7. *Project Management Software Survey* (Newtown Square, PA: Project Management Institute, 1999).

Chapter 13

Project Evaluation, Reporting, and Termination

> *We look at it and we do not see it.*

> —Lao-Tzu,
> *sixth century* B.C.

In project environments the work must be tracked, evaluated, and corrected so that schedules, expenditures, and technical performance can be kept on target. The project manager oversees the work, assesses progress, and issues instructions for corrective action. As information is received, the project manager judges the status of the project and communicates this to workers, upper management, and the client. Chapters 11 and 12 examined the kinds of information and measures used for assessing and controlling project performance. The first part of this chapter discusses how that information is reviewed and reported for evaluation and decision making purposes.

As the project draws to a conclusion, the project manager must ensure that all work is formally closed out, commitments are met or compensated for, and all remaining "loose ends" are tied up. The second portion of this chapter reviews the project manager's responsibilities in terminating the project and in performing postproject follow-up work and summary evaluation.

Projects are open systems—They are goal-oriented and utilize feedback to determine how well they are doing and when they should alter their courses of action. The primary purpose of evaluation in project management is to assess performance, reveal areas where the project deviates from goals, and uncover extant or potential problems so they can be corrected. Although it is certain that problems and deviations will occur, it is not known a priori where or when.

Evaluation also serves the purpose of summarizing project status to keep stakeholders informed. Upper management and the customer want to know how the project is progressing, and project personnel need to be kept abreast of project status and work changes. Once the project is completed, evaluation's purpose is to summarize and assess the outcome.

Two kinds of evaluation occur in projects. (1) *Formative evaluation* happens throughout the project life cycle and provides information to guide corrective action. (2) *Summary evaluation* occurs after the project is completed and focuses on the end product or result. Formative evaluation is designed to pilot the project as it progresses. It asks the questions "What is happening?" and "How is the project proceeding?" Summary evaluation is designed to appraise the project after completion. It addresses the questions "What happened?" and "What were the results?"

Project Formative Evaluation

Project formative evaluation must account for the fact that projects are complex systems: Cost, schedule, and work performance criteria are interrelated, and interdependent work packages draw from the same pool of limited resources. As a result, well-intended corrective measures directed exclusively on just one performance criteria can lead to problems in others. Similarly, attempts directed solely at improving performance in one work area can have detrimental effects on others. To provide information that realistically portrays the status of the project and enables the project manager to draw accurate conclusions, project evaluation must incorporate three performance criteria simultaneously—cost, schedule, and technical performance, and it must account for the impact that changes in any one work area will have on other related areas. The evaluation process must be able to signal potential trouble spots so action can be initiated before problems materialize. The best kind of evaluation not only reveals problems, it points out opportunities to reduce costs, speed up work, or enhance project outcomes in other ways.

Methods and Measures

A variety of methods, measures, and sources should be used to obtain evaluation information. These methods and measures should be specified before the project begins and included in the project plan. Methods and indicators for measuring schedule, cost, and technical performance were described in Chapters 10 and 11.

By relying on a variety of methods and measures (as opposed to just a few), the project manager can more readily spot problems and opportunities. Variety in the sources of information increases the validity of the evaluation, particularly when several sources all lead to the same conclusion.

The four primary ways for obtaining and/or conveying project evaluative information are graphics (charts and tables), reports (oral and written), observations, and review meetings.

Charts and tables are the most expeditious way for displaying cost, schedule, and work performance information. Their advantage is to reduce large amounts of complex information into simple, comprehensible formats. They clarify information on project progress, performance, and predictions. The charts and tables used in the previous three chapters, particularly the computer-generated ones, are good examples. When distributed and prominently displayed they allow everyone to appreciate the current status and direction of the project.

The danger of charts is that they can hide or obscure information leading to facile and erroneous conclusions. For example, it was noted earlier that because project-level charts tend to hide problems at the work package level, conclusions need to be substantiated by more detailed work package level analysis. Also, charts and tables neither reveal the underlying causes of problems nor suggest opportunities. Thus, the project manager also has to rely on additional sources of evaluative information, such as personal reports and firsthand observation. Charts and tables often require substantial time to prepare and update, and their information value has to be viewed with this trade-off in mind. Using computerized PMISs with graphics capability reduces this problem.

Oral reports about project status and performance are another source of evaluative information. These are easy and quick to obtain, but their quality and reliability depends on the interpretative and verbal skills of the presenter. Unless followed by a written report, verbal information easily gets lost or garbled.

Written reports are valuable but their quality and usefulness also varies. Written reports are most effective when they succinctly summarize information and make use of ratios and graphics to highlight important points. During the planning phase, the format and timing for all key evaluation documents for the duration of the project should be specified.

The more channels that information must pass through to travel from sender to receiver, the more distorted the information gets. The project manager can reduce information distortion by increasing firsthand observation and on-site contact with supervisors and workers. Not only does this reduce the filtering associated with upward communication, but it helps maintain the workers' sense of importance about their contribution to the project. Good project managers do not live in their offices; they are usually on-site. Of course, one person cannot be in all places at all times, and the larger and more geographically disperse the project, the relatively fewer places the project manager can visit, even on an infrequent basis.

All of these are useful and important ways to obtain and convey evaluative information. Still another way, one of the most important, is the project review meeting.

13.2 PROJECT REVIEW MEETINGS

Purpose of Review Meetings

The main function of *project review meetings* is to identify deviations from the project plan so corrective action can be quickly taken. During these meetings, participants focus on (1) current problems with the work, schedule or costs, and how they should be resolved, (2) anticipated problems, and (3) opportunities to improve project performance.

Review meetings are the managerial equivalent to the "quality circle" (QC) groups used in production environments. QC groups get the people most closely associated with the job—the workers—to (1) identify quality- and production-related problems as well as opportunities for work improvement, (2) develop ways to resolve problems and take advantage of opportunities, and (3) implement them. (In larger projects, the use of both managerial review meetings and QC groups helps to identify and resolve problems that either alone would miss.)

Review meetings can be informal and scheduled weekly, or formal and scheduled whenever needed or according to particular phases of the project. Most large projects require both kinds of reviews.

Informal Reviews

Informal reviews are held frequently and regularly, and involve a small number of people. They also are referred to as "peer reviews" because the people involved are usually members of the project team. These reviews focus on project status, special problems, emerging issues, and the performance of the project with regard to requirements, budgets, and schedules. Selection of meeting participants depends on the phase of the project and issues at hand so that only the appropriate project team members, customer representatives, functional or line managers, and project managers are chosen. Before these meetings, status reports and forecast time and cost-to-complete are updated. Also, attendees who were assigned topics in advance prepare presentations.

Attempts by the project manager to dominate meetings will be met with resistance and withdrawal. To encourage honesty and candor, the project manager should assume the role of group facilitator. Because reviews are intended to uncover problems and issues, problems and bad news should be expected and openly confronted. Finger pointing, passing blame, or smoothing over of conflict should be avoided—these reactions waste time, discourage attendance, and detract from the real value of the meetings, which is to identify problems and reach agreement on corrective action.

Formal Reviews

Besides these periodic, informal reviews, formal reviews scheduled in advance are held at critical stages or project milestones. Among the most common formal reviews conducted during project definition and execution phases are the following:

1. *Preliminary Design Review.* The functional design is reviewed to determine whether the concept and planned implementation fits the basic operational requirements.
2. *Critical Design Review.* Details of the hardware and software design are reviewed to ensure that they conform to the preliminary design specifications.
3. *Functional Readiness Review.* For high-volume products or mass-produced goods, tests are performed on the first, or early, items to evaluate the efficacy of the manufacturing process.
4. *Product Readiness Review.* Manufactured products are compared to specifications and requirements to ensure that the controlling design documentation produces items that meet requirements.

Formal *critical* reviews serve several purposes: minimization of risk, identification of uncertainties, assurances of technical integrity, and assessment of alternative design and engineering approaches. The project team assumes responsibility for accumulating information for formal reviews. Unlike in peer reviews, actual oversight and conduct is the responsibility of a group of outsiders. These outsiders, either technical experts or experienced managers, are intimately familiar with the workings of the project and the project organization, though not formally associated with the project organization or its contractors. A formal review may last for several days and require considerable preparation and scrutiny of results. The required time to prepare and conduct reviews and to obtain approvals should be allowed for in the project schedule.

Formal reviews can be a precondition for continuing the project, as in the phased project planning approach described earlier. Following formal review of the most recent project phase, a decision to continue or terminate the project is made.

Example 1: Formal Reviews and Internal Reviews in the Mars Pathfinder Project[1]

NASA conducts formal reviews for all of its major projects. Reviews that are conducted by an outside board can be extremely critical. Termination or continuance of a project depends on the board's findings. Preparation for a formal NASA review can take an enormous amount of time. Senior project management for the Mars Pathfinder project (see Example 4, Chapter 11) estimated that preparation for one such review, the *critical design review*, would require their concerted attention for as long as *6 weeks*. This would divert time from actual management of the project, which, paradoxically, could increase the likelihood of the project falling behind schedule and failing the review. To prepare for this review, project manager Brian Muirhead ordered an internal peer review.

The internal review revealed a slew of problem areas, including lack of progress in defining system interfaces (necessary for defining how parts of the system would fit together), rapid growth in the mass of the Mars lander (the latest prototype weighed too much), and a shortage of good engineers. These findings did little to inspire confidence about the project's ability to pass the critical scrutiny of the design review board.

The critical design review verdict is crucial because it represents an all-or-nothing decision. The project earns either a passing or failing grade. A failing grade initiates a cancellation review, a process that often results in project termination. A project such as Pathfinder could be canceled if budget overruns were as little as 15 percent. In this case, the design review board comprised 25 consultants and seasoned managers from NASA and JPL (Jet Propulsion Laboratory, the site doing most of the Pathfinder design work) who were not associated with the Pathfinder project.

In addition to determining the future of a project, review also serves to give it a kick in the pants if things haven't been done well. Preparation for the sessions, a laborious endeavor, forces the project team to make decisions about unresolved issues. Reviews may be held three or four times during the project.

Internal, or peer, reviews at NASA address a narrower range of topics and require only a few days preparation. The value of peer reviews lies in their ability to make sure that everyone understands what decisions are being made, nothing is overlooked, and the project is kept on track with regard to the schedule, budget, and mission requirements. Over 100 peer reviews were conducted during the 3 years of Pathfinder development.

Members of the design review board had been unhappy with many aspects of the Pathfinder project; nonetheless, they did not initiate a cancellation review. Instead, they approved the project with instructions that Pathfinder managers be more critical of designs, focus less on performance and more on cost, and discontinue obsessing over business innovations. Later, these recommendations proved useful as their implementation helped make the project one of the most successful in the history of space exploration.

A related special review, a *project audit*, provides the sponsor or customer with an independent assessment of project progress. In any project, regardless of contractual obligations, the customer should assume the ultimate responsibility as the project watchdog because it is the customer who will ultimately suffer the loss should the project get into trouble. Hence, sometimes the customer should initiate a project audit. The audit can be conducted early in the project, during design or construction, or at any time a significant change in the budget, schedule, or goals of the project occurs. Essentially, the purpose of the audit is the same as for a formal critical review: to verify project progress, examine constraints to progress, assess the effectiveness of the project organization in doing its job, and advise possible solutions to problems. An audit should scrutinize the project management and organization, project definition, schedules, budgets, constraints, and communications. An audit usually takes 1 to several weeks to conduct.

Taking Action

When problems are identified at a review, an action plan is formulated immediately or preparations are made so it can be prepared later. In the latter case, the manager responsible for the action is named and a subsequent meeting is convened with only the affected individuals.

Each action plan includes a statement of the problem, objectives for resolving it, the required course of action, a target date, and who is responsible. Figure 13-1 shows a sample action plan. To assure coordination of work and commitment to effort, approval should be sought from everyone who will contribute to or be affected by the action plan.

An example of another action plan is that of the *problem failure report*. NASA, for instance, uses such a report for tracking all problems and focusing on the most important ones. For every problem identified, a problem failure report is prepared. The problem is assigned two ratings; one to indicate its impact on mission success (1 = negligible impact; 3 = mission catastrophic); the other to indicate both certainty

Figure 13-1
Sample action plan.

Problem Area	Objective	Actions	Who	When Completed
I. Planning and scheduling	1. Establish backup support for each system.	1. (A) Discuss systems with analysts who support them; formulate plan for each system.	Project leaders and analysts	Jan. 1
	2. Review all systems. Eliminate those not used; clean up others.	2. (A) Prepare questionnaire on system status.	Ron Gilmore	Nov. 15
		2. (B) Complete questionnaires.	Analysts and programmers	Dec. 1
		2. (C) Determine status and specific actions.	PL, analysts and programmers	Jan. 31
	3. Provide information on purposes and uses of new project management system.	3. Prepare seminar on PMS and present to staff.	Joan Gibb	Before March 1

of an identified cause and confidence with a proposed solution (1 = known cause and known solution; 4 = unknown cause, unverified solution). Problems given a 2, 3, or 4 rating are those that might be potentially mission-threatening and require the project manager's personal sign-off. The problem failure report is retained electronically. On the Mars Pathfinder project, over 800 of these electronic reports were generated and subsequently evaluated.[2]

At every review meeting, problems should be documented and an action plan summary prepared. The action plan summary should indicate for each problem the actions to take, the people held responsible, and the target completion date. The status of every problem is evaluated at subsequent meetings with a review of actions taken and progress.

Project Meeting Room

Project-related meetings and conferences typically are convened in a central meeting place or project office. As described earlier, the chosen location should serve as a physical reminder of the project and provide space for storing, preparing, and displaying project information. Gantt charts, project networks, and cost charts comparing planned and actual performance are permanently displayed for easy reference.

13.3   REPORTING

Company management must be kept apprised of the status, progress, and performance of all ongoing and upcoming projects. Problems affecting profits, schedules, or budgets, as well as their expected impacts and recommended actions should be reported promptly. The customer also should be periodically updated about project status and notified whenever major problems arise. Consideration also should be given to providing status reports to other stakeholders (those who have a perceived or genuine interest in the project), weighing confidentiality and privacy issues against opportunity costs. The final choice, of course, rests with management. Stakeholders to consider include citizen, professional, and activist groups, public agencies, stockholders, and others who have a stake in project outcomes—its end-items, side effects, or spin-offs.

Reports to Top Management and the Office of Projects

Top management should be sent monthly progress reports summarizing project status. Suggested reports include[3]

1. A brief statement summarizing the project status.
2. Red flag items where corrective action has or should be taken.
3. Accomplishments to date, changes to schedule, and projections for schedule and cost at completion.
4. Current and potential problem areas and actions required.
5. Current cost situation and cost performance.
6. Manpower plan and limitations.

When several projects are simultaneously authorized or underway, management uses this information to compile monthly summaries of the relative status of all projects. For each project, the summary includes[4] the names of the customer and the project manager; the monetary and labor investment; scheduled start and finish dates; possible risks, losses, and gains; and other information requiring top management review. The summary enables top management to assess the relative performance of all projects and their combined influence on the company. It also assists the project office in planning, coordination of authorizations, and resource allocation, and it reduces the possibility of the firm overlooking key issues or overcommitting resources.

Reports to top management, prepared by the project manager or project staff, summarize the monthly status reports generated by the PCAS or PMIS.

Reports to Project and Program Managers

On large projects, the project manager receives frequent reports from work packages about the value of work completed-to-date, forecasts of costs-at-completion, and revised calendar schedules for completion (similar to Table 11-1 and Figure 11-12, aggregated up to second or third level items). The same kind of information is accumulated down to the work package level by the project manager or other control personnel in the project office. The project manager also receives monthly financial status reports showing costs incurred and cumulative planned costs versus actual costs (e.g., the information shown in Figure 12-5). These reports are also sent to the company financial manager or controller.

Reports to Functional Managers

Functional managers should be sent monthly status reports showing man-hours and costs associated with work packages in their respective areas. The reports shown in Chapter 9, Figures 9-7 through 9-11, if modified to include actual expenditures, are representative.

Reports to Customers/Users

The project manager should send monthly status reports to the customer. These reports should include recent changes as requested by the customer and changes resulting from unavoidable events that impact on work scope, schedule, or cost. The reports should be presented to the user in a clear and understandable format. Requests or questions from the user should be quickly followed up by the project manager.

Although the company marketing or customer relations director frequently is given the job of communicating any contract-related information to the customer, the project manager should take final responsibility for ensuring that the customer is well-informed about project status. The project manager, as the person ultimately accountable for project performance, must answer to the user regarding any project problems. Keeping the customer well-informed avoids later "surprises;" it helps ensure that claims are settled quickly and minimizes snags at termination.

13.4   TERMINATING THE PROJECT

Projects, by definition, are activities of limited duration; all projects come to an end. When this happens, it is the project manager who ensures that all project-related work has been completed and formally closed out by a specified date. It is the project manager's responsibility to put an end to the project—sometimes a tough requirement, especially when there is no follow-up project.

The Last Step

By the time the end-item has been delivered and installed, many people in the project team will have lost enthusiasm and be anxious to move on to something new. As a result, termination gets little attention as managers eagerly shift emphasis to upcoming projects or scan the environment for leads about potential projects. Yet, as common sense indicates, terminating a project is no less important than any other project activity. In fact (as discussed in Chapter 17), the process of terminating a project is so critical that it can determine whether, ultimately, the project is deemed a success or failure.

Termination can occur in a variety of ways; the best way involves a planned, systematic procedure; the worst, an abrupt cancellation of work, slow attrition of effort, or siphoning off resources to higher priority projects. When the project goes sour, it is either terminated before goals are reached, or allowed to "limp along" until fizzling out before completion. Unless *formally* terminated, projects have a tendency to drag on, sometimes unintentionally from neglect or insufficient resources, sometimes intentionally for lack of follow-up work. Workers remain on the project payroll for months after their obligations have been met, which can turn an otherwise successful project into financial failure. As long as the project has not been officially terminated, work orders remain open and labor charges continue to accrue.

Reasons for Termination

Project terminations essentially fall into three categories: project objectives have been achieved, it is more convenient to stop than continue, or default.[5]

Even in the first case—when projects are terminated because contractual objectives have been met—it takes a skilled project manager to orchestrate termination and ensure that no activities or obligations are uncompleted or unfulfilled. The seeds of successful termination are sown early in the project. Because termination requires customer acceptance of the project results, the criteria for acceptance should be clearly defined, agreed upon, and documented at the beginning of the project. Any subsequent changes to criteria made during the project should be approved by both contractor and customer. Throughout all phases of the project, the project manager must emphasize achievement of the customer's acceptance criteria.

Some projects never reach fruition because of uncontrollable factors in the environment. Such terminations may arise from changing market conditions, skyrocketing costs, depleted critical resources, or declining priorities that make completion infeasible or undesirable. The decision to abort before completion occurs when associated financial or other losses are less than those expected from carrying the project through to completion. The customer may simply change his mind and no longer want the project end-item.

Projects also are halted because of unsatisfactory technical performance, poor quality materials or workmanship, violation of contract, poor planning and control, bad management, or customer dissatisfaction with the contractor. Many of these reasons are the fault of the contractor and project management; they could have been avoided had management exercised better project planning and control, showed more respect for the user, or acted in a more ethical manner. These termination causes produce worse consequences, leaving user objectives unfulfilled and casting a shadow over the contractor's technical competence, managerial ability, or moral standing.

As with earlier stages of work, the project manager is responsible for planning, scheduling, monitoring and controlling activities at project termination. Some of these responsibilities listed by Archibald include[6]

A. Planning, scheduling, and monitoring completion activities by

- Obtaining and approving termination plans from involved functional managers.
- Preparing and coordinating termination plans and schedules.
- Planning for reassignment of project team personnel and transfer of resources to other projects.
- Monitoring termination activities and completion of all contractual agreements.
- Monitoring the disposition of any surplus materials and special project equipment.

B. Final close-out activities, including

- Closing out all work orders and approving the completion of all subcontracted work.
- Notifying all departments of project completion.
- Closing the project office and other facilities occupied by the project organization.
- Closing project books.
- Ensuring delivery of project files and records to the responsible managers.

C. Customer acceptance, obligation, and payment activities, including

- Ensuring delivery of end-items, side items, and customer acceptance of items.
- Communicating to the customer when all contractual obligations have been fulfilled.
- Ensuring that all documentation related to customer acceptance as required by contract has been completed.
- Expediting any customer activities needed to complete the project.
- Transmitting formal payment and collection of payments.
- Obtaining formal customer acknowledgment of completion of contractual obligations that release the contractor from further obligation (except warranties and guarantees).

The responsibility for the last group of activities, particularly those relating to payment and contractual obligations, is shared with the contract administrator or the person responsible for company-client negotiations and legal contracts. The final activity, obtaining the certificate of customer acknowledgment, may involve claims in addition to the contracted price because the customer may have failed to provide agreed-to data or support, or requested items beyond contract specifications. In such cases the contractor is entitled to compensation. In other cases, described next, the client is compensated.

Before the project is considered closed, the customer reviews the results or end-item to make sure everything is satisfactory. Items still open, in need of attention, or to be redone, and to which the contractor agrees, are recorded on a list (sometimes called a "punch list"). Items then are checked off the list by the contractor as they are rectified.

The importance of doing a good job at termination cannot be understated; neither can the difficulty. As mentioned, in the rush to finish the project and in the accompanying confusion, many of the termination responsibilities listed previously are overlooked, mishandled, or botched. To ensure they are handled properly, termination responsibilities should be systematically delegated and checked off as completed. Project termination requires the same high degree of attention and service as do other project management responsibilities. A bungled termination can bungle the project.

13.6   CLOSING THE CONTRACT

Delivery, installation, and user acceptance of the main contract end-item (the major hardware, software, or service specified by the project contract) does not necessarily mean that the project is closed. Project completion may be held up pending the contractor's delivery of necessary, ancillary articles—called *side items*—or payment of negotiated compensation for failure to meet contractual agreements.

Side Items

Effective installation, operation, maintenance, and monitoring of the contract end-item is often contingent upon availability of numerous contract *side items* such as special tools, instruments, spare parts, reports, drawings, courses of instruction, and user operating and maintenance manuals. Subcontractors usually provide side items to the prime contractor or developer. They can range from the simple and mundane to the complex and innovative. An operating manual for a network server is an example of the former; a high-fidelity computer simulator for training operators of a large chemical processing facility is an example of the latter. Simple or complex, side items are important because successful implementation of the main end-item and close-out of the project depends upon them.

Like the main end item, side items are deliverable contract items. Their cost may account for a significant percentage of the total project cost. Often, however, perhaps because they are deemed "side" items, the amount of time and effort they require is underestimated. The result is that the project cannot be completed on time even if the main contract end-item has been successfully completed. Failure to deliver side items can subject the contractor to penalties or financial loss.

Side items should be included in all aspects of project planning and control—requirements and work definition, budgeting, scheduling, and tracking. The project manager must make certain that the scope of work for side items is well understood and that qualified personnel are assigned with adequate time to fulfill requirements.[7] Side items must be looked upon as part of the scheduled contracted work, not as afterthoughts or project extensions. To ensure that the project can be closed out on schedule, side items must be given full consideration far in advance of the scheduled completion date.

Negotiated Adjustments to Final Contract

In many high-cost projects, the contractor receives payment for only a portion of the total project cost, for example 80 to 90 percent, with the remainder conditional upon the contractor's performance. Measures of performance may include the performance of equipment or service provided, the degree of contractor compliance with contractual agreements, or the quality of the working relationship maintained by the contractor.[8]

These final payment contingencies are considered postacceptance issues because they occur after the major contractual items have been accepted by the user. If the delivered equipment is satisfactory yet does not perform up to the contracted specifications, if it is found defective after a trial period due to design or production inadequacies, or if the item is delivered late, the contractor may be responsible for paying negotiated compensation to the user.

Contract sign-off might also be contingent upon how well the product functions after delivery. In that case, the project manager oversees installation, setup, and initial operation at the customer's site. The contractor might also provide on-site user support, at no additional fee, until operating deficiencies have been removed.

Sometimes it is in the best interest of the customer or contractor to negotiate aspects of the contract price or delivery date *after* the project is completed. The U.S. government and other customers retain the right to negotiate overhead rates even after the final price on a cost-plus contract has been received. Likewise, when an originally scheduled completion date has been overrun, contractors want to negotiate a revised contracted delivery date to match the actual delivery date so as to protect their reputation.

13.7 PROJECT EXTENSIONS

When additional, related work is sought that extends beyond the scope of the original project, a new, smaller project emerges. Such *project extensions* arise from the need or desire to enhance the originally funded system. There are two kinds of extensions: discretionary and essential enhancements to the original contract end item.

Discretionary enhancements are requested by the user or proposed by the contractor for the purpose of improving the operation or convenience of the original project end-item. The environment remains the same, but new and better ways are found to improve the item. In contrast, *essential enhancements* are compulsory and without them the item will cease to operate or become obsolete. When the end-item as originally planned is no longer adequate due to changes in the environment, it *must* be enhanced to remain viable.

Project extensions are originated either by a request from the user (e.g., an RFP) or with a proposal from the contractor. They represent the initial stage for a new project. Project extensions themselves become projects; they follow the stages of a development cycle and are planned, scheduled, and controlled just like the projects from which they evolved.

13.8 PROJECT SUMMARY EVALUATION

One of the final tasks of the project team, after the project has been terminated and the system is made operational, is to perform a formal evaluation. This frequently overlooked task is an essential, valuable *learning* component of project management. Without a complete, formal review of the project, there is a tendency to mentally suppress problems encountered and to understate the impact of past errors or misjudgments. ("Things weren't really so bad, now were they?")

Summary evaluation is important regardless of the outcome of project termination, even those regrettable cases where the project was ended without having achieved its goals. For project and company management to learn from past experience, it is as important to review mistakes as it is successes.

Project summary evaluation reviews the performance of the project team and the performance of the system end-item. The purpose of the review is to determine and assess what has been done and what remains to be done, not to find fault or pass blame. As mentioned earlier, finger-pointing and reprimanding are counterproductive because they encourage people to cover up the very problems and mistakes that evaluation seeks to reveal and resolve.

Postcompletion Project Review

The *postcompletion project review* (or *postmortem*) is a summary review and assessment of the project. It should be conducted after the end-item system has been implemented and the project closed out; early enough so project team members remain available to participate and retain fresh memories of their experiences. It is an important task that should be included in the project's work breakdown, budget, and schedule.[9]

The postcompletion review process should

1. Review initial project objectives in terms of technical performance, schedule, and cost; and review the soundness of the objectives in view of the problem that the system was to resolve.
2. Review the evolution of objectives through the end to determine how well the project team performed with respect to them; and review the reasons for changes, noting which changes were avoidable and which were not.
3. Review the activities and relationships of the project team throughout the project life cycle, including review of the interfaces, performance, and effectiveness of project management; the relationships among top management, the project team, the functional organization, and the client; the cause and process of termination; customer reactions and satisfaction.
4. Review the involvement and performance of all stakeholders, including subcontractors and vendors, the client, and outside support groups.
5. Review expenditures, sources of costs, and profitability; identify organizational benefits, project extensions, and marketable innovations.
6. Identify areas of the project where performance was particularly good, noting reasons for success and identifying processes that worked well.
7. Identify problems, mistakes, oversights, and areas of poor performance, and the causes.
8. Summarize the lessons learned from the project and give recommendations for incorporating them into future projects.

The review should be conducted by representatives from all functional organizations that contributed to the project—marketing, design, engineering, production, quality assurance, testing, contract administration, and so on. An outside facilitator might be selected to guide the process to ensure the review is comprehensive, unbiased, and accurate. As part of the process, each representative independently lists the things that went right and wrong with the project. Later they meet as a group, sharing their notes to create a pooled list of rights, wrongs, lessons learned, and future recommendations. (To encourage openness and candor, managers who are in a position to evaluate project team members should *not* participate in the meeting.) The completed lists of lessons learned and recommendations are then formally presented to stakeholders and other project associates, including project, functional, and senior managers, and other members of the project team.

The project postmortem review does not seek to criticize or place blame for mistakes or problems. The goal is to determine the lessons that may be learned so errors will not be repeated in the future. The thrust is to learn better methods that can be adopted for future improvements in project performance.

Project review results should be documented in a *project summary report*. This becomes the authoritative document on the project, a learning device that will help later project teams avoid making the same mistakes. The project summary report should describe the project, its evolution, and its eventual outcome. It begins with the project plan, describes how the plan worked, and where it failed. Because a project that is successful for one party may be considered unsuccessful for others, the opinions and assessments of the customer, the project team, and upper management should be considered. A project that is highly profitable for the contractor might not have effectively solved the client's problem; a project that satisfied the client might have jeopardized the financial stability of the contractor.

The project summary becomes the reference for project-related questions that might arise later. Thoroughness and clarity are essential because the people who worked on the project probably will not be available later to answer questions.

Example 2: Microsoft Postmortems[10]

Most product development projects at Microsoft conclude with a written postmortem report that is circulated to the highest levels of management, which for major projects includes to Bill Gates. A postmortem can require as much as six months to prepare and range from under ten pages to over one hundred pages in length. The general purpose is to describe what worked well in the project, what did not, and what should be improved for the next project. Descriptive information is also included such as *the size of the project team, duration of the project, aspects of the product* (size in thousand-lines-of-code [KLOC], languages and platform used), *quality issues* (number of bugs per KLOC, type and severity of bugs), *schedule performance* (actual versus planned dates), and the *development process* (tools used, interdependencies with other groups). Functional managers prepare the initial draft, then circulate it via e-mail to other team members for comment. The final draft is sent to team members, senior executives, and the directors of product development, coding, and testing.

Postinstallation System Review

Several months after its delivery, the fully operational end-item system should be evaluated to assess its performance in the user environment under ongoing operational conditions. This *postinstallation system review* provides data about the end-item system for the project team and the user. It serves a variety of purposes, such as offering maintenance information and operating data for system designers, and initiating requests for system enhancements. Using the original user requirements as the standard of evaluation, the system review attempts to answer the questions: Now that the system is fully operational, is it doing what it was intended to do? Is the user getting the benefits expected from the system? What changes are necessary to fulfill the needs or desires of the user?

The project team should make certain that the evaluated system is *unaltered* from the one delivered. Frequently the user makes system improvements after installation. Although there is nothing wrong with this per se, the system is changed physically or functionally, a fact that must be addressed when evaluating system performance.

During the course of the review the evaluation team might discover parts of the system needing maintenance. Design flaws, operating problems, or necessary enhancements—which nobody could have foreseen earlier—often become obvious after the system has been in routine operation.

Results of this review should be *documented*. The system review should describe system performance compared to system objectives, note any maintenance problems, and suggest system enhancements. Both the postinstallation system review and the project summary report should be filed and maintained for periodic reference in the planning and conduct of future projects.

13.9 SUMMARY

A variety of sources and measures are used for collecting and communicating formative evaluation information, including graphical presentations, reports, observations, and meetings. Project evaluation utilizes all of these, but the most important one is the review meeting. Most projects utilize both informal and formal reviews. Informal reviews are internal reviews held regularly and conducted by members of the project team. They address specific issues regarding project status and performance. Formal reviews are special reviews or audits held at key stages or milestones in the project, and are conducted by experienced outsiders and consultants. They provide project sponsors or customers with independent assessments of overall project performance and, sometimes, a recommendation about whether to continue the project; they also provide project management suggestions or instructions for improving the project.

A project is terminated through a series of formal procedures. The project manager oversees the planning, scheduling, and coordination of termination activities and conducts the final close out of the project. The project manager ensures delivery of side items and adjustments to the final contract. When a user request or contractor proposal is beyond the scope of the original project, a project extension is initiated.

Following project completion, the effectiveness of the project organization is assessed with a postcompletion review or postmortem. The results of this review, which considers all aspects of the project, its successes and mistakes, and lessons learned and recommendations, are compiled in a project summary report. Additionally, after the main contract end-item has been in operation for several months, a postinstallation system review is conducted to assess system performance compared to user requirements and to determine maintenance or enhancements needs. The results of the review are documented and combined with the project summary report to provide a comprehensive historical and learning document for future project teams.

The chapters in this and the previous section of the book described how project managers, organizations, and teams plan, organize, and guide projects from start to finish; they have not said much about the project managers, organizations, or teams *themselves*. The chapters in the next section of the book shift the focus from what managers and groups do in projects to important aspects of the managers and groups themselves. They address organizational behavior matters, including organization structure, leadership, managing teamwork, and managing conflict and stress, all of which are germane to the effective management of projects.

REVIEW QUESTIONS

1. Describe the difference between formative evaluation and summary evaluation in project management.
2. Why is it better to rely on a variety of information sources for evaluation than just a few? Give some examples of how several sources are used in project evaluation.
3. What are the advantages and disadvantages of the following sources of information: (a) charts and tables, (b) oral and written reports, (c) firsthand evaluation?
4. What is the purpose of internal peer reviews? When are they held? Who participates?
5. What is an action plan? What must it include?
6. What is a formal critical review? When is a formal review held and what does it look at? Why do outsiders conduct it? Why would a customer or project supporter want a formal review?
7. What should be included in summary status reports to top management? What should be included in comparative summary reports?
8. What reports should the project manager receive? How does the project manager use these reports?
9. What reports are sent to functional managers?
10. When and what kind of reports are sent to the customer? Why is reporting to customers so important?
11. What are the reasons for project termination? How can termination for reasons other than achievement of project goals be avoided?
12. What must the project manager do in the planning, scheduling, and closing out of the project?
13. What is the role of the project manager and contract administrator in receiving customer acceptance of the work and final payment?
14. What are side items? How can they delay project completion?
15. What kinds of negotiated adjustments are made to the contract, postacceptance? Why would a user or contractor want to specify the terms of a contract after the project is completed?
16. What is a project extension and how do project extensions originate? How is a project extension managed?
17. What are the differences between the two kinds of reviews in project summary evaluation: the postcompletion project or postmortem review and the post-installation system review? Describe each of these reviews.

QUESTIONS ABOUT THE STUDY PROJECT

1. How often and what kinds of review meetings were held in the project? Why were they held? Who attended them?
2. When and for what reason were special reviews held?
3. How was follow-up ensured on decisions made during review meetings?
4. Is there a project meeting room? How often and in what ways is it used?
5. Describe the kinds of project reports sent to top management and the customer. Who issued these reports? What kinds of reports were sent to project and functional managers? Who issued them?
6. How was the project terminated? Describe the activities of the project manager during the final stage of the project and the steps taken to close it out.

7. How was the contract closed out? Were there any side items or negotiated adjustments to the contract?

8. Did any follow-up projects grow out of the one being investigated?

9. Describe the project summary review (prepared at the *end* of the project). Who prepared it? Who was it sent to and how was it used? Where is it now? Show an example (or portion of one).

10. Was there a review of the product or project output after it was installed? When? By whom? What did they find? Did the client request the review or was it standard procedure?

ENDNOTES

1. Adapted from Brian Muirhead and William Simon, *High Velocity Leadership: The Mars Pathfinder Approach to Faster, Better, Cheaper* (New York: HarperBusiness, 1999): 86–89, 178–79.

2. Ibid., 179.

3. R. D. Archibald, *Managing High-Technology Programs and Projects* (New York: John Wiley & Sons, 1976): 231.

4. Archibald, ibid., 12, refers to this report as the "project register."

5. Much of the discussion in this subsection is based on D. D. Roman, *Managing Projects: A Systems Approach* (New York: Elsevier, 1986): 392–94.

6. See Archibald, *Managing High-Technology Programs and Projects*, 235–36 and 264–70, for a complete checklist of close out activities.

7. V. G. Hajek, *Managing Engineering Projects*, 3d ed. (New York: McGraw-Hill, 1984). See pp. 233–40 for a good description of monitoring and support side items for both engineering hardware and computer software projects.

8. Ibid., 241–42.

9. A complete procedure for conducting post-project reviews is discussed in Neal Whitten, *Managing Software Development Projects*, 2d ed. (New York: John Wiley & Sons, 1995), 343–57.

10. Michael Cusumano and Richard Selby, *Microsoft Secrets* (New York: Free Press, 1995): 331–34.

Organization Behavior

*P*roject outcomes depend on the way individuals and groups are organized and interact. As human endeavors, projects are both influenced by and have influence on the behavior and well-being of the
groups and individuals that belong to them.

The first three chapters in this section focus on the major organizational and behavioral issues surrounding the management of projects
and the teams and individuals that comprise them. They describe the
ways that groups are organized into projects, styles of leadership used
by project managers, roles and responsibilities of project team members, and ways groups and individuals are managed to increase effectiveness and reduce the negative consequences of working in projects.

Chapter 17 discusses failure and success in the practice of project
management. It summarizes lessons learned and ties together the major topics and tenets of the book.

Chapter 14

Project Organization Structure and Integration

> *How can you expect to govern a country that has 246 kinds of cheese?*
>
> —CHARLES DE GAULLE

*O*rganizations are systems of human and physical elements interacting to achieve goals. As with all types of systems, organizations are partly described by their *structure*—the form of relationships that bond their elements.

In all organizations two kinds of structures coexist. One is the *formal* structure, the *published* one that describes normative superior-subordinate relationships, chains of command, and subdivisions and grouping of elements. The other is the *informal structure*, the unpublished one that describes relationships that *evolve* through the interactions of people. Whereas the formal organization prescribes how people are supposed to relate, the informal organization is how they want to relate. It is the groupings, authority figures, and communication lines that exist in the organization but appear nowhere on the organization chart.

This chapter deals primarily with formal organization structure, particularly the kinds of structures applicable to projects. There is no one best way to structure project organizations, but there are structural patterns and specific roles that enhance project performance. Though project managers are seldom involved in organization design decisions, they should understand the kinds of organizational designs used in project management and their relative advantages and disadvantages. Sometimes project managers can affect the project structure, even if only through suggestions to top management.

The chapter also deals with project integration, which is the way that individual functional groups, subunits, project phases, and work tasks are interlinked and coordinated to achieve project goals. The discussion covers various kinds of integration roles used in projects, and the special case of integration in large-scale projects and development projects.

14.1 FORMAL ORGANIZATION STRUCTURE

Concepts of organizational structure apply to all kinds of organizations—companies, institutions, agencies—as well as to their subunits—divisions, departments, projects, teams, and so on. Formal organization structure is publicized in a chart such as the one for NASA in Figure 14-1; a quick glance reveals both the organizational hierarchy and groupings for specialized tasks. By looking at the chart in Figure 14-1, for example, one can see

1. The range of activities in which the organization is involved and the major subdivisions of the organization (space flight, space sciences, aeronautics and space transportation technology, space flight, etc.).
2. The management hierarchy and reporting relationships (e.g., the directors at Ames, Lewis, and Langley all report to the associate administrator for aeronautics and space technology).
3. The type of work and responsibility of each subdivision (e.g., projects at research centers focus on specific disciplines or technical goals such as space science, aeronautics and space transportation technology, space flight, and so on.)
4. The official lines of authority and communication (the administrator is the highest authority, the deputy administrator is the next highest, and so on; communication moves formally along the lines from one box to the next, up or down).

There are many things the chart does not show. For example, it does not show informal lines of communication and personal contacts whereby, for example: workers at Jet Propulsion Lab talk directly to workers at Ames Research Center on the telephone, not (as the chart implies) via the directors of these centers, nor does it indicate areas of status and power that develop at lower levels. Nonetheless, the chart does give a fundamental overview of elements and relationships of the formal organization, and in this way it is useful.

14.2 ORGANIZATION DESIGN BY DIFFERENTIATION AND INTEGRATION

There is no "best" kind of organization structure. The most appropriate structure depends on the organization's goals, type of work, and environment. Organization structures typically develop through a combination of planned and evolutionary responses to ongoing problems. Organizations create specialized roles and units, each with suitable expertise and resources needed to deal with certain classes of situations and problems efficiently. As organizations grow or the environment changes, additional subdivisions and new groupings are implemented to better handle new situations and

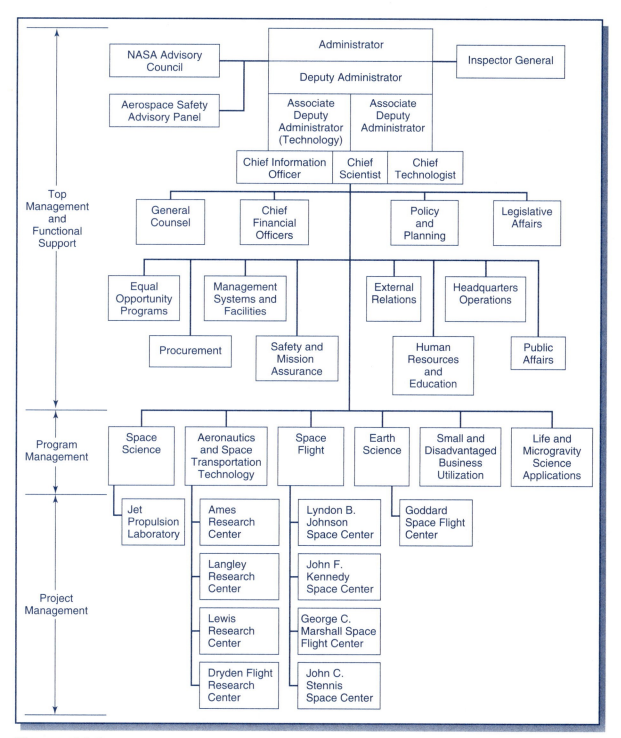

Figure 14-1
NASA organization and program chart, 1999.

emerging problems. For example, as a company increases its product line, it may subdivide its manufacturing area into product-oriented divisions to better address problems specific to just one product line. As a company expands its sales territory, it may subdivide its marketing force geographically to better handle problems of regional origin. This subdivision into specialized areas is called *differentiation*.

Obviously, subunits of an organization do not act as independent entities but must interact and support each other. The degree to which they interact, coordinate, and mutually adjust their actions to fulfill organizational goals is called *integration*.

Traditional Forms of Organization

How an organization is subdivided is referred to as the *basis* for differentiation. The six bases for differentiation are functional, geographic, product, customer, process, and project. The project form will be discussed in detail. First, however, we will look at the other five "traditional" forms of differentiation and the way subunits in each are integrated.

Functional Differentiation. The functional form of organization is so called because it is divided into functional subunits such as marketing, finance, production, personnel, and research and development; the structure of the Iron Butterfly Company in Figure 14-2 is an example. Most of the integration between subunits is handled by rules, procedures, coordinated plans, and budgets. When discrepancies occur that cannot be resolved by these integrative measures, the managerial chain of command takes over. When a problem involves several subunits, it is collectively resolved by managers of all subunits affected.

This form of organization works well in repetitive, stable environments because there is little change, and the rather low level of integration afforded by rules, procedures, and chain of command gets the job done. The functional form has a long history. The Roman army was an early organization that used functional differentiation, rules and procedures, and chain of command. The functional form remains today as the most prevalent basis for organization structure.

Geographic Differentiation. Most organizations have more than one basis for differentiation. The Roman army was also geographically differentiated; that is, structured according to region or location. Organizations subdivide according to region (e.g., Atlantic, Mid-Western, and Pacific states; European branch; Far East command;

Figure 14-2
Formal organization structure for Iron Butterfly Company showing functional breakdown.

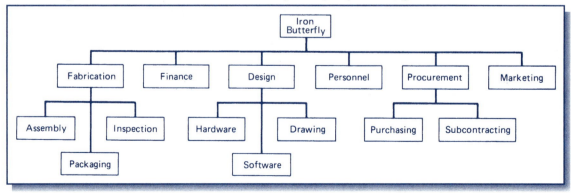

etc.) to tailor themselves to the unique requirements of local customers, markets, suppliers, enemies, and so on. Within each geographic subunit, functional differentiation is often retained. Regional subunits may operate relatively autonomously with little integration between them. Integration is usually achieved through standardized accounting and reporting procedures, simplifying upper management's need to monitor the subunits.

Product Differentiation. Firms that produce a variety of products use product-based differentiation. Corporations such as General Motors, General Foods, and General Electric are split into major subdivisions wherein each designs, manufactures, and markets its own product line. Within each subdivision is a functional, geographic, or other form of breakdown. As with geographically differentiated organizations, integration between product subdivisions tends to be limited to standardized financial and reporting rules and procedures.

Customer Differentiation. Organizations may also differentiate by customer type. For example, companies with large military sales often establish a separate division because federal requirements for proposals, contracting, and product specifications differ substantially from those for commercial customers. The level of integration between customer divisions depends on the degree of interdependency between their product lines; typically, however, integration is low.

Process Differentiation. In the process differentiated form, some logical process or sequence of steps (e.g., design, then development, then assembly, then inspection, etc.) is the basis for differentiation. Such a basis is used for the subunits in the fabrication department of Iron Butterfly, shown in Figure 14-2. A higher level of integration is required among process differentiated subunits because they are sequentially related and problems in one area directly impact the other areas. These subunits tend to rely on coordinated plans and schedules as the primary means of integration. Other means such as task forces and teams are necessary when unanticipated problems arise or as task uncertainty increases. These will be discussed later.

Drawbacks of Traditional Forms of Organization

By their very design, traditional forms of organization can address only certain anticipated, classifiable kinds of problems. As the environment changes and new kinds of problems arise, they react by further differentiating subunits and adding more rules, procedures, and levels of management. The price they pay for adding layers of management, rules, procedures, and subunits is less flexibility and greater difficulty in integrating subunits.

Most traditional organization forms work on the assumption that problems or tasks can be neatly classified and resolved within specialized areas. Thus, subunits in traditional forms tend to work independently and toward their own goals. When a problem arises that requires participation from multiple subdivisions, there may be no person or group to see that it gets resolved. Such problems fall through the cracks.

One way to handle unanticipated, unclassifiable problems is to adapt (redesign) the organization whenever they arise. However, the process of adapting organization structure to suit unique problems is slow and expensive, reflecting both the inertia of systems as well as peoples' resistance to change. The alternative to redesign is to bump problems up the chain of command. This works as long as it is not done too often because when the number of unanticipated problems becomes large, the chain of command gets quickly overloaded. Management's response to overload is to add more managers and more staff groups, which adds to the size of the management structure and eventually makes the organization even less flexible. In short, traditional organizations are not well-suited for environments where there is high uncertainty and frequent change.

14.3 REQUIREMENTS OF PROJECT ORGANIZATIONS

Project environments are characterized by complexity, change, uncertainty, and unpredictability. Projects typically require the resources and coordinated work effort of multiple people, subunits, and organizations. Each project is a new undertaking to satisfy a new goal. Subunits must work together to estimate their resource requirements, combine the requirements into a coordinated plan, and conduct work according to that plan. Changes or mistakes in one area have consequences on all others. Because each project is unique and may have no precedent, uncertainty is inherent. As the size of the project increases so do the number of subunits involved and the potential for errors or mistakes.

Projects in advanced technologies such as software development, pharmaceuticals, biomedicine, space exploration, and product and weapon systems development routinely encounter the unexpected. As a result, they need to be adjustable to changing goals and environmental forces, and deal with the uncertainty that accompanies these changes. They must be, in a word, *organic,* which means highly differentiated to accommodate a large variety of potential problems, highly integrated to respond rapidly to situations and problems that require involvement of multiple subunits, and highly flexible to alter structure as goals change.

To achieve this, all project organizations have two properties:

- They integrate subunits using horizontal relations.
- They have organization structures differentiated to suit the unique requirements of the project and the environment.

These properties are discussed next.

14.4 INTEGRATION OF SUBUNITS IN PROJECTS[1]

Traditional organizations are characterized by their verticalness, or reliance upon up-and-down patterns of authority and communication. As mentioned, this makes them clumsy, slow, and ineffective in dealing with situations with rapid change and high uncertainty. In contrast, project organizations are characterized by their *horizontalness* or use of direct communication between the parties involved in a problem. Horizontal relations cut across lines of authority and move decisions to the level of the parties affected.

All organizations have horizontal relations, most in the form of personal contacts, informal relationships, and friendships. These contacts are particularly helpful for expediting communication and getting problems resolved between subunits. For example, whenever the assembly department in Figure 14-2 experiences a minor parts shortage, George, the assembly foreman, phones Helen in purchasing for a "rush order" favor. The call bypasses the formal structure (George and Helen's respective managers) and speeds up the ordering procedure.

The drawback with informal processes such as this is that they do not ensure everyone who needs to know is involved, or that everyone who participates gets the necessary information. For example, Helen must charge all purchases to an account, but if George is not privy to the dollar amount in the account it is possible that his informal requests will deplete the account before additional funds can be credited (which involves a third party). Also, if George does not tell anyone else about the parts shortages, the reason for the problem—pilferage, defective parts, or underordering—never gets resolved. George's requests might be too late. In short, informal processes do not always occur when needed and are not fully adequate.

Project organizations improve upon informal, personal contacts by incorporating horizontal relations into the formal structure. They do this through the use of functions referred to as *integrators*. Integrators reduce the number of decisions referred up the chain of command and facilitate communication between units working together on a common task. Like informal processes, integrators bypass traditional lines of authority and speed up communication. They are better, however, because they ensure that everyone affected by a problem is involved and has the necessary information.

Several kinds of integrators are used in projects. They are listed in order of increasing authority, need, and cost. In the following list, the latter kinds take on all the authority and responsibility of the former kinds.[2]

Liaison role
Task forces and teams
Project expeditors and coordinators
Project managers
Matrix managers
Integrating contractors

14.5 LIAISON ROLES, TASK FORCES, AND TEAMS

The *liaison role* is designated to a specialized person or group that links two departments at lower levels. Figure 14-3, for example, shows the purpose of the liaison role of "inventory controller." In addition to performing other duties in the assembly department, this person links the assembly and purchasing departments by notifying purchasing of impending shortages and keeping track of orders placed. The role relieves the assembly foreman of this responsibility and, by legitimizing the process, ensures that orders get placed and are documented.

However, the liaison role is not always effective. Though the inventory controller in the example expedites parts ordering, the reason for part shortages goes unresolved. To unravel the problem it is necessary to involve people from other areas of the company. This is where the next kind of integrative function, an *interdisciplinary task force or team*, comes into play.

A *task force* is a temporary group of representatives from several areas that meets to solve a problem. For example, when a shortage problem occurs, the assembly foreman might call together liaison people from inspection, accounting, purchasing, marketing, or other areas that should be involved. The task force meets once, several times, or as needed, and after the problem is worked out it disbands. The most effective task forces are short-lived and typically have 10 members or less.[3]

To be effective, members of the task force must have information relevant to the group task and the authority to make commitments for their functional areas. If they lack information, the group's decisions will be faulty; if they lack authority, they will be unable to take action on decisions. Departments which do not have people with the knowledge and authority to serve on task forces may have to restructure themselves to develop such positions.

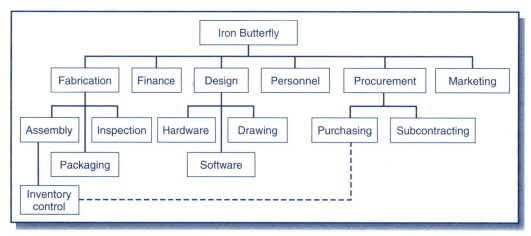

Figure 14-3
Liaison role linking assembly and purchasing departments.

Problems which are novel and need continuous coordinated interaction of sub-units require the attention of *permanent teams*. Teams have the same characteristics as task forces except they convene on a regular basis and for longer periods of time. For example, if the Iron Butterfly Company produces several products, and each requires repeated design changes throughout the year then representatives from design, fabrication, procurement, and other areas would have to meet as a team on a frequent basis. Only through repeated face-to-face association would the team be able to coordinate decisions about changes in market conditions and product design. Members may be assigned to teams part-time or full-time.

In projects there are many kinds of teams; some convene during just one stage of the project life cycle, others for the full duration of the project. One kind of permanent team in development projects is the *change board* discussed in Chapter 11, the multi-functional team that meets every week to discuss and approve changes in design. Another kind is the design-build team described later in this chapter.

Organizations are created around people, not the reverse. Therefore, it is sometimes difficult to find people with the knowledge, authority, and inclination to serve on multi-functional teams. People develop attitudes and goals oriented toward their specialization, and though this helps them to be effective in their own functional area, it restricts their ability to interact with people from other areas. For interdisciplinary teams to be effective, it is essential that members are aware of other peoples' functional orientations and receptive to their opinions and attitudes. Team-building methods described in Chapter 16 help break down barriers and forge bonds between members of cross-functional teams.

14.6   PROJECT EXPEDITORS AND COORDINATORS

Teams form the core of project organizations. The simplest projects consist of one team within a single functional area. A task force created to solve a special problem or answer a particular question is one type of project organization. The most complex projects are performed by a consortia of multifunctional teams from numerous contractors, sub-contractors, and users. Tens or hundreds of teams are created and dissolved throughout the systems development cycle. Despite the many ways to structure project teams and multiteam project organizations, the one feature common to them all is emphasis on integration. In project management, *the leader's primary role is integration*.

The simplest kind of project organization is a single, small group of people, a task force or team formed on a full- or part-time basis to perform an assignment. This kind of organization is used in projects that are important enough to warrant "disrupting" the existing organization. Project groups such as this can exist inside one functional area or span over several functional areas.

Projects within One Functional Area

It makes sense that a project that affects or is the responsibility of only one functional area should be located in that area. For example, a project to survey customer attitudes about a new product would ordinarily be placed within the marketing department because the necessary resources and expertise are located there. The team does all the tasks itself—it prepares the survey questionnaire, obtains mailing lists, distributes the survey, and processes the results. With few exceptions, these can be done by members inside the marketing department. Project teams such as this are managed by a *project expeditor*,[4] a staff assistant selected by the manager of the area wherein the project lies. The expeditor coordinates decision making, monitors schedules, makes suggestions, and keeps the executive apprised. The expeditor typically has no formal authority over team members and so must rely on persuasion, personal knowledge, and information about the project to influence team members. A single team, project expeditor organization is shown in Figure 14-4.

Multifunctional Project Teams

An example of a project that might use a *multifunctional team* is one for the development of an enterprise resource planning (ERP) system. ERP is a company or corporate wide system that ties together information about forecasting, order entry, purchasing, and inventory with functions such as accounting, finance, and human resources. This team would include representatives from all the departments that would provide inputs to the system or would utilize its outputs, such as accounting, inventory control, purchasing, manufacturing, engineering, and information technology. Sometimes representatives from suppliers and customers are also on this team. The team is responsible for establishing the system requirements and overseeing the development and installation of the system. Multifunctional teams such as this

Figure 14-4
Project within a single functional department.

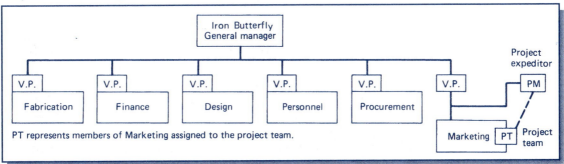

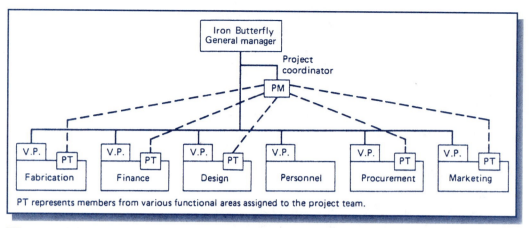

Figure 14-5
Multifunctional project team.

are typically used on projects that are large but that do not require the resources to merit a complete reorganization.

One of the best places to use multifunctional teams is in product development. By using closely knit teams of engineers, designers, manufacturers, assemblers, marketers, lawyers, suppliers, dealers, and customers, phases of the systems development cycle usually done sequentially can be done simultaneously. This approach, called concurrent engineering, eliminates cross-functional barriers and can result in higher quality and lower cost. A good example is the Ford team that created Sable and Taurus. The team not only came up with car models that won quality and design-excellence awards, but they did it for half a billion dollars under the proposed development budget.[5] Concurrent engineering is discussed later.

The multifunctional project team may be located either in the functional area most responsible for the project or at a higher-level position, such as reporting to the general manager as shown in Figure 14-5. The latter arrangement imputes greater importance to the project and improves coordination between the areas involved. The person managing such a project is designated the project *coordinator*. Though this person has no line authority over team members, he does have authority to make and execute decisions about project budgets, schedules, and work performance. Besides the high-level position of reporting to the general manager, the coordinator's influence, like that of the expeditor, originates in his project knowledge and being placed at the center of everyone involved.

14.7   PURE PROJECT ORGANIZATIONS

Projects that entail high-level complexity, major resource commitments, and heavy stakes in the outcome require a *pure project* form of organization. A pure project is a separate organization, similar to another company, especially created for and singularly devoted to achievement of the project goal. Whatever the project must have to afford it the highest priority—all necessary human and physical resources—is incorporated into the pure project organization. These organizations are able to react quickly to changing demands of the environment, the user, and the parent organization. They rely heavily on the use of liaisons, task forces, and teams.

Heading the pure object organization is the *project manager*. Unlike the coordinator, the project manager has full authority over all people and physical resources assigned to the project and, thus, maximum control. For those areas which cannot be placed under her control, the project manager has authority to contract out for resources, both from internal functional areas as well as from external subcontractors and suppliers. The pure project manager is involved in the project from start to finish: During proposal preparation, she prepares forecasts, requests plans from functional areas, and reconciles discrepancies among plans; after acceptance, she allocates budgeted money to buy resources and hire personnel; during the project, she allocates resources and approves all changes to requirements and the project plan. When personnel must be "borrowed" from functional areas, she is the one who negotiates to get the best people.

When resources are not internally available, the project manager heads selection of and negotiations with subcontractors. She oversees their work and coordinates it with other work being done. The project managers in the company relocation, and at LogiCircuit, R.L. Zept, and NASA in Chapter 2 are examples of pure project managers.

Pure Project Variations

Three common variations of the pure project structure are the *project center,* the *stand-alone project,* and the *partial project.*

In the *project center,* the structure of the parent organization remains the same except for the addition of a separate "project arm" and project manager. This form is shown in Figure 14-6 for the Logistical On-line (LOGON) project. Resources and personnel are borrowed from functional and staff areas for as long as needed. General Motors used a project center when it chose 1,200 key people from various divisions for the task of determining how to downsize all of its automotive lines. The project center developed suggestions, turned them over to the automotive divisions for implementation, and then disbanded. In another corporation, a project center was used to oversee the relocation of its offices. By creating a relocation-project center to work full-time on the tricky problems of relocation, the rest of the organization was able to continue its work as usual.

The *stand-alone project* is an organization created especially for the purpose of accomplishing the project. It does not represent only one organization but consists of members from several participating organizations. It is typically used for large-scale

Figure 14-6
Pure project as an "arm" to the functional organization.

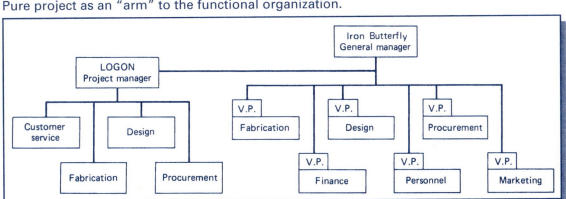

government or public works projects that involve one or more prime contractor, dozens of subcontractors, and hundreds of smaller supporting organizations, suppliers, and consultants. The international space station development program, Quebec's LaGrande hydroelectric complex, the English Channel Tunnel (Chunnel), and China's Three Gorges projects are examples. When these projects are completed, an operating function remains but the rest of the organization is dissolved. Stand-alone projects are discussed later in this chapter in the sections on integration in large-scale projects and concurrent engineering.

In a *partial project,* the functions critical to the project (such as construction or engineering) are assigned to the project manager yet other, support-oriented functions (such as procurement and accounting) remain with the functional areas. In Figure 14-6, for example, the project manager might only control design and fabrication, yet the areas of finance, marketing, and personnel give functional support. The manager of a partial project has direct control over all major project tasks, but he also receives assistance from support areas in the parent company over which he does not have control.

Disadvantages

The chief disadvantage of the pure project organization is its *cost* to the parent organization and project personnel. Because each pure project is a completely or partially independent organization, it must be fully or substantially staffed. Each project becomes a self-contained empire; between projects there is often little sharing or cross-utilization of resources. Companies with multiple pure projects may incur considerable duplication of effort and facilities.

To reduce the risk that resources will not be available when they are needed, project organizations must begin acquiring them in advance. The author was one of dozens of engineers hired in anticipation of a large government contract to ensure that the project could begin as soon as the contract was signed. However, the contract was never awarded and so eventually everyone assigned to the project was transferred elsewhere or laid off. The payroll loss alone amounted to hundreds of man-months.

This suggests still another expense: outplacement of personnel. Whenever there is no follow-up work to a project, the organization faces the problem of what to do with its workforce. Personnel on long-term projects become so highly specialized that it is difficult to place them in other projects requiring more generalized or up-to-date skills. Companies add to the cost when they delay breaking up the organization in hopes of acquiring new work. When there is no follow-up work, the only option is to release workers and sell facilities.

Pure project organizations are strictly temporary, and as the work draws to a close the uncertainty about the fate of the team leads, understandably, to a decline in morale and enthusiasm. Project managers may become so preoccupied with generating new contracts, extending old contracts, or finding jobs for themselves and the team that they neglect the project they are currently trying to complete.

14.8 MATRIX ORGANIZATION

Although the pure project form often provides the only way to do a large-scale, one-time project, its disadvantages make it impractical for businesses that *continually* operate on a project basis. Examples of such businesses include architecture and construction, where every building, bridge, dam, or highway is a new project; product development, where every product concept, design, manufacture, and promotion is a new project; information technology, where every hardware and software installation is a new project; law and accounting, where every case and audit is a new project; and aerospace, where every new aircraft and space system is a project. Though some of these projects are small enough to be handled by task forces or teams, most cannot because they are too large, too complex, and have too much at stake. In addition, most of these businesses are *multi-project* organizations, meaning they are involved in more than one project at a time. They need the capability to quickly create large project groups without the personnel and cost disadvantages associated with pure project organizations.

To achieve this capability a new form of organization was evolved. First adopted in the aerospace industry by such firms as Boeing and Lockheed-Martin, it is called the *matrix*. The matrix, shown in Figure 14-7, is a grid-like structure of authority and reporting relationships created by the overlay of a project organization on a traditional, functional organization.[6] This overlay gives the matrix three unique capabilities.

First, the functional part provides the repository for the technical expertise and physical resources needed by the project. The project manager creates a project group by negotiating with functional managers and then "borrowing" the expertise and physical resources needed for the project. Each project is composed of workers who are on loan to work together as a team during the course of the project. Because the same workforce is time-shared among several projects, duplication of effort is reduced.

Second, while in their "functional homes" workers associate with colleagues in their fields of specialization; this not only keeps them current in their profession or trade, but makes them more assignable to new projects. Each functional area has, at a given time, many individuals who are working on different projects. Sharing ideas and exchanging points of view makes them more effective in their respective projects.

Figure 14-7
Matrix form of project organization.

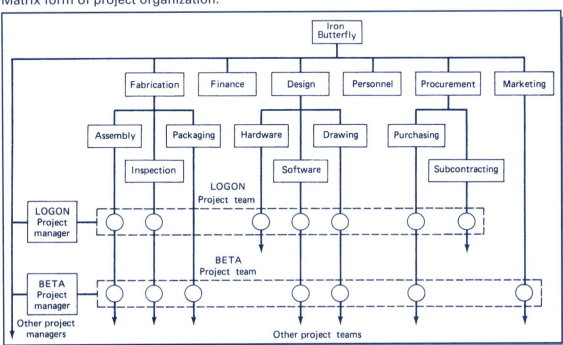

Third, when individual assignments are fulfilled or a project completed, workers return to their functional homes for a new assignment. Large fluctuations in the workforce and in worker morale and anxiety are thus reduced.

The primary effort of the project manager in the matrix (sometimes called the *matrix manager*) is integration. Typically, the project manager is considered to be on the same hierarchical level as functional managers. Functional managers provide the necessary technical counsel, advice, and support; the project manager integrates and unifies efforts of various functional areas to meet project goals. The project manager works *with* functional managers to accomplish the project.

The matrix makes it easy to create unique organizations to accomplish particular goals. It shares the virtue with the pure project organization of having dedicated resources and a project manager to give the project priority.

In multiproject organizations the matrix makes it easier to balance schedule and resource requirements among several projects at once. The prioritizing and balancing of resources between projects is the responsibility of the *manager of projects,* shown as the "vice president of projects" in Figure 14-8. The manager of projects attends to the short- and medium-term requirements of current and upcoming projects and relieves top management of most project operations responsibility.

Problems with Matrix Organizations

The strong point of the matrix organization—its combined vertical-horizontal structure—is at the same time the root cause of its problems.[7] The matrix is not just a structure but a whole different way of doing things. To be successful it must be reinforced by information systems and managerial behavior that support two-dimensional information flow and dual reporting relationships.

Figure 14-8
Location of the vice president of projects in a matrix organization.

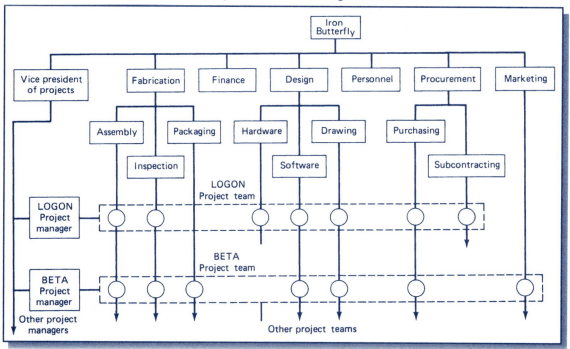

Many organizations have tried the matrix and found it impossible to implement. Most organizations are accustomed to hierarchical decision making and vertical information flow. With its emphasis on horizontal relations, lateral information flow, and decentralized decision making, the matrix is clearly contrary. It superimposes a lateral system on a functional system, so that companies adopting the matrix must add horizontal information processing systems to existing vertical accounting and command systems. This can be done, but it tends to be somewhat complicated and expensive.

In human terms, the major drawback of the matrix is that it induces conflict. Theoretically, the two-dimensional structure promotes coordinated decision making among functional areas and enables tradeoff decisions to be made for the benefit of the project. It assumes that both functional-technical and project-related issues have equal priority, and that a balance of power exists between functional and project managers. Often, however, authority in the matrix is unclear and functional and project managers jockey to control one another. Functional managers control project resources, but project managers seldom have control over functional managers. In multiproject organizations additional conflict arises over which project gets priority and which project manager gets the best resources.

Because each worker in the matrix has two bosses, one functional manager and one project-matrix manager, the matrix violates a major principle of management: single, scalar chain of command. The project manager directs the worker on a project, but the functional manager evaluates the worker's performance. The inevitable result is role conflict and confusion over allegiance to the project manager *or* to the functional manager.

The matrix strives to give equal priority to functions and projects, but sometimes both get short-shrifted. For workers to avoid chaos and confusion in the matrix, everyone must have a common reference. For this to happen, organizations must establish clear, stable values and priorities. At Boeing, for example, which has used the matrix successfully for many years, priorities are established day-to-day: People operate *either* in a project team *or* in a functional area. Whichever they are in, that is the one on which they put priority.[8]

Any attempt to adopt the matrix must be accompanied by both attitudinal and cultural change. Group and interpersonal skills to help facilitate these changes are discussed in the next two chapters.

14.9 SELECTING A PROJECT FORM

Although project managers seldom have the responsibility for designing the organizations they lead, they can offer suggestions to the managers who do. It is impossible to state which form is always best, but general criteria can help decide the most appropriate form for a given project. Figure 14-9 shows the approximate applicability of different project organization forms based upon four criteria:

- Frequency of new projects (how often, or to what degree the parent company is involved in project-related activity).
- Duration of projects (how long a typical project lasts).
- Size of projects (level of human, capital, or other resources in relation to other activities of the company).
- Complexity of relationships (number of functional areas involved in the project and degree of interdependency).

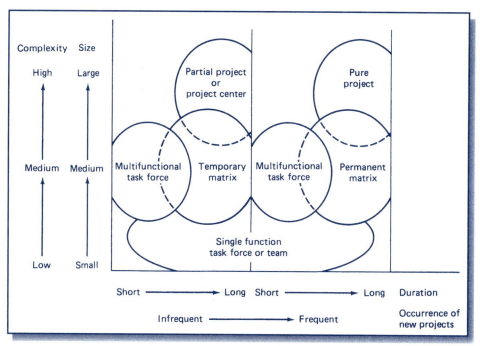

Figure 14-9
Some criteria for selecting the project organizational form.

Matrix and pure project forms are more applicable to projects of medium and higher complexity and of medium or larger size. These kinds of projects have greater resource and information requirements and need project managers and integrators with strong central authority. In particular, the matrix works best where there are a variety of different projects going on at once and where all can share functional resources on a part-time basis. In contrast, when there is less variety between projects, when specialists must be devoted full-time, and when complete project authority is desired, then the pure project form is better. Both forms are applicable when projects are an organization's "way of life," although they can also be applied temporarily to infrequent, one-shot projects when the stakes are high. As mentioned, the complexity of the matrix and the enormous human and facility requirements of the pure project can present major problems for the parent company, therefore both should be avoided when simpler forms would work as well.

For smaller projects involving several functional areas, task forces and teams that link functional areas are more appropriate. Short-term projects in one or a few functional areas can be effectively handled by part-time task forces managed by expeditors in one functional area. When several areas are involved, a multifunctional task force with a coordinator who reports to the general manager is more suitable. Projects of longer duration, but small in scope and low in complexity, are best handled by full-time project teams with coordinators. When the team size needed to accomplish the task becomes large and interrelationships become too complex, then a temporary matrix or partial project should be set up. Teams, task forces, and project centers are appropriate when the existing structure and work flow of the organization cannot be disrupted.

In selecting a project form, consider the relative importance of the following criteria: the stake of the project, the degree of technological uncertainty, the criticalness of time and cost goals, and the uniqueness of the project.[9] For example, task forces and teams are generally appropriate when the project task involves high certainty and little risk, and when time and cost are not major factors. When the risk and uncertainty is great, when time and cost goals are critical, or when there is much at stake, matrix and pure project forms better afford the obligatory high level of integration and control. When a project differs greatly from the normal business of the firm, it should be made a partial or full pure project.

These considerations all relate to the project, which, in fact, is less important at times than attributes and experiences of the parent company. For example, matrix and pure project forms are seldom used in small organizations, which usually don't have sufficient resources and managers to commit. Top management's attitudes about how much responsibility and authority is appropriate for the project manager also determines the appropriate form of organization by dictating the allowable degree of centralized project control. The most important factor is the company's experience with projects and management's perception of which project forms work best. Firms with little project experience should avoid the matrix because it is so difficult to adopt. Faced with a complex project, they might do better by adopting a partial or project center approach.

Project organization structures are not cast in concrete, though sometimes they are treated as if they are. When a project organization becomes ineffectual, it should be changed. Although restructuring causes consternation and confusion in the short run, whatever changes are necessary should be made to adapt the structure to the project requirements and resources. At Microsoft Corporation, for example, the organization of development projects is structured to mirror the products they produce.

Example 1: Product Development Organization at Microsoft[10]

A large software product-development project at Microsoft might involve 300 to 400 people, including specialists in product specification, development, testing, user education, and planning. Program managers and developers divide the project into "features," where each feature is a relatively independent building block that will be apparent to customers (e.g., printing, adding a column of numbers, or interfacing with a particular brand of hardware). They then divide the project organization into many development teams where each concentrates on one or more of these features. In essence, the project is divided into small, feature driven projects that mirror the structure of the overall product. This feature driven organization enables product functionality to be increased simply by adding more developers and more teams: The more features desired in the product, the more teams or more people on each team assigned to the project.

Each feature team consists of the program manager (who may work on more than one feature) and three to eight developers, of which one is the "lead." The lead reports to the project's development manager, who has a broad view of the product and interconnections between the features. A recent version of Excel had 10 feature teams, 8 working on the basic Excel product, 1 on a graph product, and 1 on a query tool product. Paired with the feature development teams are parallel teams responsible for feature testing. User education specialists are also assigned to work with the product group.

The philosophy for organizing projects at Microsoft is that a product tends to mirror the organization that created it. A big, slow organization will create a big, slow software product. A small, nimble group in which everyone gets along well will produce pieces of code that work together well, which is why Microsoft uses small, flexible, synchronized teams.

Although each feature team has considerable autonomy, it must follow rules to ensure its work stays coordinated with all the other teams. Each team is expected to "build" and have checked a certain amount of code each day. This forces the teams to synchronize their work at the pace of the overall project.

The term *project office* has dual meaning: it refers first to a support staff group which reports to the project manager, and second to a physical place where the project team meets. Our discussion will focus on the *project staff,* although it is stressed that all projects, even the smallest ones, should have a physical project office to serve as an information center and place where the team can meet and keep its reports.

The major purpose of a project office staff is to coordinate the project efforts of functional areas and subcontractors. The staff is responsible for planning, directing, and controlling all project activities and for linking project teams, users, and top management. When projects are small and coordinating procedures are well-established, the responsibility of the project staff falls to one person, the project manager.

Composition of the Project Office

The function and composition of the project office depends upon the authority of the project manager, and the size, importance, and goal of the project. The project office shown in Figure 14-10 is for a large-scale engineering development effort. Among the functions shown, one of the most important is planning and control. During project concept and definition, this function prepares and implements work breakdown structures (WBS), project schedules, budgets, and PERT/CPM networks. In later phases, it monitors work, forecasts trends, updates schedules and budgets, and distributes reports to functional, upper-level, and user management.

Figure 14-10
Project office for a large development project.

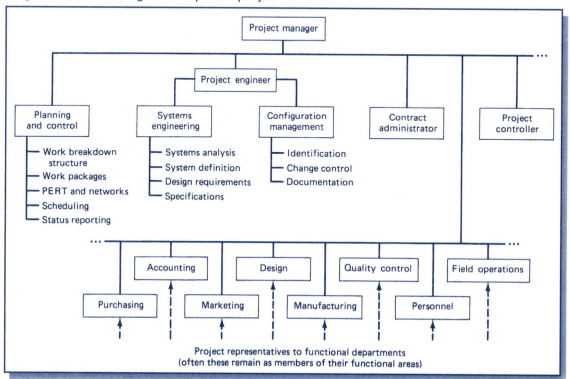

Also shown are functions for systems engineering and configuration management, both headed by the project engineer. These activities are closely tied together and to the tasks of planning and control. The systems engineering function oversees systems analysis, requirements definition, and end-item specifications (discussed in Appendix A), and furnishes inputs to both planning and control configuration management. Configuration management (discussed in Chapter 11) defines the initial product configuration and controls changes in product requirements resulting in (or from changes to) project plans and systems engineering requirements.

As shown in Figure 14-10, the project office also has functions for contracting, financial control, and for representation of all functional areas.

The project integration effort is best served when the project office is structured to mirror the functional areas it integrates.[11] This is achieved (see Figure 14-10) by having a representative from each functional area who will coordinate activities in that area with the overall project. Each representative is a specialist in a functional discipline, but while in the project office his prime charge is integrating his discipline with others in the project.

Thus, the way the project manager integrates the functional areas is by *coordinating the representatives* in the project office. She facilitates integration by, for example, having the project staff work in the same physical office, making the office open and accessible to all functional areas, and encouraging frequent meetings and using consensual decision making among representatives. Techniques for facilitating interaction are further discussed in Chapters 9 and 10.

In staffing the project office, the project manager must avoid duplicating the efforts of the functional areas. The purpose of the project office is to *coordinate* work and advise the functional areas on *what* they should do, not *how* to do it. To keep the full-time size of the project office to a minimum, on small projects all functional representatives and most specialists remain physically within their functional areas.

Office of Projects and the Program Office

Multiproject organizations also have an *office of projects* (not to be confused with the project office). This was shown in Figure 14-8 as the office of the vice president of projects. When projects are small, the office of projects substitutes for individual project offices and handles proposals, contracting, scheduling, cost control, and report preparation for every project. When projects are large or overlap, the office of projects is used *in addition* to project offices and serves to coordinate the combined requirements of all the projects.[12]

When projects are part of a program, *a program office* will ensure that the projects supplement one another and "add up" to overall program goals. The program office handles interfaces external to a project, maintains user enthusiasm and support, keeps project managers informed of potential problems, and handles interfaces and integration between projects. The NASA program office described in Chapter 2 is an example. When programs are very large, the integration work of the program office is supplemented by outside "integration contractors" to be discussed later.

14.11   THE INFORMAL ORGANIZATION

The effectiveness of the formal project organization sometimes depends on the strength and support of the emergent *informal organization*. We will consider just one facet of the informal organization, informal communication.

Informal communication—the most familiar vehicle being the *grapevine*—certainly has its drawbacks. Neither thorough nor dependable, it tends to garble messages from one person to the next (even jokes lose their punchlines after going through just a few people), and does not guarantee that people who need information will ever get it. Nonetheless, informal communication is largely beneficial and essential. It fulfills social and work needs, and conveys information more quickly and directly than most formal systems. Some management theorists posit that vast networks of informal communication are essential for organizations to perform well.

Managers cannot control informal communication, but they can influence it. Peters and Waterman describe several means of doing this.[13] One way is to remove status barriers and inspire casual conversation, particularly between managers and workers, by *insisting* on informality. For example, at Walt Disney, everyone—from the president on down—wears a name tag; at Hewlett Packard, people are urged to use first names; and at Delta Airline and Levi Strauss, the management philosophy is "open door." MBWA (management by walking around), or getting managers out of the office and talking to people (instead of relying solely on paper and e-mail reports), is another way to stimulate informal information exchange. The physical layout of the office is also instrumental. Intermingling the desks of workers from interrelated functional areas, removing walls and partitions, "family groupings" of chairs and desks, and spot placement of lounges are ways of increasing face-to-face contact.

Project management attempts to do what the informal organization sometimes does: allow the people involved in a problem or decision to directly communicate and make decisions. One way or another, people affected by a decision or problem talk about it, form ideas, and make decisions, though often the formal organization overlooks or stifles these ideas. After management has adopted the appropriate formal structure it should then encourage supportive informal processes.

14.12   INTEGRATION IN LARGE-SCALE PROJECTS

Any person or group that works toward the project goal is part of the project organization. In large-scale projects (LSP), numerous parties—sponsors, prime contractors, subcontractors, consultants, and suppliers—contribute to one effort. Figure 14-11 shows the principal contributors and relationships in an LSP. Relationships are complex and lines of authority connecting the parties are often weak (sometimes based only on contracts and purchase orders). If Figure 14-11 appears somewhat confusing, it simply reflects the fact that relationships in LSPs *are* sometimes confusing. Examples of LSPs include space systems (e.g., the international space station), construction projects (Canada's LaGrande hydroelectric venture, Holland's Delta flood control project, the English Channel Tunnel), as well as company relocations (involving the client, movers, construction companies, recruiters, consultants, and suppliers) and corporate mergers (dual sets of clients, consultants, and attorneys).

Integration between contractors in LSPs is achieved through use of project managers, coordinators, liaisons, and task forces. Notice in Figure 14-11 the relationships, both horizontal and hierarchical, among contributors' management as well as between functional areas in different organizations. Direct relationships and communication between, for instance, the sponsor's design group and the contractors' and subcontractors' design groups accelerate decision making and improve integration.

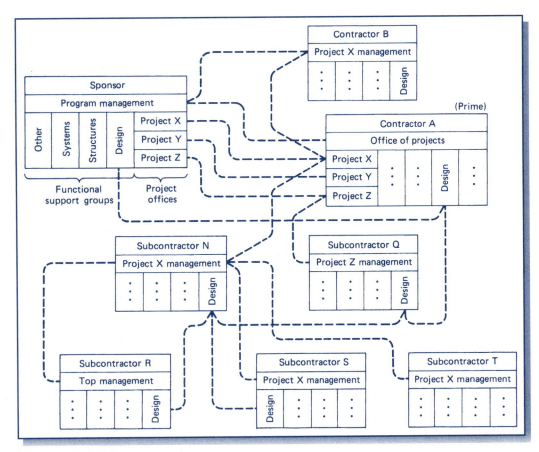

Figure 14-11
Integration relationships in a large-scale project

Most technological LSPs are devoted to development and construction of complex systems. The total effort is subdivided among a number of contributors, each responsible for a specific subsystem or component to be integrated with the others to form the overall system. Figure 14-12, for example, shows the major components in the international space station. The figure is simplified and excludes the launch vehicles to get the components in space, the support systems, and the numerous organizations working to develop, produce, launch, and integrate the components (prime contractors, subcontractors, and suppliers).

Oversight and Integration Contractors

In public works and government projects, integration is usually the responsibility of the sponsoring agency. Sometimes, however, the engineering and management tasks are quite difficult or extensive, and outside help is required.

Among the first LSPs to experience the integration problems inherent to large systems were weapons system development projects during World War II.[14] For instance, the components which made up a system such as a bomber were purchased by separate offices within, for example, the Air Force. These components—airframe, engines, and electronics—were then furnished to the airframe manufacturer to assemble. As systems grew more complex, procurement by several separate organizations no longer worked. Sometimes the subsystem interfaces were different so plugs and fasteners

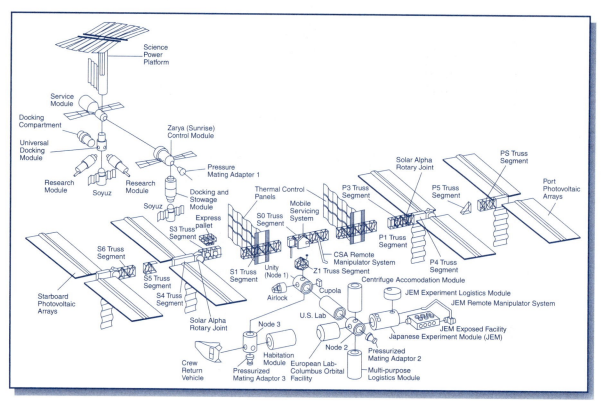

Figure 14-12
Major components in the hardware and assembly of the international space station [Diagram courtesy of NASA.]

would not fit, or the size of the components was greater than planned and the entire system had to be redesigned. To overcome these difficulties, the military established detailed specifications and committees to coordinate subsystem interfaces. This resulted in massive red tape and long delays, as exemplified by Livingston:

> A contractor wished to change the clock in an airplane cockpit from a one-day to an eight-day mechanism. A justification was written and given to the military representative, who forwarded it to the military technical group. The group requested from the contractor more detailed reasoning for the change. The contractor acknowledged and sent it to the group. The group approved the request and sent it to the change committee. The committee reviewed it, accepted the change, then sent an authorization back to the coordinator to replace the clock. This simple request took *three months* to process.[15]

Today, the integration process is expedited by giving responsibility to a single "oversight" body, similar to the role of a wedding consultant or general contractor, but on a larger scale. The job of integrating an LSP requires considerable manpower and a wide range of technical skills. Usually, the *lead* or *prime* contractor is assigned the responsibility for systems integration. Meantime, the project sponsor retains responsibilities such as contracting with *associate* contractors (subsystem manufacturers), and making major decisions, as well as resolving conflicts between the prime and associates. The associates become subcontractors to the prime contractor, taking their orders from the prime, and subjecting themselves to its surveillance and approval.

Figure 14-13 shows the relationships among the sponsor, prime, and contractors for a large urban transit project. Notice the different types of relationships.[16]

Sometimes the prime contractor is given greater responsibility, such as assisting the sponsor in selecting associates, pricing of subsystems, and allocating project funds. This presents a problem when the prime contractor and the subcontractors are competitors, because subcontractors are understandably hesitant to divulge design concepts or subsystem details, even though the prime needs them to integrate the overall system.

Sometimes even the largest prime contractors need assistance. At such times they submit a joint proposal as a *team* where one company serves as leader, assuming responsibility for systems engineering and management of the others. This appeals to small- and medium-sized firms that ordinarily would not have the resources to contract independently. The problem with this approach is that unless the lead company is strong, serious interface problems may arise. It also reduces competition, and because no team is likely to have all the best subsystems, the sponsor may require the team leader to open up the subsystem development to competition and, if necessary, change the members of the team.

When the prime contractor lacks the capability to perform the integrating work, a separate consulting firm, or *integration contractor,* is engaged entirely for providing integration and engineering advice.[17] These contractors, which sometimes employ thousands of workers, are able to quickly pull together all the necessary resources. The problem is that they often operate the same business as the contractors they integrate, which puts them in the awkward position of managing their competitors and being able to learn their secrets.

Figure 14-13
Management and authority relationships in a large construction project.

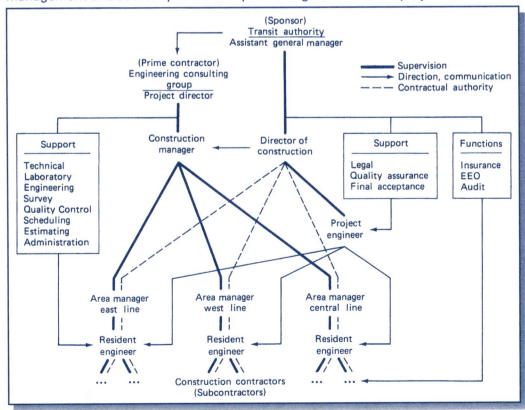

Integration in projects can be conceptualized in two ways: integration of the *functional areas* of the project organization to achieve project goals, and integration of the *phases* of the project so that issues concerning later phases influence decisions made in the early phases. The former, which has been the subject of the chapter thus far, is called *horizontal integration*; the latter is called *vertical integration* (Figure 14-14). The two aspects are not independent because integration of the project phases also usually requires integration of the functional areas.

Achieving high-level integration in LSPs can be difficult, especially in systems development projects such as new product development and software development. These projects require the efforts of many functional units to design and produce a system that will meet the exacting requirements of a customer or market. The stages in a typical development project coincide with those of the systems development cycle described in Chapter 4: conception, definition, design and development, testing, production, and installation and/or distribution.

Nonintegrated Systems Development

In a traditional development project, a different functional group handles each phase. For example, a marketing group might specify the initial concept and customer requirements, a design group might produce the technical specifications and the system design, and manufacturing and purchasing groups might determine ways to make the product and obtain parts and materials. Even when a project manager oversees the process, work at each stage is largely situated within only one functional area, receiving minimal involvement from others.

There is not much horizontal integration or vertical integration. At each new stage of the process a new functional area takes over, "inheriting" and being forced to accommodate the output of the previous stage. As a result, the design group must try to create a product design that conforms to the requirements inherited ("thrown over the wall") from marketing, and, in turn, the manufacturing group must try to develop a production process that conforms to the design inherited from the design group. The

Figure 14-14
Horizontal and vertical integration in systems development projects.

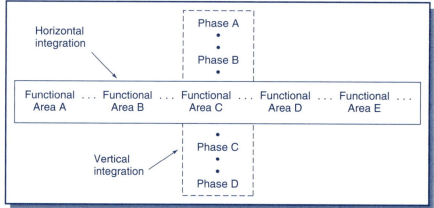

process, illustrated in Figure 14-15, involves little interaction between marketing, design, and manufacturing groups.

Decisions regarding definition, design, and production are made sequentially and independently. Information needed for decisions in each phase is not always available because not all of the right people and functional areas are involved at the time. The consequence is, for example, that marketing might fail to specify an important requirement, or else specify one that is not necessary; later, the design group might create a product design that meets requirements but is difficult or costly for the manufacturing group to produce. Each functional group taking over the process has to struggle to accommodate commitments made by earlier groups. When a group encounters commitments or design features that cannot be implemented, it must send back the design (or decision/commitment) for modification. This back-and-forth exchange between areas results in numerous *change requests*, with detrimental consequences in terms of project schedule, cost, and end-item requirements. The problem is lack of vertical integration, failure to ensure that the original requirements as defined are the ones necessary to accomplish project goals, and that all contributing functional areas will be able to fulfill those requirements.

Life Cycle Costs

Decisions made near the start of the project impact the development schedule, quality, and life cycle costs of the project end-time. *Life cycle costs* include all costs of materials, production, distribution, and operation of the end-item for as long as it continues to be produced and used. Early mistakes in design decisions become solidified. The later that problems or mistakes in design are discovered, the more costly and difficult rectification becomes. As Figure 14-16 shows, about 80 percent of a product's life cycle cost is determined in the project's conceptual and design stages, well before the product is manufactured. This means that whatever the total product cost, 80 percent is based upon choices made during the early stages of the project.[19] Unless important decisions affecting the later stages of production, system installation, and operation are made correctly at the start, grave consequences may result. These would

Figure 14-15
Traditional interaction between functional areas during phases of systems development.[18]

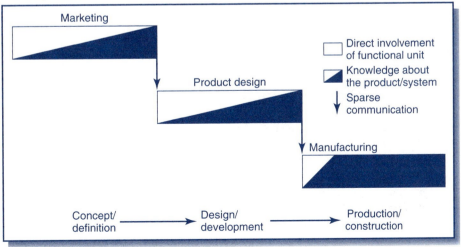

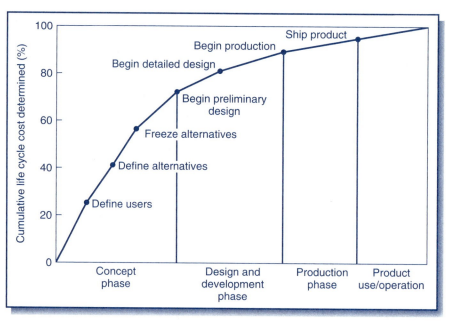

Figure 14-16
Percent of product life cycle cost set during stages of the product life cycle.

include high production costs, a protracted systems development cycle, delayed launch of the product or system, and poor quality.

Two approaches to integration in systems development projects are *concurrent engineering* and *quality function deployment*. Concurrent engineering entails an organizational approach to integration: form a single development team at the start of the project with representatives from *all* the functional areas, and have that team work on *every* stage of the development process, from concept to production and distribution. In this way, horizontal integration works in concert with vertical integration. Quality function deployment is a vertical-integration methodology: It first ensures that the right requirements are identified, and then that every functional area involved in each phase of the project can stay focused on those requirements.

14.14 CONCURRENT ENGINEERING

Many individuals and groups have a stake in the successful development, implementation, and eventual usage of any product or system. The designer asks, "What good is it if the design doesn't work?"; the salesperson asks, "What good is it if it doesn't sell?"; the finance person asks, "What good is it if it isn't profitable?"; and the manufacturing person asks, "What good is it if we can't make it?" On top of that, the customer asks, "What good is it if it costs too much, arrives too late, or doesn't meet my needs?" The term "concurrent engineering" refers to the *combined* early efforts of designers, developers, and producers to ensure that those questions get asked and answered to the satisfaction of everyone. Actually, the term is somewhat misleading because issues regarding sales, marketing, purchasing, finance, and quality—not just engineering—are all addressed from the start.

Cross-Functional Teams

Concurrent engineering is implemented with a cross-functional team. The team can be structured as a coordinated, multifunctional matrix team or as a pure-project team. Regardless, every group that is to be made responsible for part of the project or influenced by its results is given the opportunity to provide substantial early input when key decisions are formed. To encourage information sharing, the team invites different functional areas to participate as the project moves from stage to stage (Figure 14-17).

Concurrent engineering combines the interests of engineers, planners, buyers, marketers, customers, and suppliers so that the right requirements and production and procurement issues are identified early. It emphasizes both understanding of requirements and priorities and translating of requirements into product features and production processes. The result is a product or end-item design that meets customer needs and is realistic in terms of the capabilities of the manufacturer and its suppliers.

The overlap in design and production tasks reduces the time between concept formulation and product launch. For example, the production process of making dies for automobile body-panel stamping is expensive and time-consuming. With concurrent engineering, however, instead of waiting until the approach of production launch, the dies are designed and produced as soon as the body panel design has been completed. Concurrent design of panels and dies alone can reduce production preparation time for a new automobile by more than 1 year.

Concurrent engineering improves design trade-offs between product features and production capabilities. Subtle changes can be made in product design features that are transparent to the customer, but that eliminate conflicts and take advantage of existing production capabilities. Production bugs, rework, customer usage problems, and warranty claims are all reduced.

Figure 14-17
Concurrent interactions between functional areas during phases of systems development.[20]

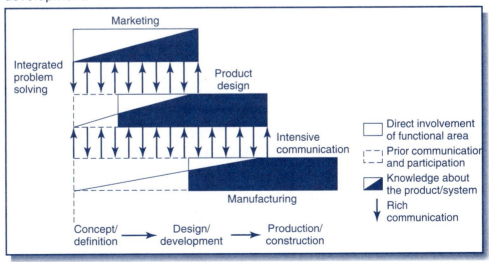

Concurrent engineering teams are sometimes referred to as *design-build teams* because they combine the interests and involvement of designers and builders into a single team effort. The following example illustrates such a joint effort.

Example 2: Design-Build Teams at Boeing[21]

At one time the Boeing factory's production plant was located on the bottom floor and the engineering group was housed on the top. Whenever a problem occurred in the plant, the engineers just walked downstairs to take a look. Today, Boeing employs well over 10,000 people at several locations, and easy interaction is impossible to achieve. Similar to other large corporations, Boeing's finance, engineering, manufacturing, and planning units had evolved into semiautonomous enclaves, each having strong self-interests and an "us versus them" attitude.

To overcome that attitude and promote functional interaction in the development program of the 777 commercial aircraft, Boeing implemented the "design-build team" concept, or DBT. This DBT concept included representatives from all involved functional units, customer airlines, and major suppliers. The concept had emerged from the simple question, "How do we make a better airplane?" The answer, Boeing managers realized, required not simply a good understanding of aircraft design, but also knowledge of things such as aircraft manufacture, operation, and maintenance. To capture knowledge about such things, Boeing developed the DBT concept wherein customers and manufacturers could join together with engineers to discuss ways of incorporating each other's objectives into the design, early in the process.

Responsibility for the airplane was assigned to DBTs based on a physical breakdown of the major components and subcomponents of the airplane. For example, the wing was divided into major subareas such as wing leading edge and trailing edge, and then further broken down into specific components such as inboard flap, outboard flap, and ailerons, before the responsibility for each component was handed to a DBT. Each DBT numbered 10 to 20 members and was run like a little company. Though initially Boeing had planned on 80 to 100 DBTs to do the job, eventually over 250 were needed. Every DBT met twice a week for a couple of hours. Each meeting was orchestrated by a team leader, followed a preset agenda, and conformed to a regimen for note-taking, making decisions, assigning responsibilities, and following up on actions. Having so many new people participate in design meetings—people from airlines, finance, production, and quality—was a totally new concept at Boeing, but with so many new people at these meetings, functional differences lessened in importance.

Almost every component in an airplane interacts with numerous other components; therefore, to ensure integration most participants in the program were assigned to multiple DBTs. The manufacturing representative, for instance, belonged to 27 different DBTs. He had responsibility for telling engineers what to expect when their elegant designs met with the realities of metal, manufacturing processes, and human assembly line and maintenance workers, and making suggestions that enabled proper manufacturing of the airplane. One suggestion he made concerned the cover on the strut-faring that would hold the engine to the wing. The faring had been designed to contain a lot of electrical and hydraulic equipment that maintenance personnel would need to access. Engineers had not noticed that the faring cover design was too small, and that removal of inside components for repair would have required removal of the entire faring. However, the manufacturing rep noticed, leading him to suggest designing two bigger doors for each side of the faring. The new design allowed greatly improved access and removal of equipment from inside the faring with minimal effort and delay.

A concurrent engineering team should be organized for maximal control over product-design decisions and facilitation of intra-team communication and commitment. Some conditions affecting the performance of concurrent engineering teams are:[22]

- Autonomy. Members placed on a concurrent engineering team should be relieved of unrelated obligations and expected to give full commitment to the development effort.

- Full time, full duration. Ideally, concurrent engineering team members should have continuous input and be party to all decisions throughout the *entire* systems development process. That's what "concurrent" means.

- Colocated. When team members work in close proximity and share one office, communication can be continuous and spontaneous. Formal meetings and reviews formerly scheduled weekly or monthly are replaced instead by numerous daily informal chats.

- Small size. The team must be small enough to allow good communication and encourage team commitment, yet large enough to include representatives of all the affected functional areas (and, perhaps, customer and suppliers also). Research shows that about six people are optimal, though as many as 10 to 20 team members can be effective. If more than 20 individuals are needed, smaller subteams should be formed and coordinated by a cross-functional core team or steering group.

- Team of doers. Though each concurrent engineering team member is a specialist in some area (design engineering, manufacturing, marketing, purchasing, etc.), each should be willing to assume a wide range of responsibilities and obligations. Concurrent engineering members must be "can do" folks who are willing to visit customers and suppliers, work on CAD/CAM, do modeling, light assembly work, or whatever else needs to be done.

Involvement in concurrent engineering requires more than just getting people together in an office. Product designers may wander through the factory to learn how their designs are manufactured and whether certain features of the design make it hard to produce. At the same time, they can explain to production engineers and assembly workers why a design feature is important and must be retained. General Motors requires that its design engineers not only roam the plant, but that they spend a full day every 3 months assembling the portion of the car they had helped design.

These are only suggestions. The ways in which organizations actually integrate functional areas and phases in the systems development process vary greatly. In example 3, you will see two companies' different approaches to systems development.

Example 3: Systems Development at Motorola and Lockheed-Martin[23]

Motorola's approach to systems development has four phases: Product definition, contract development, product development, and program wrap-up. The approach emphasizes integration of functions to develop innovative next-generation products and improved resource utilization for a speedier development process. Development projects are conducted by a core cross-functional team under the direction of a project manager. The team is responsible for most of the decisions and detailed design work, as well as for creating a work plan specifying resource requirements and performance targets. Functional units provide support to the core team.

The core team approach is used in projects where speed is critical. This includes projects that aim to create systems with entirely new product or process architectures, and those that will interface with markets that quickly change. For example, Motorola used a core team to develop a new pager system. The team consisted of a project manager and eight people from industrial engineering, robotics, process engineering, procurement, product design, manufacturing, human resources, and accounting/finance. It also included a member from Hewlett Packard, the vendor for a crucial component in the system. The team worked together in a glass-enclosed office located in the middle of a manufacturing facility. This encouraged others to "look in" on the team and offer suggestions. The team created a contract book that served as both the blueprint and work plan for the project. Senior management approved the plan, but thereafter, allowed the team responsibility for the bulk of the project. The project was completed in 18 months (half the usual time for a development effort of that size), met the cost objective (which was much lower than normal), and yielded a product of high quality and reliability.

Lockheed-Martin's advanced development division, called "Skunk Works," has a reputation for developing radical designs and breakthrough aircraft and space vehicles.[24] The term "Skunk Works" is trademarked by Lockheed, but in common usage refers to an autonomous project team working on advanced technology that can achieve results more quickly and at a lower cost than traditional development projects. For each development effort the Skunk Works forms a cross-functional team, handpicked by the project manager. Unlike the core teams at Motorola, which rely on functional teams for support, each Skunk Works team is fully autonomous and operates much like a pure-project organization. The team is similar to a separate business unit: It works largely on its own and has authority to requisition resources and subcontract work. Emphasis in Skunk Works teams is on technical excellence and speed. Although projects tend to broadly follow the phases of conception, definition, and so on, the team is free to modify the phases as well as to create procedures and standards best suited to the goals of the project. Although Motorola's core teams have broad responsibility, they remain closely linked to the existing functional areas. At Skunk Works, each team controls virtually all of the resources it needs. Members of the team are selected for high competency, broad skills, strong commitment, and ability to think on their feet. They are colocated, sometimes at an isolated site, to increase motivation and teamwork and to maintain secrecy. Aside from budgets and general procedures, the team gets minimal direction from senior management. Since its inception during World War II, Skunk Works has become a model for creating highly innovative, leading edge aircraft and space vehicles quickly and on-budget.

An example is the F117 Stealth fighter, mentioned in Chapter 11.[25] The Air Force specified rapid development of a relatively low-cost production aircraft that would be difficult to spot on radar (stealth). Although the Skunk Works team ultimately created an overall design that was radical and used new materials, it kept costs down by using an engine, computers, flight controls, and other parts from pre-existing aircraft. The project was completed in record time, only 31 months after the contract had been awarded. The cost for research, development, and production of 59 airplanes was $6.6 billion, considered low at the time when other leading aircraft programs were running at least $1 billion over budget and costing nearly $1 billion for *each plane*. Efficiency and low cost were partly attributed to the small size of the development team (only a few hundred people in the design phase), which minimized red tape, enhanced security, and allowed smooth communication and project control.

Heavyweight Teams

Motorola's core teams described in Example 3 are what Wheelwright and Clark call "heavyweight" teams.[26] The project managers are heavyweights because they are on the same level as or higher than functional managers, giving them organizational clout to exert a strong influence over everyone involved in the development effort. The autonomous teams at Skunk Works are even "heavier" in the sense that they are not required to follow a predefined development process but can craft the process and incentives to get the job done.

In general, autonomous teams can be very effective because they control the resources necessary to achieve project goals. Of course, because each team is fully accountable for results, only the team can be blamed if the project fails.

Both cross-functional core teams and autonomous teams provide strong focus on the project goal, discipline in coping with complexity, and consistency between details. Customer requirements are carefully defined, brought into focus, and translated into terms everyone on the team can understand. Elements of the process and details of the system are handled in a coherent fashion, minimizing inconsistencies and changes later on.

One disadvantage of heavyweight teams is that individual components or elements of the end-item or system might not reach the same level of technical excellence as they would if they had received attention from a traditional functional area. Although a cross-functional team might design a component that meets requirements and integrates the entire system, the component might contain flaws that only a functional team of specialists could have prevented. One way around that problem would be to involve specialists in periodic design reviews as mentioned in Chapter 13.

14.15   QUALITY FUNCTION DEPLOYMENT[27]

Quality function deployment (QFD) is a methodology for defining customer needs and requirements, as well as for keeping everyone on the project focused on them throughout the development process. It translates customer needs into specific system, product, or service characteristics, and specifies the processes and systems to produce that system, product, or service. QFD not only yields end-item results that meet customer needs, it delivers them in less time and at a lower cost than is possible with traditional product development methodologies.

QFD is a useful planning tool, and it might logically have been discussed earlier in the chapters on planning and scheduling. It is included in this chapter, however, because beyond its use as a planning tool, it represents a process for integrating cross-functional teams and project activities.

QFD was developed by Mitsubishi's Kobe Shipyards in 1972, adopted by Toyota in 1978, and soon after, implemented by many other Japanese companies. It was first adopted in the United States in 1983 by Ford to counter Toyota. QFD has since been adopted by numerous U.S. companies including General Motors, Proctor & Gamble, AT&T, Digital Equipment, Omark Industries, Hewlett-Packard, and Chrysler.

House of Quality[28]

QFD requires that the project team articulate the means by which the product or system being designed will achieve customer requirements. The QFD process starts with market needs or customer requirements, then uses a planning matrix called the *House of Quality* to translate the needs or requirements into the necessary technical requirements. The basic structure of the house of quality is shown in Figure 14-18.

- The left side of the matrix lists "what" the customer needs or requires.
- The top of the matrix lists the design attributes or technical requirements of the product; these are "how" the product can meet customer requirements.
- Additional sections on the top, right, and bottom sides show correlations among the requirements, comparisons to competitors, technical assessments, and target values.

Features of the house of quality are illustrated in Example 4.

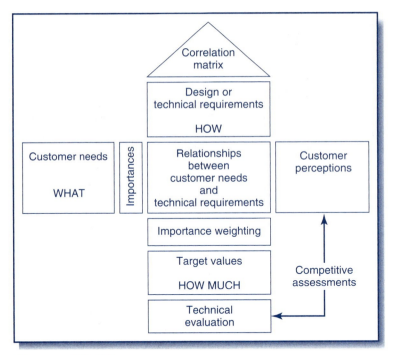

Figure 14-18
Structure of the house of quality.

Example 4: House of Quality for a TV Remote-Control Switch

Figure 14.19 is a portion of the house of quality matrix for the design of a television remote-control (RC) switch. The house is interpreted as follows:

- Rows. Listed to the left of the central matrix are *customer needs* or *requirements;* these are what customers think is important about the product. They are the product "whats."

- Importance to customer: The six requirements have been rank ordered 1-6 by customer preference; "multifunction buttons" is rated the highest; "RC easy to see/find" the lowest.

- Columns: Listed in the columns along the top of the central matrix are the *technical requirements* or *attributes* of the product; these are ways the product can meet customer requirements. They are the product "hows."

- Central matrix: Inside the central matrix are symbols showing the strength of the relationship between the whats and the hows (strong positive, positive, negative, strong negative). For example, "buttons easy to see" has a strong positive relationship to the size and color of the buttons, and a positive relationship to the size of the remote-control chassis. Note that each relationship has a numerical weighting of 1, 3, or 9.

- Importance weighting: The *weightings* of the relationships in each column are summed to determine the relative importance of the technical attributes. Thus, the most important technical attribute is "dimensions of the RC" (weight of 22), followed by "size of buttons" and "color of RC chassis" (tied at 12 each).

- Gabled roof: The "roof" on the house shows the correlations among the technical attributes. For example, "dimensions of the RC chassis" has a

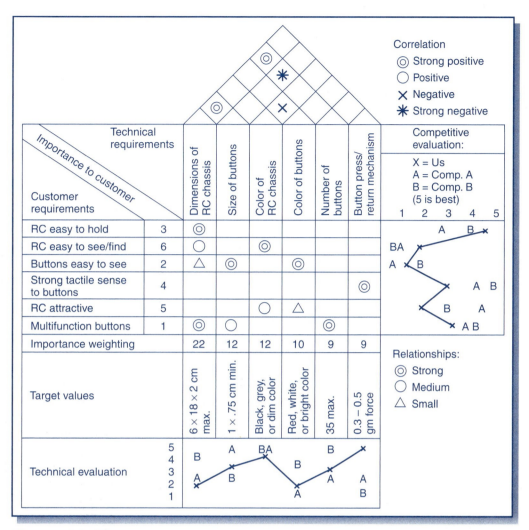

Figure 14-19
House of quality for television remote-control switch.

strong positive correlation with "size of buttons" and "number of buttons," and "size of buttons" has a strong negative correlation with "number of buttons" (smaller buttons allow space for more buttons; larger buttons, space for fewer).

- Target values: The numerical or qualitative descriptions shown in the basement of the house are design targets set for the technical attributes. One target of the design, for example, is to keep the dimensions of the RC within "6 × 18 × 2 cm."

- Technical evaluation: The graph in the subbasement compares the company ("us") against two of its competitors, A and B, on the technical attributes. For example, the company's current product does relatively poorly on the attributes of RC dimensions and button color, but fares well on chassis color and return mechanism. These evaluations are based on test results and opinions of engineers.

- Competitive evaluation: The graph on the right rates the company and its competitors in terms of customer requirements. These ratings are based on customer surveys. For example, customers think the company does best in terms of the RC being "attractive," but worst in terms of it being "easy to hold."

The house of quality suggests areas on which designers might focus the development effort to gain a market niche. For example, the rating on the right in Figure 14-19 indicates that no company does particularly well in terms of "buttons easy to see" despite the fact that customers rank that requirement second in importance. A requirement that customers rank high, yet on which they rank all companies low, suggests a design feature that could be exploited to improve a company's competitive standing. The company making the RC, for example, might try to improve the visibility of the buttons by increasing the size of buttons and/or using bright colors.

The house provides a systematic way of organizing and analyzing data to compare the hows with the whats, and prevents things from being overlooked. It justifies where to devote time and money, and where to refrain from adding resources. Still, the results of QFD are only as good as the data that go into the house. At a minimum the competitive evaluations require two perspectives: the customers' viewpoints regarding how the product compares to the competition, and the views from engineers and technicians regarding how well the product objectively meets technical requirements. The data may come from many sources, including focus groups, telephone and questionnaire surveys, experimental tests of competitors' products, and published materials.

An important system development goal is to evaluate the customer's perspective to distinguish between the *critical few* and the *trivial many* aspects of the end-item system so as to ensure that the critical ones are done right. As an example, a computer printer might have as many as 30 different design features that affect print quality. The most important feature, however, is the fusion process of melting toner on the page, which is a function of the right combination of temperature, pressure, and time. Focusing on temperature, pressure, and time narrows the design emphasis to the relatively few technical parameters of greatest importance to performance.[29] These parameters become the engineering parameters for which designers seek the "right" values. Once the right values have been set, the analysis moves on to identify important factors in the manufacturing process and the settings necessary to achieve the design requirements. In other words, the house of quality is just the first of several steps in the QFD process.

QFD Process

The QFD process employs a series of matrices in a multiphasic approach to project planning. The actual number of phases and matrices depends on the project, but Figure 14-20 shows one approach that utilizes four matrices to correspond to project phases of program planning, product design, process planning, and process control planning. The steps are as follows.

1. Create the first matrix, the "house of quality" (A). This converts customer needs and requirements into technical requirements.
2. Develop an initial version of the project plan from the house of quality (explanation follows). Although creating the house of quality can be rather time-consuming, it should not delay preparation of the project plan. A rudimentary plan should be prepared using information available from the house of quality, after which the plan can be revised and expanded when new information emerges in the updated matrix.

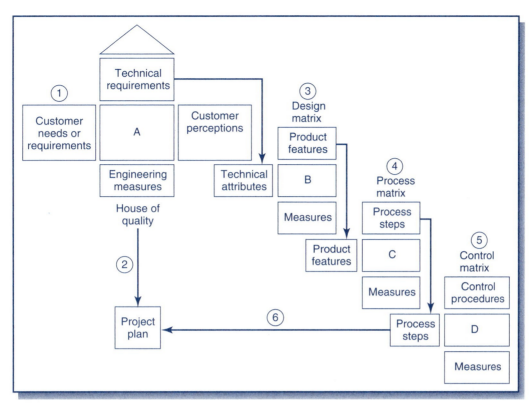

Figure 14-20
QFD multiphase, multimatrix approach.

3. Create the next matrix, the design matrix (B). This matrix converts technical requirements from the "house" matrix into product design features and requirements.
4. Create the process matrix (C). This matrix converts design features and requirements from the design matrix into process steps or production requirements.
5. Create the control matrix (D). This matrix converts process steps or production requirements from the process matrix into process tracking and control procedures.
6. Refine the project plan to incorporate aspects of the design, process, and control matrices.

The purpose of the matrices is to point out the information needed to make decisions about product definition, design, production, and delivery. The matrices link the work requirements to work tasks so that customer needs and technical requirements are translated faithfully (undistorted) into design features and production requirements. As shown in Figure 14-20, the link is achieved by taking the requirements or activities from the top of one matrix and putting them on the left side on the matrix in the next phase.

An advantage of this linking is that it ensures *traceability*, meaning that any project activity can be traced to a customer need or project requirement that it fulfills, and, conversely, every customer need and requirement can be traced to the mandatory activities. Put another way, QFD ensures that every activity serves a requirement, and every requirement is served by one or more activities. The resulting project plan, which links every task in the project with the technical requirements listed in the original house of quality, is an *integrated* project plan.

Preparing an Integrated Project Plan[30]

Much of the information needed to prepare an integrated project plan is contained in the original QFD matrix, the house of quality, including

- The goal of the end-item product or system.
- List of customer needs and requirements and their importance ranking.
- List of technical requirements to meet customer needs and their importance ranking.
- Target values for technical requirements.
- Information about congruence or conflicts between requirements.

The rankings of technical requirements in the house are especially important in project planning because they indicate which requirements are critical to fulfilling customer needs. This is necessary for allocating project resources. Although an attempt is made to plan the project such that all listed requirements are met, the ranking indicates the requirements that *must* be met for the development effort to succeed. The list of requirements also suggests whether the project is feasible. If meeting high-ranking requirements has been deemed too costly or technically challenging, then the project might simply be canceled.

The house of quality matrix requires that different functional groups work together to identify solutions, tasks, work packages, and resources. After they have identified technical requirements in the matrix, they translate them into technical approaches and then into specific tasks and work packages. Sometimes a requirement can be met by a single approach and task, and sometimes by a combination or string of tasks. The point is that the requirements become the basis for identifying the overall design approach and project tasks. Resource priority goes to the highest ranking requirements. The lowest ranking requirements are not ignored, but they receive less attention because they have the least effect on satisfying customer needs.

Each technical requirement is assigned to the manager or team that will work on the task most closely associated with the requirement. If a requirement involves several tasks and functional groups, then individuals representing all of the groups are assigned responsibility for various aspects of meeting the requirement. To ensure the overall requirement is met, one person is held accountable. The WBS approach can be used to associate tasks with requirements. Each requirement might be divided into subrequirements, which are then identified with work packages in the WBS. The result is that each requirement is associated with tasks having assigned responsibility and the appropriate resources.

The matrices in the QFD process not only connect project tasks to technical requirements and customer needs, they assist in defining the relationships among tasks and the sequence in which tasks are executed—the predecessor-successor relationships described in Chapter 8. The following simple example shows how the "roof" of the house of quality is employed in creating the project network.

Example 5: Setting Task Relationships with the House of Quality

A work breakdown analysis indicates that the five technical requirements for a product can be achieved by performing six tasks. The correspondence between technical requirements, the project tasks to achieve them, and the people responsible is:

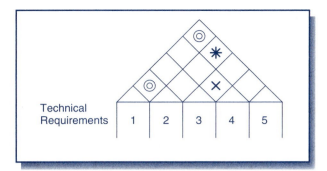

Figure 14-21
Interaction matrix from the house of quality.

Technical Requirement	Technical Task	People Responsible
1	A	JN
2	B and C	ED, BD
3	D	SH
4	E	RW
5	F	EV

The project manager and the people responsible look at the "roof" (interaction matrix) on the house of quality, shown in Figure 14-21.

The roof indicates interaction between four pairs of requirements, specifically, Requirement 1 interacts with 2 and 5, 2 with 5, and 3 with 4. Suppose the interaction is such that work associated with meeting Requirement 1 must precede work on Requirements 2 and 5, work on Requirement 2 must precede work on Requirement 5, and work on Requirement 3 must precede work on Requirement 4. Thus, the relationship between the requirements is as illustrated in Figure 14-22.

Substituting tasks for the relationships in Figure 14-22 (and assuming that tasks B and C are independent) leads to the project network in Figure 14-23.

Having defined the work packages and project network, the next steps are to develop schedules, budgets, and so on, as described in previous chapters, leading to a project plan that is integrated with customer needs and technical requirements. As shown in Figure 14-20, the project plan is first developed from the house of quality matrix, then refined and updated after completing the full series of matrices.

Although the QFD process takes longer to produce a project plan and the initial product design, it greatly reduces the time to produce the *final* design because less redesign and fewer engineering change requests are needed after the product goes into production and to the customer.

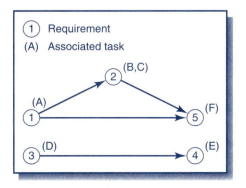

Figure 14-22
Relationship among requirements.

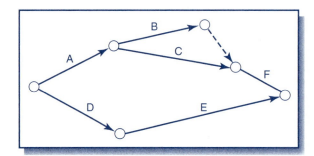

Figure 14-23
Project network.

Example 6: Chrysler Development of the LH Car Line[31]

Chrysler first applied QFD in the design and development of its LH-platform cars (Chrysler Concorde and Dodge Intrepid). Early in the product concept stage a program team was formed to establish overall design guidelines. The program team allocated responsibility for the different major automobile systems to different design groups (as did Boeing in its teams), and each group set up a QFD team to determine system-level requirements. Once requirements were set, smaller groups were formed to focus on designing the components within the system.

The QFD methodology Chrysler employed was part of a broader concurrent engineering effort yielding impressive results: The total LH design cycle took 36 months versus the historical 54 to 62 months; prototype cars were ready 95 weeks before production launch versus the traditional 60 weeks; and the program required 740 people compared to the usual 1,600 people. Customer approval ratings and sales of LH cars have been good, and the cars have received numerous awards and magazine citations for design excellence.

14.16   SUMMARY

Structure is the way organizations attempt to achieve goals and respond to problems in the environment. Two key features of structure are differentiation and integration; the former involves the subdivision of organizations into specialized subunits, and the latter links subunits to coordinate actions. Organizations traditionally differentiate along functional, geographic, customer, and process lines. They integrate subunits with rules and procedures, coordinated plans, and a chain of command. These kinds of differentiation and integration are effective when there is stability in the environment and high task certainty, but ineffective when there is frequent change, high complexity, and task uncertainty.

Projects are characterized by being able to adopt the organization structure to the unique goals. They achieve high integration through formal integration functions that emphasize horizontal relations. The simplest project organization is a task force or team with a project expeditor or coordinator to oversee and coordinate work efforts. Project expeditors and coordinators lack formal authority and must rely upon technical skills, information, and diplomacy to influence project members.

When a project task involves just one specialty, the project team comprises staff from one functional area. When it is multifunctional, members are drawn from several functional subunits and the resulting group is positioned physically outside the functional areas. The team leader reports to the chief executive overseeing the multiple areas.

When projects are large and involve substantial resource commitment and stake in the outcome, pure project organizations are used. This form commits major functional areas directly to the project and gives the project manager direct authority and control. With this form the highest priority is given to the project.

The matrix superimposes project teams on the functional organization and permits sharing of resources across projects. However, it requires two-dimensional information systems that are difficult to implement, and nontraditional dual reporting relationships that cause conflict.

Thoroughbred organizations such as those just described are seldom found. Most projects are hybrids and a pure project may be subdivided into portions that are matrixes, and vice versa. Projects are rarely the only basis for organization. Matrix forms and project centers coexist in companies that have functional, product, geographic, or customer bases, and where there are smaller project teams and task forces.

In large projects the project manager has assistance from a staff of specialists and representatives, together called the project office. This office handles tasks such as contracting, planning, scheduling, and controlling, but its major role is to integrate functional areas. Two other staff groups, the office of projects and the program office, oversee and coordinate activities in multiproject situations.

Often the project sponsor integrates the effort of multiple functional areas and organizations in large-scale, stand-alone projects. When the projects are also technically complex, the integration responsibility instead might be handled by the prime contractor or by a special integration contractor.

Project integration involves not only coordinating the efforts of multiple areas (horizontal integration), but also the phases of the project (vertical integration). In systems development projects where early commitments influence the success or failure of the effort, vertical integration happens by enabling all parties involved in, or affected by, the development effort to participate in making key project decisions at the start of the project and thereafter. One way to achieve that is through concurrent engineering, which in practice combines representatives from all areas with affected parties into a single cross-functional team. The team has the resources, authority, and autonomy to make decisions and perform or coordinate all activities to achieve project goals. Another way is through quality function deployment (QFD), a process for linking customer needs with the technical requirements, tasks, and people needed to meet them. The QFD process mandates consideration of the interaction and interrelationship between requirements, and ensures that work tasks are integrated, logically consistent, and focused on the original technical requirements.

REVIEW QUESTIONS

1. What do the terms "differentiation" and "integration" mean?
2. What are the five traditional forms of differentiation? List some companies that presently use each.
3. List the various forms of integration. Give examples of each. Which of these are lateral forms of integration?
4. What are the advantages of functional organizations? What are the disadvantages?
5. What distinguishes project forms from other forms of organization?
6. Describe the responsibility and authority for each of the following:
   Project expeditor
   Project coordinator
   Project leader in a pure project
   Project leader in a matrix

7. Describe the applications, advantages, and disadvantages for each of the following:
   Project task force
   Project team
   Pure project and project center
   Matrix

8. Give some examples of organizations where each of these project forms have been used.

9. What is the project office? Describe its purpose. Who is in the project office? How should members be selected for the project office?

10. What is meant by the informal organization? Give some examples. How does it help or hinder the formal organization? How can its beneficial aspects be influenced by the project manager?

11. Describe the role of the prime contractor and integration contractor in large projects.

12. One form of an integration contractor is the wedding consultant; another is the consultant who organizes high school reunions. For each of these
    • List the various groups, organizations, and individual parties that are involved and must be integrated.
    • Describe the relationship among these parties and how the consultant coordinates their efforts, both prior to and during the wedding or reunion.

13. An important element of informal organization not covered here is informal groups. Discuss informal groups—how they arise and why. Give some examples. How can informal groups be an asset to the project? How can they be a problem? In what ways can project managers encourage "beneficial" informal groups? How can they discourage "problematic" groups?

14. What parties should or might be included in a concurrent engineering team? What are the contributions of each? How does their inclusion in the team improve (a) the systems development process and (b) the resulting, final product?

15. What do you think are some of the major difficulties in changing from a traditional nonintegrated development approach to a concurrent design approach?

16. Breifly, define the purpose of quality function deployment (QFD).

17. In QFD, what is the source of customer needs or requirements that appear in the house of quality?

18. How do you think the QFD process can be used as part of concurrent engineering?

19. Think about the following or use whatever consumer research material available to you to define customer needs or requirements for the following:
    a. A "good" college course.
    b. Toaster (or other home appliance of your choosing).
    c. Cellular telephone.
    d. Coffee mug for your car.

    For each, define a corresponding set of physical or technical characteristics. Using the format of Figure 14-24, construct a house of quality matrix and show the relationship between the technical characteristics and customer requirements. Use the matrix in each case to "design" or suggest what the ideal product or service would be like or look like.

QUESTIONS ABOUT THE STUDY PROJECT

1. In your project, how is the parent organization organized—for example, functionally? Geographically? Show the organization chart, its overall breakdown, and relationships.

2. How does your project fit into the overall organization chart of the parent organization?

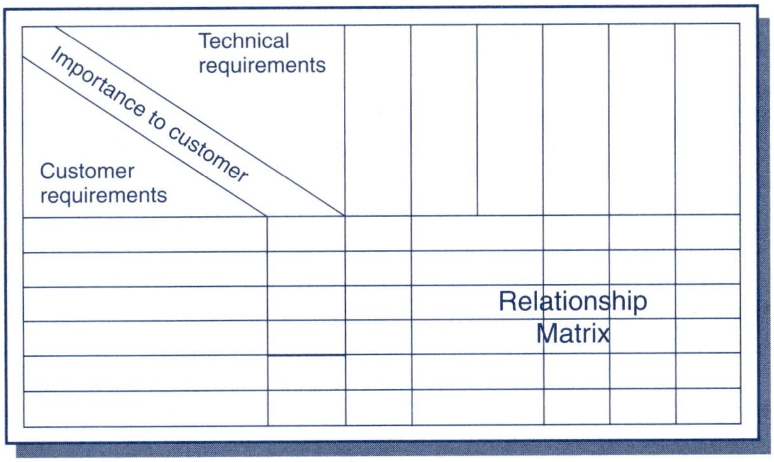

Figure 14-24
QFD matrix for Problem 19.

3. What kind of form is used in your project? Show the chart of the project organization; indicate the key roles and the authority and communication links between them.

4. How was the project structure developed? Has it "evolved" during the project? Who designs or has influence on the project structure? What role did the project manager have in its design? Is the design similar to those used in other, similar projects in the organization?

5. Critique the project design. Is it appropriate for the project goal, the parent organization, and the environment?

6. Is there a project office? Is there an office of projects or a program office? In each case: (a) Describe the physical office and how it is used; (b) describe the members of the project or program office staff—representatives, specialists, and so forth. What is the purpose of the project office staff? Describe the various tasks and functions handled by the project office. What are the members' participation in the project office (full-time, as needed, etc.)? What is the reporting relationship between the project manager and members of the project office?

7. How does the project manager integrate functional areas?

8. Are there prime and associate contractors involved? If so, what is the function of the company you are studying (prime contractor, subcontractor, or supplier) and how does it fit into the structure of all the organizations contributing to the project? If applicable, discuss the involvement of integration contractors or team leader contractors.

9. Does the project manager encourage open, informal communication? If so, in what way? If not, why not?

10. Did the project use concurrent engineering teams or quality function deployment? If so, discuss how these concepts were applied and tailored to fit the project.

Case 14-1   *The LOGON Project*

The Iron Butterfly Company is a medium-sized engineering and manufacturing firm specializing in warehousing and materials handling systems. Iron Butterfly purchases most of the subsystems and components for its product systems, then modifies and assembles them to satisfy customer requirements.

Most of its customers are in manufacturing or distribution.

Every Iron Butterfly system is made to customer specification and most of the firm's work is in system design, assembly, installation, and checkout. The firm's 250 employees are roughly divided equally among five divisions: engineering, design, fabrication, customer service, and marketing. Recently, competition has forced the firm to expand into computerized warehousing systems despite the fact that its experience and computer expertise is currently rather limited.

The company has been awarded a large contract for a robotic system for placement, storage, retrieval, and routing of shipping containers for truck and rail by the Midwest Parcel Distribution Company. This system, called the Logistical Online System, LOGON, is to be developed and installed at the company's main distribution center in Chicago. The contract is for a fixed price of $1.462 million that includes design, fabrication, and installation at the center. The contract was awarded because it was the lowest bid and because of Iron Butterfly's outstanding record for quality and customer service. A clause in the contract imposes a penalty of $1,000 daily for failure to meet the contract delivery date.

At various times throughout the estimated 47-week project, personnel will be involved from the functional divisions of design, fabrication, procurement, and customer service. Most personnel will be involved on a full-time basis for at least 4 or as many

as 18 weeks. In the past, the company has set up ad hoc project management teams comprised of a project coordinator and members selected from functional areas. These teams are then responsible for planning, scheduling, and budgeting with the actual work being done by the functional departments. Members of the teams serve primarily as liaisons to the functional areas and work part-time on the teams for the duration of the project.

The LOGON contract differs from other Iron Butterfly systems, both in its heavy usage of computer, real-time operation via remote terminals, and in its size. The company has no experience with real-time warehousing systems and has only recently hired people with the background needed for the project. (However, a contract has been signed with CRC, a major computer manufacturer, to provide hardware, programming support, and to assist with system installation and checkout.)

The LOGON contract is roughly 40 percent greater than anything Iron Butterfly has done before. At present, the company is in the middle of two other projects that absorb roughly three-fourths of its labor capacity, is winding down on a third that involves only the customer service division, and has two outstanding proposals for small projects under review.

Discuss how you would organize the LOGON project if you were the president of Iron Butterfly. Discuss the alternatives available for the LOGON project and the relative advantages and disadvantages of each. What assumptions must be made?

Case 14-2   Pinhole Camera and Optics, Inc.

Beverly is the newly appointed vice president of strategy for Pinhole Camera and Optics, Inc. (motto: "See the World through a Pinhole"), a medium-sized, privately owned, manufacturing firm. The company, now 14 years old, had experienced, up until 3 years ago, rapid growth through developing new products and optical manufacturing processes. Beverly believes that in recent years the company's market position has slipped because Pinhole has been unable to react quickly enough to changing market requirements and increasing competition. The company is divided into the traditional functional departments of research, marketing, sales, production, and so on. New product development projects are managed by handing off responsibility between managers of the departments. Beverly believes this is the greatest con-

tributor to Pinhole's inability to identify and respond to market opportunities, and she would like to create a new position, manager of new products, for the purpose of integrating departments during product development projects.

The owner of the company, Ovid Pinoli, disagrees. He contends that the managers of the functional departments, most who have been with the company since its start, are excellent managers, really know their business, and usually are able to work together. He feels there is no need to create the position, although he wonders where such a person would come from. Mr. Pinoli instead suggests that for each new project one of the current department managers should be picked to coordinate the efforts of all the departments. The manager would be selected from the department that has the biggest role in the project; in other words, according to whether the project primarily involves research, marketing, or production.

Beverly is convinced that Mr. Pinoli's idea won't improve the situation. She decides to prepare a formal written proposal that will address the pros and cons of Mr. Pinoli's suggestions and persuade him

that the new position manager of new products must be filled by someone other than a functional department manager. She also wants to describe how Pinhole's new development projects could be better organized and staffed.

If you were Beverly, what would you say in the proposal?

ENDNOTES

1. Detailed discussion of the organization structure, coordination, and integrating mechanisms in high technology environments is given by Jay Galbraith, "Environmental and Technological Determinants of Organizational Design," in *Studies in Organization Design*, J. W. Lorsch and P. R. Lawrence, eds. (Homewood, IL: Irwin-Dorsey, 1970): 113–39.

2. See Jay Galbraith, *Designing Complex Organizations* (Reading, MA: Addison-Wesley, 1973).

3. Thomas Peters and Robert Waterman, *In Search of Excellence* (New York: Warner Communications, 1984): 127–30.

4. See Keith Davis, "The Role of Project Management in Scientific Manufacturing," *IEEE Transactions of Engineering Management* 9, no. 3 (1962): 109–13.

5. Tom Peters, *Thriving on Chaos* (New York: Alfred A. Knopf, 1988): 212–13.

6. A discussion of the matrix organization, its applications and implementation is given by S. M. Davis and P. R. Lawrence, *Matrix* (Reading, MA: Addison-Wesley, 1977).

7. J. McCann and J. R. Galbraith, "Interdepartmental Relations," in *Handbook of Organizational Design* II, no. 61, P. C. Nystrom and W. H. Starbuck, eds. (New York: Oxford University Press, 1981); J. R. Meredith and S. J. Mantel, *Project Management: A Managerial Approach* (New York: John Wiley & Sons, 1985): 104.

8. Peters and Waterman, *In Search of Excellence*, 307–08.

9. See R. Thomas, J. Keating, and A. Bluedorn, "Authority Structures for Project Management," *Journal of Construction Engineering and Management* 109, no. 4 (December 1983): 406–22.

10. Michael Cusumano and Richard Selby, *Microsoft Secrets* (New York: Free Press, 1995): 74, 235–36, 248–49.

11. James Burns, "Effective Management of Programs," in *Studies in Organizational Design*, J. W. Lorsch and P. R. Lawrence, eds. (Homewood, IL: Irwin-Dorsey, 1970): 140–52.

12. See Chapter 4, "Multiproject Management," in Russell Archibald, *Managing High-Technology Programs and Projects* (New York: John Wiley & Sons, 1976).

13. Peters and Waterman, *In Search of Excellence*, 121–25.

14. This discussion is based on J. S. Livingston, "Weapons System Contracting," *Harvard Business Review* (July-August 1959): 83–92.

15. Ibid., 85.

16. Adapted from J. L. Lammie and D. P. Shah, "Construction Management: MARTA in Retrospect," *Journal of Construction Engineering and Management*, 110, no. 4 (December 1984), 459–75.

17. A more complete discussion of integration contractors is given in L. R. Sayles and M. K. Chandler, *Managing Large Systems: Organizations for the Future* (New York: Harper & Row, 1971): 253–71.

18. Adapted from Steven Wheelwright and Kim Clark, *Revolutionizing Product Development* (New York: Free Press, 1992): 178.

19. Preston Smith and Donald Reinertsen, *Developing Products in Half the Time* (New York: Van Nostrand Reinhold, 1991): 224-25.

20. Adapted from Wheelwright and Clark, *Revolutionizing Product Development*, 178.

21. Portions adapted from Karl Sabbagh, *Twenty-First Century Jet: The Making and Marketing of the Boeing 777* (New York: Scribner, 1996).

22. Adapted from John Nicholas, "Concurrent engineering: overcoming obstacles to teamwork," *Production and Inventory Management Journal* 35, no. 3 (Third Quarter 1994): 18–22.

23. Portions adapted from Wheelwright and Clark, *Revolutionizing Product Development*, 159–62, 200–03.

24. Its SR-71, a high-performance reconnaissance aircraft, was developed in the 1960s but still holds the world's speed record, three decades later. See Ben Rich and Leo Janos, *Skunk Works* (Boston: Little, Brown, & Company, 1994).

25. See David Aronstein and Albert Piccirillo, *Have Blue and the F-117A: Evolution of the "Stealth*

Fighter" (Reston, VA: American Institute of Aeronautics and Astronautics, 1997); Michael Stroud, "How the F-117A Flew On Budget, On Time," *Investor's Daily* (February 1, 1991).

26. Wheelwright and Clark, *Revolutionizing Product Development*, 194–96, 202–12.

27. Sources for this section: G. Bounds, L. Yorks, M. Adams, G. Ranney, *Beyond Total Quality Management* (New York: McGraw-Hill, 1994): 275–82; John Hauser and Don Clausing, "The house of quality," *Harvard Business Review* (May-June 1988): 63–73.

28. Portions of this section adopted from John Nicholas, *Competitive Manufacturing Manage-* *ment* (Burr Ridge, IL: Irwin/McGraw-Hill, 1998): 428–34.

29. For an example of computer printer design, see T. Greg Survant, "Changing the way we think is key to successful new products," *Target* 11, no. 2 (March/April 1995): 9–15.

30. See Barbara Bicknell and Kris Bicknell, *The Road Map to Repeatable Success: Using QFD to Implement Change* (Boca Raton, FL: CRC Press, 1995): 97–110.

31. Archie Lockamy and Anil Khurana, "Quality function deployment: a case study," *Production and Inventory Management Journal* 36, no. 2 (second quarter, 1995): 56–59.

Chapter 15

Project Roles, Responsibility, and Authority

> *All the world's a stage,*
> *And all the men and women merely players.*

—William Shakespeare,
As You Like It

When an organization wants to accomplish something new and not completely restructure itself, it uses a project team, matrix team, or task force. Responsibilities are assigned within the project, but unless it is a pure project most people are "borrowed" from other departments. Project management "gets work done through outsiders"—people from various technical, functional, and professional groups scattered throughout the parent company and outside subcontractors.[1] As Sayles and Chandler describe, project management

> calls for a new set of skills and procedures. It is dealing laterally, but not in the informal-group, informal-organization sense. It requires a capacity on the part of the manager to put together an organizational mechanism within which timely and relevant decisions are likely to be reached [as well as] a conceptual scheme for "working" interfaces . . . [It is a] dynamic, interactive, iterative, and intellectually challenging concept of the managerial role.[2]

Being a project manager means monitoring and influencing decisions without giving orders or making decisions in the same way as other managers. Most project managers have considerably more responsibility than authority, so they need different skills and approaches than traditional managers.

15.1 THE PROJECT MANAGER

Project Manager's Role

The project manager's role is so central that without it there would be no such thing as project management. The project manager is the glue holding the project together and the mover and shaker spurring it on. To be a project manager, a person wears a lot of different hats, many at the same time; they include the hats of an integrator, communicator, decision maker, motivator, evangelist, entrepreneur, and change agent.

The importance of integration in project work was emphasized earlier. Project management integrates diverse activities and scattered elements to achieve time, cost, and performance goals. As the central figure in the project, the project manager's prime role is to *integrate everything and everybody* to accomplish these goals. The project manager has been called the organizational "metronome," the person who keeps the project's diverse elements responsive to a single, central beat.[3]

The project manager is the *project communication hub,* the end of the funnel for all reports, requests, memoranda, and complaints. She takes inputs from more sources and directs information to more receivers than anyone else in the project. In between the sources and receivers, she refines, summarizes, and translates information to make sure that project stakeholders are well-informed about policies, objectives, budgets, schedules, requirements, and changes.

Being at the communication hub puts the project manager in the central position of making *decisions* such as allocating resources, setting project scope and direction, and balancing schedule, cost, and performance criteria. Even when she lacks the authority to make high-level decisions, the project manager is still best situated to influence the decisions and actions of those who do.

The prime motivational factor in any diverse group is strong commitment to a central goal. In a project organization, it is the project manager who instills a *sense of direction* and a commitment to action. There are many motivating aspects associated with project work such as spontaneity, achievement, and excitement, but these are sometimes difficult to uphold, especially in a project that is long and stressful. Lack of precedent, part-time personnel, diverse specialties, infrequent contact, and spatial distance between workers are among the factors reducing motivation in projects. Regardless, the successful project manager must foster enthusiasm, team spirit, confidence, and a reputation for excellence.

The project manager is a sort of *evangelist* who conveys faith in the project, its value, and workability. During the conceptual phase, the would-be project manager is often the only person who sees the big picture. Whether or not it gets funded depends on her ability to gain the endorsement of top management.

The project manager is an *entrepreneur,* driven to procure funds, facilities, and people to get the project off the ground and keep it flying. She must win over reluctant functional managers who will question assigning their better people to the project. Even after work is underway, the project manager must continue to champion the cause. At any stage of the project she might find herself fighting for the project's very existence. In the end, whether the project succeeds or fails, the project manager is ultimately held accountable.

Finally, the project manager is also the *change agent* who initiates passage into new and promising areas. She is always alert to developments which could impinge on the project, ready to adopt new and innovative ideas, and strives to overcome resistance to change. As the composition and size of the project (and so the communication and reporting channels) change, the project manager is the person who orchestrates and facilitates the change. At the same time, while facilitating big changes, she resists those little ones that would unnecessarily increase the scope, cost, or duration of the project.

Example 1: Gutzon Borglum: Project Manager and Sculptor[4]

If you are familiar with the carvings in Figure 15-1 then you know the handiwork of Gutzon Borglum. More than two million people a year visit Mount Rushmore National Memorial. Most of them who hear the name Gutzon Borglum think that it was he who *sculpted* the faces. And, of course, he *was* the sculptor, though not of the *actual faces* on the mountain. The contract for the project specified that the memorial was "to be carved . . . by . . . and/or under the direction of Gutzon Borglum" and that Borglum was to enjoy "full, final, and complete freedom of authority in the execution of the monument's design." He did carve the faces, but on a miniature model exactly 1/12 the size of the ones on the mountain. The model served as a guide for workers who did the actual sculpting of the monument. Much of this "sculpting" consisted of removing huge quantities of granite using dynamite and heavy drills and pneumatic jackhammers; the usual sculptor's tools of chisels and hammers were used only for detail work.

Projects of such grandiose size are never the work of just one person; however, in the case of Rushmore if anyone should get credit, it would have to be Gutzon Borglum. Although many others contributed to the project in important ways, it was Borglum's tireless efforts that yielded much of the project funding, and his genius and stubborn dedication that made it happen. He picked the site; he wrote

Figure 15-1
Gutzon Borglum's most famous work attracts millions of visitors a year. [Photo courtesy of John Nicholas.]

letters and articles, and he spoke personally to businessmen, wealthy industrialists, senators, congressman, and U.S. presidents; he determined that the faces would be of Washington, Jefferson, Roosevelt, and Lincoln; he hired and organized the work crew; he created the innovative means for transferring the design from the model to the mountain; and, *in addition to that,* he attended to myriad details, from designing the scaffolding, work platforms, tramway, hoists, and grounds buildings to orchestrating events in the pageants for the initial dedication and final unveiling ceremonies. Meantime, he also kept trying to revive his Stone Mountain project in Georgia, which he had started years earlier but had not finished. People wondered when he ever rested or if he ever slept. Of course, he was by no means perfect; he did not always have project problems under control, and his efforts were criticized for being uncoordinated and unorganized, especially in the early years. When the project began in 1927, Borglum wasn't completely sure what the monument was going to look like. At the time, however, all that mattered to South Dakotans was that it would bring recognition to their obscure state, and to Borglum that it was an opportunity to do something never before accomplished and a chance at artistic immortality.

People familiar with Borglum were impressed with his artistic talent, but they were even more impressed with his "capacity for affection, wrath, generosity, stinginess, nobility, pettiness, charm, and sheer obnoxiousness."[5] He was short on modesty and humility, and long on "mulish stubbornness." He thought big, dreamed big, talked big, and was not afraid to tackle any undertaking. His enthusiasm was contagious.

The project work crew consisted of 22 men. Most of the carving they had to do was with 80-pound drills and jackhammers while dangling on the side of a cliff. They sat in harnesses designed by Borglum that were lowered down the mountain face with hand winches. Imagine their feelings, as described by biographer Rex Smith: "You do your drilling while hanging on the side of a stone wall so lofty that you feel at first like you are hanging on the back fence of Creation. From where you sit you can look down upon mountains and plains that stretch farther than the eye can see. Surrounded by these vast spaces, suspended against a stone cliff, you feel dwarfed and insignificant . . . and uneasy."[6] Borglum was a stickler for safety, so despite the dangers there were few accidents and no fatalities throughout 14 years of work. Borglum was never chummy with his crew, but he cared and looked out for them, and, in return, they were extremely loyal to him, the project, and each other.

Seeing the monument today, we realize that its construction must have posed great challenges, but that, obviously, those challenges were overcome. Borglum, however, was never sure they would be overcome because a sculpture of such scale had never before been attempted. Although he had selected the mountain, he knew there was the risk that it might contain some disastrous hidden flaws—a crack or bad rock—that could not be worked around. In fact, besides funding, it was the shape of the mountain and its deep fissures that determined that the number of presidential busts had to be four and no more. Time and again obstacles arose, funds ran out, and the project had to be stopped. But Borglum and other believers persevered so that the project would again be revived. In the end, however, the carving was abandoned and the monument left uncompleted according to its original design because the nation was about to become embroiled in World War II and would no longer support the effort. Just months before the project was canceled, Borglum died. Up until then he had been the prominent driving force, and you have to ask, had he lived beyond the war years, how much more of the monument would have been completed? Borglum was a sculptor, but when it came to turning a mountain into a monument, he was the ultimate project manager.

Job Responsibilities

The project manager's principal responsibility is to deliver the project end-item within budget and time limitations, in accordance with technical specifications, and, when specified, in fulfillment of profit objectives. Other, specific responsibilities vary depending on the project manager's capabilities, the stage of the project, the size and nature of the project, and the responsibilities delegated by upper management. Delegated responsibility ranges at the low end from the rather limited influence of a project expeditor (where, in essence, the real project manager is the manager to whom the expeditor reports) up to the highly centralized, almost autocratic control of a pure project manager.

Though responsibilities vary, they usually include:[7]

- Planning project activities, tasks, and end results, including doing the work breakdown, scheduling, budgeting, coordinating tasks, and allocating resources.
- Selecting and organizing the project team.
- Interfacing with stakeholders:
- Negotiating with and integrating functional managers, contractors, consultants, users, and top management.
- Providing contact with the user.
- Effectively using project team and user personnel.
- Monitoring project status.
- Identifying technical and functional problems.
- Solving problems directly or knowing where to find help.
- Dealing with crises and resolving conflicts.
- Recommending termination or redirection of efforts when objectives cannot be achieved.

Spanning all of these is the umbrella responsibility for integration, coordination, and direction of all project elements and life cycle stages. This responsibility involves (1) identifying interfaces between the activities of functional departments, subcontractors, and other project contributors; (2) planning and scheduling so the efforts are integrated; (3) monitoring progress and identifying problems; and (4) communicating the status of interfaces to stakeholders, and initiating and coordinating corrective action.

Risk and uncertainty is unavoidable in project environments, and the likelihood of managerial crisis, if not a certitude, is at least substantially higher than in non-project situations. The project manager has overall responsibility for the advance planning necessary to anticipate and avoid crises.

Most project managers report in a line capacity to a senior-level executive. Their responsibility is to monitor and narrate the technical and financial status of the project and to report current and anticipated errors, problems, or overruns.

Competency and Orientation

Because project managers work at the *interface* between top management and technologists, they must generally have managerial ability, technical competence, and other broad qualifications. They must feel as much at home in the office talking with administrators about policies, schedules, and budgets as in the plant, shop, or on-site talking to specialists and supervisors about technical issues.

The relative importance of technical ability versus managerial competency depends on the project. In R&D projects, project management requires greater emphasis on the former because of the greater complexity of technical problems and the technical orientation of the project team. In product development and nontechnical projects, project management requires more emphasis on managerial ability because of the greater involvement of multiple, diverse functional areas. In general, project managers must have sufficient technical ability to understand the problem. On the other hand, too much technical emphasis can lead project managers to neglect their role as manager. There is no substitute for strong managerial competency in the role of the project manager.

Broad background is also essential. The more highly differentiated the functional areas, the more prone they are to conflict and the more resistant they are to integration. To effectively integrate multiple, diverse functional areas, the project manager needs to understand each of them, their techniques, procedures, and contribution to the project.

Studies indicate that the most effective project managers have goals, time, and interpersonal orientations intermediate to the functional units they integrate. In other words, they take a balanced outlook.[8] For instance, to integrate the efforts of a production department and a research department, the project manager's time perspective should be intermediate between production's short-term, weekly outlook and research's long-term, futuristic outlook.

Most project managers cannot be expert in all functional areas of the project, but they must be familiar enough with the areas to intelligently ponder ideas offered by specialists and to evaluate and make appropriate decisions. Along the same lines, to deal effectively with top management and the user, they must know about the workings and business of both parent and user organizations.

The project manager's broad background includes knowledge and proficiency in using management tools. Project managers have cost responsibility for the project, so they must understand the concepts of cost estimating, budgeting, cash flow, overheads, incentives, penalties, and cost-sharing ratios. They are involved in contract agreements, so they must be informed about contract terms and implications. They are responsible for the phasing and scheduling of work to meet delivery dates, so they must be familiar with the tasks, processes, and resources necessary to execute the contract. Also, they are responsible for enforcing project schedules, so they must be knowledgeable about tools and techniques for monitoring and controlling schedules. Many of these tools are covered in other parts of this book.

Project managers must also be effective communicators and listeners. They must be sensitive to the attitudes of project stakeholders regarding policies, time limits, and costs. Many members of the project team have disdain for anything nontechnical and resent the constraints imposed by schedules and budgets. Project managers must be able to convince them about the importance of project budgets, schedules, and policies.

Project managers must be able to work *with* people and delegate responsibility. They should be willing to prepare budgets and schedules with the cognizance and assistance of those who will have to live by them. Project managers must understand personalities, attitudes, and characteristics of people as team members and as individuals, and know how to best utilize talent even when it does not measure up to project requirements. Also, they must be sensitive to human frailties, needs and greed, and be interventionists skilled at resolving conflict, managing stress, and coaching and counseling. It seems like a tall order, but good project managers can do all of that.

Traditional Authority

Authority is an important subject in project management. In general, *authority* refers to a manager's power to command others to act or not to act. There are different kinds of authority, the most familiar is that conferred by the organization, called *legal authority.* Legal authority is written in the manager's job description. It refers to delegated power, hierarchical reporting, and the control of resources. Given legal authority, people in higher positions are viewed as having the "right" to control the actions of people below them. Often associated with legal authority is *reward power,* the power to evaluate and reward subordinates.

Another kind of authority, *charismatic authority,* stems from the power one gains by personal characteristics such as charm, personality, and appearance. People both in and outside the formal authority system can increase their ability to control others by being charismatic.

Traditional management theory says that authority is always greater at higher levels in the organization and is delegated downward from one level to the next. This is presumed best because managers at higher levels are assumed to know more and, therefore, are able to make decisions, delegate responsibility, and give "command" better than workers at lower levels. This point has been challenged on the grounds that modern managers, particularly in technology-based organizations, cannot possibly know everything needed to make complex decisions. They often lack the necessary technical expertise and so, increasingly, must rely upon subordinate specialists for advice. Even managers who are technically skilled cannot always manage alone; they rely upon staff groups for personnel and budgetary assistance.

Influence

It is important in project management to distinguish between legal authority and the *ability* to influence others. Managers with legal authority have the power to influence subordinates by giving orders and controlling salaries and promotions. Generally, however, the most effective managers are able to influence others *without* "ordering" them or making issue of their superior-subordinate relationship (this is especially true when subordinates are well-educated or highly experienced). Therefore, managers who rely solely on their legal authority are often relatively ineffective at influencing people.

It is possible to influence people by using other sources of influence such as (1) *knowledge* and (2) *personality.*[9] The first source of influence, *expert power,* refers to a special level of knowledge or competency attributed to the holder of the power. The recipient of the power believes that the knowledge and information possessed by the holder is relevant because he himself does not have that information. Simply, the expert power holder is seen as being right because of his knowledge, and others readily defer to his opinions or requests.

The other source of influence, *referent power,* is power derived from rapport, personal attraction, friendship, alliances, and reciprocal favors. The recipient identifies with the power holder and defers to his requests.

Given expert power and referent power, the issue of influence in organizations can be approached irrespective of the formal hierarchy and legal authority. Clearly these two kinds of power enable people to gain influence over others *despite* the formal authority system. In the informal organization, for example, they allow one member in a work group to influence all the rest (sometimes more than the group's leader).

Even within the formal organization, referent and expert power can subtly reverse the authority relationship. A subordinate may exert considerable influence over her superior if the superior comes to rely upon the subordinate for information or advice, or if a bond of trust, respect, or affection develops between them. Everyone has seen this happen, and history is replete with examples of people of "lower" social or organizational stature controlling actions of people of a higher stature: Alexandria was Queen of Russia; Rasputin was a mere priest.

Authority in Projects

Most managers rely upon multiple forms of influence—knowledge, expertise, persuasion, and personal relationships. When these fail, however, they still have their legal power to fall back on. Project managers, however, seldom have legal authority. Except in the case of the manager of a pure project, the typical project manager *lacks any form of traditional legal authority.*

Unlike traditional organizations where influence and authority flow vertically, influence and authority in project management flow horizontally and diagonally. The project manager exists *outside* the traditional hierarchy. The role is only temporary, superimposed on the existing structure, and so is not afforded the leverage inherent to a hierarchical position. Project managers work across functional and organizational lines and, except for members of the project office, have no subordinates reporting to them in a direct line capacity. The issue is further complicated in matrix organizations wherein project managers have a permanent role, yet must share formal authority with functional managers.

Thus, despite the considerable degree of responsibility they carry, most project managers lack a comparable level of formal authority. Instead they have *project authority,* meaning they can make decisions about project objectives, policies, schedules and budgets, but cannot give orders to back up those decisions.

The disparity between high formal responsibility and low formal authority has been referred to as the *authority gap.*[10] This gap means that project managers must rely on other forms of influence. "How to make friends and influence people" is not an academic issue for project managers.

Project Manager's Authority

Regardless of the size of the authority gap, most project managers handle it similarly. In cases where project managers are given no legal authority, they have no choice but to rely entirely upon influence derived from expert power and referent power. Yet even in large projects where they have some legal authority, one strong source of influence tends to arise from their professional reputations. This is so because in virtually all projects—task force, matrix, or pure project—project managers *depend* on others to get the job done. They have few resources under their direct control and must rely upon functional managers and support units for personnel and facilities. Numerous decisions must be made for which project managers lack time or expertise, so they depend upon others to investigate and suggest courses of action. To successfully implement decisions, people must be committed to supporting them. That commitment cannot be achieved through orders but must come from a personal level of mutual understanding and agreement with functional managers and supervisors.

Another source of the project manager's influence is in her network of alliances, the quality of which depends heavily upon her reputation and personal achievements. Such reputations are gained through recognition of accomplishments, not by organization charter. Even when project managers have legal authority, they seldom resort to using it because unilateral decisions and commands are inconsistent with the need for reciprocity and trade-offs in projects. Recognizing that not all information and decisions need to be channeled through them, effective project managers encourage direct contact between individuals involved, regardless of organizational level.

In summary, successful project managers tend to rely upon knowledge, experience, and personal relationships for influence (Figure 15-2). To build expert-based power, project managers must be perceived as technically and administratively competent as demonstrated by their experience and reputation. To build referent-based power, they must develop effective interpersonal, persuasion, and negotiation skills.

Sometimes the project manager possesses legal authority or the power of command. *If* the project manager has such authority, there are doubtless many instances where she will need to use it. These are situational, depending on the task at hand and the willingness of subordinates to take responsibility. This subject is discussed more in the next chapter.

Example 2: Effective Project Managers, Contrast in Styles[11]

An example of how different project managers can uniquely influence people are Kelly Johnson and Ben Rich, both former management heads of the advanced projects division of Lockheed-Martin Company, the "Skunk Works" mentioned in Chapter 14.

Kelly Johnson was a living legend, not only at the company but in the whole aerospace industry. With the help of a highly cohesive team of 150 engineers and shop workers, he created over 40 airplanes, including the fastest, highest-flying ones in the world. Yet, he was strictly business, without humor, hot tempered, and reputed to eat "young engineers for between-meal snacks." He made people with whom he had dealings sweat—whether bureaucrats or engineers—particularly excuse makers and faultfinders, so he had as many detractors as friends. Nonetheless, when someone was needed to head up the most difficult and challenging projects, company management and the military repeatedly selected Kelly. Why? Beneath the bad temper and paunchy, somewhat unkempt appearance was an unquestioned, sure-fire genius. He knew everything, it seemed, and his ability to make accurate, on-the-spot deductions was amazing. For a new engine inlet, Kelly simply glanced at the initial design and pronounced it wrong, being about 20 percent too big. His engineers worked nearly one full day to recompute the design only to discover that, sure enough, the engine inlet was 18 percent too big. In another instance, he looked at a design and said "the load here is 6.3 psi." After an

Figure 15-2
Project manager's sources of influence.

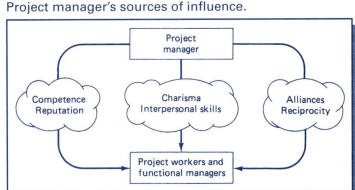

hour of complicated calculations, his people measured it as 6.2 psi. When he retired, Kelly Johnson was recognized as the preeminent aerodynamicist of his time.

As his successor, Kelly had chosen Ben Rich. Ben was the first to acknowledge that he didn't possess Kelly's genius and, therefore, would rely on his teams for most decisions. His first move was to loosen the reigns and allow the teams latitude to make most calls on their own. Ben was decisive in telling a team what he wanted, but he then let the members decide which methods and procedures to apply. He stuck to schmoozing and cheerleading through an endless supply of one-liners. As one employee put it, "Whereas Kelly ruled by his bad temper, Ben ruled by his bad jokes." Ben believed in using a nonthreatening approach. Whereas he didn't shirk from scolding deserving individuals, he preferred complimenting people and boosting morale. According to one colleague, Ben was the perfect manager: he was there to make the tough calls, defend and protect his project teams, obtain more money and new projects, and convince the government and senior management of the value of his teams' work.

Johnson and Rich led using different styles and different strengths, yet both have been acknowledged by the industry as exemplars of project managers. Kelly Johnson accomplished great things, despite his temperament, and most engineers considered it an honor to have worked with him. Competency and reputation were his strengths; people tolerated his personality. Ben Rich, no technical slouch, acknowledged that he had a few smarter people working for him. Unlike Kelly, however, he had charisma and many personal friends, and with that was able to accomplish amazing things, also.

The Balance of Power

Because project managers (with the sometime exception of the pure project managers) share authority with functional managers, what relative balance of power between them is optimal? Some theorists say that project and functional managers should share power equally. However, the concept of power has several dimensions, and according to some research not all of these dimensions should be balanced equally.[12] In the best performing projects, authority is clearly differentiated: Project managers are given the power to obtain top management backing to procure critical resources and coordinate work efforts, and to mediate conflicts; in contrast, functional managers are given power to make decisions over technical problems and the technology used.

Even in the usual circumstance where project managers do not have reward power, it is usually beneficial for them to be *perceived* by workers as having the same reward power as functional managers. Whether or not the perception is accurate, project personnel tend to follow the manager with the greatest perceived influence on salaries and promotions.

15.3 SELECTING THE PROJECT MANAGER

Four categories of qualifications can be listed for the successful project manager: personal characteristics, behavioral skills, general business skills, and technical skills.

Personal Characteristics

Archibald lists the following as essential personal characteristics.[13]

- Flexible and adaptable
- Preference for initiative and leadership
- Confidence, persuasiveness, verbal fluency
- Effective communicator and integrator

- Able to balance technical solutions with time, cost, and human factors
- Well-organized and disciplined
- A generalist rather than a specialist
- Able to devote most of his time to planning and controlling
- Able to identify problems and to make decisions
- Able to devote the time and effort and to maintain a proper balance in use of time

These characteristics are important because of the environment where the project manager works and the responsibilities and restrictions placed on the role. Obviously, project managers must be able to work in situations where there are constant deadlines, great uncertainty, start ups and close outs, and constant change in goals, tasks, people, and relationships. At the same time, they must be able to gain the respect, trust, and confidence of others.

Behavioral Skills

A project manager needs strong behavioral and interpersonal skills.[14] In particular, she must be an active listener, active communicator, and able to capitalize on informal communication channels. To be an active listener, a project manager must master the art of questioning for clarification and paraphrasing to ensure she understands verbal messages. She must know how to build trust, promote team spirit, and reward cooperation through praise and credit (often the only forms of reward she has). To be able to facilitate communication and integrate technical work she has to know the jargon of the specialists.

General Business Skills

The project manager is, after all, a *manager* and so should have general business skills also. These should include:

- Understanding of the organization and the business.
- Understanding of general management—marketing, control, contract work, purchasing, law, personal administration, and (in profit environments) the general concept of profitability.
- Ability to translate business requirements into project and system requirements.
- Strong, active, continuous interest in teaching, training, and developing subordinates.

Technical Skills

To make informed decisions, project managers must be able to grasp the technical aspects of the project. In non- or low-technology environments, understanding can be developed through experience and informal training. In high-technology projects, qualifications are more rigorous, usually including a career molded in the technology environment and a knowledge of many fields of science or engineering.[15]

Although project managers seldom do technical analysis, they must be technically qualified so as to formulate and make technical judgments. In a technical project, the project manager:

> must be capable of both integration and analysis, and must understand that the rigorous training of professional technologists with its emphasis on analysis sometimes impairs their integrative ability.[16]

To fulfill the management requirements for both technical and general business competence, projects sometimes utilize two managers—one technical and one administrative. This often happens in construction projects where the architect is responsible for technical matters while the so-called project manager handles administrative "paperwork." Having two managers tends to complicate problems of coordination, communication, and authority because both must share responsibility. Further, when the project manager becomes subservient to the architect, his ability to manage the project is compromised. This split also is common to the motion picture industry. The movie *producer* manages the resources, schedules, and budgets (in essence, the project manager), while the *director* oversees technical-artistic matters. Only occasionally are they the same person. Because the shooting of a motion picture is an artistic pursuit, directors need flexibility in budgets and shooting schedules, but costs matter too, and the producer faces the question "at what price creativity?" It comes as no surprise that the two do not always have an amicable relationship.[17] Still, the movie industry highly regards the role of the project manager. When an Academy Award is given for "Best Picture," it is awarded to the picture's producer.

Selection and Recruiting

Project managers are selected from among the ranks of product and functional managers, functional specialists, and experienced project managers. Though the last source is preferred, provided the chosen manager has a successful project record, it is often the least feasible. It is difficult to find an experienced project manager who has the right mix of qualifications and whose current project ends just before the new one begins. As a result, when experienced project managers are needed they often must be recruited from the outside. This is readily observable in the Sunday job listings of most major metropolitan newspapers (Figure 15-3 shows a sampling). One problem with recruiting outsiders is that it takes time for them to make friends, build alliances, and learn organizational procedures and policies. This problem is offset by benefits such as when the project needs an objective outsider to overhaul procedures, or when all of the inside candidates are seen as enemies.

The role of project manager is also filled by transferring or promoting functional managers. One problem with this is the difficulty some managers experience in shifting from a functional to a project perspective. A functional manager must adjust from exclusively working in one area to overseeing and integrating the work of many areas, a transition that requires considerable effort and inclination. Also, unless he has abundant, well-rounded experience he will likely be perceived by other managers as just another functional manager.

The project manager role also is filled by promoting nonmanagerial specialists (engineers, scientists, system analysts, product specialists, etc.). The problem with this is the same as with putting any nonmanager into a management role: He must first learn how to manage. Administrative and technical abilities are not the same, and just because a person is a good engineer or auditor does not mean he will be a good project manager. Besides learning how to manage, a specialist must learn how to remove himself from his area of specialty and become a generalist.

Ideally, the person selected as project manager can stay with the project for its duration and is someone for whom the assignment will not conflict with existing lines of authority or reporting relationships. It is a bad idea, for example, to put a functional specialist in a project management position that would give him authority over his former manager.

Figure 15-3
Advertisements for project management positions.

Training

Because project management skills cannot be learned quickly, organizations devote substantial time and expense in preparing individuals for careers in project management. Some sponsor internal training programs that focus on the special requirements of their organizations; others use external seminars and university programs. Recent years have seen a rapid proliferation in both kinds of training programs.

Still, there is no substitute for experience. Many organizations allow promising people who aspire to become project managers the benefit of on-the-job training.[18] As part of their career paths, technical specialists work full- or part-time as administrative assistants to experienced project managers—similar to serving an apprenticeship. In giving them such management exposure, their aptitude and talent for management can be tested. Valued specialists with little managerial aptitude or ability should be given other career opportunities commensurate with their skills and interests.

Example 3: On-the-Job Training of Project Managers[19]

Microsoft Corporation's approach to preparing project managers (which they term "program managers") is typical. There is neither an official training program for program managers nor any guidelines that spell out requirements for writing specs, scheduling projects, or making prototypes. Program managers can attend an optional, 3-week training session. Microsoft occasionally holds videotaped luncheons where managers present their experiences. The videotapes then may be circulated.

Program managers at Microsoft primarily learn the job by "doing." Microsoft carefully selects and mentors the right people, then expects them to learn on the job. For about 90 percent of program managers, training happens by pairing a new program manager with an experienced, successful program manager, whereas only 10 percent receive other, formal training.

Moving into the Role

Project management responsibilities range from few and mundane on simple projects to extensive and challenging on complex projects. Presumably, the person in the role of project manager is qualified and wants the responsibility; still, the burden of moving into the role can be eased if he has the following:[20]

- An understanding of what has to be done.
- An understanding of his authority and its limits.
- An understanding of his relationship with others in the project.
- Knowledge of the specific results that constitute a job well done.
- Knowledge of when and what he is doing exceptionally well, and when and where he is falling short.
- An awareness of what can and should be done to correct unsatisfactory results.
- The belief that his superiors have an interest and believe in him.
- The belief that his superiors are eager for him to succeed.

Not having these diminishes the project manager's effectiveness. Senior management must give the project manager the necessary assurances and information; ultimately, however, the project manager must solicit these and ensure their continuance throughout the project.

15.4 WAYS OF FILLING THE PROJECT MANAGEMENT ROLE

Organizations use various titles for the role of project manager including "program manager," "project director," "task force chairman," and others. The titles "task force coordinator" and "project engineer" also are used, though these usually imply more focused roles with less responsibility than other forms. The most effective project management role occurs when one person becomes involved during proposal preparation and stays on until the project is completed. When early in the project it is difficult to find someone available and competent enough to see the project through, the role is filled in other ways. For example, the role may be assigned to the general manager or plant manager, though these managers usually have neither the necessary time to devote to a project nor the flexibility to shift roles. Alternatively, the role may be assigned temporarily to a functional manager. Here, the consequence is that she must divide her time between the project and her department, whereby both may suffer. Also, these combination functional-project managers may have trouble gaining cooperation from other functional managers when they are seen as competitors for resources. In long-term projects, responsibility may pass from one functional manager to the next as the project progresses. The problem here is that the process lacks an oversight person who can ensure continuity from one phase to the next. Then managers at later stages inherit problems developed earlier.

Sometimes project responsibilities for scheduling, budgeting, marketing, technical performance, and so on are divided among several people. This is common practice in technological projects where, as mentioned earlier, responsibility is split between a technical project manager and an administrative project manager. The problem with this arrangement is in having two or more project management roles with no one to oversee and integrate *them.*

The project management role is optimally filled by one person, a full-time project manager, though it is okay if the manager manages multiple projects as long as the project management responsibilities of all of them are adequately fulfilled. This practice of one person managing multiple small projects can be advantageous because it puts the project manager in a position to resolve resource and priority conflicts between projects and to negotiate resources for several, simultaneous projects with functional managers.

15.5   ROLES IN THE PROJECT TEAM

In the early stages of a project, the project manager and functional managers divide the overall objective into work tasks. This division determines skill requirements and serves as the basis for personnel selection and subcontracting. Those who contribute to the project at any given time, such as people from functional support areas, contractors, and the project office, become part of the *project team.* This section describes roles and responsibilities of members of the project team.

Members Serving the Project Office

Chapter 14 described the purpose of the project office and its placement within the organization. This section focuses on specific roles of members of the project office. The example shown in Figure 15-4 is for an engineering-development project such as the one discussed in Chapter 14. In addition to the project manager and representatives from functional departments, the following other team members typically are included in the project office.

The *project engineer* shoulders responsibility for coordinating technological areas and assuring integrated design of the project end-item. The responsibility encompasses

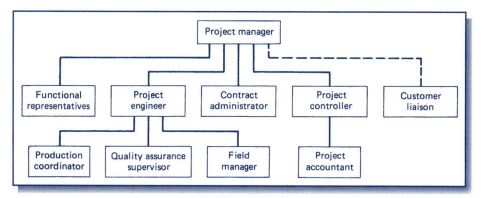

Figure 15-4
Members of the project office.

system analysis and engineering, design, interface control, system integration, and testing.[21] When several functional areas are involved, the project engineer

1. Oversees product or system design and development;
2. Translates performance requirements into design requirements;
3. Oversees communication, coordination, and direction of functional areas and subcontractors;
4. Plans, monitors, evaluates, and documents progress in design and test of subsystems; and
5. Plans, monitors, and evaluates system integration tests.

The project engineer also oversees configuration management, which means he is responsible for ensuring that activities for identifying, documenting, and controlling information related to system changes are uniform and systemic. Configuration management was discussed in Chapter 11.

The title, project engineer, sometimes denotes a person having full project manager responsibilities; commonly it refers to the more limited role described here.

The *contract administrator*[22] is responsible for project legal aspects such as authorization to begin work and subcontracting with outside firms. Contract administrators are involved in preparing the proposal, defining and negotiating the contract, integrating contract requirements into project plans, ensuring the project fulfills contractual obligations, identifying and defining changes to project scope, and communicating the completion of milestones to the customer. During closeout, they notify customers of fulfilled obligations, document customer acceptance of the end-item, and initiate formal requests for payment. They also are responsible for collecting and storing RFPs, project correspondence, legal documents, contract modifications, bills, payment vouchers, and other records and documents.

The *project controller*[23] assists the project manager in planning, controlling, reporting, and evaluation. She works with functional managers to define tasks and interrelationships on the work breakdown structure, as well as to identify individuals responsible for controlling tasks. She also maintains work package files and cost summaries, releases approved work authorization documents, monitors work progress, evaluates schedule and cost progress, and revises estimates of time and cost to complete the project. The project controller prepares and negotiates revisions to budgets, schedules, and work authorizations, drafts progress reports to users and upper management, and closes cost accounts upon completion.

The *project accountant* provides financial and accounting assistance to the project manager. He establishes procedures for utilizing the PMIS, assists in identifying tasks to be controlled, establishes cost accounts, prepares cost estimates for tasks, validates reported information, and investigates financial problems.

The *customer liaison* serves as the customer's or user's technical representative. She participates in technical discussions and ongoing reviews (within the bounds of the contract) and helps expedite contract changes. This role is important for helping maintain amicable contractor-customer relations.

The *production coordinator* plans, monitors, and coordinates production aspects of the project. Responsibilities include reviewing engineering documents released to manufacturing; developing requirements for releases, equipment, and parts; monitoring procurement and assembly of parts, materials, and processes for the end-item; monitoring manufacturing costs; developing schedules for production related activities; and serving as liaison between project management and the production department.

The *field manager* oversees installation, testing, maintenance, and handing over of the project end-item to the customer. Responsibilities include scheduling field operations, monitoring field operations costs, supervision of field personnel, and liaison with the project manager.

The *quality assurance supervisor* establishes and administers inspection procedures to ensure fulfillment of all quality-related requirements. Overall, his responsibilities encompass raising awareness of quality and instituting means for improving work methods and producing zero defects.

The project office also has *representatives* from participating functional departments and subcontractors. These people work with the project manager and others in the project office to coordinate their activities with other project team members.

Members of the office charge their work time to the project or to an overhead account. They are assigned to the office only when they must be in frequent contact with the project manager or other project office personnel, or when their services are required continuously and for an extended period. As soon as they complete their tasks, they return to their functional departments.

The project manager should try to keep the office staff small. This increases the flexibility of functional staffing to the project, minimizes duplication of personnel costs and reassignment problems, and requires less effort from the project manager. Members of the office staff contribute as needed, full- or part-time, and might be physically located in different places.

Functional Managers

Often the glamour of the work sits on the project side, and functional managers see their roles diminished. If earlier discussions have led to the impression that functional managers are somehow subservient to the project manager, that was not the intention. Both functional and project organizations depend on each other to achieve project goals. Functional managers are responsible for maintaining technical competency in their disciplines and for staffing, organizing, and executing project tasks *within their functional areas.* Together with the project manager they define tasks and develop plans, schedules, and budgets for each work package.

Because personnel in project organizations shift from one project to another, permanence may be found only in a functional "home." Unlike the project manager who tends to solicit "human resources" solely in terms of what is best for her project, a functional manager more likely looks out for the interests of the people being solicited. The functional manager is responsible for the hiring, performance reviews, compensation, professional development, and career paths of the people in his area.

In most project organizations, functional managers retain much of the same authority and responsibility as in nonproject environments. Nevertheless, some functional managers believe that the project manager undercuts their authority and that they could handle the project better if it were exclusively within their domain. Project managers who try to establish empires, undermine the authority, or otherwise confirm the suspicions of captious functional managers will have difficulty obtaining the functional support they need.

It is important that the technical role of the functional manager in project organizations not be diminished. Before a project begins, the technical responsibilities and contributions to technical content should be clearly delineated and defined for each functional manager.[24] This ensures a continued strong technical base for all projects and alleviates much of the potential animosity between functional and project managers.

Project Functional Leaders and Work Package Supervisors

In large projects each functional manager (sometimes with input from the project manager) selects someone as *project functional leader.* This person serves as the liaison between the project manager and the functional manager. This person works with the project manager, prepares his department's portion of the total project plan, and supervises project work performed by the department.

In still larger projects, the work for a project in a given department is divided into multiple, clearly defined tasks or work packages. Responsibility for each work package is delegated to a *work package supervisor* who reports to the functional leader. The work package supervisor prepares the plan, schedule, and budget for the work package, supervises the technical effort, and reports progress.

15.6   ROLES OUTSIDE THE PROJECT TEAM

Individuals and groups outside the project team can significantly influence a project's success or doom it to failure. This section discusses individuals and groups outside the immediate project team who influence the management of the project, the available resources, and project constraints (Figure 15-5). One important such role that will not be discussed in this section is that of the customer, or user. The influence and involvement of the customer or user throughout the project life cycle is covered elsewhere throughout the book, especially in chapters 4 and 5.

The Manager of Projects

The *manager of projects* (called the vice president of projects, director of projects, or other title) is positioned in the hierarchy at the same level as functional executives (refer to Figure 14-8). The manager of projects oversees multiple projects and relieves top level managers of most project related responsibilities. The manager of projects[25]

- Directs and evaluates the activities of all project managers.
- Ensures that the stream of projects is consistent with the strategic objectives of the organization.
- Works with functional heads to allocate resources and resolve priority conflicts between projects.

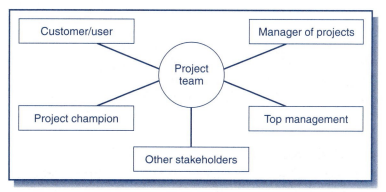

Figure 15-5
Roles outside the project team.

- Assists in development of project management policies and planning and control techniques and systems.
- Ensures consistency among projects and that any project changes are integrated with the cost, schedule, and performance objectives of the others.

In matrix organizations, the manager of projects also serves as liaison between the office of projects and top management.

Top Management

Top management ensures that projects are consistent with organizational goals and makes all final evaluations and approvals. In addition, it approves the project feasibility study, selects the project manager, and authorizes the project to begin. Top management is responsible for successful implementation of project management. For project management to be effective, top management must first[26]

- Clearly define the project manager's responsibility and authority relative to other managers.
- Define the scope and limitations on the project manager's decision making responsibilities.
- Establish policies for resolving conflicts and setting priorities.
- Prescribe the objectives against which the project manager's performance will be evaluated.
- Plan and give support to a project management system that provides information necessary for planning, control, review, and evaluation of projects.

Project managers exercise the authority granted by, and on behalf of, the senior executive or manager of projects, as stated in the organization charter. In complex situations, critical negotiations, or unresolvable conflict, top management may preempt the authority of the project manager.

Project Champion

An important role that can ultimately alter the fate of the project is that of the *project champion.* The champion is someone from outside the project team who has organizational clout and will work to ensure the project continues to get the priority and resources needed to do the job. The champion must firmly believe in the project and be willing to argue for its support, both at its start, and thereafter, as difficulties are encountered. Because the person in the champion role must have considerable formal power, she is usually in high-level management, which means she probably can't devote much time to the project. Nonetheless, the champion must be readily accessible to the project manager and readily willing to rally support whenever the project manager requests help. If the project does not already have a champion, the project manager might have to put on his evangelist hat and go scouting for one.

Other Project Stakeholders

Any group or individual that is affected by or has potential influence over the outcome of a project is a *project stakeholder.* Usually, no one associated with the project will know all the stakeholders, although some stakeholders might actively work to delay or kill it. Such stakeholders might be managers of areas that compete with the project for resources, representatives from outside environmental or political interest groups or lobbies, or anyone who perceives they have something to lose if the project goes through or win if the project is stopped. The project manager should learn who the important stakeholders are and their interests. Knowing this, she might be able to entice their support, or alter aspects of the project or its end-item to reduce their resistance.

15.7 RELATIONSHIPS AMONG PROJECT AND FUNCTIONAL ROLES

Clearly no project manager works in a vacuum. Perhaps in more than any other managerial position, the project managers' authority and responsibilities are defined by their relationships with other roles. Because the role involves multiple interfaces and has a disparity between responsibility and authority, relationships in project management are neither simple nor self-explanatory.

For example, if misunderstood or neglected, the project-functional interface can easily result in competition for resources and conflict in reporting relationships. To minimize problems and conflicts, functional and project managers should jointly participate in preparing policies that define their authority/responsibility relationships. The roles, responsibilities, and relationships in the project can then be summarized, as shown in Figure 15-6.[27] The numerous subdivision of roles and responsibilities shown in the example are for a large project; in smaller projects the relationships would be similar, but with less delegation and fewer roles. In small projects, functional managers *are* the project-functional interface and take on the responsibilities of project-functional leaders and work package supervisors.

15.8 SUMMARY

Central to project management is the role of project manager. Project managers work at the project-functional-user interface, integrating project elements to achieve time, cost, and performance objectives. They have ultimate responsibility for the success of the projects.

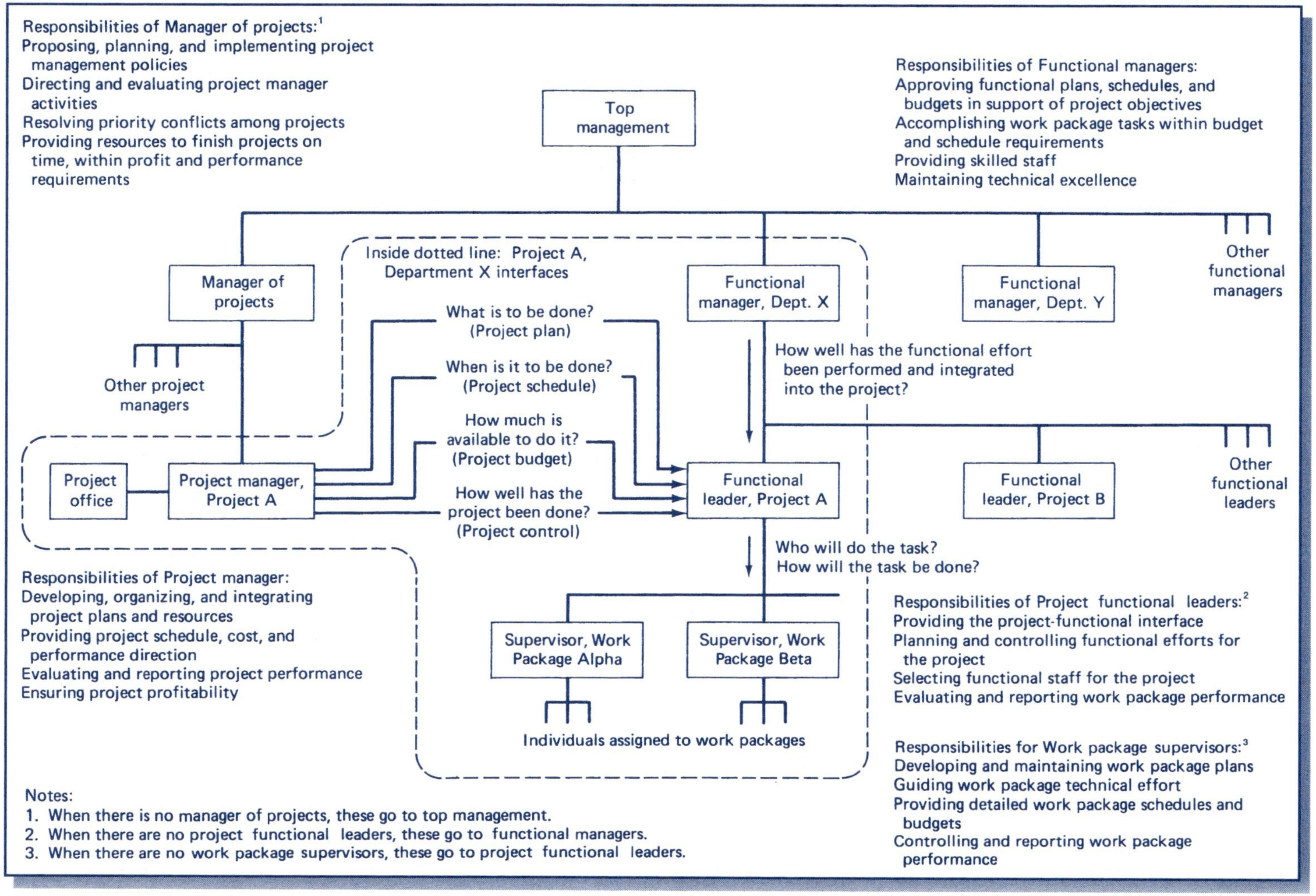

Responsibilities of Manager of projects:[1]
Proposing, planning, and implementing project management policies
Directing and evaluating project manager activities
Resolving priority conflicts among projects
Providing resources to finish projects on time, within profit and performance requirements
Top management
Responsibilities of Functional managers:
Approving functional plans, schedules, and budgets in support of project objectives
Accomplishing work package tasks within budget and schedule requirements
Providing skilled staff
Maintaining technical excellence
Manager of projects
Other project managers
Inside dotted line: Project A, Department X interfaces
What is to be done? (Project plan)
When is it to be done? (Project schedule)
How much is available to do it? (Project budget)
How well has the project been done? (Project control)
Functional manager, Dept. X
Functional manager, Dept. Y
Other functional managers
How well has the functional effort been performed and integrated into the project?
Project office
Project manager, Project A
Functional leader, Project A
Functional leader, Project B
Other functional leaders
Who will do the task?
How will the task be done?
Responsibilities of Project manager:
Developing, organizing, and integrating project plans and resources
Providing project schedule, cost, and performance direction
Evaluating and reporting project performance
Ensuring project profitability
Supervisor, Work Package Alpha
Supervisor, Work Package Beta
Individuals assigned to work packages
Responsibilities of Project functional leaders:[2]
Providing the project-functional interface
Planning and controlling functional efforts for the project
Selecting functional staff for the project
Evaluating and reporting work package performance
Responsibilities for Work package supervisors:[3]
Developing and maintaining work package plans
Guiding work package technical effort
Providing detailed work package schedules and budgets
Controlling and reporting work package performance
Notes:
1. When there is no manager of projects, these go to top management.
2. When there are no project functional leaders, these go to functional managers.
3. When there are no work package supervisors, these go to project functional leaders.

Figure 15-6
Summary of managerial roles, responsibilities, and interrelationships in project management. [Adapted with permission from David Cleland and William King, *Systems Analysis and Project Management,* 3d ed. (New York: McGraw-Hill, 1983]: 332, 353.]

Despite their pivotal role, most project managers function outside the traditional hierarchy and have little formal authority. To achieve project objectives, they tend to rely heavily upon negotiations, alliances, favors, and reciprocal agreements. Their strongest source of influence is the respect they gain through skillful and competent administration.

Project managers have influence over matters concerning critical resources and organizational support. Successful project managers are perceived as both technically and administratively competent. They have a strong business orientation as well as an understanding of the technology employed in the project. They also have strong behavioral skills and are able to function effectively in risky, changing environments.

The role of project manager is best filled by one person who becomes involved at proposal preparation and stays on until the project has been completed. Sharing or rotating the role among several people is usually less effective.

Project managers get work done through a team composed of people from various functional and support groups scattered throughout the parent company, as well as from outside subcontractors. The project office provides administrative assistance and services. Functional managers contribute primarily to the technical content of the project and also share responsibility for developing tasks, plans, schedules, and budgets for work required in their areas. They maintain the technical base upon which projects draw.

Top management, the manager of projects, and the project champion also play key roles in project management. Top management establishes the policies, responsibilities, and authority relationships through which project management is conducted. The manager of projects ensures that projects are consistent with organization goals and resolves priority and resource conflicts between multiple projects. The champion is a person with organizational clout who supports the project and works to get it the necessary priority and resources.

Many people find project work challenging, rewarding, and exhilarating; but without question, many also find it taxing, distressful, and even destructive. To increase the chances of project success—and to minimize human casualties along the way—a project manager must have the necessary behavioral skills for effectively dealing with groups and individuals. These skills include being able to assemble disparate individuals and groups into a single, cohesive team, and to recognize and handle effectively personal problems with work conflicts and emotional stress. These skills are covered in the next chapter.

REVIEW QUESTIONS

1. What is the project manager's primary role?
2. What is meant by "the project manager is an evangelist, entrepreneur, and change agent?"
3. Does the project manager's resistance to change contradict her roles as a change agent?
4. Describe the typical responsibilities of a project manager. In what ways are responsibilities such as budgeting, scheduling, and controlling considered as integration and coordination responsibilities?
5. Discuss the relative need for both technical and managerial competence in project management.
6. Why is a broad background essential for the project manager? What *is* a broad background?
7. Describe what is meant by legal authority. How does it differ from charismatic authority?

8. Describe how and in what ways people in organizations, regardless of hierarchical position, influence others.
9. How does the authority of the typical project manager differ from authority of other managers?
10. What is meant by the "authority gap?"
11. What is the most frequently used source of influence among project manages? How does the project manager use this and other sources of influence to induce functional managers to release their personnel to the project?
12. List the ideal qualifications—personal, behavioral, technical—for project managers. How do they differ from the qualifications for functional managers? How do these vary depending on the project?
13. Discuss the considerations in selecting a project manager from among each of the following groups: experienced project managers, functional managers, functional specialists.
14. Discuss the pros and cons in the various ways of filling the role of project manager (e.g., part-time, multiple project managers for one project, one manager for multiple projects, etc.).
15. How are project managers trained on the job? What are the advantages and drawbacks of relying upon on-the-job training as a source for project managers?
16. Describe the responsibilities of key members of the project office for a large-scale project.
17. Describe the responsibilities of the manager of projects.
18. Describe the project related responsibilities of top management.
19. Describe the responsibilities of the functional manager, the project leader, and the work-package supervisor in project management as well as their interfaces with one another and with the project manager.
20. Who is the project champion, and who are the stakeholders? What influence do they have on a project?

QUESTIONS ABOUT THE STUDY PROJECT

1. In your project, what is the formal title given to the role of project manager?
2. Where in the organization structure is the project manager? Show this on an organization chart.
3. Describe in one sentence the overall role for the project manager of your project. Now, list his or her *specific* responsibilities.
4. In your opinion, is the so-called project manager the *real* project manager or is someone else controlling the project? If the latter, what effect does this have on the project manager's ability to influence the project?
5. Would you describe the project manager's orientation as being more technical or more managerial? Explain.
6. Describe the project manager's professional background. Has it helped or hindered his or her ability to be a project manager? (You might pose this question to the project manager.)
7. Describe the kind of authority given to the project manager. (How much legal authority and reward power does the project manager have?) How does he or she know this; is his or her authority specified in the organization charter, the job description, or elsewhere?
8. How big would you say is the project manager's authority gap? Explain. Does the project manager have any complaints about it?

9. From where does this organization get its project managers? Does it have a procedure or seminars for training and selecting project managers? Where did the manager of your project come from?

10. How does this project manager fill the role: part- or full-time, shared or rotated with other managers, manager of several projects at once? Explain. Does the project manager have enough time to do an effective job? Would another way of filling the position be more effective?

11. Is there a project office? If not, how are the responsibilities (e.g., for contract administration) handled? If so, who is in the project office (a project engineer, contract administrator, field representative, etc.)? Are they on loan, full-time, or part-time? Describe their responsibilities.

12. What functional managers are involved in this project? Describe their responsibilities in the project, decisions they make unilaterally, and decisions they share with the project manager.

13. Is there a manager of projects? A project champion? If so, describe his or her responsibilities and influence on this particular project.

14. What has been the role of top management in your project? What, in general, is the involvement of top management in projects in this organization?

Case 15-1   The LOGON Project

Top management of the Iron Butterfly Company has decided to adopt a project-management form of organization for the LOGON project. As a consultant to top management you have been given two tasks to help implement this. First, you must develop a project management policy statement and a project manager job description. Your policy statement should define the project manager's role with respect to other functional managers, as well as clarify the role of functional managers in the project. Your job description must define the specific responsibilities and legal authority of the project manager. You should consider the reactions of functional managers to the policy statement and job description and how best to get them to "buy in." How can you give the project manager sufficient authority to manage the LOGON project without usurping the authority of other managers who must give their support (many of whom have been with the Iron Butterfly Company for over 20 years)? You should also suggest to top management what forms of evaluation can be used

on project team members as an incentive to work together toward project goals. Remember, the functional departments are also currently involved in repetitive tasks and other project activities.

Your second task is to specify and document the qualifications for the position of LOGON project manager. After considering the nature of the project (technical scope, risks, complexity, etc.) as described in the previous chapter, prepare a list of specific qualifications—general background and experience, personality characteristics, managerial, technical, and interpersonal skills—to be used to screen candidates and make the final selection. Iron Butterfly has some employees who have worked as project coordinators and expediters, but no one with experience as a pure project or matrix manager. Consider the assumptions and pros and cons of selecting a functional manager or technical specialist from inside Iron Butterfly or an experienced project manager from outside the company. A contract has been signed and LOGON is to begin in 4 months.

Case 15-2   Selecting a Project Manager at Nuwave Products Company

Nuwave Products Company is a medium-sized firm that manufactures a variety of small motors and motor parts. Nuwave recently contracted with a major software engineering firm, Manengco, to design software for a new manufacturing process to be installed at some time in the near future. The software design is part of a larger project that also involves procurement and installation of computer systems and new manufacturing equipment, and retraining of workers. The new manufacturing process will involve "lean production" concepts, which are very different from Nuwave's current processes. Some portions of the process will be highly automated, others not. Software for the new process will integrate information from the sales and finance departments with information from the manufacturing department and suppliers to create production schedules and purchase orders.

Ordinarily the manufacturing department assigns a project manager to projects that involve new processes. However, no one in the department has had experience with either a project of this scope, with the software and hardware equipment to be implemented, or with lean production concepts. The president of Nuwave thinks that in addition to designing the software, Manengco should oversee the entire project, including equipment procurement and installation and worker training. In contrast, the manufacturing department manager thinks that one of his senior engineers, Roberta Withers, could handle the project. She has a thorough knowledge of Nuwave's current manufacturing processes and experience in manufacturing machine design. Also, she is considered the department's expert in mechanical systems. Ms. Withers has a degree in mechanical engineering and has been with Nuwave for 6 years in the manufacturing department. Her boss thinks that the project would be a good opportunity for Roberta to learn about concepts such as lean production and computer integrated manufacturing systems.

QUESTIONS

1. Assume that you must act on the information available in the case. If it was your choice, who would you select to manage the project: Manengco, Roberta, or someone else? Explain.

2. If you could get more information before making a choice, what would you want to know?

ENDNOTES

1. L. R. Sayles and M. K. Chandler, *Managing Large Systems: Organizations for the Future* (New York: Harper & Row, 1971): 204.
2. Ibid., 212.
3. Ibid., 204.
4. Portions adapted from Rex Alan Smith, *The Carving of Mount Rushmore* (New York: Abbeville Press, 1985).
5. Ibid., 17–18.
6. Ibid., 164.
7. Russell Archibald, *Managing High-Technology Programs and Projects* (New York: Wiley-Interscience, 1976): 35; William Atkins, "Selecting a Project Manager," *Journal of Systems Management* (October 1980): 34; and Daniel Roman, *Managing Projects: A Systems Approach* (New York: Elsevier, 1986): 419.
8. Paul Lawrence and Jay Lorsch, *Organization and Environment: Managing Differentiation and Integration* (Boston: Graduate School of Business, Harvard University, 1967): Chap. III.
9. These bases of interpersonal power were first described by J. P. R. French and B. Raven, "The Bases of Social Power," reprinted in *Group Dynamics*, 3d ed., D. Cartwright and A. Zander, eds. (New York: Harper & Row, 1968): 259–69.
10. Richard Hodgetts, "Leadership Techniques in the Project Organization," *Academy of Management Journal*, 11 (June 1968): 211–19.
11. Ben Rich and Leo Janos, *Skunk Works* (Boston: Little, Brown & Co, 1994).
12. R. Katz and T. J. Allen, "Project Performance and the Locus of Influence in the R&D Matrix," *Academy of Management Journal* 28, no. 1 (March 1985): 67–87.
13. Archibald, *Managing High-Technology Programs*, 55.
14. J. R. Adams, S. E. Barndt, and M. D. Martin, *Managing by Project Management* (Dayton: Universal Technology, 1979): 137.
15. P. O. Gaddis, "The Project Manager," *Harvard Business Review* (May–June 1959): 89–97.
16. Ibid., 95.
17. An example is the 1984 movie *Heaven's Gate* where the director was allowed to virtually dominate the movie's producers. Originally scheduled for completion in 6 months at a cost

of $7.5 million, the production ended up being released a year late and $28 million *over* budget. The movie was a box office flop and helped clinch the demise of United Artists Corp. which had to underwrite the expense. From Steven Bach, *Final Cut* (New York: William Morrow, 1985).

18. Roman, *Managing Projects,* 439–40.

19. Michael Cusumano and Richard Selby, *Microsoft Secrets* (New York: Free Press, 1995): 105–06.

20. Harold Kerzner, *Project Management: A Systems Approach to Planning, Scheduling, and Controlling* (New York: Van Nostrand Reinhold, 1979): 99.

21. These responsibilities are for project engineers in engineering-development projects, as de-scribed in W. P. Chase, *Management of Systems Engineering* (New York: Wiley-Interscience, 1974): 25–29.

22. According to Archibald, *Managing High-Technology Programs,* 124–28, 199.

23. Ibid., 128–31.

24. Katz and Allen, "Project Performance and the Locus of Influence," 83–84.

25. David Cleland and William King, *Systems Analysis and Project Management,* 3d ed. (New York: McGraw-Hill, 1983): 358.

26. Ibid., 362–63.

27. Ibid., 332, 353.

Managing Participation, Teamwork, and Conflict

> *Eh! je suis leur chef, il fallait bien les suivre.*
> *Ah well! I am their leader, I really ought to follow them!*
>
> —ALEXANDRE AUGUSTE LEDRU-ROLLIN,
> *1857*

> *A leader is best when people barely know that he exists.*
> *Of a good leader, who talks little, when his work is done,*
> *his aims fulfilled, they will say, "We did this ourselves."*
>
> —LAO-TZU,
> *The Way of Life*

> *Kenka ryosei bai.*
> *In a quarrel, both sides are at fault.*
>
> —*Japanese proverb*

During the manned landings on the moon, a study was conducted of NASA project management by researcher Richard Chapman.[1] This was during NASA's heyday—a period marked by extraordinary achievements and a time when NASA was upheld as an example of a large agency that worked, and worked well. It is interesting and instructive to begin this chapter with a few of Chapman's comments about the project managers of that era:

[In addition to technical competence and management capacity] all agree that the project manager must have the ability . . . to build a cohesive project team. (p. 93)

Those project managers who [developed the most closely-knit project teams emphasized] decentralized decision making [and] technical problem-solving at the level where both the problem and most experience reside. [They encouraged project members] to feel a sense of responsibility for problem-solving at their respective levels, within the assigned guidelines . . . (p. 83)

Most project staffs believe that they receive generous support and attention from the project manager. Most also acknowledge that the project manager is vigorous and fair in bestowing recognition on team members and in rewarding them to the best of his capability. (p. 82)

In another study of NASA, E. H. Kloman compared the performance of two large projects, Lunar Orbiter and Surveyor. Lunar Orbiter was a success and fulfilled objectives within time and resource limits; Surveyor was not as successful and experienced cost escalation and schedule delays. The study characterized Lunar Orbiter's customer/contractor organizations as being tightly knit *cohesive* units, with good *teamwork* and mutual *respect* and *trust* for their project counterparts. In contrast, teamwork in Surveyor was characterized as "slow and fitful" to grow and "spurred by a sense of anxiety and concern."[2] Kloman concluded:

What emerges perhaps most forcefully from a broad retrospective view is the importance of the human aspects of organization and management. Both projects demonstrated the critical nature of human skills, interpersonal relations, compatibility between individual managers, and teamwork. (p. 39)

These remarks are the crux of this chapter: Behavioral issues such as decentralized decision making, interpersonal skills, supervisory support, and teamwork are important factors in effective project management. It is unfortunate that such issues are often overlooked in project practice, or given short shrift in project management education, largely because inexperienced managers and specialists in the "hard" disciplines (technicians, engineers, and businesspeople) see them as "soft" issues of little consequence and with no precise answers. However, in reality these issues are not soft. They are as hard as nails. As experienced managers know, they often have a profound effect on project performance and success.

This chapter discusses issues broached by the two studies cited previously: participative decision making, teamwork, conflict resolution, and the related matter of emotional stress in work. Behavioral scientists have been investigating practical methods for building cohesive teams, resolving interpersonal and intergroup conflict, and managing stress for many years. We will review the methods most relevant to project environments.

16.1 LEADERSHIP IN PROJECT MANAGEMENT

Leadership Style

Chapter 14 described a variety of organizational forms apropos for different purposes and types of work. Likewise, there are a variety of suitable leadership styles depending on the situation. Leadership is the ability to influence the behavior of others to accomplish what is desired; *leadership style* is the way in which a leader achieves that influence.

Leadership style can generally be divided between the two extreme approaches of *task-oriented* and *relations-oriented*. Task-oriented leaders show higher concern for the goal and the work and tend to behave in a more autocratic fashion. Relations-oriented managers show greater concern for people and tend to exercise a more democratic leadership style.

Numerous studies have been directed at discerning the most appropriate or effective leadership style. Most management theorists agree that no one leadership style is best for all situations. Effective style depends upon characteristics of the leader, the followers, the leader's interpersonal relationship with followers, and the nature and environment of the task. This perspective is called the *contingency approach* or *situational approach* to leadership. There are many different contingency models; all suggest that the leader should use the style that best fits the work situation and try not to apply the same style to all employees and situations. Brief mention will be made of two of these—those of Fred Fiedler and Hersey and Blanchard.

Contingency and Situational Approaches

According to Fiedler,[3] the three variables that most affect a leader's influence are whether (1) the work group accepts or rejects the leader, (2) the task is relatively routine or complex, and (3) the leader has high or low formal authority. Although the project manager might encounter any of these situations, the most common one (as described in the previous chapters) is likely to be:

- He has relatively low formal authority.
- He gets along with team members and is respected for his ability and expertise.
- The task is relatively complex and requires a good deal of judgment or creativity.

Fiedler's research indicates that under these three conditions a *relations-oriented* style is the most effective. The most prominent behavior in this style is the leader's positive emotional ties with and concern for subordinates.

Hersey and Blanchard[4] use a model called *situational leadership* that weighs the interplay of three variables: (1) the amount of direction and guidance a leader gives (task behavior), (2) the amount of socio-emotional support he gives (relations behavior), and (3) the readiness of followers to perform the task (maturity). The last variable, "maturity," has two aspects: the person's *skill or ability* to do something and the person's *motivation or willingness* to do something. According to the model the most effective leader behavior depends upon the maturity level of the followers. Project managers seldom manage shop-floor people. Usually they deal with technical specialists, staff personnel, managers, and other highly trained people. Thus, they tend to work with people who are either (1) able but perhaps unwilling to do what the manager wants, or (2) both able and willing to do what he wants. For Group (1) the model suggests a *participating* style as more effective. The thrust of a participative leadership style is toward facilitating, supporting, and communicating with followers. Both managers and followers share decision making.

For Group (2), the model suggests a delegating style as more effective. The manager identifies the problem or goal and gives the followers responsibility for carrying out the task. Followers are permitted to solve the problem and determine how, where, and when to do the task.

In their research on managing scientific and technical personnel, Hersey and Blanchard found that people with high levels of education and experience responded better to participating and delegating management. They also found that the same people did *not* respond well to high levels of task behavior and supervision, though sometimes they did need socio-emotional support.[5]

Of course, this is not to say that project managers never face workers who are unwilling to follow instructions or will not take initiative. In cases where delegation or diplomacy fail, a project manager with legal authority may resort to using it. Like other managers, he must occasionally cajole, give orders, and fire people to get the job done.

Project Circumstances

Effective leadership style also depends on project circumstances, especially project length and intensity. For example, a less participative, more directive style may be more appropriate when there is less time to complete the work. Thus, the work *pace* sometimes constrains the available leadership options, and in situations where there is high intensity and involvement, these incentives may act as "substitutes for leadership." People generally find it difficult to build trust and confidence when a job needs to be completed in only a few days, especially so for a job involving subcontractors, where no more than an arms-length association may exist, or where the workforce is transient and unfamiliar. In such situations the project manager may need to be more directive and assertive.[6] As with other aspects of the project manager's role, he must be adaptable—able to wear many leadership-style hats and to change them quickly.

16.2   PARTICIPATIVE MANAGEMENT

The models of both Fiedler and Hersey and Blanchard offer similar conclusions about project management situations—that the most effective leadership style for project managers is a relations-oriented style, for example, supportive, facilitative, and encouraging. As mentioned, this does not mean that project managers must never use high task behavior or tell people what to do; rather, in *most* project management situations, high relations behavior works best, even when combined with high task behavior.

This conclusion is further supported by Sayles and Chandler who reported that in large aerospace projects the preferred style of leadership is *participative management*. They observed that project managers seldom give orders to the individuals they influence, partly because most of these individuals are not subordinate to the project manager, and also because giving orders induces a "no, we won't do it" reaction. Project managers use participating management because they deal with specialists and other managers who *must* share in the decision making. Although project managers have a purview of the total system, they are farther removed from problems than the specialists and do not always know the answers to technical questions.[7]

Motivation

Project work may be stimulating, satisfying, and provide a great sense of achievement. A constant pressure to meet project goals motivates many people. Elements inherent to project management systems—contractual agreements, work breakdown structures, responsibility matrixes, and work package orders—also may be motivators. These elements provide clear goals which, when combined with financial and career rewards, motivate people in the same way as the management-by-objective approach.

But in project work there are many de-motivators, also. Too much pressure leads to stress, tension, and conflict. On large jobs individuals can lose sight of the end-item and feel alienated. Formal mechanisms of control also can be threatening. One advantage of participative decision making is that it helps overcome many potential de-motivators in projects by stimulating workers' commitment to project decisions.

Participative project managers do not relinquish responsibility, they delegate it. Even when they have legal authority, effective project managers involve others by, for example, acquainting them with problems, consulting them for their opinions, and giving them frequent feedback. Knowledgeable workers are allowed to help prepare project plans and budgets. In providing such assistance, they can appreciate how and where their work fits in; this encourages closer association with the project and greater dedication to its success. As stated earlier, people and situations vary, so the project manager must determine how much responsibility individual workers can be given and how much they have to be monitored and directed.

Management Development

Most project managers use a great deal of human-relations skills to influence actions. They work hard at being supportive, involving others in decision making, and at not being dogmatic or impatient. In projects where high potential for conflict exists, project managers need to develop good personal relationships, especially during the early phases of the project when patterns are set. To do this they have to invest considerable emotional energy in their work, be open with people, and work hard at trusting and gaining the trust of others.

Simply telling people to shift from traditional management style (high task-oriented) to project management style (high relations *and* task-oriented) is not enough. Especially in matrix organizations, unless project managers and workers receive support in adjusting to relations-oriented leadership, there is a great likelihood of failure; left alone, patterns of behavior develop naturally that can destroy participation, trust, and cooperation.[8] A planned process of individual and group development—team building and training in interpersonal skills—often is necessary to help managers and subordinates make the transition.

In the words of Bennis and Nanus, the most effective leaders are able to "align" the energies of people and groups behind the goal. They lead by "pulling rather than by pushing; by inspiring rather than by ordering"; and by creating achievable, challenging expectations and rewarding progress toward them rather than by manipulating.[9] The ample evidence, both anecdotal and empirical, is that the most effective project managers are strong leaders who utilize management.

16.3 TEAMS IN PROJECT MANAGEMENT

All project organizations, whether they be task forces, pure projects, or matrices, are comprised of groups. As Figure 16-1 illustrates, in a large project some groups comprise people from within one organization (the project office, middle level management, and functional and multifunctional work package teams), while others comprise multiple organizations (cross-organizational project management and functional groups, and so on). In many of these groups membership overlaps and people serve dual roles that link the groups together.

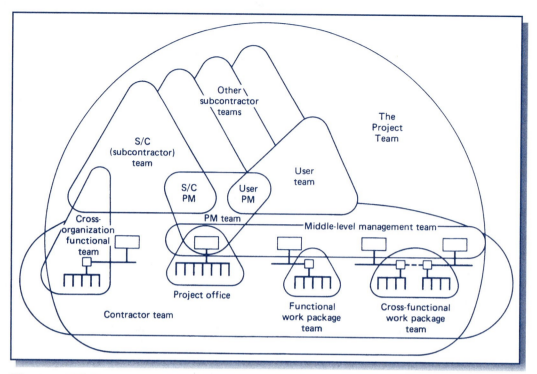

Figure 16-1
Groups comprising the project team.

The term *project team* as used here can refer to any particular group working in the project or to all groups in combination. Thus, virtually all work accomplished in a project, whether decisions or goods, is the product of teams. To be successful, however, a project needs more than teams. It needs *teamwork*.

The Trouble with Teams

Failures in projects often can be traced to the inability of a team to make the right decisions or perform the right tasks. These failures often stem from the maladies that teams suffer: internal conflict, member anxiety and frustration; time wasted on irrelevant issues; and decisions made haphazardly by senior people, by coalitions, or by default. Team members often are more concerned with getting the task *done* than with doing it *right*. Many teams never know what their *purpose* is, so they never know when, or if, they have achieved it.

In projects with multiple teams, each one might have different attitudes, orientation, and goals. Some teams might be physically isolated and maintain separate offices, creating and reinforcing separating boundaries. Or teams might develop an "us versus them" attitude leading to intergroup competition, resentment, and conflict. These occurrences make for a portentous project environment and bode ill for project success.

High Performing Teams

In contrast, successful projects are the result of the efforts of *effective* teams, those that succeed in achieving what they set out to do. Effective teams in projects mean that individuals and groups work together as a single cohesive unit.

What makes a team effective? Peter Vaill has studied a large number of effective teams, teams which "perform at levels of excellence far beyond those of comparable systems."[10] The prominent feature he found for all of them is that effective teams know their goals and commit to them. Members are never confused about why the team exists or what their individual roles are. Leaders inculcate belief in the team's purpose, transforming doubts, and embodying a team spirit. He also found that

- Commitment to the purpose of the system is never perfunctory and motivation is always high.
- Teamwork is focused on the task. Distinctions between task and process functions dissolve. Members develop behaviors that enable them to do what they must.
- Leadership is strong, clear, and never ambivalent. Leaders are reliable and predictable, regardless of style.
- The system is clearly separated from other systems; members have a consciousness that "we are different."

Vaill found three characteristics *always* present in the behavior and attitudes of leaders and members of high performing systems. He calls them *time, feeling, and focus.*

First, leaders and members devote extraordinary amounts of time to the task. They work at home, in the office, in taxicabs—anywhere. They fully commit themselves for the duration of the project. Second, they have very strong feelings about the attainment of the goal. They care deeply about the team's purpose, structure, history, future, and the people in it. And third, they focus on key issues; they have a clear list of priorities in mind. In high-performing teams, time, feeling, and focus are always found together.

Vaill encourages would-be leaders to "Seek constantly to do what is right and what is needed in the system (focus). Do it in terms of your energy (time). Put your whole psyche into it (feeling)."[11]

High-performing systems function as a whole. Everyone devotes lots of time, intensely values the system and its purpose, and is clear about priorities. Successful project organizations are high-performing systems. For project managers, Vaill's findings underscore the importance of clear definition of project objectives, clarification of the roles and tasks of team members, strong commitment to achieving objectives, strong project leadership, and a "project spirit" that bonds everyone together.

Example 1: Time, Feeling, and Focus in Project Management: Renovating the Statue of Liberty

The renovation of the Statue of Liberty is a good example of the kind of commitment and effort required for successfully managing a large-scale project.[12] Over 25 firms submitted proposals for the task of leading the team of 500 engineers, architects, artisans, and craftsmen who would do the renovation. Selected for the job was the small construction management firm of Lehrer/McGovern, Inc.

As Hofer describes the firm's partners: Lehrer is soft-spoken and generally conservative in appearance; McGovern clean-shaves his head, has a handlebar mustache, and wears cowboy boots. Despite differences in appearance, the two share similar goals and broad experience as civil engineers and construction managers.[13]

Did they devote a lot of time to the project? To coordinate the more than 50 businesses doing the job, Lehrer and McGovern worked as many as 16 hours each day. As managers they handled everything from helping architects and craftsmen implement plans, to making arrangements with subcontractors and ensuring that materials were ordered and delivered on time.

Did they instill feeling for the project? Said Lehrer, "this project is a labor of love. The spirit and pride of hundreds of men and women involved bring out the best of us as Americans."[14] They expected and they inspired feelings like that from everyone else, too. They only hired people who had "the same commitment and dedication as we do, who are aggressive and ambitious and understand that virtually nothing is impossible."[15] Before beginning this job they gave each sub-contractor a lecture about the importance of the job and that nothing be allowed to damage the "crown jewel of the United States."

Did they maintain focus? Their major emphasis was on top quality work. The two partners believe that management's close and personal involvement is crucial to quality, so they made frequent visits to the site to personally supervise or handle thousands of details.

Obviously this was an exceptional project; it was highly publicized, it faced considerable political pressure to succeed, and it had to be completed in time to celebrate the Statue's centennial anniversary. But many other prominent, highly charged projects have bombed. In this case, prominence did not negatively affect the significant roles that time, feeling, and focus had in bringing about the project's success.

Effective Project Teams

Because people in project teams have to rely on and accept one anothers' judgments, effective project work requires close collaboration: Managers share information and consult with each other to make decisions, and team members support each other and accept others' viewpoints. Individual persons, departments, or organizations must be committed to *project* objectives rather than to their own objectives. Tightly knit, highly committed project teams are essential for project success.

One way for increasing collaboration on a project team is to stimulate interaction between its members. In some cases this can be achieved by having members share office quarters. Presumably, individuals with frequent daily contact are more likely to identify with the group.

Although close physical proximity *can* increase members' affiliation with a group, alone it is insufficient to make an effective, *cohesive* team. Vaill's findings indicate that effective teams are clear about their purpose, are committed to it, know individual roles, and understand how to function as a team. However, in most projects, people have not previously worked together and do not have enough time to form friendships, develop group work habits, or build team spirit. In many projects it is common that patterns of effective group work never develop. Therefore, team building is essential in project management.

16.4   THE TEAM BUILDING APPROACH[16]

The importance of teamwork to project success has been firmly established. In a study of two NASA research centers, 36 experienced project managers were asked to rank the most important principal functions of their job. The function of collecting, organizing, directing, and motivating the *project team* and supporting groups was ranked as first in importance by 20 managers from one center and as second by 16 managers from the other center.[17] In another study involving 32 project groups in research and product development projects, the *single most* important factor to achieving project goals was found to be *group cohesiveness*.[18]

Effective groups do not just happen. Like any other purposeful system, every team and organization must be developed. This is the purpose of *team building*, a procedure whereby a team formally evaluates how it works with the purpose of improving its functioning and output. Team building considers issues such as decision making, problem solving, team objectives, internal conflict, and communication. These are called *group process issues,* referring to processes or methods by which teams get things done. Ordinarily these are responsibilities of the team leader, though many leaders ignore them. Effective groups recognize and monitor these issues, whether or not the leader is present.

The idea of formally looking at group processes is new to many people because groups rarely do it. Using the team building approach, a group explores whatever process issues its members consider important, and then *plans* for how it will resolve these issues and perform its work.

When It Is Needed

The need for team building depends on the team members and the nature of the task. Generally, the more varied the backgrounds and responsibilities of team members, the greater the need. For example, members of multidisciplinary or multiorganizational teams have different work backgrounds and goals as well as different outlooks on planning and doing work. Some members take a wider perspective, others are detail people. Team building can help both types accept differences and define common goals.

Projects involving innovation, new technology, high risks, changes in policies and procedures, tight schedules, or large investments typically place teams under heavy stress. To some extent stress may improve the output of a group, but after a point it becomes detrimental. Team building helps the group avoid conflict or deal with problems that arise from stress. With this approach, problems are disclosed and resolved as they occur, before they can escalate and interfere with team performance.

Team building efforts may be applied to experienced teams, teams of strangers, or several teams that must work together as if they were one unit.

Aspects of Team Building Efforts

The purpose of team building is to improve group problem solving and group work efforts. To this end, the approach strives to achieve norms such as the following:

1. Effective communication among members.
2. Effective resolution of group process problems.
3. Techniques for constructively using conflict.
4. Greater collaboration and creativity among team members.
5. A more trusting, supportive atmosphere within the group.
6. Clarification of the team's purpose and the role of each member.

Three features common to any team building effort are:

- It is carefully planned and facilitated, often by a human relations consultant or professional staff person.
- The consultant collects data about the group process functioning of the team in advance, then helps the group "work through" the data during a diagnostic/problem-solving workshop.
- The team makes provisions for later self-evaluation and follow-up.

Following are examples of team building as applied to three situations: current, ongoing work teams; new teams; and multiple teams that work together.

First consider how team building is applied to an experienced team within a functional or project office team that has been having problems working together. Such teams include a cross-functional management team, a design-build team, or a team of managers representing the client, contractor, and several subcontractors. Typical problems include inability to reach agreement, lack of innovative ideas, too much conflict, or complacency of team members.

Initially a human relations consultant or someone else with group processing skills is called in by the project manager, or manager of projects, to facilitate the effort. Her function is to help the group solve its own problems by drawing attention to the *way* the group's behavior is affecting its decision quality and work performance.

The consultant collects data from members using personal interviews or questionnaires. She then summarizes the data, but keeps individual sources anonymous. This summary will later be presented to the team so that members may discuss problems and analyze behavior.

The consultant first shares the results with the group leader (project manager, functional leader, or work package supervisor) and coaches him on how to prepare for the upcoming team building workshop. The consultant remains impartial to the team leader and team members. The *entire team* is her client.

The workshop is convened so that members can review and analyze the group's problems. The workshop differs from ordinary staff meetings in many ways. It convenes at an off-site location away from interruptions, may last for several days, and includes all team members. The atmosphere is open and candid, without the usual superior-subordinate restrictions. Usually the workshop is facilitated by the consultant who may alternate this role with the group leader, depending on the agenda.

The workshop specifics vary.[19] One common format is this:[20]

1. The workshop begins with an open discussion of an agenda. Team members describe what they would and would not like to have happen.

2. The consultant presents the summary results from the interviews or questionnaires. These are posted on the wall for easy reference. Discussion may be necessary to make sure everyone understands the issues. The consultant may post quotes (anonymous) from interviews. A variety of problems can be expected, for example:

   > "Our meetings are always dominated by the same two or three people."
   > "Our way of getting things done is slow and unorganized."
   > "I have no voice in decisions that affect my functional group."
   > "Even though the team leader asks for our opinions, I know she ignores them."
   > "This group works a lot of overtime because there is no scheme for how we should fit new projects into our existing workload."
   > "There is no clear cut definition distinguishing between the roles of engineers and researchers in this project."

3. Given the summary results and the time constraint of the workshop, the team sets priorities for problems it wants to resolve including additional ones generated during the workshop.

4. The group works to resolve the priority issues. In the meantime
   a. The consultant monitors the session and reports her observations, pointing out dysfunctional group behavior, encouraging members to express their

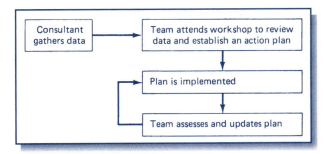

Figure 16-2
The team building cycle.

feelings, confronting behaviors of individuals that lead to defensiveness or distrust, and reinforcing effective behavior.

b. The group periodically critiques itself. After working through a problem, the group pauses to evaluate what helped or hindered the process.

c. The group prepares a formal action plan that indicates solutions, target dates, and persons responsible. The plan may include "operating guidelines" specifying *how* the group will function. (Typical guideline topics are described in Section 16.6, Step 4.)

The author has worked with project groups where problems ranging from technical issues to interpersonal conflict were resolved with team building workshops.[21]

The purpose of the workshop is twofold: It provides a structure for the team to resolve interpersonal or group process issues as well as a forum where the group examines itself as a team. Participants often find these sessions refreshing. They gain stimulating insight into group dynamics and develop a model of behavior to follow in the future.

To ensure that action steps are implemented and process issues continue to be addressed, team building always includes follow-up sessions. These take place formally at 2 to 3 month intervals or, less formally, during regular meetings. The team takes stock of its functioning, what improvements it has made, and what still is needed. As the group becomes more effective, the consultant is no longer needed and the group itself takes on the role. Whenever follow-up sessions reveal new problems on the rise, the process is repeated. The full cycle is summarized in Figure 16-2.

Two conditions are necessary for team building to succeed. First, management's *support* is needed. The team leader and upper managers must face the issues uncovered and assist in (or provide resources for) working toward solutions. Second, team members must *want* to resolve the group's problems. They must be open and honest in providing information, willing to share in the responsibility for having caused problems, and eager to work toward solutions.

16.6   BUILDING NEW TEAMS

With small variation, team building can be applied to *new* project teams. The new team might be a concurrent engineering team, a work-package team, or a management or design team with representatives from the client and contractor. The major tasks of a new team are similar to those of an experienced group—to develop a plan for working together and build both good working relationships and a good working environment. New teams have the advantage of not having established bad habits and poor working relationships.

The first task of a newly formed team is to reach agreement on its purpose, how it will achieve its purpose, and the roles of its members. It then asks itself: How can we effectively work together in a manner that will allow us to accomplish our purpose and leave us feeling good about one another?

A team building workshop facilitated by a consultant is convened to help members become acquainted, reach agreement on objectives, and decide how they will function as a team. In *Team Building: Issues and Alternatives,* William Dyer describes several workshop agendas. The following is one possible application to new project teams:[22]

Step 1: Develop a priority level. Members of the team may differ widely in the priority they place on the project goal or work task. Especially in ad hoc teams or task forces with part-time members, some members give the project high priority yet others do not. One way of acknowledging these differences is to have each member indicate on a scale of 1 to 10 the priority of the project compared to other work. Instead, each one may be asked to indicate the amount of daily or weekly time that will be devoted to the project. The information then is tallied and posted on a chart similar to Figure 16-3. A group discussion follows about commitments to the project, and about which people will accept heavier duties than others. People who so desire can explain their position on the chart. This discussion helps reduce the potential resentment of some members committing to more work than others.

Step 2: Share expectations. Each person is asked to think about the following questions: (1) What would this team be like if everything worked ideally? (2) What would it be like if everything went wrong? (3) In general, what kinds of problems occur in work groups? and (4) What actions do you think need to be taken to develop an effective team? Each person's responses are shared verbally and then posted. Concerns and answers are discussed. Differences that surface will be worked through later in Step 4.

Step 3: Clarify purpose and objectives. The team discusses and writes down its purpose and objectives. Sometimes this is straightforward, as for a work package team where the goal already has been set; other times the group will have to define the goal on its own. Either way, the purpose and objectives should be clearly defined and accepted by all members. The group objectives are the standard against which all plans and actions will be measured. The group then develops subobjectives so that members may be given specific assignments. The team objectives should complement and conform to the user and systems objectives described in Chapters 5 and 6.

Step 4: Formulating operating guidelines. Much group conflict arises over different expectations about work roles, job assignments, and how the group ought to work. Problems can be reduced by establishing group guidelines. Areas where guidelines may be formulated include:

Figure 16-3
Priority ranking for 10 team members.

1. *How will the team make decisions*—by dictate of the leader, by vote, by consensus, or by other means? Who should be involved in making decisions? Not everyone should be required to resolve all problems because some will require input from only two or three members. In most cases, the best informed people should make decisions. Total group decision making should be done only as often as necessary, but as little as possible.[23]

2. *How will the team resolve differences among members and subgroups?* Disagreements waste a lot of time, so guidelines should address the kinds of conflicts likely to arise and options for resolving them—consensus, vote, or calling in a mediator.

3. *How will the work be assigned?* The team should specify which activities the whole group will handle and which are subgroup activities. Tasks may be divided according to expertise, position of authority, or personal preference. If several people can handle a task, who will be chosen?

4. *How will the team ensure that work is completed?* One person falling behind can delay the work of others. The team must ensure that assignments and completion dates are clear and that corrective action is taken when efforts lag or are out of control.

5. *How will the team ensure open discussion?* The team must ensure that members are able to openly discuss issues so that ideas are not ignored or suppressed and that personal problems do not block team effectiveness.

6. *How frequently and where will the team meet?* What do members expect about attendance?

7. *How will the team evaluate its performance and make changes?* There should be procedures for periodic review and evaluation of the team and to allow the team to change its mode of operation and guidelines.

Teams also might discuss roles and responsibilities of group members and points of ambiguity, overlap, and conflict. This option is discussed later.

New teams do not have to wait for problems to arise before they take action; they can prevent potential problems. Team building helps members develop the common expectations necessary to build trust and mutual commitment.

Disbanding Teams

Successful teams generate close ties and strong relationships, but when projects end, so do their teams. People are usually reluctant to abandon relationships, and the breakup of a cohesive team produces feelings of loss. These feelings should be acknowledged, shared, and accepted. The disbanding of a project team may be preceded by a ceremony—a banquet, party, informal workshop or get-together—to give the team recognition for its accomplishments and to help individuals make the transition out of the team.

16.7 INTERGROUP PROBLEM SOLVING

Intergroup problem solving (IGPS) is a technique for improving working relationships *among* several teams working on a project. It permits confrontation of issues such as communicating or withholding information, competing against or collaborating with other teams or coordinating joint efforts. Following is a general design for an IGPS intervention.[24]

The two or more groups are brought together in a day-long session. They follow these steps:

1. Each group separately compiles four lists: (1) what they believe are the responsibilities of the *other* group; (2) how they feel about the other group, including its strengths and weaknesses; (3) what the group thinks are its own responsibilities; and (4) what they anticipate the other group thinks about them (strengths and weaknesses).

2. The groups meet together to share their lists. The only discussion allowed is to clarify points of disagreement, and to prioritize the items that need to be resolved.

3. The groups separate again, this time to discuss what was learned from each other's lists, to review points of disagreement, and to prioritize the items to be resolved.

4. Finally, the groups meet again to jointly discuss differences and develop a plan for resolving them.

A few weeks later at a follow-up session, they meet to determine how well their plan is working. The result of the procedure is usually a much improved understanding of what each group expects from the other and a more effective working relationship.

IGPS can be applied whenever groups interface or must work together. Examples are project and user teams, or project teams from different organizations and functional areas. Without IGPS, groups often try to optimize their *own goals*, and overall project goals suffer. One group does not understand the requirements of another group or does not share expectations about what they should do. IGPS is useful whenever there are interdependencies, deadlines, or situations that induce intergroup conflict and stress.

Participants in an intergroup session are likely to have a "gee whiz" experience. Through IGPS each group may find that their expectations are very different (and often conflicting) from the expectations of other groups. This realization is a first and necessary step to bring expectations into line and plan ways to resolve differences.

One caveat is that groups should *not* be brought together for IGPS whenever they are experiencing severe *internal* problems. A group that does not have its own internal affairs in order should first do team building for itself before it tries to resolve its relationship problems with other groups.

Example 2: Team Building and IGPS at Ruxten Software Corporation

Ron Granger is the manager of a 2-year software development project involving six programming teams at three Ruxten sites in California. Each team is headed by a team leader who reports directly to Ron on project matters. Ron also has a support staff of eight systems analysts in the project office whose function is to monitor and integrate the work of the teams. Ron and his support staff spend most of their time traveling between teams and coordinating their work.

After 8 months, the project is already running 2 months behind schedule. As Ron struggles, unsuccessfully, to get it back on track, he starts to feel that a major obstacle is the conduct of his own staff. Whereas Ron feels it might be better to give the team leaders more autonomy, his staff wants more control over them.

Ron attends a team building session for project managers at corporate headquarters and decides he should do the same for his staff. He calls in a consultant and they discuss with the staff the possibility of doing team building. The staff agrees, and the first step of the consultant is to interview each analyst about changes they want.

The first team building session lasts 2 days. It begins with the project manager asking the staff to air their complaints. The main ones are that (1) he does not back their orders to team leaders, and (2) he does not replace team leaders who they feel are "incompetent." In their view, he is a weak and indecisive project manager. Afterwards, Ron describes *his* dissatisfaction with their way of working, including their attempts to dominate the team leaders. He reasserts that their purpose is to coordinate work, not direct it.

Ron then announces his goal for team building: to get the project back on schedule. The staff agrees that his goal makes obvious sense and discusses ways to reach it. They feel that, given the importance of the team leaders' commitment to that goal, Ron should have a similar meeting with the team leaders, then a joint meeting with both team leaders and staff.

The next team building meeting includes Ron, the project staff, two team leaders, and the consultant. The two team leaders agree about the importance of putting the project back on schedule, but they feel it would be impossible given all of the specifications they have to meet. They also feel that their relationship with the eight staff members has deteriorated and would have to change first. The meeting lasts 1 1/2 days.

The third meeting includes Ron, all six team leaders, and the consultant; it lasts 2 days. Ron states that the purpose of the meeting is to break down their working relationship and put it together in a better way. He asks the team leaders to bring up any issues that bother them, including *him*. In venting their feelings, the team leaders reveal that they feel harassed by the people who are supposed to be helping them (the staff), but they are still highly motivated by the project. They discuss ways in which both the staff and members of their own teams could be more helpful to one another. Their solution is that the staff should be made *jointly* responsible with them for the performance of their teams, and that only Ron should monitor them through monthly performance reviews. Ron is not yet ready to commit to these suggestions, but after the meeting he meets with every team leader to discuss performance goals.

The final meeting is an intergroup problem solving session. The eight members of the staff, the six team leaders, Ron, and the consultant meet together for 2 days. Working in small groups, the team leaders and staff disclose what they like and do not like about their relationship and what they want to change. Each group presents the other with its complaints and suggestions for solutions. After much discussion and argument, they reach agreement on the following solutions:

1. The staff will have fewer meetings with Ron and instead associate more with the team leaders, working participatively and taking equal responsibilities.
2. The team leaders will involve their own programmers more in decision making.
3. There will be no more on-site checking by the staff. Performance will be monitored by weekly written reports from the team leaders to Ron. When necessary, Ron will make inspections and include other team leaders, but not the staff. The purpose of inspections will be to spot and solve problems, not to trap anyone or "point the finger."
4. Whenever a team leader needs help he can request the project manager to form a task force including other team leaders and members of other teams.
5. Monthly team reviews with the project manager will be conducted *with the total project group* so people can learn from each other, help one another, and maintain project team esprit de corps. The reviews will also be used to critique the progress of each team.

The changes are implemented within 2 months. This makes it possible for project members to shift their energy and talent away from policing and self-defense toward mutual assistance and problem solving. Within the year the project is back on schedule.

In all organizations, differences in objectives, opinions, and values lead to friction and conflict. Project organizations are far from the exception; if anything, they are predisposed to friction and conflict. Conflict arises between users and contractors, project staff and functional groups, and different functional departments. It occurs between people on the same team, people in different teams, and groups in different organizations. Some conflict is natural; too much is destructive.

Between User and Contractor

Seeds of conflict between the user and the contractor are sown during early contract negotiations. People representing the two parties are usually less concerned with developing trust and teamwork than with driving a hard bargain for their own best interests. The user wants to minimize cost, the contractor to maximize profit. One's gain is the other's loss. In the extreme, each side strives for an agreement which provides an "out" in case it cannot keep its part of the bargain; each makes the other side responsible in case of failure, and each gives itself final rights to all project benefits. In technology-based firms where scientists and engineers rule, the nontechnical, legal "types" who negotiate contracts may try to enlarge their function by using highly legalistic frameworks which try to cover all eventualities.[25] Says one manager,

> "You start with science and engineering, but a project, once it's decided on, has to be costed. You have to select contractors and get budgets approved. Then you turn to the contractors working with you and write contracts that say you don't trust one another. What starts as a fine scientific dream ends up being a mass of slippery eels.[26]

After negotiations are completed the contract itself becomes a source of conflict. In cost-plus agreements (see Appendix B) in which profit is a percentage of costs and there is little incentive for the contractor to control expenses, the user must closely supervise and question everything. Such scrutiny is a constant irritant to the contractor. In fixed price contracts, costs may have to be periodically renegotiated and revised upward. This is also a source of friction. Any contract that is vaguely worded or poorly specified in terms of cost, schedule, or performance is likely to have multiple interpretations and lead to disagreement and conflict.

Within the Project Organization

Functionalism is based upon and promotes differences in ideas and objectives. This is good for functional departments because it makes them better at what they do, but bad for projects because the functional areas have to work together. High-level interdependency between functional areas in projects increases the level of contact between them and, at the same time, the chances of conflict. Different functional areas have different ideas, goals, and solutions for similar problems—differences that frequently must be resolved without the benefit of a common superior.

In addition, the needs of functional areas are often incompatible with the needs of the project. Functional areas often request changes to the project plan that the project manager has to evaluate and sometimes refuse. The project manager might have to compromise the high scientific and technical standards of the research and engineering departments with time and cost considerations of the project. Even when project managers defer to the technical judgment of specialists, they often disagree over the means of implementation.

Work priorities, schedules, and resource allocations are also sources of conflict. Functional areas working in multiple projects might set priorities that conflict with priorities of project managers. Although cost estimates and schedules are originally set by functional areas, they are revised by project managers; often the final schedules conflict with other jobs, and the allocation of funds is perceived as insufficient.

In matrix organizations, functional managers sometimes see project managers as impinging on their territory, and they resent having to share planning and control with them. They might refuse to release certain personnel to projects or try to retain authority over the personnel they do release. Workers who have dual reporting relationships are often confused about priorities and loyalties.

Moreover, given that projects are temporary, goal-driven systems, workers are under constant pressure to meet time and cost objectives. People are ordinarily reluctant to accept change, yet in projects change is the norm. Expansions and contractions in the labor force make it difficult to establish obligations and reporting relationships once and for all. Administrative procedures, group interfaces, project scope, and resource allocations are always subject to change.

Finally, projects inherit feuds that have nothing to do with them. Regardless of the setting, clashes arise from differences in attitudes, personal goals, and individual traits, and from people trying to advance their careers. These create a history of antagonisms which set the stage for conflict even before a project begins.

The Project Life Cycle

Thamhain and Wilemon[27] investigated potential causes of conflict in a study of 100 project managers. They determined that, on the average, the three greatest sources of conflict are project schedules, project priorities, and the workforce—all areas over which project managers generally have limited control. Other sources of conflict identified are technical opinions and performance trade-offs, administrative and organizational issues, interpersonal differences, and costs. Costs are a relatively minor cause of conflict, the authors surmise, not because costs are unimportant but because they are difficult to control and usually dealt with incrementally over a project's life.

The study also revealed that the sources of conflict change as projects move from one phase to the next. Figure 16-4 summarizes the major sources of conflict in each phase.

Figure 16-4
Major sources of conflict during the project life cycle. [Adapted with permission from H. J. Thamhain and D. L. Wilemon, "Conflict Management in Project Life Cycles," *Sloan Management Review* (Spring 1975): 31–50.]

Start ——————— Project life cycle ————→ Finish			
Project conception	Project definition	Project execution	Project close-out
Priorities	Priorities	Schedules	Schedules
Procedures	Schedules	Technical	Personality
Schedules	Procedures	Manpower	Manpower
Manpower	Technical	Priorities	Priorities

During project conception, the most significant sources of conflict are priorities, administrative procedures, schedules, and labor. Disputes between project and functional areas arise over the relative importance of the project compared to other activities, the design of the project organization, the amount of control the project manager should have, the personnel to be assigned, and scheduling the project into existing workloads.

During project definition, the chief source of conflict remains priorities, followed by schedules, procedures, and technical issues. Priority conflicts extend from the previous phase, but new disputes arise over the enforcement of schedules and functional departments' efforts to meet technical requirements.

During the execution phase, friction arises over schedule slippages, technical problems, and labor issues. Deadlines become more difficult to meet because of accumulating schedule slippages. Efforts aimed at system integration, technical performance of subsystems, quality control, and reliability also encounter problems. Labor requirements grow to a maximum and strain the available pool of workers.

During the close-out effort, schedules continue as the biggest source of conflict as accumulated slippages make it more difficult to meet target completion dates. Pressures to meet objectives and growing anxiety over future projects increase tensions and personality related conflicts. The phasing in of new projects and the absorption of personnel back into functional areas create major conflicts in the workforce.

16.9   CONSEQUENCES OF CONFLICT

Conflict is inevitable in human systems and is not always detrimental. Properly managed, a certain amount of conflict is beneficial. Conflict helps[28]

1. Produce better ideas.
2. Force people to search for new approaches.
3. Cause persistent problems to surface and be dealt with.
4. Force people to clarify their views.
5. Cause tension which stimulates interest and creativity.
6. Give people the opportunity to test their capacities.

In fact, it is unhealthy when there is no conflict. Called *groupthink,* lack of conflict is a sign of overconformity. It causes dullness and sameness and results in poor or mediocre judgment. In contrast, conflict over differences in opinion or perspective stimulates discussion and can enhance problem solving and innovation. In project groups charged with exploring new ideas or solving complex problems, conflict is essential.

Conflict between groups in competition is beneficial because it increases group cohesion, spirit, loyalty, and the intensity of competition. However, groups in competition do not need to *cooperate.*

Conflict between project teams that should be cooperating can be devastating. Each group develops an "us versus them" attitude and selfishly strives to achieve its own objectives and block the objectives of other teams. Left uncontrolled and unresolved, destructive conflict spirals upward and creates more hostility and conflict. Conflict like this fosters lack of respect, lack of trust, and destroys communication between groups and individuals. Ideas, opinions, or suggestions of others are rejected or discredited. Project spirit breaks down and the organization splinters apart.

Microsoft forms small teams around products and then allows them to organize and work as they wish. They hire very bright, aggressive people right out of school, then push them hard to get the most and best out of them.

As author Fred Moody describes, on each product team are the designers, whose assignment is to try to pile features on the product; the developers (programmers), whose role is to resist the features for the sake of meeting deadlines; and the program manager, who tries to mediate and render verdicts. Besides having different assignments and goals, there is an enormous chasm between developers and designers in temperament, interests, and styles. Developers often feel it is impossible to make the designers understand even the simplest elements of a programming problem. Just as often, designers will spend weeks on some aspect of a product, only to be rudely told when they finally show it to a developer that it is impossible to implement. The developers see the designers as being arbitrary, fuzzy, and unstructured in their thinking. Also, they do not like relinquishing control to people they do not respect. Designers are from the arts; developers from the world of math and science. Designers tend to be female, talkative, live in lofts, and are vegetarians. Developers tend to be male, eat fast food, and talk little except to say "Not true." The way they deal with conflict differs also. Developers are given to bursts of mischievous play and will pepper a designer's door with shots from a Nerf-ball gun. Designers merely complain to their supervisor.

This adversarial relationship puts a toll on the team members, the product, the customers, and the company. Moody quotes the lead programmer on one project, who said, "I've never been through anything like this. This was the project from hell. We made the same mistakes before, and now we're making them again. Every project is like this. We keep saying that we learn from our mistakes, but we keep going through the same [expletive] over and over again."

16.10   MANAGING CONFLICT[30]

How do project managers deal with these conflicts? In general there are five ways to handle conflict; they are to

1. Withdraw or retreat from the disagreement.
2. Smooth over or de-emphasize the importance of the disagreement (pretend it does not exist).
3. Force the issue by exerting power.
4. Compromise or bargain to bring at least some degree of satisfaction to all parties.
5. Confront the conflict directly; work through the disagreement with problem solving.

All of these are at times appropriate. In a heated argument it may be best to withdraw until emotions have calmed down, or to de-emphasize the disagreement before it gets distorted out of proportion. However, this does not resolve the problem, which is likely to arise again. The project manager might force the issue by using authority; this gets the action done but it risks creating hostility. As discussed earlier, if authority must be used, it is better if it is based upon knowledge or expertise. To use bargaining or compromising, both sides must be willing to give up something to get something. Ultimately, both sides may feel they lost more than they gained, and the result is not necessarily optimal for the project. Of the five approaches, the only one which works at resolving underlying issues is *confrontation*.[31]

Confrontation

Confrontation involves recognizing potential or existing problems, then facing up to them. At the organization level this happens by having all areas involved in the project reach consensus on project objectives, administrative plans, labor requirements, and priorities. Careful monitoring of schedules, quick reallocation of resources to problem areas, close contact between project groups, and prompt resolution of technical problems are all important steps in reducing conflict.[32]

At the individual level, project managers resolve conflicts by raising confrontational questions and challenges such as[33]

> How do you know that this redesign is likely to solve the problem? Prove it to me.
>
> What have you done to correct the malfunctions that showed up on the test we agreed to?
>
> How do you expect to catch up on lost time when you haven't scheduled overtime and there is no additional staffing?

Questions such as this demonstrate that the project manager is vitally interested, alert, and that everything is subject to question. It is a crucial part of effective project management.

However, there is a catch to confrontation: The very *process* of setting plans, schedules, and priorities, and enforcing them with confronting questions is, itself, a source of conflict. Attempts to prevent or resolve conflict through planning and control become a source of conflict at the *interpersonal* level. Frequently, what begins as a conflict of schedules, priorities, or technical matters degenerates into a struggle for power and a conflict of "personalities" between parties.

Successful confrontation assumes a lot about the individuals and groups involved. It assumes that they are willing to reveal why they favor a given course of action. It assumes that they are open to and not hostile toward differing opinions. It assumes that they are all working toward a common goal. It also assumes that they are willing to abandon one position in favor of another.

The simple fact is, many groups and managers are highly critical of differences in others. Faced with differences, they tend to operate emotionally, not analytically. For individuals to use confrontation as a way to resolve conflict, they must first be able to manage their emotions. This implies fundamental changes to the interpersonal styles and processes normally used by many groups and individuals. In some cases it requires nothing short of radical change in the way people behave and in the culture of the organization.

Expectation Theory of Conflict[34]

When two people do not get along it is common to say they have a "personality conflict." The presumption is that features of their personalities—attitudes, values, experiences—are so different that they cannot possibly get along. Groups also develop personality conflicts when their values, tasks, or objectives differ.

Dyer suggests a more constructive way of looking at conflict; that it is a *violation of expectations*. Whenever a person or group violates the expectations of another, there is a negative reaction. Between groups and managers working on a project, some may feel that others are favored, have better facilities, or get more credit. When they expect more equitable treatment and do not get it, they react using verbal attacks, placing blame, or severing relations. Negative responses violate the expectations of others, who reciprocate further with more negative reactions. Team methods for resolving conflict enable groups and individuals to reach agreement on mutual expectations.

16.11   TEAM METHODS FOR RESOLVING CONFLICT

Confrontation assumes that parties can discuss issues frankly and level with one another. One way the project manager can make confrontation work is with team building. As discussed earlier, team building helps members develop attitudes more accepting of differences and leads to greater openness and trust. It attacks conflict directly by getting to the source and engaging members in problem solving. Following are team building methods that focus on conflict stemming from work roles and group interaction.

Role Clarification Technique[35]

Much conflict in projects arises because people have mixed expectations about work plans, roles, and responsibilities. In particular, disagreements arise because

- The project is new and people are not clear about what to do and what others expect of them.
- Changes in projects and work reassignments have made it unclear how functions and positions should interact.
- People get requests they do not understand or hear about things in the grapevine that they think they should already know.
- Everyone thinks someone else is handling a situation when no one is.
- People do not understand what their group or other groups are doing.

The *role clarification technique (RAT)* is a systematic procedure to help resolve these sources of conflict. The title "role clarification" suggests its goals: that everyone understand the major requirements of their own positions and duties, that others also understand everyone else's positions and duties, and that everyone knows what others expect of them.[36]

RAT has similarities with team building. It includes data collection, a meeting which lasts for 1 or 2 days, and a consultant who serves as facilitator. When incorporated as part of team building for a new team, it allows the project manager and team to negotiate team member roles. It is especially useful in participative management where responsibilities are somewhat ambiguous.

Clarifying Roles for a Team.   Role clarification for an existing team begins with each person answering a questionnaire prior to a meeting. Questions might include:[37]

1. What does the organization expect of you in your job?
2. What do you actually do in your job?
3. What should others know about your job that would help them?

4. What do you need to know about others' jobs that would help you?
5. What difficulties do you experience with others?
6. What changes in the organization, assignments, or activities would improve the work of the group?

For a new team the questions would be modified to reveal job expectations and anticipated problems.

At the start of the group meeting, the announced ground rules are that people be candid, give honest responses, express their concerns, and that everyone agrees to decisions.

The meeting begins with each person reading the answers to the first three questions. As each person reads, others have a chance to respond. It is important that each person hears how others see their job and what they expect of them.

Each person then reads the answer to Question 4 and gets responses from the people identified. Issues in Question 5 that have not already been resolved are addressed next. Throughout the process, emphasis is placed on solving problems and not placing blame. The group then discusses Question 6 and tries to reach consensus about needed changes.[38]

Clarifying the Role of One Person.   A similar process is followed for clarifying the role of just one person. It begins with the "focal person" identifying people relevant to her role—anyone who interacts with her and expects certain behavior from her to meet work obligations (boss, subordinates, members of other departments relating to the focal person). The purpose is to have these people meet together so they can clarify their expectations to the focal person.

At the meeting the focal person discusses her job responsibilities and covers topics such as those in the first five questions mentioned previously. The other people in the meeting then state their expectations of the focal person. Special attention is given to ambiguities, inconsistencies, or incompatibilities between their expectations. When consensus is reached, the focal person writes a description of her role and gives a copy to everyone. The description is reviewed to ensure that it is clear, specific, and as internally consistent as possible.

RAT is useful in matrix situations where role ambiguity can lead to power struggles between the managers and to role conflict for the workers that report to them. In projects where relationships and job descriptions are in perpetual change, a less formal procedure can be used to help redefine and reclarify roles on a frequent basis.

Intergroup Conflict Resolution[39]

When two or more groups are in conflict because of mixed expectations, a procedure similar to intergroup problem solving (IGPS) can be used. The procedure begins by each group preparing a list of what they would like the other groups to start doing, stop doing, and continue if their relations are to improve. As a variation, the groups might also guess what the others think about them and want from them. Guesses are often accurate and facilitate reaching an agreement.

The groups share their lists and negotiate an agreement stating what each will do in return for equitable changes on the part of the other. The focus is on finding solutions, not fault. A consultant may facilitate the negotiation. To increase the groups' commitment, the agreements are put in writing.

Another approach is to have Team A select a subgroup of members to represent it. Names in the subgroup are given to Team B, which selects three or four members from the Team A list. Team B also prepares a list of names and gives it to Team A. This creates a mixed team of representatives that both sides agree to. The mixed team tries to resolve problems between the teams. It can interview people in other teams, invite a facilitator, and so on. The mixed team prepares a list of actions, people to be responsible, a time frame, and ways to prevent problems from reoccurring. This is a common approach because it is easy to implement without a consultant. It requires less involvement from members than the first method, but it also tends to have less impact.

There are several preconditions for team building to be useful in resolving conflict. The conflicting parties must agree that they have problems, that the problems should be solved, that they both have a responsibility to work on them, and that they need to come together to solve them. Often it is easier to get people to deal with conflict if they realize that the goal of team building and confrontation is not to get them to like each other but to understand and work with each other.

16.12   EMOTIONAL STRESS[40]

There are numerous "down" sides to working in projects. Long hours, tight schedules, high risks, and high stakes take a toll on social and family relationships and individual mental and physical health. Projects achieve great things, but they also instigate bankruptcy, divorce, ulcers, mental breakdowns, and heart attacks. One of the major problems associated with working in projects—and which is both a contributor to and the result of individual, family, and organizational difficulties—is emotional stress. It is a problem that affects the achievement and health of project organizations and their workers, and which all project managers have to grapple with.

Factors Influencing Stress

How much emotional stress a person experiences and whether that experience is positive or negative depends upon the fit between two factors: the demands or threats of the environment and the adaptive capabilities of the person. Work-related stress depends upon a person's perception of the demands or opportunities of the job and his self-perceived abilities, self-confidence, and motivation to perform. A manager faced with impending failure to meet a deadline might experience stress if the schedule is supposed to be met, but no stress if he simply assumes the deadline will be missed. Stress is a reaction to prolonged internal and environmental conditions that overtax a person's adaptive capabilities. To feel distress, an individual's capabilities must be overtaxed for a prolonged period. Even when a person has the ability to handle a situation, he will still feel distress if he lacks self-confidence or cannot make a decision.

Stress in Projects

Among numerous causes of distress in projects are rapid pace, transient work force, anxiety over discrepancies between project performance and goals, cost overruns, and impending failure to meet schedules or contract requirements. The project manager herself is exposed to considerable stress; for example in construction, in the words of Bryman et al.:

> "The fact that the [project manager] is in the front line controlling the labor force; he's answerable to the client, to his organization at a high level; he's responsible for millions of pounds [or $] worth of work . . . In a very fragile environment he is at the mercy of the weather, material deliveries, problems with labor, and problems with getting information."[41]

The ability to cope with this stress is an aspect of project management. We will restrict discussion to three main causes of stress in projects: work overload, role conflict, and interpersonal relations.

Work overload in projects is experienced in two ways. One is simply by having too much work or doing too many things at once, with time pressures, long hours, and no letup. The other is having work that exceeds one's ability and knowledge. Overload can be self-induced by an individual's need to achieve, or it can be imposed by managers and the responsibilities of the job. Job-induced work overload is prevalent during crash efforts to recover lost ground and when projects are rushed toward completion. When work overload is in balance with abilities, it is positive and motivating. When it exceeds ability, it is distressful. A related problem, *work underload*, occurs when there is too little work, or the work is beneath a person's ability. Project workers suffer from underload whenever there is a long hiatus between projects.

Another cause of stress in projects is *role conflict*. Two or more people, for instance a functional manager and a project manager, who send contradictory or incompatible expectations cause the worker in the middle to experience stress. Role conflict is also felt when a person has two roles with incompatible requirements. A project manager, for instance, may find that he has to do things to be a good administrator that conflict with his values as a professional engineer.

A related source of stress is *role ambiguity*. This results from inadequate or confusing information about what a person needs to do to fulfill his job, or about the consequences of failing to meet requirements of the job. Role ambiguity is stressful because the person knows neither where he stands nor what to do next.

Role conflict and role ambiguity are common in projects because people have to interact with and satisfy the expectations of many others. Role ambiguity causes greater stress among managers because typically they have lower tolerance for uncertainty. Project managers in particular might find their work frustrating and stressful because the authority they need to carry out project responsibilities is often unclear or inadequate.

Stress also develops from the demands and pressures of *social relations*. Having a boss or partner who is self-centered and authoritarian causes stress. Irritable, abrasive, or condescending personalities are hard to work with; they make others feel unimportant and provoke anxiety (which people try to suppress and it builds up internally) or anger and outbursts (which generate still more tensions).

In summary, the typical project has many environmental stressors, and emotional stress is inevitable. Like conflict, however, there are ways to manage stress to reduce its negative consequences.

16.13   Stress Management

Most people accept distress as the price of success. Although stress is inevitable, distress is not. Project managers must be able to anticipate which work demands are most stressful and know how to ameliorate the negative effects.

In general, means for reducing negative stress at work are aimed either at changing the organizational conditions that cause stress or at helping people to better cope with stress. Because stress results from the interaction of people with their environment, both are necessary. Organizational level means are aimed at task, role, physical, and interpersonal stressors; individual level means are aimed at peoples' ability to manage and respond to stressful demands. Following are some methods which can readily be applied by project managers.

Organizational Level Means[42]

One way to reduce worker distress in projects is to create a less distressful project environment. Various avenues include

1. Setting reasonable work plans and schedules.
2. Delegating responsibility and increasing individual autonomy.
3. Clarifying responsibilities, authority, and performance criteria.
4. Clarifying goals, procedures, and decision criteria.
5. Giving consideration and support in leadership.

The first way calls for preplanning and scheduling to allow for reasonable work hours and time off. Good planning and scheduling helps balance work loads and familiarizes workers with what is expected. It helps avoid ambiguity in expectations, work overload, and the "crunch" that precedes milestones and project close-out.

Good planning and scheduling are "technical" means for reducing stress; these methods and procedures are described elsewhere in this book. The other ways on the list are "behavioral" means for managing stress. They consist of ways for altering work demands, relationships, and individual behavior, and center around participating management, team building, and conflict resolution.

Modifying Work Demands Through Participation. The distressful influence of some kinds of leadership styles is well-known. Dictatorial, self-centered leaders (the too bossy boss) cause frustration, annoyance, and stress; the opposite kind, the do-nothing, understimulating boss is just as bad. In contrast, it makes sense (and there is supporting research) that the participating style of leadership is the least stressful.[43] Most projects are demanding; one way to reduce distress is to give project workers decision latitude and autonomy commensurate with work demands and their ability. Participating leaders set goals and define task limits, but allow greater freedom about how goals will be achieved. This latitude gives workers greater flexibility and results in less anxiety and tension.

Modifying Work Relationships. In project environments where there is considerable change and complexity, distress is caused by confusion, ambiguity, and conflict about work roles. One means for reducing role-related work stress is the role analysis technique described previously. By clarifying role demands and minimizing contradictions in role expectations, stress originating from role conflict and role ambiguity is reduced. Like good project planning, this should be done early so that work roles and expectations are clear from the beginning.

Social Support. Another way to reduce stress arising from work roles and relationships is to increase the *social support* within project teams. Social support is the assistance one gets through interpersonal relationships. Generally, people are better able to cope with stressful situations when they feel others care about and are willing to help them.[44] Social support at work comes in the form of giving emotional support (listening and caring), appraising performance and behavior, and giving advice, information, and direct assistance in a task.

Vital sources of social support are family, close friends, a supportive boss, and good relations with coworkers and subordinates. Social support from managers and coworkers does not necessarily alter the stressor but it does help people to better cope. Supportive managers act as a barrier against destructive stress, and their subordinates are less likely to suffer harmful consequences than those with unsupportive managers.[45] Coworker social support in groups is equally important, though often group supportiveness correlates with the amount of support modeled by the leader. Caught between the conflicting expectations of a functional manager and project manager, a person who has supportive coworkers will be better able to deal with the conflict and feel less troubled by her inability to meet both expectations.

How do people become supportive? Simply telling someone to be supportive does not work. Even when managers try to be supportive by giving advice they often leave the distressed worker worse off. Giving someone physical assistance is easy, but true emotional support is difficult and more subtle. Empathic listening, understanding, and real concern are essential parts of support often missing in naive efforts to help. Usually it is necessary to provide training in social support skills, then reinforce and reward the usage of these skills. Unfortunately, as with many other behavioral aspects of management, empathy and sensitivity are considered "soft" issues and are often devalued as "nonproductive."

Individual Level Means

In high stress project environments, project managers are advised to implement a *stress management program.* Such programs vary widely in focus; some are aimed at altering the perception of potential stressors, others at treating stress-induced problems. They range from training in relaxation and personal coping to lifestyle management and physical exercise.

Comprehensive stress management programs are directed at three levels: perceived stressors in the environment, people's responses to stress, and clinical treatment. Techniques at the first level aim to reduce stressors in the environment. Because something must first be perceived as stressful to actually become stressful, one way to reduce stress is to alter perceptions. By developing creative perceptual frames of reference people can learn to face problems in ways that are not psychologically destructive. For example, people in stressful decision making positions are encouraged to think "I will give this project all I have to offer, but if I make a mistake it will not be the end. I don't have to be liked by everyone to be effective. It is enough to do my job well and be respected."[46] Individuals learn to interpret situations in ways that increase their resistance to stress.

Techniques at the second level are directed at improving the way people respond to stressful situations. They include, for example, relaxation training (meditation, Zen, biofeedback, relaxation response, and other techniques), and physical and emotional outlets such as sports, relaxing with friends and family, and diversions from work-related problems.

Third level methods are directed at reducing the physical effects of distress. They include counseling, psychotherapy and medical care. Most stress management programs emphasize the first two levels to try to minimize the need for third-level steps.

Stress management programs should involve everyone in the project team who needs help from distress. Project managers are among the most stressed individuals because they are caught in the middle and are under pressure from everyone else. They usually need a stress management program as much or more than anyone.

16.14 SUMMARY

According to contingency theories of leadership the most effective style in project management is relations-oriented. Effective project managers often use participating decision making because they must rely upon the decisions and opinions of specialists and other managers to gain commitment to action. Research suggests that participation is the preferred and most common style among project managers.

Project organizations comprise teams. A significant factor in superior project performance is cohesive project teams and close teamwork. Teamwork must be developed and nurtured. Especially when a project comprises team members from divergent backgrounds or exposes members to high stress, groups need help in developing effective teamwork. Team development methods are applicable throughout all phases of the systems development process. Team building is useful for resolving problems in experienced teams and for building teamwork in new groups. Intergroup problem solving is useful for building teamwork between two or more groups. With slight variation these methods may be adapted to bring users, subcontractors, and suppliers together at the start of a project. They also may be used to unify work groups following changes in project organization or plans, and to prepare team members for new job assignments just before a project is completed.

Conflict is inevitable in organizations and, properly managed, it is beneficial. In projects, the primary sources of conflict are schedules, priorities, manpower levels, technical opinions, administrative issues, interpersonal conflicts, and costs. The relative importance of these varies with the stage of the project life cycle.

Conflict is generally best dealt with through confrontation. Confrontation examines the underlying issues and attempts to resolve the conflict at its source. It presumes, however, that people will be open, honest, and willing to work together to resolve the conflict. Lacking these conditions or poorly handled, confrontation can lead to hostility and personality conflicts.

Conflict often occurs because of a violation of expectations between parties. Sharing, clarifying, and mutual agreement of expectations is one way to eliminate such conflict. This is the basis for conflict resolution using the role analysis and intergroup conflict resolution techniques.

Stress in projects is inevitable, though distress is not. Stress induces energy, increases vitality, and helps people deal with the demands of work. However, stress from too few or too many work demands can be debilitating. In projects, the main sources of stress are demanding goals and schedules, work tasks, roles, and social relations. Good project planning helps reduce many technical sources of stress. Participating management, role analysis, and social support help reduce destructive stress from work tasks, roles, and social relations.

As leaders, project managers share responsibility for the physical and emotional health of project team members. In high stress projects, managers can sponsor stress management programs and set an example by taking advantage of these programs. Project managers may be in the best position to diagnose the stress of the organization by using their own stress level as a barometer.

REVIEW QUESTIONS

1. Explain the difference between task-oriented and relations-oriented leadership styles.
2. Describe the contingency approach to leadership. According to this approach, what is the best way to lead?
3. What are the differences between the leadership models of Fiedler and Hersey-Blanchard? What do they say about leading in the situations faced by project managers?
4. In what ways is participative management useful for motivating and gaining commitment?

5. Why is teamwork important in projects? Isn't it enough to have individual workers who are highly skilled and motivated?

6. What characteristics are common to Vaill's high-performing systems?

7. What is meant by group process issues? What kinds of issues do they include?

8. What is the purpose of team building? Where is team building needed?

9. Outline the steps in a team building session for a group that has been working together. Outline the steps for building a new project team.

10. Outline the steps in the IGPS process.

11. What conditions of management and the participating members are necessary for team building interventions to succeed?

12. Describe some situations that you know of where team building could be used.

13. What do you think are the reasons why team building is not used more often? What barriers are there to applying team building?

14. What are the sources of conflict between the user and the contractor? How do contracts lead to conflict?

15. What are the sources of conflict between parties in the project organization?

16. Describe how the sources of conflict vary with the phases of the project life cycle.

17. What are the negative consequences of conflict in projects?

18. Explain why some conflict is natural and beneficial.

19. Describe five ways of dealing with conflict.

20. Explain how the project manager uses confrontation to resolve conflict.

21. What are the assumptions in using confrontation (i.e., what conditions must exist for it to be successful)?

22. Describe the "expectation theory" of conflict. How does the expectation theory compare with your experiences of conflict in work situations?

23. Describe the role analysis technique. What sources of conflict does it resolve?

24. Describe what happens in intergroup problem solving. What sources of conflict does it resolve?

25. Describe each of these major sources of stress in project environment: project goals and schedules, work overload, role conflict and ambiguity, and social/interpersonal relations. Describe your work experiences with these sources of stress.

26. Describe the means by which (a) participating management and (b) role analysis help to reduce work stress.

27. What is "social support?" What are the sources of social support? How does social support reduce job stress?

28. What are some ways of improving social support among project team members?

29. Name some techniques that individuals can use to manage or reduce their stress levels.

30. Investigate further, through outside reading or discussion, the techniques listed in Question 29.

QUESTIONS ABOUT THE STUDY PROJECT

1. How would you characterize the leadership style of the project manager in your project? Is it authoritarian, laissez faire (do nothing), or participative? Is the project manager more task- or more relations-oriented, or both?

2. What kind of people must the project manager influence? Given the theories of this chapter, is the style of leadership used appropriate? Despite the theories, does the style used by the project manager seem to be effective?

3. What do you think are the primary work motivators for people in this project? Discuss the relative importance of salary, career potential, formal controls, and participation in decision making.

4. Describe the different groups (management teams, project office, functional groups) that comprise the project team in this project.

5. What mechanisms are used to link these teams—for example, coordinators, frequent meetings, or close proximity?

6. What kinds of formal and informal activities are used to increase the cohesiveness of the project team? Can any of these be termed as team building?

7. What kinds of activities are used or steps taken to resolve problems involving multiple groups?

8. How would you characterize the level of teamwork in this project?

9. Ask the project manager if he or she knows about formal team building and intergroup problem solving procedures like those described in this book.

10. At the end of this (or other projects), what does the organization do to disband a team? Are there any procedures for giving recognition or dealing with members' feelings about disbanding?

11. How prevalent is conflict and what effect does conflict have on individual and project performance?

12. What responsibility does the project manager take in resolving these conflicts?

13. How does the project manager resolve conflict? Is confrontation used?

14. Are any formal procedures used, such as RAT or IGPS, to resolve conflicts?

    Emotional stress is a personal issue and most people are hesitant to speak about it other than on a general level. Still, you might ask the project manager or other team members about stresses they personally feel or perceive in the project.

15. Is this a high stress or low stress project? Explain. If it is a high stress environment, is it taken for granted that that is the way it must be or do people feel that steps could be taken to reduce the stress?

16. Does the project manager try to help team members deal with job stress? Explain.

17. Does the organization make available to its employees programs on stress management?

Case 16-1   Mars Climate Orbiter Spacecraft[47]

NASA designed the Mars Climate Orbiter spacecraft to collect data about Mars' atmospheric conditions and serve as a data relay station. Instruments aboard the Orbiter would provide detailed information about the temperature, dust, water vapor, and carbon dioxide in Mars' atmosphere for approximately 2 Earth years. The Orbiter would also provide a relay point for data transmissions to and from spacecraft on the surface of Mars for up to 5 years.

The Orbiter was launched in December of 1998 and arrived in the vicinity of Mars 9 months later, firing its main engine to go into orbit around the planet. Everything looked normal as it passed behind Mars as seen from the Earth; after that the Orbiter was never heard from again; it had, presumably, crashed into the planet. Paraphrasing project manager Richard Cook, "We had planned to approach the planet at an altitude of about 150 kilometers, but upon review of data leading up to the arrival, we saw indications that the approach altitude was much lower, about 60 kilometers. We believe the minimum survivable altitude for the spacecraft would have been 85 kilometers."

Later, an internal peer review attributed the $280 million mission loss to an error in the information passed between the two teams responsible for the spacecraft's operations, the Climate Orbiter spacecraft team in Colorado and the mission navigation team in California. In communicating back and forth, one team had used English units (inches, feet, pounds), while the other used metric units (meters, grams). Without knowing it, the two teams were using different measurement systems for information critical for maneuvering the spacecraft into proper Mars orbit.

QUESTIONS

1. How could such a mistake have occurred between the two teams?
2. What does the mistake suggest about the degree of interaction and coordination between the teams?
3. How might this problem have been prevented?

ENDNOTES

1. Richard L. Chapman, *Project Management in NASA: the System and the Men* (Washington, D.C.: NASA SP-324, NTIS No. N75-15692, 1973). The project team Chapman refers to is the project office staff which numbered from one or two members on small matrix projects to as many as 70 in large pure project organizations.
2. E. H. Kloman, *Unmanned Space Project Management* (Washington, D.C.: NASA SP-4102, 1972), 23.
3. Fred Fiedler, *A Theory of Leadership Effectiveness* (New York: McGraw-Hill, 1967).
4. P. Hersey and K. Blanchard, *Management of Organization Behavior: Utilizing Human Resources,* 4th ed. (Upper Saddle River, NJ: Prentice Hall, 1982): 150–73.
5. Paul Hersey and Kenneth Blanchard, "Managing Research and Development Personnel: An Application of Leadership Theory," *Research Management* (September 1969).
6. A. Bryman, M. Bresnan, A. Beardsworth, J. Ford, and El. Keil, "The Concept of the Temporary System: The Case of the Construction Project," *Research in the Sociology and Psychology of Organizations* 5 (1987): 253–83.
7. L. R. Sayles and M. K. Chandler, *Managing Large Systems: Organizations for the Future* (New York: Harper & Row, 1971): 219.
8. For a discussion of the interpersonal and leadership requirements for the matrix, see S. M. Davis and P. R. Lawrence, *Matrix* (Reading, MA: Addison-Wesley, 1977): 108–09.
9. Warren Bennis and Burt Nanus, *Leadership: Strategies for Taking Charge* (New York: Harper & Row, 1985): 224–25.
10. Peter Vaill, "The Purposing of High-Performing Systems," *Organizational Dynamics* (Autumn 1982): 23–39.
11. Ibid., 38.
12. This discussion is largely based on W. Hofer, "Lady Liberty's Business Army," *Nation's Business* (July 1983): 18–28; see also Alice Hall, "Liberty Lifts Her Lamp Once More," *National Geographic* (July 1986): 2–19.
13. Hofer, ibid.
14. Ibid., 28.
15. Ibid., 21.
16. John Nicholas, "Developing Effective Teams for System Design and Implementation," *Production and Inventory Management* (Third Quarter 1980): 37–47; and John Nicholas, "Organization Development in Systems Management," *Journal of Systems Management* 30, no. 11 (November 1979): 24–30. Much of the following discussion is derived from these sources.
17. See Chapman, *Project Management in NASA,* 59–62. The other functions of project management were defined to be project planning, information and control, and consultation.
18. R. T. Keller, "Predictors of the Performance of Project Groups in R&D Organizations," *Academy of Management Journal* 29, no. 4 (December 1986): 715–26.
19. See, for example, William Dyer, *Team Building: Issues and Alternatives,* 2d ed. (Reading MA: Addison-Wesley, 1987) and Nicholas, "Organization Development in Systems Management," 24–30.
20. A. J. Reilly and J. E. Jones, "Team Building," in *Annual Handbook of Group Facilitators,* eds. J. W. Pfeiffer and J. E. Jones (LaJolla, CA: University Associates, 1974).
21. Nicholas, "Organization Development in Systems Management."
22. This discussion is largely based on Dyer, *Team Building,* 100–06.

23. Davis and Lawrence, *Matrix*, 134.
24. R. R. Blake, H. A. Shepard, and J. S. Mouton, *Managing Intergroup Conflicts in Industry* (Houston: Gulf Publishing, 1965).
25. Sayles and Chandler, *Managing Large Systems*, 277–78.
26. Ibid., 278.
27. H. J. Thamhain and D. L. Wilemon, "Conflict Management in Project Life Cycles," *Sloan Management Review* (Spring 1975): 31–50; and H. J. Thamhain and D. L. Wilemon, "Diagnosing Conflict Determinants in Project Management," *IEEE Transactions of Engineering Management* 22 (February 1975).
28. W. H. Schmidt, "Conflict: A Powerful Process for (Good or Bad) Change," *Management Review* 63 (December 1974): 5.
29. Fred Moody, *I Sing the Body Electronic* (New York: Viking, 1995): 110–15.
30. This section focuses on managing conflict from a group level perspective. For an individual level perspective, see Marc Robert, *Managing Conflict from the Inside Out* (Austin: Learning Concepts, 1982).
31. It is not only the best approach, it is also the one most favored by project managers (followed by compromise, then smoothing, then forcing and withdrawal). See Thamhain and Wilemon, "Conflict Management in Project Life Cycles," 42–44.
32. Ibid., 46–47.
33. Sayles and Chandler, *Managing Large Systems*, 216.
34. This discussion is based upon Dyer, *Team Building*, 116–18. See Herb Bisno, *Managing Conflict* (Newbury Park, CA: Sage, 1988) for another perspective.
35. This discussion is based upon Dyer, *Team Building*, 109–16.
36. Ibid., 111.
37. Ibid., 112.
38. Ibid., 113–14.
39. Ibid., 116–17, 135.
40. Portions of this section are adapted from E. F. Huse and T. G. Cummings, *Organization Development and Change*, 3d ed. (St. Paul: West, 1985): Chap. 12; J. C. Quick and J. D. Quick, *Organizational Stress and Preventive Management* (New York: McGraw-Hill, 1984): and J. C. Williams, *Human Behavior in Organizations*, 2d ed. (Cincinnati: South-Western, 1982): Chap. 9.
41. A. Bryman et al., "The Concept of the Temporary System: The Case of the Construction Project," *Research in the Sociology and Psychology of Organizations* 5, (1987): 253–83.
42. Portions of this section are adapted from Huse and Cummings, *Organization Development and Change*; Quick and Quick, *Organizational Stress and Preventive Management*; Williams, *Human Behavior in Organizations*; J. S. House, *Work Stress and Social Support* (Reading, MA: Addison-Wesley, 1981); and L. J. Warshaw, *Managing Stress* (Reading, MA: Addison-Wesley, 1982).
43. See research cited in Quick and Quick, *Organizational Stress and Preventive Management*, 170.
44. House, *Work Stress and Social Support*, 22–26, 30–38.
45. Ibid., 98, 99.
46. Williams, *Human Behavior in Organizations*, 221.
47. NASA Web site, December 1999.

Chapter 17

Project Failure, Success, and Lessons Learned

> *Fools you are to say you learn by your experience. I prefer to profit by others' mistakes and avoid the price of my own.*
>
> —Otto van Bismark-Schönhausen

> *Failure is God's way of saying "Excuse me, you're heading in the wrong direction."*
>
> —Oprah Winfrey

Now that you are familiar with the terminology, concepts, and methodology of project management, it is a good time to review the tenets of this book.

Experienced project managers will tell you that the failure or success of a project has quite a lot to do with its management. In this chapter, the practices of project management have been classified, rather broadly, into those contributing to project failure and to project success. The classification is the result of an informal survey of project management literature over the last 30 years; it includes findings from academic studies as well as the opinions of project managers from various industries—construction, research and development, information technology, and product development. The survey affirms that project failure and success do depend on project management a great deal. It also shows there is considerable consensus among industries about the project management practices that influence project outcomes the most.

This chapter is a review of the core issues of this book—the must "don'ts" as well as the must "dos" of project management. We look at project failure (the must don'ts) first.

17.1   PROJECT FAILURE

Why Talk about Failure?

By looking at failure it is not the intent of this chapter to finish the book on a sour note; rather, we look at failure for one reason: to learn from past mistakes. Some philosophers (notably Karl Popper) say that knowledge advances not through success, but through failure.[1] In science it is largely in those situations where theories fail to give reliable and accurate predictions that scientists are forced to advance new and better theories. Newton's theories were supplanted by those of Einstein because they failed to explain certain phenomenon; now Einstein's are being modified. It happens with common practice, also. Whenever underlying causes (or theories) are advanced about why a failure occurred, others can take actions to prevent similar failures from recurring. Many newsworthy project failures—those involving loss of life or significant resources—are followed by an inquiry or investigation, the results of which may be made public. Most failures do not receive full investigation, even when they should. It is in the spirit of learning and improvement that we examine project failure.

What Is Project Failure?

No failure occurs in isolation. All failures are *system failures* in the sense that they are actually the *output* of a particular system. That is to say, there are features or defects in the system that *produced* or allowed the failure.[2] Broadly speaking, a system fails if it meets either of two criteria:[3]

1. It does not satisfy the requirements of those involved with the system—management, users, or other affected parties. Project failure usually implies not meeting cost, schedule, performance, quality, safety, or related objectives.
2. It produces results that are undesirable to those involved with it. A failed project does not meet user or developer expectations, or leaves them worse off than before.

The criteria of project failure can be viewed from the two perspectives illustrated in Figure 17-1. As examples:

1. When a fixed price project has a cost overrun, the developer must absorb the excess cost, suffering a loss or reduced profit. From the developer's perspective, the project is a failure.
2. The project end-item is not accepted or utilized even though it was delivered on schedule, under budget, and according to specifications. This is a project failure experienced by the user or other project recipients.

The two kinds of failure can be mutually exclusive: while one of the parties experiences failure, the other experiences success. For example, even though project cost overruns might drive a developer into bankruptcy, the user may derive considerable benefit from the end-item; in contrast, the developer might earn handsome profits from the project, yet the user is disappointed with or never uses the end-item.

Figure 17-1
Perspectives of project failure.

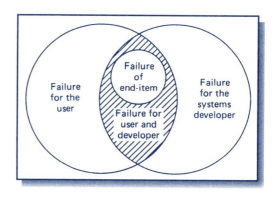

As Figure 17-1 shows, however, the two kinds of failure are sometimes interlinked, as when the project end-item itself fails. For example, the collapse of a building during construction and any injury or loss of life it causes represents a "project failure" for everyone—the user, project team, contractor, and others involved. Such a failure adversely influences all parties by increasing project costs and schedules and adding to human suffering. Similarly, everyone is affected when rising costs or poor performance force either the system developer or the user to withdraw from the project. Then the remaining party is left in the predicament of holding an "unfinished project."

Causes of Failure

Some failures are unavoidable because they are beyond anyone's ability to anticipate, avoid, or influence. Examples are failures caused by weather or labor problems, intractable technical difficulties, or other forces neither foreseeable nor controllable. But, perhaps surprisingly, these are not the causes of a great number of project failures. Rather, failure usually is caused by "defects" in (1) the project and user organizations—attitudes, practices, and structure, or (2) the project end-item—hardware, software, and component parts. These defects often are interlinked. For example, although hardware failures result from defects in components and procedures, these defects can usually be traced to mistakes in the design, which, in turn, can be traced to defects in the *design and management process* that allowed mistakes to go uncorrected. That is to say, defects in the system that plans and controls the project—the project management system—can allow and lead to poor design, poor quality control, inadequate inspection, and, ultimately, failure in the end-item itself ("hardware" or "component" failures).

A case in point is the tragic loss of the space shuttle *Challenger* and its seven astronauts. Although faulty hardware design directly caused the explosion, the root causes were management ineptitude and flaws in the project organization that permitted design errors to go uncorrected. The Challenger accident was directly attributed to defective O-rings—seals in the booster rocket that allowed hot exhausts to leak out and trigger an explosion in the external fuel tank. However, it was known and well-documented that the seals would perform poorly under certain temperatures and, therefore, constituted a serious risk to flight safety. On the day of the tragedy, several engineers warned that the seals might fail. Earlier decisions to retain the suboptimal seals and the approval to go ahead for launch, despite warnings, were management judgments that ignored abundant information to the contrary. It can easily be argued that the accident was the output of a defective management system.

In a similar, more general vein, whenever a user fails to accept or utilize a project end-item (called "implementation failure"), the reason is typically because the end-item did not satisfy the user's requirements or because it was not needed to start with.

This is a common failure in information systems project wherein systems are installed, then seldom used thereafter. Sometimes the problem is that the *true user* of the system was misidentified. Regardless, failure to meet user needs rests with project management for allowing such a state of affairs to develop.

The point is this: *The root cause of many project failures is not intractable technical problems, nor uncontrollable forces, nor the user, but simply bad project management.* This kind of failure is the output of a defective project management system—organizations, practices, or procedures.

17.2 PROJECT MANAGEMENT CAUSES OF PROJECT FAILURE

Figure 17-2 shows 14 factors—inadequacies or defects in project management—which are sources of project failure as identified in the survey.[4] Although having any of these factors in a project does not necessarily mean that the project will fail, however,

Figure 17-2
Project management causes of project failure.

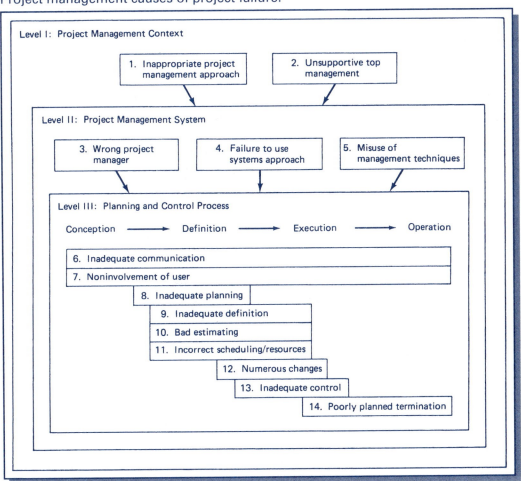

appearance of such is an *inauspicious sign* because any can increase the chances of failure. The factors are categorized into three levels: the environment or context of the project, the project management system, and the project planning and control process.

Level I: Failures in the Project Management Context

These are sources of failure traceable to the inappropriate "fit" of the project organization to project objectives, project tasks, top management, and the larger environment. They include the use of a project management approach or model that is incorrect for the project objectives and environment, and lack of top management support for the project.

1. Inadequate Project Management Approach. The project does not have the right organization structure, project manager, or team (in terms of skills, experience, authority, formality, or complexity) to "fit" the project. For example:

a. The project organization structure, planning, and controls are incongruent or incompatible with the project situation, the philosophy of the project manager, or corporate culture and objectives.
b. More emphasis is placed on keeping the team busy than on results. Members of the team are assigned to the project without regard to appropriate skills and experience.
c. Either no one is held accountable for the entire project, or the responsibility, expectations, and authority of the project manager are unclear or undefined.
d. A project team, project manager, or project structure that was successful in the past is "plugged" into a new project without considering the unique requirements of the project or distinguishing characteristics of its environment.

2. Unsupportive Top Management Top management does not give the active and continued support necessary to achieve project goals. This is revealed in many ways. For example:

a. Top management does not yield adequate responsibility or authority to the project manager, or back the project manager's decisions or actions.
b. The company does not make policy and procedural changes (budgeting, planning, and control systems, reporting and authority relationship, etc.) needed to conduct effective project management.
c. Top management does not participate in reviewing project plans and progress.

Level II: Failures in the Project Management System

These are sources of failure traceable to project leadership, philosophy, and practice. They include the wrong project manager, neglect of the systems approach in the project life cycle, and misuse of project management techniques.

3. The Wrong Project Manager. The person in the role of project manager does not have the background, skills, experience, or personality to lead and manage the project. For example:

a. The project manager is unable to confront conflict. She does not ask tough, probing questions, and cannot effectively argue for the best interests of the project.
b. The project manager cannot make the adjustment from a traditional work environment to the change and uncertainty of projects. She lacks the ability to function effectively under short time frames and stressful situations.

c. The project manager is not well-rounded in technical and managerial skills. Sometimes this arises from a variation of the so-called Peter Principle: putting a good technician into a managerial role about which she knows nothing. In other cases, the project manager has managerial skills, but is so preoccupied with administrative details that she ignores critical technical matters. She lacks the skills and charisma to command the respect of the project team.

4. Ignoring the Systemic Nature of Projects.   The project is not treated as a system. Elements and processes of the project are compartmentalized without regard to their interaction. For example:

a. Hardware, software, resources, and facilities are viewed independently without regard to their relation to overall project objectives. Emphasis is placed on individual activities rather than on project objectives.

b. The evolutionary process of systems development is viewed piecewise, one step at a time, without regard to subsequent or previous stages. This is evident by poor planning for future stages and inadequate evaluation of past stages. Problems are passed from one phase to the next.

5. Inappropriate or Misuse of Management Techniques.   Project management techniques are misunderstood or improperly employed. The problem lies with the project manager, the project team, or the techniques themselves. For example:

a. The project manager fails to distinguish nonproject techniques of planning, coordinating, and control from those necessary for project activities. The project manager or his team do not understand the need for tools such as PERT, WBS, performance analysis, conflict confrontation, and team building; these techniques are used incorrectly or not at all.

b. The project manager does not attend to the human/behavioral side of projects; he does not build a project team, help team members understand the project goal, nor inspire them to work together toward the goal.

c. The techniques used are too sophisticated or otherwise inappropriate for the particular project. Schedules and reports are too detailed or insufficiently detailed for project decisions. Manual techniques that are simpler, more appropriate, and better suited for small projects are bypassed in favor of sophisticated (but unwieldy or unnecessary) computerized reporting systems.

Level III: Failures in Planning and Control Processes

These sources of failure rest in the project planning and control process. As shown in Figure 17-2, some, like poor communication and inadequate user participation, can occur anytime in the project and require continuous attention. Others, such as inadequate definition, estimation, scheduling, or control occur primarily during certain phases of the project.

6. Inadequate Communication in the Project.   These are problems that stem from lack of information quality, accuracy, or timeliness, poor data collection and documentation, or inadequate distribution of information to those who need it. For example:

a. Early in the project, information about objectives, responsibilities, and acceptance criteria is not documented. No attempt is made to identify information and sources that will be needed during the project. Parties that "need to know" are not identified or kept informed.

b. During the project there is no posting or reporting of information about project status or about changes to the plan or end-item.

c. Insufficient meetings are convened to collect and disseminate information. Reviews do not delve deeply enough nor ask probing questions. No project log or audit trail of project development is kept.

d. The quality and quantity of information gradually lessens as the project progresses because "there is not enough time." Communications are not documented so it is difficult to distinguish facts from assumptions.

7. Failure to Involve the User.   The user or customer does not participate in the planning/definition/design/implementation process, and user needs are disregarded. This is one of the most frequently mentioned sources of project failure. Failure to involve the user early in the project results in lack of agreement about requirements, numerous change requests later, and conflict between the user and project team during implementation. Even when users do participate in defining requirements, without continued involvement they cannot visualize the appearance or functioning of the final end-item and are dissatisfied when they see the result. Problems are aggravated and more difficult to solve when there are multiple users. Both the user and project management are to blame:

a. The user may feel awkward or uncomfortable and try to minimize his involvement. Some users resist participation, even when invited.

b. The behavior of the project team discourages user involvement. Members of the project team may behave arrogantly and make the user feel ignorant or inferior. Such behavior delimits user/project team trust and strains communication.

8. Inadequate Project Planning.   Analysis and planning of project details is inadequate and sloppy; reports and recommendations from previous projects are ignored. Instead of preparing in advance, management reacts to things as they occur.

Although poor project planning by itself is a major reported source of project failure, also cited are three particular features of planning—definition, estimating, and scheduling.

9. Inadequate Project Definition.   Vague, wrong, misleading, or absence of project definition is a frequently mentioned cause of failure. There is no formal definition of technical requirements, tasks, or project scope. Definition problems result from:

a. Lack of, or a poorly prepared proposal, WBS, responsibility matrix, or work role definitions.

b. Lack of user involvement in defining project scope, tasks, and requirements. The project team never becomes familiar with the user's operation and cannot construct a design that relates to user requirements.

10. Bad Estimating of Time and Resources.   Estimates of resource requirements, activity durations, and completion dates are unrealistic. Bad estimating occurs because:

a. Standards or files of similar projects are not used to estimate how long the project should take.

b. Estimates are made without regard to the experience of the workers. It is assumed that all personnel are "experts" and that they will perform the work without a hitch.

c. Estimates are prepared by people unfamiliar with details and problems; those responsible for the work are not involved.

d. Not enough time is allowed for estimating.

e. The user exerts pressures to get the project done quickly; this results in setting unrealistic deadlines and eliminating "unnecessary" tasks such as documentation.

11. Incorrect Scheduling and Handling of Resources. Scheduling and allocation of resources are incorrect; assignments are not anticipated; resource skills and capabilities are unknown; and resources for backup are unavailable. The problem begins during planning and continues throughout the project:

a. Resource requirements are not anticipated and scheduled, and resource issues are addressed only as they occur. There is no skills inventory showing who is available for the project.

b. Project personnel are reassigned or turned over without readjusting the schedule to allow for lost time or the learning curve.

12. Numerous Changes during the Execution Phase. Changes are made to the original requirements without corresponding changes to the schedule, budget, or other elements of the plan. This oversight leads to inadequate project communication, poor project definition, lack of user involvement, and sloppy project control.

13. Inadequate Control. Project management does not anticipate problems but reacts after they arise; control is focused on daily issues without looking ahead to potential problem situations; management waits until near the completion date to see if the project is on time. Sources of control problems include:

a. Definition of work tasks that are too large to be effectively controlled, work packages and work groups that are too large to be supervised, and milestones that are too far apart to permit stepwise monitoring of the percentage of project completed.

b. No adherence to standards or specifications for design, documentation, testing, or evaluation. Auditors do not perform careful evaluation, and evaluation is not used to determine why problems arise.

c. No attempt to resolve emerging problems early in the project. Instead of being prospective and preventive, the control process is retrospective and curative.

d. No forecasting or planning of the funds needed to guarantee completion of project objectives.

e. The management system takes on greater importance than the people in the system or the project end-item. This exacerbates peoples' tendency to resist controls and encourages them to circumvent or sabotage control procedures.

14. Project Termination is Poorly Planned. It is not known what constitutes project completion or the end-item, what the acceptance criteria are, or who must sign off the project; there is no formal termination procedure addressing objectives, performance, end products, and maintenance issues; the impact on users is not predicted; personnel are not evaluated for their performance; there is no post installation survey addressing system bugs, necessary or already made changes, results, or usefulness.

This problem is often related to poor project definition and lack of user involvement:

a. When project termination is not clearly defined, the project is allowed to continue even after it has long ceased to make cost-effective progress.

b. When users are not involved in planning, there is greater chance of disagreement over final conditions acceptance. After acceptance, problems with the end-item go unidentified or are permitted to continue despite user dissatisfaction.

Bad project termination has negative consequences beyond failure of the immediate project. When no attempt is made to review project performance, it is unlikely that any knowledge can be gained to transfer to other projects. Recommended enhancements to the system go undocumented and are lost forever. When project personnel are not evaluated at the end of the project, their work performance is forgotten and there is no accurate basis upon which to make future work assignments.

Interdependency of Factors

Figure 17-2 implies that an inadequacy at one level has negative impact on the next lower level. For example, selecting an inappropriate project management approach (Level I) may cause project systemic features to be ignored, the wrong project manager to be chosen, or project management techniques to be misused (Level II); in turn, these lead to poor communication, inadequate definition and scheduling, and other problems in planning and control (Level III).

Figure 17-2 also implies a hierarchy of effects; a problem at higher levels (I or II) increases the chance of project failure even when there are no inadequacies at Level III. For example, strong user involvement or good planning (Level III) alone are probably not enough to prevent failure if the project manager is unskilled or a poor leader (Level II). Similarly, even an exceptional project manager will have trouble preventing failure if top management does not support the project (Level I).

Thus, there is good reason for strong emphasis on Levels I and II because, generally, correct action at these levels helps eliminate or mitigate problems at lower levels. For example, using the appropriate project management model and having top management support tends to encourage (or mitigate the problems of) selecting the right project manager, using the structured systems approach, and using the right management techniques; these, in turn, tend to mitigate problems and reduce sources of failure further down in the planning and control process.

The caveat is that while eliminating sources of failure at higher levels tends to reduce failure at lower levels, the precaution does not guarantee success. Given the uncertainty of projects, causes for failure can develop at any level at any time. Management must continuously monitor and address all failure risks and new problems.

Does Eliminating Failure Guarantee Success?

Though the fourteen factors in Figure 17-2 are frequently cited as sources of project failure, they are not universal verities. Their validity and importance must be weighed and assessed in each project.

Because in most human endeavors absence of failure does not equate to success, mere absence of the previously stated factors, itself, will probably not make a project a "success." Sources of failure are similar to Herzberg's "hygiene" factors: although eliminating the problem factors reduces the chances of failure, this alone will not guarantee success.[5] For a project to be successful, other factors (similar to Herzberg's "motivators") must also be present in the project.

17.3 PROJECT SUCCESS

What Is Project Success?

A project is considered successful when it satisfies project objectives. Project objectives, however, commonly involve multiple dimensions or criteria (e.g., the time/cost/performance triad often mentioned in this book), and many "average" projects, although not considered failures, do not satisfy objectives in all dimensions. Project management usually makes trade-offs, and if the trade-offs are mutually agreed upon by the developer and the user, the project might still be successful even when portions of the objectives were not met. Many firms measure success by considering only the highest priority criteria and give lesser weight to time and cost measures. For example, in aerospace the primary success criteria is engineering performance; at Walt Disney it is safety.[6]

In a study of "successful" projects, Ashley, Lurie, and Jaselskis asked eight companies to select successful and average projects for purposes of comparison.[7] Based upon interviews with project personnel, "successful" projects were judged to be those doing "better than average" on the criteria of cost, schedules, and satisfaction of key project participants (client, project manager, project team, and system developer). Their findings are consistent with fields such as R&D and information technology, which make similar, frequent reference to budgets, schedules, and developer/user satisfaction as criteria of project success. Other frequently mentioned success measures include "within original scope or mutually agreed upon scope changes," and "without disturbing the corporate culture of values."[8] Considering only project cost, schedule, and performance specifications as measures of unequivocal success may be misleading. The requirements for a project might have been met exactly, yet if they were incomplete or poorly defined, the result would not have met user needs and the project would be judged a failure.

Study findings of Shenhar, Levy, and Dvir[9] suggest that both the stage of the project and life cycle of the end-item must be incorporated into project success criteria. For example, when the project end-item is a product or operational system, the project's ultimate success rests upon whether the end-item fulfilled customer needs. Simply, was the customer satisfied with the project end-item? Obviously, the answer cannot be determined until some time *after* the project has been completed. Another measure of project success that must be postponed until later, perhaps a year or longer after project completion, is assessment of the project's impact on the business or organization. Did the project ultimately improve operations, sales, income, or profit margins? These long-term impacts are especially relevant for both process reengineering and product-development projects.

In general, the best overall criterion for project success, regardless of industry, is the satisfaction of the parties involved. By most accounts, if the client, end-user, project manager, and developer all feel that their expectations were met or exceeded, the project must be considered a success.

17.4 PROJECT MANAGEMENT CAUSES OF PROJECT SUCCESS

The characteristics of project management frequently associated with successful projects are shown in Figure 17-3.[10] These characteristics, identified from a survey of articles that discuss successful projects, are broadly classified into three categories: project participants, communication and information sharing and exchange, and the project management/systems development process.

Project Participants

Two ingredients frequently identified as essential for project success are the *commitment* and *involvement* of key project participants such as top management (the developer), the project manager, the project team, and the user.

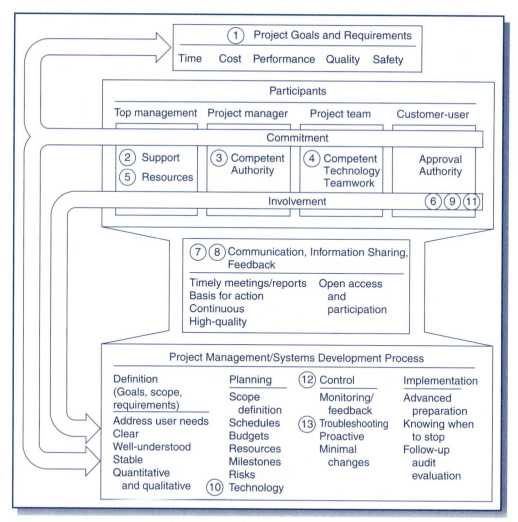

Figure 17-3
Project management causes of project success.

Earlier it was stated that for a project *not* to fail, it must have goals that are clear and well-defined. However, for a project to be successful, it needs more than that: it needs strong *commitment* from all of the participants fulfilling these goals. Everyone must understand and be motivated to achieve the goals of the project.

Second, project participants must be committed to the planning and control process. They must understand the concept of project management, its purpose and goals, and be committed to following steps and procedures for carrying it out.

Additionally, they must be *involved* in the project. They must be given the opportunity and have the desire to provide inputs (e.g., ideas, evaluation, and final approval) at key stages of the project life cycle.

The following sections focus on these and other aspects of project participants' roles in successful projects.

Top Management.   Top management commitment is essential to project success because it influences acceptance or resistance from others on the project. Management shows commitment by supporting the project—allocating necessary resources, giving the project manager adequate authority and influence (e.g., to select subcontractors, approve overtime, select team personnel, relax specifications, etc.), and backing the project manager in times of crisis. In successful projects, the project manager is confident about top management's support and satisfied with the levels of responsibility and authority conferred to him.

Often top management shows commitment by appointing a *project sponsor* to champion the project. This person interfaces with users, project and functional managers, and top management to expedite responses to potential problems. She is involved from the early planning stages and ensures that company and project management values are incorporated into project plans.

Project Manager. Project managers of successful projects are committed to meeting time, cost, safety, and quality goals. They are deeply involved in the project from beginning to end. They have sufficient authority to oversee development of plans and schedules, make additions or changes, and carry them out.

In successful projects, project managers are experienced and capable in administration, technology, communication, and human relations. Usually it is more important that they have a basic understanding of the technology rather than a command of it. However, in some high-tech projects they may need expertise in the technology. In either case, they must be both people-oriented and results-oriented, diplomatic and hard driving.

Good project managers have leadership styles that allow them to compensate for any "gap" between their authority and responsibility. They are able to utilize styles of leadership appropriate for their workers, even though they may only have a short time to get familiar with workers.

The best project managers get more done by being both efficient and effective. They set up the system of roles, responsibilities, and communication patterns, and then manage it. They trust the skills of their team members and delegate work to them.

They also make vigorous use of management by walking around (MBWA). They are accessible, familiar, and on a friendly basis with people in the project. They keep people talking to each other because they know that "it is usually less necessary to get people to work hard than to get them to work together."[11] The best project managers are intimately familiar with all aspects of the project. They know not only what is going on in the laboratory or shop, but in marketing and manufacturing, also.

Project Team. In successful projects, the project team is committed both to the goals of the project and to the project management process. The whole team is involved in estimating, setting schedules and budgets, helping solve problems, and making decisions—a process that helps develop positive attitudes about the project, build commitment to project goals, and motivate the team.

Commitment to project management is enhanced by a corporate culture that understands and supports project management. Kerzner reports that in companies with a "culture of project management," workers are trained to report to multiple bosses; functional managers and project managers maintain a balance of power; both project and functional managers are committed to the job; top managers understand their interface role with project managers; and functional managers are trusted by project managers to get the work done.[12]

In successful projects, the project team is staffed with the necessary expertise and experience. The team has the requisite skills and knowledge, and is provided adequate resources and technology to perform its functions.

In successful projects, there is close teamwork, confidence, trust, and understanding of everyones' roles. Team building is employed to define roles and delegate authority and responsibility. To foster good relations that carry through to the workplace, team members are encouraged to mix socially.

Customer-User. In successful projects, there is no question about who the customer and end-user are. The customer pays for the project, and the user is the ultimate recipient or operator of the end-item. Sometimes they are the same, sometimes not. We refer to both as the client. The project team identifies these parties before the project begins and understands what they want.

In successful projects, the client is strongly committed to project goals and is involved in the project management process. The customer has the authority and influence to share in making decisions, authorizing changes, and helping select subcontractors. Through client involvement in planning and design the project team can better determine what the client wants and can set specific goals and criteria. The customer-user is involved in the implementation process and gives final approval for the installed end-item.

Communication and Information Sharing Exchange

Successful projects are characterized by good communication and high-quality information sharing and exchange. As shown in Figure 17-3, good communication implies a mechanism for effectively integrating the efforts of all project participants and for facilitating project management and the development process. In successful projects, there is continuous, clear communication between all personnel within the project/user/top management team. Good communication is maintained throughout all stages of the project, from conception through completion.

Good communication partly depends on the quality and quantity of face-to-face meetings. In successful projects, there are frequent review meetings to exchange information and instructions about project objectives, status, policies, and changes. Meetings are accessible and everyone is encouraged to attend. At meetings it is specified which parties have priority, and leading roles change hands as required. Personnel are committed to addressing problems and quickly resolving them. Frequent "teach-ins" are held so participants at various stages of the project (e.g., planners, designers, and builders) can better understand one another. Meetings are informal, people trust each another, and project managers *listen* to people.

Project Management and Systems Development

In successful projects, several factors relate to project management functions and to elements of the systems development process. These factors include project definition, planning, control, and implementation.

Definition. In successful projects, there is complete and clear definition of project scope, objectives, and work to be done. Project responsibilities and requirements are clearly defined and well-understood by everyone involved. Clarity of definition produces common expectations among the participants.

Although some flexibility in definition is desirable, goals and requirements need to be relatively stable. It is difficult to proceed when there is persistent change in goals, scope, or requirements. Changes require adjustments to be made to plans and communicated to participants.

In successful projects, goals and requirements are quantified wherever possible, but important qualitative aspects of project performance are also included.

Planning. In successful projects, plans are related to time, cost, and performance goals. The plans include scope and work definition, schedules, networks, milestones, cost estimates, cash flow analyses, labor and equipment requirements, and risk analysis. Plans ensure that the hard things—things that people want to avoid thinking about—get done first. In successful projects, the technology has been carefully considered and the problems anticipated and understood. Safety is also an issue, and plans include requirements and means for ensuring participants' safety.

Peoples' behavior and attitudes are important, too. People are more likely to follow plans when they personally helped develop the schedules and plans. Good planning takes into consideration those who will be affected by the project and seeks their participation and approval.

In successful projects, the plans provide detailed descriptions of the stages of the project, ways to measure performance, and arrangements for project control and trouble shooting.

Control. Successful projects have a control and reporting system that provides for monitoring and feedback at all stages, and enables comparison of schedules, budgets, and team performance with project goals.

The control system uses checks and balances. It supplies information that is timely, meaningful, free of irrelevant details, yet covers everything. It enables ongoing assessment of the effectiveness of the project team, how well objectives are being met, and the likelihood of success.

In successful projects, the control system is proactive and forward-looking. It allows time to anticipate problems, foresee and forestall them, and to react as problems arise. Schedule slippages and cost growth are taken as early warning indicators of problems.

The project manager and project team in successful projects are committed to the control process. The project manager looks for problems just emerging, and the team takes quick action to resolve problems. The project manager openly discusses problems with the user and the team.

In successful projects, minimal changes are allowed except when essential to safety, to facilitate the job, or to meet user needs. Most changes are made on paper, early in the job, not later. Pressure is put on planners and designers to produce complete, finished designs before building or fabrication begins.

Implementation. In successful projects, preparation for implementation is done in advance. It is addressed in the initial plan and throughout the project. There is a strong liaison between the project team and the user about implementation details. Work is paced to minimize the downstream adverse impacts on people.

In successful projects, the originally authorized plan spells out how and when the project should be terminated. The project is not allowed to drift from earlier goals, exceed goals, or to do too much or go on for too long.

Even in success there is room for improvement. In successful projects, the team learns from its experience. When the work is finished the team assesses its experience, evaluates its performance, and applies the learnings to subsequent projects.

What is the relative importance of the success factors listed in Figure 17-3? We can get a partial answer from looking at a survey on information systems projects conducted by Jang, Klein, and Balloun[13] that asked users and developers in 50 firms to rank 13 factors according to their importance in determining project success. The participants ranked the factors as follows (and noted in Figure 17-3):

1. Clearly defined goals.
2. Support of top management.
3. Competent project manager.
4. Competent team members.
5. Sufficient project resources.
6. Client involvement in defining needs and requirement.
7. Adequate communication channels.

8. Involvement of all parties in project review and corrections.
9. Consulting with users and keeping them informed.
10. Technology being implemented has been reviewed and critiqued, and works well.

11. Clients understand the usefulness of the project.
12. Control measures to keep project on track.
13. Daily troubleshooting and resolution of problems.

17.5 A MODEL AND PROCEDURE FOR ANALYZING PROJECT PERFORMANCE

The following sections discuss an approach for using the factors described previously, to improve project performance.

Project Force Field Analysis

Many years ago, social scientist Kurt Lewin proposed a method for analyzing problem situations and determining alternative courses of action.[14] The method organizes information pertaining to organizational improvement into two categories: those "forces" at work that restrain improvement, and those that facilitate it. In theory, the state of affairs of any situation is allowed to persist because the restraining and facilitating forces are in equilibrium (Figure 17-4). If the restraining forces should increase, the state of affairs will worsen. Conversely, if the facilitating forces are strengthened the state of affairs will improve.

This dichotomy of forces is utilized in a so-called "force field analysis" to determine the best way to improve a situation. Force field analysis begins by identifying all of the restraining and facilitating forces in a situation and the relative strength of each. This makes it possible to then determine which restraining forces must be weakened or which facilitating forces must be strengthened to move the situation toward the ideal state.

Although the technique was originally proposed as a means for overcoming resistance to change, it can be used by managers in other applications. In project management, the technique can be used to investigate forces acting on a current project or that might influence an upcoming project, and to determine where emphasis is

Figure 17-4
Force field analysis.

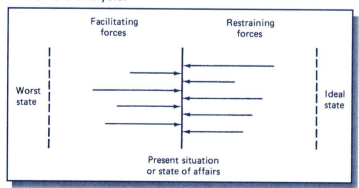

needed to increase the project's likelihood for success. The factors discussed earlier about project failure and success are the "forces" that influence a project and are somewhat controllable. A general force field analysis of project management using these factors is shown in Figure 17-5.

Some important features should be noted about the forces in Figure 17-5. First, notice that many of the forces affecting project performance are potentially either facilitating *or* restraining. This means that, for example, "top management commitment" is a restraining force when it is lacking but a facilitating force when it is present. It does not mean, however, that the forces are "binary." When there is weak or no management commitment, project performance is restrained. However, when commitment *is* present, its facilitating influence depends on its strength and visibility. When top management provides necessary resources, bestows adequate authority on the project manager, and appoints a sponsor to the project, it provides a stronger facilitating force than if it did only one of these.

Figure 17-5
General force field analysis of project performance.

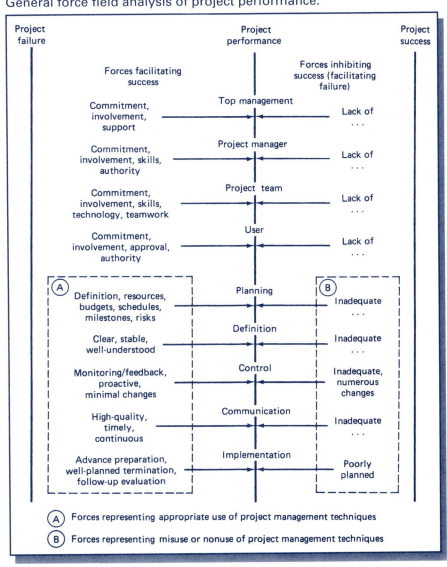

Second, not all forces are equal; some are of generally greater importance and influence than others. For example, the commitment and support of top management, the project manager, or the user are potentially greater forces than all others combined. Without commitment, involvement, and support, increasing other facilitating forces will offer little help.

Finally, the forces are not independent. Referring back to our discussion of Figure 17-2, some of the forces—such as having top management support or the right project manager—tend to impact other forces. Improving or strengthening these facilitating forces has a ripple effect on other facilitating forces.

Implementing the Analysis

A force field analysis can be used in particular cases for determining which forces might hinder a new project, or for analyzing the forces acting on a current project. The value of the technique, even if not strictly followed, is that it systematizes thinking and organizes information about project problems and causes.

The analysis begins by gathering information through questionnaires or interviews about the forces facilitating and hindering project performance. The forces shown in Figure 17-5 represent general categories of forces; for individual projects it is necessary to identify *specific* forces—procedures, systems, or behavior and attitudes of individuals and groups that help or hinder the project. The survey should include all parties involved in the project or affected by project problems—management, the project team, and users.

The results of the survey are discussed at a meeting where members examine, clarify, and reach agreement about them. Forces that seem to involve multiple issues are broken down and listed as separate forces. The list of forces is posted and arrows are drawn from each force, similar to Figure 17-5. Members are asked to judge the strength of the forces, and the length of each arrow is drawn to reflect the consensus.

The forces then are ranked so that the strongest are given highest priority. They also are rated for solvability. Those rated "unsolvable" (such as imposed by the environment) are noted in order to avoid argument over unsolvable problems.

The final step is to generate actions for reducing the "solvable" restraining forces with the highest priority, and for increasing the facilitating forces. Plans are prepared showing objectives, actions, target dates, and people responsible for each.

This last step recognizes that actions are tentative and that problem solving is part of the project control process, and, therefore, ongoing. Periodic follow-up meetings are convened to evaluate the status of the forces and to modify actions. The process can be incorporated in the team building efforts described in Chapter 16.

The utility of the force field analysis process is the systematic framework it provides for viewing problems and identifying solutions with the highest likelihood of success. Some people might resist this procedure as irrelevant or silly, so it is most important not to simply list forces and draw arrows, but to move toward identifying key stumbling blocks, prioritizing them, taking action, and evaluating results. Force field analysis is just a convenient way to get the process started.

17.6   EPILOGUE

In a sense, the answer to the issue posed in this chapter—how to avoid failure and get success—has been the subject of this entire book. Although factors such as management support and client involvement are crucial for success, it is often the use or misuse of the procedures, methodologies, and systems of project management—tools described in this book—that make the difference between success and failure. In project management, it's only *success* that counts.

It is not success at all costs, however. Project management should strive to deliver the end-item to the user's satisfaction, but, as implied elsewhere in this book, it should do so *in an aboveboard and ethical manner*. From the beginning of the project, the contract defines project specifications according to the requirements of (presumably) both the client and the developer. Methods of project management seek to fulfill that contract and provide an end-item that is satisfying to the client and the developer. Ideally, they do it in a way that also rewards and enriches the quality of work life of the participants.

This book has given you the project management tools and the guidelines about how and where to use them. Now comes the hard part—which is up to you: deciding which tools are necessary, desirable, or inappropriate for the goals, resources, constraints, and organization of each particular project. No tool works equally well in all situations, and appropriate use of any tools depends first on selecting the right ones. Many of the tools in this book have more universal application than others, yet not every project requires them or would benefit from their usage.

In applying project management, you can expect resistance—particularly at first. Project management organization structures, leadership styles, and information, planning and control systems are departures from traditional management. People tend to resist change because they find it risky and threatening. To most people, project management represents a major change, especially if it is implemented all at once.

But seldom is it necessary to implement it all at once. Only in larger projects are all or most of the tools mentioned in this book needed. In small projects, only certain ones apply or are necessary. It is better to introduce project management with a small demonstration project and a limited number of project management tools, making sure you include the essential ones. A force field kind of analysis will help you decide which tools are essential and which can be left out. A small demonstration project will give you the opportunity to try out certain techniques, to build competency, and to show off the results.

Implementing project management is itself a project. As with all projects, implementing project management should follow a logical sequence of development. To make it work you should have well-defined goals and requirements about what you want to accomplish. You also have to have the commitment and involvement of your top management and the project team. Of course, you need a list of tasks, responsibility assignments, a schedule, a budget, a system for reporting and control, and an implementation plan. How you do it is the subject of this book. After that, in the words of the sage Hillel,[15] "All else is commentary."

REVIEW QUESTIONS

1. What are the two criteria of system failure? Describe a recent example for each of a project that failed.
2. Give specific examples (other than those cited in this chapter) of project failures experienced exclusively by either the client or the developer. Give some specific examples of projects where failure was experienced by both.
3. Explain how defects in the project end-item are caused by defects in the project management system.
4. How can the user's failure to accept or utilize a system (implementation failure) be blamed on project management?

5. Describe each of the following Level I factors and discuss how they contribute to project failure. Cite examples.
   a. Inappropriate project management model
   b. Unsupportive top management

6. Describe each of the following Level II factors and discuss how they contribute to project failure. Cite examples.
   a. Wrong project manager
   b. Ignoring systemic nature of projects
   c. Inappropriate or misuse of management techniques

7. Describe each of the following Level III factors and discuss how they contribute to project failure. Cite examples.
   a. Inadequate communication in the project
   b. Failure to involve the user
   c. Inadequate or lack of planning
   d. Inadequate project definition
   e. Bad estimating of time and resources
   f. Incorrect scheduling and handling of resources
   g. Numerous changes during the acquisition phase
   h. Inadequate control
   i. Project termination is poorly planned

8. Discuss how the factors are interrelated. Which of the factors tend to carry greater weight in influencing project failure? Which factors tend to impact other factors?

9. What are the criteria for project success? How do they vary depending on the industry or project?

10. Discuss the importance of commitment and involvement to project success. An important issue not addressed in this chapter is how to build commitment; discuss how it is done.

11. Discuss the role of project participants in achieving project success. Discuss the skills, knowledge, functions, attitudes, behavior, or other factors—where appropriate—necessary from each of the following for projects to succeed:
    a. Top management
    b. Project manager
    c. Project team
    d. Users or customers

12. Discuss the importance of communication and information exchange to project success. What are the crucial features and elements of effective communication and information exchanges in successful projects?

13. Discuss the following points of project management and systems development and how they are essential to project success:
    a. Definition
    b. Planning
    c. Control
    d. Implementation

14. What is a force field analysis? Describe a force field analysis procedure for investigating particular projects.

15. Why might you expect resistance to using project management for the first time? Discuss how you might overcome that resistance. (You might find helpful the team building and conflict resolution methods that are described in Chapter 16.)

QUESTIONS ABOUT THE STUDY PROJECT

1. If the project you are studying is a current project, review the factors of success and failure described in this chapter and, based upon your evaluation of their presence and strength in the project, estimate the project's chance of success or failure. What other unique factors are influencing the project? In your evaluation, you might want to involve the project manager and team members and include their opinions.

   Use a force field analysis to determine which factors or forces (restraining or facilitating) might be altered to improve project performance. Discuss your findings with the project manager.

2. If the project you are studying has been completed, was it a success or failure? Did *everyone* consider it a success? To answer this, try to determine how satisfied the developer, the project team, and the client were with the project. Review the factors of project success and failure described in this chapter and determine which were present and how strong they were. How much did they contribute to its overall success or failure? What other factors influenced project performance?

   Using a force field analysis, determine which factors or forces (restraining or facilitating) might have been altered to improve project performance.

3. Prepare a short, formal proposal describing the results of the analysis and how to improve the performance of the project you are studying. (If the project has been completed, describe how it could have been improved.) The proposal should indicate the actions, anticipated results, estimated costs, and benefits.

4. If your proposal includes project management techniques not currently being used in the organization, consider how they might be implemented. How will you "sell" management on these techniques and convince them that they will be an improvement? How will you ensure that the people to implement or use the techniques will accept them and practice them faithfully? As with any plan, your proposal is a "request for change" and should address the issue of human resistance to change.

ENDNOTES

1. Karl Popper, *The Logic of Scientific Discovery* (New York: Harper & Row, 1968).
2. J. Naughton and G. Peters, *Systems Performance: Human Factors and Failures* (Milton Keynes, Great Britain: The Open University Press, 1976).
3. Ibid., 60.
4. See S. Alter and M. Ginzberg, "Managing Uncertainty in MIS Implementation," *Sloan Management Review* (Fall 1978); Ivars Avots, "Why Does Project Management Fail?" *California Management Review* 12, no. 1 (Fall 1969): 77–82; T. Guimaraes, "Understanding Implementation Failure," *Journal of Systems Management* (March 1981): 12–17; L. Holt, "Project Management Principles Succeed at ICI," *Industrial Management and Data Systems*, (March/April 1983): 4–9; S. P.

Keider, "Why Projects Fail," *Datamation* 20, no. 12 (December 1974): 53–55; M. Lasden, "Effective Project Management," *Computer Decisions* (March 1980): 49–57; J. G. Shanks, "Inflating or Deflating Projects Depends on the 'Big Four'," *Data Management* (August 1985): 18–22; W. C. Wall, "Ten Proverbs for Project Control," *Research Management* (March 1982): 26–29.

5. Herzberg's theory considers various factors that impact worker motivation. The theory says that there are some factors—"motivators"—the presence of which genuinely serve to increase workers' motivation. There are other factors however, "hygiene" factors, that are needed just to prevent motivation from deteriorating. Although the presence of these does nothing to

increase motivation, the absence of them results in decreased motivation. See F. Herzberg, B. Mausner, and B. Snyderman, *The Motivation to Work,* 2d ed. (New York: John Wiley & Sons, 1959).

6. H. Kerzner, "In Search of Excellence in Project Management," *Journal of Systems Management* (February 1987): 30–39.

7. D. B. Ashley, C. L. Lurie, and E. J. Jaselskis, "Determinants of Construction Project Success," *Project Management Journal* 18, no. 2 (June 1987): 69–79. Also see J. K. Pinto and D. P. Slevin, "Project Success: Definitions and Measurement Techniques," *Project Management Journal* (February 1988): 67–71.

8. See Kerzner, "In Search of Excellence in Project Management."

9. A. Shenhar, O. Levy, and D. Dvir, "Mapping the Dimensions of Project Success," *Project Management Journal* (June 1997): 5–13.

10. See D. B. Ashley, C. L. Lurie, and E. J. Jaselskis, "Determinants of Construction Project Success"; H. Kerzner, "In Search of Excellence in Project Management," 30–39; L. Holt, "Project Principles Succeed at ICI"; M. Lasden, "Effective Project Management"; W. A. Norko, "Steps in Successful Project Management," *Journal of Systems Management* (September 1986): 36–38; J. K. Pinto and D. P. Slevin, "Critical Factors in Successful Project Implementation," *IEEE Transactions on Engineering Management* EM–34, no. 1 (February 1987): 22–27; W. A. Randolph and B. Z. Posner, "What Every Manager Needs to Know About Project Management," *Sloan Management Review* (Summer 1988): 65–73; W. C. Wall, "Ten Proverbs for Project Control"; M. F. Wolff, "Rules of Thumb for Project Management," *Research Management* 27 (July–August 1984): 11–13.

11. Wolff, "Rules of Thumb for Project Management."

12. Kerzner, "In Search of Excellence in Project Management," 33.

13. J. Jang, G. Klein, and J. Balloun, "Ranking System Implementation Success Factors," *Project Management Journal* (December 1996): 49–53.

14. K. Lewin, *Field Theory in Social Science* (New York: Harper & Row, 1951).

15. The words as used here, of course, are in a different context than he intended.

Appendix

Systems Engineering Process

*D*ifferent industries and organizations use different plans and procedures for conducting systems engineering. Despite variation in particular stages and terminology, almost all of them include various activities that coincide with the five major stages of concept, analysis, design, implementation, and operation.[1] One particular plan for the application of systems engineering is shown in Figure A-1. This plan covers the primary stages of systems concept, definition/preliminary design, detailed design/development, construction/production, and operation, as well as a "prestage" of needs identification and a "throughout stage" of evaluation. In addition to addressing the objectives and characteristics of the operating (end-item) system, the plan identifies characteristics of the support system necessary to execute and maintain the operating system.

STAGE 0:   IDENTIFICATION OF NEED

Systems engineering is associated with poorly defined problems. The customer may feel that something is wrong or recognize a need for something new, but might be unclear about the extent or source of problem or need, how the system should look, or what it should do. This makes defining the performance requirements of the system and telling the customer what to expect difficult.

Before any work can begin on the system it is necessary to develop a clear conception of the problem and to estimate the value of the desired system. The process begins by asking some basic questions:[2]

1. How did the problem or need arise?
2. Who believes it to be a problem or feels the need?
3. Why is a solution important? How much money (or time, etc.) will it save? What is the value of the system?
4. Is it the root problem or need, or is it a manifestation of some other, deeper problem? Would greater benefits accrue if other problems or needs were addressed instead?

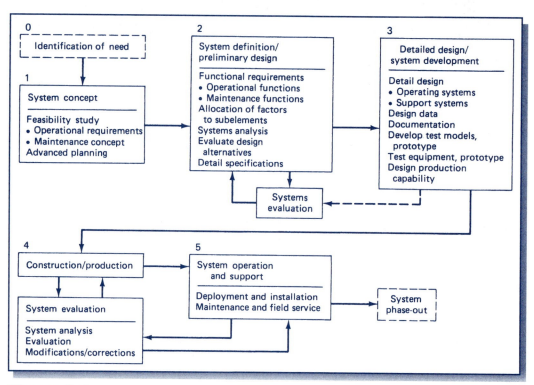

Figure A-1
Systems engineering process. [Adapted from B. Blanchard and W. Fabrycky, *Systems Engineering and Analysis* (Upper Saddle River, NJ: Prentice Hall, 1981): 238.]

5. In which scenario will the return on efforts be the greatest—where resources are applied to this system or where they are applied to another problem or need?

The customer and the systems engineer or contractor answer these questions interactively. First the customer states the "felt" need, then the contractor prepares a refined statement of the need and a preliminary description of the system, including performance requirements, cost, and schedule. The customer reviews the system description and redefines the need; then the contractor redetermines the system descriptions, performance requirements, schedule, and cost. The process continues back and forth until the parties agree upon a system description.

During this stage, the value and need of the system relative to the cost is examined. It must be established that the system will perform a needed or desired function and be justified in comparison to alternative systems or investments. Justification for the system does not have to be in economic terms: Many large-scale military and space systems, for example, have been justified more on strategic defense or world opinion than on economic grounds.

Once the value and need for the system have been established, the cost and time to produce the system is estimated. Although the actual cost will seldom be as first quoted, a cost estimate for the given value of the system is necessary to justify proceeding to the next stage. The cost estimate assumes that the system can be produced and operated within a reasonable time period. The time estimate assumes specified performance requirements, reliability, and cost, any of which might be modified depending on the time available to produce the system.

Stage 1: System Concept

During Stage 1, a feasibility study is undertaken to more precisely formulate and define the system. The systems engineering process creates a system to meet a set of requirements; The purpose of the concept stage is to distill a concise set of requirements, concepts, and criteria upon which to base all remaining design and developmental work. Operational requirements for the system are defined for physical parameters, performance factors, effectiveness characteristics, system utilization, and operational environment. At the same time, a system maintenance concept is developed to address issues and policies of operational support, maintenance, repair, and logistics.

The feasibility study is a preliminary systems analysis that develops goals for hardware, software, support, and other elements of the system. The study's results include design requirements and criteria for the overall system as well as a preliminary definition of the functional configuration and physical characteristics of the system; these become the basis for the preliminary system design and serve as reference for comparison with the final, actual system.

The results are reviewed in terms of political, ecological, economical, social, and related issues. This review may indicate that the proposed system is incompatible with the ecological, political, or economical environment.

Stage 2: System Definition and Preliminary Design

The concepts, criteria, and requirements for the overall system are grouped and translated into functions. A function is a specific action required to achieve a specific objective. The list of functions outlines the operations necessary to fulfill system requirements. For example, on most long distance, high-volume transport vehicles for humans (airplanes, trains, etc.) there is need for power generation, comfort, food preparation, waste management, and so on. Objectives and requirements are set for each of these, and then functions are defined as a means of attaining them. A function often implies eventual insertion of a piece of equipment with appropriate characteristics; for example, engines, seats, fuel lines, lights, and lavatories.

The process begins by identifying the major functions of the system as laid out by the requirements in Stage 1. Functional flow charts and block diagrams (Figure A-2) are developed to portray system design requirements showing relationships, hierarchy, and interfaces. Analysis is performed (1) on each operational function to reflect the various modes of system operation and utilization, and (2) for each maintenance function to reflect considerations of effectiveness and supportability. To avoid making the system description too complex, the breakdown starts with a simple representation and elaborates only where necessary.

Initially, the system description must be sufficiently flexible to permit changes as knowledge and experience is gained during the project. Machine-machine and man-machine interfaces and requirements for subsystems are identified in terms of power, light, temperature, signals, sensing, and so on. Initially, no attempt is made to identify the specific hardware, software, people, or facilities that will comprise the system.

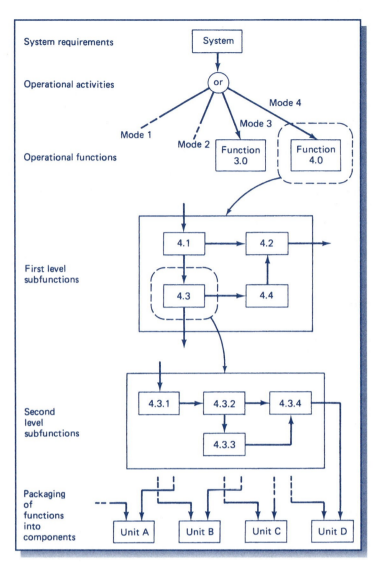

Figure A-2
Functional block flow diagram.

Later in this phase, systems analysis is performed on each block in the flow diagram to determine technical requirements and the most reliable and effective ways to satisfy them. Factors for each level of the system are allocated among subelements to provide guidelines for designers. For example, if a system is to weigh 5000 pounds, and cost $50,000, it must be determined how much each of the subelements should weigh and cost. In turn, the subelements' requirements are subdivided among assemblies, subassemblies, component parts, and so on. Operational requirements are analyzed for hardware, software, people, and facilities, and detailed specifications are laid out. Procedural support needs also are determined wherever people interface with the system (e.g., instructions for installing, operating, troubleshooting, inspecting, and repairing the system). Finally, a schematic block diagram is prepared that ties all items together in a system-installed configuration. This diagram indicates specifications along with the flows, sequencing, and interface requirements with which to evaluate the system design.

A similar procedure is conducted concurrently on the support system: Functional flow diagrams are prepared showing all scheduled and unscheduled support functions for correcting malfunctions or performing scheduled maintenance. Each block of the diagram is analyzed in detail to determine the most feasible, reliable, and economic means for supporting the operating system and minimizing downtime. This analysis may lead to additional operating system features to facilitate testing or parts replacement, or redesigning subsystems and equipment to reduce maintenance.

The functional breakdown and allocation of system requirements establishes boundaries and constraints on each functional block. For each function several satisfactory designs might be identified. Alternative designs are analyzed using mathematical models.

The final proposed operating/support system is synthesized and evaluated. The system synthesis combines the performance, configuration, and arrangement of the system and its subelements along with techniques for test, operation, and life cycle support. A dynamic analysis and evaluation is performed by simulating all units on a computer or subjecting selected units to mathematical analysis. Several iterations may be required before detailed design specifications about the system and satisfactory input-output requirements of subsystems can be made.

The result of Stage 2 is a list of specifications for system design. The customer review team studies the design recommendations and decides to approve, reject, or request changes. Designing a system in detail can be very expensive, so detailed design usually does not begin until after system development has been authorized and funds allotted.

STAGE 3:   DETAILED DESIGN AND SYSTEM DEVELOPMENT

The process of detailed design involves further description of subsystems, units, assemblies, lower level parts, and components of the prime mission operating equipment and support items. Decisions are made about whether subsystems and components will be manual, automatic, or semiautomatic; whether components will be electronic, mechanical, or hydraulic; whether input-output devices will be manual, keyboard, magnetic tape, disks, or other. This detailed description results in design documentation for all elements of the system: specifications, analysis results, study results, detailed drawings, materials and parts lists, and so on. Computer software also is developed at this time.

Everything up to this point has been analytical in nature. The next step is to move from "concepts on paper" to a configuration that is ready for fabrication or production. Commercially available component parts are selected on the basis of surveys and comparison testing in a laboratory. Components that must be developed from scratch are tested experimentally using "breadboards." A breadboard is a test model or assembly of components that enables design effectiveness to be verified by trial and error. Portions of the system may require redesign based upon the outcome of breadboard tests. Breadboards are used to develop individual pieces of equipment that will subsequently be mated and integrated for overall systems development. A nearly complete or "prototype" system, assembled for purposes of developmental testing, may then be used to evaluate the overall system in terms of satisfying customer requirements.

System development and design testing and evaluation includes[3]

1. Checking the operation of subsystems when combined in a complete system.
2. Evaluating the validity of assumptions made in the systems analysis.
3. Paying close attention to
   a. "cross talk" among subsystems
   b. power couplings
   c. feedback among subsystems
   d. adjustments and calibrations
   e. serviceability and maintenance

The system must be thoroughly checked under a variety of conditions so deficiencies can be corrected. Notable problems previously overlooked in the design process will come to light during testing and evaluation. Modifications often are required to correct for oversights, eliminate deficiencies, or simply improve the system.

When there is insufficient time and money to prepare a prototype for system development, the first few production models manufactured are subjected to developmental testing and design evaluation. Gradually, as minor modifications are made and the design is approved, full-scale production begins. Design and development testing is phased out and quality control testing begins. Quality control testing looks at the manufacturing system to ensure it is producing according to design specifications. It continues for as long as the system is operated.

The design of the production capability (facilities and related resources) to make the system also begins during this phase so that by the time the system is fully developed it can be produced (Stage 4). Called "process design," it includes the design of new (or redesign of old) facilities and manufacturing processes, selection of specific materials and pieces of equipment, and preparations for production control, quality testing, manufacturing tooling, product transportation, personnel hiring and training, and data collection and processing.

STAGE 4: SYSTEM CONSTRUCTION AND/OR PRODUCTION

During Stage 4, the system is either (1) mass produced (i.e., assembly line production systems), (2) produced in limited quantities with different features (i.e., job-shop production systems), or (3) built as a single item (e.g., a large ship or other one-of-a-kind item). This stage begins as soon as the design is frozen. (In less complex systems, the process may skip the development stage and jump directly here from Stage 2.) Stage 4 involves acquiring materials, maintaining adequate inventory, and controlling production/construction operations to uphold product performance, quality, reliability, safety, and other criteria. Stages 3 and 4 are sometimes referred to as the "acquisition" phase—the phase where the system physically comes into being and system objectives are accomplished.

STAGE 5: SYSTEM OPERATION AND SUPPORT

Stage 5 completes the life cycle of the system. Here the customer operates the system until it ultimately wears out or becomes obsolete. The support system is utilized in three ways: assistance in deploying, installing, and checking out the system; field service and maintenance support in assisting day to day operation, and modification and enhancement of the system to ensure continued satisfaction; and support in phasing out or disposing of the system at the end of its life cycle.

THROUGHOUT: SYSTEM EVALUATION

Although system evaluation is the major activity of Stage 3, it is an ongoing, interactive process throughout the entire systems engineering process as well. The role of system evaluation is summarized in Figure A-3.

During Stages 1 and 2, system evaluation utilizes conceptual, mathematical models to refine system definition and select design alternatives. In Stage 3, evaluation relies upon physical test models and mock-ups to test how well designs satisfy requirements. Prototype and production models are evaluated to test total system design assumptions and integration. During Stage 4, production models are evaluated on-site or through sample testing. Finally, during operation in Stage 5, the overall

Figure A-3
System data analysis and evaluation. [Adapted from Wilton Chase, *Management of Systems Engineering* (New York: John Wiley & Sons, 1974): 76–77, with permission.]

System Engineering Steps	Unit of Measure	Data Baseline	Approach
Definition of operational requirements	System and subsystems	System performance effectiveness criteria	System mathematical models
Determination of functional requirements	Subsystems and end-items	Operational performance requirements	Functional requirements analysis
Preliminary design of system and subsystems	End-items and components	Proven technology Research data / Functional flow diagrams / Allocation of requirements to end-items and components	Schematic diagrams of system and component interactions / Computer simulation / Design/tradeoff analysis
Detailed design of end-items	Components and parts	System schematics	Engineering drawings / Mock-ups
Fabrication of end-items	Components	Engineering drawings / End-item design characteristics and performance requirements	Simulation of development models under operational loads and environments
Installation and checkout of end-items	Components and end-items	Assembly, integration, and test procedures	Testing end-items both alone and when integrated in the operating system
System integration tests	Subsystems and system	Operation and maintenance procedures	Quality tests Monitoring of system status to verify performance, effectiveness of system concept/design
Operational testing of system	System and operations	Production end-items, procedures, personnel, logistics, support	

system is evaluated within the operating environment for its ability to satisfy original requirements.

Systems engineering deals with the total system and its complete life cycle. To accomplish overall system objectives, a system must be designed, tested, and supported as a complete entity. The "system" must be seen as including not only prime mission equipment—hardware and software—but everything needed to make it work, including (1) supporting information and equipment for production, control, testing, training, and maintenance; (2) facilities to produce and operate it; (3) selection and training of personnel to produce, operate, and maintain it; and (4) management policies and programs to implement, operate, and support it.

No two systems are ever alike, but systems engineering remains a process for making logical systems design decisions regardless of size, purpose, or complexity.

ENDNOTES

1. For examples, see Walter Beam, *Systems Engineering: Architecture and Design* (New York: McGraw-Hill, 1990); and Jeffrey Grady, *Systems Requirements Analysis* (New York: McGraw-Hill, 1993).

2. G. W. Jenkins, "The Systems Approach," in *Systems Behavior,* 2d ed., John Beishan and Geoff Peter, eds. (London: Harper & Row for the Open University, 1976): 88.

3. Harold Chestnut, *Systems Engineering Methods* (New York: John Wiley & Sons, 1967): 33.

Appendix B

Types of Contracts

A contract is an agreement between two parties wherein one party (the contractor) promises to perform a service, and the other party (the client) promises to do something in return—typically make payment for the service. Both the service requirements and the payment must be clear and unequivocally spelled out in the contract. An ambiguous or inconsistent contract is difficult to understand and enforce.

Different kinds of contracts provide different advantages to the client and the contractor. Depending on the risk of the project and the degree of difficulty in estimating costs, the client and contractor try to negotiate the type of contract that best serves their own interests. In some cases, for example, the client can protect herself by imposing penalty clauses or incorporating incentives into the contract.

The two fundamental kinds of contacts are *fixed price* and *cost-plus* contracts. In the fixed price contract, the price is agreed upon and remains fixed as long as there are no changes to the scope or provisions of the agreement. In the cost-plus contract, the contractor is reimbursed for all or some of the expenses incurred during the performance of the contract, and as a result, the final price is unknown until the project is completed. Within these two types, several variations exist including some with built-in incentives for the contractor to meet cost, time, or performance targets.[1]

Variables

The variables specified in a contract may include the following:

C_{ex} and C_{ac}	Target (expected) cost and actual cost. "Cost" represent monies expended by the contractor in performing the work. C_{ex} and C_{ac} are the negotiated target cost and the actual cost of the project under normal circumstances.
Fee	Amount paid to the contractor in addition to reimbursable costs.
Price	The price the client pays for the project. Price includes reimbursable costs (or a percentage thereof) incurred by the contractor, plus the contractor's profit or fee.

CSR   The cost sharing ratio. When costs are to be shared by the client and the customer, this is the percentage of the cost that each agrees to share (the sum is 100 percent).

FIXED PRICE CONTRACTS

Fixed Price Contract (FP)

Under an FP or "lump sum" agreement, the contractor agrees to perform all work at a fixed price. Clients are able to get the minimum price by putting out the contract to competitive bidders. The contractor must be very careful in estimating the target cost because, once agreed upon, the price cannot be adjusted. If the contractor overestimates the target cost in the bidding stage, he may lose the contract to a lower priced competitor; if the estimate is too low, he might win the job but make little or no profit.

Example 1: Fixed Price Contract

Contract agreement:

$$Cost\ estimate,\ C_{ex} = \$100,000$$
$$Fee = \$10,000$$
$$Price = \$110,000$$

Whatever the project actually ends up costing (C_{ac}), the price to the client remains $110,000.

When a project can be readily specified in detail, an FP contract is preferred by both client and contractor. From the client's point of view, there is less need to supervise the project because she does not have to be concerned with project costs to the contractor. She need only monitor work progress to see that it meets contractual completion date and performance specifications. Under an FP agreement, clients are less likely to request changes or additions to the contract.

The disadvantage of an FP contract is that it is more difficult and more costly to prepare. Because the contractor can make larger profits by reducing its costs, there is some incentive to use cheaper quality materials, perform marginal workmanship, or extend the completion to his own gain. The client can counteract these tendencies by stipulating rigid end-item specifications and completion dates as well as by supervising the work. Of course, the contractor also runs the risk of underestimating. Furthermore, if the project gets into trouble, bankrupts the contractor, or is left incomplete for other reasons, the client may be subject to legal action from other involved parties.

Fixed Price with Redetermination[2]

Contracts with long lead times such as construction and production may have *escalation provisions* which protect the contractor against cost increases in materials, labor rates, or overhead expenses needed to perform the work. For example, the price may be tied to an inflation index so it can be adjusted in the advent of inflation, or it may be *redetermined* as costs become known. In the latter case, the initial price is negotiated with the stipulation that it will be redetermined at intervals so that the price can reflect actual cost data. A variety of redetermination contracts are used: some establish a ceiling price for the contract and permit only downward adjustments, others permit upward and downward adjustments; some establish one readjustment period at the end of the project, others use more than one period. Redetermination contracts are appropriate where engineering and design efforts are difficult to estimate, or in long-term quantity production contracts where the final price cannot be estimated for lack of accurate cost data.

The redetermined price may apply to items already produced as well as future items. Because the only requirement to renegotiate the price is substantiating cost data, redetermined contracts tend to induce inefficiencies. After negotiating a low initial price, the contractor may produce a few items and then "discover" that the costs are much higher than expected. The contract thus becomes a "cost plus" kind of contract and is subject to abuse.

COST-PLUS CONTRACTS

When it is difficult to achieve accurate cost estimates in the early phases of work, such as in R&D or advanced technology projects, a type of contract called cost-plus permits work to begin before the costs are fully specified.

Cost Plus Fixed Fee (CPFF)

Under a CPFF contract, the contractor is reimbursed for all direct allowable costs plus an additional, fixed amount to cover overhead and profit. This is justified when costs rise due to increases in the scope of work or escalate because of factors beyond the contractor's control. Regardless of the cost, the fee specified remains the same. Usually the fee is a negotiated percentage of the C_{ex}, though often it is allowed to increase in proportion to actual costs up to a percentage ceiling.

Example 2: Cost Plus Fixed Fee Contract

Contract agreement:

Cost estimate, C_{ex} = $100,000, but all "allowable" costs will be reimbursed
Fee = $10,000
Target Price = $110,000

All allowable costs (perhaps "all" costs, C_{ac}), will be reimbursed in addition to the fee. Thus, if the project ends up costing C_{ac} = $200,000, the price to the client is $210,000.

In contrast to the FP contract, a CPFF agreement puts the burden of risk on the client. The contract does not indicate what the project is going to cost until the end of the project, and it provides little incentive for the contractor to control costs, finish on time, or do anything beyond minimum requirements because he gets paid the same fee regardless. The major factor motivating the contractor to control costs and schedules is the negative effect overruns have on his reputation. Another is that as long as the contractor's workforce and facilities are tied up, he cannot work on other projects.

Because of the risks to the client in a CPFF agreement, she must exercise substantial *external* control to ensure the project is done efficiently, meeting technical, time, and cost targets. She may specify who is to be the project manager or have her own project manager on-site to work with the contractor's project manager.

Despite the risk, the client might have to resort to a CPFF contract when estimating costs is difficult and few contractors are willing to take the project.

Time and Materials Contract (TM)

A TM contract is a simple form of agreement that reimburses the contractor for labor costs and materials as incurred. It provides for payment of direct labor hours at an hourly rate which includes the direct labor cost, indirect costs, and profit. Sometimes a ceiling price is established which may be exceeded, depending on the agreement. Charges for private consultants and other services (electricians, carpenters, etc.) are usually based on time and materials.

INCENTIVE CONTRACTS

When the contractor is unwilling to enter into an FP agreement and the client does not want a CPFF contract, an alternative is to use an incentive arrangement. This has features of both kinds of contacts: It is similar to CPFF in that costs are reimbursed, but the amount reimbursed is based on an incentive formula called a *cost sharing ratio* (CSR). A CSR of 80/20, for example, indicates that for every dollar spent on costs, the client pays 80 cents and the contractor pays 20 cents. It is beneficial to the contractor to keep costs low because he pays 20 cents on every dollar spent above C_{ex} (thus making 20 cents less profit), but earns 20 cents more on every dollar saved below C_{ex}. As further incentive to keep costs down, the ratio might be accelerated at costs above C_{ex} so that the contractor has to pay a higher percentage.

Cost Plus Incentive Fee Contract (CPIF)

A CPIF contract alleviates some of the disadvantages to the client of a fixed price contract because it offers a profit incentive for the contractor to reduce costs and improve efficiency. The project price in a CPIF contract is based on a percentage of the actual cost, C_{ac}, using a CSR. The contract specifies the target costs, C_{ex}, and the CSR specifies how any cost savings or overruns will be shared between the client and the contractor.

Example 3: Cost Plus Incentive Fee Contract

Contract agreement:

Cost estimate, C_{ex} = $100,000, but all "allowable" costs will be reimbursed.
Fee = $10,000
Target Price = $110,000
Cost sharing: CSR = 50/50, therefore
if C_{ac} < $100,000, client will reimburse C_{ac} plus
50% of amount below $100,000.
if C_{ac} > $100,000, client will reimburse $100,000 plus
50% of amount above $100,000.

The incentive is for the contractor to keep costs below or not too far above $100,000. Suppose C_{ac} is only $80,000 ($20,000 under C_{ex}). The contractor gets paid $80,000 plus $10,000 (50 percent of the savings) plus the $10,000 fee. Total price to client: $100,000. The client sees a $10,000 savings on the price, and the contractor gets a $10,000 bonus. The client must be vigilant in checking to see that the incentive to minimize cost doesn't lead the contractor to "cut corners" on work and materials.

Now suppose C_{ac} is $200,000 ($100,000 over C_{ex}). The contractor gets paid $100,000 ($C_{ex}$) plus $50,000 (50 percent of the overrun) plus the $10,000 fee. Total price to client: $160,000. The contractor is $200,000 − $160,000 = $40,000 in the red.

Fixed Price Incentive Fee Contract (FPIF)

A FPIF contract is similar to a CPIF contract, but it puts a ceiling on the price and profit. The contractor negotiates to perform the work for a target price based upon a target cost (C_{ex}) plus a fee. A maximum price and a maximum profit are also negotiated. If the total cost ends up being less than the target cost, the contractor makes a higher profit, up to the maximum. If there is a cost overrun, the contractor absorbs some of the overrun.

Example 4: Fixed Price Incentive Fee Contract

Contract agreement:

Cost estimate, C_{ex} = $100,000, but all "allowable" costs will be reimbursed.
Fee = $10,000
Target Price = $110,000
Maximum Price = $125,000 (fee + reimbursement), client will pay no more than this
Maximum Profit = $15,000, contractor profit cannot exceed this
Cost sharing: CSR = 50/50, therefore
if C_{ac} < $100,000, client will reimburse C_{ac} plus an additional 50% of amount below $100,000, as long as the additional amount does not exceed $5000
if C_{ac} > $100,000, client will reimburse $100,000 plus an additional 50% of amount above $100,000, but the total reimbursement cannot exceed $115,000

The incentive again is for the contractor to keep costs below or not far above $100,000. However, because the contractor cannot earn a profit of more than $15,000, there is less of a tendency for the contractor to cut corners to increase profits. Suppose C_{ac} is only $80,000 ($20,000 under C_{ex}). The contractor gets paid $80,000 plus the $10,000 fee, but only an additional $5000 for the cost savings (50 percent of the $20,000 savings is $10,000, but only $5000 is allowed because that plus the fee equals $15,000, the maximum allowable profit). Total price to client: $95,000, a $15,000 savings from the target price.

Now suppose C_{ac} is $200,000 ($100,000 over C_{ex}). Fifty percent of the overrun is $50,000, but the client will pay at most $125,000. This is the maximum price and is what the contractor receives. The client pays only $15,000 above the target price, so the contractor suffers a $200,000 − $125,000 = $75,000 loss.

The FPIF applies to long duration or large production projects. It is not applicable to R&D or other projects where the target cost is difficult or impossible to estimate.

FPIF contracts are not true fixed price contracts. They invite contractors to negotiate unrealistically high C_{ex}s so that extra profits can be made through the incentive features. However, unlike cost-plus contracts, they provide some assurance about a maximum price and that the contractor will not cut corners to gain a hefty profit.

Multiple Incentive Contracts[3]

Multiple incentive contracts attempt to relate profits to the uncertainties associated with achieving time, cost, and performance goals in large-scale development programs. The intent is to reward contractors that are able to set and achieve realistic targets for *all three* criteria.

Fee weights assigned to the three criteria are used to determine the amount of "fee swing" allocated to each criterion. Consider the example shown below where the cost-fee structure is similar to the previous CPIF example. Here the "fee swing" is between 2 percent and 14 percent, or a total of 12 percent.[4]

$$C_{ex} = \$100{,}000$$
$$F_{ex} = \$8\ (8\%)$$
$$F_{max} = \$14\ (14\%)$$
$$F_{min} = \$2\ (2\%)$$

The 12 percent fee swing is then divided among the three criteria:

CRITERION	WEIGHT	FEE SWING
Performance	0.5	6%
Cost	0.25	3%
Time	0.25	3%
Total	1.00	12%

In engineering contracts, typically the largest weight is given to performance, followed by time and cost. For performance several measures might be used at once, such as accuracy, range, reliability, and speed, in which case a point system is devised so all attributes can be represented as a single performance factor using one curve.

In this example, the performance factor is given a weight of 0.5, which yields a profit swing of 6 percent; time and cost are given weights of 0.25, so each have a profit swing of 3 percent. The profit percentage is computed as a function of these three criteria, as shown in Figure B-1, according to the formula

$$P = (8 + x + y + z)\%\ (C_{ex}).$$

Because these criteria tend to be interrelated (e.g., performance targets can be surpassed, but at the expense of time and cost, and so on), structuring the contract is a complicated issue. As computations and legal terms can be tricky, this type of contract is seldom used.[5]

Figure B-1
Multiple incentive contract.

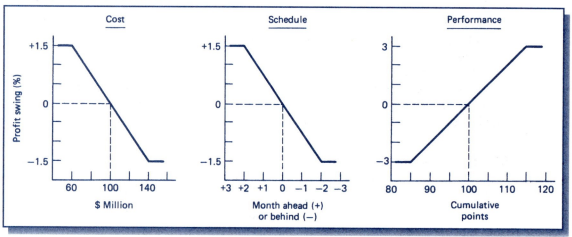

ENDNOTES

1. A more complete description of contracts is given in William Hirsch, *The Contracts Management Deskbook,* Rev. ed. (New York: Amocom, 1986): 43–75.

2. V. G. Hajek, *Management of Engineering Projects,* 3d ed. (New York, John Wiley & Sons, 1984): 82–83.

3. R. W. Miller, *Schedule, Cost, and Profit Control with PERT* (New York: McGraw-Hill, 1963): 173–184.

4. Example from ibid., 174–75.

5. See Miller, ibid., 183–96, for a more complete discussion of multiple incentive contracts, their usage in PERT systems, and their development and application to program control.

Appendix C

Logistical On-Line System Project Master Plan

Attachments

Item 1. Robot transporter
Item 2. MPD site layout
Item 3. Storage rack assembly
Item 4. LOGON organization chart
Item 5. Project responsibilities
Item 6. Principal subtasks
Item 7. Project schedule
Item 8. LOGON project cost estimate

Iron Butterfly, Corp.

Elegant design. Built to last.

To: SEE DISTRIBUTION   Ref. Job No.: 904-01

From: Frank Wesley, Project Manager   Date: 1-3-05

Subject: Logistical Online System Project

<u>Project Summary Plan</u>

The Project Summary Plan for the Logistical Online System Project for the Midwest Parcel Distribution Company's Chicago distribution center has been modified to include your suggestions and approved by everyone in distribution. Copies of this document are herewith sent for use in the performance of contract requirements.

FW:es
Enclosure

<u>Distribution:</u>

    Julia Melissa, Project Engineer
    Sam Block, Fabrication Manager
    Noah Errs, Quality Control Supervisor
    Larry Fine, Software Manager
    Sharry Hyman, Design Manager
    Brian Jennings, Assembly Supervisor
    Frank Nichol, Site Operations Manager
    Emily Nichol, Assembly Supervisor
    Robert Powers, Drawing Supervisor
    Burton Vance, Purchasing Manager

LOGISTICAL ONLINE SYSTEM
PROJECT SUMMARY PLAN

I. MANAGEMENT SUMMARY

On September 5, 2004, Iron Butterfly Company (IBC) was awarded the contract by the Midwest Parcel Distribution (MPD) Company of New York for the Logistical Online (LOGON) System Project. The system is to be installed at MPD Co.'s main Chicago distribution facility.

The project consists of designing, fabricating, and installing a parcel transport, storage, and database system, for automatic placement, storage, and retrieval of standardized shipping containers. The system uses an overhead conveyor track system, conveyor-robot transporter units, racks with standard size shipping containers and storage buckets, and a computerized database for automatic placement and retrieval of parcels and record keeping.

Iron Butterfly is the prime contractor and is responsible for the design of hardware and software, fabrication of component parts, system installation, and checkout. The major subcontractors are Creative Robotics, Inc. (CRI), Steel Enterprises, Inc. (SEI), United Plastics Co. (UPC), and CompuResearch Corp. (CRC). Iron Butterfly will provide overall project management between CRI, SEI, and UPC Corp. and related contract administration; legal, accounting, insurance, auditing, and counseling services as may be required. The project manager is Mr. Frank Wesley, and the project engineer is Ms. Julia Melissa.

The project will commence with basic design on or before May 6, 2005; installation at the site will begin on or before January 9, 2006; and final system approval by MPD Co. will be made on or before April 7, 2006. The principle subtasks are shown in the schedule, Item 7.

The price of the contract is $1,452,000, fixed fee with limited escalation, based on a target final approval date of April 7, 2006. Total expenses, tabulated in Item 8, for labor, overhead, materials, subcontracting, and general/administrative are $1,319,518. The agreement provides for an escalation clause tied to inflation indices for material expenses for the steel conveyor track and rack support systems. Because the facility will be unusable for MPD Co. during most of the later part of the project, an agreed-to penalty of $1,000 a day will be imposed on IBC for target completion overruns. Contingency arrangements in the agreement allow for reconsideration of the penalty in event of disruption of work for labor dispute with management.

II. PROJECT DESCRIPTION

On September 5, 2004, Iron Butterfly Company (IBC) was awarded the contract for the Logistical Online System Project. The award followed a 4-month competitive bidding review by the Midwest Parcel Distribution (MPD) Company of New York. The system is to be installed at MPD Co.'s main Chicago distribution facility.

The project consists of designing, fabricating, and installing a parcel transport, storage, and database system, hereafter called LOGON, for automatic placement, storage, and retrieval of standardized shipping containers. The system will substantially improve the speed of parcel handling, increase the utilization of storage facility space, enhance record keeping, and reduce labor costs at the facility. Anticipated ancillary benefits include reduced insurance premium and shrinkage costs.

The system uses an overhead conveyor track system, conveyor-robot transporter units, racks with standard size shipping containers and storage buckets, and a computerized database for automatic placement and retrieval of parcels and recordkeeping.

The LOGON system works as follows:

Upon a parcel's arrival at the distribution center receiving dock, it is placed into one of three standard-sized parcel "buckets." The buckets are electronically coded as to parcel item and shipping destination. This code is relayed to a master database from any of four terminal work stations located at the dock. The work stations are connected via a DEM-LAN network to a CRC Model 4000 server. The Model 4000 has 64 GB storage with backup for retaining information about parcel description, status, storage location, and destination. The system keeps track of available, remaining storage space, and, if need be, reallocates buckets for optimal space utilization. The CRC4000 will also provide reports about system status and performance on request by management.

The parcel buckets are manually attached to a robot transporter mounted on an overhead track-conveyor system (Item 1). The robot transporter carries the bucket to a "suitable" vacant storage slot within a shipping container located on a rack in the facility. The computer determines which shipping container has a vacant slot of sufficient size and containing parcels going to the same or nearby destination as parcels in the transporter's parcel bucket. The robot transporter then conveys the bucket to the appropriate shipping container and unloads it into the vacant slot. Shipping containers are stacked three high in seven rows of racks (Items 2 and 3). The storage facility has capacity for 400 shipping containers, each with 150 cubic feet of storage capacity.

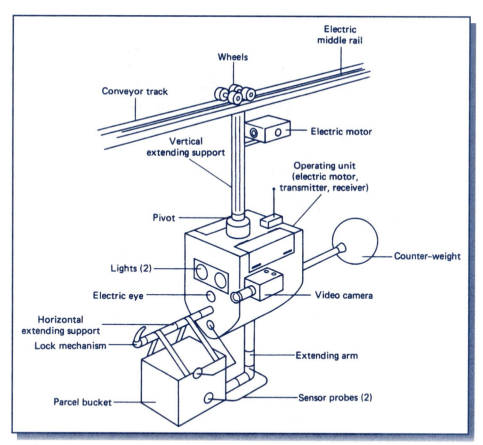

Item 1
Robot transporter.

Item 2
MPD site layout.

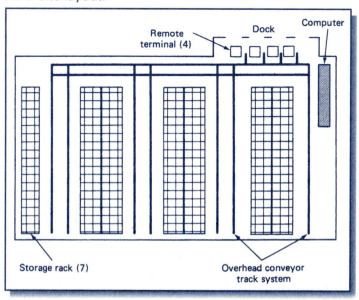

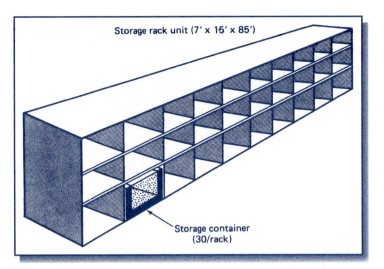

Storage rack unit (7' x 15' x 85')

Storage container
(30/rack)

Item 3
Storage rack assembly.

When a truck or rail car going to a specific destination is to be loaded, the destination is keyed in at the dock terminal workstation so the database system can identify all shipping containers having buckets with parcels going to the same or nearby destinations. The system then routes the robot transporters to the appropriate shipping containers for retrieval of parcel buckets. The system has four robot transporters that operate independently and simultaneously. The robot transporters retrieve the buckets and transport them back to the loading dock for placement of parcels into departing truck or rail cars. The longest specified retrieval time in the system is 8 minutes.

Iron Butterfly is the prime contractor and is responsible for the design of hardware and software, fabrication of components parts, system installation, and checkout. The major subcontractors are Creative Robotics, Inc., which will supply the major components for the robot transporters; Steel Enterprises, Inc., which will supply the parts for the overhead track-conveyor system and storage racks; United Plastics Co., which will supply the shipping containers and parcel buckets; and CompuResearch Corp. (CRC) which will supply the terminal workstations, DEM-LAN network, and CRC4000 computer. CRC will also provide support for software development and installation of all computer hardware items.

Structural tests performed by M&M Engineering Corp. indicate that the present ceiling structure of the facility can support additional loads of up to 600 psi. The LOGON system would add a maximum of 325 psi, including parcel weight, and thus can be installed directly to the existing ceiling frame without additional reinforcement. Structural tests performed on walls and floors also indicate sufficient strength to support the system

Appendix C   Logistical On-Line System Project Master Plan

with a safety factor of 2.1. The system can be directly connected to the existing main electrical harness hookup.

During system installation MPD has arranged for alternate, temporary storage at another facility and rerouting of most parcel traffic to its other sites.

As much as possible, design information about existing systems, such as MPD's Tulsa facility, will be utilized to try to initially move the project to an advanced stage. Remaining design work will use as much as possible of work that has been done already, without compromising confidentiality of clients, on previous, similar projects.

III. ORGANIZATION SECTION

III.1 Project Administration

All correspondence on project matters will be between the project manager for IBC and the project director for MPD. When specifically authorized, project personnel may correspond directly with the client or subcontractors for information, keeping the project manager and project director informed with copies of all correspondence and memos of telephone conversations.

The account number assigned to the LOGON project is 901-0000. Work packages and tasks will be assigned subaccount numbers at the time when work package instructions and schedules are authorized. A single invoice for the project accounts as a whole is acceptable for billing at monthly intervals.

III.2 Project Organization and Responsibility

The organization of Iron Butterfly Company for the performance of the LOGON project is shown in Item 4. Specific administrative and managerial responsibilities are summarized in the responsibility chart, Item 5.

The project manager, Mr. Wesley, is responsible for managing project work, which includes all client contact, reporting of progress, adherence to contractual commitments regarding schedule and technical performance, and monitoring of budgetary expenditures. Changes in scope of contractual services will be recorded in communications with the client. He and his staff will report directly to Mr. Ed Demerest, vice president and project director for MPD Co.

The project engineer, Ms. Melissa, is responsible for establishing specifications and ensuring system delivery to meet technical requirements. She will supervise the preparation of design requirements and drawings depicting system elements, estimate

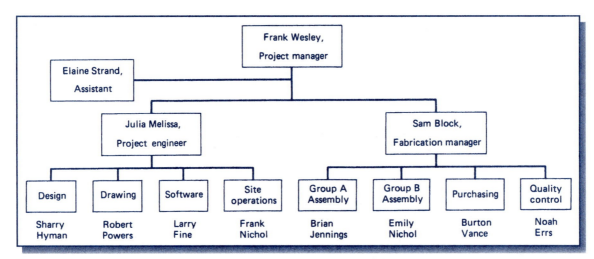

Item 4
LOGON organization chart.

quantities, check drawings and requirements calculations, and ensure that system technical requirements are fulfilled at the site.

The fabrication manager, Mr. Block, is responsible for managing procurement, assembly and related work at the IBC plant. He will direct procurement and assembly operations, ensure that the quality of delivered parts from subcontractors meets requirements, coordinate assembly operations of robotic transporters, track conveyor, and storage rack subsystems, and sign off final approval for assemblies prior to shipment to the MPD site.

III.3 Subcontractor Administration

The four primary subcontractors of the project are Creative Robotics, Inc. (CRI), Steel Enterprises, Inc. (SEI), United Plastics Co. (UPC), and CompuResearch Corp. (CRC). Key personnel associated with each are:

Bill Plante	Project coordinator, CRI
Terry Hemmart	Manager, manufacturing, SEI
Delbert Dillert	Customer representation, UPC
Lynn Duthbart	Systems engineering representative, CRC
Elmer Hyman	Customer representative, CRC

Changes or modifications to the respective agreements requested by a subcontractor or by IBC will be acted upon by the IBC project manager, Mr. Wesley, upon receipt of a written proposal from the subcontractor.

Persons responsible

Responsibility code

- P Primary responsibility
- S Secondary responsibility
- N Must be notified
- A Must give approval

Project Task or Activity	Project manager		Project engineer — Design					Project engineer — Drawing				Project engineer — Software					Site operations					Fabrication manager — Assembly A					Assembly B		Purchasing
	F.W.	J.M.	S.E.H.	R.L.G.	P.J.	D.V.R.	R.I.P.	O.E.M.	P.V.R.	D.M.N.	R.L.	L.S.F.	L.L.L.	J.R.S.	D.V.Q.	F.W.N.	J.M.N.	L.O.T.	A.U.A.	D.A.R.	S.O.B.	E.N.	G.G.F.	R.T.T.	B.V.L.	B.J.	T.T.Y.	H.R.D.	B.V.
Project coordination	P	S																		S									
Project development	A	P	A	P	S	S										A				N	N							N	
Project design	A	A	A	P	S						N					N				N									
H Basic design	N	A	A	P	S		N				N					A				N									
I Hardware Design A		A	A	P	S																								
J Hardware Design B		A	A	P	S																								
K Drawings B		N	A				A	S	P											N									
L Software specs		N										A	P	S	S					A									
M Parts Purchase B																												P	
N Parts Purchase A							A	A	S	P										A	N							P	
O Drawings A							A	A	S	P										N	A								
P Installation drawings																N													
Q Software purchase															N	N				A	A							P	
U Assembly A															N	N				A	N	A	A	P	A			P	
V Assembly B															A	A				N	N	P	S	S	P				
W Test A															A	A			S	A	A		S	S		S	S		
X Test B																			S	A	P					P			
Y Final installation																													
Z Final test																													

Item 5
Project responsibilities.

579

Correspondence to subcontractors concerning technical matters will be directed to the previously named first four parties or their substitutes. Software specifications related work with CRC will be coordinated by, and communications should be directed to, the CRC customer representative. Project telephone conversations between IBC and subcontractors shall be noted in handwritten memos and copies sent to the IBC project engineer.

Progress reports shall be prepared by Mr. Plante, CRI project coordinator, Ms. Hemmart, SEI manufacturing manager, Mr. Dillert, UPC customer representative, and Mrs. Duthbart, CRC systems engineering representative for presentation at weekly meetings to be held at IBC's Chicago office for the duration of scheduled involvement as noted in the respective agreements. Other meetings may require attendance by other individuals as required by the subcontractors or requested by the project manager. The following number of meetings have been included in the respective subcontractor agreement budgets.

CRI   5 meetings
SEI   3 meetings
UPC   2 meetings
CRC   5 meetings (software development)
CRC   8 meetings (site system integration)

The subcontractors will provide information and perform services on the project as follows:

1. CRI will perform all elements of work associated with procurement, manufacturing, and component functional tests of parts and subassemblies according to specifications, plans, and drawings provided by IBC. Parts and components for four robotic-transporters will be delivered to IBC according to the criteria and dates specified in the agreement.

2. SEI will perform all work associated with procurement, manufacturing, and component functional tests of parts and subassemblies according to the specifications, plans, and drawings provided by IBC. Parts and components for the complete overhead conveyor track system and seven storage racks will be delivered to IBC according to the criteria and dates specified in the agreement.

3. UPC will perform all work associated with procurement, manufacturing, and component functional tests of parts and subassemblies according to the specifications, plans, and drawings provided by IBC. Plastic containers and parcel buckets will be delivered to the MPD Chicago distribution facility in quantities and according to dates specified in the agreement. One plastic container and one each of three size parcel buckets will be delivered to the IBC facility for tests according to the date specified in the agreement.

4. CRC will perform all work associated with development, programming, and tests of LOGON system robotic transporter control software, system database, and reporting functions according to the specifications provided by IBC. Software will be delivered to the IBC facility according to dates specified in the agreement.

5. CRC will transport, install, and perform component and integration tests for checkout of four terminal work stations, DEM-LAN network, CRC4000 server, printer, backup system, and related hardware according to criteria and dates specified in the agreement.

Iron Butterfly will provide overall project management between CRI, SEI, and UPC Corp. and related contract administration, legal, accounting, insurance, auditing, and counseling services as may be required by the project.

III.4 Client Interface

Key personnel associated with the project for MPD Company are:

Ed Demerest	Project director, Chicago
Lynn Joffrey	Administrative assistant, Chicago
Cecil Party	Financial manager, Chicago
Mary Marquart	Operations manager, New York

Changes or modifications to the agreement requested either by MPD or by IBC will be acted upon by the operations manager, Mrs. Marquart, upon receipt of a written proposal from IBC.

All correspondence with MPD regarding the project will be directed to the project director, Mr. Demerest. If he requests our contacting another person or contractor, he will receive a copy of each item of correspondence between parties. Project telephone conversations between IBC and outside parties shall be noted in handwritten memos and copies sent to Ms. Joffrey.

Progress reports shall be prepared by Mr. Wesley, IBC project manager, for presentation at monthly meetings to be held at MPD Co.'s Chicago office. Other meetings may require attendance by other individuals as required by MPD or requested by Mr. Wesley. Mr. Wesley shall also convene two other meetings, a mid-project review and a project summary, at the New York office of MPD. A total of 15 meetings are included in the agreement budget. MPD Co. will provide information and perform services on the project as follows:

1. MPD will perform all elements of work associated with vacating the site prior to the date in the agreement for commencing of system installation.

2. MPD will provide surveys, design criteria, drawings, and preliminary plans prepared under previous agreements or received through requests for proposals for the LOGON system.

3. MPD will provide design criteria, drawings, and plans prepared for the automated parcel storage and retrieval system at MPD Co.'s Tulsa facility.

4. MPD will obtain all internal, municipal, state, and federal approvals as may be necessary to complete the project.

5. MPD will provide overall project management between MPD, IBC, and CRC Corp.; contract administration; legal, accounting, insurance, auditing, and consulting services as may be required by the project.

The contract administrator is the operations manager. Changes or modifications to the agreement with MPD, requested either by MPD or IBC, shall be subject to a written proposal by IBC to MPD's contract administrator through Mr. Demerest.

The financial manager, Mr. Party, is responsible for approvals of monthly expense summaries provided by STING and monthly payment to IBC. MPD is responsible for securing necessary support from electrical and telephone utilities for system hookup, and for making available to IBC all criteria, drawings and studies prepared for the Chicago site facility and the Tulsa facility automated system.

III.5 Manpower and Training

No additional manpower requirements beyond current staffing levels are envisioned to perform services for this project. Five personnel from the design group for this project have been enrolled in and will have completed a robotics seminar at a local university before the project begins.

III.6 User Training

Two systems operations manuals and 16 hours of technical assistance will be provided. Thereafter, ongoing operator training will be the responsibility of MPD Co.

IV. TECHNICAL SECTION

IV.1 Statement of Work and Scope

The major tasks to be performed are the design, fabrication, installation, and checkout of the LOGON system for the Chicago distribution center of MPD Co. The work will be executed in accordance with the terms, conditions, and scope as set forth in the applicable drawings and specifications prepared by IBC in the written proposal and confirmed in the agreement.

Subtasks required to perform the major tasks noted above are shown on the network in Item 6. The major subtasks are (letters refer to task designations on Item 6):

1. Perform basic design of overall system. (H)

2. Prepare detailed design specifications for robotic transporter, conveyor track, storage rack systems, and shipping and parcel containers to be sent to Creative Robotics, Steel Enterprises, and United Plastics, subcontractors. (J, I, M, N)

3. Prepare specifications for the software system and for DEM-LAN and CRC 4000 system interface. (L)

4. Prepare detailed assembly drawings for robotic transporter units, conveyor track system, and storage rack system. (O, K)

5. Prepare drawings and a master plan for system installation and test at the site. (P)

6. Fabricate robotic transporter units, conveyor track, and rack support subassemblies at IBC facility. (U,V)

7. Perform preliminary functionality tests on robotic transporter units at IBC facility. (X)

8. Perform structural and functional tests of conveyor track and storage rack systems at IBC facility. (W)

9. Perform installation of all subsystems at MPD Chicago facility site. (Y)

10. Perform checkout of subsystems and final checkout of overall system at MPD facility site. (Z)

IV.2 <u>Schedule and Calendar</u>

The project will commence with basic design on or before May 15, 2005; installation at the site will begin on or before January 9, 2006; and final system approval by MPD Co. will be made on or before April 14, 2006. The project master schedule for the most significant portions of the project is given in Item 7. The significant project milestones indicated are:

1. Commence basic design   May 16, 2005
2. Basic design review   July 26, 2005

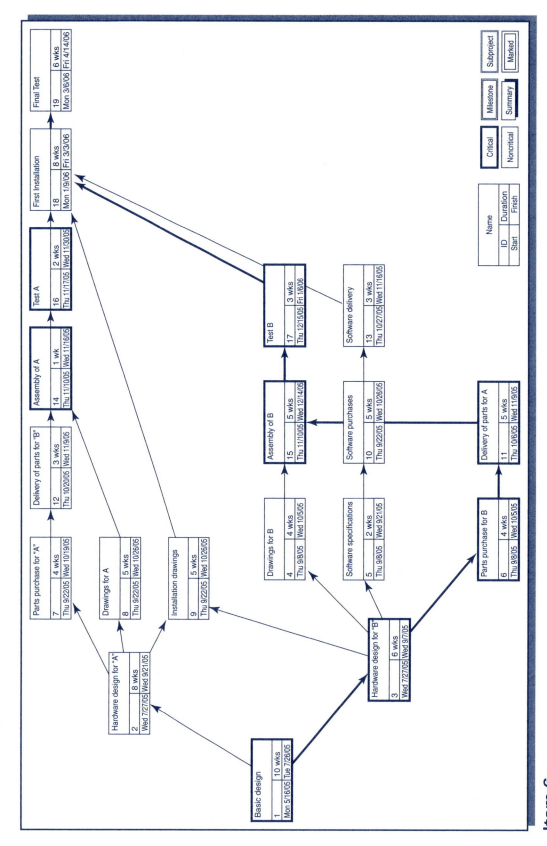

Item 6
Principal subtasks.

584

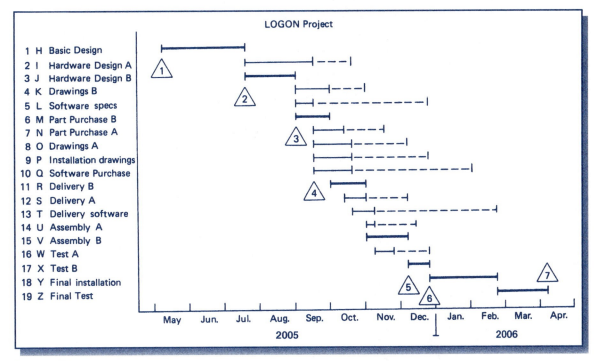

LOGON Project

1	H	Basic Design
2	I	Hardware Design A
3	J	Hardware Design B
4	K	Drawings B
5	L	Software specs
6	M	Part Purchase B
7	N	Part Purchase A
8	O	Drawings A
9	P	Installation drawings
10	Q	Software Purchase
11	R	Delivery B
12	S	Delivery A
13	T	Delivery software
14	U	Assembly A
15	V	Assembly B
16	W	Test A
17	X	Test B
18	Y	Final installation
19	Z	Final Test

May Jun. Jul. Aug. Sep. Oct. Nov. Dec. | Jan. Feb. Mar. Apr.

2005   2006

Item 7
Project schedule.

3. Transporter and conveyor
   design review   September 7, 2005
4. Computer system specs review   September 21, 2005
5. Hardware group A & B review   November 30, 2005
6. Begin installation at site   January 9, 2006
7. Final user approval   April 14, 2006

Starting dates for activities dependent on the results of reviews will be adjusted to make allowances for significant
changes in the length of predecessor activities, although no adjustments are anticipated.

Work package instructions and a detailed schedule for basic
design has been distributed. Subsequent schedule and work package information will be distributed and discussed at review
meetings.

The schedule of contract deliverables is given in Section
IV.9.

IV.3 Budget and Cost

The price of the contract is $1,452,000, fixed fee with limited
escalation, based on a target final approval date of April 14,
2006. Expenses and fees will be billed and are payable monthly
as incurred. The agreement provides for an escalation clause

tied to inflation indices for material expenses for the steel conveyor track and rack support systems. Because the facility will be otherwise unusable for MPD Co. during the last 5 months of the project, completion by the contracted date is imperative. An agreed-to penalty of $1,000 a day will be imposed on IBC for target completion overruns. Contingency arrangements in the agreement allow for reconsideration of the penalty in event of disruption of work for labor dispute with management.

Principal tasks, subtasks, man-hours, and dollars to perform them have been estimated. Total expenses, as tabulated in Item 8, for labor, overhead, materials, subcontracting, and general/administrative are $1,319,518.

Expenditures of direct labor, the largest single cost factor, are under immediate control of department heads in design, fabrication, procurement, and customer service departments because they assign personnel to the project.

Responsibility for expenditures of man-hours and direct expenses belongs to the project manager, who receives biweekly accounting of all expenditures of time and money.

IV.4 Information Requirements

Most of the information required by IBC to perform under the terms of the agreement has been supplied by MPD Co. A limited amount of site information will be obtained from additional required surveys performed by an IBC survey party. MPD has expressed a willingness to dispatch some of its own personnel for minor survey work to expedite the project.

IV.5 Documentation and Maintenance

Minutes and action plans of review meetings will be formally documented and sent to the project manager. Biweekly expense and progress reports will be sent from functional managers to the project manager. Monthly project summary reports will be sent from the project manager to functional managers and to other managers and supervisors listed in distribution.

Cost, performance, and progress documentation will be maintained and reported through the company project cost accounting system.

A final summary report will be prepared by the office of the project manager for the company archives.

The project manager is responsible for maintenance of all project files. All copies of project documents sent outside IBC will leave only under his direction.

Task	Labor Time	Labor Rate	Labor Cost	O/H @ 0.25	Materials	S/C	G/A @ 0.10	Total
Project coordination	2,000	28	56,000	14,000				
	2,000	12	24,000	6,000				
		Total	80,000	20,000	2,000		10,200	112,200
Project development	400	28	11,200	2,800				
	400	20	8,000	2,000				
		Total	19,200	4,800	4,500		12,850	31,350
Project design	50	28	1,400	350				
	150	24	3,600	900				
	150	12	1,800	450				
		Total	6,800	1,700	6,00		1,450	15,950
H Basic hardware	300	30	9,000	2,250				
	1,600	24	38,400	9,600				
	1,400	15	21,000	5,250				
		Total	68,400	17,100	5,410		9,091	100,001
I Hardware Design A	180	26	4,680	1,170				
	1,100	24	26,400	6,600				
	900	15	13,500	3,375				
		Total	44,580	11,145	2,450		5,818	63,993
J Hardware Design B	250	26	6,500	1,625				
	1,350	24	32,400	8,100				
	1,300	20	26,000	6,500				
		Total	64,900	16,225	6,150		8,728	96,003
K Drawings B	160	26	4,160	1,040				
	160	18	2,880	720				
		Total	7,040	1,760	5,740		1,454	15,994
L Software specs	160	28	4,480	1,120				
	240	24	5,760	1,440				
	240	20	4,800	1,200				
		Total	15,040	3,760	2,330	11,600	3,273	36,003
M Parts Purchase B	2	28	56	5				
	16	24	384	96				
		Total	440	101	25	75,800	7,637	84,003
N Parts Purchase A	4	28	112	28				
	20	24	480	120				
		Total	592	148	35	71,950	7,273	79,998
O Drawings A	650	26	16,900	4,225				
	700	18	12,600	3,150				
		Total	29,500	7,375	8,580		4,546	50,001
P Installation drawings	450	28	12,600	3,150				
	600	26	15,600	3,900				
	700	18	12,600	3,150				
		Total	40,800	10,200	3,540		5,454	59,994

LOGON Project Cost Estimate (in dollars)

Item 8
LOGON project cost estimate.

Appendix C Logistical On-Line System Project Master Plan

LOGON Project Cost Estimate (in dollars)

Task	Labor Time	Labor Rate	Labor Cost	O/H @ 0.25	Materials	S/C	G/A @ 0.10	Total
Q Software	8	28	224	56				
purchase	16	24	384	96				
			0	0				
			608	152	160	71,800	7,272	79,992
U Assembly A	10	28	280	70				
	100	24	2,400	600				
	120	20	2,400	600				
		Total	5,080	1,270	6,400		1,275	14,025
V Assembly B	100	28	2,800	700				
	1,100	24	26,400	6,600				
	1,100	20	2,200	5,500				
		Total	51,200	12,800	8,700		7,270	79,970
W Test A	20	26	520	130				
	300	24	7,200	1,800				
	300	20	6,000	1,500				
		Total	13,720	3,430	4,700		2,185	24,035
X Test B	30	26	780	195				
	450	24	10,800	2,700				
	450	20	9,000	2,250				
		Total	20,580	5,145	7,000		3,273	35,998
Y Final	320	28	8,960	2,240				
installation	1,200	24	28,800	7,200				
	900	22	19,800	4,950				
		Total	57,560	14,390	12,100	10,500	9,455	104,005
Z Final test	200	28	5,600	1,400				
	1,000	24	24,000	6,000				
	600	21	12,600	3,150				
		Total	42,200	10,550	1,250	6,000	6,000	66,000
		Total	568,240	140,633	87,070	247,650	104,501	1,319,518

Item 8
(continued)

IV.6 Work Review

Internal review of work produced in each of the design, fabrication, procurement, and customer service divisions is a responsibility of the division head for each of the functional disciplines.

IV.7 Applicable Codes and Standards

Track conveyors, storage racks and supporting structures, electrical harnesses, and radio transmitters are to be designed to the applicable standards of AATOP, ASMER, OSHA, the Illinois Building Requirements Board, and the City of Chicago.

IV.8 Variations, Changes, Contingencies

The agreement with MPD defines the conditions for considering a change in compensation or penalties due to a change in the scope of work or cost of steel-fabricated materials, or unanticipated stoppage of work for labor dispute. It describes the procedure whereby authorization for such a change may be obtained from MPD.

The agreement, Paragraph 9.2, under prime compensation, states:

"Whenever there is a major change in the scope, character, or complexity of the work, or if extra work is required, or if there is an increase in the expense to the CONTRACTOR for steel-fabricated materials as negotiated in the agreement with the responsible SUBCONTRACTORS, or if there is a stoppage of work resulting from a labor dispute with management, the CONTRACTOR shall, upon request of the CLIENT, submit a cost estimate of CONSULTANT services and expenses for the change, whether it shall involve an increase or a decrease in the Lump Sum. The CLIENT shall request such an estimate using the form provided herein (Attachment F). Changes for reasons of labor dispute with management will be reviewed and determined according to the conditions specified (Attachment G)."

During system installation and tests, MPD has made arrangements to reroute about 70 percent of its Chicago parcel business to other distribution centers. The remainder will be stored at an alternate facility near Chicago. In the event of an unforeseen schedule overrun, the reroute plan will remain in effect. MPD requires 30 days notice of anticipated schedule overrun to extend the agreement with the alternate Chicago storage facility.

IV.9 Contract Deliverables

All items are to be assembled, installed, and in operation at the site in accordance with technical specifications in the agreement.

Transport of components and parts from subcontractors to the IBC plant will be scheduled by subcontractors. The respective agreements specify the following items as deliverable to IBC:

Item	Date
Parts and components for robot-transporters from CRI	Nov. 1, 2005
Parts and components for overhead conveyor track and storage rack systems from SEI	Nov. 4, 2005
One shipping container and one each of three-size parcel buckets from UPC	Nov. 10, 2005
Robotic-transporter system control software from CRC	Oct. 27, 2006

Transport of Group A and Group B subassemblies from the IBC plant to the MPD site will be accomplished in one-half day. Agreement for delivery is with Acme Systems Contractor, Co.

Following are the items identified in the agreement as deliverable to MPD:

Item	Date
Hardware (Group A):	
7 storage racks, 10´ × 15´ × 6´	
Installed at site	Nov. 16, 2005
Final structural, functional checkout	Nov. 30, 2005
Delivered 400 shipping containers	
Installed at site	Dec. 1, 2005
Delivered 1000 size D43A parcel buckets	Dec. 10, 2005
Delivered 600 size D25B parcel buckets	Dec. 10, 2005
Delivered 600 size D12C parcel buckets	Dec. 10, 2005
Overhead track conveyor system	
(1567´ noncontiguous linear section,	
18 crossover points, distribution uniform	
balance, weld supported at 6″ intervals)	
Installed at site	Nov. 1, 2005
Final structural, functional checkout	Nov. 5, 2005
Hardware (Group B):	
4 robot transporter units	
(each 300 lb. max. load capacity compatible	
with three-size parcel buckets, 380 Mh,	
retrieval at farthest point 8 min.)	
Installed at site	Nov. 10, 2005
Four unit functional checkout	Nov. 12, 2005
Integration checkout, groups A and B	Jan. 5, 2006
Software Group:	
Submission of software specifications	
to CompuResearch Corp. (CRC)	Sept. 21, 2005
(Installation of DEM-LAN network, four	
CRC2950 workstation terminals and CRC4000	
server, all performed by CRC)	February 10, 2006
(Software-integration checkout, performed by CRC)	March 6, 2006
Final checkout:	
Two copies, system operation/maintenance manuals	March 6, 2006
Robot-transporter/CRC4000 integration	April 1, 2006
Benchmark systems test, with parcels	April 5, 2006
User training	April 12-13, 2006
Final system checkout, user	April 14, 2006

AUTHOR INDEX

591

Toffler, A., 34, 50
Tomczak, D., 50

V

Vaill, P., 509, 510, 532,
VanSlyke, R., 260
Vazsonyi, A., 267

W

Wakabayashi, H., 339
Wall, W., 553, 554

Walker, M., 267
Warshaw, L., 533
Waterman, R., 452, 475, 476
Weist, J., 228, 267, 305, 382
Wheelwright, S., 462, 476
Whitten, N., 156, 339, 429
Wileman, D., 519, 533
Willard, R., 67, 82
Williams, J., 533
Wilson, T., 305
Wolff, M., 554
Wood, M., 50

Y

Yorks, L., 476
Yourdan, E., 156, 339

Z

Zander, A., 501

SUBJECT INDEX

Polaris missile program, 230
Popper, Karl, 535
Postcompletion project review, 425–426
Postcompletion project summary, 143, 163, 425–426
    for risk identification, 309–310
Postinstallation system review, 143, 426–427
Postmortem, project, 146, 425–426
Power, managerial, 483–484, 486
Precedence, 193–194
Precedence diagraming method (*See* PDM)
Predecessors, 195
    immediate, 195–196, 199, 201, 205
    redundant, 201, 203
Preliminary design review, 416
Price, project, 563, 564–568
Primavera, 390
    (*illus.*), 398–399, 401–402
Priority
    resource, 247
    risk, 318–319
    scheduling, heuristics for, 251–252
    team members', 414
Probabilistic analysis
    in GERT, 254–258
    in PERT, 232–234
    simulation for, 235–236
Probability
    distribution
        beta, 231–233, 238
        normal, 233–234
    vs. likelihood, 338
    of output, 254–255
    of target completion date, 232–233
Problem formulation
    in project feasibility, 105
    in systems analysis, 71
Process, system, 56
Process design, 560
Process differentiation, 437
Process flow diagram, 25
    schematic (*illus.*), 104
Procrastination, work, 351
Proctor & Gamble Corp., 463
Procurement management, 97
Producer, motion picture, 488
Product development (*See also* Systems development)
    conflict during, 521
    interaction design, 135–136
    organization at Microsoft, 449
    projects, examples, 8, 36–37, 145
    QFD use at Chrysler, 469–470
Product differentiation, 437
Product management, 35
Product readiness review, 416
Production
    capability, 560
    planning for, 137–138
Production/build in systems development, 138–141
Production/fabrication, 75, 92
Productivity software, 406–407

Profit and billing, 238
Program
    examples, 33, 42–45
    (*illus.*), 33
    vs. project, 50
    in systems development cycle, 90
Program evaluation and review technique (*See* PERT)
Program management, 32–33
    examples, 42–45
Program manager, 45
    reports, 420
Program office, 451
Project (*See also individual subjects, e.g.:* Project accountant; Project audit; etc.)
    antiquity, examples, 1–3, 24–25
    authority, sources of, 484–486
    (*illus.*), 485
    budget (*See* Budgets)
    characteristics, 4, 22
    contingency amount, 279
    duration, 205–207, 220–221
        reducing, 238–240
        shortest, 240–242
    evaluation, 414–415
    examples, familiar, 4–9, 30–31, 36–45
    extensions, 424
    failure, 535–542
    force-field analysis, 548–550
        (*illus.*), 549
    functional managers and leaders, 493–494
    internal conflict, 518–519
    meeting room, 419
    vs. nonprojects, 5, 7, 25
    postcompletion review, 426–427
    review meetings, 415–419
    risky, 307
    success, 542–548
    summary evaluation, 424–427
    systems nature of, ignoring, 539
    termination, 420–424
    typology of (*illus.*), 6
Project accountant, 269, 493
Project audit, 417–418
Project center, 443
Project champion, 495–496
Project charter, 160
Project close-out (*See* Termination)
Project control
    change control, 371–375
    and contracts, 375–376
    emphasis, 349–356
    failure, source of, 541
    forecasting to-complete, 365–369
    index monitoring, 369–370
    internal vs. external, 342
    performance analysis, 356–365
    PERT/Cost systems for, 343–344
    problems with, 376–377
    process, 345–349
    subsystem, 63
    success, factor in, 547
    variance limits, 370–371
Project controller, 492

Project coordinator, 26, 442, 493
Project cost
    direct, 238–242
    indirect, 242–243
    optimum, 243
    overhead, 282–283, 433–345
Project cost accounting system (PCAS) 284–286, 420
    (*illus.*), 285
    and cost accounts, 286–287, 290
Project contracting (*See* Contracting)
Project engineer, 491–492
Project expeditor, 26, 440–441
Project feasibility (*See* Feasibility)
Project form, selection of, 447–449
    (*illus.*), 448
Project goals: time, cost, technical performance, 5, 10, 88
    (*illus.*), 10
Project initiation, 91, 95–96
Project initiation, proposal, and authorization process, 115
    (*illus.*), 115
Project integrators, 439
Project life cycle, 87, 90
    conflict, sources within, 519–520
        (*illus.*), 519
    managing, 88–89
    PMIS applications during, 407–409
        (*illus.*), 408
    risk during, 307–308
Project management
    in aircraft development, example, 59–62
    applicability of, 27–29
    in auditing, example, 40–41
    commercial and for-profit, 35
    as a common approach, 29
    computer-based applications, 386–389 (*See also* PMIS)
    in disaster recovery, example, 47–48
    environments of, 35–36
    ethical conduct in, 551
    failure, causes of, 537–542
        (*illus.*), 537
    features of, 11–12, 22–24
    forms of, 31–34
    in fundraising, example, 42
    getting started, 551
    government and nonprofit, 35
    history, 24–26
    in industrial settings, 36–40
    in management consulting, example, 41–42
    in manufacturing, example, 39–40
    military, 35–36
    misuse of techniques, 539
    need for, 7–9
    philosophy, 12–13
    in R&D, example, 39–40
    as risk management, 323–326
    in service sector, example, 40–42
    in small projects, example, 40
    software, 25 (*See also* PMIS)
    success, causes of, 543–548
        (*illus.*), 543